Women's International Thought: Towards a New Canon

This first anthology of women's international thought explores how women transformed the practice of international relations, from the early to middle twentieth century. Revealing a major distortion in current understandings of the history and theory of international relations, this anthology offers an alternative "archive" of international thought. By including women as international thinkers it demonstrates their centrality to early international relations discourses in and on the Anglo-American world order and how they were excluded from its history and conceptualization.

Encompassing 104 selections by 92 different thinkers, including Anna Julia Cooper, Margaret Sanger, Rosa Luxemburg, Judith Shklar, Hannah Arendt, Merze Tate, Susan Strange, Lucy P. Mair, and Claudia Jones, it covers the widest possible range of subject matter, genres, ideological and political positions, and professional contexts. Organized into thirteen thematic sections, each with a substantial introductory essay, the anthology provides intellectual, political, and biographical context, and original arguments, showing women's significance in international thought.

PATRICIA OWENS is Professor of International Relations at the University of Oxford. Her previous publications include *Economy of Force* (2015), winner of BISA's Susan Strange Prize, *Between War and Politics* (2007), and, as co-editor, *The Globalization of World Politics* (2020). She is a former fellow of the Radcliffe Institute for Advanced Study and Proctor Fellow at Princeton University

KATHARINA RIETZLER is Senior Lecturer in American History at the University of Sussex. She is currently completing a book on American philanthropy, International Relations, and the problem of the public, 1913–1954. Her work has appeared in journals such as *Modern Intellectual History*, *Diplomatic History*, and the *Journal of Global History*. She is a former Mellon Fellow in American History at the University of Cambridge.

KIMBERLY HUTCHINGS is Professor of Politics and International Relations at Queen Mary University of London. She is the author of works including *Kant, Critique and Politics* (1996), *International Political*

Theory (1999), *Hegel and Feminist Philosophy* (2003), *Time and World Politics: Thinking the Present* (2008), and *Global Ethics: An Introduction* (2nd edition, 2018) and co-author of *Violence and Political Theory* (2020) with Elizabeth Frazer.

SARAH C. DUNSTAN is a Leverhulme Early Career Fellow and Lecturer in the International History of Global Human Rights at the University of Glasgow. She is the author of *Race, Rights and Reform* (2021). Her work has also appeared in journals such as the *Journal of Modern History*, the *Journal of the History of Ideas*, the *Journal of Contemporary History*, and *Gender & History*.

Women's International Thought: Towards a New Canon

Edited by

Patricia Owens
University of Oxford

Katharina Rietzler
University of Sussex

Kimberly Hutchings
Queen Mary University of London

Sarah C. Dunstan
University of Glasgow

CAMBRIDGE
UNIVERSITY PRESS

CAMBRIDGE
UNIVERSITY PRESS

University Printing House, Cambridge CB2 8BS, United Kingdom

One Liberty Plaza, 20th Floor, New York, NY 10006, USA

477 Williamstown Road, Port Melbourne, VIC 3207, Australia

314–321, 3rd Floor, Plot 3, Splendor Forum, Jasola District Centre, New Delhi – 110025, India

103 Penang Road, #05–06/07, Visioncrest Commercial, Singapore 238467

Cambridge University Press is part of the University of Cambridge.

It furthers the University's mission by disseminating knowledge in the pursuit of education, learning, and research at the highest international levels of excellence.

www.cambridge.org
Information on this title: www.cambridge.org/9781316518243
DOI: 10.1017/9781009004978

First published 2022

Printed in the United Kingdom by TJ Books Limited, Padstow Cornwall

A catalogue record for this publication is available from the British Library.

Library of Congress Cataloging-in-Publication Data
Names: Owens, Patricia, 1975– editor.
Title: Women's international thought : towards a new canon / [edited by] Patricia
   Owens, Katharina Rietzler, Kimberly Hutchings, Sarah C. Dunstan.
Description: New York : Cambridge University Press, 2021. | Includes biblio-
   graphical references and index.
Identifiers: LCCN 2021005338 (print) | LCCN 2021005339 (ebook) |
   ISBN 9781316518243 (hardback) | ISBN 9781108999762 (paperback) |
   ISBN 9781009004978 (epub)
Subjects: LCSH: International relations–History. | Women–Political activity. |
   Women–Intellectual life. | Feminism–History. | Internationalism–History.
Classification: LCC JZ1253.2 .W683 2021 (print) | LCC JZ1253.2 (ebook) |
   DDC 327.1092/52–dc23
LC record available at https://lccn.loc.gov/2021005338
LC ebook record available at https://lccn.loc.gov/2021005339

ISBN 978-1-316-51824-3 Hardback
ISBN 978-1-108-99976-2 Paperback

Contents

6. Diplomacy and Foreign Policy

7. World Peace

8. World Economy

Preface and Acknowledgments

All scholarship is a collective endeavor, but this book, and the context in which it was completed, has taught us more about the necessities of collective intellectual work, and its material and emotional conditions, than we would have liked. The COVID-19 pandemic and first national lockdown came to our cities just as we completed the first draft of the book, but with a lot more work to do. We began copy-editing and proof-checking during our third lockdown. Even before the coronavirus, we were conscious of the extent to which intellectual labor depends on other forms of labor, often unacknowledged and provided by others. We would thus like to begin, rather than end, these acknowledgments by expressing our gratitude to our parents, partners, children, friends, and colleagues who allowed us to complete this work under multiple lockdowns and deliver it to the Press.

Women's International Thought: Towards a New Canon is the companion volume to *Women's International Thought: A New History*, a multidisciplinary collection of in-depth essays on over a dozen of the thinkers included here.[1] We would strongly encourage readers to consult those essays, written by some of the leading historians and IR scholars working today. In their different ways, individually and collectively, these essays have deepened our understanding of the practices and locations of international thought and immeasurably improved the curation of this anthology. We thus acknowledge and thank Lucian M. Ashworth, Keisha N. Blain, Catia Confortini, Geoffrey Field, Kimberly Hutchings, Andrew Jewett, Helen M. Kinsella, Vivian M. May, Tamson Pietsch, Or Rosenboim, Barbara Savage, Robbie Shilliam, Glenda Sluga, Imaobong Umoren, and Natasha Wheatley.

---

[1] Patricia Owens and Katharina Rietzler (eds.), *Women's International Thought: A New History* (Cambridge: Cambridge University Press, 2021). They include Anna Julia Cooper, Rosa Luxemburg, Simone Weil, Eslanda Robeson, Elizabeth Lippincott McQueen, Amy Ashwood Garvey, Elizabeth Wiskemann, F. Melian Stawell, Emily Greene Balch, Merze Tate, Barbara Wootton, Vera Micheles Dean, and Krystyna Marek, among others.

As stated in the preface to the first volume, *A New History* is not the last word, but a beginning. We feel this even more strongly about this second volume. Its subtitle – *Towards a New Canon* – is the result of lengthy discussions and a compromise with the Press. We are very conscious of the limitations of thinking in terms of canonical thinkers and texts. As we discuss in more detail in the Introduction to this work, canons are the product of deeply biased selection and reception processes. Even efforts to expand intellectual canons are beset with problems. We thus strongly emphasize the "*Towards*" in our subtitle, with its implication of movement, and thus travel, interchange, and exchange. It would go against the very spirit of our historical and theoretical project to seek to secure and fix a new canon of international thought.

This book is the second major publication of our Leverhulme Trust Research Project on Women and the History of International Thought (RPG-2017-319). We are grateful to the Trust for its generosity, affording us some of the time we have spent on this work but also, even more tangibly, the funds necessary to republish some of the works included here. May we also take this opportunity to acknowledge again those who supported and advised us during the initial application to the Trust, including our three Project Advisors, David Armitage, Robert Vitalis, and Penny Weiss, as well as Duncan Bell, Lene Hansen, Andrew Hurrell, Helen McCarthy, Iain McDaniel, Susan Pedersen, Jan Selby, Glenda Sluga, and Rorden Wilkinson.

The Radcliffe Institute for Advanced Study at Harvard University extended its generosity to us once again with funds to workshop this book in March 2020, though this event had to be cancelled due to the COVID-19 pandemic. We nonetheless thank Radcliffe and wish to recognize its hitherto unacknowledged part in the history of international thought. We also want to acknowledge and thank the many people who devoted time in support of the planned workshop: David Armitage, our Harvard co-sponsor and Project Advisor, Wendy Frohlich and Maura Madden, for administrative support, and all the participants, Keisha N. Blain, Catia Confortini, Adom Getachew, Helen M. Kinsella, Craig Murphy, Robbie Shilliam, Hilda Smith, Robert Vitalis, and Joanna Wood. For sending detailed comments on draft portions of the book we're especially grateful to David Armitage, Keisha N. Blain, Molly Cochran, Catia Confortini, Adom Getachew, Helen M. Kinsella, Helen McCarthy, Vanessa Ogle, Barbara Savage, Robbie Shilliam, and Natasha Wheatley.

We also wish to thank the organizers and participants of the invited talks, workshops, and conferences where we have presented ideas that have fed into this volume, including at Cambridge University, Duke

University, Sydney University, Freie Universität Berlin, Oxford University, London School of Economics, University of Glasgow, University of Sussex, University of Kent, the Society for the History of Women in the Americas, the British Association of American Studies, the British International Studies Association, and the United Nations Library in Geneva, as well as events that had to be cancelled due to COVID-19, including in Oxford, Durham, Edinburgh, and Glasgow, and an International Studies Association Annual Convention.

Very special thanks must also go to our project administrators, Sharon Krummel and Dawn Tohill, for their major work in pursuing and securing the permissions to republish the selections that comprise the majority of this volume. In particular, many archivists were extraordinarily helpful, and we wish to thank Sue Donnelly at the London School of Economics Library; Wendy E. Chmielewski, curator of the Swarthmore College Peace Collection; and Ellen M. Shea, Head of Research Services at the Schlesinger Library on the History of Women in America. So too would we like to thank Maureen Moynagh, Professor of English at St. Francis Xavier University, for her help in securing certain selections. We did experience some frustrations. We were refused permission to republish from Elizabeth Fisher Read's 1925 book *International Law and International Relations*. This was first published by the American Foundation for Studies in Government, an interest group founded by Read's partner Esther Lape to support US involvement in a world court. At some point, Cengage Global, a major multinational education company, acquired the rights to this "product" and refused our repeated requests to republish on the basis of a "business decision" that would not be further explained. We are grateful to all the very many other archivists, publishers, and other permissions holders for responding so positively and constructively to requests. In this regard, we are particularly grateful to the holders of the copyright of the image on our front cover. The image is a reproduction of a work by Harlem Rennaissance sculptor Augusta Savage. Commissioned for the 1939 World's Fair in New York, the original was a 16-foot sculpture, "Lift Every Voice and Sing," also known as "The Harp," or "Harp of Humanity." As Augusta Savage was unable to afford to have the work cast in bronze, it was destroyed at the end of the Fair. For permission to use this reproduction we are grateful to the Eartha M. M. White Collection, Thomas G. Carpenter Library, University of North Florida, Jacksonville, Florida.

It continues to be an absolute pleasure to work with our editors at Cambridge University Press. We're extraordinarily grateful to the enthusiasm, professionalism, and vision of Liz Friend-Smith and Atifa Jiwa as well as the four anonymous reviewers of the original proposal. We also wish to thank our production editor, Natasha Whelan, and copy-editor, Steven Holt, for the attention and care they have shown towards this work. We decided not to correct or comment on grammatical and related errors in the source texts, leaving them as they were in the original work.

Patricia Owens, Katharina Rietzler, Kimberly Hutchings, and Sarah C. Dunstan

Permissions

Every effort has been made to contact the relevant copyright holders for the extracts reproduced in this book. In the event of any error, the publisher will be pleased to make corrections in any reprints or future editions. The publishers and the editors are grateful for permission to reproduce the extracts found in this book:

Field and Discipline

Jessie W. Hughan (co-authored with Nicholas Kelley), "A Course in International Relations," *Intercollegiate Socialist*, 3:3 (February–March 1915): 14–15.

Committee on the Bureau of International Research in Harvard University and Radcliffe College (n.d. *c.* 1923), "Foundation for Instruction in International Affairs," Schlesinger Library, Radcliffe Institute for Advanced Study, XIXB, Series 1, Minutes 1924–42. By permission of the Schlesinger Library, Harvard University.

Extracted from F. Melian Stawell, *The Growth of International Thought* (London: Thornton Butterworth, 1929), 7; 18–26.

Lucy Philip Mair, "International Relations as an Independent Subject," 20 February 1934, 1–3. LSE\LSE School History \Box 10 Chairs. Reproduced under the UK Orphan Works Licensing Scheme. License OWLS000293-3 https://www .orphanworkslicensing.service.gov.uk/view-register/details?owls Number=OWLS000293-3&searchQuery=lucy%20philip% 20mair&filter=All.

Merze Tate, "Teaching of International Relations in Negro Colleges," *The Quarterly Review of Higher Education among Negroes*, 15 (July 1947): 149–153. By permission of the university archivist at Johnson C. Smith University (publisher of *The Quarterly Review of Higher Education among Negroes*).

Agnes Headlam-Morley, "Idealism and Realism in International Relations," an Inaugural Lecture delivered before the University of Oxford, 6 May 1949, 3–14. By permission of Agnes Headlam-Morley's nephew and copyright holder, Peter Headlam-Morley.

Annette Baker Fox (co-author with William T. R. Fox), "The Teaching of International Relations in the United States," *World Politics*, 13:3 (1961): 339–343. Reproduced with permission of Cambridge University Press through PLSclear.

Rachel Wall, "The Nature of Contemporary History," Radio Broadcast, 16 May 1966, recorded 18 March 1966.

Geopolitics and War

Extracted from Ellen Churchill Semple, *Influences of Geographic Environment on the Basis of Ratzel's System of Anthropo-Geography* (New York: Henry Holt & Co., 1911), 1–3; 12–13; 30–31.

Sylvia Pankhurst, "The Fascist World War (Ethiopia and Spain)," *New Times and Ethiopia News*, 1 August 1935, reprinted in *The Sylvia Pankhurst Reader*, ed. Kathryn Dodd (Manchester: Manchester University Press, 1993), 214–216. By permission of the Sylvia Pankhurst Literary Estate.

THE MEDITERRANEAN IN POLITICS by Monroe (1938) 1,300w from pp. 66–69. In abridged form by permission of Oxford University Press.

Harold Sprout, Margaret Sprout, *Toward a New Order of Sea Power: American Naval Policy and the World Scene, 1918–1922* (London: H. Milford, Oxford University Press, 1940), 18–33. Republished with permission of Princeton University Press; permission conveyed through Copyright Clearance Center.

Extracted from Claudia Jones, "What We Must Now Do about India," *Weekly Review*, 25 August 1942, 8–10.

Excerpt(s) from THE PROMISE OF POLITICS by Hannah Arendt, copyright © 2005 by The Literary Trust of Hannah Arendt and Jerome Kohn. Used by permission of Schocken Books, an imprint of the Knopf Doubleday Publishing Group, a division of Penguin Random House LLC. All rights reserved.

Pearl Harbor: Warning and Decision, Roberta Wohlstetter, Copyright © 1962 by the Board of Trustees of the Leland Stanford Junior University. Renewed 1990. All rights reserved. Used with the permission of Stanford University Press, www.sup.org.

Mary McCarthy, *Vietnam* (New York: Harcourt, Brace & World, 1967), 11–20. By permission of the Mary McCarthy Literary Estate.

Imperialism

Extracted from Jessie Fauset, "Impressions of the Second Pan-African Congress," *Crisis. A Record of the Darker Races*, 23:1 (November 1921): 12–18. Du Bois, W. E. Burghardt (editor), New York: National Association for the Advancement of Colored People.

Lillian M. Penson, "The London West India Interest in the Eighteenth Century," *The English Historical Review*, 36:143 (1921): 373–392. In abridged form by permission of Oxford University Press.

Anna Julia Cooper, *Slavery and the French and Haitian Revolutions* (New York: Edwin Mellen Press, 1988. Reprint 1925). By permission of the Edwin Mellen Press.

Extracted from Lilian Knowles, "Leading Features of the Economic History of the Great Powers in the Nineteenth Century," *Economic Development in the Nineteenth Century: France, Germany, Russia, and the United States* (London: Augustus M. Kelley, 1932), 3–13.

NATIVE ADMINISTRATION IN NIGERIA by Perham (1937) 3,240w from pp. 350–360. In abridged form by permission of Oxford University Press.

Extracted from Sibyl Crowe, "Introduction," *The Berlin West African Conference, 1884–1885* (London: Longmans Green and Co., 1942), 3–7. Reproduced under the UK Orphan Works Licensing Scheme. License OWLS000293-4. https://www.orphanworkslicensing.service.gov.uk/view-register/details?owlsNumber=OWLS000293-4&searchQuery=crowe&filter=All.

Extracted from Amy Jacques Garvey, "Chinese Milk Africans in the Carribbean," *The African* (January 1946).

Mary Macdonald Proudfoot, *Britain and the United States in the Caribbean: A Comparative Study in Methods of Development* (Faber & Faber, 1954), 245–248. Republished with permission of ABC-CLIO, LLC; permission conveyed through Copyright Clearance Center.

Anticolonialism

Jane Nardal, *La Dépêche africaine* (15 February 1928): 5–6. Translated in T. Denean Sharpley-Whiting, *Negritude*

Women (Minneapolis, MN: University of Minnesota Press, 2002), 105–107. Copyright 2002 by the Regents of the University of Minnesota.

Extracted from Dorothy Macardle, *The Irish Republic* (London: Victor Gollancz, 1937), 143–152.

Una Marson, "To Joe and Ben" (1937), *Selected Poems*, ed. Alison Donnell (Leeds: Peepal Tree Press, 2011), 133–136. Permission granted by Peepal Tree Press.

Nancy Cunard, interview with George Padmore, *The White Man's Duty: An Analysis of the Colonial Question in Light of the Atlantic Charter* (London: W. H. Allen & Co., 1942). Permission granted by the Literary Estate of Nancy Cunard.

Simone Weil, "The Colonial Question and the Destiny of the French People," in *Simone Weil on Colonialism: An Ethic of the Other*, trans. J. P. Little (New York: Rowman & Littlefield Publishing Co., 2003), 102–117. Reproduced with permission of Rowman and Littlefield Publishing Group Inc. through PLSclear.

Suzanne Césaire, "Le grand camouflage," *Tropiques* 13–14 (September 1945): 267–273. Translated in T. Denean Sharpley-Whiting, *Negritude Women* (Minneapolis, MN: University of Minnesota Press, 2002), 135–140. Copyright 2002 by the Regents of the University of Minnesota.

Eslanda Robeson, *African Journey* (London: Victor Gollancz, 1946), 28–29. Republished with permission of ABC-CLIO, LLC; permission conveyed through Copyright Clearance Center.

Extracts reprinted with permission from Ayebia Clarke Publishing Ltd © *Claudia Jones: Beyond Containment* Edited by Carole Boyce Davies (Ayebia: 2011 Oxfordshire UK).

International Law and International Organization

Extracted from Mary Parker Follett, *The New State* (New York: Longmans, Green & Co., 1918), 350–356.

Extracted from Sarah Wambaugh, *A Monograph on Plebiscites* (New York: Oxford University Press, 1920), 27–33.

Extracted from Lucie A. Zimmern, *Must the League Fail?* (London: Martin Hopkinson, 1932), 25–33, 60–63. Reproduced under the UK Orphan Works Licensing Scheme. License OWLS000293-5. https://www.orphanworks licensing.service.gov.uk/view-register/details?owlsNumber= OWLS000293-5&searchQuery=OWLS000293-1&filter=All.

Extracted from Barbara Wootton, "Socialism and Federation" (1941), reprinted in Patrick Ransome (ed.), *Studies in Federal Planning* (London: Macmillan, 1943 [reprint: London, Lothian Foundation, 1990]), 286–292.

Krystyna Marek, *The Identity and Continuity of States in Public International Law* (Geneva: Droz, 1954, 2nd ed. 1968), 1–3. By permission of Librairie Droz S.A.

Extracted from M. Margaret Ball and Hugh B. Killough, *International Relations* (London: Stevens & Sons, 1956), 13–23. Reproduced under the UK Orphan Works Licensing Scheme. License OWLS000293-1. https://www.orphanworks licensing.service.gov.uk/view-register/details?owlsNumber= OWLS000293-1&searchQuery=OWLS000293-1&filter=All.

Pauli Murray (co-written with Leslie Rubin), *The Constitution and Government of Ghana* (London: Sweet & Maxwell Limited, 1961), v, 32–33, 39–40, 152–157. Reproduced with permission of Thomas Reuters (Professional) Ltd through PLS Clear.

Louise W. Holborn, *Refugees: A Problem of Our Time* (Metuchen, NJ: Scarecrow Press, 1975). Permission granted by Professor Hannah H. Gray, Louise Holborn's niece and copyright holder.

Diplomacy and Foreign Policy

Extracted from Margaret Lambert, "The Problem," *The Saar* (London: Faber and Faber, 1934), 1–11. Reproduced by permission of Katia Marsh, executor of the Enid Marx Estate.

Extracted from Merze Tate, "The War Aims of World War I and World War II and Their Relation to the Darker Peoples of the World," *Journal of Negro Education* 12:3 (1943): 521–523; 531–532.

THE ROME–BERLIN AXIS: A HISTORY OF THE RELATIONS BETWEEN HITLER AND MUSSOLINI by Wiskemann (1949) 3,150w from pp. 339–346. In abridged form by permission of Oxford University Press.

Extracted from Vera Micheles Dean, "Preface," *Foreign Policy without Fear* (New York: McGraw-Hill, 1953), vii–x.

Adda B. Bozeman, "India's Foreign Policy Today: Reflections upon Its Sources," *World Politics* 10:2 (1958): 261–266, 267–273. Reproduced with permission of Cambridge University Press through PLSclear.

Extracted from Judith Shklar, "Decisionism," in Carl J. Friedrich, ed., *Nomos VII: Rational Decision* (New York:

Atherton Press, 1964 [Reprint: London: Routledge, 2017]),
11–17.

Extracted from Coral Bell, "The Debate," in *The Debatable
Alliance: An Essay in Anglo-American Relations* (Oxford:
Oxford University Press, 1964), 1–7.

Agatha Ramm, "War and Revolution: Germany 1909–1919," in
Germany 1789–1919: A Political History (London: Methuen,
1967), 417–420. Reproduced with permission of Informa UK
Limited through PLSClear.

World Peace

Extracted from Bertha von Suttner, "Universal Peace – From a
Woman's Standpoint," *North American Review* 169 (July
1899): 50–69.

Extracted from Emily Greene Balch, "The Time for Making
Peace," in Jane Addams, Emily G. Balch, and Alice
Hamilton (eds.), *Women at the Hague: The International
Congress of Women and Its Results* (New York: Macmillan,
1915), 111–123.

Extracted from Helena Swanwick, "Women and War," pamphlet for Union of Democratic Control (1915), 1–14.

Extracted from Mary Church Terrell, "Speech and Resolution
Presented at International Women's Congress, Zurich,
in German and French," 1919. Mary Church Terrell
Papers: Speeches and Writings, 1953; 1919, Library
of Congress.

Jane Addams, *Peace and Bread in Time of War* (New York: King's
Crown Press, [1922] 1945), 132–133. Reproduced by permission of the US section of the Women's International League
for Peace and Freedom.

Vera Brittain, "Peace and the Public Mind," in Margaret Storm
Jameson, ed., *Challenge to Death* (New York: 1935), 47–55.
Permission granted by Mark Bostridge and T. J. Brittain-
Catlin, Literary Executors for the Estate of Vera Brittain.

Helene Stöcker, "Review of *The Twenty Years' Crisis, 1919–1939*
by E. H. Carr" (1940), unpublished manuscript, Swarthmore
College Peace Collection. By permission of the Swarthmore
Peace Collection.

Edith Sampson, "Address by the Hon. Mrs. Edith Sampson,"
Washington University, St. Louis, Missouri, 26 October
1952. Edith Sampson Papers, Schlesinger Library, Harvard
University. Permission granted by Judge Thomas Spurlock,

Edith Sampson's nephew, and Schlesinger Library, Harvard University.

World Economy

Rosa Luxemburg, "Protective Tariffs and Accumulation," [1913]), 426–433. Reproduced from ACCUMULATION OF CAPITAL RC, 1st Edition by Rosa Luxemburg, published by Routledge. © Routledge 2003, reproduced by arrangement with Taylor & Francis Books UK.

Extracted from Persia Campbell, "Foreign Competition for Chinese Labour," in *Chinese Coolie Emigration to Countries within the British Empire* (London: P. S. King and Son, 1923), 86–96.

Lilian M. Friedländer, "Labour Problems in Two Worlds," *Economica*, 25 (April 1929): 4–14. Reproduced by permission of John Wiley & Sons Limited through PLSClear.

Extracted from Eleanor Lansing Dulles, *The Bank for International Settlements at Work* (New York: Macmillan, 1932), vii; 1–4.

Ursula K. Hicks, "Learning about Economic Development," *Oxford Economic Papers*, 9:1 (1957): 1–8; 13. In abridged form by permission of Oxford University Press.

Sudha R. Shenoy, "The Coming Serfdom in India," *The Freeman*, 8 (1966): 35–39. Abridged, under Creative Commons license.

Edith Penrose, *The Large International Firm in Developing Countries: The International Petroleum Industry* (London: Allen & Unwin, 1968), 80–86. Permission granted by Allen & Unwin.

Susan Strange, "Targets and Parameters," in *Sterling and British Policy: A Political Study of an International Currency in Decline* (Oxford: Oxford University Press, 1971), 334–337. Reproduced with permission of Chatham House through PLSClear.

Men, Women, and Gender

Anna Julia Cooper, "Woman versus Indian," *A Voice from the South* (Oxford: Oxford University Press, 1988 [1892]), 118–124. Reproduced with Permission of Oxford University Press through PLS Clear.

Extracted from Vernon Lee, "The Economic Parasitism of Women" (London and Leipzig: T. Fisher Unwin, 1908), 136–141; 148–150; 154–157.

Extracted from Ellen Churchill Semple, "Geographical Research as a Field for Women," *The Fiftieth Anniversary of the Opening of Vassar College October 10–13, 1915* (Boston, MA: D. B. Updike, Merrymount Press, 1916), 70–80.

Extracted from Emily G. Balch, "Women's Work for Peace," *The World Tomorrow*, 4–5 (1922): 334–336.

Virginia Woolf, *Three Guineas* (London: Hogarth Press, 1938), 191–198. By permission of the Society of Authors as the Literary Representative of the Estate of Virginia Woolf.

Extracted from Pearl S. Buck and Eslanda Robeson, *American Argument* (London: Methuen & Co., 1950), 67–69. With permission of Edgar S. Walsh, the sole trustee of the Pearl S. Buck Literary Trust.

Excerpt from THE SECOND SEX by Simone de Beauvoir and translated by Constance Borde and Sheila Malovany-Chevallier. Used by permission of Alfred A. Knopf, an imprint of the Knopf Doubleday Publishing Group, a division of Penguin Random House LLC. All rights reserved. From *The Second Sex* by Simone De Beauvoir published by Vintage Classics. First published as *Le deuxième sexe* by Simone de Beauvoir © 1949 by Éditions Gallimard, Paris. Translation copyright © 2009 by Constance Borde and Sheila Malovany-Chevallier. Reprinted by permission of The Random House Group Limited.

Jeanne Vialle, 'Femmes africaines/African Women', *Civilisations* 1:4 (1951): 55–58. By permission of the journal *Civilisations*.

Public Opinion and Education

Extracted from Nannie H. Burroughs, "The Colored Woman and Her Relation to the Domestic Problem," in I. Garland Penn and J. W. E. Bowen (eds.), *The United Negro. His Problems and His Progress, Containing the Addresses and Proceedings the Negro Young People's Christian and Educational Congress, Held August 6–11, 1902* (Atlanta, GA: D. E. Luther Publishing, 1902), 324–329.

Extracted from Fannie Fern Andrews, "The Relation of Teachers to the Peace Movement," *Education* 28 (1908): 279–282.

Extracted from Eileen Power, "The Teaching of History and World Peace," in F. S. Marvin (ed.), *The Evolution of World Peace* (London: Humphrey Milford/Oxford University Press, 1921), 179–191.

Virginia Gildersleeve, "The Creation of the International Mind" (*c.* 1931/1932), Gildersleeve Papers, Columbia University, Box 62 – Speeches at UN, AAUW, & IFUW, Education & International Subjects, Folder: Some Speeches on World Peace and International Subjects, Rare Book & Manuscript Library, Columbia University in the City of New York.

Extracted from Merze Tate, *The Disarmament Illusion: The Movement for a Limitation of Armaments to 1907* (New York: MacMillan Company, 1942), 151–155; 157–161.

Extracted from Margaret Read, *Problems of Mass Education*, Current Affairs No. 33 (London: Bureau of Current Affairs, 1947). Reproduced under the UK Orphan Works Licensing Scheme. License OWLS000296. https://www .orphanworkslicensing.service.gov.uk/view-register/details?owls Number=OWLS000296-1&searchQuery=OWLS000296& filter=All.

Extracted from Dorothy Fosdick, *Common Sense and World Affairs* (New York: Harcourt, Brace, 1955), 181–182; 185–193. Reproduced under the UK Orphan Works Licensing Scheme. License OWLS000293-6. https://www .orphanworkslicensing.service.gov.uk/view-register/details?owls Number=OWLS000293-6&searchQuery=OWLS000293-1& filter=All.

Amy Ashwood Garvey, "The Birth of the Universal Negro Improvement Association," in Tony Martin (ed.), *The Pan-African Connection: From Slavery to Garvey and Beyond* (Dover, MA: The Majority Press, 1983), 223–226. Reproduced by permission of the Majority Press.

Population, Nation, Immigration

Rosa Luxemburg, "The Right of Nations to Self-Determination," in *The National Question – Selected Writings by Rosa Luxemburg*, ed. Horace B. Davis (New York: Monthly Review Press, 1976). By permission of the Monthly Review Press.

Extracted from Margaret Sanger, "Conscripted Motherhood," in *Pivot of Civilization* (New York: Brentano, 1922), 28–32; 48–53.

Extracted from Annie Marion Maclean, *Modern Immigration* (Philadelphia, PA: J. B. Lippincott Co., 1925), 211; 213–218; 228.

Extracted from Caroline Playne, *Neuroses of the Nations* (London: George Allen and Unwin, 1925), 54–61.

From Luisa Moreno, "Caravans of Sorrow: Noncitizen Americans of the Southwest," Address delivered to the Fourth Annual Conference of the American Committee for Protection of the Foreign Born, Washington DC, 3 March 1940.

Extracted from Shirley Graham, "Minority Peoples in China," *Freedomways*, 1:1 (Spring 1961): 95–101.

Technology, Progress, and Environment

Extracted from Bertha von Suttner, *The Barbarization of the Skies* (1912), trans. Belinda Cooper, ed. Hope Elizabeth May (Mount Pleasant: The Bertha von Suttner Project, 2016), 1–7.

Elizabeth Lippincott McQueen, "Air-Mindedness," Address to the Women's Aeronautic Association of California, 1934, USC 55, Box 3/Folder 4 – WIAA Events Pamphlet, [pamphlet], 1–5.

Extracted from Margaret Mead, section on bringing modern technologies into traditional cultures in Margaret Mead (ed.), *Cultural Relations and Technical Change: A Manual Prepared for the World Federation on Mental Health* (UNESCO: Paris, 1953), 309–315.

Religion and Ethics

Zora Neale Hurston. Renewed 1966 by Joel Hurston and John C. Hurston. Used by permission of HarperCollins Publishers.

Simone Weil, *Letter to a Priest*, trans A. F. Mills, introduction by Mario van der Ruhr (London and New York: Routledge, 2002. Reprint, 1951), 15–19; 51–55. Reproduced with permission of Informa UK Limited through PLSClear.

Extracted from Barbara Ward, *Faith and Freedom: A Study of Western Society* (London: Hamish Hamilton, 1954), 237–241; 266–269.

G. E. M. Anscombe, *Mr Truman's Degree* (Oxford: Oxonian Press, 1956), 6–12. Permission granted by Elizabeth Anscombe's literary executor, Dr. M. C. Gormally.

Introduction

Women defined and transformed the substance and practice of international relations as it emerged as a separate intellectual field examining
the relations between peoples, empires, and states at the turn of the
twentieth century. They engaged the international politics of their time
in the context of diverse colonial and anticolonial struggles, inter-
imperial wars and superpower rivalry, and nationalist, ideological, and
political conflict. They addressed war, racial hierarchy and immigration,
labor organization and world economy, colonial administration, foreign
policy and diplomacy, international law and organization, religion and
ethics, technological transformation, and environmental destruction.
This wide-ranging work took many forms and genres and was produced
in a variety of professional and intellectual contexts. It was well known
and influential in its time. And, yet, examining the contemporary field of
international relations, its history and scholars, it is as if this past had
never existed, as if women had hardly lived, thought, and practiced as
scholars, as advisors and policy makers, as journalists, and as public
intellectuals.[1] This anthology proves this conventional version of international relations history wrong.

This is the first anthology of women's international thought, focusing
on Anglo-American locations from the late nineteenth century to the
long mid-twentieth century. That this is the first such volume reflects two
things: first, the centrality of women to early international relations
discourses and, second, the erasure and exclusion of women from its
history and conceptualization. Partly due to the novelty of the subject
matter, the fluidity of its intellectual boundaries, and its co-emergence
with the expansion of women's higher education at the turn of the
twentieth century, large numbers of women scholars and teachers were
formative in the intellectual and institutional development of the study of
international relations. Women founded or co-founded some of its

---

[1] Patricia Owens and Katharina Rietzler (eds.), *Women's International Thought: A New
History* (Cambridge: Cambridge University Press, 2021).

1

earliest teaching and research centers, including the Harvard/Radcliffe Bureau of International Research and the Geneva School of International Studies. They worked in and moved between foreign affairs think tanks or in other institutional locations such as women's colleges. Others wrote on international relations from parallel professional contexts outside academe, such as journalism, activism, social work, and teaching.[2] International relations was crucial to the work of many canonical women intellectuals. Indeed, these women helped to produce the very notion of international relations during the twentieth century.

Nonetheless, this vast store of ideas and contexts is almost completely absent from existing international intellectual histories and even from histories of the academic discipline of International Relations (IR). Contemporary historians and scholars of international relations are aware of how major global developments are produced in and through the terms of gender, race, and class.[3] Yet international intellectual and disciplinary histories have lagged. It is as if there is something unthinkable about historical women's thought on international relations, something distinctive about the strictures imposed on these thinkers and responses to their work. Indeed, there is: a structural and disciplinary production of women as incapable of and incidental to knowledge about international relations except in highly specific ways or at certain moments in time. We see this in current surveys and anthologies of international thinkers, which imply that women in the past never engaged intellectually with world politics until the 1980s and the re-emergence of feminist IR.[4]

---

[2] Valeska Huber, Tamson Pietsch, and Katharina Rietzler, "Women's International Thought and the New Professions, 1900–1940," *Modern Intellectual History*, 18:1 (2021): 121–145; Katharina Rietzler, "U.S. Foreign Policy Think Tanks and Women's Intellectual Labor, 1920–1950," *Diplomatic History*, 46:3 (2022, in press).

[3] Cynthia Enloe, *Bananas, Beaches and Bases: Making Feminist Sense of International Politics* (Berkeley, CA: University of California Press, 1990); Ann Towns, *Women and States: Norms and Hierarchies in International Society* (Cambridge: Cambridge University Press, 2010); Helen M. Kinsella, *The Image before the Weapon: A Critical History of the Distinction between Combatant and Civilian* (Ithaca, NY: Cornell University Press, 2011); Julie V. Gottlieb, *"Guilty Women," Foreign Policy, and Appeasement in Inter-War Britain* (London: Palgrave, 2015); Glenda Sluga and Patricia Clavin (eds.), *Internationalisms: A Twentieth-Century History* (Cambridge: Cambridge University Press, 2017).

[4] Patricia Owens, "Women and the History of International Thought," *International Studies Quarterly*, 62:3 (2018): 467–481. Some IR scholars have focused on historical women thinkers, usually feminist work. See Lucian M. Ashworth, "Feminism, War and the Prospects for International Government: Helena Swanwick (1864–1939) and the Lost Feminists of Interwar International Relations," *International Feminist Journal of Politics*, 13:1 (2011): 24–42; Catia Confortini, *Intelligent Compassion: Feminist Critical Methodology in the Women's International League for Peace and Freedom* (Oxford: Oxford University Press, 2012); Molly Cochran, "The 'Newer Ideals' of Jane Addams's Progressivism: A Realistic Utopia of Cosmopolitan Justice," in Molly Cochran and Cornelia Navari (eds.), *Progressivism and US Foreign Policy between the World Wars* (New York: Palgrave

Despite women being at the forefront of international thought throughout the twentieth century, their ideas were often stolen and, if not, then ignored. The very use of the English term "international thought" can be traced to Florence Melian Stawell's *The Growth of International Thought*, published in 1929. Her work is the first of a highly distinctive genre: surveys of canonical "international" thinkers, a genre from which, ironically, she and all women and people of color were later omitted.[5] Indicating so much of the fate and contingency of women's international thinking, Stawell's idea to write the book came from her mentor, liberal internationalist Gilbert Murray, after he reviewed Stawell's proposal for a different book on the League of Nations. Murray appropriated Stawell's idea for himself and proposed that she write a history of international thought instead.[6] In republishing an extract from Stawell's book, we are retrieving and honoring the unintended effect of an intellectual theft at the origin of twentieth-century Anglophone histories of "international thought."[7] More broadly, this volume reveals a major distortion in current understandings of histories of this interdisciplinary field, of how international relations was conceived, and does so, in part, by expanding its archives to include a wide variety of genres, and professional and intellectual contexts.[8]

Much of this important and wide-ranging work is little known, difficult to access, or out of print, further contributing to the marginalization of

Macmillan, 2017), 143–165; J. Ann Tickner and Jacqui True, "A Century of International Relations Feminism: From World War One Women's Peace Pragmatism to the Women, Peace and Security Agenda," *International Studies Quarterly*, 62:2 (2018): 221–233; Jan Stöckmann, "Women, Wars, and World Affairs: Recovering Feminist International Relations, 1915–39," *Review of International Studies*, 44:2 (2018): 215–235.

[5] Kimberly Hutchings and Patricia Owens, "Women Thinkers and the Canon of International Thought: Recovery, Rejection and Reconstitution," *American Political Science Review*, 115.2 (2021). 347–359.

[6] Glenda Sluga, "From F. Melian Stawell to E. Greene Balch: International and Internationalist Thinking at the Gender Margins, 1919–1947," in Patricia Owens and Katharina Rietzler (eds.), *Women's International Thought: A New History* (Cambridge: Cambridge University Press, 2021), 223–243.

[7] For a wider study of such phenomena see Dale Spender, *Women of Ideas and What Men Have Done to Them: From Aphra Behn to Adrienne Rich* (London: Ark Paperbacks, 1983).

[8] There is also a wider historical literature on women's formative role in international organizations, networks, and diplomacy. For a selection see Linda Schott, *Reconstructing Women's Thoughts: The Women's International League for Peace and Freedom before World War II* (Stanford, CA: Stanford University Press, 1997); Christine von Oertzen, *Science, Gender, and Internationalism: Women's Academic Networks, 1917–1955* (London: Palgrave, 2012); Helen McCarthy, *Women of the World: The Rise of the Female Diplomat* (London: Bloomsbury, 2014); Karen Garner, *Women and Gender in International History* (London: Bloomsbury, 2018).

women's international thought. Some of it can be found only in institutional or other archives and took many forms, including speeches, journalism, letters, novels, lectures, radio broadcasts, internal memoranda, funding bids, book reviews, poems, and memoirs, a selection of which appears in this volume, alongside scholarly monographs and articles. The use of different genres reflects not just opportunity or its absence, but also intellectual and political choice. Rosa Luxemburg, Amy Jacques Garvey, and Amy Ashwood Garvey, among others, formulated their analyses of world order in pamphlets and newspapers to quickly and inexpensively circulate their ideas to the audiences they wished to reach and mobilize. Una Marson and Jane Vialle used poetry and short-form essays to lay bare the cultural as well as political workings of empire in a way that other genres could not.[9] Retrieving and analyzing this work prompts deeper reflection on the dynamics of knowledge production in histories of international thought, a field that always existed at the interstices of theory and practice.

This intellectual production and its practical applications were recognized in its own time, both outside and inside academe, and often centrally so in fields that either pre-dated or were adjacent to the academic discipline of IR. In making selections of this work available in anthology form, some of it for the first time, we begin the necessary and basic work of recovery, reconstruction, and analysis of these international intellectual histories without being defined by the history and current terms of reference within the discipline of IR. In so doing, we model a different approach to histories of international thought, international theory, and pedagogy.[10] Gendered, racialized, sexual, and class hierarchies have been a fundamental enabling and disabling condition for the production and reception of all knowledge about international relations. Hence the exclusion of historical women from histories of international thought does not only concern the past of international thinking or only "women." It has shaped *all* international thought and is implicated in a range of academic practices today, from teaching methods and syllabus

---

[9] On the potential of poetic knowledge as political thought see Gary Wilder, *Freedom Time: Negritude, Decolonization and the Future of the World* (Durham, NC: Duke University Press, 2015), 1–16.

[10] Recent works in histories of international thought include Edward Keene, *International Political Thought: A Historical Introduction* (Cambridge: Polity, 2005); David Armitage, *Foundations of International Thought* (Cambridge: Cambridge University Press, 2013); Lucian Ashworth, *A History of International Thought: From the Origins of the Modern State to Academic IR* (London: Routledge, 2014); Duncan Bell, *Reordering the World: Essays on Liberalism and Empire* (Princeton, NJ: Princeton University Press, 2016); Or Rosenboim, *The Emergence of Globalism: Visions of World Order in Britain and the United States, 1939–1950* (Princeton, NJ: Princeton University Press, 2017).

design to citation practices. Like canon formation, anthologizing is fundamentally pedagogical and often conservative, but not without radical potential.[11]

At the turn of the twentieth century, the study of international relations was a wide-ranging field drawing on methods and approaches from History, Classics, Colonial Administration and Anthropology, Economics, Law, and Political Science. IR developed as a separate subdiscipline of Political Science in the United States during the 1950s and from the 1970s in Britain.[12] Recognizing the scholarly and popular circulation of women's writings in their time, both as a broad interdisciplinary field and then later as a separate academic discipline, raises serious questions about the politics of IR's disciplinary formation and the appropriation and/or erasure of this large body of international thought.[13]

Canons are formed to establish and legitimize new academic disciplines or intellectual fields, outlining their central questions and providing for their pedagogical reproduction. Heavily influenced by Political Theory's canon, the proliferation of works seeking to establish the legitimacy of disciplinary IR from the 1950s focused on a number of all-male "Fathers" of international thought.[14] This is nowhere more evident than in the subsequent proliferation of eponymous "schools" of international theory, Hobbesian, Lockean, Kantian, Marxian, Foucauldian, and so on. The existing canon of "great" thinkers and texts was constructed as a conversation by, for, and between white men. These homosocial

---

[11] See, for example, Nancy Cunard (ed.), *Negro: An Anthology* (London: Wishart, 1934), discussed later in this volume. Also see Peggy McIntosh, *Interactive Phases of Curricular RE-Vision: A Feminist Perspective*. Working Paper No. 124 (Wellesley, MA: Wellesley College Center for Research on Women, 1983); Joan Wallach Scott, *Gender and the Politics of History*, revised ed. (New York: Columbia University Press, 1999).

[12] There is much contestation around the periodization. Nonetheless, we draw a fundamental distinction between histories of the wider field of international relations and the academic discipline of IR as well as wider histories of international thought by figures who had no, or very little, relationship to IR inside the academy. The selections in this volume encompass each domain, as well as thinkers who worked across both. See the discussion between Robert Vitalis and Nicolas Guilhot in "H-Diplo/ISSF Roundtable Review on Nicolas Guilhot (ed.). *The Invention of International Relations Theory: Realism, the Rockefeller Foundation, and the 1954 Conference on Theory.*" Available at http://h-diplo .org/ISSF/PDF/ISSF-Roundtable-3-5.pdf.

[13] Owens and Rietzler (eds.), *Women's International Thought*.

[14] Kenneth W. Thompson, *Fathers of International Thought: The Legacy of Political Theory* (Baton Rouge, LA: Louisiana State University Press, 1994). See also Hans J. Morgenthau and Kenneth W. Thompson (eds.), *Principles and Problems of International Politics: Selected Readings* (New York: Knopf, 1950); Stanley Hoffman, *Contemporary Theory in International Relations* (Englewood Cliffs, NJ: Prentice Hall, 1964); M. G. Forsyth, H. M. A. Keens-Soper, and P. Savigear (eds.), *The Theory of International Relations: Selected Texts from Gentili to Treitschke* (London: Routledge, 1970).

relationships may not have been sexual, though they often involved intellectual crushes.[15] They took a fraternal and mentoring form, and always involved the acknowledgment of "forefathers," even if the intention was patricidal.[16]

This process of IR's canon formation erased women and people of color, leading to an inaccurate and deficient account of the history of international thought.[17] This is no surprise. As feminist historians and theorists have long shown, canon formation is not a neutral exercise in which only the worthiest thinkers and genres are singled out. Expectations about intellectual greatness are highly gendered, racialized, and classed such that even the mediocre work of white men can be celebrated and canonized and the exceptional work of those gendered female and racialized as non-white can be ignored, appropriated, and/or maligned. Thinking with individual intellectuals and evaluating their work is necessary to understanding the history of international ideas. But it is not sufficient if it is premised on a narrow swath of individuals and scholarship and if it is retrospectively bounded by the received histories and contemporary assumptions of the contemporary academic discipline of IR. Rather, we need to recognize the diverse scholars and practitioners of international relations who, in turn, were grounded in distinct genres of writing, arrays of publications, actions, identities, and subject positions as fundamental to the histories of international thought.[18]

---

[15] Eve Kosofsky Sedgwick, *Between Men: English Literature and Male Homosocial Desire* (New York: Columbia University Press, 1985).

[16] Berenice A. Carroll, "The Politics of 'Originality': Women and the Class System of the Intellect," *Journal of Women's History*, 2:2 (1990): 147. So-called critical international theory also assumes a patrilineal history of international thought where inquiry into the IR canon is "generational in nature – and perhaps patricidal in execution." James Der Derian, "Introduction: Critical Investigations," in James Der Derian (ed.), *International Theory: Critical Investigations* (New York: New York University Press, 1995), 3.

[17] Hutchings and Owens, "Women Thinkers"; for analysis of the comparable process in History and Sociology see Gerda Lerner, "How the Historical Profession Became a Male Preserve," *Journal of Women's History*, 11:2 (1999): 221–223; Mary-Jo Deegan, "Early Women Sociologists and the American Sociological Society: Patterns of Exclusion and Participation," *American Sociologist*, 16 (1981): 14–24.

[18] Studies of Black women's international thought are by far the most advanced in this regard. See Barbara Ransby, *Eslanda: The Large and Unconventional Life of Mrs. Paul Robeson* (New Haven, CT: Yale University Press, 2003); Gerald Horne, *Race Woman: The Lives of Mrs. Shirley Graham Du Bois* (New York: New York University Press, 2002); Carol Boyce Davies, *Left of Karl Marx: The Political Life of Black Communist Claudia Jones* (Durham, NC: University of North Carolina Press, 2007); Gregg Andrews, *Thyra J. Edwards: Black Activist in the Global Freedom Struggle* (Columbia, MI: University of Missouri Press, 2011); Keisha N. Blain, *Set the World on Fire: Black Nationalist Women and the Global Struggle for Freedom* (Philadelphia, PA: University of Pennsylvania Press, 2018); Keisha N. Blain and Tiffany M. Gill (eds.), *To Turn the Whole World Over: Black Women and Internationalism* (Chicago, IL: University of Illinois Press, 2019).

This volume builds on and extends to histories of international thought work in the fields of women's and gender history and feminist theory, particularly Black feminist intellectual history and feminist political theory.[19] For some time, scholars in these fields have shown that it is not enough to simply add a few notable, almost always elite white or Ashkenazi Jewish women to existing canons. As we have seen in IR, recent efforts to expand the canon have included one or two historical women, those working before the late twentieth century, but never more than two in one volume. These figures are presented as exceptional individuals (Hannah Arendt, Susan Sontag) and/or primarily concerned with gender (Virginia Woolf, Simone de Beauvoir).[20]

Though a necessary and perhaps inevitable first step, this belated compensation for past neglect does little to expose the appropriations and omissions on which the slightly amended canon was built. It does not address how the production and reception of intellectual labour is deeply gendered, racialized, and classed. It does not account for the intimate and relational nature of intellectual production, for example the work of "canon-adjacent" figures or "wives of the canon," collaborators who were central to the production of "great texts" by "great men" but are erased in canon-formation.[21] And it rarely centers the multiple genres through which people thought about international relations. In other words, it is limited in its modifications and methods because it does not center gender, race, and class substantially, empirically, theoretically, and methodologically.

---

[19] See, especially, Hilda L. Smith and Bernice A. Carroll (eds.), *Women's Political and Social Thought: An Anthology* (Bloomington, IN: University of Indiana Press, 2000); Penny A. Weiss, *Canon Fodder: Historical Women Political Thinkers* (University Park, PA: Pennsylvania University Press, 2009) and Mia Bay, Farah J. Griffin, Martha S. Jones, and Barbara D. Savage (eds.), *Toward an Intellectual History of Black Women* (Chapel Hill, NC: University of North Carolina Press, 2015); Blain and Gill, *To Turn the Whole World Over*. Also see Gerda Lerner, *The Majority Finds Its Past: Placing Women in History* (Oxford: Oxford University Press, 1981); Joan Wallach Scott (ed.), *Feminism and History* (Oxford: Oxford University Press, 1996). Within international intellectual history see Glenda Sluga, "Turning International: *Foundations of Modern International Thought* and New Paradigms for Intellectual History," *History of European Ideas*, 41:1 (2015): 103–115.

[20] See Cerwyn Moore and Chris Farrands (eds.), *International Relations Theory and Philosophy: Interpretive Dialogues* (London: Routledge, 2010); Henrick Bliddal (ed.), *Classics of International Relations* (London: Routledge, 2013); Richard Ned Lebow, Peer Schouten, and Hidemi Suganami (eds.), *The Return of the Theorists: Dialogues with Great Thinkers in International Relations* (London: Palgrave, 2016). For analysis of women as "exceptional" see Joanna Russ, *How to Suppress Women's Writing* (London: Women's Press, 1983), 80.

[21] Jennifer Forestal and Menaka Philips, "Gender and the 'Great Man': Recovering Philosophy's 'Wives of the Canon,'" *Hypatia*, 33:4 (2018): 587–592.

Asking questions about women and histories of international thought allows us to identify and trace how these axes of difference organized intellectual production and reception of work on international relations. We refer to "historical women" to indicate both our temporal focus on the late nineteenth to long mid-twentieth centuries, and also to signal the discursive and historical constructs ("women") emergent from the sex/gender binary and intersecting axes of difference.[22] We understand "women" not as a biological category or ontological designation, but as an historical and intersectional identity which shapes and is shaped by racialized, national, class, and sexual identities and relations. This challenges any essentialization of gender or naturalization of "white women's IR."[23] There is no single axis of subordination that affected the production of international thought. Hence, there can be no such thing as a women's *tradition* of international thought, given the multiple intersecting relations of power that shape intellectual production.[24]

Thus, in this volume, we adopt a capacious understanding of the gendered history of international thought. Through the twentieth century, norms around gender and sexuality came under greater scrutiny and repeatedly shifted in ways that reflected and reinforced racial and class hierarchies.[25] Indeed, the deliberate exclusion of African Americans from IR's intellectual and disciplinary histories was constitutive of "American IR" because the early science of international relations was the science of race relations, taking the form of racism and white supremacy.[26] Black scholars were excluded as active agents and

---

[22] Kimberlé Crenshaw, "Demarginalizing the Intersection of Race and Sex: A Black Feminist Critique of Antidiscrimination Doctrine, Feminist Theory and Antiracist Politics," *University of Chicago Legal Forum*, 1 (1989): 139–167; Patricia Hill Collins, *Black Feminist Thought: Knowledge, Consciousness, and the Politics of Empowerment* (New York: Routledge, 1991). For a recent account of intersectionality as a tool against structural domination see Barbara Tomlinson, *Undermining Intersectionality: The Perils of Powerblind Feminism* (Philadelphia, PA: Temple University Press, 2018); Jennifer C. Nash, *Black Feminism Reimagined: After Intersectionality* (Durham, NC: Duke University Press, 2019).

[23] Owens, "Women and the History of International Thought," 467.

[24] Hutchings and Owens, "Women Thinkers."

[25] See Christina Crosby, *The Ends of History: Victorians and "The Women Question"* (New York: Routledge, 1991); Anne McClintock, *Imperial Leather: Race, Gender and Sexuality in the Colonial Context* (New York: Routledge, 1995); Leila Rupp, "Outing the Past: U.S. Queer History in Global Perspective," in Leila J. Rupp and Susan Kathleen Freeman (eds.), *Understanding and Teaching U.S. Lesbian, Gay, Bisexual, and Transgender History*, 2nd ed. (Madison, WI: University of Wisconsin Press, 2017), 17–30.

[26] Robert Vitalis, *White World Order, Black Power Politics: The Birth of American International Relations* (Ithaca, NY: Cornell University Press, 2015); Vineet Thakur and Peter Vale, *South Africa, Race and the Making of International Relations* (London: Rowman and Littlefield, 2020).

producers of international thought while people of color were objects of study and thought, as in works by Margery Perham, Lucy Philip Mair, Annette Baker Fox, and many others in this volume. Since international relations meant race relations, explicitly so in the first half of the twentieth century, international thinking itself is implicated in producing the meanings of racialized difference in the Anglo-American world, including that of a white "Anglosphere."[27] Many of the thinkers in this volume were African American. Still more were neither racialized as white nor born in the United States or Britain, but through migration from the Caribbean and elsewhere shaped international thought in Anglo-American locations.

Significantly, most of the figures in this volume possessed something that made them members of a small minority, a university degree, often a doctorate. Into the twentieth century, husbands and fathers held patriarchal legal control over women's professional and educational lives. Yet the extension of white women's social and political rights in the United States and Western Europe opened the doors of university education to a privileged few, some of whom rose to the most senior positions, such as Agnes Headlam-Morley, who took the Montague Burton Professorship of IR at Oxford in 1948.[28] Black women's educational opportunities in the United States were even more limited and often confined to those institutions built up by African American thinkers and educators, such as Anna Julia Cooper, Nannie Helen Burroughs, and Mary Church Terrell.[29] Among university students in general, women were a minority before the late twentieth century, and they suffered multiple forms of discrimination. Many institutions established separate women's colleges or institutes that were fundamental to supporting and circulating women's international thought, though they remain peripheral in IR's existing disciplinary and intellectual histories.[30] Formal higher education

[27] Srdjan Vucetic, *The Anglosphere: A Genealogy of a Racialized Identity in International Relations* (Stanford, CA: Stanford University Press, 2011); Duncan Bell, *Dreamworlds of Race: Empire and the Utopian Destiny of Anglo-America* (Princeton, NJ: Princeton University Press, 2020).

[28] Oliver Janz and Daniel Schönpflug (eds.), *Gender History in a Transnational Perspective: Networks, Biographies, Gender Orders* (New York: Berghahn Books, 2014); Anne Oakley, *Women, Peace and Welfare: A Suppressed History of Social Reform* (Cambridge: Polity Press, 2018).

[29] Stephanie Y. Evans, *Black Women in the Ivory Tower 1850–1954: An Intellectual History* (Gainesville, FL: University Press of Florida, 2007).

[30] On co-education in the United States see Nancy Weiss Malkiel, *"Keep the Damned Women Out": The Struggle for Coeducation* (Princeton, NJ: Princeton University Press, 2016); Lynn Gordon, *Gender and Higher Education in the Progressive Era* (New Haven, CT: Yale University Press, 1990), 13–51.

was an admission ticket to intellectual recognition, mentorships, and publishing, but it was hard to attain before mass entry to higher education late into the twentieth century.[31] The significance of the co-emergence of the field of international relations and the expansion of women's higher education is a crucial area of ongoing research.[32]

Critically linked to access to higher education, and the material resources it required, is the privileged class position of most of the thinkers in this volume, especially when it influenced their position in racial and/or international hierarchies. Literacy, the time to write, and access to publication opportunities have often been the domain of a privileged few.[33] At times, class power shaped women's international thought in very tangible ways. Born into the upper echelons of society in the British Empire and the daughter of an English Viscount, Margaret Lambert used her connections to conduct interviews and fieldwork in the borderlands of 1930s Europe. Similar class privileges were afforded to Bertha von Suttner. Born into the princely Czech House of Kinsky, she later married an Austro-Hungarian baron. F. Melian Stawell was the daughter of a British colonial statesman and a Chief Justice of the Supreme Court of Victoria, Australia.

Marriage or patronage could facilitate entry into educational and political worlds.[34] Yet, for university women, marriage to a male academic could be a distinct disadvantage as anti-nepotism rules in the United States meant that women married to male faculty were often denied academic jobs. And the intellectual credentials of Agnes Headlam-Morley and her Oxford colleague Sybil Crowe were sometimes disparaged because they were daughters of prominent diplomats.[35] Thus, while filial and marital relationships could constrain intellectual

---

[31] Britain followed broader trends in Western Europe. In 1900, university students made up less than one percent of their age cohort (between 20 and 24), rising to just over two percent by 1940. The United States offered more access to higher education. In 1900, 2.3 percent attended university and by 1940 the figure was 9.1 percent. Hartmut Kaelble, *Social Mobility in the Nineteenth and Twentieth Centuries: Europe and America in Comparative Perspective* (New York: St. Martin's Press, 1986), 42–43.

[32] Joanna Wood, D.Phil. dissertation in progress, University of Oxford.

[33] Valentine Cunningham, *British Writers of the Thirties* (Oxford: Oxford University Press, 1988), 308.

[34] Paula E. Stephan and Mary Mathewes Kassis, "The History of Women and Couples in Academe," in Marianne A. Ferber and Jane W. Loeb (eds.), *Academic Couples: Problems and Promises* (Urbana, IL: University of Illinois Press, 1997), 59; Linda M. Perkins, "For the Good of the Race: Married African-American Academics, a Historical Perspective," in Marianne A. Ferber and Jane W. Loeb (eds.), *Academic Couples: Problems and Promises* (Urbana, IL: University of Illinois Press, 1997), 80–105.

[35] Carroll Quigley, *The Anglo-American Establishment: From Rhodes to Cliveden* (New York: Books in Focus, 1981), 310.

production, women's international thought could also flourish in that context, providing access and sometimes credibility.[36] Occasionally, heterosexual marriages provided a congenial working relationship with both partners achieving recognition, even if unequally attributed, and even just in a preface. Arguably the two most influential works of post-war "American IR" were produced in collaboration with an unnamed "wife" who did "more than keep the children quiet and move commas around, more than criticize and read proof [sic]; she did most of the research for one chapter and contributed ideas and information to all of them."[37] Other relationships were marked by intellectual exploitation and partner abuse. The best documented case of abuse is E. H. Carr's treatment of his wives, including Cambridge historian Betty Behrens.[38]

There is a great number of intellectual "power couples" in this volume, heterosexual unions in which both were international thinkers: Lucie and Alfred Zimmern, Shirley Graham and W. E. B. DuBois, Amy Ashwood and later Amy Jacques and Marcus Garvey, Margaret and Harold Sprout, Suzanne Roussy Césaire and Aimé Césaire, Eslanda and Paul Robeson, Annette Baker and William T. R. Fox, Roberta and Albert Wohlstetter, and Edith and Ernest Penrose. Gender structured these intellectual–intimate partnerships in conventional and unconventional ways. Lucie Zimmern co-founded and ran one of the most successful internationalist education projects of the 1920s and 1930s and may have been the most reviled woman in interwar international studies. She was bitterly resented for her outspokenness and the access her marriage gave to high-level meetings and conferences.[39] Some thinkers left a high-profile marriage but continued the intellectual engagement with their ex-partner's ideas. Amy Ashwood Garvey's divorce from Marcus in 1922 by no means ended her struggles with Pan-Africanism and Black

---

[36] Robert Shaffer, "Women and International Relations: Pearl S. Buck's Critique of the Cold War," *Journal of Women's History*, 11:3 (1999): 157.

[37] Kenneth N. Waltz, *Man, the State, and War* (New York: Columbia University Press, 1959), n.p. The preface to Waltz's *Theory of International Politics* also notes that "Through many discussions, mainly with my wife and with graduate students at Brandeis and Berkeley, a number of the points I make were developed": Kenneth N. Waltz, *Theory of International Politics* (London: Addison-Wesley Publishing, 1979), n.p. The unnamed wife was Helen "Huddle" Waltz, *née* Lindsley.

[38] David Pryce-Jones, "Unlimited Nastiness," *The New Criterion*, December 1999. Available at https://newcriterion.com/issues/1999/12/unlimited-nastiness. Jonathan Haslam, *The Vices of Integrity: E. H. Carr, 1892–1982* (London: Verso, 2000); Betty Behrens papers, Churchill College, Cambridge.

[39] Patricia Owens and Katharina Rietzler, "The Lucie Zimmern School of International Studies," work in progress.

patriarchy.[40] During Marcus's imprisonment, his second wife, Amy Jacques Garvey, became de facto leader of the Universal Negro Improvement Association and worked to keep his Pan-Africanist ideas alive following his 1940 death.[41] A prolific writer and intellectual in her own right, she is nonetheless often dismissed as a "supportive wife" or "helpmeet." Roberta and Albert Wohlstetter, both RAND Corporation thermonuclear strategists, projected a public profile that linked 1950s domesticity to an aggressive Cold War doctrine that countenanced the first use of nuclear weapons.[42] William T. R. Fox coined the phrase "superpower," while Annette Baker Fox became a specialist on small and middling powers.

Not all women international thinkers were attracted to or married men. Others in same-sex relationships were not permitted to marry even if they wanted to. Jane Addams, Vernon Lee, and Margaret Lambert had rich intellectual collaborations with same-sex partners. Elizabeth Fischer Read directed research for the American Foundation for Studies in Government, founded by her lover and partner, Esther Lape.[43] Other unmarried "college women" such as Headlam-Morley, Crowe, Lillian Penson, and Emily Greene Balch dedicated themselves to teaching international history and to the life of their educational institutions. Women's colleges and settlement houses were also settings for "romantic friendships," such as Addams's with Mary Rozet Smith or F. Melian Stawell's with Clare Reynolds and Mary Parker Follet.[44] Sylvia Pankhurst refused the institution of marriage. Still others, such as Margery Perham and Simone Weil, chose a celibate life.[45] These lives were not necessarily ones of solitude; many were enmeshed in "women's culture," and this often impacted on intellectual work. It is hard to conclusively assess how the absence or presence of intimate

---

[40] Robbie Shilliam, "Theorizing with Amy Ashwood Garvey," in Patricia Owens and Katharina Rietzler (eds.), *Women's International Thought: A New History* (Cambridge: Cambridge University Press, 2021), 158–178; Blain, *Set the World on Fire*, 19, 146–151.

[41] Ula Taylor, *The Veiled Garvey: The Life and Times of Amy Jacques Garvey* (Chapel Hill, NC: University of North Carolina Press, 2002); Blain, *Set the World on Fire*, 35.

[42] Ron Robin, *The Cold World They Made: The Strategic Legacy of Roberta and Albert Wohlstetter* (Cambridge, MA: Harvard University Press, 2016).

[43] Reid was the author of *International Law and International Relations* (New York: American Foundation, 1925). As explained in the acknowledgments, we were not permitted to reprint this work.

[44] Dáša Frančíková, "Romantic Friendship: Exploring Modern Categories of Sexuality, Love, and Desire between Women," in Leila J. Rupp and Susan Kathleen Freeman (eds.), *Understanding and Teaching U.S. Lesbian, Gay, Bisexual, and Transgender History*, 2nd ed. (Madison, WI: University of Wisconsin Press, 2017), 143–152.

[45] C. Brad Faught, *Into Africa: The Imperial Life of Margery Perham* (London: I. B. Tauris, 2011).

relations – sexual or otherwise – directly shaped international thinking, not least due to homophobia, "closeted" sexualities, and the contingent and shifting ideas about the appropriate division of intellectual labor in various kinds of relationships. Nevertheless, ignoring the ways in which intimate relationships could influence and inform the possibility and reception of international thought would be remiss, especially as many of our thinkers subjected them to critical scrutiny.

Of course, class position, as well as intimate relations, can be ambiguous. Several thinkers came from comfortable families but regarded themselves as thinkers of the proletariat, such as Rosa Luxemburg. Others may have become middle-class due to their education and profession. Anna Julia Cooper was born into slavery, but, though never well-off, belonged to the small early-twentieth-century African American middle class as an educator, institution-builder, public intellectual, and Black club woman.[46] Others began life in middle- or even upper-middle-class families but struggled financially in later life, including Luisa Moreno, Una Marson, Emily Greene Balch, and Elizabeth Wiskemann. The gendered double burden of paid work and care work also shaped intellectual lives. After divorcing her first husband, Shirley Graham Du Bois struggled to support herself and two sons, relying on family members for childcare while she worked multiple jobs.[47] Migration and the complexity of the global color line impacted economic status. Amy Ashwood Garvey came from a middle-class Jamaican family but was a working-class intellectual in the United States.[48] Migration status and political persecution could heighten precarity. As a foreign-born resident, Claudia Jones was deported from the United States to Britain for her radical left and anti-racist work. Material precarity did not determine ideology, of course. Adda Bozeman endured difficult circumstances in youth but hailed from a quasi-aristocratic family. She never held intellectual positions that would place her in the labor movement or indicate a commitment to socialism.

There are fewer thinkers in this anthology who can be regarded as working-class intellectuals. The paradigmatic example might be Claudia Jones, an autodidact who came from a poor Caribbean family that emigrated to the United States after economic collapse.[49] She became

---

[46] Vivian M. May, *Anna Julia Cooper, Visionary Black Feminist: A Critical Introduction* (New York: Routledge, 2007), 14–37.

[47] Gerald Horne, *Race Woman: The Lives of Shirley Graham Du Bois* (New York: New York University Press, 2000).

[48] Tony Martin, *Amy Ashwood Garvey: Pan-Africanist, Feminist and Mrs. Marcus Garvey Number 1 (Or A Tale of Two Amies)* (Dover, MA: Majority Press, 2007).

[49] Sarah C. Dunstan and Patricia Owens, "Claudia Jones, International Thinker," *Modern Intellectual History*, First View (2021): 1–25.

a committed trade unionist and member of the National Association for the Advancement of Colored People (NAACP) and the Communist Party of the United States (CPUSA), dedicating her intellectual life to the education and politicization of Black and working people.[50] That she did so in a particular historical moment, during the mass mobilization and radicalization of workers between the two world wars, is no accident. Self-education via Black and working-class print cultures and other forms of associational life was key for thinkers such as Jones. After the Second World War, large numbers of American workers entered higher education, which, paradoxically, dismantled many arenas for working-class intellectual formation.[51] Certainly, with the educational reforms of the late nineteenth century, working-class people had greater recourse to the written word for capturing and sharing their ideas. However, huge barriers to the publication and circulation of their writing remained. Just as the proper study of working-class and much Black and women's thought requires analyzing unconventional genres such as letters, radio transcripts, newspaper articles, and speeches alongside more traditional forms, this also holds true for international thought.[52]

There are multiple and complex connections between sex/gender, race, class, and international thinking for those speaking from what Vernon Lee called the "over-sexed" position of "women."[53] One could not write and think about international relations from this subject position without being read through a sex/gender lens, even if some figures, such as Pauli Murray and Simone Weil, were gender non-conforming.[54]

---

[50] Boyce Davies, *Left of Karl Marx.*

[51] Tobias Higbie, *Labor's Mind: A History of Working-Class Intellectual Life* (Urbana, IL: University of Illinois Press, 2019). More generally, the study of working-class thought is a conundrum for intellectual history given its emphasis on tracing ideas through written documents. Histories of reading have been at the forefront of scholarship on working-class intellectual life. Elizabeth McHenry, *Forgotten Readers: Recovering the Lost History of African American Literary Societies* (Durham, NC: Duke University Press, 2002); Jonathon Rose, *The Intellectual Life of the British Working Classes* (New Haven, CT: Yale University Press, 2008).

[52] Chris Hilliard, *To Exercise Our Talents: The Democratization of Writing in Britain* (Cambridge, MA: Harvard University Press, 2006), 4; Brent Hayes Edwards, *The Practice of Diaspora: Literature, Translation, and the Rise of Black Internationalism* (Cambridge: Cambridge University Press, 2003); Brittney C. Cooper, *Beyond Respectability: The Intellectual Thought of Race Women* (Illinois, IL: University of Illinois Press, 2017).

[53] Vernon Lee, "The Economic Parasitism of Women," in *Gospels of Anarchy and Other Contemporary Studies* (London and Leipzig: T. Fisher & Unwin, 1908, reprinted Whitefish, MT: Kessinger Publishing, 2004), 148.

[54] On Pauli Murray's struggles with gender identity, see Rosalind Rosenberg, *Jane Crow: The Life of Pauli Murray* (New York: Oxford University Press, 2017); Cooper, *Beyond Respectability*, chapter 3. Murray's life and thought has been studied extensively, see e.g. the contributors to "Dialogue: Pauli Murray's Notable Connections," *Journal of Women's History*, 14:2 (2002), 54–87.

In turn, some women explicitly situated themselves in gendered and racial terms and approached international questions from this standpoint. They made connections between international relations and their own sexed/gendered/racialized subject-positions, analyzing how they supported or subverted national and imperial structures, including their own reception as scholars. Others were less keen to position themselves as "women" intellectually even as they wrote on the "woman question" and were more likely to adopt an ethno-cultural identity such as "Jewish."[55] Of course, while even the most canonical – Arendt, Luxemburg, de Beauvoir – have had undue attention devoted to their personal lives, and the obverse is rarely the case for men, we do not naïvely endorse this difference. Rather, as we have suggested, there are structural reasons why familial relationships, sexual and/or life partners, class, and racial hierarchies are explored at greater depth in histories of thought that center gender.

This is one of the largest anthologies of international thought ever compiled, if not the largest currently in print. It is organized thematically and encompasses 104 selections by 92 different thinkers. Yet, even excluding all those who fall outside our spatial and temporal scope, there were numerous other figures that could have been included.[56] In deciding the content of the anthology, we prioritized representing the scope and diversity of international thought within our location and period, Britain and the United States from the late nineteenth century to the long mid-twentieth century. We were determined to include the widest

[55] Kimberly Maslin, "The Gender-Neutral Feminism of Hannah Arendt," *Hypatia*, 28:3 (2013): 585–601; Milen Jissov, "The Self and History: Hannah Arendt and the Perplexities of Jewish Identity," *Canadian Journal of History*, 52:1 (2017): 54–79; Patricia Owens, *Between War and Politics: International Relations and the Thought of Hannah Arendt* (Oxford: Oxford University Press, 2007).

[56] For example, two thinkers that fall outside our temporal scope are Jeane Kirkpatrick (1926–2006) and Jean Bethke Elshtain (1941–2013) as their main contributions appeared at the end of the twentieth century. See Jean Bethke Elshtain, *Women and War* (New York: University of Chicago Press, 1987); Jeane Kirkpatrick, "Dictatorships and Double Standards," *Commentary Magazine*, 68:5 (1979): 34–45. Others within our scope include, but are not limited to, Elise M. Boulding, Maria Montessori, Rebecca West, Thyra J. Edwards, Marthe Rajchman, Paulette Nardal, Gertrude Bell, Gwendolen M. Carter, Edith Ware, Ruth Savord, Jessie Barnard, Sonia Z. Hyman, Mary Agnes Hamilton, Susan Lawrence, Kathleen Courtney, Harriet Wanklyn, Annie Besant, Caroline Ware, Barbara Tuchman, Yuri Kochiyama, Mary McLeod Bethune, Elaine Windrich, Anna Arnold Hedgeman, Ida B. Wells, Miriam Camps, Sheila Patterson, Vijaya Lakshmi Pandit, Amelia Johnson, Charlotte Perkins Gilman, Clara Zetkin, Maymi L. T. De Mena, Mittie M. L. Gordon, Ellen Swallow Richards, Mary E. Townsend, Dorothy Kenyon, Florence Wilson, Margarete Rothbarth, Dorothy Thompson, Sigrid Schultz, Elspeth Rostow, Florence Tuttle, Rachel Crowdy, Williana Burroughs, Bessie Louise Pierce, Laura Cornelius Kellogg, Gertrude Simmons Bonnin (Zitkála-Šá), and Ellen Wilkinson.

possible range of subject matter, genres, and ideological/political positions, as well as professional locations. Given the influence of European traditions on Anglo-American international thought, we include a small number of non-Anglophone and émigré thinkers, including seven translated texts, three newly commissioned for this volume.[57]

In the process of selection, we became ever more aware of all that we could have included, as we excavated the vibrant and rich history of international thought. Most obviously, our narrow geographic but broad temporal scope reflects the prevalence of Anglophone writers in existing histories, and how this intellectual world was structured by US and British world power. The very task of tracing and shaping the contours of women's international thought remains necessarily incomplete. Indeed, this anthology not only allows us to identify how incomplete it is, but also enables other projects that seek in-depth recoveries, analyses, and contextualization of international thought in other locations and periods, and to discover that which is not yet known. The intellectual traditions represented in this volume are multiple yet provincial. They are nonetheless fundamental to understanding twentieth-century international thought in and on the Anglo-American world.

The thirteen thematic sections are derived from our readings of women's international thought and its imbrication in the core questions of the time on this vast subject of international relations, as delineated in our introductory essays for each section. The essays also contain original arguments, and all are contributions to the history of international thought. Our research has shown that, while there is such a thing as distinctly international thought, reflection on the relations between peoples, empires, and states, it does not exist in a vacuum and draws from and overlaps with political, economic, legal, anthropological, and geographic thought. Many thinkers in this volume worked on core international relations questions in fields adjacent to or preceding the establishment of International Relations as a separate academic discipline. Thus, we draw no clear lines between disciplines, themes, or thinkers; several selections and thinkers cut across subject matter and a small number appear in more than one section. Crucially, each selection only captures a thinker's ideas at specific moments in time and should not be read as representing the totality or culmination of their thought. Many, if

---

[57] Jane Nardal, Jane Vialle, Mary Church Terrell, Simone Weil, and Simone de Beauvoir, translated from French; and Bertha von Suttner and Helene Stöcker translated from German, with the translations of Stöcker, Terrell, and Vialle commissioned for this volume. On the influence of émigré thinkers see Felix Rösch (ed.), *Émigré Scholars and the Genesis of American International Relations: A European Discipline in America?* (London: Palgrave, 2014).

not all, shifted their views, and for a variety of reasons. Each thematic section contains eight selections and begins with a substantial introductory essay, providing intellectual, political, and biographical context. We now briefly introduce these themes, outlining the structure of the rest of the book.

The first section, Field and Discipline, contains selections from thinkers not only active in but formative to both the study of international relations as an interdisciplinary field, drawing on questions and methods in History, Classics, Colonial Administration and Anthropology, Economics, and Political Science, and a would-be separate academic discipline in its own right much later in the twentieth century. The selections illuminate how women founded or co-founded some of the most important internationalist educational and research projects, taught in the earliest IR departments, and wrote some of the first surveys of international thought. They intervened in, shaped, and often defined still on-going and highly contentious debates about IR's proper methodology and academic location; its early relationship to Diplomatic and Contemporary History; the distinctiveness of IR as a separate university subject; and how it should be taught in the then still racially segregated colleges in the United States.

Until very recently, intellectual and disciplinary histories portrayed IR as a response to the First World War, largely preoccupied with war and peace, side-lining the field's fundamental concern with colonial administration and imperial rivalry. To the limited extent that women appeared in these war-centered histories they were associated with feminist peace movements. As demonstrated later in the volume, thinkers associated with peace activism generated deep and enduring analyses of war-preparation and fighting. But large numbers of women with no association with peace movements also thought deeply about war and the geopolitical context in which wars occurred, the theme of this second section. We feature both academic and non academic thinkers writing in a variety of genres on the unfettered violence endemic not just to war, but to international politics, and the geopolitical tradition of thought that was so influential on international intellectual and disciplinary history.

From at least the nineteenth century, understandings of racial difference were used to justify the theory and practices of imperialism, which organizes the third section of the anthology. As already indicated, numerous scholars in this volume operated within intellectual worlds structured by racial–imperial thought. The selections here range from analyses of how imperialism created and perpetuated a racialized global politics to how to improve the efficiency of colonial administration, and to how empire as a putative instrument of human development is dependent on race relations and imperial policies.

The fourth section, Anticolonialism, collects writings by thinkers reflecting on and practicing wide-ranging forms of anticolonial international thought, with a particular focus on analysis and critique of the British and French empires. We include an early articulation of Black feminist internationalism; analysis of anticolonial warfare; critiques of the mobilization of race in the service of imperialism; and alternate visions for dismantling the imperial world system. In many respects these differing perspectives, largely written by thinkers outside academe, follow the chronology of the twentieth century, from the heyday of empire through to the post-Second World War context of decolonization. They also encompass multiple genres, from scholarly monographs through magazine articles and poetry.

International Law and International Organization, our fifth section, deals with two crucial subjects in the emerging field of international relations in the early twentieth century, subjects that were also closely tied to questions of women's political rights such as retention of nationality after marriage or suffrage. Women thinkers interrogated the nature of state sovereignty and proposed concrete processes for how it could be transferred and repurposed. The selections chart the growth and achievements of international organizations but also reflect on problems of representation and how international law ought to deal with differences in national character, culture, and class. Assessments of international law's ability to order international relations and to regulate international conflict in a world of declining European empires and superpower conflict ranged from the skeptical to the enthusiastic. We also include writing on the question of federation as an alternative to international governance and a form of regional ordering that enabled postcolonial states to challenge a hierarchical world order.

There is remarkable continuity between the international thought in this volume and IR's core subject matter today. This is nowhere more evident than in work on Diplomacy and Foreign Policy, our sixth section. To a great extent, especially in Britain, early international relations was a branch of History, focused on the study of diplomats and high politics. By the 1970s in Britain, IR's belated professionalization as a social science involved a conscious break away from old-school diplomatic history. In American IR, the analysis of foreign policy and diplomacy became influenced by an anti-legalist shift to realist theory and social scientific models. Our selections often juxtapose a focus on the corridors of power with the messy realities of mass politics. We include examples of traditional and still influential forms of foreign policy analysis but also of those thinkers who had already taken a broader view of what the study of diplomacy might entail, including analyses of the psychological, intellectual, and cultural influences on foreign policy. For others, foreign policy analysis took a more public and obviously political turn with all its attendant risks.

Just as the study of international relations was shaped in the context of catastrophic world wars, so too was it shaped by the competing intellectual traditions of pacifism and visions of world order that would support peace. The selections in our seventh section, World Peace, include advocates for peace in the context of the Great War and of international institutions as the most efficacious means of creating peace. Sometimes women thinkers admonished men for their perceived failure to acknowledge the inherently gendered character, burden, and consequences of warfare. Some understood women to play a particular role in peacemaking, emphasizing how the capacity for motherhood and maternal work could alter understandings of war. Others focused specifically on the relationship between state sovereignty as a fundamental tenet of international law and efforts towards disarmament. Clearly, "peace" was racially charged, inextricable from notions of imperialism and Third World "development."

It is no surprise that a great deal of women's international thought centred on World Economy, the subject of our eighth section. Indeed, the two most recognized women in existing international and disciplinary histories were economic thinkers, Rosa Luxemburg and Susan Strange.[58] That the other thinkers in this section remain largely unknown underscores the general neglect of historical women, the tokenization of a select few, and also the way in which economic histories of empire were written out of histories of international thought in post-war disciplinary IR, and the relative dominance of war and national security. All these factors marginalized figures selected here who were often highly influential in wider public and policy debates on international economic life, including on international finance and banking, multinational corporations, the organization and regulation of labour, post-imperial economic decline, and the economic development of colonial and postcolonial nations.

As already indicated, gender was often an explicit theme or structure of analysis in writing about international relations. For the thinkers in our ninth section, Men, Women, and Gender, the presence of women, as authors and as subject matter, not only made gender visible, but also highlighted the intersectionality of gender with racial and class

---

[58] Owens, "Women and the History of International Thought," 470.

distinctions and the role of gendered ideology and divisions of labor in structuring and legitimating international politics. The selections here are diverse. They include nineteenth-century white middle-class views of gender, which resonate with a version of a "standpoint" position in which women have specific insights into the world; claims that gendered ideologies sustained war and inter-state competition; and efforts to complicate the idea of a women's or feminist standpoint by drawing attention to the raced and classed nature of suffrage movements, and the complicity of some white feminisms with militarism and racism.

The international dimension of educational philosophy and practice was a core theme of early international thought. Our tenth section, Public Opinion and Education, revives this subject, showing how education is connected to some of the essential elements of democratic and international theory, including the role of public opinion in foreign policy. Women thinkers embraced positions that ranged from public opinion optimism to profound skepticism regarding both the popular control of policy makers and the extent to which popular prejudices could be manipulated. Black women educators were the first to analyze education as a problem in international-relations-as-race-relations, while white educators stressed their own role in advancing world peace, feeding into liberal internationalism. Others recognized the importance of education in underpinning transnational movements for anticolonial liberation. Education had ambivalent potential. It could empower publics to question foreign policy and the prevailing international order but could also be used paternalistically to quell such opposition. Our selections recognize both tendencies, ranging from optimistic assessments of how education might create race consciousness to stark distinctions between education "at home" and "in the colonies."

The relationships between population, nation, and immigration are questions at the heart of international relations, and the themes of our eleventh section. The boundaries of the categories of population and nation were hugely in flux throughout the twentieth century, shifting with trends around immigration to the colonial and postcolonial metropole as well as mass migrations prompted by the conflicts of the First and Second World Wars. The thinkers here explored the question of minorities within nation-states, parsing how racial and ethnic identity mapped onto state belonging and status in racist and civilizational rhetoric. In some cases, this thinking reflected prevailing notions of racist and classist hierarchies. In others, thinkers offered a transformative way of understanding difference in relation to national belonging. Often, family figured as an object of analysis and as a source of metaphors and analogies. Some thinkers took explicitly gendered positions to argue for changes to state and international organization that specifically reflected the socio-biological function of citizens. We have selected a cross-section of these views and multiple genres, from activist pamphlets to speeches and scholarly articles and monographs.

Our penultimate section analyzes questions of technology, progress, and environment, including the revolutionary potential of air power, the consequences of the atomic bomb, and ideas of modernization, "development," and "delayed industrialization" in so-called economically "backward" states. Some thinkers explored how the mediation of photographic technologies in war shifts political imagination. Some pioneered the ecological critiques of dependence on industrial technologies, whilst others unapologetically castigated the regressive nature of environmentalist politics and firmly defended the industrial revolution. Technology narratives tended to swing between utopian hopes of technological fixes to problems of war and development and apocalyptic scenarios of nuclear annihilation or environmental destruction. Although some thinkers fall into the utopian versus apocalyptic camps, most of the arguments are more nuanced or ambivalent, and none of the thinkers embraced technological determinism.

The study of international relations has always contained religious and explicitly normative strands, from Christian realism to just war theory. But a century of total war and genocide, and the discrediting of Western normative traditions, raised particularly urgent moral and spiritual questions. Visions of global order increasingly acknowledged that if international norms were to have religious grounds, then multiple traditions would have to be considered. Women were central in formulating these challenges to international theorizing. Some became public moralists. Others warned that religion could be instrumentalized to justify militarism, imperialism, and paternalism. In our last section, Religion and Ethics, we feature thinkers who engaged with several traditions, ranging from nonconformist Protestantism to Catholicism and Voodoo. Frequently, they criticized the failure of organized religion to be a positive force in world politics. But normative engagement with international questions could also lead to intellectual innovation in the form of new approaches to moral reasoning.

We are only now beginning to come to terms with the implications of the expropriation and erasure of women's international thought and, as a result, what its recovery, reconstruction, and analysis might mean for intellectual and disciplinary history and international theory. Anthologizing is not a solution to the problem that precipitated and justifies this volume; namely, historical women's radical exclusion from histories of international thought. Presenting "women's international thought" in anthology form risks enabling tokenism, the add-on of a few new names as a minor correction to existing ways of teaching and researching international history and theory. We hope that the way we have selected, curated, and introduced this work will reduce what – to some extent and in some contexts – is probably inevitable. In the end, we believe that such an anthology is necessary. But its publication does not represent the culmination of thinking, just a moment in time within a continuing conversation. In no sense is this work complete, and nor are the history and meanings of our central organizing concepts – women, international, and thought – fixed. Instead we seek to deepen and expand understandings of what international thinking was, is, and could be.

1

Field and Discipline
Introduction by Patricia Owens

Recent revisionist histories of the academic discipline of International Relations (IR) have radically undermined the notion that it emerged as a noble venture in response to the horrors of the First World War.[1] In its most influential Anglo-American locations, international relations developed both as an interdisciplinary subject and as a separate academic discipline fundamentally shaped by inter-imperial rivalry, inter-racial hierarchy, world economy, colonial administration, and new international organizations to manage global structures. Yet, to date, both conventional and revisionist historiography has revealed a justifiably unflattering but also quite partial portrait of "white man's IR."[2] We have very little sense of women's foundational role in the history of academic IR, a story that is not entirely of "white women."[3]

In the third decade of the twenty-first century, IR remains one of the least racially and intellectually diverse social science disciplines.[4] For structural reasons related to racial, class, national, and gendered politics, there were relatively few women of color in academic IR in the early to long mid-twentieth century. Yet, as we demonstrate in this volume,

---

[1] For recent revisionist disciplinary history see Robert Vitalis, *White World Order, Black Power Politics: The Birth of American International Relations* (Ithaca, NY: Cornell University Press, 2015); Vineet Thakur and Peter Vale, *South Africa, Race and the Making of International Relations* (London: Rowman and Littlefield, 2020). For more conventional histories of IR see Brian Porter (ed.), *The Aberystwyth Papers, 1919–1969* (Oxford: Oxford University Press, 1972); William C. Olson and A. J. R. Groom, *International Relations Then and Now: Origins and Trends in Interpretation* (London: Unwin Hyman, 1991).

[2] David Lake, "White Man's IR: An Intellectual Confession," *Perspectives on Politics*, 14:4 (2016): 1112–1122; Peter Vale and Vineet Thakur, "IR and the Making of the White Man's World," in Arlene B. Tickner and Karen Smith (eds.), *International Relations from the Global South: Worlds of Difference* (London: Routledge, 2020).

[3] On "white women's IR" see Patricia Owens, "Women and the History of International Thought," *International Studies Quarterly*, 62:3 (2018): 467.

[4] Paula D. McClain, Gloria Y. A. Ayee, Taneisha N. Means, Alicia M. Reyes-Barriéntez, and Nura A. Sediqe, "Race, Power, and Knowledge: Tracing the Roots of Exclusion in the Development of Political Science in the United States," *Politics, Groups, and Identities*, 4:3 (2016): 467–482; Isaac A. Kamola, *Making the World Global: U.S. Universities and the Production of the Global Imaginary* (Durham, NC: Duke University Press, 2019).

23

women of color produced some of the most powerful international thinking, albeit unrecognized in Anglo-American academe. Indeed, much of this international thought may have been so powerful precisely because it emerged free of the conforming strictures of the ivory tower. Nonetheless, as a relatively novel field, research and teaching in IR allowed large numbers of middle- and upper-class women to break new ground within the institutionally racist and patriarchal setting of the university.[5] The first African American woman to earn a graduate degree from Oxford as well as Oxford's and Edinburgh's first women professors were IR scholars.

Women thinkers were active, even formative, in IR both as an early-twentieth-century interdisciplinary subject or field, co-founding research centers as early as 1924, and as the earliest beginnings of a separate academic discipline in its own right from the 1950s in the United States and from the 1970s in Britain. In both field and discipline and in both locations, women initiated and intervened in still on-going and highly contentious debates about IR's proper subject matter, method-ology, and academic place. To illustrate, we include in this section writings on pilot IR syllabi, a funding bid for a new international relations research center, work mapping the history of international thought and the distinctiveness of IR as a separate university subject, and the racial politics of how it should be taught. We also include writing on IR's relationship to Political Science in the United States and Diplomatic and Contemporary History within Britain. To capture the range and the contestation around what IR was and should be, we include a variety of genres, not only journal articles and books but course syllabi, internal university memoranda, a radio broadcast, and an inaugural professorial lecture.

We begin this section with the syllabus for a 1915 "Course in International Relations," co-written by Jessie W. Hughan (1875–1955) with Harvard's Nicholas Kelley. This was commissioned by and pub-lished in the influential *Intercollegiate Socialist*, the journal of the Intercollegiate Socialist Society,[6] suggesting a much wider set of ideo-logical influences within early American IR than is usually found in

---

[5] Cf. a similar process in Anthropology reviewed by Deborah L. Nichols, "Women in Anthropology," *American Anthropologist*, 98:2 (1996): 405–408.

[6] For discussion see Craig N. Murphy, "Relocating the Point of IR," in Synne L. Dyvik, Jan Selby, and Rorden Wilkinson (eds.), *What's the Point of International Relations?* (London: Routledge, 2017), 71–82; also see Max Horn, *The Intercollegiate Socialist Society, 1905–1921: Origins of the Modern American Student Movement* (Boulder, CO: Westview Press, 1979).

existing disciplinary histories.[7] The course covered seven substantive topics, Modern World Commerce, the Causes of Modern War, The Facts of War and Militarism, the Peace Ideal and Nonresistance, International Law and Arbitration, Proposed Remedies and Palliatives for War, and Socialism and War. Apart from the emphasis on socialism, the course content is not dissimilar from introductory syllabi today, though, given its date, it is noticeable that imperialism and anticolonialism are missing. This omission may indicate the ambivalent relationship between white socialist internationalism, which did not always oppose imperialism, and Black and anticolonial internationalisms, also represented in this volume.[8]

Jessie W. Hughan is an important and prolific figure in the history of popular international thinking in the early-twentieth-century United States. According to contemporary IR scholar Craig N. Murphy, a focus on the relations between war, imperialism, and poverty and exploitation both in the metropole and in the colonies made Hughan and the circle around her representative of "the best of the early IR scholars." The core intellectual concerns of this group, which included W. E. B. DuBois, "remained at the center of IR until the Cold War," during which many radicals were drummed out of the US academy, with African American intellectuals also disproportionately affected.[9] Born in New York, and studying at Barnard and Columbia, Hughan was one of the leading US pacifists of her day, opposing US entry into the First World War and founding the War Resisters League. In 1924, she published *A Study of International Government*, also written for a popular audience, which included a discussion of the limits on international cooperation under capitalism. Hughan was a member of the Socialist Party of America and an officer of the Intercollegiate Socialist Society, a forum for the discussion of socialism on college campuses, and its successor the League for Industrial Democracy.[10] Hughan regularly ran for public office, not expecting to win but to increase engagement with socialist ideas and

---

[7] Olson and Groom, *International Relations Then and Now*; Torbjørn L. Knutsen, *A History of International Relations Theory*, 3rd ed. (Manchester: Manchester University Press, 2016).

[8] Robbie Shilliam, "Decolonizing the Manifesto," in Terrel Carver and James Farr (eds.), *The Cambridge Companion to the Communist Manifesto* (Cambridge: Cambridge University Press, 2015), 195–213.

[9] Murphy, "Relocating the Point of IR," 71–82.

[10] Jessie Hughan's other works, all written for popular audiences, include *The Facts of Socialism* (New York: John Lane Co., 1913); *What about Spain?* (New York: War Resisters League, 1937); *The Beginnings of War Resistance* (New York: War Resisters League, 1937); *A Preface to Post-War* (New York: War Resisters League, 1943); *New Leagues for Old: Blueprints or Foundations?* (New York: Plowshare Press, 1945).

possible co-optation of socialist policies. During the first Red Scare, Hughan was on the list of "dangerous radicals" in the 1919 Congressional enquiry into domestic radicalism and, along with Emily Greene Balch, who appears later in the volume, was pushed out of her university position. Not only her gender, but also her socialist politics, ensured Hughan's erasure from histories of US international thought.

One of the most neglected factors influencing early international thinking was its co-emergence with the vastly increased numbers of women entering higher education.[11] As Joanna Wood has argued, the vision for the Radcliffe Bureau of International Research, founded in 1924, was for all college-educated women to receive instruction in a field that – because of its relative novelty and the fluidity of its boundaries with other fields – provided unique intellectual and professional opportunities for elite, mostly white women.[12] It is difficult to overstate the importance of Radcliffe's support for women's research on international relations in the 1920s and 1930s. Much of the international thought in this volume was supported by Radcliffe College or the Bureau, including works by Mary Parker Follett, M. Margaret Ball, Merze Tate, Fannie Fern Andrews, Vera Micheles Dean, Eleanor Lansing Dulles, Louise W. Holborn, and Sarah Wambaugh.

The volume and quality of this research is some fulfillment of the vision of the two academic entrepreneurs who negotiated the establishment of the Bureau and directed a substantial amount of funds towards women: Ada Louise Comstock, the first full-time president of Radcliffe College, and Bernice Brown Cronkhite, dean of Radcliffe and scholar of international law. The initial proposal to the Laura Spelman Rockefeller Memorial envisioned support for graduate research in international relations, law, or institutions; a course in international relations for women teachers and other professionals; and conferences on international relations subjects open to the public. As a women's college, and given the recent history of women's international cooperation and federation, Radcliffe was envisaged as ideally suited to developing and hosting courses in international relations and international law. The Rockefeller

---

[11] Mary Ann Dzuback, "Gender, Professional Knowledge and Institutional Power: Women Social Scientists and the Research University," in A. M. May (ed.), *The "Woman Question" in Higher Education: Perspectives on Gender and Knowledge Production in America* (Cheltenham: Edward Elgar Publishing, 2008), 52–73; Katharina Rietzler, "Experts for Peace: Structures and Motivations of Philanthropic Internationalism in the United States and Europe," in Daniel Laqua (ed.), *Internationalism Reconfigured: Transnational Ideas and Movements between the World Wars* (London: I. B. Tauris, 2011), 48.

[12] Joanna Wood, D.Phil. dissertation in progress, University of Oxford.

Memorial awarded $50,000 per year between 1924 and 1939. Around eleven percent went to women's research.[13]

But what and where is "international thought"? As noted in the introduction to this volume, the first use of the English term can be traced to Florence Melian Stawell's (1869–1936) 1929 work *The Growth of International Thought*. Despite this heritage, the first close reading of Stawell's work appears only now, in an essay by Glenda Sluga in the companion volume to this anthology.[14] The youngest daughter of ten children, Stawell was among the first of six women permitted to attend the University of Melbourne, Australia which her father, Sir William Stawell, had co-founded. She came from a wealthy and political family; her father was Chief Justice and Lieutenant-Governor of Victoria. Her comings and goings in England were dutifully reported in the Australian press. Stawell had traveled to Britain for graduate research at Newnham College, Cambridge, where she befriended Mary Parker Follett, sparking Follett's own important work on international organization, excerpted later in this volume. Set for an illustrious academic career, Stawell's Cambridge lectureship was cut short due to ill health. After moving to London, where she participated in the League of Nations Union, Stawell was on the edge of the Bloomsbury circle, associating with Gilbert Murray but also Virginia Woolf, Bertrand Russell, and G. Lowes Dickinson.[15] Stawell's internationalist ideas were developed for popular audiences and with a pedagogic purpose. She taught Ethics at Morley College in London, where Virginia Woolf and Lucy Philip Mair also taught.

Like so many interwar international thinkers, Florence Melian Stawell combined her interest in contemporary world politics with classical training and scholarship, writing prolifically on both.[16] *The Growth of*

---

[13] Dzuback, "Gender, Professional Knowledge and Institutional Power," 61.

[14] Glenda Sluga, "From F. Melian Stawell to E. Greene Balch: International and *Internationalist* Thinking at the Gender Margins, 1919–1947," in Patricia Owens and Katharina Rietzler (eds.), *Women's International Thought: A New History* (Cambridge: Cambridge University Press, 2021), 223–243.

[15] Karen Levenback, *Virginia Woolf, Melian Stawell and Bloomsbury* (London: Cecil Woolf, 2017).

[16] Her works include *Homer and the Iliad* (London: J. M. Dent, 1909); "History and the League of Nations," *History*, 3:12 (1918): 224; *Patriotism and the Fellowship of Nations: A Little Primer of Great Problems* (London: J. M. Dent, 1916); *The Price of Freedom: An Anthology for All Nations Chosen by F. Melian Stawell* (London: Headley, 1917); and, with F. S. Marvin, *The Making of the Western Mind* (London: Methuen, 1924). On the influence of classical training on early-twentieth-century British international thought, especially Alfred Zimmern and Gilbert Murray, see Jeanne Morefield, *Covenants without Swords: Idealist Liberalism and the Spirit of Empire* (Princeton, NJ: Princeton University Press, 2005); and *Empires without Imperialism: Anglo-American Decline and the Politics of Deflection* (Oxford: Oxford University Press, 2014), chapter 1.

International Thought located in Antiquity the germ of two ideas that Stawell claimed would be the foundation for international peace in the twentieth century, "arbitration between equals and confederacy on equal terms" (42). Yet, she lamented, any cooperation among Greek city states only seemed possible when they were "united against another enemy, the Persian ... 'the foreigner'" (42). Yet race and empire were also the foundation of Stawell's own Eurocentric and teleological account of the history of international thought in which colonized populations were "savages" and the underlying principles of true internationalism had "been felt, sometimes clearly, more often dimly, by all the best thinkers of Europe" (41). More surprising, and perhaps more fruitful for international theory, is Stawell's feminist account of the Peloponnesian War. Stawell described Thucydides' history as "one of the strongest indictments against war ever written" (41). More intriguingly, she turned to the equally powerful "voice of reason and pity" (42) in Euripides' play *The Trojan Women*, which famously recounted the War from the perspective of the Melian women survivors of the massacres and slaughter, the "conquered ... are the heroic figures in the drama" (42). Since even Stawell's middle name recognized the conquered inhabitants of Melos, her feminist reading of the "Greeks" prefigures more recent calls for "a Melian security studies."[17]

As should be clear, in the early twentieth century, the study of international relations was an interdisciplinary field, drawing on questions and methods associated with Classics, History, Economics, and Colonial Administration and Anthropology, as much as Political Science and Law. Thus, retrieving and reading historical women allows us to see the range of such work in light of contemporary debates about IR's nature and purpose and to consider which fields and approaches were marginalized when IR later formed as a separate academic discipline. As well as producing and shaping their subject, women international relations scholars reflected on the nature of that subject. Our fourth selection is from a scholar that straddled IR as both a field and a slowly emerging discipline, Lucy Philip Mair, who in 1934 authored an internal university memorandum, "International Relations as an Independent Subject," published here for the first time. Mair was among the first cohort of scholars hired in the Department of International Studies established in 1927 at the London School of Economics (LSE). She followed a

---

[17] Tarak Barkawi and Mark Laffey, "The Postcolonial Moment in Security Studies," *Review of International Studies*, 32:2 (2006), 351. See, for example, Eva C. Keuls, *The Reign of the Phallus: Sexual Politics in Ancient Athens* (Berkeley, CA: University of California Press, 1985).

remarkably similar trajectory to Stawell, studying Classics at Cambridge, working for Gilbert Murray at the League of Nations Union, and teaching world politics at Morley College the same year that she joined the faculty of LSE.

Lucy Philip Mair lectured extensively on Colonial Administration before the Second World War, with all courses listed under IR, teaching a large percentage of the international relations students in one of its largest academic centers in the world. It is most likely that the occasion for the memorandum, excerpted here, was to intervene in discussions about the reorganization of subjects and departments at the LSE in the context of the economic crisis of the 1930s. However, beyond the institutional background, the memorandum can also be read as an early example of a concern, even paranoia, about IR's intellectual and disciplinary status, whether it was a distinctive subject in its own right or a subfield of Political Science or Economics. For example, a very large proportion of what is still considered core IR subject matter was taught by women Economic Historians from as early as 1904, when Lilian Knowles began teaching imperial and great power economic history and, later, Eileen Power taught world history in the Economic History department at the LSE.

In that context, Mair wrote one of the earliest critiques of what would later be known as the "domestic analogy" in international theory,[18] "the dangerous fallacy of re-arming by analogy, of supposing that one can draw data as to relations between individuals, conclusions regarding relations between groups" (46). The single most powerful justification for a separate university subject of international relations was the irreducible difference between relations *within* highly organized groups and those *among* them. "This problem is absolutely *sui generis*," Mair wrote. "It cannot be understood or solved by a process of facile generalization from the history of political development within individual states" (46).

But what is the subject of international relations? Mair's answer was shaped by internationalist efforts at global reform, her own earlier work for the League of Nations Union, and her current scholarship, which included analysis of the new "mandates" system for administering the former colonies of the empires defeated in the First World War.[19]

---

[18] Hedley Bull, "Society and Anarchy in International Relations," in Herbert Butterfield and Martin Wight (eds.), *Diplomatic Investigations* (London: Allen & Unwin, 1966), 35.

[19] For some of her early work see Lucy Philip Mair, *The Protection of Minorities: The Working and Scope of the Minorities Treaties under the League of Nations* (London: Christophers, 1928); Lucy Philip Mair, "Colonial Administration as a Science," *Journal of the Royal African Society*, 32:129 (1933): 366–371; Lucy Mair, *Welfare in the British Colonies* (London: Royal Institute of International Affairs 1944); Lucy Mair, *Australia in New*

Writing the same year that the Soviet Union joined the League, Mair suggested that IR's central focus should be "analysis of those organs of international government which were established at the close of the last war" (47), specifically the League of Nations. Yet international relations approaches to studying "the practice" of international institutions was broader than the older field of International Law because it was concerned with "the whole range of relations between those organised political entities we call nations" (47).

After the Second World War, Mair migrated from the International Studies Department to Anthropology, the field that would come to specialize in subjects such as "race relations" and "development" that were core international relations topics in the first half of the twentieth century (their post-war articulation can be found in the sections on Imperialism and on Population, Nation, Immigration). The later erasure of colonial administration and race relations from IR's intellectual and disciplinary history also contributed to the erasure of figures such as Mair and Margery Perham, perhaps the most well-known and influential international thinker in the post-war British academy before Susan Strange, both of whom appear later in this volume.

As with both Mair's work on colonies and Stawell's on international thought, seemingly "progressive" international reform in the 1920s and 1930s was founded on racial hierarchy. Yet, numerous African American scholars mounted devastating critiques of global white supremacy in the first decades of the twentieth century. Robert Vitalis has recently suggested that arguably the "most accomplished international relations scholar"[20] at the historically Black Howard University was Merze Tate. An alumna of the Lucie and Alfred Zimmern School of International Studies in Geneva and student of Agnes Headlam-Morley at Oxford, Tate became the first African American woman to earn a graduate degree from Oxford in 1935 and, in 1941, to gain a PhD in government from Harvard. In 1947, *The Quarterly Review of Higher Education among Negroes* invited Tate to describe IR teaching in Black colleges. For Tate, the only difference between white and Black colleges was the need for "the constant reminder that the American Negro is only one of many minorities in the world and that his problem is not unique but only one phase of a much larger issue" (49).

Guinea (London: Christophers 1948). For a lengthier discussion of Mair see Owens, "Women and the History of International Thought," 476–479.

[20] Vitalis, *White World Order*, 161. Also see Barbara Savage, "Professor Merze Tate: Diplomatic Historian, Cosmopolitan Woman," in Mia Bay, Farah J. Griffin, Martha S. Jones, and Barbara D. Savage (eds.), *Toward an Intellectual History of Black Women* (Chapel Hill, NC: University of North Carolina Press, 2015), 252–270.

Tate defined IR's core subject matter as "power politics," which she understood to be fundamentally "geopolitical."[21] She understood geopolitics in the broadest sense, as the "geographic study of the state from the view point of foreign policy" (50). "One cannot teach 19th and 20th century imperialism, the partitioning of Africa, of Asia, of the Pacific, of the Arctic and Antarctic regions, and the scramble for world markets and spheres of economic penetration," Tate wrote, "without a background in geography," or for that matter, political economy, international law, and new approaches to political philosophy (49). More broadly, the field incorporated the study of "imperialism, political philosophy, economics, political science and history" (51). Military strategy and political leadership were forms of applied geopolitics. In stark contrast to the dominant geopolitical approaches of her day, Tate pursued what Barbara Savage calls an "anti-racist geopolitics."[22]

For Tate, IR was inherently multidisciplinary, a field that crossed the social sciences and humanities, including historical and cultural fields of research. But Tate's humanistic, anti-racist and historical approach did not take root in the wider IR discipline as it developed within American Political Science. This was not due to racism alone, nor in Britain to the downgrading of historical research, but to the dominance of behavioral social science in the United States. Given its size, ubiquity, and influence, IR became "an American specialism," identified thus by Annette Baker Fox and her co-author husband sixteen years before Stanley Hoffmann's much-cited claim that IR was an "American social science."[23] After meeting William T. R. Fox at graduate school in Chicago, Annette became the quintessential "trailing spouse," following his various career opportunities. Her first book was a study of colonialism in the Caribbean. She later became an expert on "small" and "middle" powers, pioneering this field, while William worked on and coined the term "superpower,"[24] a highly suggestive narrative of the gendering of

[21] Merze Tate, *The Disarmament Illusion: The Movement for a Limitation of Armaments to 1907* (New York: Macmillan, 1942); *The United States and the Hawaiian Kingdom: A Political History* (New Haven, CT: Yale University Press, 1965); *Hawaii: Reciprocity or Annexation* (East Lansing, MI: Michigan State University Press, 1968).

[22] For analysis see Barbara Savage, "Beyond Illusions: Imperialism, Race and Technology in Merze Tate's International Thought," in Patricia Owens and Katharina Rietzler (eds.), *Women's International Thought: A New History* (Cambridge: Cambridge University Press, 2021), 266–285.

[23] Stanley Hoffmann, "An American Social Science: International Relations," *Daedalus*, 106:3 (1977): 41–60.

[24] Annette Baker Fox, *Freedom and Welfare in the Caribbean: A Colonial Dilemma* (New York: Harcourt, Brace and Co., 1949); *The Power of Small States: Diplomacy in World War II* (Chicago, IL: University of Chicago Press, 1959).

power in world politics and divisions of labor within one of post-war IR's leading "power couples."[25]

In one of their intellectual collaborations excerpted here, the Foxes argued that by the 1960s IR scholars in the United States were busy making "their subject more 'scientific,'" demonstrating "the same enthusiasm for empirical, behavioral, and quantitative research, the same effort to discover uniformities in state or national behavior, and the same interest in choosing ... problems whose study would clarify questions of public policy" (68). In the context of decolonization, the expansion of nationalism and democracy, scientific and technological revolutions, regional organizations and "peace time" military alliances, nuclear arms races, and foreign aid, IR's subject matter also stretched far beyond Lucy Philip Mair's focus on international institutions to regulate the relations between imperial states and colonial administration of the rest of the world. The study of colonial administration, a subject Annette Baker Fox knew well, morphed into "area studies," "the intensive study of one or more areas formerly thought exotic" (67). In the nuclear age, academic IR was dominated by national security and military strategy.

Given its size, resources, and geopolitical position, "American IR" began to acquire a more secure and prominent position within the academy from the 1950s, in part through carving out a distinctive place for itself within Political Science.[26] Still, in 1960s Britain, there was no "discipline" beyond the university teaching of international relations, usually by trained historians. As various efforts to forge a disciplinary identity began to coalesce, one frequently stated motivation was the need to move beyond the way in which many historians had approached international relations to date, through the analysis of diplomatic history, especially interwar diplomacy. At the time, many historians were professionally ill-disposed towards the sweeping theoretical generalizations about "power politics" or "international society" that others, often with a background in law, thought necessary for a "theory" of international relations.[27]

One proponent of conventional diplomatic history was the first woman to hold a professorship at Oxford, Agnes Headlam-Morley, who took the

---

[25] Katharina Rietzler, "IR's 'Power Couples,'" Women and the History of International Thought Blog. Available at https://whit.web.ox.ac.uk/article/irs-power-couples.

[26] Brian Schmidt, *The Political Discourse of Anarchy: A Disciplinary History of International Relations* (Albany, NY: SUNY Press, 1998).

[27] For a discussion see Ian Hall, *Dilemmas of Decline: British Intellectuals and World Politics, 1945–1975* (Berkeley, CA: University of California Press, 2012), 86–87. See, for example, Georg Schwarzenberger, *Power Politics* (London: Stevens and Son, 1951); C. A. W. Manning, *The Nature of International Society* (London: Bell and Sons, 1962).

prestigious Montague Burton Chair in 1948.[28] Like Tate, whom she taught, Headlam-Morley attended the Zimmern School in Geneva. Her father was James Headlam-Morley, an historian and senior civil servant who helped draft the Treaty of Versailles. Headlam-Morley's inaugural professorial lecture, "Idealism and Realism in International Relations," excerpted here, illuminates her approach both to these now clichéd terms and to diplomatic history in what she saw as "an age of great events ... which has produced an unusual number of great men" (55).

Through a critique of Woodrow Wilson's single-minded support for the League of Nations, Hitler's world policy, and communist ideology, Headlam-Morley suggested that the definitions of and distinction between realism and idealism "breaks down." They "are differences of degree, not of kind" (60). "The Communists call themselves realists. But if you happen not to accept their philosophy you think of them as perverted idealists. The French nationalists too took pride in their realism. But we cannot say that Clemenceau or Barthou had no ideal. They strove to keep safe the heart of European civilization" (60). With her apologetics for Britain's interwar diplomacy, Headlam-Morley's lecture reflects the influence of conservatism on the outlook of many who professed IR as a university subject at this time.

Such an outlook also shaped Headlam-Morley's response to the demands of writing contemporary international history, by which she meant the story of the major events and personalities within the living memory of historians. The problem, as she saw it, was that "when we plodding historians indulge in flights of fancy, it is ten to one not because we have any deeper insight, but because we wish to fit the facts into our preconceived ideas. The story must [invent] a moral. It is then that we become tedious" (56). She concluded that the best approach to writing international history was distinctly British, exemplified by the volumes of historical works by Winston Churchill, "who does not play about with

---

[28] The Lithuanian-born Montague Burton, who made his money through menswear and was knighted in 1931, established several professorships in international relations, including in Jerusalem, in Oxford, at the LSE, and in Edinburgh. Burton was among a number of prominent wealthy landowners and entrepreneurs in interwar Britain who increased their fortunes by pioneering certain tax avoidance strategies to reduce liability to tax, through the use both of domestic schemes and of offshore tax havens. See the "Memorandum Prepared for Board's Committee on Evasion of Income Tax and Sur-Tax," September 1933, British National Archives, IR 40/4574. Burton was an early adopter of what would later become a central means to avoid taxes on European-owned assets after decolonization. On the wider history see Vanessa Ogle, "'Funk Money': The End of Empires, the Expansion of Tax Havens, and Decolonization as an Economic and Financial Event," *Past & Present*, 249:1 (2020): 213–249.

abstract truth and absolute reality. He tells us how things appear to him, with all his cranks and foibles and pre-judgements" (64).

As evidenced by Tate's anti-racist geopolitics, not all early IR women with historical training adopted such a constricted and nationalistic approach to diplomatic history. Still others practiced what became known as "contemporary history," a *seemingly* less Eurocentric version advocated by Rachel F. Wall, holder of Oxford's first university lecture-ship in IR and a specialist on East Asia.[29] Like Susan Strange and several others, Wall combined her graduate studies at the LSE with work at Chatham House, co-authoring the 1955–6 *Survey of International Affairs*.[30] Chatham House, which had been established after the First World War, was more open to women researchers in the interwar years and early Cold War than its US equivalent, the Council on Foreign Relations.[31] In a 1966 radio address for the BBC, Wall argued that "the diplomacy of the twenties and thirties, which still looms so large in conventional accounts of the period, contributes little to our understanding of the present" (70).[32] The first decades of the twentieth century had inaugurated a revolutionary change in world politics. The end of European domination was "a central fact in world history" (72), which called for an equally radical change in the categories and procedures of historical research.

Declining sovereignty, new federalist solutions to world order, Europe's loss of political and ideological power, and the technological

---

[29] Rachel F. Wall, *Japan's Century: An Interpretation of Japanese History since the Eighteen-Fifties* (London: Historical Association, 1964). For a discussion of the Eurocentrism of advocates of world history, particularly in the context of analyses of Asian nations, but focusing on G. P. Gooch and H. G. Wells, see Chika Tonooka, "World History's Eurocentric Moment? British Internationalism in the Age of Asian Nationalism, c. 1905–1931," *Modern Intellectual History* (2019): 1–26 (firstview). For a brief discussion of Wall see Martin Caedel, "The Academic Normalization of International Relations at Oxford, 1920–2012," in Christopher Hood, Desmond King, and Gillian Peele (eds.), *Forging a Discipline: A Critical Assessment of Oxford's Development of the Study of Politics and International Relations in Comparative Perspective* (Oxford: Oxford University Press, 2012), 197–198.

[30] Geoffrey Barraclough and Rachel F. Wall, *Survey of International Affairs, 1955–1956* (Oxford: Oxford University Press, 1960). Wall's approach to contemporary history was influenced by Geoffrey Barraclough, *An Introduction to Contemporary History* (Harmondsworth: Penguin, 1988 [1964]).

[31] Inderjeet Parmer, *Think Tanks and Power in Foreign Policy: A Comparative Study of the Role and Influence of the Council on Foreign Relations and the Royal Institute of International Affairs, 1939–1945* (London: Palgrave Macmillan 2004).

[32] For a discussion of the relationship between contemporary history and early IR in Britain see Geoffrey Field, "Elizabeth Wiskemann, Scholar-Journalist, and the Study of International Relations," in Patricia Owens and Katharina Rietzler (eds.), *Women's International Thought: A New History* (Cambridge: Cambridge University Press, 2021), 198. Also see Rachel Wall, "New Ways in History," *Times Literary Supplement*, 7 April 1966.

and economic shrinking of space all undermined national or even regional approaches to history. Contemporary history "must be international or world history" (71), a less Eurocentric history that was genuinely "world-wide in both its outline and its relevance" and which emphasized the *interaction* of world regions (71). Wall gave the example of the political projects of pan-African and pan-Arab unity, which, she reminded her listeners, had been sneered at in the West. With proposals for reconstituting international order around regional federations, postcolonial leaders and intellectuals challenged neo-colonialist orders in a way deeply threatening to British, French, and US foreign policy visions.[33] Yet "what's of interest to the contemporary historian," Wall maintained, "is that Nkrumah and Nasser should have thought along non-national lines at all" (71). Contemporary history emerged in parallel with but then later diverged from much of the more theory-driven work that became most influential in later British IR, a divergence not helped by Wall's early retirement from Oxford due to ill-health.

The history of international thought inside the Anglo-American academy is an obviously important part of the story of how women in the past thought about relations between peoples, empires, and states. Among other things, it sheds light on the assumptions about the fields and approaches through which a separate IR discipline was formed. The vast majority of early "IR women" in the academy, certainly in Britain and to a significant degree in the United States, were trained as historians engaged in often very practical and always empirically grounded research. The professionalization of academic IR involved a conscious break away from historical approaches and a reorganization around a set of ideological "isms" and (all-male) eponymous "Schools" founded by "great white fathers."[34] In the process, historians were often caricatured as incapable of advancing "theory" and thinking at the level of abstraction necessary for a distinct theory of the "international system." This marginalized women practicing IR as a wider interdisciplinary field, including some of the most important and influential international thinkers of the twentieth century.

Several years into what has been described as IR's "historical turn" this now appears ironic. Historians have long moved away from the study of diplomatic relations, narrowly conceived, towards the historical

---

[33] Adom Getachew, *Worldmaking after Empire: The Rise and Fall of Self-Determination* (Princeton, NJ: Princeton University Press, 2019).

[34] Robert Vitalis, "Beyond Practitioner Histories of International Relations: Or, the Stories That Professors Like to Tell (about) Themselves," in Synne L. Dyvik, Jan Selby, and Rorden Wilkinson (eds.), *What's the Point of International Relations?* (London: Routledge, 2017), 99.

understanding of international and global dynamics, working with and sometimes generating the many thematic, conceptual, and theoretical moves that contemporary IR scholars regularly import from other fields and disciplines but rarely, if ever, export. If there ever was a time that IR could point to the outmoded character of diplomatic history as the *raison d'être* for a separate academic discipline that time has long passed. As IR continues to move beyond and slowly recover from its "grand theory wars," embracing mixed methods and genuine interdisciplinarity, it could do worse than enter into new and productive conversations with earlier generations of thinkers who were constitutively marginalized in the process of what should be, but is not *yet*, the academic home of the best international relations scholarship.

Patricia Owens

Jessie W. Hughan

**From "A Course in International Relations"
(co-authored with Nicholas Kelley) (1915)**

Note: The following tentative course on International Relations has been prepared by Jessie W. Hughan, Ph.D., and Nicholas Kelley, of the Executive Committee. While the committee, in the short time at its disposal, was unable to prepare a course with any claim to scientific completeness, it yet seems advisable to suggest to the chapters some readings on the general subject of war and peace. International relations are not a part of Socialism, though the topics overlap to a great extent, and we believe that these relations can be logically approached only through the Socialist method of the economic interpretation of history.

1. Modern World Commerce
   Norman Angell – *The Great Illusion. I*
   Norman Angell – *International Polity*, Chap. 3 (Arms and Industry)
   David Starr Jordan – *The Unseen Empire*
   Sereno Pratt – *Finance and Commerce*
2. Causes of Modern War
   Kirkpatrick – *War, What For!* Chap. 3
   G. B. Shaw – *Common-Sense About the War*
   Usher – *Pan-Germanism*
   Bemhardi – *Germany and the Next War*, Chap. 5
   Angell – *The Great Illusion*
   Hillquit – *The Metropolitan*, Dec., '14
3. The Facts of War and Militarism
   Kirkpatrick – *War, What For!* Chaps. 4–5
   Blioch – *The Future of War*
   A. T. Mahan – *Armaments and Militarism*
   A. W. Allen – *The Drain of Armament*
   W. P. F. – *Social Wastage of War* – Report of Mass. Commission on The Cost of Living, May, 1910, p. 198, R.

L. A. Mead – *Swords and Ploughshares*, Chap. 4
Angell – *International Polity*, Chaps. 4–5 (Arms and Industry)
4. The Peace Ideal and Non-Resistance
    L. N. Tolstoi – *Bethink Yourselves*
    Jane Addams – *Newer Ideals of Peace*, Chaps. 1, 8
    L. A. Mead – *Swords and Ploughshares*, Chaps. 10–12
    Wm James – *The Moral Equivalent of War*
    Nicholas M. Butler – *The International Mind*
    D. S. Jordan – *War and Waste*
4. International Law and Arbitration
    John B. Moore – *Digest of International Law*
    John B. Moore – *American Diplomacy*, Chap. 8
    General Arbitration Treaties of 1911 – A. A. I. C.
    The Commission of Inquiry – W. P. E.
    Mead – *Swords and Ploughshares*, Chaps. 13, 15
5. Proposed Remedies and Palliatives for War
    Hillquit – *The Metropolitan*, Jan., '15
    The Hague Conference – Instructions to American Delegates,
        1907 – W. P. F. Record of the Hague
    W. P. F. Hudson Maxim – *Peace Through Preparedness*
    Hamilton Holt – The Independent
    Alllan Benson – Pearson's Magazine, Nov. Manifesto of American
        Socialist Party, December, 1914
    Programs of World Peace Foundation. National League for the
        Limitation of Armament
    The Federalist
6. Socialism and War
    Karl Kautsky – *Krieg und Kapitalismus*
    Kirkpatrick – *War, What For!* Chap. 10
    Gustav Herve – *My Country, Right or Wrong*
    Manifesto of American Socialist Party – The American Socialist,
        January, 1915
    Manifestoes of the European Socialist Groups – The
        Intercollegiate Socialist, Oct.–Nov., 1914
    War Year-Book of the I. S. 5. (announced)
    Untermann – The Dick Militia Law

The files of *The New Review*, *The International Socialist Review*, *The American Socialist*, *The New York Call (Sunday Magazine)*, etc., contain illuminating articles on this subject. The *Atlantic Monthly*, *Pearson's*, *The Metropolitan*, *New Republic*, *The Independent* and *Harper's Weekly* are also well worth perusal. The initials "W. P. F." stand for the World Peace Foundation, with headquarters at 40 Mt. Vernon Street, Boston; the initials "A. A. I. C." for The American Association for International Conciliation.

Committee on the Bureau of International Research in Harvard University and Radcliffe College (n.d. *c.* 1923)

From "Proposal for a Foundation for Instruction in International Affairs" and "Foundation for Instruction in International Affairs"

The proposed Foundation for Instruction in International Affairs would enable Radcliffe College to offer first, advanced instruction to competent graduate students, second, systematic instruction to mature non-collegiate women and, third, lectures open to the public.

Inasmuch as women are now voters, it is important that they should be given an opportunity long since open to men, to inform themselves on international questions. Such a plan would become a factor in promoting good relationships among nations and would serve to illustrate how institutions of higher learning might help to solve the great human problem of bettering international relations.

Radcliffe College, which at present offers courses in international law and diplomacy, is especially fitted to carry out such a plan. It has already shown a genuine interest in promoting such a study. It has a well established program, the services of eminent professors teaching at Harvard and Radcliffe [   ]. The Olivart collection of international law, one of the largest in the world, is in the Harvard Law School library while the Wheaton collection of international texts is available at Brown University. Radcliffe's location in a cosmopolitan district gives it an advantage in carrying out a program for the non-collegiate public.

A woman's college is selected as the first to try the plan because of the interest among college women in federating internationally, as illustrated by the International Federation of University Women. This society, made up of seventeen national organizations, has as its aim "to promote understanding and friendship between the university women of the nations of the world, and thereby to further their interests and develop between their countries sympathy and mutual helpfulness."

In the present year 212 women are engaged in graduate study at Radcliffe. These students come from 55 institutions of learning and from foreign countries.

With a fund such as is proposed, Radcliffe might develop a center for study in international law unique in the country and in the world.

The importance of such a graduate center in offering opportunities for the highest scholastic attainments in this field is obvious, as likewise the advantage of carrying out the full program in one college for the purpose of showing the complete possibilities of the plan.

A somewhat similar plan is that now known as the Institute of Politics at Williamstown. This covers a four weeks period and costs between $25,000 and $35,000.

The Council of Radcliffe College will welcome a study of the resources and conditions favorable to the development of such a foundation as is proposed.

F. Melian Stawell

From *The Growth of International Thought* (1929)

"Shall I bring to the birth, and not cause to bring forth?" Said the Lord.

Underlying this book is the conviction that a sane nationalism, when it understands itself, points the way to internationalism at its completion. The principle that builds the single State cannot end with the single State. This has been felt, sometimes clearly, more often dimly, by all the best thinkers of Europe. The lesson has been hard; indeed, it has never been learnt, but it ought to be learnt and it could be learnt. Gradually the sense of its need has grown and in that growth lies hope. The survey which follows has been, for reasons of space, confined on the whole to Europe, but the same factors are and always have been at work in all nations.

[...]

The gods had no mercy. The Peloponnesian War ended with the fall of Athens, and though she rose again there was never heart enough in the people to make the effort necessary for federation. How great an effort was needed may be felt from Thucydides' own account of the civil war in Corcyra, oligarchs against democrats, where there was "every form of murder and every extreme of cruelty," "where the father slew the son and the supplianto were torn from the temples." It is one of the strongest indictments against war ever written, stronger for the understanding Thucydides had of the weakness as well as the wickedness of men. The prime cause of the fighting is the lust for power and gain. But once war is begun "men are tempted by dire necessity." "War is a hard master and most men grow like the lives they lead." So it goes on till there is nothing but suspicion everywhere. "There was no treaty binding enough to reconcile opponents: every one knew that nothing was secure and therefore he thought only of his own safety; he could not afford to trust another."

Yet this was the age that produced a Thucydides, and his was not the only voice of reason and pity. The play of "The Trojan Women" by

Euripides was performed the year after Melos had been sacked when "the men were killed, the women and children sold into slavery," and no play gives a more moving picture of the conquered. It is they who are the heroic figures in the drama; all the glory is for Hecuba and Andromache and Cassandra, shamed and tortured, not for their Greek conquerors. And the brilliant comedy of the "Lysistrata" in and through its reckless indecency strikes a note that is almost as touching. Lysistrata, whose name means "the Peacemaker," and whose character is as winning as her name, determines to band the Theban and Spartan women together with the Athenian in a vow that they will have nothing to do with men until the senseless war is ended. And when the others shrink from the sacrifice it is the Spartan who supports her. "The one true woman among you all!" cries Lysistrata. "Stand by me, and we shall save Greece yet, we two."

They did not save Greece, neither they nor their creator Aristophanes. His limitations are plain enough. Even the lovely choruses of peace between enemies with which the "Lysistrata" closes sing of Athens and Sparta united indeed, but united against another enemy, the Persian. And this is always the way through all the dreams and efforts of classic Hellas. When Isocrates half a century later once again implores them to unite, the union at which he aims is still to be pointed against "the foreigner." None the less, if the Athenians had listened to Euripides, Thucydides and Aristophanes and not to Alcibiades and Cleon, if they had taken the advice of Cimon against his stately stern opponent, Pericles, and refused all attempts at crippling Sparta that could only "leave Greece lame in one leg," they might have opened an era in the history of their country that would have set a priceless example for all the others that have followed. Because they had, in germ at least, the two ideas of arbitration between equals and confederacy on equal terms, ideas which the long bitter experience of ages is at last teaching us are essential if nations are to be saved from the curse of war. One of the most admirable devices for civic life at Athens, and the Athenians were fertile in such, was the custom of submitting every quarrel between citizens that did not involve a serious crime to the good offices of an arbitrator, before it came into court at all.

If both parties accepted the award, and they often did, the quarrel was at an end. And this excellent plan they prepared to use between States. At the very opening of the Peloponnesian War the Spartans are felt to be at least formally in the wrong because they do not accept the offer made by Pericles.

Not that the historian makes Pericles pacific, far from it, in his justification of war for the sake of Empire, though it is Empire as the basis for a lofty culture. Pericles is made to use words almost as tyrannical as those of Cleon, his successor, and, in a sense, his Nemesis. It is all the more remarkable that an offer of arbitration should have been made and recorded, even if it were only offered to conciliate the public opinion of Greece. Plutarch even ascribes to Pericles a proposal, before the war broke out, for a Pan-Hellenic congress with delegates chosen from all the States. Thucydides, however, mentions nothing of the kind, while Plutarch is writing nearly four hundred years later and himself doubtful of Pericles' good faith. But that Plutarch should make the statement at all throws light on what was felt to be possible in antiquity, although it was never achieved.

It is significant that the great grievance against the Athens of Pericles was that she turned the Delian confederacy, intended to be of equals, herself merely the leader, into a despotic Empire, "enslaving free cities contrary to treaty."

Cicero, looking back as Plutarch did through a haze of distance, spoke of the Amphictyonic Council as the common council of Greece. We know now that it was far from being that. Still, there is importance in the mere fact that twelve of the leading "tribes" did unite on an equal basis for common purposes, even if that common purpose was limited to the care of the Delphic territory and the observance of certain rules in battle. Delegates were chosen, two for each "tribe," and the arrangements were such that as regard the voting "Athens, Sparta and Thebes had no more influence that the humblest Ionian, Dorian or Boeotian city." Moreover, the Amphictyons will always deserve a place in any review of Internationalism because theirs was the first Council in Europe, so far as we know, to attempt a definite limitation of cruelties in war. No Amphictyon, according to the ancient oath, could annihilate another's city nor cut off the water, "neither in time of peace nor in time of war." The same spirit is shown by the Platonic saying in the *Republic*, even though Plato limits the compassion of it to the Greeks, that men should never make war without remembering that one day the enemy will become a friend.

Sayings and agreements like these, even though they were never followed up, exhibit that Hellenic balance and humanity of judgement which point out of a way of progress more practicable than the advice of extremists. No pure Greek appears ever to have advocated either non-resistance to oppression or the attempt to shorten war by making it as horrible as possible. To the Greek intellect, alert both in theory and practice, it would have seemed absurd to suppose that tyrants would become less tyrannical by being allowed to have their own way, and sophistical to argue that because war was a resort to force it meant that the force must be unlimited. On the contrary, to find the right limit in war, as elsewhere, was to a thoughtful Greek the problem of problems.

That they never did find this limit was due, not to a lack of insight so much as to a lack of determination and endurance among the common people. And so we turn back to their writers for inspiration, when we are tempted to turn away from their history in despair.

It should be added, if only to avoid misunderstanding, that, for all their treachery and instability, the Greeks were the most humane people of antiquity, beyond Semites, Egyptians and Romans as they were beyond the Italians and Spaniards of the Renaissance.

To a born conqueror, an explorer, and organizer such as Alexander, Greece in her weakness and disunion might well have seemed half-derelict and the Near East entirely so. The powerful days of Babylonia, Assyria and Egypt were in the past; the power of Persia was plainly weakening. The thought that it might be possible to conquer them all must have been intoxicating to a man as restless and ambitious as he was able.

But many scholars have believed that he may also have felt a finer ambition and dreamed of welding the peoples together. It is far from unlikely. He certainly assumed Persian dress and manners and yet he claimed as jealously as his father Philip that a Macedonian was also a Hellene. The largeness of the idea would appeal to a man of his constructive audacity who delighted to open pathways between East and West and recognized merit wherever he came on it, founding new cities in lands that might have seemed worn out, patronizing and encouraging the despised Jews. Moreover, the Persian civilization had always attracted the Greeks even when they fought against it. The whole of Herodotus' history turns on the contrast between the two civilizations, the Greek and the Persian, the free and the despotic, and Herodotus is at pains to show the generous and royal side even of the despotism that he opposes. The figure of Darius in Aeschylus' "Persians," play of triumph though it is, stands out as noble and impressive. Even the "Medizing" of traitors among the Greeks bears witness to the charm. And half-way between Aeschylus and Alexander we have Xenophon, taking for his ideal prince the legendary figure of Cyrus the Great and emphasizing the humane and broad-minded spirit of one who was to rule over many peoples.

But, if it is true that Alexander did have such an aim, he took the wrong way to realize it. The characteristic Greek ideal was, that at least a substantial nucleus of the citizens must be free, and by this they meant that they must share both in administering and in making the laws. This was their right and not a favour. Philip and Alexander inaugurated the era of great despotisms, where the last word rests with the sovereign and those whom he has chosen. And the word is backed by force. The ordinary citizen has no more control over the military power than he has over the laws. The union that is possible under these conditions, in losing freedom, loses the elasticity which gives the spring to internationalism.

Lucy Philip Mair

From "International Relations as an Independent Subject" (1934)

It is sometimes argued that there is no room for a special study of international relations since the whole subject matter is covered elsewhere in economics and politics, of which international relations merely represents the international aspect. This view has a certain superficial attractiveness, but I do not think it is really justified.

It is true that the most extensive international contacts are economic, and that a high proportion of present-day international problems arise from the political control of this form of international relation; but it does not follow from this that the nature of such problems will reveal itself spontaneously to the student as a by-product of his studies of the theory of government, or of international trade. To hold this view is to fall into the dangerous fallacy of re-arming by analogy, of supposing that one can draw from data as to relations between individuals, conclusions regarding relations between groups, or that, because the name "government" is applied to the political organisation both of individuals and of states, an analysis of national government can explain the international community.

The claim of any branch of the social sciences to be regarded as an autonomous subject seems to depend on two questions: whether its subject matter can be clearly differentiated from those of other branches, and whether it is too wide for the field to be satisfactorily covered by the student unless he makes it a special study. International Relations fulfils both these requirements. In its present-day form the study must centre around the problem of the attempt to unite in a collective system a number of communities which are highly organised politically with a view to independent action. This problem is absolutely *sui generis*. It cannot be understood or solved by a process of facile generalisation from the history of political development within individual states. To the sociologist the relevant consideration in studying the relations between organised groups of individuals is just that they are groups, and that the nature of their organisation conditions their interaction. The international institutions which we have owe their peculiar form to the circumstances that they deal with already existent organised groups, and this fact, together with the fact that the application of coercion to such groups is a process which must differ not only in kind but also in degree from the coercion of the individual within the state, means that their development or failure to develop must follow lines peculiar to itself.

The study of international relations is in essence the study of these institutions and their functioning, and of these fields in the relations between States where organisation is felt to be necessary but is at present lacking. It centres round the analysis of those organs of international government which were established at the close of the last war – the League of Nations and its subsidiary organs and the Permanent Court of International Justice, though it has to deal also with less well-known institutions such as the diplomatic machine and the various organs which exist for international co-operation in technical matters. Its approach to these institutions is along broader lines than that of international law, for it is concerned not only with law as a body of rules but with the extent to which it is effective, the forces which make its acceptance or rejection, for the further development or restriction of the sphere of legal obligation. It is concerned with the practice of international institutions as well as their constitution, and must study this in the wider context of the whole range of relations between those organised political entities which we call nations. This subject matter is certainly extensive enough to promise a special study extending over a two years' course.

It is sometimes argued, on the other hand, that the sound understanding of international relations requires too great a background of general knowledge for it to be suitable as an undergraduate study at all, that it should be left for post-graduate students who have already taken a full course in economics, politics or history. This is an argument which would be equally applicable to all undergraduate studies. Only those who make academic work their profession, and a few others whose work leaves them time to extend their range of general knowledge, learn in later years how far the best undergraduate training is for providing the key to understanding of the world around him which the student so often thinks he has acquired. This is an argument for less and not more specialisation at the undergraduate stage. The majority of students, after all, are not destined to the furtherance of knowledge by research or teaching. For them the gain to be derived from a study of the social sciences will not consist in a detailed study of one branch, but rather in the attainment of an objective attitude towards those problems of economics and politics in which the modern world is interested, and of the understanding of sufficient elementary facts about their nature to enable them to withstand the fallacies of the popular press. From this point of view the desirability of being able to offer to the student an explanation of the fundamental facts of the international situation surely requires no stressing.

Merze Tate

From "Teaching of International Relations in Negro Colleges" (1947)

I was invited to discuss with you the teaching of International Relations in Negro Colleges. I have changed my subject to the Teaching of International Relations. There is no justification for teaching International Relations in any different way in a Negro College from the way it should be taught in a white college. In teaching at Howard University I present the same material in the same manner as I would at Michigan, Radcliffe, Smith, Wellesley, Indiana State, or Ohio State. The only departure that I feel is justified is the constant reminder that the American Negro is only one of many minorities in the world and that his problem is not unique but only one phase of a much larger issue. The teacher of international relations at the College level has an opportunity to draw on several fields of learning for there are many facets to power politics. These may be economic, political, historical, cultural, geographic, ideological, etc. Consequently, all the social sciences provide basic material. If the particular course in international relations at Howard University happens to be History 202A – European Diplomatic Relations 1870–1941 or 202B – Problems of Modern Europe 1914–1941 we will find economics, geography, political science, political philosophy, international law and geo-politics inextricably interwoven with the history of these periods. One cannot teach 19th and 20th century imperialism, the partitioning of Africa, of Asia, of the Pacific, of the Arctic and Antarctic regions, and the scramble for world markets and spheres of economic penetration without a background of geography. An examination of 19th and 20th century laissez-faire liberalism, leads inevitably to a consideration of the last phases of capitalism and a study of scientific socialism or Marxism; while a history of 20th century Russia and the U.S.S.R. compels one to examine Lenin's great contribution to socialism in deciphering the "dictatorship of the proletariat" through the device of the soviet.

49

International law embellishes the study of modern arbitration, the Hague Conferences and Conventions, the problems of neutrality during 1914–1917 and 1935–1941; the drafting of the Covenant of the League of Nations, of the Charter of the United Nations, and of the statutes of the Permanent Court of International Justice and the International Court, the post World War I war crimes fiasco and the Nuremburg Trials.

The teaching of international relations offers an opportunity to present new philosophies in the field of politics. For example, the philosophy of Existentialism best expounded in the thought of Jean-Paul Sartre, represents contemporary shattered post-war Europe. At the heart of this philosophy is the concept of man as liberty, man who has full freedom to create himself and his values as he wills. Sartre maintains that Existentialism inspires man to positive action, in giving him the full measure of his liberty and in refusing to permit refuge in false security. This philosophy has been attacked from both the Left and the Right. Communists find Existentialism the expression of a decadent bourgeois culture, the philosophy of a hopeless, unhealthy world. Conservative Christians attack it because of its uncompromising atheism, its denial of transcendent values, its obsession with perversion, and moral and physical ugliness. Clerics called it "materialistic."

A field of international relations which gained much vogue during World War II was geopolitics. The word: "Geopolitik," coined by the Swede, Rudolf Kjellen, was before this decade a new word to the average American. The prefix "geo" which preceded "politik" means much and relates politics to the soil. Geopolitics is primarily concerned with a consideration of the political state in its geographical environment, but the study of neither geography nor political science alone is sufficient for the understanding of geopolitics. A knowledge of both the earth and the state is a prerequisite. The Geopolitical Institute at Munich, headed by Major General Karl Haushofer, popularized the word and contributed several definitions, such as: "Geopolitik is the doctrine of the power of the state on earth"; "Geopolitik is the doctrine of the earth relations of political developments"; "Geopolitik is the science which deals with the political organisms of space and their structure"; "Geopolitik is the scientific foundation of the art of political action in the life and death struggle of state organisms for Lebensraum." Haushofer says "Geopolitik grew out of political geography. It activates the latter's fund of knowledge and puts it at the service of the political leader." The German theory of Geopolitics leads to war. The broader interpretation of geopolitics is the geographic study of the state from the viewpoint of foreign policy.

Thus the stress is placed on the geographic aspect of international relations. Geopolitics from a broad viewpoint is scientific only in so far as it seeks to study the geographical aspects of the state in an objective manner. But geopolitics differs from geography; the former is a dynamic study ... dealing with what the state wishes to become ... while geography is static and considers the state in its material environment from the viewpoint of an objective analysis.

Geopoliticians always draw lessons from the military events of the past. The study of military, naval, and air strategy is therefore an important source for geopolitics. Needless to say, the lessons of the Second World War regarding land, sea, and air power are important material for the study of geopolitics. Geopolitics draws upon imperialism, political philosophy, economics, political science and history. The teacher of the subject can find a wealth of material for enriching the course from the above listed fields. In fact, some geo-politicians interpret history as "geography in action." The elements of history are man, place, and time, while the elements of geopolitics are the earth and the state. The word "state" is frequently used in geopolitics. This is the concept of the self-governing state possessing the rights of sovereignty. The dynamic nature of geopolitics is found in the adjustment of the state to the natural environment. This dynamic nature is also revealed in the German definition of frontiers as lines of battlefield.

Geopoliticians may be considered not only from the viewpoint of contributors to geopolitical theory like Ratzel and Sir Halford Mackinder, but also from the point of view of leadership in applied geopolitics. James Monroe for his statement of regionalism or the doctrine of two spheres; Theodore Roosevelt by his acquisition in 1903 of the Canal Zone across the Isthmus of Panama; Secretary Seward by his purchase of Alaska and his attempts to have the United States acquire Iceland and Greenland and F. D. Roosevelt, for his over-age destroyer and air base deal were leaders in applied geopolitics. Likewise, Benjamin Disraeli by his purchase for Great Britain in 1875 of a substantial portion of the shares of the Suez Canal Company; Cecil Rhodes, who planned to make Britain supreme from Cape to Cairo on the continent of Africa; Otto von Bismarck, who succeeded in uniting Germany under one flag by three successive wars; and Adolf Hitler were all geopoliticians of the first order. Mussolini's efforts to control the "waist" of the Mediterranean, to make that sea "mare nostrum" and to build an Empire in Africa indicated his geopolitical interests. Baron Tanaka, as Prime Minister of Japan, is alleged to have presented to the Emperor in 1927 the geopolitical ideas of a New Order in Greater East Asia. Geopolitics has proved that the study of both history and geography is necessary to understand the events of the past and the problems of the future.

Today, Sir Halford Mackinder's geopolitical concept of the Heartland, open to some qualifications, is being developed as never before. Mackinder's three point thesis which has recently become familiar to Anglo-American, is terrifying to the United States. As early as 1904 Mackinder stated:

> Who rules East Europe commands the Heartland;
> Who rules the Heartland commands the World Island;
> Who rules the World Island commands the World.

The teacher of international relations is therefore bound to point out the real results of the two World Wars. The defeat of the Central Powers was not the most significant event of the first World War. The outstanding result was the Bolsheviki organization of the U.S.S.R. Similarly, the defeat of Germany, Italy and Japan in World War II were only incidental events. The overwhelming result of that great struggle is the rise to preeminence in world affairs of Soviet Russia. The world balance of power has been overset in favor of the pivot state, which is now expanding over the marginal lands of Euro-Asia.

The Empire of the world may soon be in sight. There is fear that the world island may become such a huge base for naval, land and air power that the rest of the world may be overcome.

The geographic study of the state from the viewpoint of foreign policy yields certain contributions which the teacher of international relations must indicate. These are:

1. The elements forming the basis of the world power of a state are sixfold: location, size and shape, climate and climatic energy, population and manpower, natural resources and industrial capacity, and social and political organization. All these are essential for world power.
2. The concept of regionalism must be given some consideration. Regionalism as a principle in international relations is the attempt to organize large areas of the world, usually but not necessarily continental in extent, into economic and cultural units under the leadership of a dominant power.
3. The Arctic will be the future air Mediterranean. Consequently, the foreign policy of the states near the Arctic Ocean may be vitally affected. Since three fourths of the land area of the earth lies in the Northern Hemisphere centered around the north pole, certain Arctic areas will become extremely significant as bases in the air age. The great circle routes from Chicago to Berlin or London from New York to Moscow, pass over Labrador. Likewise, a great circle air route from

New York City or Chicago to Tokyo, from Kansas City to Shanghai or from Seattle to Chungking crosses Alaska.

4. World War II proved the importance of bases ... land, sea and air ... in the study of strategy. The determination of the United States to retain captured islands in the Pacific as bases proves the value of this emphasis upon bases. The foreign policy of many states in the post-war world may result in a scramble for bases.

5. The geopolitical concepts of defense in depth and selling of space to gain time which proved so important in World War II have lost much of their significance in the atomic age. Today a great power faces annihilation with as much anxiety as does a small state. Today no power can be saved by its isolated position or remoteness from a powder keg: by its industrial potential ... the capacity to prepare for war: by its defense in depth or extensive terrain which permits the selling of space to gain time. These advantages of the pre-atomic age no longer exist.

Today there is no isolated location, no remoteness, no defense in depth for there is no space, no industrial plant that cannot be reached and destroyed by the enemy. Tomorrow time will be measured in the twinkle of an eye. Stratospheric projectiles and jet-propelled superbombers carrying atomic bombs at supersonic speeds will become the competitive weapons of pre-armed nations against which there is no defense, except to use them. Therefore, we argue that our security lies in keeping our research going, regardless of cost and effort, so that we can maintain the lead and stay ahead of the world in the development of atomic energy. Thus a competition in a new and awesome field threatens to supersede the old race in armaments.

The teacher of international relations should continually emphasize that excessive armaments of any nature are not the primary cause of war; the political, economic, and psychological causes must first be removed, before states will disarm. The failure of the great powers to agree on a plan for the control of atomic energy for military purposes is a matter of confidence. With good faith, either the American or the Russian plan, or a synthesis of the two, could be made to work. But on each side confidence is lacking in the intentions and policies of the other party. Finally, it should be realized that the control of atomic energy is only one phase of the limitation of armaments.

Scientists have evolved new chemical, bacteriological, and biological weapons and they are experimenting with the cosmic ray. Science left free can destroy mankind. Thus any effectual plan for the control of atomic energy should be adopted and extended to cover other weapons of mass destruction. But mere outlawry of atomic weapons by legislative fiat before the establishment of an effective system of inspection and control will raise technical problems of inspection and control which are inordinately difficult but not beyond solution if there is a will to solve them.

In the past statesmen have been guided by the assumption that states were sovereign entities. But the Baruch plan for the control of atomic energy cuts athwart the concept of sovereignty which for centuries has governed the thinking of nations, "Physical science has made the sovereign national state a fearful anachronism." There can be no sovereignty in its absolute sense in the atomic age. The word has lost its meaning in an era where the choice is between international cooperation or international disintegration, between world peace and world destruction, between "the quick and the dead."

Agnes Headlam-Morley

**From "Idealism and Realism in International Relations,"
an Inaugural Lecture (1949)**

But when on hearing of my own appointment I gave further thought to
my doubts and hesitations, I found that they did not spring entirely from
a fitting modesty. I was appalled by the amount of history that goes on, by
the sheer weight of knowledge that is accumulated from day to day, by
the books that I would have to read; worse still by the books which
I might be expected to write. In this lamentable state, my mind echoed
the cri de Coeur of Linklater's disreputable Italian count, "I don't want
books stuffed full of the world's calamities – give me one book about a
man who strangled his mistress with her hair on a dark night".

We live in an age of great events, events that may be horrible, strange,
fantastic, but not surely without dramatic interest. It is an age moreover
which has produced an unusual number of great men, Lenin, Hitler,
Churchill, Roosevelt, Stresemann, Weizmann, good or evil their
achievement is at least remarkable. And behind them is a host of others,
human, often tragic, each in their own way significant, Wilson,
Masaryk, Briand, Benes, Brüning, Mussolini, Stalin, Tito, Neville
Chamberlain. The raw material of this history is voluminous, it makes
tough reading but it is interesting enough – far more interesting than the
books which the historians write. For when we come to recount these
events, to describe these personalities, for the most part we make a sorry
business of it.

From this perplexity I could find no escape, so I gave it up and read a
different kind of book. There surprisingly I found the answer. Catharine
Moreland wished she were more fond of history. "I read it a little as a
duty, but I find little that does not either vex or weary me. The quarrels of
Popes and Kings, with wars and pestilences on every page – and yet I find
it odd that it should be so dull, for a great deal of it must be invention".
"Historians you think", said Miss Tilney, "are not happy in their flights
of fancy, they display imagination without raising interest".

A great deal of it must be invention. I do not think that historians to-day are tempted to invent facts. They are trained not to do so, and in any case there are plenty of experts about to catch them out if they do. No historian has all the facts before him. But the writer of recent history has a great many more facts to work on, more than have those who deal with earlier periods. It is just because there is so much material and because somehow he must make sense of it all that he is perhaps more tempted to invent explanations to attribute motives. Miss Austin complains not that the historians use their imaginations, but that, when they do so they are dull. This she found surprising. The imagination as she knew it, as all artists know it, is a faculty which enables them to penetrate below the surface of events, to an inner truth, a deeper reality. But when we plodding histor-ians indulge in flights of fancy, it is ten to one not because we have any deeper insight, but because we wish to fit the facts into our own precon-ceived ideas. The story must have a moral. The moral is not always easy to see. So we invent one. It is then that we become tedious. For truth is always more interesting than our invention.

When I started to write this lecture I thought that I would practice what I preached; that I would allow the characters to speak for themselves; the events to tell their own story. Then, God willing, the moral would emerge. Having chosen Idealism and Realism as my theme it seemed reasonable to begin with President Wilson. Here was an idealist on a grand scale, all I had to do was to describe him; to tell you as accurately as I could what he thought and said and did. I soon came to a stop. Wilson was a man who thought a lot about politics, a man whose speeches had great influence on their time. What he said was, in many ways, as important as what he did. But when I came to analyse his thoughts, I found that everything I put down was misleading. Wilson hardly ever said anything without qualifying it. But having made what were in fact incompatible statements, he did not take up the challenge and pursue his thoughts to a conclusion. It was not that he expressed himself badly. He had a sense of words. He could coin a striking phrase. Often enough he would take some rigmarole that Col. House had written and reduce it to a few terse sentences. None the less he remains elusive. If you try to think yourself into his mind; to discover what he really meant by the League of Nations, by International Law, by Self Determination, by the Freedom of the Seas, you find yourself more and more befogged. It is impossible to paraphrase what he said, and to give an endless string of quotations would scarcely make a good beginning to a lecture of this kind.

So there seemed nothing for it but to begin the other way round. What is meant by Idealism and Realism in politics? Why am I so sure that President Wilson was an idealist? Ideal and Real. The philosophers know what they mean by those words. But as we use them in a popular not a philosophic sense, they are difficult to define. Still they and their derivations are commonly used, and they do appear to convey some meaning. Lord Robert Cecil discussing the early proposals for the League of Nations pointed out that it would be a mistake to trust utilitarian motives, "All this will fail as a unifying force unless we add something more. It is a delusion to suppose that the pursuit of material wealth tends to peace. What is wanted is a great ideal and that must be found in the Old Hebrew – and let me add Christian conception of the reign of peace". Here at least is something definite. An Idealist is one who sees things, not only as they are, but as what they should be. He believes that we will achieve no part of the good that we desire unless we aim high and relate the means to the end. A realist, I suppose, is one who sees the world as it is. He will not admit that something which he recognizes as good is for that reason attainable. "I like the League of Nations", Clemenceau used to say, "but I don't believe in it". The realist too, if he is wise, will relate the means to the end, but maybe he will think that as regards method he has more scope than the idealist.

Wilson undoubtedly believed that a better world was possible and that it was his mission to bring it into being. Not only was he an idealist, but he believed in ideas. He thought that an idea once it is launched into the world will act on its momentum, for good or for ill. He put the point fairly clearly before the League Commission at Paris. "We have said that this war was carried on for a vindication of democracy". Then follows the qualification. "This statement did not create the impulse, but it brought it to consciousness". He goes on, "as soon as it was stated that the war was being waged for a vindication of democracy, a new spirit came into the world". He represented the mightiest of all nations. None the less he would say that the Idea, (not the fact but the Idea) of the great powers and of the balance of power has always produced only aggression and selfishness and war.

If Wilson had looked squarely at the facts he would have found good cause for hope. Lloyd George believed no less firmly than he in the principle of self determination. In this he was supported by his experts in the British delegation. In my father's unpublished diary of the Peace Conference, I find constant references to the difficulties that arise when economic interests cut across national aspirations. Again and again he comes back to the point that frontiers must be drawn in accordance with the wishes of the people. "We must settle the frontiers on national grounds and then do everything to encourage free commercial intercourse between nations". These Englishmen thought of Europe as a comity of nations, great and small. They did not think it necessary that political boundaries should be an obstacle to trade. In spite of all that has happened I think that they were right. They acted on the principle of respect for the individual human personality.

Lloyd George did not pin his faith to the League of Nations. But he gave a free hand to Lord Robert Cecil who did more than any one else at Paris to secure a workable machinery for the peaceful settlement of disputes. Lloyd George saw that it would be futile to set up International Institutions unless there were a firm foundation of political agreement. There could be no stability in Europe unless Germany were allowed to take her proper place as a great power. There could be no lasting peace unless we were just in our dealings with the defeated enemy and applied our own principles with impartiality. He worked for these ends with the utmost tenacity and spent a great deal of energy trying to undo the harm he had done by his original dishonesty about reparations.

But Wilson had decided before he ever came to Paris that the only thing that mattered was the League of Nations. He told the American delegation that no matter how satisfactory the peace treaties might be in their territorial and economic aspects, they would be futile for the preservation of future peace unless they provided for the League. Over and over again he compromised on other points in order to win support for the Covenant.

The League, as Wilson conceived it, could not solve the problems of Europe. He did not want an international government. In spite of all he said about covenants for mutual protection, it is clear that he did not even want a treaty of alliance. None the less he tried to win Clemenceau over by telling him that the league would give security. When Lloyd George proposed an Anglo American Guarantee he agreed without demur. Col. House noted at the time that he did not think the Senate would accept it (he does not seem to have thought this important). But Wilson gave no warning to his colleagues at Paris.

Later, before the Foreign Relations Committee of the Senate, he said that the guarantee treaty involved nothing more than was already contained in the Covenant. It was a moral not a legal obligation. When they asked what this meant, he said that a legal obligation binds you to do a particular duty under certain sanctions; a moral obligation is of course superior, but there is always an element of judgment. It was one of the senators who suggested that a treaty imposes a legal obligation to which there is only a moral sanction. This Wilson welcomed as a new idea. Then he added, "You see we are talking of different things, in international law the word "legal" does not mean the same as in national law. So the language does not fit". Here he had perhaps hit on something – but he did not follow it up.

I do not think that at that time it was possible for the Americans to undertake definite military commitments in Europe. A nation does not so easily depart from its accustomed paths. The time was not ripe for the overthrow of well established traditions. But amazing though it is, Wilson does not appear to have realized the nature of the problem by which he was faced. Faith can remove mountains, but one must at least recognize there is a mountain to be moved. Wilson did not take seriously the French demand for security. He did not even take seriously the fact of American isolationism. He seems to have thought that once the Covenant came into being the evocative effect would be so great that all the problems would melt away – quite irrespective of what was contained in the Covenant.

British policy was, I think, essentially sound; to rebuild the concert of Europe: to heal the breach between France and Germany. Later there was a statesman in Germany, Gustav Stresemann, who had the clarity of vision to see things as they were. He would have pursued such a policy, at first for the sake of his own country, then in the interests of Europe. He had enduring courage. But we, after Locarno, did not carry it through with sufficient resolution.

Wilson's personal failure is easy enough to explain. The defect in character is so obvious, the lack of humility so startling. He was a shallow thinker. In thought as in action he stopped half way. Rationally he could carry nothing to a conclusion, intuitively he could not penetrate below the surface of men's minds. He voiced ideas which the majority of well meaning people accepted. He never probed to the springs of action. In much of the popular idealism of the nineteen twenties we find the same easy assumption that any amount of superficiality is justifiable in a good cause.

We have allowed our spiritual faculties to become so numb that we think of good in a feeble attenuated form. But we still live in the shadow of the mountain of paradise. It is even more difficult for us to understand evil. We know now what Hitler did, we can follow every twist and turn of his policy, we can assess every step in his progress to power and to destruction. But for all that I doubt if we understand him better than did Brüning or Treviranus or Schleicher or Papen or any of the others who failed to stop him in Germany. In judging him now we would not make the same mistakes as they. We may value others that are just as bad, but we cannot leave it alone. We have to have an explanation. Some say it was Fichte, some say it was Wagner, some say it was Hegel (this is obvious nonsense). Some put it all down to Nietzsche.

> Die Krähen schreien
> Und ziehen schwirren Flugs zur Stadt:
> Bald wird es schneien –
> Wohl dem, der jetzt noch – Heimat hat!

In the tormented poet there was more human feeling than Hitler ever showed. In any case what Nietzsche meant by force was not what Hitler meant, and what Nietzsche meant by the superman was not at all what Hitler meant by the Aryan race. Hitler was not a creative thinker. He used and distorted the thought of others. As one would expect they were mostly, though not all, German thinkers. But the impulse of his action did not come from them. He was an angler in the lake of darkness. We can only probe about in the mire.

National Socialism was inherently irrational. For that very reason it was the most repellent, the most terrifying of heresies. Communism if once you accept the materialist premise is consistent, intellectually satisfying. But I do not think that this is the source of its strength. You can explain religion and art, psychology and biology in materialist terms. You can destroy one civilization and built [sic] up another in its place. But "the new hygienically conditioned, artificially lit city of man" will rest on foundations that are shallow and unsafe. It is not the apparent rationalism, or the materialism which give to revolutionary communism its dynamic force. It is the doctrine of historical determinism which appeals to something deeply rooted in human nature. Once he accepts this doctrine man no longer thinks of himself as a self contained entity controlling his environment by the use of reason. He becomes the instrument of a transcendent power – the dominating force of history.

[...]

It is not Marx and Lenin whom we are told to obey. They are the high priests of the Moloch of history.

[...]

The upshot of it all is that my original definition breaks down. There is no clearer distinction between realists and idealists. Some pursue a relatively higher, some a lower, aim; some have more, some less, confidence in their ability to alter facts. But these are differences of degree, not of kind. The Communists call themselves realists. But if you happen not to accept their philosophy you think of them as perverted idealists. The French nationalists too took pride in their realism. But we cannot say that Clemenceau or Barthou had no ideal. They strove to keep safe the heart of European civilization. Every historian must try to make sense of his history. So every statesman must have a purpose to his policy. Opportunism of aim hardly exists. Hitler perhaps came nearest to it. Even in Laval there was an underlying consistency of aim, the physical survival of the State of France.

But what about the method as distinct from the purpose of policy. Hitler claimed to be a realist. By this he meant that he would use any means that came to his hand. He would have entire freedom of action.

He would be limited by no moral scruples, by no pity, by no loyalty. Hitler, an extreme revolutionary, never openly disclosed his revolutionary purpose. He was an opportunist towards his own people no less than in foreign policy. In *Mein Kampf* he wrote, "The Germans have not the faintest notion of the way the nation has to be swindled if one wants to win mass support". (The sentence was left out in later editions).

He told the Germans that he asked only for peace and justice. He would right the wrongs of Versailles. He would never lead them into war. After every act of violence he assured the world that this was the last. In spite of all the evidence to the contrary, he gave the impression of sincerity. He had the power to convince, and yet he was unable to understand the motives of those who took him at his word. Chamberlain did not understand Hitler. It is equally clear that Hitler did not understand Chamberlain. When Chamberlain flew to Berchtesgaden Hitler thought that he had come to do a deal. It did not occur to him that Chamberlain might think there was justice in the German claim for treaty revision. After the invasion of Prague Hitler was genuinely surprised at the reaction in this country. And yet although it was obvious now that no one believed in his assurances – he continued to use the same method.

[...]

From 1930 to 1939 Hitler achieved astonishing results by cool calculation and unlimited daring. During the early stages of the war he showed a real grasp of strategy. One would have supposed that he, above all men, understood the art of force, its effect and limitations. In time he lost even this. Then the cataclysm began. He became the slave of his own will. The instrument of his own technique. He lived in a world of fantasy.

> It all ended in nothing.
> So much for Hitler's realism.

The Communist use of the word opportunist is interesting. Marxist-Leninist theory is concerned not only with the purpose of policy; it also lays down a detailed technique of action. An opportunist is one who deviated from this rigidly prescribed method. But this applies only to the inner working of the Communist movement. In dealing with non Communist governments expediency is the only rule. In the interests of the Soviet Union – the land of Socialism – any alliance, any bargain, any twist or turn of policy is permissible. To strengthen and preserve the Communist parties in Capitalist countries, the pretence of co-operation with Bourgeois democratic parties may from time to time be adopted. In August 1939 Molotov told Schulenburg, the German Ambassador, that the principle of peaceful existence of various political systems side by side represented a long established principle of the foreign policy of the U.S.S.R. This, of course, had it been true, would have meant a complete denial of Marxist-Leninist doctrine. It behoves us to be cautious.

Unlimited opportunism is in the end self destruction. Stalin it would seem has so far retained sufficient statesmanship, sufficient sense of reality to know this. During the war the Englishmen and Americans who came into contact with him were convinced he would not make a separate peace. In his first interview with Harry Hopkins he said that there must always be maintained a minimum standard of morality between nations.

This the Germans had broken. It may have been said to please an American, but somehow it rings true. Probably he only meant that there must be some honour among thieves. If you engage on a common purpose, you must carry it through to the end. To Cordell Hull he said that the Russians had waited fifty years for a chance to crush Germany. Now it had come, they would not throw it away. That I think explains it. Stalin can understand nationalism – he is not a Russian for nothing. In spite of Marx he can use it, adopt it, come to terms with it. He can understand imperialism. But the principle of individual liberty which lies at the root of western civilization, is to him a sham and a pretence. He can despise those who stand by this principle, he can oppose them, but never in the long run co-operate with them.

For Great Britain deliberate opportunism is impossible. When you state a moral principle you are stuck with it – as Hopkins so succinctly put it – however many fingers you may have crossed at the time. This of course is true only because the moral sentiments which we so freely express are at bottom sincere. We can compromise, hedge, prevaricate, surrender, we can never throw them off – except in war. In July, 1939, a German Foreign Office official pointed out to the Russian Charge d'Affaires that England had nothing to offer Russia but participation in a European conflict, Germany could promise her neutrality and an understanding on mutual interests, "which just as in former times would work out to the advantage of both countries" – a new partition of Poland and Russian domination of the Baltic States. This I think was the crux of the matter. Whatever mistakes Chamberlain may have made in his negotiations with Russia, the fact remains that an alliance on their terms was not possible. We could not go to war for the defence of our own freedom and the liberties of Europe and at the same time agree to force upon these small states a Russian occupation to which they would not agree.

Winston Churchill has suggested that in dire necessity we should have come to some arrangement which left the details to be settled after war began. "In such circumstances different temper prevails. Allies in war are inclined to defer a great deal to each other's wishes, the flail of battle beats upon the front and all kinds of expedients are welcomed which, in peace, would be abhorrent". This was not practicable. The Russians wanted a clear statement in black and white and they got it from the Germans.

But Churchill was right about war. Then all one can hope to do is avoid commitments which prejudice the peace. This time we could not manage it. In a vain attempt to reconcile the Russian and Polish governments, we agreed, indeed proposed, an arrangement by which great areas of German territory were handed over to Poland. Whole cities were depopulated, millions of people were deprived of all they possessed and driven starving into the overcrowded Western zone. It would have happened in any case. We had no power to prevent it. Now a few years later we find it necessary to give elaborate justifications because we have made some adjustments in the frontiers of Western Germany and have handed over a few thousand inhabitants to the benevolent rule of Holland.

There are two limitations of policy. The limitation of power and the limitation imposed by our own ethical conceptions. The false idealist ignores the one, the false realist despises the other. The true realist knows that however noble his purpose, he will profit nothing by it, if, even unwillingly, he turns away from justice and from mercy.

To the Christian it must always seem that he is concerned more with means than with ends. He can be satisfied with no half way man made ideal. But he does not know the time or manner of the coming of the Kingdom that he seeks. All that he can do is try to discern God's will for himself, and for himself alone. In accordance with that will he must try to act and he must not trouble overmuch about the consequences – for "the result is in other hands".

So it is in thought no less than in action. Burchardt, the historian of the Renaissance, refused to adopt a philosophy of history. He did not say so, but I think he meant, that if we embark on a philosophy we end by making our own moral rather than attending on God's purpose. But Burchardt did once say that the great periods of civilization are those in which every faculty of the human mind is fully engaged. For that reason he came to put the Middle Ages above the Renaissance.

If we would write the history of our own times, we must be at once more humble and more ambitious. I told you at the beginning that it was President Wilson who cured me of my presumption. Now it isn't just Wilson that is indescribable. The truth of the matter is that there is nothing more difficult than to describe any person or any event. A person is perhaps a little easier because if you stick to his lifetime and use a biographical form there is a certain limitation both natural and conventional. But if you start off on an event, however small, however concrete it may seem, you will find that you are tangled up in all the past and all the present.

To begin with I think we must get rid of the idea that we can write about things as they are. Only the very greatest artists can see things apart from themselves and see them whole. It seems unlikely that we should be able to do what only Shakespeare and perhaps Dante and Tolstoy could accomplish. We can describe things only as they appear to us – as we are – with all our curious lopsided experiences and prejudices. For this we are not to blame. But what is inexcusable is to start writing, talking, teaching until we have had a good look at the facts even though our vision is distorted. If we look hard enough we may perhaps learn at least one thing – that is to distinguish the facts that are fixed from the facts that can be changed. All great statesmen and soldiers learn to make this distinction. There are plenty of you here in Oxford who have experienced this discipline in action. That is why you are better fitted to write this history than I shall ever be – and I see signs that it is going to happen. That is why Winston Churchill is so good a writer. He does not play about with abstract truth and absolute reality. He tells us how things appear to him, with all his cranks and foibles and pre-judgements. But he does look hard at the facts and he does what Burchardt would have us do. He uses all his faculties at once. He does not allow the pretentiousness of reason to deaden his imagination or his spiritual intuition, so being what he is, everything he touches comes to life. But there is the other difficulty. The subject is too big for us. We historians are always tempted – as I have been tempted to-day – to bite off more than we can chew. In this too, the artists may help us, for they are concerned not only with content but with form. It is this sense of form which enables them to make their self imposed limitations a source of strength. We do not know God's purpose in history. But we do know that all truth is one. So it does not matter how narrow or how wide are the bounds that we set – so long as we accept the limitations of our capacity. We have not all got Winston's gift of imagination – perhaps that is as well. But we are all made in the image of God, we have all got some measure of spiritual understanding, if only we will use it.

Whatever we choose, it may be the history of three thousand years or more, it may be a bit of economic analysis, it may be an intricate diplomatic negotiation, it may be the life of an obscure official – it does not matter so long as we bring all our powers to bear on the subject. If we do so perhaps now and then we will pierce below the surface and experience for a moment the joy of discovery. For reality is always more wonderful than our imagining, and to the faithful in action and to the faithful in thought, perhaps it be given to see the great, flowing cross of courage, to hear the beating of eternal wings.

Annette Baker Fox

From "The Teaching of International Relations in the United States" (co-authored with William T. R. Fox) (1961)

International relations, as a subject of instruction, has flourished more in the United States than elsewhere and more in recent years than ever before. What forces explain its growth and its present shape? How have methods of teaching it been affected by the goals of the teacher, by his relation to research, and by the formal organization of international studies in American colleges and universities? To what extent is the American experience so rooted in uniquely American conditions that it is unlikely to be repeated elsewhere? These questions will be considered in turn.

Professor Alfred Grosser, in a penetrating review of a number of international relations works of ambitious scope, has asked if the study of international relations is not an American specialty. Americans who are teaching, researching, and publishing in the field of international relations are so numerous and so ubiquitous that it is not easy to escape that impression. There are about twenty general textbooks on international relations of American origin currently in print. In addition to *Foreign Affairs* and the specialized journals, *International Organization, American Journal of International Law,* and those devoted to the problems of particular geographic areas, there are three journals primarily [...] addressed to the professional student of international relations: *Conflict Resolution, Orbis, and World Politics.*

The American study of international relations reflects a "voluntaristic" attitude toward questions of foreign policy: a belief that Americans can, by the foreign policy choices they make, be masters of their own destiny.[35]

---

[35] Reinhold Niebuhr has written of "the error of excessive voluntarism" of those who assume that "it would be a fairly easy achievement for nations to abridge their sovereignty in favor of a new international authority" (*The Children of Light and the Children of Darkness* (New York: Scribner's, 1944), 169). [...]

Arnold Wolfers, writing about the attitude in our handling of foreign affairs, has described an Anglo-American "philosophy of choice," which he contrasts with a Continental European "philosophy of necessity."[36] It certainly used to be true that insular location, a naval defensive screen, and great war potential combined, prior to our own century, to permit Britain and the United States a genuine freedom to maintain low levels of peacetime defense mobilization, to eschew defensive alliances, and to postpone both decisions to intervene in European wars and decisions to mobilize to make that intervention effective. In this former era of insularity, American students of international relations could write in time of peace as if the imperatives of national security set few limits on American freedom of action. Many of them did not view the European "balance of power" state system as a legitimate order to be lived with and adapted to. They saw in that order the focus of infection for the war disease – a disease to be cured or, if that were not possible, to be quarantined.

The great transformations of twentieth century world politics have drastically changed the focus and content of the typical international relations course without essentially modifying the reformist or, at any rate, meliorist attitudes of the teachers and writers.[37] It is now accepted that loss of insularity has taken away from the American people their freedom to choose to remain aloof from the politics of Europe, Africa, and Asia. There remains, however, the conviction that what the United States does or does not do makes a difference. American professors of international relations, no matter how little policy-oriented their intellectual interests may be, generally believe that deeper and more widespread knowledge of international relations will somehow result in better public policies and therefore in a better world for Americans to live in. They now know that even a superpower does not have unlimited choice,[38] but they by no means see the future as wholly predetermined.

A list of these great transformations would include: (1) the expansion of the European state system into a world system, with the superpowers peripheral to Europe playing unprecedented roles in a bipolar system; (2) the diffusion outward from Europe to the Afro-Asian world of

---

[36] "Political Theory and International Relations," introductory essay in Arnold Wolfers and Laurence W. Martin (eds.), *The Anglo-American Tradition in Foreign Affairs* (New Haven, CT: Yale University Press, 1956), ix–xxvii.

[37] [...]

[38] Former members of the policy-planning staff of the Department of State have produced a series of books stressing the "realities" and therefore the limits of choice in American foreign policy. See Louis J. Halle, *Dream and Reality* (New York: Harper, 1959); George F. Kennan, *Realities of American Foreign Policy* (Princeton, NJ: Princeton University Press, 1955); Charles B. Marshall, *The Limits of Foreign Policy* (New York: Henry Holt, 1954).

nationalism and of demands for rising living standards and the dignity of participation in the political process; (3) the democratization of the control of foreign relations at the same time that the widened sphere of state activity has made the conduct of foreign relations ever more complex and difficult; (4) the sudden emergence of science and technology as great and semi-independent variables in the equations of world politics; (5) the drawing-together of the old states of Europe and the transoceanic states of European culture in varying forms of association, such as the European Coal and Steel Community, the British Commonwealth, and NATO; and (6) the new necessity, especially for the superpowers, to do things in peacetime which many states formerly did only in war – maintain a high level of defense mobilization, engage in coalition military planning, finance a massive foreign aid program, and develop a vigorous psychological strategy.

The study of international relations has been reshaped in an effort to clarify American choices as to how to counter, or adapt to, or give direction to these transformations.[39] The bipolar system and the concern for the new policy problems of the Far East, the Middle East, and Africa have caused a tremendous upsurge of area studies. Typical leading American universities have each developed programs for the intensive study of one or more areas formerly thought exotic.[40] There is new interest in regional organization and the conditions under which the leaders of sovereign states most readily permit decisions to be made by regional organizations which the state has joined.[41] There is also an intensified interest in the international social forces which are operating in the turbulent half of the world now in a state of constitutional flux.[42] The inappropriateness of the new instruments of mass destruction for any socially acceptable purpose but deterrence has had two quite separate impacts: study by the civilian student of international relations of questions of military strategy and even of pure strategic theory,[43] and a renewed interest in finding technically well-founded bases for arms limitation which would lend added stability to the "balance of terror"

---

[39] [...]

[40] Columbia University, for example, has a Russian Institute, an East Asian Institute, and a Near and Middle East Institute. Each has meant a permanent expansion of the faculty by several professorships, and in each case one of the added professors has specialized in the international relations of the area.

[41] E.g., Ernst B. Haas, *The Uniting of Europe* (Stanford, CA: Stanford University Press, 1958); [...]

[42] Dankwart Rustow is, for example, an "associate professor of international social forces" at Columbia University. [...]

[43] Cf. Bernard Brodie, *Strategy in the Missile Age* (Princeton, NJ: Princeton University Press, 1959) [...]

and lessen the threat of the accidental or the catalytic war.[44] Finally, with the recognition of the importance of lengthened lead-times in arms production, the enhanced role of force in peace and of limited-war capabilities, and the need for military policies to be continuously co-ordinated with economic policies and information policies, there is sharply increased attention to national security policy, civil–military relations, and the interplay of domestic and foreign politics.[45]

The American study of international relations has been modified not only in the light of the great transformations of twentieth-century world politics but also in the light of emerging trends and changing fashions in social science, and particularly political science, research. Scholars in international relations have shown the same concern as scholars in domestic politics in endeavoring to make their subject more "scientific,"[46] the same enthusiasm for empirical, behavioral, and quantitative research,[47] the same effort to discover uniformities in state or national behavior,[48] and the same interest in choosing for investigation problems whose study would clarify questions of public policy.[49] This last interest is not a threat to objectivity so long as the preferences of the disciplined scholar are permitted to operate only in the selection of the problem and not in the mode of observation and analysis.

---

[44] [...]

[45] See, e.g., Samuel P. Huntington, *The Soldier and the State* (Cambridge, MA: Harvard University Press, 1957); and Walter Millis (with Harvey C. Mansfield and Harold Stein), *Arms and the State* (New York: Twentieth Century Fund, 1958). The Social Science Research Council has for several years had a Committee on National Security Policy Research.

[46] For a discussion of the distinction between scientific and other scholarly writing in international relations and a survey of the former, see Harold D. Lasswell, "The Scientific Study of International Relations," *Yearbook of World Affairs*, xii (1958): 1–28.

[47] See Karl W. Deutsch, *Nationalism and Social Communication* (New York: John Wiley, 1953) [...]

[48] [...] Two recent books which describe uniformities of state behavior observed in a series of case studies are Annette B. Fox, *The Power of Small States* (Chicago, IL: University of Chicago Press, 1959), and Paul Kecskemeti, *Strategic Surrender* (Stanford, CA: Stanford University Press, 1958).

[49] E.g., Klaus Knorr (ed.), *NATO and American Security* (Princeton, NJ: Princeton University Press, 1959); and Arnold Wolfers (ed.), *Alliance Policy in the Cold War* (Baltimore, MD: Johns Hopkins Press, 1956).

Rachel Wall

From "The Nature of Contemporary History" (1966)

History is traditionally concerned with the remote past. Today that's no longer good enough. The world of the nineteen sixties is so different from that of even ten or twenty years ago that many people who'd have previously been quite unconcerned, today want to know how these changes have come about. It's some indication of this interest in the recent past, that this year a new journal was launched, especially concerned with contemporary history. And this provides an opportunity to ask some searching questions. First and foremost, what do we mean by contemporary history?

All centuries of course, have been periods of change, although in some it's been more apparent at the time than in others. But in this respect the twentieth century's been outstanding. In the last few decades we've seen the consummation of a period of revolutionary change which has certainly had no equal in intensity in European history since the Renaissance and which because of its world-wide scope may well be unprecedented. It's because of the revolutionary nature of change in the recent past that a new form of historical approach has become essential. And it's this that I call contemporary history. Putting it briefly, contemporary history tries to put the world of today into a coherent historical setting. The contemporary historian takes his bearings from the contemporary situation, and looking back over the past half-century or so, distinguishes between those factors which characterised the old world which was passing and those which throw light on the new world which was coming into existence.

For as in other periods of transition the two developments have been going on side by side. This idea of relevance in terms of the present is the distinguishing characteristic of the new history and it's this that determines the historian's attitudes towards his material and his period of study. In most history, the problem of what is relevant presents few real difficulties. Either the material has been pre-selected by the accident of survival, or by what contemporaries thought it was important to record;

or alternatively – as for example, in respect to the history of the nineteenth century, where we have a wealth of material – the problem of what is relevant is helped by the fact that we know the outcome of events. For example, the outcome of the movement for German unification in the nineteenth century was Bismarck's empire and so it's natural to interpret the history of Germany in the nineteenth century in terms of the empire created by Bismarck in 1871. Contemporary history, on the other hand, is what we call open-ended. That's to say, that in most problems of contemporary history, the outcome is quite uncertain. The consequences of events such as the Sino-Soviet dispute are unpredictable and it's no part of the job of the contemporary historian to attempt to give an answer in advance. But he *is* concerned to explain why such problems are relevant at all.

In some cases of course problems which are actual today have substantial origins in the nineteen forties. But in others it may be necessary to go back more than a century. For example, a question such as the rivalry between the United States and the Soviet Union in Asia has its origins at least as early as the mid-nineteenth century. Already in 1853, the American representative in China was arguing that 'almost any sacrifice should be made by the United States to keep Russia from spreading her Pacific boundary, and to avoid her ... interference in Chinese domestic affairs'. And the beginning of the interest of both countries in Asia goes back further still. But the point I want to make is this: what differentiates contemporary history from other sorts of history is that instead of working forward from a given point in the past with the 'answers' already in mind, it's the historian's own choice of subject which determines the period studied.

Similarly, events are not necessarily relevant because they are recent. Contemporary history is the history of those developments and movements which characterise the world we live in and a great deal which has happened in the past half century is simply irrelevant to the world of today. For example, much of the diplomacy of the twenties and thirties which still looms so large in conventional accounts of the period, contributes little to our understanding of the present situation. Whereas, there's an *immediacy* about some of the problems of those years which has all too often been overlooked – about Britain's loss of naval supremacy for example and China's struggle to rid itself of its semi-colonial status. Today, we can't fail to be interested in the views of men like Paul Reinsch, who, in 1918, when people were preoccupied with the problems facing the Peace Conference in Paris wrote 'there is no single problem in Europe which equals in its importance the future peace of the world, the need of a just settlement of Chinese affairs' [sic].

What then are the features of the contemporary world which determine the character of contemporary history? One of the most striking is, I suppose, the fact that the world of today is one world, so that contemporary history must be international or world history. This has come about, as we all know, because of the decreasing significance of distance. This meant that even at the height of the Cold War, it wasn't possible to isolate one region from another and it's characteristic of the situation in the sixties that China, the Soviet Union and the United States, are all concerned with events in Africa. In the contemporary world, not only are problems world-wide in their implications, but so are the consequences of action taken with regard to them. Today it's not only possible to have instantaneous communication across the world; the development of the destructive power of weapons and the accuracy of delivery systems means that universal destruction too could be instantaneous. If nothing else, this situation in itself underlines the need for a type of history that's world-wide in both its outlook and its relevance.

Moreover, the contemporary historian looks at the recent past in a different way from a historian interested in a particular nation state. And in so far as he may be concerned with a particular nation state, his concern will be directed towards different aspects of its history. For example, he is not interested in many men who will find a place in national histories – men like President Harding in the United States, or Baldwin in England, or Halenkoff in the Soviet Union; whereas others, such as Jean Monnet, who has had a key part in the movement for European unity, or William Burghardt Du Bois, who inspired the Negro revival and the early Pan-Africanism, have a more positive significance in contemporary history than they have in their national histories.

But if contemporary history is international it is also sub-national or a-national. For me one of the most striking features of the contemporary period, compared with the situation after 1919, is the reduced relevance of national frontiers. I am not talking here in military terms, although clearly developments in weaponry are one factor, for most nations can no longer take meaningful decisions about even their *own* defence. What is interesting, is the very multiplicity of such factors at work. As we all know, many people nowadays question the validity of state sovereignty. At the same time, there's widespread interest in federal-type solutions – the United Arab Republic, for instance, or the European Common Market. Moreover, none of the major powers today – neither the United States, the Soviet Union nor China are national states in the accepted sense of the word. There's also the whole question of ideology. At least since 1917, ideologies have cut across frontiers and the like-minded have supported each other to an extent unparalleled in the heyday of the nation state, you've only to think of such characteristically twentieth century movements as Fascism and Communism, of anti-colonialism and attempts to end racial discrimination. It's easy to denigrate the achievements of Pan-Africanism or of the search for Arab unity but what's of interest to the contemporary historian is that Nkrumah and Nasser should have thought along non-national lines at all. And a look at the social history of the recent past shows similar trends at work. There's little that can be identified as exclusively characteristic of one nation or another about recent styles of dress, or of contemporary design in buildings or in the attraction of particular forms of mass entertainment.

A second major characteristic of contemporary history as compared with the history of the later modern period is the change in the balance of significance between events in Europe and those in the extra-European world. We can, of course, trace the origins of this situation back into the late nineteenth century but it's only in the recent past that it's become a central fact in world history. You've only to turn to the *Times* review of the important events of 1929 to see how completely attitudes have changed. *The Times* wrote then: 'Except for sundry disturbances which were confined to localities, such as the civil war in Afghanistan, conflicts between Jews and Arabs in Palestine, and continued marching and counter-marching of armed forces in China, the year 1929 was passed everywhere in tranquillity ...' How utterly different is the reaction which disturbances in these parts of the world provoke today. One has only to think of the war in Kashmir, of the Arab–Israeli conflict which culminated in the intervention of the great powers at Suez in 1956, or of the importance which we now attach to anything that happens in China. In any attempt to explain current problems *far* more attention must be given to the study of the extra-European world than was usual even a decade or so ago.

The obvious increase in the importance of the extra-European world has given rise to an interest in extra-European history for its own sake. But there's a tendency to think that it's adequate to discuss extra-European history in regional terms.

In fact, in contemporary history it's the interaction between regions which is the characteristic phenomenon. For many years there's been fine specialist work done on areas outside Europe but its relevance to European history, or to that of other areas, has been almost entirely ignored. What is required is not more work of an exclusive specialist nature but the integration of specialist work in one field with that in another. If this is to be done, there will have to be a greater interest in bridge building from all sides.

You may wonder what's the point of identifying contemporary history as a distinctive form of history in its own right. It's often suggested that contemporary history is simply a continuation of later modern history and that nothing's to be gained by treating it as anything else. This problem is due partly to the confusion which arises from the many uses of the word 'contemporary'. But this isn't really the essence of the point at issue. Those people who think of contemporary history as merely the most recent period of later modern history, fail to identify the recent past as a period of transition and evidently believe that it's affected by the same issues and ideas as the nineteenth century. This is far from being the case. To take one more striking example. When in the nineteenth century, countries like China and Japan began to modernise, and to bring their political, economic and legal institutions up to date, they thought in terms of European ideas and institutions and in particular in terms of the ideas of the western liberal state. At the turn of the century, revolutionaries like Sun Yat-sen were dedicated to the liberal republican tradition and at least a part of the White Man's burden was to carry parliamentary-type government to the furthest corners of the earth.

Later, when anti-liberal ideologies, such as Fascism and Communism, predominated in Europe, these also, to some extent, provided a model for reformers and revolutionary leaders elsewhere. Peron is, perhaps, the best known example. Today there's a dramatic contrast and it's evident that the very relevance of the European example, be it liberal or anti-liberal, is itself in question. It's characteristic of the current situation that in 1962 Che Guevara shrugged off any association between Communism and the Cuban revolution, saying, 'In our revolution we found we had done just what Mao wrote – without even reading him – it's common-sense in any country of our type'. In short, modernisers of today approach current problems without any over-all assumptions about the merits of particular ideological systems. And in so far as ideological concepts are themselves rooted in the European tradition, the reduced significance of ideological considerations in the world at large, is a further indication of the change in the influence of Europe, and with it of the radical change in the nature of history of the recent past compared with that of the period of European predominance. Perhaps, more than any other single factor, it's this change in the significance of Europe and of European ideas in the contemporary world which forces the contemporary historian to set up new categories and to establish new 'rules of procedure'.

Looked at with these criteria in mind, I find the new *Journal of Contemporary History* very disappointing. I can't help wondering how far the editors have made any really strenuous scrutiny of their assumptions about the nature of contemporary history. The first three issues of the Journal are devoted to European topics – to Fascism, to the Left-Wing intelligentsia between the wars and to the year 1914. Indeed, the editorial in the first issue explained that 'the field of study and discussion of the Journal will be Europe in the twentieth century', on the grounds of the 'conviction that contemporary Europe is a legitimate subject of study and debate, requiring no special defence or explanation'. But in saying this the editors have missed the opportunity of explaining how 'contemporary Europe' is related to 'the contemporary history' of the title of the Journal.

Of course contemporary Europe is a legitimate subject of study and debate. Indeed, Europe's changing relations with the extra-European world must be one of the major themes, in any assessment of the twentieth century. But as I've tried to show, it's only *one* aspect of a process which is at least two-sided. Moreover, in discussing Europe in the contemporary world you've got to remember that this isn't the world of thirty years ago. If topics like Fascism are to be of anything other than parochial, antiquarian interest, it's no good rehearsing the arguments of contemporaries, you've got to make a case for your choice of subject in terms which are meaningful today. And one of the conclusions from studying contemporary history is this: that it's as misleading to concentrate on Europe in the inter-war years, as it's impossible to do so in the post-war period. But treating the history of the twentieth century in the way I've suggested tonight, gives coherence to both.

Contemporary history, then, is *not* concerned with the twentieth century for its own sake but because the study of the recent past throws light on the world we live in. In this way, contemporary history restores a social function to history at a time when it's important that it should have one. And in this connection, it's important to remember that most of the people now studying weren't even born on V-J Day. This fact has implications far wider than those usually associated with differences in generations. It means that they were born into a world in which the explosions over Hiroshima and Nagasaki had *already* blasted us, however unwillingly, into a new age. An age in which the only certainty is the certainty of change itself. *This* is the basic reason why the demand for contemporary history, as an explanation of our current predicament, continues to grow.

2

Geopolitics and War
Introduction by Patricia Owens

At the turn of the twentieth century, empires were enmeshed in a world-wide zero-sum competition over territory, peoples, and natural resources. With the closing of imperial frontiers, and at a time when international relations explicitly meant race relations, there was increasing anxiety in the imperial core about the implications of rising Asian powers. In this context, distinctly "geopolitical" thought emerged as a response to more intense inter-imperial rivalry, legitimizing the expansionist aims of the European and US empires in terms of a social Darwinist struggle. Geopolitical thought was a response to increasing contacts across races, anxieties about the longevity of global white supremacy, socialist revolution, and calls for women's suffrage.[1] Indeed, it offered the first historical–sociological explanation of international relations itself. In Halford Mackinder's words, worldwide political plurality was generated from the interaction of uneven geographical features, the "grouping of lands and seas, and of fertility and natural pathways," and the evolution of different racial and civilizational groups.[2] States and empires were like organisms whose territorial boundaries could not be fixed or permanently contained.

Through the twentieth century, women were at the forefront of geopolitical thinking and they wrote powerful analyses of war, the organized, reciprocal killing and maiming of people and destruction of things. In this section, we pair writing on geopolitics with writing on war, selecting work that addresses these core subjects from myriad angles, philosophical and practical, historical and contemporary, cultural and ethical. The works were written in different professional contexts, from academe,

---

[1] Lothrop Stoddard, *Rising Tide of Color: The Threat against White World Supremacy* (New York: Charles Scribner's Sons, 1920); Anna Julia Cooper, who appears in this volume, critiqued Stoddard's white supremacism in her PhD dissertation, posthumously published and translated as *Slavery and the French and Haitian Revolutionists*, ed. Frances Richardson (Lanham, MD: Rowman & Littlefield, 2006).

[2] Halford Mackinder, *Democratic Ideals and Reality: A Study in the Politics of Reconstruction* (New York: Henry Holt, 1942 [1919]), 2.

journalism, activism, and think tanks. They also represent and respond to the widest range of political and intellectual positions in the Anglo-American world during the early to middle twentieth century, from conservative geopolitics, fascist internationalism, liberal imperialism, anticolonialism, Black, socialist, and feminist internationalism, and proto-neoconservatism. They also cross genres, from philosophical treatises to works of history, political essays, and polemics, and are aimed at diverse audiences, from policymakers and academe to highbrow or working-class publics. We include theoretical work on some of the epistemological and ontological questions about the nature of both war and geopolitics as well as more practical and empirical analyses of particular wars and geopolitical contexts from the period 1911 to 1968.

One of the most influential proponents of geopolitical thought in the United States, author of an original and comprehensive theory of how geography shaped international politics, was Ellen Churchill Semple (1863–1932). Here we excerpt her 1911 magnum opus, *Influences of Geographic Environment on the Basis of Ratzel's System of Anthropo-Geography*. In Semple's work, international thinking is the study of interactions between the physical environment and the historical evolution of competing civilizations, some more or less civilized, more or less savage. Semple intended her scholarship to have influence outside academe. She wrote policy briefs for Woodrow Wilson on the boundaries of new nations after the First World War and advised the Japanese government on its colonial strategy in Korea. Today, Semple is best known in Geography, but almost completely absent in intellectual and disciplinary histories of IR.[3] Her marginalization is primarily the result of her gender – she is treated as Ratzel's "disciple" rather than an independent thinker, unlike *her* students and successors[4] – but also discomfort with German geopolitical thought, particularly its association with Nazism.[5] Nonetheless, the historical and contemporary influences of the geopolitical thought that she developed in the United States include Cold War

---

[3] For a discussion and analysis of Semple's reception in IR see Kimberly Hutchings and Patricia Owens, "Women Thinkers and the Canon of International Thought: Recovery, Rejection, and Reconstitution," *American Political Science Review*, 115:2 (2021): 347–359; also see Innes M. Keighren, *Bringing Geography to Book: Ellen Semple and the Reception of Geographical Knowledge* (London: I. B. Tauris, 2010).

[4] John Hobson, *The Eurocentric Conception of World Politics: Western International Theory 1760–2010* (Cambridge: Cambridge University Press, 2012), 261.

[5] This is also partly true of the Cambridge-based British political geographer Harriet Wanklyn (1906–1990), who also wrote a biography of Ratzel in which she sought to rehabilitate him from much of the association with Hitler's regime. Harriet Wanklyn, *Friedrich Ratzel: A Biographical Memoir and Bibliography* (Cambridge: Cambridge University Press, 1961).

doctrines of containment and the domino theory, as well as the "realist" tradition of IR.[6]

Before Merze Tate, excerpted elsewhere in this volume, most if not all geopolitical thought was a highly conservative and obviously racist form of international thinking. Adherents to the classical geopolitical tradition offered an intellectual alternative to Marxist-Leninist proletarian internationalism, Wilsonian "liberal" internationalism, anticolonial ideas and movements, and non-Western imperial thought. Yet, as discussed in the previous section, Merze Tate articulated IR's core subject matter as fundamentally geopolitical, which she understood more generically as the relationship between geography and history on a world-wide scale. In that essay, which should be read alongside this section, Tate described the elements of "international history" as "man, place, and time, while the elements of geopolitics are the earth and state. The dynamic nature of geopolitics is found in the adjustment of the state to the natural environment" (51).

From the 1940s, Tate pursued a consciously anti-racist geopolitical research program inside the academy. In Anglo-American academic IR outside the Black academy, such a commitment was unusual, to say the least, even though open statements about the racial superiority of white nations declined through the century. This more generic mode of geopolitical analysis which began to develop from the 1930s and 1940s is represented here by Elizabeth Monroe's (1905–1986) 1938 work *The Mediterranean in Politics* and Margaret Sprout's (1903–2004) study of naval power, co-authored as one of IR's earliest "power couples."[7] Outside academe, the Marxist journalist Claudia Jones (1915–1964) offered a radical alternative vision of the significance of the relations between populations, territory, and resources in her left anti-racist and anti-fascist geopolitical analysis of the Second World War, which we also excerpt.

Monroe's career was typical of a generation of mid-century British women international thinkers, crossing international organizations, think tanks, journalism, and academe. After studying at Oxford University, she worked for the secretariat of the League of Nations and then the London think tank Chatham House, where she co-wrote a book on the 1935 "Abyssinian Crisis" caused by the Italian invasion of Ethiopia, and which

---

[6] Lucian M. Ashworth, *A History of International Thought: From the Origins of the Modern State to Academic IR* (London: Routledge, 2014).

[7] Katharina Rietzler, "IR's 'Power Couples,'" Women and the History of International Thought Project Blog, https://whit.web.ox.ac.uk/article/irs-power-couples (accessed November 8, 2019).

several other figures in this volume addressed.[8] *The Mediterranean in Politics*, based on Monroe's research in the Middle East and North Africa and funded by the Rockefeller Foundation, was a study of the competing imperialisms of Britain, France, Italy, Turkey, and Spain. The analysis represents both the British establishment's view of its rule in the Middle East and the Chatham House specialty of producing knowledge that was useful for policymakers: no matter how terrible the experience of British imperialism for those subjected to it, "the work of the man on the spot, often provide a record of disinterested service" (96). Britain was in the Middle East for three reasons, Monroe argued: prestige, military-strategic, and commercial. She was skeptical of the notion that moral duty played any role, with one exception; moral duty was Britain's "first consideration ... towards the Palestinian Jews" (95). Later, Monroe became head of the British government's Middle East Division at the Ministry of Information in the Second World War, then diplomatic correspondent for *The Observer* and Middle East correspondent for *The Economist*. On leaving journalism, she took a research post at the Middle East Centre at St. Antony's, Oxford, creating its archive.

By the 1940s, the sanitization of geopolitical thought was evident not only in descriptions of imperial world politics but also in new writing on the history of geopolitical thought. During the nineteenth century, the racial anxieties triggered by Japanese expansion had a profound effect on American naval officer Alfred Thayer Mahan's influential 1889 work *The Influence of Sea Power upon History*. Mahan argued that the United States could no longer slumber in relative isolation with rising barbaric civilizations in "the East." In Margaret and Harold Sprout's analysis of Mahan in their 1943 *Toward a New Order of Sea Power* and in Margaret's seminal essay "Mahan: Evangelist of Sea Power," Mahan's racial anxiety is sublimated and American imperial expansion normalized.[9] "Conquest of Spain's West Indian islands and provision for a naval base in a nominally independent Cuba," wrote the Sprouts, "insured American dominance in the Caribbean. Annexation of the Hawaiian Islands in 1898, and partition of the Samoan archipelago the following year, foreshadowed a similar primacy throughout a vast triangle in the eastern Pacific" (101).

The Sprouts made a number of important and lasting contributions to the study of IR in the US academy, but only Harold held a formal

---

[8] A. H. M. Jones and Elizabeth Monroe, *A History of Ethiopia* (Oxford: Clarendon Press, 1935).

[9] Margaret Tuttle Sprout, "Mahan: Evangelist of Sea Power," in Edward Mead Earle (ed.), *Makers of Modern Strategy: Military Thought from Machiavelli to Hitler* (Princeton, NJ: Princeton University Press, 1941), 415–445.

academic post at Princeton University. During the Second World War, Margaret and Harold collected and edited the most widely used textbook of early post-war IR in the United States, *Foundations of National Power*.[10] Margaret participated in Edward Mead Earle's Princeton seminars, which helped foster behavioral approaches to international relations.[11] And as early as the 1950s, they introduced environmental problems to IR.[12] With Nicholas Spykman and Harold Lasswell, Margaret and Harold Sprout are considered among "the earliest and most important of the revolutionaries" in the study of international affairs in the United States during the 1940s and 1950s.[13] They influenced generations of IR scholars, including through helping to side-line explicit discussions of racial hierarchy in world politics.

Claudia Jones (1915–1964) was born in the Caribbean island territory of Trinidad and Tobago, then controlled by the United States under the "tutelage of Mahan" (Sprout, 100). The global economic decline devastated the Trinidadian economy, leading her family to migrate north, to Harlem, New York in 1924, when she was nine years old. After graduating from high school, where she was active in the junior NAACP, Jones worked in a laundry and millinery; "college was out for me and I had to … contribute to the family larder."[14] She thus received no further formal education beyond high school and never enjoyed the security of

---

[10] William C. Olson and A. J. R. Groom, *International Relations: Then and Now: Origins and Trends in Interpretation* (London: HarperCollins Academic, 1991), 105. Among the authors of the eighty-five selected works in *Foundations of National Power*, there are only four women. But almost half the volume was co-authored by Margaret Sprout in the form of the extensive introductions/commentaries on each section. In one of these extensive introductions, the Sprouts cite extensively from Monroe's *The Mediterranean in Politics*. However, despite Monroe being listed in the "author index" for the volume, the Sprouts did not select Monroe's writing for the anthology. Harold Sprout and Margaret Sprout (eds.), *Foundations of National Power: Readings on World Politics and American Security* (Princeton, NJ: Princeton University Press, 1945), 263, 279, 280.

[11] Torbjørn L. Knutsen, *A History of International Relations Theory*, 3rd ed. (Manchester: Manchester University Press, 2016), 261 262.

[12] Harold Sprout and Margaret Sprout, "Environmental Factors in the Study of International Politics," *Conflict Resolution*, 1:4 (1957): 309–328. The International Studies Association has a Harold and Margaret Sprout Award, established in 1972, for the best book each year on international environmental problems.

[13] James N. Rosenau, Vincent Davis, and Maurice A. East (eds.), *The Analysis of International Politics: Essays in Honour of Harold and Margaret Sprout* (New York: Free Press, 1972), 1–2. For an excellent discussion see Or Rosenboim, "The Value of Space: Geopolitics, Geography and the American Search for International Theory in the 1950s," *The International History Review*, 42:3 (2020): 639–655.

[14] Claudia Jones, "Autobiographical History," in *Claudia Jones: Beyond Containment*, ed. Carole Boyce Davies (Oxford: Ayebia Clarke, 2010), 13. Also see Marika Sherwood, *Claudia Jones: A Life in Exile* (London: Lawrence and Wishart, 1999); Carole Boyce Davies, *Left of Karl Marx: The Political Life of Black Communist Claudia Jones* (Durham, NC: Duke University Press, 2008).

an academic post. Yet, in terms of access to the means of disseminating her ideas, Jones was in a relatively privileged position compared with other Black and working-class women. She had a column for the "Negro nationalist" newspaper of the Federated Youth Clubs of Harlem.[15] She wrote for the CPUSA paper, the *Weekly Review*, rising to editor, and for the *Daily Worker*, and wrote regular essays for *Political Affairs*. After her deportation to Britain under the McCarran Act for "subversive" activity, Jones founded *The West Indian Gazette* and London's Notting Hill Carnival. She played an important role in shaping how thousands of ordinary African Americans and British West Indians thought about international politics, "establish[ing] political thinking for minority people in Britain."[16] Jones's life and work illustrate the centrality of journalism for activist-intellectual production, a relatively neglected genre in histories of international thought.

Claudia Jones's international thinking was shaped both by the CPUSA and by Black radical traditions, as well as her response to what she called "the new realignments ..., on an international as well as on a domestic scale."[17] We have chosen a *Weekly Review* article from 1942, "What We Must Now Do about India," because it encapsulates core aspects of Jones's left geopolitical analysis and anti-imperial strategic thinking. In a series of *Weekly Review* articles during this period, Jones focused on the strategic questions of population and natural resources but also centered the power and agency of colonized populations.[18] Initially opposed to US entry into the "predatory"[19] inter-imperialist war between Germany, Britain, and France, Jones supported US entry after the Nazi invasion of the Soviet Union in 1941 in order to create a second front against the Axis powers. Jones consistently read military strategic questions through the eyes of colonial peoples and the coming post-colonial international order. In the article below, written in the context of Britain's violent crackdown on the Indian independence movement, her analysis of India's strategic significance centered on the relations between territory, population, and resources. Yet the relationship between states and empires, and the wars that they fought, were fundamentally shaped by

[15] Jones, "Autobiographical History," 13.
[16] Nia Reynolds (director), *Looking for Claudia Jones* (documentary) (London: Black Stock Films, 2013).
[17] Claudia Jones, "How Is Morale in America's Army?," *Weekly Review*, August 26, 1941, 6, 15.
[18] For a more in-depth discussion see Sarah C. Dunstan and Patricia Owens, "Claudia Jones, International Thinker," *Modern Intellectual History*, First View (2021): 1–24.
[19] Claudia Jones, "Quiz: Wasn't the Bourgeois Democracy of the British ...," *Weekly Review*, December 9, 1941, 14.

the world-wide capitalist system. She thus articulated popular geopolitical framings of the war within a Marxist-Leninist lexicon of historic stages.

Central to Jones's earlier politicization was the Italian invasion and colonial occupation of Ethiopia in October 1935, which culminated in the overthrow of Emperor Haile Selassie in 1937 and the extension of Mussolini's Fascist International to Africa. One of Jones's first jobs in journalism was writing summaries of the editorial positions of commercial, Black, trade union presses on the Ethiopian war. "To my amazement ... I saw my boss reading my précis to the applause and response of thousands of community people in Harlem, ... [and] the next day ... come in and tell me what a 'big Negro' he was."[20] Italy's annexation and occupation of Ethiopia was an epochal event, exposing the hypocrisy of the leading imperial powers' appeasement of what George Padmore called "colonial fascism" and the inadequacy of the collective security mechanism of the League of Nations when sanctions against Italy were voted down. It galvanized Black internationalist and anticolonial activists, sharpening their analyses of global white supremacy, the politics of international organization, and the limits of the European left.[21] We include a number of Black internationalist and Pan-Africanist thinkers in this volume. Perhaps their most committed white English feminist ally was the communist, anti-fascist, and pan-Africanist Sylvia Pankhurst (1882–1960) born in Manchester, England. Her 1935 essay "The Fascist World War (Ethiopia and Spain)," excerpted below, offers a critical analysis of the fascist preoccupation with people and land.[22] Pankhurst wrote this short polemic, which was published in *New Times and Ethiopia News*, a journal she founded in response to the invasion of Ethiopia, to draw attention to the white supremacy that allowed international leaders to stand by "while Ethiopia was vanquished: this is only Africa; this is not a White Man's country. They listened to the Italian propaganda; these are primitives, their customs are barbarous" (92–93).

Both her parents, Richard and Emmeline Pankhurst, supported women's suffrage. Emmeline founded the Women's Social and Political Union (WSPU) and raised her daughters to be its future leaders.

---

[20] Jones, "Autobiographical History," 13.
[21] Neelam Srivastava, *Italian Colonialism and Resistances to Empire, 1930–1970* (London: Palgrave, 2018); Adom Getachew, *Worldmaking after Empire: The Rise and Fall of Self-Determination* (Princeton, NJ: Princeton University Press, 2019), 7.
[22] On Pankhurst's role in metropolitan anticolonialism, including her partnerships with Black intellectuals, see Priyamvada Gopal, *Insurgent Empire: Anticolonial Resistance and British Dissent* (London: Verso, 2019), 292–296, 316–317.

But Sylvia was not just "a Pankhurst" or Manchester radical.[23] A much more militant feminist and radical socialist, Sylvia was arrested on multiple occasions, imprisoned, and repeatedly force-fed during hunger strikes. Fabian socialist feminists criticized Pankhurst's revolutionary communism; she was subsequently expelled from the WSPU. In response, Pankhurst established the East London Federation of Suffragettes in 1914, traveled to Moscow, where she met Lenin, and theorized domestic labor and the possibilities for democracy under communism. She was expelled from Britain's Communist Party for refusing to relinquish control of the newspaper *The Workers' Dreadnought*, which she had founded.[24] She was a supporter of anticolonial causes, writing on Ireland and India as well as Ethiopia. Her opposition to the First World War and support for the Women's International Peace Conference at The Hague led to a further split from her mother and sister, both of whom supported the war. Like Claudia Jones, Pankhurst created her own platform to disseminate her ideas, founding the *New Times and Ethiopia News*, which she edited for two decades. She moved to Ethiopia in 1956, working on education and development projects, and editing the *Ethiopia Observer*. She died in Addis Ababa in 1960, received a state funeral, and is buried alongside the patriots of "the Italian war."

Clearly, diverse forms of anti-fascist politics were the context for much international thought in the 1930s and 1940s, including the most influential political thinkers. Hannah Arendt's (1906–1975) political thought was fundamentally rooted in her political analysis of total war and her experience as a persecuted and stateless Jew.[25] Born in Hanover, Prussia to a secular, middle-class family, Arendt studied Classics, Christian theology, and philosophy. In response to the growing tide of

[23] Rachel Holmes, *Sylvia Pankhurst: Natural Born Rebel* (London: Bloomsbury, 2020).

[24] Pankhurst was a prolific writer, including Sylvia Pankhurst, *Rebel Ireland* (London: Workers' Socialist Federation, 1919); *The Truth about the Oil War* (London: Dreadnought Publishers, 1922); *India and Earthly Paradise* (London: Sunshine Publishing, 1926); *Delphos: The Future of International Language* (London: Kegan Paul, 1927); *The Suffragette Movement: An Intimate Account of Persons and Ideals* (London: Longmans, 1932); *Ethiopia and Eritrea: The Last Phase of the Reunion Struggle* (London: Lalibela House, 1953); *Ethiopia: A Cultural History* (London: Lalibela House, 1955). Also see Kathryn Dodd, "Introduction: The Politics of Form in Sylvia Pankhurst's Writing," in *The Sylvia Pankhurst Reader* (Manchester: Manchester University Press, 1993), 1–30.

[25] Arendt's writing on war has received book-length treatment in the field of IR and this is the only IR monograph to date on an historical woman. For an account of how Arendt's political thought was fundamentally rooted in war and its political significance see Patricia Owens, *Between War and Politics: International Relations and the Thought of Hannah Arendt* (Oxford: Oxford University Press, 2007). For biographical and contextual analysis see Elizabeth Young-Bruehl, *Hannah Arendt: For the Love of the World* (New Haven, CT: Yale University Press, 1982).

anti-Semitism in the 1920s and 1930s, she became increasingly active in Jewish and leftist politics. After having been arrested by the Gestapo, she fled Germany. Imprisoned again in France, she escaped to the United States, where she completed her monumental study *The Origins of Totalitarianism*. *Origins* famously located the seeds of European fascism in the imperial expansion of the late nineteenth century. The scramble for Africa, Arendt argued, "became the most fertile soil for the flowering of what later was to become the Nazi elite. Here they had seen with their own eyes how peoples could be converted into races and how ... one might put one's own people into the position of the master race."[26] Virtually all of Arendt's major contributions to twentieth-century political thought were generated through her experiences of and reflections on international phenomena, among them statelessness and exile, imperialism and totalitarianism, world wars and genocide, and threats of nuclear annihilation.[27]

The selection we have chosen here is a lesser known piece, from Arendt's posthumously published material for a book she never completed on the political implications of total wars of annihilation. Epitomized by the Holocaust, and the imminent danger of a worldwide nuclear conflagration that could wipe out all life on earth, "the razing of entire civilizations ... had at one fell swoop thrust themselves back into the ominous realm of the all-too-possible" (111). With total war, and with nuclear weapons, "the limits inherent in violent action had been overstepped" (111). What was uniquely wrong about wars of annihilation, Arendt claimed, was not just the numbers of the dead or the destruction of entire cities, but the destruction of an "historical and political reality ... that cannot be rebuilt because it is itself not a product ... [the] action and speech created by human relationships" (111). In an effort to articulate an alternative way of thinking and talking about war, of transforming wars of annihilation into wars in which post-war alliances were still possible, Arendt returned, in allegorical and Eurocentric style, to "the ur-example of a war of annihilation," the Trojan War.[28]

---

[26] Hannah Arendt, *The Origins of Totalitarianism* (New York: Harcourt Brace Jovanovich, 1966 [1951]), 206.

[27] Patricia Owens, "The International Origins of Hannah Arendt's Historical Method," *Political Power and Social Theory*, 32 (2016): 37–62.

[28] A. Dirk Moses, "*Das römische Gespräch* in a New Key: Hannah Arendt, Genocide, and the Defense of Republican Civilization," *The Journal of Modern History*, 85:4 (2013): 867–913; Patricia Owens, "Racism in the Theory Canon: Hannah Arendt and 'the One Great Crime in Which America Was Never Involved,'" *Millennium*, 45:3 (2017): 403–424.

One of Arendt's many legacies on post-war thought was the language of "totalitarianism," in which people become masses and commonplace territorial or "geopolitical" expansion gave way to fantasies of world domination. This discourse of "totalitarianism," which Arendt did not intend to become a tool of Cold War propaganda, nonetheless helped to sustain and justify the newly expanded American national security state and its response to the emergence of a rival nuclear "superpower" supporting anticolonial movements around the world. Geopolitical competition between the United States and the USSR was supplanted by visions of a new global spatial order in which the nuclear revolution made territory and distance almost insignificant. What if a "totalitarian aggressor" launched a pre-emptive nuclear strike against the United States just as Japan, against all expectations, had launched the attack on Pearl Harbor in 1941?

At the forefront of this new mode of strategic theorizing was Roberta Wohlstetter (1912–2007). Her Bancroft Prize-winning 1960 book, *Pearl Harbor: Warning and Decision*, was required reading in Donald Rumsfeld's Department of Defense after the 9.11 attacks, "a sacred text" of his emerging neoconservative philosophy.[29] Wohlstetter had studied at the women's colleges Vassar, Radcliffe, and Barnard, taught at the University of Southern California, and worked at the RAND Corporation. Originally commissioned as a RAND report, *Pearl Harbor* was a study of the American military intelligence failures leading to Japan's surprise attack. Wohlstetter argued that the United States had systematically underestimated the Japanese enemy. But this was not a mere intelligence failure; "the uncertainty of strategic warning is intrinsic" (117), fundamental to the human psyche. Wohlstetter's findings articulated the historical and psychological grounds for a radical new approach to US nuclear strategy. She was *The Los Angeles Times* "woman of the year" in 1963 and received the Presidential Medal of Freedom from Ronald Reagan in 1985.

In later co-authored work with her husband, Albert, Roberta Wohlstetter rejected the doctrine of Mutual Assured Destruction, in which both the US and the USSR were deterred from first use of nuclear weapons given the devastating effects of inevitable nuclear retaliation. Instead US national security required an assiduously aggressive posture, a willingness to fight and win a nuclear war: atomic weapons should be viewed as usable. As a recent major treatment of Roberta and Albert suggests, "When the scales of gender conventions are peeled back,

---

[29] Ron Robin, *The Cold World They Made: The Strategic Legacy of Roberta and Albert Wohlstetter* (Cambridge, MA: Harvard University Press, 2016), 284.

Roberta appears as an equal contributor to the major themes that pre-occupied the Wohlstetters," perhaps the most influential US strategic thinkers of the Cold War.[30]

We conclude this section with a study of one of the defining military campaigns of the so-called "Global Cold War," the New York intellectual Mary McCarthy's (1912–1989) report on the United States' pacification war in Vietnam.[31] Raised in an abusive Catholic family, McCarthy left the Church, becoming atheist and communist in the 1930s. She later rejected Soviet Communism, but remained a socialist through her life. She studied at Vassar and made a living as a novelist, critic, and public intellectual.[32] With Hannah Arendt, McCarthy was a central figure in the New York intellectual scene of the 1950s and 1960s. She traveled to Saigon in 1967 and to Hanoi in 1968 to report on the United States' war on Vietnam for the *New York Review of Books*. Joining critics such as Hans J. Morgenthau, Noam Chomsky, and Susan Sontag, McCarthy not only indicted the US military campaign, a war of aggression aimed at over-turning the leaders of Vietnam's independence war from colonial France, but also condemned the modern capitalist society, national security state, and Cold War social scientific ideology that led the United States into that war and shaped how it was conducted and justified. The selection we have chosen focuses on the so-called "other war," President Johnson's name for the military campaign to deprive insurgents of cover and support. Millions of Vietnamese people were forcibly and deliberately removed into camps and their homesteads burned down. McCarthy wrote caustically about the civilian and military personnel overseeing this brutal pacification, those "springy, zesty, burning-eyes warriors" (125). They preferred to imagine what they were doing as "more congenial … than the war they are launching from the skies. Americans do not like to be negative, and the 'other' war is constructive." Under the expert guidance of leading social scientists, "brimming with public spirit," "charts and graphs and maps and symbols" were produced to demonstrate the successes of pacification (121–122).

War and geopolitics, and the relationship between them, are major structuring features of world order. They intersect with, generate, and

---

[30] Robin, *The Cold World They Made*, 5. This is a compelling intellectual history of a partnership that profoundly shaped both US Cold War military strategy and neoconservative support for so-called "preventive" wars.

[31] Arne Westad, *The Global Cold War* (Cambridge: Cambridge University Press, 2007).

[32] Mary McCarthy, *Hanoi* (New York: Harcourt Brace and World, 1968); also see Frances Kiernan, *Seeing Mary Plain: A Life of Mary McCarthy* (New York: W. W. Norton 2000); Sabrina Fuchs Abrams, *Mary McCarthy: Gender, Politics, and the Postwar Intellectual* (New York: Peter Lang, 2004).

are shaped by other major themes in this book because they are so defining of twentieth-century international relations: imperialism, anticolonialism, technology and "progress," world peace, and world economy. The writings below are from some of the most influential thinkers in their respective fields and were recognized as such in their day. Yet in contemporary International Relations and international intellectual history, only Margaret Sprout and Roberta Wohlstetter have some recognition as war theorists. Hannah Arendt's wide-ranging engagements with war and other international relations questions have only recently begun to receive the recognition they deserve in political theory and the history of political and international thought. Claudia Jones has been described as "one of the most brilliant, innovative black feminist and radical thinkers of the twentieth-century," but histories of international thought have ignored her.[33] Interestingly, all figures in this section wrote for wide and overlapping audiences, which in Ellen Churchill Semple's case was intended to be field-defining. They had very particular and broader audiences in mind. Thus, all of these texts were political interventions. Exemplified by Jones and Sylvia Pankhurst, women often turned to journalism to mobilize and organize political action. They took on explicitly educative roles. But even the most philosophical and abstract works selected here are grounded in and a response to some of the defining military and "geopolitical" events of the twentieth century.

Patricia Owens

---

[33] Erik S. McDuffie, *Sojourning for Freedom: Black Women, American Communism, and the Making of Black Left Feminism* (Durham, NC: Duke University Press, 2011), 8.

Ellen Churchill Semple

From *Influences of Geographic Environment on the Basis of Ratzel's System of Anthropo-Geography* (1911)

Man is a product of the earth's surface. This means not merely that he is a child of the earth, dust of her dust; but that the earth has mothered him, fed him, set him tasks, directed his thoughts, confronted him with difficulties that have strengthened his body and sharpened his wits, given him his problems of navigation or irrigation, and at the same time whispered hints for their solution. She has entered into his bone and tissue, into his mind and soul. On the mountains she has given him leg muscles of iron to climb the slope; along the coast she has left these weak and flabby, but given him instead vigorous development of chest and arm to handle his paddle or oar. In the river valley she attaches him to the fertile soil, circumscribes his ideas and ambitions by a dull round of calm, exacting duties, narrows his outlook to the cramped horizon of his farm. Up on the windswept plateaus, in the boundless stretch of the grasslands and the waterless tracts of the desert, where he roams with his flocks from pasture to pasture and oasis to oasis, where life knows much hardship but escapes the grind of drudgery, where the watching of grazing herds gives him leisure for contemplation, and the wide-ranging life a big horizon, his ideas take on a certain gigantic simplicity; religion becomes monotheism. God becomes one, unrivalled like the sand of the desert and the grass of the steppe, stretching on and on without break or change. Chewing over and over the cud of his simple belief as the one food of his unfed mind, his faith becomes fanaticism; his big special ideas, born of that ceaseless regular wandering, outgrow the land that bred them and bear their legitimate fruit in wide imperial conquests.

Man can no more be scientifically studied apart from the ground which he tills, or the lands over which he travels, or the seas over which he trades, than polar bear or desert cactus can be understood apart from its habitat. Man's relations to his environment are infinitely more numerous and complex than those of the most highly organized plant or animal.

So complex are they that they constitute a legitimate and necessary object of special study. The investigation which they receive in anthropology, ethnology, sociology and history is piecemeal and partial, limited as to the race, cultural development, epoch, country or variety of geographic conditions taken into account. Hence all these sciences, together with history so far as history undertakes to explain the causes of events, fail to reach a satisfactory solution of their problems largely because the geographic factor which enters into them all has not been thoroughly analysed. Man has been so noisy about the way he has "conquered Nature," and Nature has been so silent in her persistent influence over man, that the geographic factor in the equation of human development has been overlooked.

In every problem of history there are two main factors, variously stated as heredity and environment, man and his geographic conditions, the internal forces of race and the external forces of habitat. Now the geographic element in the long history of human development has been operating strongly and operating persistently. Herein lies its importance. It is a stable force. It never sleeps. This natural environment, this physical basis of history, is for all intents and purposes immutable in comparison with the other factor in the problem – shifting, plastic, progressive, retrogressive man.

History tends to repeat itself largely owing to this steady, unchanging geographic element. If the ancient Roman consul in far-away Britain often assumed an independence of action and initiative unknown in the provincial governors of Gaul, and if, centuries after, Roman Catholicism in England maintained a similar independence towards the Holy See, both facts have their cause in the remoteness of Britain from the center of political or ecclesiastical power in Rome. If the independence of the Roman Consul in Britain was duplicated later by the attitude of the Thirteen Colonies toward England, and again, within the young Republic by the headstrong self-reliance, impatient of the government authority, which characterized the early Trans-Allegheny commonwealths in their aggressive Indian policy, and led them to make war and conclude treaties for the cession of land like sovereign states; and if this attitude of independence in the over-mountain men reappeared in a spirit of political defection looking toward secession from the Union and a new combination with their British neighbour on the Great Lakes or the Spanish beyond the Mississippi, these are all the identical effects of geographical remoteness made yet more remote by barriers of mountain and sea. This is the long reach which weakens the arm of authority, no matter what the race or country or epoch.

[...]

These complex geographic influences cannot be analysed and their strength estimated except from the standpoint of evolution. That is one reason these half-baked geographic principles rest heavy on our mental digestion. They have been formulated without reference to the all-important fact that the geographical relations of man, like his social and political organization, are subject to the law of development. Just as the embryo state found in the primitive Saxon tribe has passed through many phases in attaining the political character of the present British Empire, so every stage in this maturing growth has been accompanied or even preceded by a steady evolution of the geographic relations of the English people.

Owing to the evolution of geographic relations, the physical environment favourable to one stage of development may be adverse to another, and *vice versa*. For instance, a small, isolated and protected habitat, like that of Egypt, Phoenicia, Crete and Greece, encourages the birth and precocious growth of civilization; but later it may cramp progress, and lend the stamp of arrested development to a people who were once the model for all their little world. Open and wind-swept Russia, lacking these small, warm nurseries where Nature could cuddle her children, has bred upon its boundless plains a massive, untutored, homogeneous folk, fed upon the crumbs of culture that have fallen from the richer tables of Europe. But that item of area is a variable quantity in the equation. It changes its character at a higher stage of cultural development. Consequently, when the Muscovite people, instructed by the example of western Europe, shall have grown up intellectually, economically and politically to their big territory, its area will become a great national asset. Russia will come into its own, heir to a long-withheld inheritance. Many of its previous geographic disadvantages will vanish, like the diseases of childhood, while its massive size will dwarf many previous advantages of its European neighbors.

This evolution of geographic relations applies not only to the local environment, but also to the wider world relations of a people. Greeks and Syrians, English and Japanese, take a different rank among the nations of the earth to-day from that held by their ancestors 2,000 years ago, simply because the world relations of civilized peoples have been steadily expanding since those far-back days of Tyrian and Athenian supremacy. The period of maritime discoveries in the fifteenth and sixteenth centuries shifted the foci of the world relations of European states from enclosed seas to the rim of the Atlantic. Venice and Genoa gave way to Cadiz and Lagos, just as sixteen centuries before Corinth and Athens had yielded their ascendency to Rome and Ostia. The keen but circumscribed trade of the Baltic, which gave wealth and historical pre-eminence to Lübeck and the other Hanse Towns of northern Germany from the twelfth to the seventeenth century, lost its relative importance when the Atlantic became the maritime field of history. Maritime leadership passed westward from Lübeck and Stralsund to Amsterdam and Bristol, as the historical horizon widened. England, prior to this sudden dislocation, lay on the outskirts of civilized Europe, a terminal land, not a focus. The peripheral location which retarded her early development became a source of power when she accumulated sufficient density of population for colonizing enterprises, and when maritime discovery opened a way to trans-oceanic lands.

Meanwhile, local geographic advantages in the old basins remain the same, although they are dwarfed by the development of relatively greater advantages elsewhere. The broken coastline, limited area and favourable position of Greece make its people to-day a nation of seamen, and enable them to absorb by their considerable merchant fleet a great part of the trade of the eastern Mediterranean,[34] just as they did in the days of Pericles: but that youthful Aegean world which once constituted so large a part of the *oikoumene,* has shrunken to a modest province, and its highways to local paths.

[...]

The earth is an inseparable whole. Each country or sea is physically and historically intelligible only as a portion of that whole. Currents and wind-systems of the oceans modify the climate of the nearby continents, and direct the first daring navigations of their peoples. The alternating monsoons of the Indian Ocean guided Arab merchantmen from ancient times back and forth between the Red Sea and the Malabar coast of India. The Equatorial Current and the northeast trade-wind carried the timid ships of Columbus across the Atlantic to America. The Gulf Stream and the prevailing westerlies later gave English vessels the advantage on the return voyage. Europe is a part of the Atlantic coast. This is a fact so significant that the North Atlantic has become a European sea. The United States also is a part of the Atlantic coast: this is the dominant fact of American history. China forms a section of the Pacific rim. This is the fact back of the geographic distribution of Chinese emigration to Annam, Tonkin, Siam, Malacca, the Philippines, East Indies, Borneo, Australia, Hawaiian Islands, the Pacific Coast States, British Columbia, the Alaskan coast southward from Bristol Bay in Bering Sea, Ecuador and Peru.

As the earth is one, so is humanity. Its unity of species points to some degree of communication through a long pre-historic past. Universal

---

[34] Hugh Robert Mill, *International Geography,* p. 347. New York, 1902.

history is not entitled to the name unless it embraces all parts of the earth and all peoples, whether savage or civilized. To fill the gaps in the written record it must turn to ethnology and geography, which by tracing the distribution and movements of primitive peoples can often reconstruct the most important features of their history.

Anthropo-geographic problems are never simple. They must all be viewed in the long perspective of evolution and the historical past. They require allowance for the dominance of different geographic factors at different periods, and for a possible range of geographic influences wide as the earth itself. In the investigator they call for painstaking analysis and, above all, an open mind.

Sylvia Pankhurst

From "The Fascist World War (Ethiopia and Spain)" (1935)

We are in the world war of Fascism against Democracy. The Italian Dictator's other term for this war already in swing, is the war of the 'Dissatisfied Nations' against the 'Satisfied Nations.'

This war began in Ethiopia; now it has spread to Spain, where the Government democratically elected by the Spanish people, in constitutional form, is being attacked by the Fascists, who were defeated at the ballot box. The Spanish Fascists would already have been defeated in the test of force which they have chosen, were it not that they are being assisted by the Fascist powers outside. Italy and Germany are assisting them. [...]

The Air Arm

It is the air arm which counts in Spain, as it counted in Ethiopia, and there is evidence that the Italian dictatorship is supplying its Fascist ally with aeroplanes, and that the German ally is supplying its Fascist ally with aeroplanes, and that the German ally is supplying cash. One of the first to publish the news was the Antwerp correspondent of the Paris newspaper *Populaire*, which reported that the Spanish Fascist leader, General Franco, had made an important transaction in gold at Hamburg to buy twenty-four aeroplanes from Italy.

What more natural, given Signor Mussolini's often-declared determination to create a Fascist International for war on the rest of the world? Italy has the planes accumulated for exterminating Ethiopians immobilised by the rains of that much tortured country: therefore she is able to lend them to her Fascist ally!

People Stood by

People stood by while Ethiopia was vanquished: this is only Africa; this is not a White Man's country. They listened to the Italian propaganda;

these are primitives, their customs are barbarous. Now people stand by again; they do not like Spanish politics; these are a disorderly people, fighting amongst themselves; they are Anarchists, Socialists, Reds, strikers; it does not matter to us.

Meanwhile the Fascists consider it does matter and are supplying all they can to their own side.

It was the same in Italy when Fascism started the civil war there: the Christian Democrats of Don Sterzo's Popolari, the old Liberals of Giolitti, the Free Masons, the old, tolerant type of Conservatism, all said: it is only the Socialists and the other Reds, the Trade Unionists and the Co-operators, who are attacked; then, one by one, each of them went down before the bludgeon, the rifle and the repressive antics of Fascism; their organisations were suppressed, their leaders imprisoned or compelled to flee [...]

Divide and Conquer

The policy of the Fascist government is based consistently on the old maxim: 'Divide and Conquer.' To the conservatives of France, Britain and every country, it represents itself as the Party which opposes Bolshevism, and organises and disciplines the disorderly and selfish ranks of labour. Hence on the French Bourse spirits rose, and prices ascended with a rush for Spanish securities when an unfounded rumour flashed through that Madrid had fallen to the rebels. Hence, too, we find certain Members of Parliament becoming indignant at the notion that this country might perhaps be supplying arms to the Government of Spain which has been elected by due process of electoral law and is now fighting a life and death struggle against the Fascist International. It is on class and party prejudice that the Spanish Fascists rely when they broadcast appeals for help in their rebellion to the British, German and Italian Governments. [...]

The People of Spain

The people of Spain have rallied with amazing spontaneity against the rebel lawbreakers. Let pressmen and detractors say what they will, the photographs published in every newspaper record uncontrovertibly the fact that men and woman [sic] have rushed to the barricades by the thousand, to defend their liberty at the risk of death. They are no embittered fanatic groups, these crowds of men and women, old and young; they are the average people, who have left their work and play, their domestic joys and cares to defend a cause which to them over masters all.

Elizabeth Monroe

From *The Mediterranean in Politics* (1938)

Out of four Mediterranean territories, therefore, only one presents Great Britain with any real difficulty, but that one offers a problem so formidable as to endanger reputation, not only in the Mediterranean, but in more than half the countries in the world. In Gibraltar, Malta, and Cyprus, goodwill is something tangible which her money can help buy; in Palestine, it is elusive and unobtainable until her Government is ready to admit that the problem has surpassed the stage at which it can be solved by mere administration, and until she summons the courage to handle a political problem in a political way. In the pass to which Palestine has brought her, unequivocal definition of her intentions seems to be the only means of recapturing the reputation she has already lost. Come what may in the way of recriminations, she will at least occasion a certain respect if she ceases to beat about the bush, and presents the world with a policy which is frankly based upon that soundest and best-understood of all aims – the improvement of her own security.

[...]

'The Mediterranean – main artery of the British Empire.' This familiar tag, sadly overworked at political meetings, is in fact a little misleading, for the metaphor implies life-blood, and therefore a channel of vital supply. To Great Britain, the Mediterranean is not this, for she can do without the commercial route if need be, indeed she is more and more easily able to do so as modern invention lessens the distance by the ocean routes which she can use instead.

Her chief reason for maintaining her Mediterranean strength is in order to increase her voice in the councils of Europe, and to uphold her prestige in a belt of territory where 'face' counts – namely, in the desert region which she must cross in her day-to-day contact with her eastern Dominions and India, and which is also one of the world's great oil areas.

Her second reason is strategic. In the event of war, her fortresses in the Mediterranean increase her mobility for purposes of imperial defence. They also enable her to get at her adversary in an area where he is highly vulnerable – in the Grand Canal running from Gibraltar to Aden, where the U-boats of twenty years ago and the pirate sub-marines of to-day have successfully demonstrated that defence is difficult and attack easy. Her third reason is commercial; as one of the world's greatest traders, she finds that it pays to advertise along one of the world's main highways.

Here are three motives for remaining in the Mediterranean. Some Englishmen like to add a fourth, which is that Great Britain is bound by duty to the peoples who inhabit her Mediterranean dependencies. But examination proves that this theory does not everywhere apply. Were Great Britain to abandon the Mediterranean, the Arabs of Palestine would be delighted to see her go. The Cypriot Greeks, too, would vote joyfully for union with Greece, provided that they could do so without losing the protection of British arms; on the other hand, they would regret their vote if they woke to find that the British forces had sailed away, and left them exposed to annexation by Turkey or Italy. With the Maltese, her relation is different, both because of their loyalty, and because they came voluntarily into the British Empire. No doubt Great Britain's feelings towards them weigh less with her than does her need of their island as a base, but this does not alter the fact that many Maltese have worked actively on her behalf against alien influence, and that (judging by precedents in Ethiopia and Austria) she would be playing them a shabby trick were she to leave them to the mercies of a newcomer. Towards one people, however, moral duty is her first consideration – namely, towards the Palestinian Jews.

When the British begin to talk of the moral obligations of empire, foreigners always hide a smile, seeing in the statement but another example of the perfidy of Albion. Thus, when the Englishman asserts that British forces remain in the Mediterranean partly because Great Britain is committed to 400,000 Jews settled under her guarantee in the midst of an inimical Arab world, the foreigner replies: 'Thou hypocrite!' He contends that she is thinking not of moral duty but of the dissatisfaction in Lombard Street, and of the havoc which the wrath of the great Jewish financial houses could wreak in the City. There is some truth in the allegation, but, at the same time, the man who makes it is failing to give the British people their due. Any suggestions that the Jewish National Home in Palestine should be left to sink or swim would cause a feeling of revulsion among large numbers of Englishmen; already outraged at the treatment which a great race is receiving in certain states of Europe they would be loth to countenance any action which exposed more Jews to oppression, or which smacked of deserting the Jewish people in one of the black moments of its history.

To sum up, then: Diplomatic influence, imperial strategy, national prosperity, a sense of obligation to the Jews. These reasons, in order of importance, help to explain why Great Britain is 'quitting nothing' in the Mediterranean. All but one are highly material, for material reasons are undeniably at the bottom of every nation's imperialism. But to strike a solely material note is to give a false idea of the qualities which make the strength of a successful empire. However self-interested the original motives for which Great Britain grabbed her colonies, her subsequent handling of them, and in particular the work of the man on the spot, often provide a record of disinterested service. Palestine is a blot on her escutcheon, and her handling of Cyprus is not a very creditable performance, but penetrate a little farther and you will gain a more just impression of her Empire as a whole. When you see the Sudan, or Transjordan, or the mark which she has left in Egypt, you realize that a Cromer or a Macmichael could not have won the name he has made had British material interests been his only inspiration.

To say this is to make no unique claim for Great Britain; the same applies, in the French Empire, to the work of a man like Lyautey. Nor is it to deny that material motives usually underly [sic] a government's imperial policy. Great Britain could abandon her Mediterranean dependencies without causing bodily harm to any of their inhabitants except the Jews and, no doubt, those Maltese who have worked openly in her interests. She does not do so, partly from the instincts that prompt the holding of possessions and the finishing of a job once begun, but chiefly because her presence there affords her standing and influence in Europe and Asia, and enables her to do the buying and selling upon which depends the high standard of living to which her people have become accustomed in their over-populated British Isles.

Margaret Sprout

From *Toward a New Order of Sea Power*
(co-authored with Harold Sprout) (1940)

Mahan's master work on sea power, and the subsequent books and essays that streamed from his hurrying pen, had world-wide repercussions on naval development and world politics. Mahan's interpretation of history excited expansionist forces already stirring in Europe, in America, and in the Far East. His strategic ideas, derived largely from the history of British naval policy and operations, were accepted as precepts from universal application and utility, without qualification as to time and place. And the impact of these ideas was widely felt in accelerated naval development which, inside of two decades, was profoundly to alter the balance of naval power, with political repercussions on every ocean and continent.

This changing order of sea power was but one of the many shifts in international power relations which followed the spread of the industrial revolution. For more than a century, British manufacturing and related industries had dominated the world economy. But similar industries had gradually taken root elsewhere, often with the direct aid of English capital. And these came in time to be serious rivals of the mines and factories of Great Britain.

The growth of mutually competitive industrial economies on the European continent, in America, and in other lands, inaugurated a new era of imperialism which in certain respects closely resembled the mercantilistic expansion of the eighteenth century. This neo-mercantilistic imperialism received in the 1890's a tremendous stimulus from the vision of power, glory, profit, and moral destiny, set forth with crusading zeal in Mahan's prolific writings. These as well as the trend of political and economic events, stimulated the growth of navies which supported and at the same time fostered the new imperialism. The rising wave of imperialism further accelerated the pace of naval expansion the world over. And this in turn undermined the historic world-wide naval dominance of Great Britain.

That dominance rested not only upon the greater material strength and the peculiar strategic doctrine of the British Navy, but also upon the incomparable geographic position of the British Isles and upon the configuration of the narrow seas. [...]

The rise of Japanese naval power undermined England's strategic dominance, and hence political influence, in the Far East. Through one of the ironies of history, Englishmen themselves contributed materially to this result. British shipyards in the 1880's and 1890's built one warship after another for Japan. And British naval officers were loaned to the Mikado's Government to teach the elements of naval science and administration. [...]

Meanwhile, parallel developments were taking place in the Western hemisphere. Prior to the Civil War, the United States had both a navy and a naval policy. But neither affected the main currents of world politics in any large or continuing manner. [...] After a brief war-induced growth, the American Navy passed into a prolonged eclipse. Reconstruction commenced in the early 'eighties, and by 1890 was acquiring some momentum. Mahan's writings, in conjunction with other influences, accelerated the pace and changed the direction of American naval development. [...]

Acceleration of the naval building pace in Europe, especially the very rapid growth of the German Navy after 1900, threatened England's historic dominance in European waters. So instead of strengthening its overseas squadrons, the British Government had progressively to deplete them in order to maintain a safe margin of superiority in the narrow seas and eastern Atlantic. [...]

Great Britain's growing commitments in Europe and shrinking power overseas profoundly affected international politics in the Far East. Security for British interests in Asia was sought through a multilateral equipoise stable enough to support the status quo in that remote sector. Englishmen encouraged our annexation of the Philippine Islands in 1898, regarding the United States as a friendly steadying influence in the Far East. When they failed to secure a formal alliance with the United States, they entered into a military partnership with Japan, directed first against Russia, later against Germany. And in various other ways they labored to fashion a political substitute for their former naval dominance in the Far East.

In the Western Hemisphere Great Britain followed a radically different course. Here the materials were lacking for a political equipoise, or balance of power. British statesmen had either to resist or to accept the naval primacy of the United States. Necessarily they chose the latter. [...]

The implications of all this are clearer in retrospect, of course, than they were in prospect. With increasing difficulty the British Government did manage to keep a margin of naval superiority that seemed to assure its hold on the sea approaches to Europe. [...] However, the ability to maintain such a blockade would thereafter depend not only on Britain's naval dominance in European waters but also on the attitude and policy of the transoceanic naval Powers, Japan and the United States.

[...] Great Britain's world-wide command of the seas had vanished, and with it the historic balance wheel of the vast, intricate, and swiftly moving machinery of that advantageous world economic community and quasi-political order which British sea power had fostered and supported during the preceding century.

America's Continental Fortress

The changing order of sea power improved the already strong defensive position of the continental United States. From the standpoint of resistance to external aggression, Continental America, then as today, bore a superficial, often remarked, and very much overstressed resemblance to the British Isles. [...] Bodies of water separated both countries from other centers of military power. In both, as a result, sea power had traditionally played a larger role than land power in the conception and practice of statecraft. But there the similarity ended.

Owing to the immense width of the oceans, as well as to the inherent military weakness of all other countries in the Western hemisphere, the American position was immeasurably stronger than England's for purposes of defense against armed aggression from overseas. [...]

From the standpoint of world politics, and for the purposes of waging war offensively in distant seas, however, the American position was infinitely weaker than England's. [...] [T]he geographical location of the British Isles, the early seizure of Gibraltar, and the possession of a superior navy had given Great Britain an invincible grip on the ocean portals of Europe. [...]

For geographical reasons, obvious though too often ignored by empire-minded Americans, no exercise of sea power within the Western Hemisphere would possibly produce world results in any way comparable to those which flowed from England's historic command of Europe's narrow seas. There were no commercial bottlenecks in the New World comparable to the English Channel and the Strait of Gibraltar. [...]

Military control of the Caribbean, as well as of the Atlantic and Pacific approaches to the United States, might be imperatively necessary to render the continental homeland of the American people invulnerable to external pressure and armed aggression. That idea in one form or another was historically one of the foundation stones of American diplomacy. It was the very essence of the Monroe Doctrine. American statesmen and their naval advisers might, and did, conclude under the tutelage of Mahan that military control of these waters required building a fleet of capital ships and adopting England's strategic doctrine. But it was difficult to see, Mahan and his disciples notwithstanding, how any fleet, however strong, or any strategic doctrine, however sound, could give the United States Government a leverage on world politics even remotely approaching that exercised by Great Britain down to the end of the nineteenth century. [...] The growing complexity of war technology [...] steadily narrowed the range of major fleet operations and raised up new obstacles in the way of landing and maintaining large expeditionary forces on distant hostile shores. [...] The revolutionary rise of submarine and air power in particular, while progressively undermining the security of England's island base just off the coast of Europe, actually strengthened the defences of our continental base three thousand miles from Europe and farther still from Asia. [...]

By the end of the last century, the United States had evolved into an immense, compact, united country with varied and abundant resources, accumulated wealth, diversified industries, superior technology, and excellent internal communications. These all contributed to making the United States virtually proof against sea-blockade, even if there had existed anywhere in the world a Power with the naval forces and freedom of action necessary to undertake so herculean a task. [...]

At the same time, Great Britain's recurrent preoccupation with balance-of-power politics in the Old World [...] repeatedly frustrated England's own imperial ambitions in this hemisphere. [...] And there was never a time from then until the World War of 1914, when either Great Britain or any other European country enjoyed the political freedom of action necessary to challenge in this hemisphere the rapidly rising naval power of the United States. [...]

The defensive position of the United States was still further strengthened, down to 1898, by a truly remarkable dearth of oversea commitments and responsibilities. [...] We had no detached possessions except Alaska which then lay beyond the grasp of any potential aggressor. Non-intervention, neutrality, and no "entangling alliances" were the guiding principles of America's relations with Europe. [...]

The naval implications of all this were clear to Mahan. As he frankly admitted in 1890, for a country situated as the United States then was, the primary object of naval policy was neither to defend a scattered empire nor to support a program of expansion overseas, but rather to insure to merchant shipping safe and uninterrupted access to its home ports in war as well as in peace. [...]

To realize this objective, Mahan continued, there was needed a navy capable of driving any hostile forces from the sea approaches to the continental United States. It was not sufficient merely to provide local harbor defences and land forces to stop the enemy at the coastline. [...] Only a fighting fleet could drive off hostile blockading squadrons. And that fleet, in Mahan's judgment, must include battleships, as powerfully armed and as stoutly armored as any capital ships in existence.

While Mahan fervently hoped in 1890, that the time was not far distant when the United States would embark upon oversea expansion which in turn would necessitate a still greater navy, he recognized that American requirements were for the time being comparatively modest. [...]

Our position in this hemisphere was still further buttressed by the insular accessions which resulted directly and indirectly from the war with Spain. Conquest of Spain's West Indian islands, and provision for a naval base in a nominally independent Cuba, insured American dominance in the Caribbean. Annexation of the Hawaiian Islands in 1898, and partition of the Samoan archipelago the following year, foreshadowed a similar primacy throughout a vast triangle in the eastern Pacific. [...]

Completion of the Panama Canal in 1914 transformed the Caribbean into a world thoroughfare as Mahan and others had foreseen; but a thoroughfare under the exclusive, undisputed, and undisputable control of the American Navy. [...]

America's "Achilles Heel" in the Western Pacific

The war with Spain resulted also in the annexation of Guam and the Philippine Islands. The latter lay in the far western Pacific, nearly 5,000 nautical miles beyond Hawaii, more than two weeks continuous steaming for the fastest ships then in service. And as a glance at the political and military geography of the western Pacific readily shows, these accessions radically altered and unbelievably complicated the hitherto relatively simple defense problem of the United States. [...]

Under conditions prevailing down to 1914, possession of Wake, Guam and the Philippines gave the United States a position of some potential military strength in the western Pacific. Development of a properly equipped and adequately fortified base, probably in Guam, would have transformed this position from one of potential into actual strength. [...] And this, for better or for worse, would have given the United States, on the critical eve of World War, a considerably greater leverage on international developments in the Far East.

Actually, very little was done to improve our strategic position in either Guam or the Philippines. Experts disagreed as to proper location of dockyards and defensive works. There was considerable popular opposition in America to any action which seemed to envisage our permanent occupation of those distant islands. Members of Congress, with their eyes on patronage, the pork barrel, and the next election, were chiefly interested in public works nearer home. As a result, our military road across the Pacific faded out a thousand miles or so West of Hawaii. American diplomacy in the Far East lacked the support of readily available superior force. And American insular possessions in the western Pacific remained a remote and indefensible salient, virtually a hostage to Japan, or, as Theodore Roosevelt aptly said of the Philippines, the "Achilles heel" of the United States.

It is difficult to reconcile this inaction with the trend of American political commitments in eastern Asia. Since before the middle of the nineteenth century, American statesmen had stood for equality of commercial opportunity in the Far East. But they had rarely shown any disposition to back this up with anything stronger than words. Following the war with Spain, however, the United States Government, with verbal encouragement and support from London, assumed leadership and a degree of responsibility for maintaining this open-door principle as against Japan and the Continental European Powers which were moving in from all directions on the moribund Chinese Empire. This undertaking, springing partly from expectations of pecuniary gain, and partly from conceptions of moral duty, entailed large risks and paid dividends chiefly in ill will. The trend toward conflict in the Pacific was accentuated by recurring difficulties arising from the entry and settlement of Japanese subjects in the United States. And at no time after 1905 could American statesmen entirely ignore either the possibility of war with Japan or the certain repercussions in the Far East of a general war in Europe.

The possibility of the latter was especially disquieting, or should have been, because of a fateful strategic decision embodied in the peace settlement of 1898 with Spain. Whether it was wise for the United States to retain any of the Spanish islands in the western Pacific is certainly a debatable question. But it is clear in retrospect at least, that it was a strategic mistake to take only Guam and the Philippines, leaving the rest to fall into the hands of some other first-class Power.

Throughout a distance of approximately fifteen hundred miles, these islands – the Caroline and Marianas groups – crowded the southern flank of the sea route to the Philippines and Far East by way of Hawaii and Guam. In Spanish hands these islands presented no serious threat, for

Spain was no longer a power with which to reckon. But their cession from Spain to one of the Great Powers would inevitably alter the strategical situation, and might, under readily conceivable circumstances, undermine the entire military position of the United States in the western Pacific. [...]

The disposition to be made of these western Pacific islands was also extensively discussed within the United States during the summer and autumn of 1898. The religious press urged their annexation as a means of fostering missionary enterprise. Others emphasized their value in connection with various trans-Pacific cable projects. Here and there someone grasped their geomilitary bearing on American plans and policies in the Far East. But the military argument seems to have made but little impression either on the public mind or on national policy. The Caroline Islands were discussed at the peace conference, but the question was not pressed in the face of Spanish resistance. The American commissioners demanded and secured the Philippines and Guam. The remainder were left in Spanish hands. [...]

Early in 1899, the Spanish Crown liquidated the last remnant of its shattered Pacific empire by ceding the Caroline and Marianas Islands to Germany which already held the Marshall group still farther to the east. Years afterward, Mahan recalled that "when the Caroline and Ladrone Islands were about to be ceded to Germany by Spain ... I received more than one letter urging me to use any influence I could exert to induce our government to resist the step. My reply was that, besides having no influence, I saw no sufficient reason for our opposition." [...] This was also the official view, and German forces took possession with the full acquiescence of the United States.

Under conditions prevailing in 1899, this doubtless seemed to be a safe enough national policy. Germany was a strong and rapidly growing Power. But Germany's European entanglements and England's command of the European seas precluded any concentration of German naval strength in the Pacific Ocean. What this complacent view ignored was the possibility of a further transfer at some later date from Germany to Japan. Such a transfer would instantly alter the strategical situation to the serious disadvantage of the United States. It would jeopardize the security of American insular possessions in the western Pacific and weaken American influence throughout the Far East, since Japanese imperialists had large ambitions in that region and the steadily growing naval power of Japan was and would remain concentrated in the Pacific.

The possibility that the Marshall, Caroline, and Marianas Islands might eventually pass into the hands of Japan began to take shape after the formation in 1902 of the Anglo-Japanese Alliance.

That possibility markedly increased when Germany succeeded Russia as the primary object against which that Alliance was directed. And the dangers inherent in that possibility grew steadily larger as Japan advanced step by step in Asia, as Japan's Navy rose in strength and prestige, as Japanese–American relations surmounted one diplomatic crisis after another, and as the European Powers hurried on to war and disaster.

What lay in the future, no one could wholly foresee. The rise of American naval power, together with the conception of national security embodied in the Monroe Doctrine, seemed to assure a fair degree of international stability within the Western Hemisphere, *come what might in Europe*. But a combination of conditions, circumstances, and events had thus far prevented any single Power from succeeding to Great Britain's former primacy in the Far East. And it required no prophetic gift to foresee that war in Europe might well lead to chaos in Asia, with the United States drifting toward armed conflict with a militant expanding Japan, bent on establishing political hegemony in the Far East, and naval dominance in the western Pacific.

Claudia Jones

From "What We Must Now Do about India" (1942)

THE world spotlight, focused-on the India crisis, has brought about an unprecedented discussion about India. Among anti-fascists, such discussions do not conjure up mental pictures about a "FABULOUS, MYSTERIOUS" India; they do not call up visions of an India which is the "PEARL OF THE BRITISH EMPIRE" – rather such discussions are, in the main, based on viewing India and her nearly 400 million people from the deep life and death relationship which she occupies today. The entire anti-fascist world has been shocked by the reviving of the old whiplash and terror, rule of British colonial rulers and the British Cabinet against the Indian people.

It is all the more significant that the India crisis occurs at a time when the war has reached its over-all crisis, upon whose victory depends the opening of the Second Front Now. It is doubly significant that the India crisis has come at a time when we celebrate the first anniversary of the Atlantic Charter which has as its declared aim "THE RIGHT OF ALL PEOPLES TO CHOOSE THE FORM OF GOVERNMENT UNDER WHICH THEY WILL LIVE."

Despite this realization, nearly the entire press of the nation has cloaked the real issues of the India crisis with the same attitude as that of the Colonial rulers, who under the guise of "law and order" are using guns and bullets against the Indian people. It is for these main reasons that it is important to establish what the real issue is in India; and why it is important for us to immediately act to bring about a speedy solution of this crisis, which is inseparably connected with the whole cause of victory.

The cause of victory needs India, because India represents an important bastion for us both militarily and politically. India is in the path of Axis aggression. Hitler is moving in the direction of Asia Minor, helped by Rommel in the East, thus hoping to conquer the Caucasus. Japan is showing signs of moving upon Soviet Siberia and India. The consequences of such a juncture through India could not but have terrible results for the Indian people, as well as the cause of victory. For the aim of the Axis powers is to separate the Soviet Union and China from their allies. Politically, India's importance lies in the fact that the mobilization of her nearly 400 million people is needed now in our battle of freedom in order to stop Japan and Hitler.

India's fate is directly connected with the fate of the colonial peoples. Freedom for India may decide whether or not we will have on our side powerful allies to stop Japan and halt Hitler's advance in the Middle East. It is actually a test as to whether we will really fulfill our war aims – the freedom and independence of all peoples everywhere. It is for this reason the whole colonial world in Asia, Africa, Latin America, as well as the Negro people of our own country, anxiously watch to see what the position of London and Washington will be. By now we should have learned that the way to mobilize the peoples of the Far East, as well as the whole colonial world, is through the mobilization of the people THEMSELVES to defend their own homelands.

It is in this deep sense that we must recognize that freedom for India as well as the opening of the Second Front NOW, are two parts of the single key to victory.

Why then has India not been mobilized? The British colonial rulers and the continued stand of the British Cabinet to maintain the old policy of colonial rule (refusal to arm the people, etc.) are responsible. These colonial rulers, who, only six months ago, proved their complete inadequacy to mobilize the people for defense in Burma and Malaya, now are attempting through "law and order" to attempt to "organize" the people for effective resistance against the enemy. How can the colonial rulers, after 300 years, proven incapable to solve the problem by "law and order," solve it now? We know that a people only fight if they are convinced that this is their war of liberation. It is for that reason too, that we cannot ask the Indian people to "put aside" their struggle for independence, in the interest of victory. In the first place, this war has proven, as in China and the Soviet Union, that only an armed people supporting the army is capable of defeating the fascists. Secondly, such an approach is the direct opposite to achieving full and complete participation of India against fascism, for the only way such mobilization can be achieved is through freely permitting India to mobilize in its own defense. Only then can we really win them as allies.

This, in essence, is the stand of the overwhelming majority of the All-India Congress leaders and the Indian people. The Indian people have seen the effects of the colonial policy in Burma and Malaya.

They have also seen the other road – in China.

Despite the confusion in the press, it is obvious that the All-India Congress and the Indian people are aware of the fact that the Axis must be defeated in order to save India. This was shown in the rejection by the Congress Working Committee (prior to the All-India Congress meeting) of Ghandi's resolution. This resolution was one which insinuated that the whole India nationalist movement is ready to sell out to Japan.

Moreover, at the time when the British colonial rulers descended with their rule of terror against the leaders of the All-India Congress and the Indian people, Nehru and the other Congress leaders (as distinct from Ghandi) re-emphasized that their demand for a National Government responsible to the people was a war demand, a military measure, to assure the most effective mobilization of the people for the defense of India, in cooperation especially with China, the Soviet Union, England and the United States.

Even more clearcut is the stand of India's Communist Party which has put to the fore as India's supreme need the defense of their country, calling on the people to unite and take their full part in the just war against fascism. Stating unequivocally that the "policy of the British government perpetuating the enslavement of India" is to be condemned, it points out that it should not be permitted to prevent the Indian people from adopting a correct attitude toward the war and from mobilizing the power of the people. They urge the recognition of the independence of India and state: "The establishment of a provisional National Government, enjoying the confidence of the people and the realization of democratic liberties are essential to transform our general support of the war into an active and effective material cooperation."

From this we can see that Ghandi does not represent the All-India Congress nor the sentiments of the Indian people. As a matter of fact, there has been going on for some time a sharp struggle against the dangerous "non-violent resistance, non-cooperation with Britain" stand of Ghandi. The suppression of the Indian people and the Congress, who are moving away from Ghandism, can only serve to strengthen Ghandi's hand, and thus endanger the whole course of India's freedom, as well as the United Nations.

An example of the bankruptcy of British colonial rule in India in this present crisis is to be seen in an article printed in the April issue of "The Student," organ of the All-India Student Federation.

Describing the situation in Calcutta which students found upon returning from the All-India Students Conference in Patha, the article points out the "utter inadequacy" of the arrangements for defense of the city; the "insolence" of local British authorities to keep the PEOPLE out of it. Entitled "If Moscow, Chungking, London Can – Calcutta, Too, Can Take It," it describes the work of the students coming at the imminent fall of Singapore and Rangoon.

The description of what the students did, how they organized the Civil Defense, how they inspired the people, their belief and understanding of the issues involved, is stirring testimony of the ability and will of the Indian youth and their people to defend their nation, and in turn the cause of the United Nations.

"Students came back filled with the 'New Life' the 'New Line' had given them. One thought was in every mind. Will the fascist hordes over-run our fair land – when in the Russian snows, the Chinese loess caves, the desolate Balkan countryside, men, women and even children were holding fast? Shall we lose the first round against the invader, when the Chinese people had not lost it in ten years?

"Calcutta was a dismal sight ... We got the 'New Line' in a flash! We stopped trying to 'understand' it through tortuous clumsy efforts to 'reason out' how this was the Soviet's war, Europe's war, and 'therefore' 'our war,' in our interest. One look at our beloved city, where Bankin roused slumbering India to a flaming patriotism, where Rabindranath stood his full height, the tallest among men, where Deshbandhu Das, our greatest orator, commanded India's millions to remain forever true to unflinching patriotism – one look at the stark nakedness of our city was enough ... We took a patriot's oath to keep the Japanese jackal out of the city.

"Who said 'Imperialism' was 'our ally'? The Civil Defense arrangements were made by riff-raffs of questionable character for the most part, the imperialist's insolence made him keep the PEOPLE out of it. The utter inadequacy of these arrangements, the cynical indifference of the bureaucrats even at this twilight time, reduced our people to utter hope-lessness. The panicky editorials in our dailies – written by men who should have known better – added to the confusion. On top of it all, the silver-haired custodians of our education failed to stand their ground as fearless, dignified patriots. The result was crowded railway stations, deserted streets, deserted colleges and schools – for the authorities closed the institutions indefinitely and encouraged the students to evacuate."

The article goes on to describe how they issued a stirring appeal which ran:

For all self-respecting men and women, the issue is clear. For us there is no escape. Either we stand and FIGHT, or we go down in history as the blackest traitors. To remain at our post is the sacred duty, the task of the moment ... to rouse the people, to organize and lead them into active resistance, we have to inspire them, awaken in them the spirit of resistance that is slumbering. We have the perspective before us of the day when hundreds of thousands of youth are in the streets educating and inspiring the inhabitants of this great city, when they have made every man a soldier and every house a barricade against fascism …

The results which they got, through carrying through study courses on Civilian Defense within a week, were 300 volunteers enrolled within a week and 1,000 to be gotten by the end of the month! – showing the potentialities that India's millions have to organize in defense of their own land.

Of course, this is not to imply that there aren't many complex problems in India. We do not help by wringing our hands over Ghandi – or dwelling on "India's differences." For the path to the solution of these inner problems are [sic] in the first place the job of the people of India. Our role is to help to influence the direction of that struggle, to help achieve what is needed now: the full mobilization of the people of India for resistance to the Axis. For as proven by China and the Soviet Union, national consciousness of a people grows, once they are given the perspective and means to accomplish that unity.

We know that there two paths open to the solution of this issue. We have already discussed some of the consequences of the path being followed by British colonial leaders – the path of Burma. To allow this to happen is to strengthen colonialism. It is to allow the fifth column and defeatists to seek to use the India crisis as another false argument against opening the vitally needed Second Front. The very crisis in India has come at this time due to the delay in opening the Second Front, enabling Hitler to freely continue his drives and Japan to become more bold as a result.

Not to enable a free India to mobilize in her own defense is to renounce the aims for which we are fighting – for freedom and independence of peoples everywhere.

On the other hand, we can play an important role in the crisis. In fact, we must. That is by action. By urging (as has already been suggested by Pearl Buck, and increasingly being voiced by labor, youth and other progressive organizations) President Roosevelt to intervene in the India Crisis, to urge the British government to immediately resume negotiations with the Indian people. Such negotiations, unlike the Cripps Mission, must come to terms WITH India, instead of laying down terms TO India.

This is a test of everything we are fighting for. It is up to each and every one of us by boldly speaking – as we are doing on the Second Front – to speak out for India's freedom, to help pave the way for complete victory now.

Hannah Arendt

From "The Question of War" (1958–1959)

Surely no one now doubts that, as the logical outcome of such possibilities, a third world war can hardly end in anything but the annihilation of the loser. We are already so in the thrall of total war that we can scarcely imagine a war between Russia and America in which the American Constitution or the current Russian regime would survive defeat. But that means that a future war will not be about a gain or loss of power, about borders, export markets, or *Lebensraum*, that is, about things that can also be achieved by means of political discussion and without the use of force. It means that war has now ceased to be the *ultima ratio* of negotiations, whereby the goals of a war were determined at the point where negotiations broke off, so that all ensuing military actions really were nothing but a continuation of politics by other means. What is now at stake is something that could, of course, never be a matter for negotiation: the sheer existence of a nation and its people. It is at this point – when war no longer presumes the coexistence of hostile parties as a given and no longer seeks simply to put an end to the conflict between them by force – that war first truly ceases to be a means of politics and, as a war of annihilation, begins to overstep the bounds set by politics and to annihilate politics itself.

This concept of what is now called "total war" originated, as we know, in those totalitarian regimes with which it is inextricably linked; a war of annihilation is the only war appropriate to a totalitarian system. Total war was first proclaimed by nations under totalitarian rule, but in doing so they inevitably forced their own principle of action onto the nontotalitarian world. Once a principle of such vast scope enters the world, it is of course practically impossible to limit it, for instance, to a conflict between totalitarian and nontotalitarian nations. This became clear when the atomic bomb, which was originally produced as a weapon against Hitler's Germany, was dropped on Japan. A cause of outrage, though not the sole cause, was that although Japan was indeed an imperialist power, it was not a totalitarian regime.

Common both to a horror that extended beyond all political or moral considerations and to an outrage that was itself an immediate political and moral reaction was the realization of what total war actually means and the awareness that total war was now a fait accompli, not only for countries under totalitarian rule and the conflicts they had brought about, but also for the whole world. The extermination of entire peoples and the razing of entire civilizations – which, because such things no longer occurred at the heart of the civilized world, had seemed impossible both in principle since the days of the Romans and de facto over the last three or four centuries of the modern era – had at one fell swoop thrust themselves back into the ominous realm of the all-too possible. And although it arose as a response to a totalitarian threat – insofar as surely not one of these scientists would have thought of producing an atomic bomb if he had not feared that Hitler's Germany might produce and use the bomb – this possibility had instantly become a reality that had hardly anything to do with what had called it into existence.

Here, for perhaps the first time in the modern era though hardly recorded and remembered history, the limits inherent in violent action had been overstepped – limits that declared that the destruction brought about by brute force must always be only partial, affecting only certain portions of the world and taking only a certain number, however that number might be determined, of human lives, but never annihilating a whole nation or a whole people. But it has happened often enough in history that the world of an entire people has been levelled, the walls of its city razed, the men slain, and the rest of the population sold into slavery, and only over the last centuries of the modern era have people wanted to believe that such things could no longer occur. We have always more or less explicitly known that this was one of the few mortal sins of politics. This mortal sin, or, less loftily, this overstepping of the limits inherent in violent action, consists of two things. First, murder is no longer about a larger or smaller number of people who must die in any case, but rather about a whole people and its political constitution, both of which harbour the possibility – and in the constitution's case, the intention – of being immortal. Second, and closely linked to the first point, violence is applied here not only to things that have been produced, which also arose by means of force, but also to a historical and political reality housed in this world of products, a reality that cannot be rebuilt because it is itself not a product. When a people loses its political freedom, it loses its political reality, even if it should succeed in surviving physically.

What perishes in this case is not a world resulting from production, but one of action and speech created by human relationships, a world that never comes to an end and that – though spun of the most ephemeral stuff, of fleeting words and quickly forgotten deeds – is of such incredible, enduring tenacity that under certain circumstances, as for example in the case of the Jewish people, it can outlive by centuries the loss of a palpable manufactured world. That, however, is the exception, and ordinarily this system of relationships established by action, in which the past lives on in the form of a history that goes on speaking and being spoken about, can exist only within the world produced by man, nesting there in its stones until they too speak and in speaking bear witness, even if we must first dig them out of the earth. This entire truly human world, which in a narrower sense forms the political realm, can indeed be destroyed by brute force, but it did not arise from force, and its inherent destiny is not to perish by force.

This world of relationships most certainly does not arise out of the strength or energy of the individual, but rather out of the many, and it is out of their being together that power arises, a power that renders even the greatest individual strength powerless. This power can be weakened, just as it can be renewed, by all sorts of factors; it can be destroyed for good and all only by brute force, if that force is total and literally leaves no stone atop another, no human being alongside another. Both these possibilities are inherent in totalitarian rule, which is not satisfied with intimidating individuals at home but also uses systematic terror to destroy all inter-human relationships. This terror finds its equivalent in total war, which is not satisfied with destroying strategically important military targets, but sets out to destroy – because it now technologically can seek to destroy – the entire world that has arisen between human beings.

It would be relatively easy to prove that Western civilization's political theories and moral codes have always tried to exclude a war of annihilation from the arsenal of political tools; and it would presumably be easier still to show that such theories and demands have proved to be less than effectual. Oddly enough, it is to the nature of such things – which in the broadest sense concern the civilized behaviour that man demands of himself – that something Plato once said does indeed apply: that poetry, together with the images and models it offers us, "educates our progeny by embellishing the thousand deeds of our ancestors" (*Phaedrus*, 245a). In the ancient world, at least in purely political terms, the greatest subject for such pedagogical embellishments was the Trojan War, in whose victors the Greeks saw their ancestors and in whose vanquished the Romans saw theirs. And thus they became the "twin peoples" of antiquity, as Mommsen liked to call them, because the same single enterprise was held to be the beginning of their historical existence. And even today, the Greeks' war against Troy, which ended in such a total destruction of that city that until recent times it was possible to believe that it had never existed, can probably still be considered the ur-example of a war of annihilation.

Thus, in contemplating the political significance of the war of annihilation that once again threatens us, let us permit ourselves first to think about this most ancient of examples and its embellishments – above all because, in embellishing this war both Greeks and Romans, sometimes in agreement on many levels but just as frequently in opposition, also defined, for themselves and thus to a certain extent for us – what politics actually means and what place it should have in history. First, then, it is of crucial importance that Homer's song does not pass over the van-quished man in silence, that it bears witness as much on behalf of Hector as of Achilles, and that although both the Greeks' victory and Troy's defeat had been irrevocably preordained by the decree of the gods, that did not make Achilles the greater man or Hector the lesser man, or the Greeks' cause more just or Troy's self-defense less just. Homer cele-brates this war of annihilation, already centuries old by his time, in such a way that, in a certain sense – that is, in the sense of poetical and historical recollection – he undoes that very annihilation. Homer's grand impartial-ity is not value-free objectivity in the modern sense, but rather a perfect freedom from particular interests and complete independence from the judgment of history, and, in contrast to history, he depends on the judgment of those involved and of their concept of greatness. His impar-tiality stands at the beginning of all historiography and not just that of the West. For what we understand by history had never existed anywhere before, nor has any history been written since that is not influenced at least indirectly by the Homeric example. We find the same idea in Herodotus when he says that he wants to prevent "great and wondrous deeds, some performed by Hellenes, some by the barbarians, from being relegated to oblivion" (I, i) – an idea that, as Burckhardt once correctly remarked, "would never have occurred to any Egyptian or Jew" (*Griechische Kulturgeschichte*, III, p. 406).

As we know only too well, the Greek effort to transform wars of annihilation into political wars never went any further than Homer's historical recollection and decidedly poetical rescue of those who were defeated and destroyed, and ultimately it was the inability to make such a transformation that led to the ruin of the Greek city-states. By defining the political in the way it did, the Greek polis chose a different path when it came to war. As we've seen, the Greeks formed the polis around the Homeric agora, the place where free men assembled and conversed, and by doing so centered what was truly "political" – that is, what belonged to the polis and was therefore denied to all barbarians and other unfree people – on this world of coming together, being together, speaking about something with one another; and they saw this entire arena under the sign of divine *Peithō*, the power to persuade and influence, which reigned among equals and determined all things without force or coercion. War, and the brute force it entailed, was, on the other hand, entirely excluded from what was truly political, which arose and had its validity among the citizens of the polis. In dealing with other states or city-states, the polis as a whole acted with force, and thus in its own eyes acted "unpolitically." In consequence, and indeed of necessity, such military action invalidated the basic equality of citizens, who were neither rulers nor subjects. Because war cannot be waged without command and obedience, and because military decisions cannot be a matter of debate and persuasion, war belonged, as the Greeks saw it, in a non-political sphere. Everything we understand as foreign policy belonged in that same sphere. Here, war is not the continuation of politics by other means, but just the opposite: negotiation and the conclusions of treaties are understood merely as a continuation of war by other means, the means of cunning and deception.

The impact of Homer on the development of the Greek polis did not exhaust itself, however, in what was really only a negative exclusion of force from the political arena, the consequence of which was simply that war continued to be waged as before according to the principle that the stronger does what he can and the weaker endures what he must (cf. Thucydides, v, "The Melian Dialogue"). The full Homeric effect of the poet's depiction of the Trojan War can be found in the way in which the polis incorporated the concept of struggle into its organizational form, not only as a legitimate pursuit, but also, in a certain sense, as the highest form of human communal activity. What is commonly called the agonistic spirit of the Greeks – and what doubtlessly helps us explain (if such things can ever be explained) the fact that within the few centuries of Greece's golden age we find a greater and more significant concentration of genius in every intellectual field than anywhere else in history – is by no means simply a striving to prove oneself always and everywhere the best, a subject about which Homer himself speaks and which indeed had such meaning for the Greeks that the verb for it in their language, *aristeuein* (to be the best), could be understood not merely as an endeavour but also as an activity that makes up the whole of life. The model for such rivalry among men was still seen as the combat between Hector and Achilles, which, quite apart from who wins or loses, gives each the opportunity to show himself as he really is, that is, by appearing in reality to become fully real. It is much the same with the war between the Greeks and the Trojans, which for the first time gives them both the opportunity to really show themselves. The war also mirrors the quarrel of the gods, which not only gives its full meaning to the battle raging on earth, but also clearly reveals that there is an element of divinity on both sides, even when one is doomed to perish. The war against Troy has two sides, and Homer sees it no less through the eyes of the Trojans than through those of the Greeks. This Homeric way of showing that all things with two sides make their real appearance only in struggle also lies behind Heraclitus' statement that war is "the father of all things" (Fragment B53). Here, the brute force of war in all its horror is derived directly from the strength and might of men, who can display their inherent energies only if something or someone opposes them and tests their mettle.

Two elements that appear almost undifferentiated in Homer – the sheer strength of great deeds and the ravishing power of the great words that accompany them and sway the assembly of men who see and hear them – can later be seen very clearly separated from each other: in athletic contests, which provided the only opportunity for the Greeks to come together and admire a display of nonviolent strength, and in oratorical contests and those never-ending verbal exchanges that took place within the polis itself. In the latter, the two-sided aspect of things, which in Homer is inherent in man-to-man combat, takes place solely in the realm of speech, where every victory can prove as equivocal as Achilles' and every defeat as praiseworthy as Hector's. But oratorical contests do not remain limited to the two sides taken by the orators, who, to be sure, reveal themselves as persons in the sides they take, for every speech, however "objective" it pretends to be, also inevitably discloses its speaker in a way that is difficult to define but nonetheless part of its compelling nature. Here, the same two-sidedness that Homer provided in his poem of the Trojan War takes on the tremendous manifold of the topics addressed, which, insofar as they are spoken about by so many people in the presence of so many others, are drawn into the public light of day, where they are forced, as it were, to reveal all their aspects. Only in such a manifold can one and the same topic appear in its full reality, whereby what must be borne in mind is that every topic has as many sides and can appear in as many perspectives as there are people to discuss it. Since for the Greeks the public political space is common to all (*koinon*), the space where the citizens assemble, it is the realm in which all things can first be recognised in their many-sidedness. This ability to see the same thing first from two opposing sides and then from all sides – an ability ultimately based in Homeric impartiality, unique in antiquity, and whose passionate intensity is unexcelled even in our own time – also underlies certain tricks of the Sophists, whose importance in liberating human thought from the constrictions of dogma we underestimate if, in following Plato, we condemn them on moral grounds. And yet their extraordinary skill in argumentations is of secondary importance to the first successful creation by the polis of a political realm. The crucial factor is not that one could now turn arguments around and stand propositions on their heads, but rather that one gained the ability to truly *see* topics from various sides – that is politically – with the result that people understood how to assume the many possible perspectives provided by the real world, from which one and the same topic can be regarded and in which each topic, despite its oneness, appears in a great diversity of views. This is considerably more than our simply putting aside personal interests, which results only in a negative gain; moreover, in cutting ties to our own interests, we run the danger of losing our ties to the world and our attachment to its objects and the affairs that take place in it. The ability to see the same thing from various standpoints stays in the human world; it is simply the exchange of the standpoint given us by nature for that of someone else, with whom we share the same world, resulting in a true freedom of movement in the physical one. Being able to persuade and influence others, which was how the citizens of the polis interacted politically, presumed a kind of freedom that was not irrevocably bound, either mentally or physically, to one's own standpoint or point of view.

The Greeks' unique ideal, and thus their standard for an aptitude that is specifically political, lies in *phronēsis*, the insight of the political man (the *politikos*, not the statesman, who did not even exist in this world), which has so little to do with wisdom that Aristotle could explicitly define it in contradistinction to the wisdom of the philosophers. Such insight into a political issue means nothing other than the greatest possible overview of all the possible standpoints and viewpoints from which an issue can be seen and judged. Over the ensuing centuries, hardly anyone speaks of *phronēsis*, which for Aristotle is the cardinal virtue of the political man. We do not run across it again until Kant, in his discussion of common sense as a faculty of judgment. He calls it an "enlarged mentality" and explicitly defines it as the ability "to think from the position of every other person" (*Critique of Judgment*, 40).

Roberta Wohlstetter

From *Pearl Harbor: Warning and Decision* (1960)

The history of Pearl Harbor has an interest exceeding by far any tale of an isolated catastrophe that might have been the result of negligence or stupidity or treachery, however lurid. For we have found the roots of this surprise in circumstances that affected honest, dedicated, and intelligent men. The possibility of such surprise at any time lies in the conditions of human perception and stems from uncertainties so basic that they are not likely to be eliminated, though they might be reduced.

It is only to be expected that the relevant signals, so clearly audible after an event, will be partially obscured before the event by surrounding noise. Even past diligence constructs its own background of noise, in the form of false alarms, which make less likely an alarm when the real thing arrives: the old story of "cry wolf" has a permanent relevance. A totalitarian aggressor can draw a tight curtain of secrecy about his actions and thus muffle the signals of attack. The Western democracies must interpret such signals responsibly and cautiously, for the process of commitment to war, except *in extremis*, is hedged about by the requirements of consultation. The precautions of secrecy, which are necessary even in a democracy to keep open privileged sources of information, may hamper the use of that information or may slow its transmission to those who have the power of decision. Moreover, human attention is directed by beliefs as to what is likely to occur, and one cannot always listen for the right sounds. An all-out thermonuclear attack on a Western power would be an unprecedented event, and some little time (which might be vital) would surely have to pass before that power's allies could understand the nature of the event and take appropriate action.

There is a good deal of evidence, some of it quantitative that in conditions of great uncertainty people tend to predict that events that they want to happen will actually happen. Wishfulness in conditions of uncertainty is natural and is hard to banish simply by exhortation – or by wishing. Further, the uncertainty of strategic warning is intrinsic, since an enemy decision to attack might be reversed or the direction of the attack changed; and a defensive action can be taken only at some cost. (For example, at Pearl Harbor, flying a 360-degree reconnaissance would have meant sacrificing training, would have interrupted the high-priority shipment program to the Philippines, and would have exhausted crews and worn out equipment within a few weeks.) In general, an extraordinary state of alert that brings about a peak in readiness must be followed by a trough at a later date. In some cases the cost of the defensive actions is hard to estimate and their relevance is uncertain. Therefore the choice of action in response to strategic warning must also be uncertain. Finally, the balance of technical and military factors that might make an attack infeasible at one time can change swiftly and without notice to make it feasible at another. In our day such balances are changing with unprecedented speed.

Pearl Harbor is not an isolated catastrophe. It can be matched by many examples of effective surprise attack. The German attack on Russia in the summer of 1941 was preceded by a flood of signals, the massing of troops, and even direct warnings to Russia by the governments of the United States and the United Kingdom, both of whom had been correctly informed about the imminence of the onslaught. Yet it achieved total surprise. [...] Soviet arguments current today that Stalin and Marshal Zhukov, his Chief of the General Staff, knew and failed to act have obvious parallels with the accusations about President Roosevelt's conspiracy of silence. These Soviet reinterpretations of history aim not only to downgrade Stalin, but also to establish that Soviet leaders were not *really* surprised in 1941, and the Soviet Union can therefore count on adequate warning in any future conflict. [...] But the difficulties of discerning a surprise attack oneself apply equally to totalitarian and democratic states.

The stunning tactical success of the Japanese attack on the British at Singapore was made possible by the deeply held British faith in the impregnability of that fortrees. As Captain Grenfell put it, newspapers and statesmen like their fortresses to be impregnable. "Every fortress," he wrote, "that has come into the news in my lifetime – Port Arthur, Tsing Tao, the great French defensive system of the Maginot Line – has been popularly described as impregnable before it has been attacked. ... One way or another it became virtually accepted fact in Britain and the Dominions that Singapore was an impregnable bastion of Imperial security."[35] Yet the defences of Singapore were rendered useless by military surprise in the form of an attack from an unexpected, northerly direction.

---

[35] Russell Grenfell, *Main Fleet to Singapore* (New York: Macmillan, 1952), 64.

More recently, the Korean War provided some striking examples of surprise. The original North Korean attack was preceded by almost weekly maneuvers probing the border. These regular week-end penetrations built up so high a level of noise that on June 25, 1950, the actual initiation of hostilities was not distinguished from the preceding tests and false alarms. The intervention of the Chinese, at a later stage of the Korean War, was preceded by mass movements of Chinese troops and explicit warnings by the Chinese government to our own, by way of India, that this was precisely what they would do if we crossed the 38th parallel. Nonetheless, in important respects, we were surprised by the Chinese Communist forces in November, 1950. [...]

How do matters stand with reference to a future thermonuclear aggression by a totalitarian power? Would such an attack be harder or easier to conceal than the Japanese aggression against Pearl Harbor? There have been many attempts in recent years to cheer us with the thought that the H-bomb has so outmoded general war that this question may appear unimportant. However, such attempts to comfort ourselves really beg the question. The question is, Will it be possible in the future for a totalitarian power so to conceal an impending attack on the forces that we have disposed for retaliation as to have a high probability of virtually eliminating them before they receive warning or have time to respond to it? In this connection it is important to observe that there is no cause for complacency. In spite of the vast increase in expenditures for collecting and analysing intelligence data and in spite of advances in the art of machine decoding and machine translation, the balance of advantage seems clearly to have shifted since Pearl Harbor in favour of a surprise attacker. The benefits to be expected from achieving surprise have increased enormously and the penalties for losing the initiative in an all-out war have grown correspondingly. In fact, since only by an all-out surprise attack could an attacker hope to prevent retaliation, anything less would be suicidal, assuming that some form of attack is contemplated by one major power against another.

In such a surprise attack a major power today would have advantages exceeding those enjoyed by the Japanese in 1941. It is a familiar fact that with the ever-increasing readiness of bomber and missile forces, strategic warning becomes harder and harder to obtain; and with the decrease in the flight time for delivery of massive weapons of destruction, tactical warning times have contracted from weeks to minutes. It is no longer necessary for the aggressor to undertake huge movements of troops and ships in the weeks immediately preceding an all-out war, such as we described in our account of the Japanese war plan. Manned bombers capable of delivering a blow many times more devastating than anything dreamed of by the Japanese might be on their way from bases deep inside their homeland without yielding any substantial intelligence warning; they might conceivably follow routes that, by avoiding detection or at least identification among friendly and unknown traffic appearing on radars, would be unlikely to give even tactical warning. Submarines might be kept on station several hundred miles off our coast during years of peace and might launch ballistic missiles on the receipt of a prearranged signal. Finally, intercontinental ballistic missiles might be kept for years at a high degree of readiness, and, if there were enough of them, they might be launched after simply being "counted down," with no further visible preparation. Total flight time for such rockets between continents might be less than fifteen minutes and radar warning less than that. Most important, such blows, unlike those leveled by the Japanese at Pearl Harbor, might determine the outcome not merely of a battle, but of the war itself. In short, the subject of surprise attack continues to be of vital concern. This fact has been suggested by the great debate among the powers on arms control and on the possibilities of using limitation and inspection arrangements to guard against surprise attack. The very little we have said suggests that such arrangements present formidable difficulties.

This study has not been intended as a "how-to-do-it" manual on intelligence, but perhaps one major practical lesson emerges from it. We cannot *count* on strategic warning. We *might* get it, and we might be able to take useful preparatory actions that would be impossible without it. We certainly ought to plan to exploit such a possibility should it occur. However, since we cannot rely on strategic warning, our defences, if we are to have confidence in them, must be designed to function without it. If we accept the fact that the signal picture for impending attacks is almost sure to be ambiguous, we shall prearrange actions that are right and feasible in response to ambiguous signals, including signs of an attack that might be false. We must be capable of reacting repeatedly to false alarms without committing ourselves or the enemy to wage thermonuclear war.

It is only human to want some unique and univocal signal, to want a guarantee from intelligence, an unambiguous substitute for a formal declaration of war. This is surely the unconscious motivation of all the rewriting of Pearl Harbor history, which sees in such wavering and uncertain sources of information as the winds code and all of the various and much-argued MAGIC texts a clear statement of Japanese intent. But we have seen how drastically such an interpretation oversimplifies the task of the analyst and decision maker. If the study of Pearl Harbor has anything to offer for the future, it is this: We have to accept the fact of uncertainty and learn to live with it. No magic, in code or otherwise, will provide certainty. Our plans must work without it.

Mary McCarthy

From *Vietnam* (1967)

The war, they say, is not going to be won in Saigon, nor on the battle-field, but in the villages and hamlets. This idea, by now trite (it was first discovered in Diem's time and has been rebaptized under a number of names – New Life Hamlets, Rural Construction, Counter Insurgency, Nation-Building, Revolutionary Development, the Hearts and Minds Program), is the main source of inspiration for the various teams of missionaries, military and civilian, who think they are engaged in a crusade. Not just a crusade against Communism, but something *positive*. Back in the fifties and early sixties, the war was presented as an invest-ment: the taxpayer was persuaded that if he stopped Communism *now* in Vietnam, he would not have to keep stopping it in Thailand, Burma, etc. That was the domino theory, which our leading statesmen today, quite comically, are busy repudiating before Congressional committees – sud-denly nobody will admit to ever having been an advocate of it. The notion of a costly investment that will save money in the end has a natural appeal to a nation of homeowners, but now the assertion of an American "interest" in Vietnam has begun to look too speculative as the stake increases ("When is it going to pay off?") and also too squalid as the war daily becomes more savage and destructive. Hence the "other" war, proclaimed by President Johnson in Honolulu, which is simultaneously pictured as a strategy for winning War Number One and as a top priority in itself. Indeed, in Vietnam, there are moments when the "other" war seems to be viewed as the sole reason for the American presence, and it is certainly more congenial to American officials, brimming with public spirit, than the war they are launching from the skies. Americans do not like to be negative, and the "other" war is constructive.

To see it, of course, you have to get out of Saigon, but, before you go, you will have to be briefed, in one of those new office buildings, on what you are going to see. In the field, you will be briefed again, by a military man, in a district or province headquarters, and frequently all you will see of New Life Hamlets, Constructed Hamlets, Consolidated Hamlets are the charts and graphs and maps and symbols that some ardent colonel or brisk bureaucrat is demonstrating to you with a pointer, and the mimeographed handout, full of statistics, that you take away with you, together with a supplement on Viet Cong Terror. On paper and in chart form, it all sounds commendable, especially if you are able to ignore the sounds of bombing from B-52's that are shaking the windows and making the charts rattle. The briefing official is enthusiastic, as he points out the progress that has been made, when, for example, the activities organized under AID were reorganized under OCO (Office of Civilian Operations). You stare at the chart on the office wall in which to you there is no semblance of logic or sequence ("Why," you wonder, "should Youth Affairs be grouped under Urban Development"), and the official rubs his hands with pleasure: "First we organized it *vertically*. Now we have organized it *horizontally!*" He does not say that one of the main reasons for the creation of the OCO was to provide a cover for certain CIA activities. Out in the field, you learn from some disgruntled officer that the AID representatives, who are perhaps now OCO representatives without knowing it, have not been paid for six months.

In a Saigon "backgrounder," you are told about public-health measures undertaken by Free World Forces. Again a glowing progress report. In 1965, there were 180 medical people from the "Free World" in Vietnam treating patients; in 1966, there were 700 – quite a little escalation, almost four times as many. The troop commitment, of course, not mentioned by the briefer, jumped from 60,000 to 400,000 – more than six-and-a-half times as many. That the multiplication of troops implied an obvious escalation in the number of civilian patients requiring treatment is not mentioned either. Under questioning, the official, slightly irritated, estimates that the civilian casualties comprise between 7½ and 15 per cent of the surgical patients treated in hospitals. He had "not been interested particularly, until all the furore," in what percentage of the patients were war casualties. And naturally he was not interested in what percentage of civilian casualties never reached a hospital at all.

Nor would there have been any point in asking him what happens to the Viet Cong wounded – a troubling question I never heard raised in nearly a month in Vietnam. A very few are in hospitals – some have been seen recently by a journalist in Can Tho – and the mother of a marine killed in action has made public in a Texan newspaper a letter from her boy telling how he felt when ordered to go back to the battlefield and shoot wounded VC in the head (prompt denial from the Marine Corps). But American officials on the spot are not concerned by the discrepancy between estimated VC wounded and estimated VC in hospitals:

225 being treated in U.S. medical facilities in one week in May, whereas at the end of April an estimated 30,000 to 35,000 had been wounded in action since the first year.

But – to return to the "backgrounder" – the treatment of war victims, it turned out, was not one of the medical "bull's-eyes" aimed at in the "other" war. Rather, a peacetime-type program, "beefing up" the medical school, improvement of hospital facilities, donation of drugs and antibiotics (Which, as I learned from another source, are in turn *sold* by the local nurses to the patients for whom they have been prescribed), the control of epidemic diseases, such as plague and cholera, education of the population in good health procedures. American and allied workers, you here, are teaching the Vietnamese in the government villages to boil their water, and the children are learning dental hygiene. Toothbrushes are distributed, and the children are shown how to use them. If the children get the habit, the parents will copy them, a former social worker explains, projecting from experience with first-generation immigrants back home. There is a campaign on to vaccinate and immunize as much of the population as can be got to co-operate; easy subjects are refugees and forced évacués, who can be lined up for shots while going through the screening process and being issued an identity card – a political health certificate.

All this is not simply on paper. In the field, you are actually able to see medical teams at work, setting up temporary dispensaries under the trees in the hamlets for the weekly or biweekly "sick call" – distributing medicines, tapping, listening, sterilizing, bandaging; the most common diagnosis is suspected tuberculosis. In Tay Ninh Province, I watched a Philcag (Filipino) medical team at work in a Buddhist hamlet. One doctor was examining a very thin old man, who was stripped to the waist; probably tubercular, the doctor told me, writing something on a card which he gave to the old man. "What happens next?" I wanted to know. Well, the old man would go to the province hospital for an X ray (that was the purpose of the card), and if the diagnosis was positive, then treatment should follow. I was impressed. But (as I later learned at a briefing) there are only sixty civilian hospitals in South Vietnam – for nearly 16 million people – so that the old man's total benefit, most likely, from the open-air consultation was to have learned, gratis, that he might be tubercular.

Across the road, some dentist's chairs were set up, and teeth were being pulled, very efficiently, from women and children of all ages. I asked about the toothbrushes I had heard about in Saigon. The Filipino major laughed. "Yes, we have distributed them. They use them as toys." Then he reached into his pocket – he was a kindly young man with children of his own – and took out some money for all the children who had gathered round to buy popsicles (the local equivalent) from the popsicle man. Later I watched the Filipino general, a very handsome tall man with a cropped head, resembling Yul Brynner, distribute Têt gifts and candy to children in a Cao Dai orphanage and be photographed with his arm around a little blind girl. A few hours earlier, he had posed distributing food in a Catholic hamlet – "Free World" surplus items, such as canned cooked beets. The photography, I was told, would help sell the Philcag operation to the Assembly in Manila, where some leftist elements were trying to block funds for it. Actually, I could not see that the general was doing any harm, whatever his purposes might be, politically – unless not doing more is harm, in which case we are all guilty – and he was more efficient than other Civic Action leaders. His troops had just chopped down a large section of jungle (we proceeded through it in convoy, wearing bulletproof vests and bristling with rifles and machine guns, because of the VC), which was going to be turned into a hamlet for resettling refugees. They had also built a school, which we stopped to inspect, finding, to the general's surprise, that it had been taken over by the local district chief for his office headquarters.

The Filipino team, possibly because they were Asians, seemed to be on quite good terms with the population. Elsewhere – at Go Cong, in the delta – I saw mistrustful patients and heard stories of rivalry between the Vietnamese doctor, a gynaecologist, and the Spanish and American medical teams; my companion and I were told that we were the first "outsiders," including the resident doctors, to be allowed by the Vietnamese into *his* wing – the maternity, which was far the cleanest and most modern in the hospital and contained one patient. Similar jealousies existed of the German medical staff at Hue. In the rather squalid surgical wing of the Go Cong hospital, there were two badly burned children. Were they war casualties, I asked the official who was showing us through. Yes, he conceded, as a matter of fact they were. How many of the patients were war-wounded, I wanted to know. "About four" of the children, he reckoned. And one old man, he added, after reflection.

The Filipinos were fairly dispassionate about their role in pacification; this may have been because they had no troops fighting in the war (those leftist elements in the Assembly!) and therefore did not have to act like saviors of the Vietnamese people. The Americans, on the contrary, are zealots – above all, the blueprinters in the Saigon offices – although occasionally in the field, too, you meet a true believer – a sandy, crew-cut, keen-eyed army colonel who talks to you about "the nuts and bolts" of the program, which, he is glad to say, is finally getting the "grass roots" support it needs. It is impossible to find out from such a man what he is doing, concretely; an aide steps forward to state, "We sterilize the area prior to the insertion of the RD teams," whose task, says the colonel, is to find out "the aspirations of the people." He cannot tell you whether there has been any land reform in his area – that is a strictly Vietnamese pigeon – in fact he has no idea of *how* the land in the area is owned. He is strong on co-ordination: all his Vietnamese counterparts, the colonel who "wears two hats" as province chief, the mayor, a deposed general, are "very fine sound men," and the Marine general in the area is "one of the finest men and officers" he has ever met. For another army zealot every Vietnamese officer he deals with is "an outstanding individual."

These springy, zesty, burning-eyed warriors, military and civilian, engaged in AID or Combined Action (essentially pacification) stir far-away memories of American college presidents of the fund-raising type; their diction is peppery with oxymoron ("When peace breaks out," "Then the commodities started to hit the beach") like a college president's address to an alumni dinner. They see themselves in fact as educators, spreading the American way of life, a new *propaganda fide*. When I asked an OCO man in Saigon what his groups actually did in a Vietnamese village to prepare – his word – the people for elections, he answered, "We teach them Civics 101."

The American taxpayer who thinks that aid means help has missed the idea. Aid is, first of all, to achieve economic stability within the present system, *i.e.*, political stability for the present ruling groups. Loans are extended, under the counterpart-fund arrangement, to finance Vietnamese imports of American capital equipment (thus AIDing, with the other hand, American industry). Second, aid is *education*. Distribution of canned goods (instill new food habits), distribution of seeds, fertilizer, chewing gum and candy (the Vietnamese complain that the G.I.'s fire candy at their children, like a spray of bullets), lessons in sanitation, hog-raising, and crop rotation. The program is designed, not just to make Americans popular, but to shake up the Vietnamese, as in some "stimulating" freshman course where the student learns to question the "prejudices" implanted in him by his parents. "We're trying to wean them away from the old barter economy and show them a market economy. Then they'll really *go*."

"We're teaching them free enterprise," explains a breathless JUSPAO official in the grim town of Phu Cuong. He is speaking of the "refugees" from the Iron Triangle, who were forcibly cleared out of their hamlets, which were then burned and levelled, during Operation Cedar Falls ("Clear and Destroy"). They had just been transferred into a camp, hastily constructed by the ARVN with tin roofs painted red and white, to make the form, as seen from the air, of a Giant Red Cross – 1,651 women, 3,754 children, 582 men, mostly old, who had been kindly allowed to bring some of their furniture and pots and pans and their pigs and chickens and sacks of their hoarded rice; their water cattle had been transported for them, on barges, and were now sickening on a dry, stubbly, sandy plain. "We've got a captive audience!" the official continued excitedly. "This is our big chance!"

To teach them free enterprise and, presumably, when they were "ready" for it, Civics 101; for the present, the government had to consider them "hostile civilians." These wives and children and old fathers of men thought to be at large with the Viet Cong had been rice farmers only a few weeks before. Now they were going to have to pitch in and learn to be vegetable farmers; the area selected for their eventual resettlement was not suitable for rice-growing, unfortunately. Opportunity was beckoning for these poor peasants, thanks to the uprooting process they had just undergone. They would have the chance to buy and build their own homes on a pattern and of materials already picked out for them; the government was allowing them 1,700 piasters towards the purchase price. To get a new house free, even though that would seem only fair in the abstract, would be unfair to them as human beings, it was explained to me: investing their own labor and their own money would make them feel that the house was really *theirs*. "The Lord helps those who help themselves" – the social worker's Great Commandment – is interpreted in war-pounded Vietnam, and with relentless priggery, as the "U.S. helps those who help themselves."

3

Imperialism
Introduction by Sarah C. Dunstan

The practice of empire and its effects on world order has been a, if not the, central preoccupation of international thought.[1] The works in this section range in focus from studies of the economic dynamics of imperialism through to efforts to improve the efficiency of colonial administration to critiques of empire as a political system. Unsurprisingly, "race" and "racism" as ordering principles of international relations run through all of these works. Some thinkers, such as Anna Julia Cooper, identified racism as a problematic at the heart of international relations at a deep structural level. Others, like Margery Perham and Mary Macdonald Proudfoot, reflected what might be considered British "white women's IR" in this period: the view of empire as an instrument of development necessitated by racial difference, and elaborated their visions of race relations and imperial policies accordingly.[2] In many respects these differing perspectives follow the chronology of the twentieth century, from the heyday of imperialism through to post-Second World War decolonization, and from the height of the British Empire through to the rise of American hegemony.

The writings here also encompass multiple genres and methodologies, from the accessible and activist magazine articles of Jessie Fauset and Amy Jacques Garvey through the sweeping and perspicacious histories of Cooper and Lilian Knowles and the policy-oriented monographs of Margery Perham and Mary Macdonald Proudfoot. As the field of international relations moved away from studies of the mechanics of imperialism, so too did later histories of IR as an academic discipline tend to elide its origins in and focus on imperialism. This has contributed to the neglect of the thinkers included here precisely because their

---

[1] David Long and Brian C. Schmidt (eds.), *Imperialism and Internationalism in the Discipline of International Relations* (Albany, NY: SUNY Press, 2005); Sankar Muthu (ed.), *Empire and Modern Political Thought* (Cambridge: Cambridge University Press, 2012).

[2] Patricia Owens, "Women and the History of International Thought," *International Studies Quarterly*, 62:3 (2018): 467–481.

intellectual contributions are inextricable from the preoccupation with empire. It is also because they are made in the register of history. Five of the authors in this section were trained as historians, reflecting the influence of historical approaches in early international thought, a point also made elsewhere in this volume.

The first selection of this type, "The London West India Interest in the Eighteenth Century," was published in 1921 by the British historian Dame Lillian Margery Penson (1896–1963). Penson received her PhD in modern history from the University of London in 1921, one of the first to receive the degree from that institution. Prior to embarking on her postgraduate study, she worked as an editor of the peace handbooks prepared for the Paris conference of 1919. In 1930, at the age of thirty-four, she was appointed to the Professorial Chair of modern history at Bedford College in London, Britain's first higher education college for women. Penson's academic research focused on the foreign policy of European powers and the last Victorian Prime Minister, Lord Salisbury. In addition to her own publications, she also worked closely with the Cambridge diplomatic historian Harold Temperley. Together they co-authored *The Foundation of British Foreign Policy* and co-edited *A Century of Diplomatic Blue Books, 1814–1914*. In the 1940s, she also acted as a policy advisor, working on the commission for higher education in the colonies chaired by Sir Cyril Asquith. In the following decades, she traveled extensively through Africa, establishing colleges on the continent that were initially branches of the University of London. Penson was particularly involved in the University of Khartoum and the University College of Rhodesia and Nyasaland.[3] Her dedication to the development of colonial education was a common expression of international thought in this period, as highlighted in the section on Public Opinion and Education. In 1948, she became the first woman to serve as Vice-Chancellor of the University of London. The article excerpted here was published early in Penson's career, in 1921, in the *English Historical Review*. In the context of a post-war resurgence of British trade in the West Indies, Penson focuses on the British economic operation in the region, making the case that the economic rapprochement between British West Indian planters and London merchants allowed these West Indian interests to "exert an influence over British politics far greater" than that of other contemporary West Indian colonies (152). This influence was of great significance to British foreign policymaking in the context of economic investment in the region and included

---

[3] F. M. L. Thompson, "The Humanities," in F. M. L. Thompson (ed.), *The University of London and the World of Learning, 1836–1986* (London: Hambledon, 1990), 71.

establishing an agricultural college in Trinidad and a British–Canadian weekly freight, mail, and passenger service.

The history of British imperial economic development and the relations between imperial states were Lilian Knowles's (1870–1926) primary research focus. Knowles, Britain's first fulltime lecturer in Economic History, had read History and Law at Girton College, Cambridge, receiving Firsts in both subjects in 1894. At the time, Cambridge did not confer degrees to women, so Knowles became one of the 700 so-called "Steamboat Ladies" able to receive their degrees *ad eundem* between 1904 and 1907 by traveling from Oxford or Cambridge to Trinity College, Dublin. In 1904, Knowles was appointed to the LSE, where she spent her entire career.[4] Reflecting the core premise of the study of international relations and more recent work in "global economic history," Knowles argued that British history had to be understood as part of a "great system of world exchange of peoples and goods" (163). "England" was "part of a great Western civilization acting on other Powers and being reacted on in turn by them."[5] Although she has not received the scholarly attention afforded her better known colleague at the LSE, Halford Mackinder, Knowles was also an influential pioneer of neo-mercantilist and imperialist thought. As Maxine Berg has pointed out, in the early twentieth century, "the LSE was not so much socialist and Fabian, as is often assumed, but rather … inclined to favour radical Milnerite conservatism and opposition to free trade."[6]

Knowles's posthumously published *Economic Development in the Nineteenth Century* demonstrates her thinking in this regard. The book itself is a grand narrative history of "that almost incredible and romantic development of the interiors of continents and the new wanderings of the peoples" that resulted in "world interdependence", again presaging by decades IR's recent (re)discovery of the importance of "the nineteenth century" for modern international relations.[7] Clearly reflecting her

[4] Among her books are *The Industrial and Commercial Revolutions in Great Britain during the Nineteenth Century* (London: G. Routledge & Sons, Ltd, 1921), *The Economic Development of the British Overseas Empire* (London: G. Routledge, 1924), and two posthumously published volumes, including *Economic Development in the Nineteenth Century: France, Germany, Russia and the United States* (London: Routledge, 1932).

[5] C. M. Knowles, "Professor Lilian Knowles, 1870–1926," in L. C. A. Knowles and C. M. Knowles, *The Economic Development of the British Overseas Empire*, vol. 2 (London: Routledge, 1930), vii–xxiixv.

[6] Maxine Berg, "The First Women Economic Historians," *The Economic History Review*, 45:2 (1992): 316.

[7] Knowles, *The Economic Development of the British Overseas Empire*, 5; 10; Barry Buzan and George Lawson, *The Global Transformation: History, Modernity and the Making of International Relations* (Cambridge: Cambridge University Press, 2015).

political position, Knowles presented "English invention" as the catalyst for this vibrant new world order. She was a "country tory, patriot, and imperialist" who credited France with the establishment of the "great liberal treaty system of Europe ... completed between 1860 and 1870."[8] Knowles argued, however, that it was England that had really transformed the world with innovations "that provided the mechanism and much of the capital for transforming agricultural into industrial states" all over the world (162). Part and parcel of this network of industrialized economic relations was the "new imperialism" that sought "new sources of raw material" and "the development of the unoccupied spaces suitable for settlement by the white races." This had the effect of "transforming Germany and Russia, spreading to the United States, permeating South America, impinging upon Africa and reconstructing India and Japan, reacting on China, colonizing Australia and making its influence felt on remote Pacific islands" (162). Empire, for Knowles, was a major source of innovation and human development.

We find a similar view in Sybil Eyre Crowe's 1942 book *The Berlin West African Conference, 1884–1885*, but with a greater focus on the diplomacy of imperial international relations. Crowe was a Cambridge-trained scholar who had been first a lecturer and then tutor in politics at St. Hilda's in Oxford until her retirement in 1975. During the Second World War, she worked as a research assistant for the British Foreign Office. Despite her own intellectual *bona fides*, her academic and policy work was overshadowed by the specter of her father, the British diplomat Eyre Crowe. Although born in Germany, Eyre Crowe had enjoyed an extensive tenure at the British Foreign Office. His biography became Sibyl Crowe's magnum opus, a remarkable work reliant upon her privileged access to her father's papers.[9] The work that follows here is less well known, but her remarks about the Minotaur wearing a Prussian soldier's *Pickelhaube* in the labyrinthine world of high imperialist conference diplomacy should be read in the context of her father's complicated relationship with Germany. During his time at the British Foreign Office he had become the archetypal anti-German voice.[10]

Published in the midst of the Second World War, Crowe's account of the Berlin West African Conference of 1884–1885 does not delve into the colonial horrors that would follow – King Leopold of Belgium is only briefly mentioned. Instead Crowe's analysis of the conference is an

---

[8] Berg, "The First Women Economic Historians," 316.

[9] Sibyl Eyre Crowe and Edward Corp, *Our Ablest Public Servant: Sir Eyre Crowe GCB, GCMG, KCB, KCMG 1864–1925* (Braunton: Merlin Books, 1993).

[10] Steiner has revealed recently in an interview that Sibyl Crowe refused Steiner access to crucial sources from Eyre Crowe's private papers. Sarah C. Dunstan, interview with Zara Steiner, November 11, 2019, Cambridge, United Kingdom.

exercise in skepticism of supposedly enlightened diplomacy. Rather than advancing a common understanding among all the major players regarding international norms on international public law, trade, slavery, or colonial administration, what was produced at Berlin, according to Crowe, was a mere but momentous shift in diplomatic alliances. When the representatives of the British and German empires "sat down calmly at a conference table," they realized "that their interests were practically identical" (175). She produced this narrative of the Berlin conference at the tail end of two decades that had been obsessed with European summitry. Moreover, she had been trained – and was still writing – in a context in which the imperial world order, however crisis-riddled, remained authoritative. This is clear in her description of the Conference as a moment "in which African and colonial questions generally are still subordinate to European in world diplomacy, colonial issues being more affected by European than European by colonial" (174). Insofar as Crowe's analysis was concerned, the experience or perspective of colonial subjects was not relevant to the ordering of the international world. As Knowles had done before her, she saw imperialism as the natural mode of powerful states.

Unlike Knowles, Penson, and Crowe, the African American teacher and writer Jessie Fauset (1882–1961) questioned the morality of the colonial world order and the hierarchies of race it engendered. In the selection included here, Fauset describes the discussions and efforts of the 1921 Pan-African Congress to identify the problems of existing practices of colonial administration and to suggest avenues for improvement. The first Pan-African Congress of this kind had been organized in Paris in 1919 by W. E. B. Du Bois, Blaise Diagne, and Gratien Candace to coincide with the peace negotiations following the First World War. The organizers and delegates had hoped to intervene in discussions around the future of Germany's colonies in Africa, as well as to assert a Black presence in the international order more broadly. In so doing they sought to shed light on racism within the United States and to dismantle notions of Black racial inferiority by asserting their own assimilation into Western nations.[11] The second Congress, held in 1921, was co-organized by Du Bois and Jessie Fauset herself. One hundred and ten delegates from around the world attended across the three sessions held in London, Brussels, and Paris.[12] At least twelve of the attendees were women, many of whom delivered papers, including Fauset herself, Helen

[11] See Sarah C. Dunstan, "Conflicts of Interest: The 1919 Pan-African Congress and the Wilsonian Moment," *Callaloo*, 39:1 (Winter 2016): 133–150.
[12] "110 Delegates to the Pan-African Congress by Country," *Crisis*, 23:2 (December 1922): 68–69.

Curtis (an African American activist and representative of the International Council of the Women of the Darker Races), and Florence Kelley (an American social reformer).[13]

In the excerpt below, Fauset positions Africa as a source of revitalization for a Europe "depleted ... through the ages by war and famine and plague" (146). Rather than seeking to overthrow empire entirely, she sought to reconfigure the imperial relationship into a mutually beneficial exchange. Whilst Europe could offer scientific knowledge and financial aid, Africa could supply access to natural resources as well as cultural renewal in the form of "the inherent artistry of the African" (146). Like the three sessions of the Congress themselves, Fauset's intention was simultaneously to assert the value of "what colored people had achieved in the different parts of the world" and to highlight the conditions they lived in due to racism and a badly implemented colonial administration. It seemed to her that the "black colonial's problem" was "the same intrinsically" as the African American's situation, although it "wore on the face of it a different aspect." A key difference lay in the "smothering power" of the Belgian and French imperial forces, a power that prevented the "frank" discussion of the problems that the Americans preferred. Despite the United States' withdrawal from the League of Nations, Fauset saw the work of the Pan-African association and the League of Nations as ideologically aligned, writing that their positions "differed not a whit in essential methods" (150). Indeed, the Congress resulted in a petition to the floor of the League of Nations' Assembly by the Haitian diplomat to France, Dantès Bellegarde, although it ultimately had little direct impact.

Fauset was no stranger to the difficulties of racial politics. The valedictorian of her class when she graduated from the Philadelphia High School for Girls, she is believed to have been the school's first African American graduate.[14] Although she ultimately won a scholarship to study classical languages at Cornell, she had originally hoped to take her degree at the women's college of Bryn Mawr, an institution reluctant to admit Black students. For most of her life, Fauset worked as a French teacher in the segregated public schools of Washington, DC and New York. She was also a novelist, publishing four books in the 1920s and the 1930s during the period that has retrospectively become known as the Harlem Renaissance. Fauset was a leading figure in the Renaissance due to her

---

[13] For a detailed discussion of the 1921 Pan-African Congress, see Hakim Adi, *Pan African: A History* (London: Bloomsbury, 2018), 57–63.

[14] Kathryn West, "Fauset, Jessie Redmon," in Cary D. Wintz and Paul Finkelman (eds.), *Encyclopedia of the Harlem Renaissance* (New York: Routledge, 2004), 363.

work as a literary editor for the National Association for the Advancement of Colored People's journal, *Crisis*. The article included here was published in that journal, which, from its inception, had aimed "to set forth those facts and arguments which show the danger of race prejudice."[15]

Pan-Africanist thinker and teacher Anna Julia Cooper (1858–1964) also published in *Crisis* throughout her long career. She had wanted to attend the 1921 Congress, but her teaching commitments prevented her. Born into slavery in North Carolina, Cooper nonetheless became the fourth African American woman to gain a doctoral degree.[16] For most of her life she taught in the segregated school system in North Carolina and then Washington, DC, not completing her PhD until she reached her sixties and could take leave from her teaching position. The excerpt here is drawn from her doctoral dissertation, *L'Attitude de la France à l'égard de l'esclavage pendant la Révolution*, which she completed at the Sorbonne in 1925 as the first Black woman to be awarded the degree from that institution. Her dissertation, and subsequent book, examined the French position on slavery between 1789 and 1848, arguing that the dynamics of imperialism – slavery chief amongst them – had created and perpetuated a global politics of modernity structured around racism. Despite the pioneering nature of this historical work, Cooper has been entirely elided from histories of international thought, her work an uneasy fit for a discipline so long predicated on white supremacist thought.[17]

Cooper adopted an analytic frame that gave agency to the free and enslaved Black peoples, and the *gens de couleur* of Haiti. This was a radical departure from the existing scholarship on the so-called Age of Revolution which erased the experiences of the people of St. Domingue (now Haiti) and instead glorified French Enlightenment republicanism.[18] An original thinker, Cooper's sophisticated analysis pre-dated better-known studies by intellectuals such as Trinidadian historian C. L. R. James and the African American scholar

---

[15] W. E. B. Du Bois, "Editorial," *Crisis* (November 1910), 10.

[16] See Mark S. Giles, "Special Focus: Dr. Anna Julia Cooper, 1858–1964: Teacher, Scholar, and Timeless Womanist," *The Journal of Negro Education*, 75:4 (Fall 2006): 621–634.

[17] Some work has begun to rectify this erasure. See Vivian May, "Anna Julia Cooper on Slavery's Afterlife: Can International Thought 'Hear' Her 'Muffled' Voice and Ideas?," in Patricia Owens and Katharina Rietzler (eds.), *Women's International Thought: A New History* (Cambridge: Cambridge University Press, 2021), 53–85; Vivian May, *Anna Julia Cooper, Visionary Black Feminist: A Critical Introduction* (New York: Routledge, 2007); Kimberly Hutchings and Patricia Owens, "Women Thinkers and the Canon of International Thought: Recovery, Rejection, and Reconstitution," *American Political Science Review*, 115:2 (2021): 347–359.

[18] May, "Anna Julia Cooper," 75.

W. E. B. Du Bois. Not just an important intervention into the historiography of the French and Haitian Revolutions, Cooper's work provides an innovative way into understanding the ways in which racism underpins the global history of capitalism.

On the other side of these formulations of race and empire in the interwar period were those who developed colonial administrative practices. Within the Anglo-American field of international relations, as elsewhere, knowledge production was deeply enmeshed with the contemporary imperial order.[19] Often operating in male-dominated academic arenas, women were nonetheless among the most influential thinkers and policy advisors in this context. An exemplar of this is Dame Margery Perham (1895–1982), an expert on British imperialism in Africa. At Oxford in the late 1930s, Perham taught at the Summer School on Colonial Administration and, following the war, she ran the Devonshire Courses designed to train British Colonial administrators. Her 1937 book, *Native Administration in Nigeria*, was "required reading" for those in the Colonial service.[20] At its founding in 1939, she was the first (and, at the time, only) woman Fellow at Nuffield College, Oxford, and was also the first director and one of the founders of the (then) Institute of Colonial Studies at Oxford. In the 1940s, this academic work translated into practice when she became the key policy advisor within Whitehall, sitting on a number of government committees and working closely with Arthur Creech Jones, Labour's Colonial Secretary between 1945 and 1950.[21] Perham's influence in mid-century Britain as the African expert cannot be underestimated. For the forty years of her career, she brought her views on African Affairs to a broader public through a large number of articles and letters for *The Times*.[22] She was the first woman to be asked to deliver the BBC Reith Lectures in 1961.[23]

In the foreword to *Native Administration in Nigeria*, Perham described her aim as an effort to "clothe the skeleton of the administrative system with flesh and blood."[24] This work, based on a nine-month period of

[19] David Engerman, "American Knowledge and Global Power," *Diplomatic History*, 31 (2007): 599–622.

[20] C. Brad Faught, *Into Africa: The Imperial Life of Margery Perham* (London: I. B. Tauris, 2011).

[21] Cherry Gertzel, "Margery Perham's Image of Africa," *The Journal of Imperial and Commonwealth History*, 19:3 (1991): 37–40.

[22] Alison Smith and Mary Bull, "Introduction," *Journal of Imperial and Commonwealth History*, 19:3 (1991): 4.

[23] Margery Perham, *The Colonial Reckoning: The Reith Lectures, 1961* (London: Collins, 1961).

[24] Margery Perham, *Native Administration in Nigeria* (Oxford: Oxford University Press, 1937; reprint 1962), xiv. For a selection of other works by Perham see *African Discovery*

study funded by the Rhodes Trustees, as well as the extended periods she had spent in Africa from 1921, draws explicitly upon both government sources and the limited anthropological work on different Nigerian tribes at that time.[25] The extract here focuses on the systems of indirect rule set up in Northern Nigeria by Lord Frederick Lugard, a British colonial administrator who had been the last Governor (1912–1914) and first Governor-General of Nigeria (1914–1919). Perham defines indirect rule "as a system by which the tutelary power recognizes existing African societies and assists them to adapt themselves to the functions of local government."[26] Whilst in the earlier part of this chapter, Perham focuses on what she perceives to be the merits of this approach, this extract contains her critique as well as some recommendations for future development. She listed the problems at the heart of the system, from the revolving door of Governors and other Colonial officials with a tendency to view Nigeria "as a stage set for an individual career" through to the investiture of "individual native agents … with extraordinary powers" regardless of their qualifications (168). Most crucial, from the perspective of the British officers, was the lack of both expert "knowledge and interest" in all areas of the colonial service. In part, it was this gap that Perham sought to fill. This lack of understanding only compounded what she called the "abnormality" of a situation in which "a handful of officials has almost complete control over the lives of millions of another race" (169). Perham was a strong believer in British intervention to create a "proper sphere in which" Africans could "develop," an image of Africa that perpetuated racial hierarchies. Her work reflects an important strand of the history of international thought, and the norms of her nation, class, and institution.

The same can be said of Mary Macdonald Proudfoot, who also worked at the interstices of academia and policy. Like Sybil Crowe, Proudfoot began her career as a research assistant for Perham prior to becoming a lecturer in modern history at Oxford in the late 1930s. Her first book, published in 1946, was a study of the democratic institutions of

(London: Faber and Faber, 1942, 1946, 1949, 1957, 1963; Harmondsworth: Penguin Books, 1948); *African Facts and American Criticism* (New York: Council on Foreign Relations, Inc., 1944); *Africans and British Rule* (London: Oxford University Press, 1934, 1941); *The Colonies and the Colonial Future* (London: Edinburgh House Press, 1942); *The Economics of a Tropical Dependency*, 2 vols. (London: Published under the auspices of Nuffield College by Faber and Faber, 1946–1948).
[25] Women were ineligible at this time for the more famous Rhodes Scholarship but they could, as Perham did, access some funding from the Rhodes Trustees for academic research and travel.
[26] Perham, *Native Administration in Nigeria*, 345.

Austria.[27] During the war she had enlisted in the army, ultimately working on the refugee crisis as part of the Supreme Headquarters Allied Expeditionary Force.[28] When she married a colleague from the force, an American geographer at Northwestern University, she moved to the United States and shifted her research interests to the Caribbean.[29] The book that resulted, *Britain and the United States in the Caribbean: A Comparative Study in Methods of Development*, appeared in the Oxford University Press series Studies in Colonial Legislature, edited by Perham. The series also included books by a scholar far better known in IR, Martin Wight. Wight had worked for Perham at Oxford, in his case researching colonial institutions during the Second World War. The two books he contributed to Perham's series, *The Development of the Legislative Council 1606–1945* (1946) and *The Gold Coast Legislative Council* (1947), were the fruits of that work.

In her volume for the series, Proudfoot addressed what she believed was "the major problem" of her time: "the relationship between the developed and the undeveloped areas of the world" (181). She began by detailing the trajectory of this relationship from the *"laissez-faire"* policies of non-annexation in place at the end of the nineteenth century through the notion of trusteeship advanced most prominently in the British case by Lord Salisbury, Joseph Chamberlain, and Lord Lugard. She then described the contemporary moment as a period that required "a new method ... whereby undeveloped areas may be developed without conquest, and without the establishment or continuance of any form of paternal overlordship" (181). In this, the Great Powers could learn from each other. Her book was an effort towards such a partnership, a case study contrasting the British administration of Jamaica, Barbados, Trinidad, and St. Lucia with the United States' administration of Puerto Rico.

Proudfoot's work is evidence of the extent to which racialized philosophies penetrated international thinking in this period. She expressed doubt that development was possible in the British West Indies because "its teeming millions of backward and primitive peoples ... would make any ... theory of equality self-evidently ludicrous" (184). Unlike

---

[27] Mary Macdonald Proudfoot, *The Republic of Austria, 1918–1934: A Study in the Failure of Democratic Government* (London: Issued under the auspices of the Royal Institute of International Affairs by G. Cummerlege and Oxford University Press, 1946).

[28] Margery Perham, "Editor's Introduction," in Mary Macdonald Proudfoot, *Britain and the United States in the Caribbean: A Comparative Study in Methods of Development* (London: Faber & Faber, 1954), vii.

[29] Robert E. Scott, *The Annals of the American Academy of Political and Social Science*, 298 (1955): 188.

Perham's work, which showed some level of respect, albeit limited and imperialist, for colonized populations, Proudfoot exemplifies a much more rigid bifurcation of the world into "backward" and "advanced" peoples.[30] Yet she grounded her theory of "development" in self-sufficiency, pointing to the failures of the charity-based system employed in the British West Indies that was never "commensurate with the needs of the people" (186). She contrasted this unfavourably with the US approach of drawing up "federal 'hand-out' legislation" from the mainland to Puerto Rico. This substantially raised the standard of living, but the population still remained dependent on the United States. Reflecting then prevalent ideologies of colonial welfarism, Proudfoot argued that the establishment of an effective welfare state in Caribbean nations required "the production and the increase of wealth" rather than just the immediate alleviation of the symptoms of poverty.[31] She credited the Americans with their placement and encouragement of social work professionals but questioned their assimilative tendencies. In contrast, the British understood the difference between "their culture" and that of the islanders in terms of the latter requiring the same level of amenities.

In many regards, Proudfoot's comparison of the British and United States' presence in the Caribbean reflected a broader shift in thinking about imperialism. The "assimilative" tendencies of the United States were symptomatic of the neo-imperialist world order that would be ushered in as colonial territories gained their independence from older forms of empire. The Jamaican activist Amy Jacques Garvey (1895–1973) identified the changing nature of imperial dynamics in the Caribbean in her 1946 article "Chinese Milk Africans in the Caribbean." Unlike Proudfoot, Jacques Garvey saw beyond "the teeming millions" to identify the very different situations of various groups operating within the Caribbean, focusing in particular upon the Chinese communities there. She noted the historical arrival of Chinese workers in Jamaica, Trinidad, and British Guiana and then traced their trajectory as a community from indentured labours to flourishing capitalists with a monopoly on "both the retail and whole grocery trade" (178). Such success was the result of a community-centered economic strategy. Within their own networks Chinese workers operated closed communal banks (*fui*) which selectively financed Chinese business. The banks were further

---

[30] See Duncan Bell, "Empire and Imperialism," in Gregory Claeys and Gareth Stedman Jones (eds.), *The Cambridge History of Nineteenth-Century Political Thought* (Cambridge: Cambridge University Press, 2012).

[31] Mary Macdonald Proudfoot, *Britain and the United States in the Caribbean* (London: Faber & Faber Ltd, 1954), 249.

supplemented by two illegal lottery systems, "Pekka Pow" and "Drop Pan," that operated at the expense of Black Jamaicans. Jacques Garvey pointed to the way that the profits from these initiatives were invested back into the Chinese community and also sent home to China itself. Such loyalty, she argued, was the product of the Chinese citizenship laws that made any child of a Chinese citizen Chinese themselves, regardless of race. Jacques Garvey declared that even "[t]he darkest looking ones of black mothers are recognized equally as Chinese, sent to Chinese schools." This was very different from the complicated and racialized hierarchies of citizenship involved in belonging to the British Commonwealth or, indeed, the United States. The Chinese citizens in the Caribbean, in turn, "show[ed] their allegiance to China in a financial way" (180). As a result, the resources of the Caribbean became the resources of China, leaving the Black Jamaican peoples to exist in poor conditions where problems such as malnutrition ran rife. Jacques Garvey framed these Chinese successes in terms of the rise of a new economic imperialism, concluding her article with the following questions: "Are they just 'colonies' of Chinese in the Caribbean now? Or will they be colonies of China later on?" (180).

Almost two decades later, in her 1961 Reith Lectures for the BBC, Margery Perham would ask similar questions about the Chinese and Russian economic efforts in African territories that had once been part of the British Empire.[32] Jacques Garvey, however, was asking these questions from a very different vantage point. Born into a middle-class family, Amy Jacques was one of the very few Jamaican children of her generation to finish high school. Upon graduating in 1912 she worked as a legal clerk until she moved to New York in 1917.[33] Once in New York, Amy Jacques became involved in Marcus Garvey's Universal Negro Improvement Association (UNIA). There she drew upon her experience at the law firm to act as one of the organization's legal advisors, as well as the associate editor for the UNIA newspaper, the *Negro World*, and as Marcus Garvey's private secretary.[34]

Founded in 1914 by Marcus and his first wife Amy Ashwood Garvey, UNIA was a Black nationalist organization dedicated to overcoming racism via a number of programs premised on racial pride and economic self-sufficiency. Most famous of these was its "Back to Africa" movement, which called for the formation of an independent United States

[32] Margery Perham, "Lecture 6: Prospects for the Future," Reith Lectures 1961: The Colonial Reckoning, December 21, 1961, Home Service, 5–6.

[33] Carole Boyce Davies, *Encyclopedia of the African Diaspora: Origins, Experiences, and Culture, Volume 1* (Santa Barbara, CA: ABC-CLIO, 2008), 458.

[34] Amy Jacques Garvey, *Garvey and Garveyism* (Kingston, Jamaica: United Printers, 1963), 106.

of Africa. The program appealed primarily to a membership drawn from the Black urban working class in the United States, but by 1920 it had chapters in over forty countries and counted its membership at over one million worldwide. Amy Jacques very quickly became one of the most prominent activists in UNIA, not least because of her 1922 marriage to Marcus Garvey after his divorce in 1922 from Amy Ashwood, whose work we excerpt elsewhere in this volume. When he was indicted and jailed for mail fraud in 1923, she acted as his representative and the organization's *de facto* leader. At the same time, she worked to popularize his thought, editing two volumes of the *Philosophy and Opinions of Marcus Garvey* (one published in 1923, and the second in 1925), as well as two volumes of his poetry.[35]

Scholars have long relegated Jacques Garvey to the role of Marcus Garvey's spouse and supporter.[36] Whilst she indubitably did a great deal of work to propagate her husband's thinking, the reality is that she was a prolific writer herself and played an active role in UNIA's leadership in her own right. At the *Negro World*, Jacques Garvey was responsible for the "Women's Page," a section where she regularly published sophisticated analyses of the operation of race and empire in the United States and worldwide. Unlike Marcus Garvey, she consistently drew attention to women's involvement in emancipatory movements and underlined the convergence of racism, sexism, and classism in Black women's lives and in their experience of empire.[37] Moreover, after his death in 1940 she continued her activism and journalism, writing on anti-imperialism, racism, and Garveyism as a philosophy.[38] The extract included here is indicative of her incisive thinking about the dynamics of race and imperialism.

Whilst sophisticated critiques of racism and ethnic nationalism such as those found in the work of Cooper and Jacques Garvey were hardly dominant in bastions of empire such as the British Foreign Office or Oxford and Cambridge, they were nonetheless a force to be reckoned

---

[35] Karen S. Adler, "'ALWAYS LEADING OUR MEN IN SERVICE AND SACRIFICE': Amy Jacques Garvey, Feminist Black Nationalist," *Gender & Society*, 6:3 (September 1992): 346–375.

[36] See Judith Stein, *The World of Marcus Garvey* (Baton Rouge, LA: Louisiana State University Press, 1986), 151; Tony Martin, *Marcus Garvey, Hero* (Dover, MA: Majority Press, 1983), 67.

[37] See Amy Jacques Garvey, "What Some Women of the Race Have Accomplished," *Negro World*, June 7, 1924; "Black Women's Resolve for 1926," *Negro World*, January 9, 1926; "A Woman's Hands Guide the Indian National Congress," *Negro World*, August 28, 1926; "Scanty Clothes Make Hardy Women," *Negro World*, November 27, 1926.

[38] Amy Jacques Garvey, *Garvey and Garveyism; Black Power in America: Marcus Garvey's Impact on Jamaica and Africa* (Kingston, Jamaica: Self-published by Amy Jacques Garvey, 1968).

with on the international stage. The kind of policy work around colonialism that gave impetus to the research of thinkers such as Proudfoot and Perham was slowly subsumed by efforts towards decolonization. Moreover, the post-war realities of empire saw scholars of colonial administration transition in their focus from effective colonial administration to the relationship between Britain and its Commonwealth. We can see this clearly in Proudfoot's work for the Colonial Office in the 1960s. Hired to advise on the development of a new constitution in the British Virgin Islands, Proudfoot authored the 1965 "Proudfoot Report" for the Office. This report was far more progressive than her 1954 work had been, arguing that British Virgin Islanders possessed the "evident ability and seriousness" necessary for self-government. In her view "the British pattern of government – a Legislature and Executive, a small cabinet group, however styled can ... work as well as – perhaps better than – it now works at Westminster."[39] Proudfoot's position was based on the assumption that British political institutions were "part of the heritage of" Virgin Islanders in their position as "fellow members of the Commonwealth."[40]

Whilst Proudfoot's work in 1965 concentrated on a Commonwealth population that remained distant, other scholars of colonial administration focused on changes occurring at the heart of empire, in Britain itself. As the population of Black people in Britain rose from 74,500 in 1951 to 500,000 by 1962, this work was particularly concerned with what was referred to as "race relations."[41] British universities in particular became locations where empire's integrity was challenged by the increasing presence of African students.[42] Perham, for example, grew concerned about the "warping" effect upon Black male students in Britain who were potentially able to achieve the "supreme racial compensation" of sleeping with white women.[43]

Perham's thinking reflected a broader theme amongst those who had worked on questions of colonial administration, wherein concerns for the

---

[39] "Proudfoot Report," British Virgin Islands: Report of the Constitutional Commissioner, 1965 / [Colonial Office]. Great Britain. Colonial Office (London: HMSO, 1965), 10–11. There is a critical discussion of her role in Eugenia O'Neal, *From the Field to the Legislature: A History of Women in the Virgin Islands* (Westport, CT: Greenwood Press, 2001), 66–68.

[40] "Proudfoot Report," 11–12.

[41] Chris Waters, "'Dark Strangers' in Our Midst: Discourses of Race and Nation in Britain, 1947–1963," *Journal of British Studies*, 36:2 (1997): 209.

[42] See Stuart Hall, *Familiar Stranger: A Life between Two Islands*, ed. B. Schwarz (Durham, NC: Duke University Press, 2017), 158–170.

[43] Jordanna Bailkin, *The Afterlife of Empire* (Berkeley, CA: University of California Press, 2012), 110.

fragility of imperial relations rested upon the consequences of Black students' experiences of racial discrimination in Britain, a subject we discuss in our section on Population, Nation, Immigration. Such worries were multi-faceted, premised on racist distaste for this new proximity of formerly colonial subjects and false conceptions about Black intellectual inferiority, as well as fears that such experiences might lead to a rejection of British values and the Commonwealth itself.[44] These concerns were difficult to reconcile in the context of Britain's economic dependence upon Commonwealth resources and labour. Racism did not inspire the same kind of economic loyalty that Chinese policies of inclusion described by Jacques Garvey seemed to elicit. In surveying the contexts in which each of the thinkers included in this section operated, it is evident that the question of imperialism took on vastly different forms throughout the first half of the twentieth century. The common thread throughout their thought was the issue of race.

Sarah C. Dunstan

---

[44] Robbie Shilliam, "Behind the Rhodes Statue: Black Competency and the Imperial Academy," *History of the Human Sciences*, 32:5 (2019): 15–16.

Jessie Fauset

From "Impressions of the Second Pan-African Congress" (1921)

THE dream of a Pan-African Congress had already come true in 1919. Yet it was with hearts half-wondering, half fearful that we ventured to realize it afresh in 1921. So tenuous, so delicate had been its beginnings. Had the black world, although once stirred by the terrific rumblings of the Great War, relapsed into its lethargy? Then out of Africa just before it was time to cross the Atlantic came a letter, one of many, but this the most appealing word from the Egyptian Sudan: "Sir: We cannot come but we are sending you this small sum ($17.92), to help toward the expenses of the Pan-African Congress. Oh Sir, we are looking to you for we need help sorely!"

So with this in mind we crossed the seas not knowing just what would be the plan of action for the Congress, for would not its members come from the four corners of the earth and must there not of necessity be a diversity of opinion, of thought, of project? But the main thing, the great thing, was that Ethiopia's sons through delegates were stretching out their hands from all over the black and yearning world.

II

THEN one day, the 27th of August, we met in London in Central Hall, under the shadow of Westminster Abbey. Many significant happenings had those cloisters looked down on, but surely on none more significant than on this group of men and women of African descent, so different in rearing and tradition and yet so similar in purpose. The rod of the common oppressor had made them feel their own community of blood, of necessity, of problem.

Men from strange and diverse lands came together. We were all of us foreigners. South Africa was represented, the Gold Coast, Sierra Leone and Lagos, Grenada, the United States of America, Martinique, Liberia.

No natives of Morocco or of East Africa came, yet men who had lived there presented and discussed their problems. British Guiana and Jamaica were there and the men and women of African blood who were at that time resident in London.

That was a wonderful meeting. I think that at first we did not realize how wonderful. The first day Dr. Alcindor of London and Rev. Jernagin of Washington presided; the second day Dr. DuBois and Mr. Archer, ex-Mayor of Battersea, London. Of necessity those first meetings had to be occasions for getting acquainted, for bestowing confidences for opening up our hearts. Native African and native American stood side by side and said, "Brother, this is my lot; tell me what is yours!"

[...]

We listened well. What can be more fascinating than learning at first hand that the stranger across the seas, however different in phrase or expression, yet knows no difference of heart? We were all one family in London. What small divergences of opinion, slight suspicions, doubtful glances there may have been at first were all quickly dissipated. We felt our common blood with almost unbelievable unanimity.

Out of the flood of talk emerged real fact and purpose for the American delegate. First, that West Africa had practically no problems concerning the expropriation of land but had imminent something else, the problem of political power and the heavy and insulting problem of segregation. The East African, on the other hand, and also the South African had no vestige of a vote (save in Natal), had been utterly despoiled of the best portions of his land, nor could he buy it back. In addition to this the East African had to consider the influx of the East Indian who might prove a friend, or might prove as harsh a taskmaster as the European despoiler.

Through the inter-play of speech and description and idea, two propositions flashed out – one, the proposition of Mr. Augusto, a splendid, fearless speaker from Lagos, that the Pan-African Congress should accomplish something very concrete. He urged that we start with the material in hand and advance to better things. First of all let us begin by financing the Liberian loan. Liberia is a Negro Independency already founded. "Let us," pleaded Mr. Augusto, "lend the solid weight of the newly-conscious black world toward its development."

The other proposition was that of Mr. Marryshow, of Grenada, and of Professor Hutto of Georgia. "We must remember," both of them pointed out, "that not words but actions are needed. We must be prepared to put our hands in our pockets; we must make sacrifices to help each other."

"Tell us what to do," said Mr. Hutto, "and the Knights of Pythias of Georgia stand ready, 80,000 strong, to do their part."

Those were fine, constructive words. Then at the last meeting we listened to the resolutions which Dr. DuBois had drawn up. Bold and glorious resolutions they were, couched in winged, unambiguous words. Without a single dissenting vote the members of the Congress accepted them. We clasped hands with our newly found brethren and departed, feeling that it was good to be alive and most wonderful to be colored. Not one of us but envisaged in his heart the dawn of a day of new and perfect African brotherhood.

III

DOWN to Dover we flew, up the English Channel to Ostend, and thence to Brussels. Brussels was different. How shall I explain it? The city was like most other large cities, alive and bustling, with its share of noise. All about us were beautiful, large buildings and commodious stores, except in the public squares where the ancient structures, the town hall and the like, centuries old, recalled the splendor and dignity of other days. But over Brussels hung the shadow of monarchical government. True London is the heart of a monarchy, too, but the stranger does not feel it unless he is passing Buckingham Palace or watching the London Horse Guards change. At first it was not so noticeable.

We had been invited by Paul Otlet and Senator LaFontaine and had been helped greatly by M. Paul Panda, a native of the Belgian Congo who had been educated in Belgium. The Congress itself was held in the marvellous Palais Mondial, the World Palace situated in the Cinquantenaire Park.

We could not have asked for a better setting. But there was a difference. In the first place, there were many more white than colored people – there are not many of us in Brussells [sic] – and it was not long before we realized that their interest was deeper, more immediately significant than that of the white people we had found elsewhere. Many of Belgium's economic and material interests centre [sic] in Africa in the Belgian Congo. Any interference with the natives might result in an interference with the sources from which so many Belgian capitalists drew their prosperity.

After all, who were these dark strangers speaking another tongue and introducing Heaven only knew what ideas to be carried into the Congo? Once when speaking of the strides which colored America had made in education I suggested to M. Panda that perhaps some American colored teachers might be induced to visit the Congo and help with the instruction of the natives. "Oh, no, no, no!" he exclaimed, and added the naïve explanation, "Belgium would never permit that, the colored Americans are too malins" (clever).

After we had visited the Congo Museum we were better able to understand the unspoken determination of the Belgians to let nothing interfere with their dominion in the Congo. Such treasures! Such illimitable riches! What a store-house it must plainly be for them. For the first time in my life I was able to envisage what Africa means to Europe, depleted as she has become through the ages by war and famine and plague.

In the museum were the seeds of hundreds of edible plants; there was wood – great trunks of dense, fine-grained mahogany as thick as a man's body is wide and as long as half a New York block. Elephants' tusks gleamed, white and shapely, seven feet long from tip to base without allowing for the curve, and as broad through as a man's arm. All the wealth of the world – skins and furs, gold and copper – would seem to center in the Congo.

Nor was this all. Around us in the spacious rooms were the expression of an earlier but well developed art, wood-carvings showing beyond the shadow of a doubt the inherent artistry of the African. Dearest of all, yet somehow least surprising to us, was the number of musical instruments. There is not a single musical instrument in the world, I would venture to say, of which the Congo cannot furnish a prototype. Native wealth, native art lay about us in profusion even in the museum. Small wonder that the Belgian men and women watched us with careful eyes.

The program in Brussels was naturally different from that in London. We undertook to learn something of the culture which colored people had achieved in the different parts of the world, but we hoped also to hear of actual native conditions as we had heard of them in the first conference. M. Panda spoke of the general development of the Congo, Madame Saroléa of the Congolese woman. Miss Fauset told of the colored graduates in the United States and showed the pictures of the first women who had obtained the degree of Doctor of Philosophy. Bishop Phillips of Nashville and Bishop Hurst of Baltimore greeted the assembly. Mrs. Curtis told of Liberia, the presiding officer of the Conference, M. Diagne, and his white colleague M. Barthélemy from the Pas de Calais, in the French Chamber of Deputies, ably assisted.

Belgian officialdom was well represented. General Sorelas of Spain spoke of the problem of the mixed race. Another General, a Belgian, splendid in ribbons and orders, was on the platform, and two members of the Belgian Colonial Office were present, "unofficially."

There was no doubt but that our assembly was noted. A fine, fresh-faced youth from the International University gave us a welcome from students of all nations; we were invited to a reception at the Hotel de Ville

(City Hall) in the ancient public square, and on the last day General Sorelas and his beautiful wife and daughters received us all in their home.

And yet the shadow of Colonial dominion governed. Always the careful Belgian eye watched and peered, the Belgian ear listened. For three days we listened to pleasant generalities without a word of criticism of Colonial Governments, without a murmur of complaint of Black Africa, without a suggestion that this was an international Congress called to define and make intelligible the greatest set of wrongs against human beings that the modern world has known. We realized of course how delicate the Belgian situation was and how sensitive a conscience the nation had because of the atrocities of the Leopold regime. We knew the tremendous power of capital organized to exploit the Congo; but despite this we proposed before the Congress was over to voice the wrongs of Negroes temperately but clearly. We assumed of course that this was what Belgium expected, but we reckoned without our hosts in a very literal sense. Indeed as we afterward found, we were reckoning without our own presiding officer, for without doubt M. Diagne on account of his high position in the French Government had undoubtedly felt called on to assure the Belgian Government that no "radical" step would be taken by the Congress. He sponsored therefore a mild resolution suggested by the secretaries of the Palais Mondial stating that Negroes were "susceptible" of education and pledging co-operation of the Pan-African Congress with the international movement in Belgium.

When the London resolutions (which are published this month as our leading editorial), were read, M. Diagne was greatly alarmed, and our Belgian visitors were excited. The American delegates were firm and for a while it looked as though the main session of the Pan-African Congress was destined to end in a rather disgraceful row. It was here, however, that the American delegates under the leadership of Dr. DuBois, showed themselves the real masters of the situation. With only formal and dignified protest, they allowed M. Diagne to "jam through" his resolution and adjourn the session; but they kept their own resolutions in place before the Congress to come up for final consideration in Paris, and they maintained the closing of the session in Brussels in order and unity. I suppose the white world of Europe has never seen a finer example of unity and trust on the part of Negroes toward a Negro leader.

But we left Belgium in thoughtful and puzzled mood. How great was this smothering power which made it impossible for men even in a scientific Congress to be frank and to express their inmost desires?

Not one word, for instance, had been said during the whole Congress by Belgian white or black, or French presiding officer which would lead one to suspect that Leopold and his tribe had ever been other than the

Congo's tutelary angels. Apparently not even an improvement could be hinted at. And the few Africans who were present said nothing. But at that last meeting just before we left, a Congolese came forward and fastened the button of the Congo Union in Dr. DuBois' coat. What lay behind that impassive face?

IV

At last Paris!

Between Brussels and the queen city of the world we saw blasted town, ravaged village and plain, ruined in a war whose basic motif had been the rape of Africa. What should we learn of the black man in France?

Already we had realized that the black colonial's problem while the same intrinsically, wore on the face of it a different aspect from that of the black Americans. Or was it that we had learned more quickly and better than they the value of organization, of frankness, of freedom of speech? We wondered then and we wonder still though Heaven knows in all humility.

But Paris at last, with its glow and its lights and its indefinable attraction!

We met in the Salle des Ingénieurs (Engineers' Hall) in little Rue Blanche back of the Opera. Logan was there, Béton and Dr. Jackson, men who had worked faithfully and well for us even before we had come to Paris. And around us were more strange faces – new types to us – from Senegal, from the French Congo, from Madagascar, from Annam. I looked at that sea of dark faces and my heart was moved within me. However their white overlords or their minions might plot and plan and thwart, nothing could dislodge from the minds of all of them the knowledge that black was at last stretching out to black, hands of hope and the promise of unity though seas and armies divided.

On the platform was, I suppose, the intellectual efflorescence of the Negro race. To American eyes and, according to the papers, to many others, Dr. DuBois loomed first, for he had first envisaged this movement and many of us knew how gigantically he had toiled. Then there was M. Bellegarde, the Haitian minister to France and Haitian delegate to the assembly of the League of Nations. Beside him sat the grave and dignified delegate from the Liga Africana of Lisbon, Portugal, and on the other side the presiding officer, M. Diagne and his colleague, M. Candace, French deputy from Guadeloupe. A little to one side sat the American Rayford Logan, assistant secretary of the Pan-African Congress at Paris and our interpreter. His translations, made off-hand without a moment's preparation, were a remarkable exhibition.

In the audience besides those faithful American delegates[45] who had followed us from London on, were other friends, Henry O. Tanner, Captain and Mrs. Napoleon Marshall, who had joined us in Paris, Bishop and Mrs. Hurst, who had come back from Brussels to Paris with us, Captain and Mrs. Arthur Spingarn, white delegates from America, who had attended the conferences regularly and had laughed and worked with us in between whiles.

The situation in Paris was less tense, one felt the difference between monarchy and republic. But again the American was temporarily puzzled. Even allowing for natural differences of training and tradition, it seemed absurd to have the floor given repeatedly to speakers who dwelt on the glories of France and the honor of being a black Frenchman, when what we and most of those humble delegates wanted to learn was about us.

The contrast between the speakers of the Eastern and Western hemispheres with but two exceptions was most striking. Messieurs Diagne and Candace gave us fine oratory, magnificent gestures – but platitudes. But the speeches of Dr. DuBois, of Edward Frazier, of Walter White, of Dr. Jackson, of a young and and [sic] fiery Jamaican and of M. Bellegarde, gave facts and food for thought. The exceptions were the speeches of M. Challaye, a white member of the Society for the Defense of African Natives, and those of the grave and courtly Portuguese, Messieurs Magalhaens [sic] and Santos-Pinto.

But this audience was different from that in Brussells [sic]. To begin with, its members were mainly black and being black, had suffered. More than one man to whom the unusually autocratic presiding officer had not given the right to speak said to me after hearing Dr. DuBois' exposition of the meaning and purpose of the Pan-African Congress, "Do you think I could get a chance to speak to Dr. DuBois. There is much I would tell him."

France is a colonial power but France is a republic. And so when our resolutions were presented once more to this the final session of the Pan-African Congress, that audience felt that here at last was the fearless voicing of the long stifled desires of their hearts, here was comprehension, here was the translation of hitherto unsyllabled, unuttered prayers. The few paragraphs about capitalism M. Diagne postponed "for the consideration of the next Pan-African Congress." But the rest that yearning, groping audience accepted with their souls. The last session of the last day was over. It was midnight and spent and happy we found our way home through the streets of Paris which never sleeps.

[45] A list of delegates will be published later.

V

YET after all the real task was at Geneva. The city struck us dumb at first with its beauty of sky and water – the blue and white of the September heavens above, Lake Geneva and the Rhone River gliding green and transparent under stone bridges, black and white swans, red-beaked, floating lazily about green baby islands, and above and beyond all in the far distance Mont Blanc rising hoary, serene and majestic. In the sunset it looked like burnished silver.

But scant time we had for looking at that! The Assembly of the League of Nations was on. A thousand petitions and resolutions were in process of being presented. Delegates from many nations were here and men of international name and fame were presiding. How were we to gain audience? Fortunately for us Dr. DuBois' name and reputation proved the open sesame. He had not been in the city two hours before invitations and requests for interviews poured in. [...]

VI

RESULTS are hard to define. But I must strive to point out a few. First then, out of these two preliminary conferences of 1919 and 1921, a definite organization has been evolved, to be known as the Pan-African Congress. There will be more of this in these pages. Naturally working with people from all over the world, with the necessity for using at least two languages, with the limited detailed knowledge which the black foreigner is permitted to get of Africa and with the pressure brought to bear on many Africans to prevent them from frank speech – action must be slow and very careful. It will take years for an institution of this sort to function. But it is on its own feet now and the burden no longer is on black America. It must stand or fall by its own merits. We have gained proof that organization on our part arrests the attention of the world. We had no need to seek publicity. If we had wanted to we could not have escaped it. The press was with us always.

The white world is feverishly anxious to know of our thoughts, our hopes, our dreams. Organization is our strongest weapon.

It was especially arresting to notice that the Pan-African Congress and the Assembly of the League of Nations differed not a whit in essential methods. Neither attempted a hard and fast program. Lumbering and slow were the wheels of both activities. There had to be much talk, many explanations, an infinity of time and patience and then talk again. Neither the wrongs of Africa nor of the world, can be righted in a day nor in a decade. We can only make beginnings.

The most important result was our realization that there is an immensity of work ahead of all of us. We have got to learn everything – facts about Africa, the difference between her colonial governments, one foreign language at least (French or Spanish), new points of view, generosity of ideal and of act. All the possibilities of all black men are needed to weld together the black men of the world against the day when black and white meet to do battle.

God grant that when that day comes we shall be so powerful that the enemy will say, "But behold! these men are our brothers."

Lillian M. Penson

From "The London West India Interest in the Eighteenth Century" (1921)

The character of society in the West India Islands in the eighteenth century was, in some respects, very similar to that of Maryland, Virginia, and the Carolinas. Their trade was not competitive with that of the mother country; they had a staple product, sugar; their cultivation was carried on by slave labour. But between the society of the West India Islands and that of the southern colonies of North America there were two principal differences: in the West India Islands there was greater disproportion between the negro and the white populations, and amongst the proprietors of the plantations absenteeism was far more rife. These differences made the protection given by the mother country essential to the islands, as preventing not only foreign aggression, but also rebellion at home. The prevalence of absenteeism had also another result. The absentees formed at home a wealthy and influential body of men. In the London West India organizations of the eighteenth century they were an element which can have existed only to a very small degree in the societies connected with the North American colonies. The amalgamation of the West India planters in England with the London merchants trading to the West Indies gave to the society which they formed a strength that enabled it to exert an influence over British politics far greater than that of its contemporaries. And that society has had a continuous life to the present day, through all the economic and political changes through which the West India colonies have passed.

Certain definite results can be traced to this influence in the eighteenth century. Professor Pitman[46] has indicated its importance in the cases of the Molasses Act of 1733 and the Sugar Act of 1739,[47] and it was seen again in 1764 when the policy of the act of 1733 was further developed.[48]

---

[46] *The British West Indies*, pp. 254–63, 181–3, 187.   [47] 6 Geo. II, cap. 13.
[48] 12 Geo. II, cap. 30.

152

Yet, if these acts could have been enforced, the result to the prosperity of the New England colonies would have been serious. With the same object in view – the maintenance of the prosperity of the sugar plantations by increasing the demand for British sugar – opposition, by this time no longer uniformly successful, was organized to Pitt's Irish resolutions of 1786,[49] to the founding of a British company for trading at Sierra Leone in 1791,[50] and to the introduction of East India sugar in 1792.[51] Two other important objects of the West India interest can be traced in the eighteenth century. In time of war, constant representation to ministers of the danger to the islands, the necessity for increased squadrons and for convoys for the trade, had at any rate a considerable part in saving the islands from foreign conquest. And in the latter years of the century from 1788 onwards the whole force of the West India interest was employed to oppose the attacks then made on the slave-trade.[52]

Of this West India interest there were, as has already been indicated, two main sections, the planters resident in England and the London merchants trading to the islands. A third element must be mentioned, connected sometimes with one or the other of these two, that is the colonial agents. The first colonial agent[53] of any West India island appears to have belonged to Barbados. The history of his appointment is interesting.

[...]

It does not appear probable that in the early years of the eighteenth century these agents and planters and merchants had any permanent organization. When necessity arose meetings were held so that joint action could be taken, but there was no continuity in their history. Before a permanent society could come into existence there were several interests which had to be reconciled one to another. There had to be harmony between the resident planters, whose representatives the agents were, and the absentees; and between the absentee planters and the merchants. There had, moreover, to be unanimity between those

---

[49] 4 Geo. III, cap. 15.

[50] Chatham Papers, 352 (Public Record Office), Resolutions of West India Planters and Merchants, 24, 26 February, 9 March, 22 April, 6 May 1785. Also Standing Committee's Minutes, vol. i, 18, 31 May, 7, 14 June 1785. See also Holland Rose, *William Pitt and the National Revival*, pp. 255, 260.

[51] Standing Committee's Minutes, vol. i, 11, 13, 14, 17, 18, 19, 20, 23 May 1791.

[52] *Ibid.*, vol. i, 14, 20, 24, 28 February, 9–12 March, 17, 19, 20, 22, 31 March 1792.

[53] A sub-committee was appointed at a meeting of 7 February 1788 to deal with this matter, and its sittings are recorded at various periods during the remainder of the century (Standing Committee's Minutes, vols. i and ii).

concerned in the various islands: no evidence has been found that the last point was the occasion of any difficulty.[54]

The only institution connected with the West India interest which is known to have been in existence at this time was the Jamaica Coffee House, in St. Michael's Alley, Cornhill, whose foundation dates probably from the last decade of the seventeenth century.[55] Here the masters of ships engaged in the Jamaica and Guinea trade called to collect letters, and were to be seen by merchants or others at stated hours. To this coffee house letters were addressed to the agents and probably to other merchants and planters from their correspondents in Jamaica,[56] and no doubt meetings were sometimes held here, to consult on the business of the island. But there is no indication that there was any regular organization for the transaction of affairs.

[...]

This organization was generally known as the Society of West India Merchants, a title that suggests analogy to the Society of London Merchants trading to Virginia and Maryland which seems to have developed at about the same time.[57] The first reference that has been found relates to the year 1760.[58] Under that date there is a letter among the Newcastle Papers in the British Museum in which it is stated that 'The Agents of the Colonies and the West India Merchants' wished to be permitted to wait on the duke of Newcastle with a memorial. The letter is signed 'Beeston Long, Chairman of the West India Merchants'.[59] Six years later the West India merchants invited the duke of Newcastle to a dinner, and a letter on the subject has been preserved from the duke of Newcastle to Mr. Long.[60] These letters could not perhaps be taken as proof of the existence of a permanent and organized society of the West India interest if it were not that from 1769 onwards there have been

---

[54] A possible source of difference is indicated in a letter-book of Messrs. Lascelles and Maxwell, 1752–4, letter dated 1 May 1753 to Thomas Stevenson & Sons: 'a Bill is ordered ... for the better peopling and Cultivating the Lands of the Island of, Jamaica, which the Ministry seems to have much at heart. If that can be compassed effectually, a plenty of sugar may hurt yours and the Leeward Islands in time.'

[55] *General Advertiser*, Tuesday, 18 December 1750. Notice headed 'To all Persons Concerned in the Jamaica Trade', where reference is made to the existence of the coffee house for sixty years past.

[56] *Ibid.*, and Brit. Mus., Add. MS. 12431, fos. 116–17, 120–1.

[57] Reference to this society is made in the Chatham Papers, 95. See also Merchants' Minutes, vol. i, meeting of 4 July 1769.

[58] It is possible that the society had been in existence since 1746 or earlier, and that only its political activities are now in 1760; see below, p. 383, n. 5.

[59] Brit. Mus., Add. MS. 32902, fo. 458.

[60] Brit. Mus., Add. MS. 32975, fos. 416, 430. See also letter from Stephen Fuller, agent for Jamaica, Add. MS. 32975, fo. 400.

preserved the minutes of its meetings. These are now in the possession of the direct descendant of the society – the West India Committee.

The first entry in the minute books is under date 11 April 1769. By that time it is evident that the society has been in activity sufficiently long for its constitution to be taken as a matter of course. All our conclusions as to the form of the society have to be deduced from a study of the business transacted, the methods by which the society worked, and the information given as to the persons present at the meetings. It is characteristic of the whole development of the organized West India interest that there is no trace throughout the eighteenth century of any rules other than those of custom: in 1829 and again in 1843 there were constitutional reforms, but these are the earliest on record. Nevertheless, we can get from the minutes a tolerably clear and detailed account of the nature of the society. The meetings were held normally once a month, but departures from this practice appear to have been frequent. There was no regular locality for the meetings, a room at the office of the Marine Society[61] being the most usual meeting-place. The exact basis of membership of the society is difficult to determine; probably there was no definite system of admission until the last ten years of the century.[62] By 1792 it had become usual for the names of new members to be proposed and seconded by existing members at a meeting of the society, and then after the lapse of a few weeks the new members were declared to be admitted. The title of the society indicates that the membership was confined to merchants. No doubt this was so, but it is very difficult to make any further decision as to the scope of the membership. A consideration of their own interests would probably, however, lead all the prominent merchants to attend the meetings. The attendance varied considerably; there were six or eight members in the early years of the society who were usually present, and there were also a very large number who attended more rarely, some very seldom indeed.

From the rule that all members of the society should be merchants even the colonial agents do not appear to have been exempt. One of the most constant attendants at the meetings was Stephen Fuller, the agent for Jamaica, and Richard Maitland, agent for Grenada, St. Vincent, and Tobago,[63] was also a member; but the agent for Barbados, George

---

[61] A charitable organization for ministering to the widows and orphans of seamen: it was established in 1756; its present office is Clark's Place, Bishopsgate.

[62] At a meeting of 2 April 1771 it was resolved that 'the question of the admission of members to this meeting' should be considered next month, but when the time came the matter was postponed (Merchants' Minutes, vol. i, meetings of 2 April and 7 May 1771).

[63] Tobago after 1772.

Walker, does not appear.[64] Stephen Fuller and Richard Maitland we know to have been merchants, and George Walker was an absentee planter, so it seems safe to assume that the agents were admitted as merchants and not in virtue of their agency. Nevertheless, the merchants who were also agents had a very prominent place in the society, and matters were frequently referred to them on the grounds of their position as agents.

[64] George Walker and his successor Samuel Estwick appear later when there are joint meetings of planters and merchants.

Anna Julia Cooper

From *Slavery and the French and Haitian Revolutions* (1925)

In the European colonies of America, black slavery was an institution founded solely on the abuse of power. In all aspects created by a barbarous and shortsighted politics, and maintained by violence, we shall see that it could be abolished by a stroke, a simple legislative measure when the people it dishonored felt that they could no longer violate moral laws. Precisely because of its artificial character, Negro slavery appeared more odious than any other, for it meant the exploitation of man by man. It was done without pretext and without excuse. And only in the name of the right of the strongest.

We have to look for the origins of this latest form of slavery in the customs of the Spanish and of the Portuguese, who were little inclined to manual work, and who were too indolent to do it for themselves.

It was a slavery incomparably more cruel than that which was rampant in antiquity and which is still perpetuated in our day in Muslim countries. The Iberian peoples early found it profitable to combine the trade in slaves with all the other trade they engaged in along the length of the African coasts.

For a long time they undertook this commerce on a small scale for their own colonies in the new world. They would voyage to the coasts of Africa to buy the blacks, then transport them across the Atlantic. But later they did this in order to sell the blacks to the English and French colonies. The notorious Prince Henri was already using his influence to protect a company that had been formed at Lisbon, and the market of that town had already become very important even before the discoveries of Christopher Columbus opened an unexpected new area of trade.

In 1503 several black slaves were first taken to Hispaniola; it was immediately apparent that they were much more vigorous and very much hardier than the native Indians, especially for the exhausting work in the mines. The celebrated Bishop Las Casas, protector of the unhappy Indians who were perishing by the thousands because they were driven

157

to excessive labor, then proposed to the Regent – Cardinal Ximenes that a black population be systematically organized to do the work of the mines – but Ximenes refused. Yet Charles the Fifth was to show fewer qualms: After 1517 he accorded to a Flemish gentleman formal permission to bring 4000 African slaves every year to the islands of Porto Rico, Hispaniola, Cuba and Jamaica, and the origin of the Negro slave trade can be traced to this concession. The commerce was very lucrative and it was to spread; the complement of slave ships promptly multiplied in European ports. England, France and Holland took an active part in the trade, and, not satisfied to transport slaves only to their own colonies, they all fought for the trade of the Spanish colonies of Central and South America. It was estimated that at the time of the French Revolution 74,000 [sic] Negro slaves were transported each year to America; 38,000 were taken there by the English, 20,000 by the French, 4,000 by the Dutch and 2,000 by the Danes. This constant and terrible replenishment was necessary because of the excessive mortality of the slaves – almost three times their birth-rate.

At that these 74,000 [sic] blacks who arrived in the colonies were but a negligible percentage of the victims of this barbarous commerce in human lives. For every one imported, four had already died, succumbing to the perils of the passage, during which the poor souls had been chained and penned like cattle. Above all they died in the course of the fearful man-hunts organized on the African continent to supply the demands of the African slave traders. As the devastation gradually extended the villages disappeared, and the populations were slaughtered in the resistance or sold. The slave trade was a catalyst for the plunder, the atrocious wars, and the anarchy which for three centuries desolated western Africa, giving reign to savagery, and impeding the progress of all civilization. [...]

Despite some material gains, such crimes could only arouse a general condemnation. The humanitarian ideals of the eighteenth century were too flagrantly offended; indignant protests became current everywhere. A methodical campaign for the universal recognition of the most sacred human rights would be organized against this evil institution. The Revolution would finally bring about what even the principles of Christianity had been unable to achieve. The supremely philosophic century was to shake the conscience of all Europe.

The United States, where the principles of liberty were applied for the first time, above all the Southern States which had already suffered from the curse which slavery brought to them, had on several occasions demanded the abolition of the slave trade. At first the English mother-country turned a deaf ear: she profited too much from the traffic to be willing to suppress it.

Then, when the independence of the English colonies of America was recognized and the new constitution was drafted, even the most honest and conscientious men of the nation felt fearful before the magnitude of the problem which they would have to solve if they took up such a burning question. Whether from excessive and mistaken patriotism or from moral weakness they allowed to persist an already established state of affairs which was to remain a living negation of their noble principles. A philanthropic movement favoring the emancipation of the Negroes nonetheless made itself felt throughout the United States, thanks to the Quakers, a sect which since 1774 had expelled from their society all those found interested in the slave trade, and thanks to such men as John Woolman, Benezet, and Warner Miflin [sic].

This movement resulted in the enactment of certain measures against the importation of Negroes in nine of the newly recognized states, as well as the emancipation of all the blacks born in Pennsylvania after 1776.

In England the demand for abolition of the slave trade had been heard since 1780. And although the colonial slave-holders sought in 1784 to safeguard their interests from the consequences of this movement by the Passage of the Consolidated Slave Act, William Pitt dared to speak openly in Parliament in 1788 for abolition of the trade.

The English philanthropist Ransay, Granville Sharp, and especially Thomas Clarkson, the young and brilliant Professor of Cambridge University, stirred up English opinion at that time by writing pamphlets exposing colonial practices. The abolitionists liked to buttress their arguments with that famous phrase uttered in 1772 by Lord Mansfield:

> The air of England has long been too pure for a slave, and
> every man is free who breathes it. Every man who comes into
> England is entitled to the protection of the English law.

In 1783 as [sic] association had been formed in London as much for the deliverance of the slaves of the Antilles as for the discouragement of the traffic on the coasts of Africa. Two years later Dr. Pinkard, the Vice-Chancellor of Cambridge University, proposed as a subject for the Latin prize "Is it proper to make men slaves without their permission?" Clarkson, who was then a student, won the prize, and the following year published a work titled *Essay on the Slavery and Commerce of the Human Species*. This book marked a turning point in the struggle against slavery. In 1787 Granville Sharp became president, and William Wilberforce and Clarkson the guiding spirits of the anti-slavery society formed in 1783; it reorganized on a serious basis with the aim of suppressing the slave trade.

Meanwhile, it was in France that the first flash of the philosophic ideal capable of awakening the entire world burst forth. Montesquieu,

Rousseau, Voltaire, Filangieri and Raynal thundered the most forcefully against the odious traffic. It was in France that official acts striking a death blow to the most unjust of institutions would be announced for the first time. The honor of having voted the deliverance of the slaves in all the French colonies belongs to the National convention of the French Republic. It did this at the meeting of the 16 pluviose [sic], year II. [...]

It certainly is true that slavery has the most disastrous effect on intelligence and customs, not only for slaves but for their masters. Not simply the moral order but also the very economic order of civil societies is seriously damaged by it. Public welfare is corrupted at its sources. The exploitation of man by man, be it that of the weak by the strong, or of the poor by the rich, is always egotistical and thoughtless of others. Slavery is therefore a supreme crime against humanity; it is logical and just that it should carry its punishment in itself.

Lilian Knowles

From *Economic Development in the Nineteenth Century* (1932)

DURING the nineteenth century two great economic forces were at work in the world – English invention, which for the first time gave man a control over nature, and the French conception of economic liberty which followed on the French Revolution.

The English had by the end of the eighteenth century attained a degree of personal freedom undreamed of by other nations, and England's continental colonies on the mainland of North America, which became the U.S.A. in 1783, had necessarily followed its tradition of individual freedom and initiative. Far other was the development of the continental countries still sunk in serfdom and feudalism in the eighteenth century. The peoples looked to the feudal lord or king for guidance and leadership, and what was done in Europe was done mainly by autocratic monarchs acting according to their own ideas or those of some prominent minister.

In England, Burghley and Elizabeth worked after this fashion, so did Henry IV of France and Sully, Louis XIV and Colbert, but as late as the last quarter of the nineteenth century one finds that Kaiser William I and Bismarck and the Czar and Witte in Russia were the arbiters of the economic life of their countries. In England, after the execution of Charles I, changes came from below and were due to individual initiative. On the continent they still came from above and varied according to the ideas of monarchs.

With the French Revolution there came a great uprising from below, which represented an attempt to attain by revolution and suddenly that personal freedom which in England had been attained by an evolutionary process. Wherever the French armies went under their revolutionary leaders or under Napoleon, they freed serfs, abolished gilds [sic, throughout], introduced new laws of property, organized mediaeval countries on new lines, and made it necessary for monarchs who wished to retain their thrones to attempt to do from above what France had done from below, that is to say, introduce personal freedom.

The interest of the evolution of Europe lies in the attempts of Central and Eastern European governments to remodel their economy under the stimulus given by the French invasions and French ideas. In so far as their evolution demanded machinery and railways, they borrowed their economic equipment from England. The two influences were, however, interdependent. It would have been impossible to fill factories, work blast furnaces, build and operate railways with a people who were tied to the soil or prevented from settling in new places. French influence provided the people, English invention their occupations. It was the French revolutionary ideas of personal freedom that gave the great impetus to the reforms of the period 1806–65 which abolished serfdom in Central and Eastern Europe. It was due to French initiative that the great liberal treaty system of Europe was completed between 1860 and 1870 which meant the abolition of so many commercial and colonial restrictions. It was England, however, that inaugurated the new employments for the people who were now able to migrate; it was England that provided the mechanism and much of the capital for transforming agricultural into industrial states; and above all, it was England that provided in mechanical transport the means for that almost incredible and romantic development of the interiors of continents and the new wandering of the peoples. Railways opened up inland countries; steamship companies advertised for and moved people in millions to the New World; the continent of Africa became the object of intense competition; and the whole world entered into a new economic phase. It is the play of the ideas and inventions of the two giants, England and France, on the feudal agricultural Empires of Central and Eastern Europe, that constitutes much of the fascination of the nineteenth century. It is, further, the reaction of the Old world on the New, transforming the United States, a great empty continent, into a huge food-producing and industrial entity, and the reaction of this New World with its grain and meat exports on the Old, which again helped to alter the whole character of the economic development of Europe after 1870. These stupendous world movements emanating from England and France, transforming Germany and Russia, spreading to the United States, permeating South America, impinging upon Africa and reconstructing India and Japan, reacting on China, colonizing Australia and making its influence felt in remote Pacific islands, constitute the world revolution we have to examine.

Our subject, therefore, embraces first of all the establishment of personal freedom, freedom to move, freedom to buy and sell, free choice of an occupation. After that comes the adoption of machinery, creating new classes, new towns, new wants in raw material, and new facilities of transport. Then follows the railway, making continental areas as accessible and as valuable as countries with large coastlines; and after that follows the steamship, aiding the great migration to those countries and linking up the world in a system of common economic relationships. Inside this great system of world exchange of peoples and goods are the nations, and each nation has its own idea of what should be its proper policy with regard to its own people now that railways and steamships have made new things easily available and men have become capable of a new mobility. It has to develop a new policy for the purpose of expanding its own type of civilization and selling its own goods. Protection or free trade, colonies and markets, raw materials and food stuffs, coal and iron, the creation and control of mechanical transport by sea and land, the regulation of capital and labour – all these become increasingly the object of national concern. The feudal states were naturally the first to evolve state direction in these matters, but the individualist states did not lag far behind. The nineteenth century witnesses first of all a repudiation of state action and a general belief that the state can do no good thing, and ends with a violent reaction from laissez-faire to state control in most spheres of economic life.

The Great Powers fall into two distinct groups, the individualist and the feudal. The individualist countries are the United Kingdom[65] and the United States; and the feudal countries are France, Germany, and Russia with their tradition of royal control. Not merely did the upheaval in France against feudalism react powerfully on the other two, but it occurred just at the time when English mechanism provided new careers and the Americas new outlets. The feudal countries with their backward agricultural populations could not leave things to individual initiative, as did England and the United States. The direction and assistance from above was necessarily greater. Moreover, with the exception of Great Britain, and to a less degree Germany, the Great Powers even to-day are primarily agricultural communities, and agriculture and agricultural problems have been their main concern. The settling of the questions arising out of the abolition of serfdom, the alteration of the whole methods of agricultural production in the change involved from serf to free labour, the introduction of intensive agriculture – all these questions, remote from England, have been of primary importance on the continent of Europe. The task of England, with her engineering and machine production and her labour questions, has been to work out the problems connected with the new industrial and urban developments. She invented the factory inspector and main

---

[65] Dealt with by Professor Knowles in her *The Industrial and Commercial Revolutions in the Nineteenth Century*.

drainage, the Factory Acts, trade unions, and co-operation. The task of Continental Europe has been, mainly, to solve the questions connected with a backward peasantry just out of serfdom and increased home production in agriculture, combined with protection from American imports. All this has meant in these countries a necessary continuance of direction from above. England, on the other hand, went over to free trade in 1846 and relied on imported foodstuffs. She was not preoccupied until after 1914 about her home production of food.

This late emancipation from feudalism and serfdom on the continent has had very important results in stimulating both co-operative societies and the amalgamation of businesses to form combinations. Accustomed to work together for common cultivation on a manor, co-operative societies in agriculture are almost natural to peasants in feudal countries such as Denmark, Germany, and Russia. Accustomed to being organized from above, businesses will fall easily into line for common action to regulate production or stimulate the export trade. The slow growth of co-operation and combination in England may be ascribed to its historical training in individual action. In the United States co-operation hardly makes any headway, while the typical combination there is the trust or single firm, not as in Germany a combination of firms all retaining their individuality but co-operating for common purposes.

Another grouping of the Powers is, however, possible. Instead of classing them as feudal or individualist states, they may be divided according to whether they are primarily agricultural or primarily industrial states. This brings into one category the two most industrialized Powers, England and Germany, in contrast with the two great agricultural Empires, the United States and Russia, while France holds a position midway between them.

Each of these Powers has become conscious of its economic wants and each believes that it has a civilizing mission in the world. Hence the great expansion of Russia in Siberia; of the United States in Mexico, Alaska, the Philippines, and the region of the Panama Canal; of France with its great colonial Empire in Indo-China, Madagascar, in the Sudan and west Africa, to say nothing of its Mediterranean colonization in Algeria, Tunis and Morocco; and England with its quarter of the globe. The Pacific became a new object of rivalry and spheres of influence in China were a manifestation of the new economic imperialism. Thus the various national policies were reinforced by a policy of expansion for national purposes.

Thus it is seen that personal freedom, involving agricultural reconstruction, engineering and machine production, mechanical transport, and national expansion for markets and raw materials, are the main economic features of the nineteenth century.

The attainment of personal freedom meant the final abolition of serfdom in France in 1789, in Germany and Austria-Hungary between 1806 and 1848, and in Russia between 1861 and 1865. The abolition of slavery in the British Empire in 1833, in the French dominions in 1848, and in the United States in 1862–3 followed as a matter of course. As, however, the feudal lord had been judge and administrator of his district, the abolition of his power over the serfs meant a complete recasting of the administration in rural districts. In the towns the gilds had restricted the choice of an individual's occupation and had circumscribed settlement within the urban areas. Personal freedom did not merely mean the abolition of serfdom; it meant the overhauling and liberalizing of gild restrictions.

The gilds had, however, been largely responsible for town administration and their reform meant also the reconstruction of urban governments. Even free men, that is to say, men who were not serfs, had been prevented from moving from place to place by settlement laws. The food supply of each area was so precarious that all districts resented the intrusion of new comers and the gilds were always afraid of rural craftsmen who might work more cheaply and undercut prices; it is a phase of the perennial duel between town and country. It was characteristic of the trend towards personal freedom that, during the nineteenth century, these restrictions on movement were modified. The general result was free movement and free choice of an occupation, an intensified migration and the growth of towns. This new personal freedom meant in Europe a complete reconstruction of agricultural life. Agriculture had been mainly based on the communal cultivation of strips in the open fields supplemented by great wastes for fuel and fodder when the crops were growing. With the abolition of serfdom there came the break-up of the communal system, the enclosure of the strips, the break-up of the wastes, and the introduction of separate and individual ownership and intensive cultivation with greatly increased yields. Agricultural tenures were altered no less than agricultural methods. In the United States the freeing of the slaves meant the break-up of the large estates of the South and equally a new system of agricultural tenures and methods. Everywhere the law had to be recast to fit the new conditions of ownership designed for persons who were free to buy and sell, free to move, free to acquire land, free to leave it by will, free to marry and free to emigrate, all of which things were new for the bulk of population [sic] in the nineteenth century, and it is in this direction that the influence of France has been paramount. Serfdom was inconsistent with liberty, equality, and fraternity. In his Codes, Napoleon provided a new legal basis on which the new systems of personal freedom could rest.

The industrial revolution hinged on the development of steam power, the use of coal, the smelting of iron, the rise of engineering, machines and machine tools, and the development of industrial chemistry. The two most highly industrialized nations in 1815 were England and France. Germany was purely agricultural, divided by innumerable internal tariff barriers and bad roads. She was a very poor country with little or no capital. Russia was a self-sufficing Empire, dependent upon serf labour for agriculture and for her industrial production upon serf workshops.

The United States were, in 1815, a strip of Western territory bordering the Atlantic, cultivating cereals and exporting tobacco and cotton, and relying on imports for the bulk of their manufactured articles. The nineteenth century witnessed the inauguration of industrialism in these three great agricultural states. All three developed coal and iron, engineering and machine making; all three developed the textile manufactures; all three developed the inevitable concomitant of machine production, namely, mechanical transport, more particularly railways. The industrial revolution is a marked feature in New England after 1840, in Germany after 1860, and in Russia after 1890.

The industrial changes gave rise in each country to a new labour movement. The old gilds decayed, trade unions arose, and new theories for the reconstruction of society were enunciated to which were given the comprehensive title of Socialism. Alongside these new theories there developed an industrial code of great elaborateness and intricacy, designed to prevent some of the worst evils of the change. Just as the agricultural changes had meant a new legislation, so the industrial changes meant a new administration by inspectors, a new code of industrial legislation and a new educational system.

Mechanical transport, by means of the railway and the steamship, meant the penetration of great land with the result that new Empires and new international rivalries were created. There was a new mobility of goods and bulky articles, and foodstuffs like wheat and meat were moved for the first time in large quantities.

There was also a new mobility of persons, and that not merely of Europeans but of Asiatics, creating new problems of race exclusion and colour rivalry and new questions as to the maintenance of the standard of life. Americans and Australians were faced with the necessity of preserving their standards of life as against Eastern European immigrants with their lower standards, and have had to devote much thought to the question of the exclusion of Japanese and Chinese.

Margery Perham

From *Native Administration in Nigeria* (1937)

Some of the weaknesses of the Colonial Service arise from conditions which can hardly be changed. Yet it is better to recognize them if only to maintain a constant effort to mitigate their pathological effects upon Native Administration.

Chief among them is the temporary nature of the officers' service. They are passing only the central years of their lives in a strange country, and it is too much to expect that all of them will take its fortunes and future very deeply to heart. If this is true of Administrative Officers who generally pass their whole service in one territory, it is much more true of governors and senior departmental officers who pass from one territory to another. The Administrative Officer's service, moreover, is cut into numerous fragments as he moves about from place to place and tribe to tribe. Nothing is more deadening and more destructive to good work than these perpetual changes of posting. The tour in Nigeria is, for reasons of health, necessarily short. If, as so often happens, it is passed in two or more different stations, or even if the expectation of such a transfer hangs over the officer, it is impossible for him to feel a serious sense of responsibility for the people in his charge or to make that extra effort which is required to study their customs and language.

It is therefore possible that at any given moment a large proportion of the Service, from the highest to the lowest, may be deficient both in knowledge and interest, and content themselves with taking short views about the problems of the territory. For the average man there is a tendency, of which he may be unconscious, to regard the country not as it is or might be but as the stage set for an individual career. Where this is so, the unambitious will be content with the minimum of work by which a presentable routine can be maintained, while the ambitious will express his energy in impressive schemes of reform or, at least, of change. Not only ambition but beneficence may urge an officer who is conscious of the limits of time, but not of the human conditions in which he works, to cultivate that most abundant and illusory African crop of quick results upon paper.

The pressure of our administrative conditions in Africa is towards a superficially competent Government acting through African subordinates who, whether or not they are the natural leaders, become by our use of them a class whose interests and standards separate them from the mass of the people. All African governments are tempted to invest individual native agents, who may or may not be indigenous authorities, with extraordinary powers for the rapid enforcement of measures which we regard as necessary to efficient administration. At best this method is politically sterile. At worst it may lead to gross hidden oppression which may not stop short – I write advisedly – of torture and murder. To penetrate to the masses and discover their needs and the effects upon their lives of our measures is an exacting task which produces few results for presentation in annual reports.

It may, indeed, oblige District Officers to proffer the unpopular advice that schemes of development initiated by higher officials should be slowed down or abandoned. The docility of the Africans and the apparent plasticity of their social life is a further encouragement to superficial plans. Africans do not immediately register our mistakes but allow them to accumulate until those responsible for them have long since left the province, if not, indeed, the country.

So long as the obvious results of mishandling the human factor are not immediately apparent, it is to be feared that sociological investigation will remain the last of the many inquiries which African Governments finance. There is a disposition among Englishmen who pride themselves upon being practical to regard any deliberate concern with the psychological aspect of affairs as academic – using the word in a depreciatory sense – or sentimental. When, as so frequently occurs, by our misunderstanding of this factor, we find ourselves in very practical and expensive difficulties, we extricate ourselves by means of a common sense which prompts us to use the minimum of coercion and to combine it with investigation. We do not, however, seem to acquire the foresight which is the obvious lesson of these events.

In Northern Rhodesia, Nyasaland, and Zanzibar, our attention has lately been called to the unfortunate results of administrative mistakes due largely to inadequate knowledge of the subject people. We have seen the part played by this cause in the Aba riots. The Nigerian Government has, perhaps, gone farther than most in its employment of anthropology, and in promoting investigation by its officers, which, though its scientific value may be limited, brings them into more intimate and sympathetic contact with their people than is possible in the ordinary course of their work. Yet Nigeria's achievement is still small beside the great need for knowledge. It may, therefore, be accounted in Nigeria's favour that some of her people are less tractable than in the east and south of Africa, and therefore supply a partial check upon faulty administration.

The Development of Native Society

Fuller knowledge would affect the whole tone of our administration by giving us a greater realization of its difficulties. The situation in which a handful of officials has almost complete control over the lives of millions of another race is accepted by most Englishmen as a perfectly normal situation for which a suitable routine can be devised. If its abnormality were more often recognized, our governments would be less complacent and exacting, and their servants would have less hesitation in reporting an inevitable measure of failure.

The African situation is, indeed, not so simple as it appears even for those governments, British or foreign, which aim at a clear-cut objective of economic self-interest or assimilation and have absolved themselves from any obligation to study native facts and feelings. Indirect rule offers a more complex problem, not because it is less clear in its aims, but because these envisage a synthesis between European and African culture which has to be developed rather than defined.

To maintain the conditions in which this development is possible is the great problem of indirect rule. By its success in this it must stand or fall. Those who believe that human, and especially, perhaps, primitive, society is organic expect it to live and grow in any conditions by some mysterious natural law. Unfortunately history teaches that there are circumstances in which men cannot achieve effective social organization. In Africa we are setting heavy burdens upon native institutions which have been weakened by the abnormal strain of the last thirty or forty years. The internal effects of this strain, which escape the eye of the administrator, have lately been investigated by the anthropologists. It is not possible to discuss here the valuable evidence they have already collected. Speaking generally, they reveal to us small groups which were held closely together by the internal needs of an almost self-contained economy, and by the pressure of external forces, human and physical. These have suddenly found themselves embraced by a world economy and an imperial order. The pressures have been relaxed and the healthy tension in which the entire social organization was held has been slackened. Some, perhaps most, of the purposes which these institutions were designed to meet are now fulfilled for them by external agency. Their members, yesterday active, independent, and self-reliant, have passed under the control of foreigners remote in culture from them-selves, and suffer to-day a sense of bewilderment and inferiority that diminishes their full human stature. Yet the groups do not, as some critics of indirect rule assume, dissolve. Their institutions, even if weakened, persist, and their members remain united by their culture, their language which is part of their culture, and their common associ-ations and territory. A wider sense of civic obligation does not conveni-ently spring into being to fit the new political and economic boundaries, and it is the main belief underlying indirect rule that this sense can best be developed through a gradual extension of existing social conceptions. These small societies will not grow and adjust themselves unless their members are given a sphere for the display of initiative. Yet the tendency of all our African administration is to narrow this sphere almost to nothing by over-regulation, and only in one or two parts of Africa has a conscious effort been made to preserve it. Even in Nigeria the margin in which Native Authorities can exercise choice is narrow. In the Emirates there is always the danger that the Native Administrations will become bureaucracies, to which the whole motive power is supplied by British officials. Inquiry, for example, elicits few items in the estimates which are due solely or even mainly to native initiation.

Mr. Victor Murray claims that the degree of independence demanded by Khama and Moshesh comes nearer to the ideal of indirect rule than anything found in the home of that doctrine.[66] This sugges-tion contains sufficient truth to make it worth consideration by the Nigerian authorities. But it over-simplifies the problem. We must remember, firstly, that the Bamangwato and Basuto chiefs have not been able to retain all the powers claimed by their great predecessors. Secondly, that their powers, because they have been subject to little study or guidance by officials, have not been used to help the people to adapt their lives to changing conditions. It is true that the Protectorates are in an especially vulnerable position owing to their relationship with South Africa, but it is doubtful whether any African tribe can make the adjustment which conditions demand unless more active European guidance is given to the process. The vast majority of Africans are not able to understand the new world of which they have been made members. They cannot even define the stresses to which their own societies are being subjected.[67]

---

[66] 'Education under Indirect Rule', *Journal of the Royal African Society*, July 1935, pp. 245–7.

[67] For a discussion of these problems in the Protectorates, see *The Protectorates of South Africa*, by M. Perham and L. Curtis, 1935.

We have here the main difficulty in Native Administration. A mean has to be found between the over-regulation which, even under a system of indirect rule, can drain the remaining sense of responsibility from tribal communities, and, upon the other hand, a laisser-faire attitude which allows them to drift into unforeseen maladjustments or even dangers. I believe that almost everywhere in Africa, even in Nigeria, we err upon the side of over-regulation. We are tempted farther along this path by the impressive results that can be obtained by compulsion, or something very near it. There is, indeed, real difficulty in judging whether the material benefits to the people for which, at best, this compulsion is used, out-weigh any invisible injuries it inflicts upon their social character. It may be too soon to judge of these effects; it is certain that we make insufficient attempt to do so.

The government that decides to allow Africans scope for choice and adjustment must, as Lord Lugard pointed out in his Memoranda, be prepared to take risks and to tolerate much that we regard as abuse. The head of such a government may be obliged to take a stand against criticism, even from England, where that is offered in ignorance of the African background, and to refuse to follow some single regrettable incident by general restrictions that would weaken the educational value of the whole system. Yet, as Sir Donald Cameron taught, it must not go so far in this direction as to resign its own leadership towards civilization.

The mean between the extremes is clearly not an easy one to find, and it should be constantly shifting as the people advance in civilization. No formula can be of help: the decision for each group will be found only by good judgement based upon sufficient knowledge.

Sibyl Crowe

From *The Berlin West African Conference, 1884–1885* (1942)

This study is primarily a diplomatic not a legal one, its object being to set[68] the Berlin West African Conference of 1884–5 in its true relation to contemporary history. The importance of the conference[69] as a landmark in international law, has in fact been exaggerated, for when its regulations are studied it can be seen that they all failed of their purpose. Free trade[70] was to be established in the basin and mouths of the Congo; there was to be free navigation of the Congo and the Niger.[71] Actually highly monopolistic systems of trade were set up in both these regions.[72] The centre of Africa was to be internationalised.[73] It became Belgian.[74] Lofty ideals and philanthropic intentions were loudly enunciated by delegates of every country to the conference.[75] Only the vaguest and most unsatisfactory resolutions were passed concerning the internal slave trade, the one humanitarian question of any importance to be discussed at its sittings; whilst the basin of the Congo, if not the Niger became subsequently, as everyone knows, the scene of some of the worst brutalities in colonial history.

---

[68] Cf. Appendix I.

[69] Cf. J. S. Reeves, *The International Beginning of the Congo Free State*, p. 50 (though afterwards he contradicts, p. 65). H. E. Yarnall, *The Great Powers and the Congo Conference, 1884 to 1885*, pp. 76, 78. A. B. Keith, *The Belgian Congo and the Berlin Act*, p. 57. E. Banning, *Le Partage Politique de l'Afrique*, pp. 5–6, 91–2, 154–5.

[70] Cf. General Act, Chapters iv and v. (Accounts and Papers LV, 1884–5: C. 4361: C. 4739. Documents Diplomatiques – Affaires du Congo et de l'Afrique Occidentale 1885 (Livre Jaune). E. Hertslet, *Map of Africa by Treaty*, Vol. I, pp. 21–45).

[71] General Act, Chapter ii.

[72] Cf. For *Congo* – J. S. Keltie, *The Partition of Africa*, pp. 215–16, 219–22. Reeves, p. 8. Keith, pp. 79, 81–2. H. H. Johnston, *Colonisation of Africa by Alien Races*, p. 348.

For *Niger* – Johnston, p. 192. Keltie, pp. 274–5. W. N. M. Gear, *Nigeria under British Rule*, pp. 183, 187–8.

[73] Cf. Protocols of Conference (Accounts and Papers LVI, 1884–5: C. 4361), Protocols IX and X. L.J., Congo, 1885. Cf. ALSO Reeves, pp. 73–4. Keltie, p. 214. Keith, pp. 64–5.

[74] Keltie, pp. 201–2, 215–16. Keith, pp. 66–7, 137–44.

[75] General Act, Chapter ii. Cf. below, p. 103.

As regards the more distant future, it was originally stipulated that the Conventional Basin of the Congo,[76] a huge area, which, besides the Congo Free State, comprised parts of French equatorial Africa, of German Cameroons, of Portuguese Angola, of the future British colony of Rhodesia, of Italian Somaliland, and of territories of the Sultan of Zanzibar (which later became British and German East Africa),[77] should be neutralised in time of war. Actually it was found necessary to make neutrality optional. Only the Congo Free State opted for neutrality,[78] and this neutrality was violated by Germany in 1914.

Last but not least, and this is the feature of international law most commonly associated with it, the conference made an attempt to regulate future acquisitions of colonial territory on a legal basis. But here again, its resolutions, when closely scrutinised, are found to be as empty as Pandora's box. In the first place,[79] the rules laid down concerning effective occupation, applied only to the *coasts* of West Africa, which had already nearly all been seized, and which were finally partitioned during the next few years; secondly, even within this limited sphere the guarantees given by the powers amounted to little more than a simple promise to notify the acquisition of any given piece of territory, *after* it had been acquired, surely on every ground a most inadequate piece of legislation.

Important questions of a territorial nature which may have avoided serious conflict,[80] and in this sense made a real contribution to international law, were undoubtedly settled whilst the conference was sitting. But they were officially outside its programme, were not once mentioned during its meetings and formed no acknowledged contribution to the act which embodied its results.[81] It is true that the conference also facilitated, *after* it had broken up, a series of bi-lateral agreements made between 1885 and 1886 by powers interested in Africa. These agreements may also have avoided friction, and may therefore also be considered to form a contribution to international law. But they were essentially a continuation of the earlier "ex officio" achievements of the conference, not of its actual work. Besides this they covered a very short span of time, and must not be confused with any far-reaching effect which the conference may have had, even *indirectly*, on international rivalry in Africa during the next fifty years or so. This appears to have been negligible.

---

[76] Cf. G. L. Beer, *African Questions at the Peace Conference*, pp. 196–7. Banning, *Partage*, p. 90.
[77] Cf. below, pp. 135–9.   [78] Cf. Beer, p. 263.   [79] General Act, Chapter vi.
[80] Cf. below, Part II, Chapter v, pp. 152–75.   [81] Cf. Banning, *Partage*, pp. 8–88.

The legal significance of the conference, therefore, *dwindles*, when viewed in true historical perspective. But what, for want of a better term, must be styled its immediate diplomatic and political significance, seems, on the contrary, to grow in importance, the closer it is examined, throwing valuable light on historical problems of the first magnitude, and it is for this reason that it has been chosen as the subject of the present study.

This will be divided into two parts:

> The history of events leading up to the conference.
> The history of the conference itself.

Certain main threads will be found running through both, the essentials of the situation being these:

The conference, the first big colonial one in modern times, was held at Berlin between November 15th, 1884, and February 26th, 1885, to discuss outstanding problems connected with West Africa. It was attended by every power in Europe (except Switzerland) as well as by the United States – in all, fourteen powers. Of these fourteen powers only five were of real importance. These were – France, Germany, Great Britain, Portugal, and an ambiguous body called the International Association of the Congo, which had no legal representation there at all, and which was in reality only a cloak to hide the ambitions of Leopold II, King of the Belgians. Its history, therefore, resolves itself principally into the interplay of these five powers. Of these five again, three are more important than the rest. They are France, Germany, and Great Britain. The period under consideration is one in which African and colonial questions generally are still subordinate to European in world diplomacy, colonial issues being more affected by European than European by colonial. Consequently the part played by the *major* European powers is of *major* interest, that of the *minor* ones of *minor* interest.

Amongst these powers again Germany held the commanding position. Hence the importance of an understanding of the policy of Germany, whose immediate interest in the issues at stake is not always clear. The dominating figure in Europe at the time was Bismarck, and it was Bismarck who held the balance between France and England. Not only was Germany dominant in Europe, she was desirous in Africa, and it is in this combination of circumstances that the *raison d'être* of the conference must be found.

Its history bears an intimate relation to the Anglo-German colonial quarrel of 1884–5, and its corollary, the Franco-German entente of the same year (the first and last since 1870), from which the conference sprang. Its conception, it is no exaggeration to say, evolves literally step by step with the growth of friction between England and Germany. It is at once the epitome of, and the index to the outcome of that friction. Each successive stage of Anglo-German tension produced fist vague, then ever more determined approaches of Germany to France. These at first took the form of projects concerned entirely with a conference on the Congo; they were then extended to the Niger; then to the general question of effective occupation on the coasts of West Africa; and finally to an understanding (of which the acknowledged "Anknüpfungspunkt"[82] was hostility to England, on the double basis of Egypt and West Africa.

The Anglo-German quarrel of 1884–5[83] was not only unfortunate but unnecessary. This being so, it is to be expected that the history of the conference should reflect something of its superfluous – perhaps even its mistaken nature – and this is indeed what it does. Arising out of a misunderstanding based on false postulates, it is itself an illustration of the mistakes of that misunderstanding. Its diplomatic results were the exact opposite of what had been contemplated. It was the fruit of a Franco-German entente directed against England. It resulted in a weakening of that entente, and, within the charmed walls of the conference room,[84] though without them the colonial conflict still raged, of a rapprochement between England and Germany on all the most important points at issue, it being discovered, when the representatives of the two countries sat down calmly at a conference table to discuss them, that their interests were practically identical.

This aspect of the conference is of course not the only one of diplomatic significance, but it does seem to be the most important, and the one of greatest general interest, and will for this reason occupy the fullest attention here. The part played by Leopold of the Belgians will take a second place not only because it has hitherto been much more fully dealt with by historians, but also because it is considered that this is where it really belongs. By this it is not meant to minimise, or in any way to overlook, Leopold's role, in the history of the conference. He emerged from it, as Bismarck did not, as a real, perhaps its greatest victor (although this was only realised later). That he did so was due to the mixture of astuteness and energy, comparable in quality, though not, by the necessities of the case, in actual power, to Bismarck's own, with which he succeeded in deceiving all the great powers, including Germany, as to the real nature of his aims. Owing to the skill with which he did this, his sometimes appears as the guiding hand in the very

---

[82] Cf. below, p. 63.   [83] Cf. below, Chapter iii, pp. 34–49.

[84] Cf. R. S. Thomson, *Fondation de l'Etat Indépendant du Congo* (who also comments on this). Also G. Königk, *Die Berliner Kongo-Konferenz, 1884– 5*, p. 185.

complicated negotiations from which he gained so signal a triumph. Nevertheless his activities were always on a secondary plane.

Ultimately the deciding factor in the whole situation was the general trend of Bismarck's policy, both colonial and European. It was no accident that the conference should have been held at Berlin: no accident either that German restlessness should have been the yeast fermenting the mixed African and European leaven in the years 1884–5. Germany, at that time, was the arbiter, in a very real sense, of colonial destinies. With this Ariadne-like caution the reader is now invited to enter the diplomatic labyrinth, where, if he does not succeed as seeing himself as Theseus, he will at least, it is hoped, be prepared to find the Minotaur wearing a Pickelhaube.

Amy Jacques Garvey

From "Chinese Milk Africans in the Caribbean" (1946)

"Life of the people compromises the livelihood of the people, the existence of Society, the welfare of the Nation, and the life of the Masses."   Dr. Sun Yat Sen

Newspaper headlines have a way of sparking inquisitive thoughts, which when satisfied are revealing and for the benefit of those grievously concerned should be well publicized, so that unconscious apathy should not be made a plea for lack of remedial measures.

Two such headlines in a Jamaica newspaper recently deserve our study: "Chinese Here Gave One Hundred Thousand Pounds ($500,000) for Their Wounded Soldiers," and "Nutrition Report Has Startling Findings."

The malnutrition refers to one million black people of this Caribbean Island, and the contributions to China were from seven thousand Chinese. How come? Because Jamaicans (people of African descent) are being used to underwrite these magnificent contributions. Similar conditions prevail in Trinidad and British Guiana.

Chinese Retail Monopoly

How did they get to the Caribbean? What has been their process of financial development?

After the emancipation of black slaves, plantation laborers were scarce, and some indentured ones were imported from India, but in 1845 this immigration was stopped, and the Sugar Planters succeeded in getting Government permission to import indentured Chinese laborers to the Islands.

The first batch landed in 1853. Trinidad got 990. British Guiana got 647. Jamaica got 472 from Colon, but they were rather worn-out by hard work on the Panama Railway.

In 1884, another batch landed in Jamaica, a total of 696 including 109 women consigned to the Sugar Estates. In the course of years, they deserted the Estates, tried their hands at retail grocery trading instead of manual labor, and now monopolize both the retail and whole grocery trade.

Oriental Technique

What then is this technique they employed to accomplish this, seeing that they were comparatively few in numbers in alien countries, and handicapped by language? Clannishness, still tongues but active brains; and a pooling of all their resources for their individual good, and common interest.

Communal Banks (Fui) are operated among themselves, so as to finance individuals in business, by group systems excluding the Islanders.

Two other forms of painless, but painfully effective draining of the finances of these Caribbean Territories are "Drop Pan" and "Pekka Pow" games of chance, not legalized, therefore not supervised by the government, nor does the government get one cent in revenue from their operations.

Lottery Banks

In Jamaica alone there are nine banks under the Pekka Pow system, similar to the numbers racket in the U.S.A., with "Drawings" twice daily. If one hits 8, the top score for say one pound ($5.00), the banker is likely to disappear for a time.

The player has no recourse to law, as the game is illegal; anyway, he buys his mark from an agent, who pretends to keep a grocery shop, as a blind for the more lucrative business of "Pow."

The agents have runners (Jamaicans) who usually get caught with the slips by police, and have convictions recorded against their names. The agents have dispatchers who rush all monies to the bankers, so the police won't get the cash, even when they are raided [sic].

As for the bankers, they are barricaded behind zinc fences, steel-barred windows, iron doors with electrical bells to the inner chambers, and rumor says, under-ground passages and vaults, so that if the police succeeded in breaking in the outer chamber, he would see an innocent Chinese sipping tea.

Expanding Monopolies

The average intake from the most popular and prosperous banks is one thousand pounds **($5,000, approx.)** each daily. As one "Powist" said "your estimate is conservative, but how can I stop when I have dropped so much in it already?"

With such a steady flow of capital into their coffers, they not only control the wholesale and retail grocery trade, but are stealthily entering the manufacturing field as well, in such commodities as soft drinks, liquors, butter-fat products and ice cream.

Before the war, they dictated prices on groceries, which are wholly imported, so that the consumer was held to pay for the goods his people derived no benefit from by way of employment, nor for commercial expansion, or cultural development [sic].

Build Modern Homes

They no longer live behind their shops, but have built two-storied buildings – living upstairs, and dividing downstairs into grocery and liquor bars – the latter trade they are trying to monopolize too. During the war when groceries were scarce, importation and prices controlled by the government, the majority of these groceries were sectioned off and used as ice cream parlors.

In country districts, impoverished small planters, harassed by drought and hurricanes, are forced sometimes to swap their produce for groceries at give-away prices, so as to provide themselves with urgent necessities, thus enabling the Chinese grocer to become a produce dealer at a handsome profit [sic].

Panama Curbs Chinese

Similar conditions obtained in Panama, but being a republic and not under alien absentee control, she restricted Chinese immigration, but they took advantage of loop-holes and continued to get into the country as picture-brides and British subjects from Hong Kong [sic].

Further laws were made prohibiting their entry. Between 1940–41, laws were made to nationalize commerce, and enforce the employment of Panamanians in their commerce and industry.

These laws have caused many Chinese businesses to close down; those who acquired Panamanian wives transferred their businesses to the latter, or to their Panamanian-born sons.

Retains Racial Ties

"Organic laws make a child born of Chinese parent or parents a Chinese, no matter where born," so says a Chinese official, and they live up to this.

The darkest looking ones of black mothers are recognized equally as Chinese, sent to Chinese schools, and show their allegiance to China in a financial way. Thus, they swell their numbers and financial power, at the expense of Africa, and peoples of African descent. Voluntarily, they support their Consuls and the branches of the Kuomintang Party networked in these areas [sic].

Future Expansion

They are planning as soon as shipping permits to send for more of their people in these already overcrowded Islands, where thousands of the Islanders are returning from farms in the U.S.A. and from the battle-fronts of the world [sic].

What will be the out-come? What are the underlying motives of these people, who owe all to the Islands, and yet give all to China?

Dr. York C. T. Shen, China's Minister to Panama, gives us an inkling of his message on the occasion of the celebration of their republic, when he said:

Diplomatic Analysis

"The Chinese government deeply appreciates the patriotic activities and great amount of contribution from the **Overseas Chinese, including our dear colonies in the Caribbean area** ... The far East, and the Caribbean are in reality getting nearer and closer to each other."

They waited until the Chungking government gave the order to celebrate V-J Day for 3 days, then, every Chinese and half-Chinese, British-born and Chinese-born, closed all their businesses, ceased all work, to parade, celebrate, and to give more money to China. Are they just "colonies" of Chinese in the Caribbean now? Or will they be colonies of China later on?

Mary Macdonald Proudfoot

From *Britain and the United States in the Caribbean* (1954)

The relationship between the developed and the relatively undeveloped areas of the world is now generally recognized as one of the major problems of our time. In the past the strong spilled out over their weaker neighbours, often invigorating those able to survive the ordeal. By these means the backward countries sometimes became, in their turn, the leaders in the march of civilization. Public opinion in the democracies of the west has long ceased to commend these ancient and ruthless processes. The alternative policy of the nineteenth century was the doctrine of *laissez faire*, every state, as every individual, being left to work out its own salvation. The political complement of *laissez faire* was the policy of non-annexation, individuals and societies being left to develop in a condition of free competition. But already, before the end of the century, the more thoughtful were beginning to discover that *laissez faire* provided no real solution because the undeveloped countries could not advance except by contact with those more fully developed. In the nineties the positive conception of trusteeship, first enunciated by Burke, was being advanced by ministers – notably Lord Salisbury and Joseph Chamberlain – and by administrators led by Lord Lugard, in the direction of developing backward areas in the interests at once of their own inhabitants and of the world in general. But just as, formerly, the old annexationist process fell into disrepute, so the philosophy of trusteeship, implying as it did a paternal relationship between advanced and backward peoples, has now been discarded as undemocratic. All states must be treated as equal in status, however unequal in fact. A new method has therefore to be evolved whereby undeveloped areas may be developed without conquest, and without the establishment or continuance of any form of paternal overlordship.

This difficult problem has acquired a much greater urgency within the last decade, because formerly separated and self-sufficient parts of the world are being linked swiftly together by scientific and other discoveries, so that the enormous disparity in standards of living, as between the inhabitants of the few advanced and the many backward areas, becomes ever more apparent. And, as it becomes more apparent, it becomes also more ominous, for just as a handful of rich men cannot long live happily, or, indeed, safely, surrounded by slums, so the very small minority of relatively advanced countries can no longer isolate themselves and hide their riches from their hungry neighbours. The advanced countries must, in fact, for their own safety, develop the undeveloped areas.

The present relationship between the metropolitan or colonial powers and their own dependent areas is one facet of this much wider problem. It would be generally admitted that so far no satisfactory solution has been evolved, either by the United Kingdom, with its long and varied experience as an imperial power, or by the United States, with its great wealth and its enlightened determination, in the years since the ending of World War II, to use a great part of that wealth to eliminate the slum areas of the world. It would seem highly desirable that these two Great Powers, each shouldering heavy responsibilities, should pay close attention to each other's methods, so that each may derive the maximum benefit from the experiences of the other.

The object of this study is to focus attention upon a very small area, viz, the British and American Caribbean islands, in an attempt to review these different methods in some detail, and to determine what has been, in each case, the results. This book is not, however, intended as an exhaustive area study, the basic material for which is not yet available. Indeed, the paucity and uneven value of this material are major handicaps for any study of West Indian affairs today. For instance, although a good deal of valuable economic data can be obtained, very little basic research has been done by anthropologists or sociologists and relatively little information of any kind is available relating to the smaller islands.

[...]

The Attitude of the Metropolitan Powers Towards Social Problems

This situation constitutes a challenge to the metropolitan powers, both of whom have been much disturbed, and particularly over the last decade, by the prevailing state of affairs. In the United Kingdom, the full revelation of conditions laid bare by the Report of the Moyne Commission in 1939 caused the British government much anxiety, an anxiety shared by public opinion in general when the Report was officially released in 1945. The B.W.I. includes some of Britain's oldest colonies, and it was felt to be particularly unfortunate that conditions should be so bad in territories which had been in some cases for centuries under British rule. In any case it was considered essential that since self-government was the avowed goal, every effort should be made to raise existing low social standards as a preliminary to the successful working of self government. This was the *raison d'être* for the establishment of the D.W.O. The same anxiety to improve social conditions was prevalent in the United States. Here, however, it stemmed from rather different causes. There was no intention in Washington at the beginning of World War II that the status of the dependent territories should be changed, and thus no theorizing as to whether it would be practicable to give political independence to societies where social standards were low and economic dependence very marked. On the other hand, the conviction grew, from the beginning of the New Deal era in the thirties, that the inhabitants of a United States dependency were entitled, by a kind of moral law, to enjoy the same standard of living as inhabitants of the continental United States.[85] It would, in fact, be hard to base particular policies on this theory, since standards of living vary very greatly within the United States, and it is doubtful whether, for instance, a Negro agricultural labourer in Mississippi has ever had appreciably better prospects than the average agricultural labourer, whether white or Negro, in Puerto Rico. None the less this theory, if it can be so described, has been most valuable, particularly to the Puerto Ricans, as a slogan, because it has resulted in very general acceptance by progressive groups in the United States of the claim made by the dependencies that whenever federal 'hand-out' legislation benefiting states of the Union is passed by Congress, this should, in equity, be made applicable to Dependencies.[86] The Virgin Islands of the United

---

[85] See Pamphlet, *Social Security for Puerto Rico*, Antonio Fernos-Isern. Resident Commissioner for Puerto Rico in Washington (1949). 'It is only fair to extend to Puerto Rico all federal grant-in-aid and social security laws, in order to give every citizen in Puerto Rico the same chance in life as is given to every citizen in the States.'

[86] The decision of the Senate Finance Committee in May 1950, to exclude Puerto Rico and the Virgin Islands from expanded federal social security benefits, occasioned a storm of protest from city officials, labour leaders, civic organizations, and leading churchmen, who assailed the action as 'un-American' and 'openly discriminatory'. *New York Times*, 14 May 1950. It may be noted, however, that protests of this kind commonly stem from New York, where there is general desire not to increase the already large Puerto Rican community by any further widening of the already yawning gulf between the generous social services offered in the city and the somewhat meagre ones available on the island. There are also Puerto Rican votes to be considered. See Ch. VII.

States bases its claims to federal assistance on similar grounds,[87] but is usually less successful in persuading Congress of their validity. Few of the groups who sponsor this idea take into account the fact that the Caribbean dependencies do not, as do the states of the Union, pay federal income tax, and that they are assisted by the federal government in a variety of ways that the states of the Union are not.

On the British side, the size of the Colonial Empire, with its vast areas either still to be developed or more usually incapable of development, and its teeming millions of backward and primitive people, many of them still in the tribal stage, would make any such theory of equality self-evidently ludicrous. Because of this, there is perhaps a greater readiness in Whitehall than in Washington to accept existing conditions or, at any rate, to be ready to work from one decade to the next at slow and unspectacular improvements, without the stimulus of the hope that if sufficient energy is expended a new world can be created overnight. At best, the British attitude will in the long run pay dividends in terms of gradual but lasting progress; at worst it can result in a complacent contentment with things as they are. At best, the American attitude gives birth to a fierce determination to raise standards, and, if possible, to do so overnight. Enthusiasm is catching, and part of the present success of the Puerto Ricans in 'Operation Bootstrap' is a result. Few Americans have, however, much sense of time and when the impossibility of achieving desirable reforms overnight becomes too clearly apparent, the reaction is sometimes the lethargy of despair.

Both metropolitan powers at first attempted a solution to their common problem of a very low living standard in the dependencies by pouring in financial assistance to help build up the exiguous social services available. Both, however, came to realize that more effective if less immediate assistance could be given by developing the economies of the dependencies in the hope that their peoples would, in the end,

---

[87] See, for instance, the testimony given by Mr. Roy W. Bornn, Director of Social Welfare, Virgin Islands of the United States, before the Ways and Means Committee of the House of Representatives, on the importance of extending further titles of the Social Security Act to his islands. May 1949. Mr. Bornn drew attention to the disparity between old age assistance payments in the United States and in the Virgin Islands. '... old age assistance payments last December in the United States under the Social Security programme ranged from $16.38 a month in Mississippi to $78.18 a month in Colorado. Note this figure – the continental low of $16.38 a month in Mississippi is nearly four times the $4.62 old age average in the Virgin Islands! The continental high, in Colorado, of $78.18 per person per month is seventeen times the Virgin Islands rate.'

be able to support for themselves the social services they desired.[88]
This standpoint has been adopted with enthusiasm by the present
leaders in Puerto Rico, although it would seem that the concurrent
attempt to get Puerto Rico included in federal 'hand-out' legislation of
all kinds has already resulted in the building up of a standard of living
for at least some sections of the Puerto Rican people which cannot be
maintained without substantial mainland aid. The peoples of the
British dependencies have been, with a few exceptions, much less
enthusiastic in their attempts to create a new world for themselves,
and the sense of urgency and determination characteristic of dominant
groups in Puerto Rico is as a rule conspicuous by its absence in the
British islands.

In the British territories, the United Kingdom pattern has been
followed in that, by tradition, reliance has been, until very recent times,
placed primarily on private charity,[89] voluntary service[90] and self-help,
for the solution of social difficulties, territorial governments standing by,
as it were, ready to assist in so far as they were able in real emergencies if
all other sources failed.

[88] See, for instance, the conclusions reached by the Comptroller for Development and
      Welfare, on the housing problem in the British West Indies: 'The housing problem in the
      West Indies cannot be solved by subsidies under the Colonial Development and Welfare
      Acts of 1940 and 1945. If all the funds available over the next ten years were devoted to
      housing improvement, conditions would still be far from satisfactory. This stark fact has
      to be faced in forming a housing policy. In any country, economic improvement is the
      forerunner of housing improvement, and consequently Development and Welfare policy
      aims at concentration of capital expenditure on "development" projects calculated to
      raise the general standard of living: the emphasis lies on welfare through development.
      Until economic planning of regional and local resources improves the bulk and
      distribution of wealth, there is no hope for widespread housing improvement in the
      West Indies.' D.W.O. Report, 1945–1946, p. 117.
[89] For instance, between 1667–1732, 218 endowments were left in trust by Jamaican
      settlers for the maintenance of schools and churches; and there are still in Jamaica
      today some fifteen endowed secondary schools. In Antigua estates were donated in the
      seventeenth century from the profits of which medical missionaries were to be trained to
      minister to the slaves. There are many other examples. Even today, local planters and
      merchants donate substantial sums of money for charitable purposes, such as orphan
      children's homes, almshouses, and the like.
[90] Voluntary service has, however, always been of a somewhat abbreviated variety. Wives of
      the planters, and of expatriate business men and officials, have never, apparently, felt
      obligated to undertake the kind of social work which would even today be accepted as a
      normal duty in any English rural community. The Moyne Report of 1939 remarked on
      the fact that '… people of leisure show little interest in social welfare', Ch. XI, para. 28.
      See also address given by Miss Dora Ibberson, C.B.E., at the University of Puerto Rico
      in 1946, reprinted in *The Welfare Reporter*, vol. V, no. 18, September 1946. Monthly
      magazine of Jamaica Welfare (1943) Ltd.

These extra-governmental sources have never, it need hardly be said, been in any way commensurate with the needs of the people and the most cursory study of the reports of successive governors, officials, missionaries, and emissaries of the home government ever since Emancipation indicate [sic] the anxiety felt at one time or another by responsible people in all callings over every facet of B.W.I. life.

4

Anticolonialism

Introduction by Sarah C. Dunstan and Patricia Owens

Interdisciplinary scholarship on the intellectual history of imperialism is a thriving subfield in studies of political thought.[1] Indeed, to a large degree, the history of international thinking is a history of imperial and inter-imperial thought and practice.[2] If early international relations meant race relations, then *anti*colonialism, the intellectual and political project of understanding, resisting, and transforming global racial and colonial exploitation, is also fundamental to the history of international thought and practice. Both imperial and anti-imperial thought were published in the earliest journals on international relations.[3] Yet, anticolonialism was later constituted as a discourse outside and implicitly against the formal institutionalization of the academic discipline of International Relations (IR) in the second half of the twentieth century. Today, work on the intellectual and political history of anticolonialism is flourishing, alongside and often in conversation with scholarship on the closely related history of Black internationalisms.[4] Within these literatures, the most developed engagement with historical women's thought has been scholarship on Black feminist internationalism within the United States.[5] There is also a body of scholarship on Francophone

---

[1] Jennifer Pitts, *A Turn to Empire: The Rise of Imperial Liberalism in Britain and France* (Princeton, NJ: Princeton University Press, 2005); Duncan Bell, *Reordering the World: Essays on Liberalism and Empire* (Princeton, NJ: Princeton University Press, 2016); Adom Getachew, *Worldmaking after Empire: The Rise and Fall of Self-Determination* (Princeton, NJ: Princeton University Press, 2019).

[2] David Long and Brian Schmidt, *Imperialism and Internationalism in the Discipline of International Relations* (Albany, NY: SUNY Press, 2005); Robert Vitalis, *White World Order, Black Power Politics: The Birth of American International Relations* (Ithaca, NY: Cornell University Press, 2015); Vineet Thakur and Peter Vale, *South Africa, Race and the Making of International Relations* (London: Rowman and Littlefield, 2020).

[3] W. E. B. DuBois, "Worlds of Color," *Foreign Affairs*, 3:3 (1925): 423–444.

[4] Pankaj Mishra, *From the Ruin of Empire: The Revolt against the West and the Remaking of Asia* (London: Picador, 2012); Priyamvada Gopal, *Insurgent Empire: Anticolonial Resistance and British Dissent* (London: Verso, 2019).

[5] Cheryl Higashida, *Black Internationalist Feminism: Women Writers of the Black Left, 1945–1995* (Champaign, IL: University of Illinois Press, 2011). On the decisive role of

Black women's anticolonial thought which attained wider influence through anticolonial activism and the crises of the world wars.[6]

Women were central to theorizing and resisting colonialism in its diverse forms and locations. Yet, very little, if any, of this work has influenced contemporary international theory or histories of international thought given the gendered and racialized politics of expectations surrounding intellectual worth and appropriate genre.[7] Indeed, if there is a structural and disciplinary production of women as incapable of generating knowledge about international relations, then the strictures imposed on women of color are still graver. Even work that centers on anticolonialism rarely focuses on women's thought and practice. The very political stakes that led women to deploy genres that allowed them to reach broader audiences with the aim of dismantling imperialism further contributed to their exclusion from even the most serious treatments of anticolonialism. As the selections here illuminate, the choice of genre was often itself an act of anticolonial resistance. The use of media such as poetry or travel memoir enabled thinkers to emphasize the human impact of imperialism and sometimes to avoid government surveillance. So too did it indicate an understanding of the workings of colonialism as simultaneously political and cultural. Empire had to be fought on both fronts. Here we include a wide selection of such work primarily from thinkers working outside academe, though often with advanced degrees, and in

women in the transnational Black nationalist movement in the United States, focusing on the 1920s–1960s and the thinkers Amy Ashwood Garvey, Amy Jacques Garvey, Ethel Collins, Maymie Leona Turpeau De Mena, Mittie Maud Lena Gordon, and Ethel Waddell see Keisha N. Blain, *Set the World on Fire: Black Nationalist Women and the Global Struggle for Freedom* (Philadelphia, PA: University of Pennsylvania Press, 2018). For an account of activist and intellectual movements between 1945 and 1979 of notions of the military "negro domestic" to Black revolutionary woman to African and pan-African woman to Third World Black woman see Ashley D. Farmer, *Remaking Black Power: How Black Women Transformed an Era* (Chapel Hill, NC: University of North Carolina Press, 2017).

[6] See T. Denean Sharpley-Whiting, *Negritude Women* (Minneapolis, MN: University of Minnesota Press, 2002); Jennifer M. Wilks, *Race, Gender, and Comparative Black Modernism: Suzanne Lacascade, Marita Bonner, Suzanne Césaire, Dorothy West* (Baton Rouge, LA: Louisiana State University Press, 2008); Annette K. Joseph-Gabriel, *Reimagining Liberation: How Black Women Transformed Citizenship in the French Empire* (Champaign, IL: University of Illinois Press, 2020).

[7] For extremely rare exceptions see Shiera S. el-Malik, "Intellectual Work 'In-the-World': Women's Writing and Anti-colonial Thought in Africa," *Irish Studies in International Affairs*, 24 (2013): 1–20; and Patricia Owens and Katharina Rietzler (eds.), *Women's International Thought: A New History* (Cambridge: Cambridge University Press, 2021), which includes essays on anticolonial and Black internationalist thinkers, such as Anna Julia Cooper, Simone Weil, Eslanda Robeson, Amy Ashwood Garvey, Mittie Maude Lena Gordon, and Merze Tate.

diverse genres, including journalism, memoir, and poetry, in addition to traditional essay forms.

It is also important to note that all of these selections were published after the First World War and the so-called "peace" that followed, appearing between 1928 and 1964. In many ways, this war was a turning point in anticolonial thinking because it laid bare the fault lines of the so-called "civilizing mission" of European empire.[8] The peace treaties invited a re-imagining of world orders that opened up new avenues for transnational collaboration.[9] In the ensuing decades, anticolonial vocabularies and arguments were fundamentally shaped by these new relationships, as well as reactions to the changing nature of empire and imperialism, the onset of the Second World War, and the political project of decolonization. We can see these contours of anticolonial thought in the following selections, three of which are in translation from the original French, a reflection of the wider influences upon anticolonial thinkers operating in Anglo-American contexts.

Our first selection is one of the earliest theorizations of "Black Internationalism," Jeanne "Jane" Nardal's (1900–1993) "Internationalisme noir," published in 1928. Black internationalist consciousness, she argued, had its origins in the global conflict of the First World War. The widespread experiences of total war mirrored the experiences of Black populations around the world, yet the violence of war, and a disenchantment with the possibility of civic equality in the metropole, led to a rediscovery of African culture, of *la vogue nègre*. Nardal grew up in the French colony of Martinique, before moving to Paris to study literature and French at the Sorbonne in 1923 (she and her sister, Paulette, were the first Antillean women to be admitted).[10] Extreme racism and sexism in the imperial capital prompted their involvement in anti-racist movements. For Jane Nardal, this activism manifested itself primarily through her journalism and editorial work, much of which sought to show that imperial and racist hierarchies would be overcome

---

[8] See Michael Adas, "Contested Hegemonies: The Great War and the Afro-Asian Assault on the Civilizing Mission Ideology," *Journal of World History*, 15 (2004): 31–63.

[9] See Erez Manela, *The Wilsonian Moment: Self-Determination and the International Origins of Anticolonial Nationalism* (New York: Oxford University Press, 2007).

[10] Paulette Nardal, who in 1946 became the first woman of color appointed to the Division of Non-Self Governing Territories at the United Nations, was also a committed activist and intellectual. Her work could equally well have been included in this section, but this particular text by Jeanne Nardal best speaks to the internationalist focus of this volume. See Emily Musil Church, "In Search of Seven Sisters: A Biography of the Nardal Sisters of Martinique," *Callaloo*, 36:2 (2013): 375–390; Emmanuel Kwaku Akyeampong, Henry Louis Gates, and Steven J. Niven (eds.), *Dictionary of African Biography* (New York: Oxford University Press, 2012), 390–392.

only when Black peoples were recognized as co-contributors to their respective national cultures. To this end, she advocated the production of literature and art that married what she saw as the best of French culture, *latinité*, with the best of African culture, *Africanité*.

Nardal's essay articulated ideas about race that were central to *négritude*, an influential French political cultural movement of the 1930s, and appeared in the newspaper Nardal had co-founded, *La Dépêche africaine*,[11] which was published primarily in French but with a regular English section. Its circulation peaked at around 10,000 in its four-year run.[12] *La Dépêche africaine*'s mission was to serve as "an independent journal of correspondence between blacks, for the moral and material interests of the indigenous populations, through the objective study of the larger colonial questions considered from political, economic, and social points of view."[13] Nardal's article was an unusual foray into cultural nationalism for the periodical, but it nonetheless fit directly into *La Dépêche africaine*'s efforts to intervene in the contemporary imperial order. Nardal was read by influential African American intellectuals such as Eslanda Robeson, who also appears here, as well as Alain Locke and W. E. B. Du Bois, all of whom advanced anti-racist and anticolonial theory.

In style and substance, Suzanne Roussy Césaire's analysis of international order was not dissimilar to Nardal's, and the two moved in similar intellectual circles in Paris in the 1930s. However, Césaire's work was far more engaged with the contemporary French movement of surrealism. Born in the French territory of Martinique in 1913, Césaire studied literature at university in Toulouse and then Paris at the École normale supérieure. In the middle to late thirties, she became involved in the cultural political movement of *négritude* and worked with the poets and politicians Léopold Sédar Senghor and Aimé Césaire on the groundbreaking Black activist journal *L'Étudiant noir*.[14] Suzanne's intellectual work has long been overshadowed by Aimé, whom she married in 1937. Nevertheless, the essay excerpted here, "The Great Camouflage," needs to be understood in relation to their intellectual collaboration on the

---

[11] For more on her activism see Jennifer Ann Boittin, "In Black and White: Gender, Race Relations, and the Nardal Sisters in Interwar Paris," *French Colonial History*, 6 (2005): 120–135.

[12] T. Denean Sharpley-Whiting, "*Femme négritude*: Jane Nardal, *La Dépêche africaine*, and the Francophone New Negro," *Souls: Critical Journal of Black Politics & Culture*, 2:4 (Fall 2001): 11; Sharpley-Whiting, *Negritude Women*.

[13] "Notre but – Notre programme," *La Dépêche africaine*, February 15, 1928, 1.

[14] For more on this see Sarah C. Dunstan, *Race, Rights and Reform: Black Activism in the French Empire and the United States from World War I to the Cold War* (New York: Cambridge University Press, 2021).

relations between race, culture, and human freedom. The piece appeared in 1945 in *Tropiques*, a journal they helped to launch under the Vichy regime in Martinique during the Second World War. *Tropiques* was explicitly intended as an assertion of Black cultural originality, an attempt to meet the challenge laid down in Nardal's "Internationalisme noir." "The Great Camouflage" is filled with a surrealist poetic language unlike the more academic tones of the contemporary colonial policy theorists in our section on Imperialism. Césaire's tone and form was partly a reaction to the colonial context in which her work was circulated: despite its explicitly political nature, *Tropiques* managed for some years to pass under the radar of the Vichy regime as it was dubbed a magazine of "folklore." International political thought was disseminated under the guise of cultural and literary writing, a technique common in francophone anticolonial thinking in this period.

Césaire paints a picture of the Antilles as the product of centuries of French colonialism and slavery. This history cut both ways, placing the islands in a position of eternal struggle. For the Antillean who is the "great-grandson of a colonist and a black slave woman," the sense of belonging to France is always undercut by racialized identity. French colonial officials demarcated the boundaries of French belonging in Martinique. Yet they were filled with dread by their "colored descendants." By blood and education, Antilleans are French, yet also not considered part of "Western civilization" due to the colonial logics of race (227). In tension with this tangled colonial dynamic is the ever-present conflict between the processes of modernization epitomized by the United States and the tentacles of "the old continent," Europe (226). In both cases, people of color suffer, but "blacks in America … suffer most" due to a "day-to-day humiliation" that knows no bounds. As remedy to this tug of war and the Antillean struggle, Césaire proposed African solidarity as a source of revitalization because it had endured, despite European imperialism. In explicitly gendered language, she wrote, "Africa is there, present, that she waits, immensely virginal despite the colonization, turbulent, devourer of whites" (228).

En route to Africa in 1936, Eslanda Goode Robeson (1895–1965) stopped in Paris, where she interviewed the French-Congolese politician Jane Vialle (1900–1993). Vialle, who appears later in this volume, shared Robeson's sense that only women took a serious interest in the plight of other women, and that international solidarity was the only way to improve the conditions of women of color around the world.[15] White

[15] Jane Vialle to Eslanda Robeson, *Africa Diary*, no. 2, July 4, 1946, Eslanda Robeson Collection, Moorland Spingarn Research Center, 123–124. On their exchange see Sarah

supremacy permeated world order and had to be dealt with in international terms. Born to a middle-class family in Washington, DC, Robeson began her intellectual training as a chemist, completing a degree at Columbia University in 1923. She married Paul Robeson, the hugely influential singer, actor, and political activist, which both enabled and constricted Eslanda's political and intellectual work and recognition. In the 1930s, she studied at the London School of Economics with celebrated Polish anthropologist Bronisław Malinowski, and in 1946 she gained a doctorate in Anthropology from Hartford Seminary. She credited her move to London for sparking her interest in African diaspora and countries.[16] The London circles in which she moved certainly exposed her to the dynamics of empire and a critical anti-imperialism: she was friends with, among others, Trinidadian intellectuals and activists Claudia Jones, who appears later in this section, C. L. R. James, and George Padmore.[17] During her residence in London, Robeson took her first trip to Africa in 1936, accompanied by her young son. Her 1945 travel memoir *African Journey*, excerpted here, was based on her research for and diary of the trip.

The travel memoir is not a genre conventionally recognized in international intellectual history. Nonetheless, the text is inflected with Robeson's anthropological training and keen sense of the mechanisms of racism in the contemporary world order, of her experiences as an active participant in international affairs, as well as a critical observer. As she wrote, "the Negro problem was not only the problem of the 13 million Negroes in America, but was and is the far greater problem of the 150 million Negroes in Africa, plus the problem of the 10 million Negroes in the West Indies."[18] In other writings, Robeson elaborated her call to internationalism in explicitly gendered terms.[19]

Unlike Robeson, Nardal, or Césaire, Claudia Jones (1915–1964) did not have access to higher education, but nonetheless successfully

---

C. Dunstan, "'Une Nègre de drame': Jane Vialle and the Politics of Representation in Colonial Reform, 1945–1953," *Journal of Contemporary History*, 55:3 (2020): 645–665.

[16] Eslanda Robeson, *African Journey* (New York: John Day, 1945), 13. For other work by Robeson see Pearl S. Buck with Eslanda G. Robeson, *American Argument* (London: Methuen & Co., 1950); Eslanda Goode Robeson: *Paul Robeson, Negro* (New York: Harper Brothers, 1930).

[17] Barbara Ransby, *Eslanda: The Large and Unconventional Life of Mrs. Paul Robseon* (New Haven, CT: Yale University Press, 2013), 85–90.

[18] Robeson, *African Journey*, 13–14.

[19] For more on Robeson see Imaobong Umoren, "Ideas in Action: Eslanda Robeson's International Thought after 1945," in Patricia Owens and Katharina Rietzler (eds.), *Women's International Thought: A New History* (Cambridge: Cambridge University Press, 2021), 93–114.

combined theoretical innovation with anticolonial praxis.[20] Following the economic crash in Trinidad, Jones's family migrated to Harlem, New York in 1924. After graduating from high school, she worked low-wage jobs to support her family. She joined the Young Communist League and by 1936 was writing for the Communist Party (CPUSA) newspapers the *Daily Worker* and the *Weekly Review*, an article from which appears in our section on Geopolitics and War.[21] By 1945, Jones was editor of the "Negro Affairs" unit at the *Daily Worker* and became active in national women's movements.[22] Between 1947 and 1952, she worked on the National Peace Commission of the CPUSA, focusing on the US–Korean War.[23] As the international landscape crystallized into the Cold War and the domestic political climate increased pressure on those with communist affiliations, Jones was arrested several times between 1948 and 1955 and served eighteen months in prison before her deportation to Britain in 1955. In London, she continued her writing and activism, launching her own newspaper in 1958, the *West Indian Gazette*, which she ran until her early death in 1964.

Jones's essay in this section was first published in *Freedomways*, an African American political and cultural journal founded by W. E. B. and Shirley Graham Du Bois, among others, in 1961. From the beginning, the journal took strong anticolonial and anti-racist positions, reporting on the American Civil Rights Movement as well as movements for independence around the world. Jones's article is a searing assessment of the international and imperial forces that prompted the emigration of over a quarter of a million people from the newly independent West Indies to Britain in the decade spanning from 1954 to 1964. Their presence tested the British Government's commitment to a "multi-racial" Commonwealth and exposed the ongoing racist legacies of imperialism, which are discussed in our section on Population, Nation, Immigration.[24] Jones's observations on the intersections between racial identity, national belonging, and access to citizenship rights are predicated on an analysis of the continuing impact of imperialism upon

---

[20] Sarah C. Dunstan and Patricia Owens, "Claudia Jones: International Thinker," *Modern Intellectual History*, First View (2021): 1–24.

[21] The definitive biography remains Carole Boyce Davies, *Left of Karl Marx: The Political Life of Black Communist Claudia Jones* (Durham, NC: Duke University Press, 2008).

[22] Claudia Jones, "Dear Comrade Foster: The Following Is the Autobiographical (Personal, Political, Medical) History That I Promised … Comradely, Claudia Jones (December 6, 1955)," *American Communist History*, 4:1 (2005): 89.

[23] Cristina Mislán, "Claudia Jones Speaks to 'Half the World': Gendering Cold War Politics in the *Daily Worker*, 1950–1953," *Feminist Media Studies*, 17:2 (2017): 281–296.

[24] Colin Grant, *Homecoming: Voices of the Windrush Generation* (London: Vintage, 2019).

international and "domestic" orders. Her writing illuminates how imperialism shifted when the "empire came home" in "post-war" Britain.

One of Jones's intellectual heroes was the abolitionist Frederick Douglass, who, as she noted more than once, went to Ireland to express solidarity with the struggle for independence against British colonial rule, a solidarity not always reciprocated by Irish-Americans.[25] Unsurprisingly, Nardal's observation of the upending effects of the First World War also applied to Ireland's struggle. Here the Irish revolutionary intellectual Dorothy Macardle (1889–1958) details the situation in 1916, in the middle of the inter-imperial war with Germany. Britain had introduced military conscription to Ireland, in addition to espionage and surveillance, arrests and prosecutions, and the violent and nonviolent suppression of dissidents. Macardle joined the armed struggle against British rule, becoming an active member of the *Cumann na mBan*, the women's auxiliary corps of the Irish Volunteer Forces, and was arrested and interned during the Irish War of Independence (1919–1921).

The Irish Republic, first published in 1937 but released in multiple subsequent editions, is still considered an authoritative history of the violent conflicts in Ireland during the 1919–1923 period, encompassing the War of Independence, the founding of the Irish Free State, and the subsequent Civil War. Macardle opposed the Anglo-Irish Treaty, which partitioned Ireland and betrayed the republican cause. The Free State remained a dominion within the British Empire and Northern Ireland, settled by royalist/loyalist Protestants, remained part of what the British state referred to as "the United Kingdom," a term that republicans continue to reject. The subsequent civil war between pro- and anti-Treaty forces resulted in a victory for the pro-Treaty side due to military support from the British. In our selection from *The Irish Republic*, Macardle analyzes the major political, military, and diplomatic events immediately leading up to the armed insurrection that became known as the Easter Rising of April 1916 and the proclamation of the Irish Republic. She conveys the political and military dilemmas; divisions within the republican-nationalist movement; the role of Irish American organizations; and the alliance of convenience with Britain's enemy, Imperial Germany, in hope of weapons and military training.

In the 1930s, Macardle worked as a journalist at the League of Nations, taking a far stronger anti-fascist, anti-Nazi position than the Irish government, which pursued a policy of neutrality in the Second

---

[25] Noel Ignatiev, *How the Irish Became White* (London: Routledge, 1995); Claudia Jones, "The Spirit of Frederick Douglass," *Weekly Review*, March 17, 1941.

World War, in order to avoid another civil war.[26] Una Marson
(1905–1965), Jamaican feminist and pan-Africanist intellectual,
developed her international thinking before the rise of fascist
internationalism but, as seen in the excerpt below, became intensely
involved in anti-fascist anticolonialism, particularly after the Italian invasion of Ethiopia in 1935.[27] Born in Jamaica to middle-class parents,
Marson, like Jones, had no formal education beyond high school. Yet,
in 1926, she became an editor of *Jamaica Critic*, and later edited and
produced her own magazine, *The Cosmopolitan*, while publishing critically acclaimed feminist poetry.[28] She moved to London in 1932, though
she frequently traveled back to Jamaica, becoming an active member of
the League of Coloured People, the British Commonwealth League, and
the International Alliance of Women. Marson worked at the League of
Nations headquarters in Geneva prior to taking up a post at the Ethiopian
ministry in London, which included administrative work for Emperor
Haile Selassie and the Ethiopian minister, Charles Martin.

We have excerpted Marson's poem "To Jo and Ben," which appeared
in *The Moth and The Star*, dedicated to Charles Martin's sons, who, as
the poem's dedication describes, were "brutally murdered in April
1937 at Addis Ababa by the Italians." "Bombs rained/ From hell's
corsairs/ Upon You/ But you were still/ Unscathed. /Conquered your
land/ But Still/ With the unconquered/ Band of gallant warriors/ You
stood … To free the land/ That gave you birth/ From savagery's dark
reign." Like several other thinkers in the volume, Marson can be situated
within Black internationalist traditions, specifically as a leading member
of the West Indian intellectual tradition in Britain. Poetry was frequently
used as a medium of political protest within anticolonial and anti-
imperial movements, in part because it was not usually subject to police
or state surveillance and less likely to end in reprisal. Whilst Marson did
not make her choice for this reason, it is nonetheless important to observe

---

[26] Also see Dorothy Macardle, *Children of Europe: A Study of the Children of Liberated Countries; Their War-Time, Their Experiences, and Their Needs, with a Note on Germany* (London: Gollancz, 1949). For biographical and contextual analysis see Nadia Clare Smith, *Dorothy Macardle: A Biography* (Alstead, NH: Woodfield Press, 1999); Leeann Lane, *Dorothy Macardle* (Dublin: University College Dublin Press, 2019).

[27] Also see Sylvia Pankhurst's article on the Italian invasion of Ethiopia in the section on "Geopolitics and War."

[28] Delia Jarrett-Macauley, *The Life of Una Marson 1905–65* (Manchester: Manchester University Press, 1998); also see Alison Donnell, "Una Marson: Feminism, Anti-colonialism and a Forgotten Fight for Freedom," in Bill Schwarz (ed.), *West Indian Intellectuals in Britain* (Manchester: Manchester University Press, 2003), 114–131; Imaobong D. Umoren, "'This Is the Age of Woman': Black Feminism and Black Internationalism in the Works of Una Marson, 1928–1938," *History of Women in the Americas*, 1:1 (2013): 50–73.

that this poem is part of a much larger tradition of anti-imperial protest, particularly in the Caribbean, in which she was a leading figure.[29] As the first Black female producer for the BBC, Marson developed the hugely influential Caribbean Voices, a weekly feature within the Calling the West Indies series, the BBC's first program for Caribbean listeners. In its run from 1943 to 1958, the program was a critical platform for Caribbean writers and poets. In the words of Barbadian poet Edward Kamau Brathwaite, Marson's Caribbean Voices was "the single most important literary catalyst for Caribbean creative and critical writing in English."[30]

The only daughter of Sir Bache Cunard – the heir to the British Cunard shipping line – and the American-born London socialite Mary Alice Cunard (née Burke), Nancy Cunard (1896–1985) was an unlikely anticolonial thinker. And yet, in all her professional endeavors, including activism, poetry, journalism, and publishing, she forcefully rejected the gendered and classed trappings of her birth. Yet her relationship to empire, anticolonialism, and the question of racial difference was defined by her identity as a wealthy white woman.[31] Cunard was to some extent conscious of her own positionality. She adopted an anti-racist platform, explicitly disavowing whiteness, or particular versions of whiteness that emphasized racial otherness.[32] She also used her privilege to amplify Black critiques of racism and imperialism.

Cunard is perhaps best known for editing the 1934 volume *Negro: An Anthology*, an 855-page collection of essays, short stories, sheet music, drawings, and poems from over 150 Black thinkers and artists, with some white contributors. The volume was explicitly designed to assert the diversity and reality of Black humanity, including a significant number of women. Two contributors, Zora Neale Hurston and Pauli Murray, also appear in this volume.[33] Cunard's anthology was an impressive and significant intervention into interwar discussions about race.[34] She laid out her own thinking on racism and colonialism, arguing that "it is

---

[29] See Sarah C. Dunstan, *Race, Rights and Revolution: Black Activism in the French Empire and the United States from World War One to the Cold War* (New York: Cambridge University Press, 2021).

[30] Edward Kamau Brathwaite, *History of the Voice: The Development of Nation Language in Anglophone Caribbean Poetry* (London: New Beacon, 1984), 87.

[31] Jane Marcus, *Hearts of Darkness: White Women Write Race* (New Brunswick, NJ: Rutgers University Press, 2004), 7.

[32] Maureen Moynagh, *Nancy Cunard: Essays on Race and Empire* (Peterborough: Broadview, 2002), 35.

[33] Nancy Cunard, *Negro: An Anthology* (London: Wishart Press, 1934).

[34] Thabisile Griffin, *"I Seem to Be Thinking of Africa All the Time": Nancy Cunard's "Negro: An Anthology,"* Master's thesis, University of California, Los Angeles, 2014, ii.

Communism alone which throws down the barriers of race as finally it wipes out class distinctions."[35] The essay we extract here, from Cunard's 1942 *White Man's Duty: An Analysis of the Colonial Question in the Light of the Atlantic Charter*, is less obviously communist. However, Cunard adopts a similar framing to *Negro: An Anthology*, setting out her argument in the preface before showcasing the thought of George Padmore, one of the most influential Black and Trinidadian thinkers and activists of the twentieth century.

Padmore had worked in the United States and Europe as a Communist organizer before breaking with the Comintern to pursue Pan-Africanist organizing in Britain. Cunard and Padmore became friends and collaborators through his involvement with *Negro: An Anthology*. The bulk of *White Man's Duty* comprises the transcript of Cunard's conversation with Padmore. She prompts him to explain "his analysis and solution of the problem" of world peace and empire, including reaction to the 1941 Atlantic Charter, President Roosevelt and Prime Minister Churchill's statement on their goals for the post-war order. Neither Cunard nor Padmore believed that the Charter's rosy vision of freedom included people of color or colonial subjects. In particular, Britain's plan for peace had to properly address the question of Empire. Instead of maintaining the racialized norms of empire – which were also manifested in Britain through an unofficial color bar – Cunard urged her readers to force Britain to "become the *real* British 'Commonwealth'" in which all members had equal rights.

Literary scholar Maureen Moynagh has described Cunard as a kind of "political tourist," noting that her work took on the aspect of both the imperial gaze of an aristocratic white woman and the commitment of a political activist.[36] As a collector of African art in the 1920s – most famously her collection of African jewellery – Cunard's interest in Africa and the African diaspora was heavily embedded in the contemporary *vogue nègre*. This was symptomatic of the Parisian landscape she inhabited in this period: many of her friends and lovers were important figures in surrealism and modernism, both movements that took inspiration from imperial imaginaries of Africa. In the late 1920s, Cunard developed friendships with African American writers visiting Paris, such as novelist Langston Hughes. This opened her eyes to the realities of racism in the United States. Her burgeoning awareness was cemented when, in 1928, she began a romantic relationship with the jazz musician

---

[35] Nancy Cunard, "Introduction to Negro: An Anthology," in *Negro: An Anthology* (London: Wishart Press, 1934), 14.
[36] Moynagh, *Nancy Cunard*, 14.

Henry Crowder. The mixed-race couple were often refused entry to restaurants in Britain, and they were often the object of scorn in public.[37] Indeed, *Negro: An Anthology* was funded by the damages Cunard won from a libel suit against the British press for the racial slurs used to describe their relationship.

Our final selection comes from another white woman whose eyes were opened to the horrors of colonialism and racism, Simone Weil (1909–1943). Primarily through the work of Helen M. Kinsella, Weil is one of the few historical women to receive minor acknowledgment in IR's existing canon.[38] Yet this attention is meager relative to her influence, particularly for her best-known work on the concept of power and the question of rights. Weil's anticolonialism emerged from her political experiences as a teacher and activist in imperial France. Born in Paris to secular Jewish parents, Weil originally trained as a philosopher, and was the only woman in her class at the École normale supérieure. Upon graduation in 1931, she worked as a teacher at *lycées* and became active in labor unions, teaching philosophy to workers and protesting for better conditions. Drawn to Marxism, she took a sabbatical from teaching in 1934 to work as a member of the class she saw as most oppressed, unskilled women factory workers, and participated in the infamous 1936 Paris factory strikes. However, by 1931, after reading reports of French colonial reprisals in response to the Yên Bái uprising in Indochina, Weil became increasingly critical of French colonialism and drew comparisons between the oppression of the working classes in France and France's colonial subjects.[39]

Weil's sense of these parallels deepened after the fall of France in September 1939. Initially moving with her family to Vichy France, she worked for the Resistance, distributing one of its more influential newspapers, *Les Cahiers de témoignage chrétien*. Eventually she was forced to leave France for New York, before moving to London to work

[37] Nancy Cunard, *These Were the Hours* (Carbondale, IL: Southern Illinois University Press, 1969), 148.

[38] See Helen M. Kinsella, "Simone Weil: An Introduction," in Felix Rösch (ed.), *Émigré Scholars and the Genesis of American International Relations: A European Discipline in America?* (London: Palgrave, 2014), 176–197; and Helen M. Kinsella, "Of Colonialism and Corpses: Simone Weil on Force," in Patricia Owens and Katharina Rietzler (eds.), *Women's International Thought: A New History* (Cambridge: Cambridge University Press, 2021), 72–92. For a selection of Weil's work see Simone Weil, *Letter to a Priest* (New York: Routledge, 2014 [1951]); Simone Weil, *The Need for Roots* (London: Routledge, 2002 [1952]); Simone Weil, *Selected Essays* (London: Oxford University Press, 2015 [1962]); Simone Weil, *Simone Weil on Colonialism: An Ethic of the Other* (Lanham, MD: Rowman & Littlefield, 2003).

[39] Simone Pétrement, *Simone Weil: A Life*, trans. Raymond Rosenthal (New York: Pantheon Books, 1977), 218, 284–285.

with the Free French Forces. The article below was written from London in 1943 not long before her death from tuberculosis. "The Colonial Question and the Destiny of the French People" is one of thirteen articles she wrote questioning the ethics of colonialism. It combines Weil's analysis of the legitimate uses of force and individual freedom with a stark critique of European imperialism through a comparison of French colonialism to the German occupation of France. Complaints about Germany's infringement of French sovereignty could logically be applied to the French military occupation throughout its empire. "If the methods of colonial conquest are examined in detail," Weil wrote, "the analogy with Hitlerian methods is obvious" (221). Only a twisted logic premised on false racial hierarchies could provide support for imperialism. Even if such racial logics were accepted, Weil argued, then "the force upon which a colonial empire rests is a naval fleet." "If it is force that decides, France has lost hers; if it is a question of rights, France never had the right to determine the destiny of non-French peoples" (221).

In the Introduction to the ground-breaking volume *Non-Western Thought and International Relations*, Robbie Shilliam suggests that "It is trite, but necessary, to state that women thinkers have been central to – and often originators of – the many projects undertaken to understand and transform a global modernity defined by imperialism and colonialism." Yet, "no women thinkers" are included in the volume, leading Shilliam "to consider how unexpectedly – but smoothly – the same exclusion of the agency of women enacted by imperial and colonial powers can be unintentionally repeated in projects such as this."[40] Given the location and positionality of the editors, as well as the volume's temporal and geographic focus, we also reproduce imperial and colonial exclusions in this anthology. As indicated in the Introduction, our main focus is international thought in Anglo-American locations, but we have included some continental European thinkers given the influence of European – and, in this case, specifically Francophone – traditions on Anglo-American international thought. The selections here are not comprehensive. There were numerous women anticolonial thinkers and activists in other colonial locations where the influence of their ideas was curtailed. Reading this work, largely by non-Anglophone and émigré thinkers, in conjunction with the writing in the preceding section on "Imperialism," should give many of us pause. The relatively small

---

[40] Robbie Shilliam, "Non-Western Thought and International Relations," in Robbie Shilliam (ed.), *Non-Western Thought and International Relations: Imperialism, Colonialism and Investigations of Global Modernity* (London: Routledge, 2010), 10.

numbers of women of color writing about international relations in the Anglo-American academy can be explained by the racial, class, and gendered hierarchies of and exclusions from higher education. The relative absence here of Anglophone white anticolonial thinkers cannot be so easily explained away.

Sarah C. Dunstan and Patricia Owens

Jane Nardal

From "Internationalisme noir" (1928)

There is in this postwar era a lowering or the attempt at a lowering of the barriers that exist between countries. Will the various frontiers, custom duties, prejudices, cultural mores, religion, and languages allow this project to be realized? We want to hope for this, those of us who note at the same time the birth of a movement not at all opposed to this first one. Blacks of all origins, of different nationalities, mores, and religions vaguely feel that in spite of everything they belong to one and the same race. Previously the more assimilated blacks looked down arrogantly upon their colored brethren, believing themselves surely of a different species than they; on the other hand, certain blacks who had never left African soil to be led into slavery looked down upon as so many base swine those who at the whim of whites had been enslaved, then freed, then molded into the white man's image.

Then came war, dislocation, blacks from every origin coming together in Europe, the sufferings of war, the similar infelicities of the postwar period. Then snobs – whom we must thank here – and artists launched Negro art. They taught many blacks, who themselves were surprised, that there existed in Africa an absolutely original black literature and sculpture, that in America poetry and sublime songs, "the Spirituals," had been composed by wretched black slaves. Successively revealed to the white world as well as the black was the plasticity of black bodies in their sculptural attitudes, giving way without transition to an undulation, or to a sudden slackening, under the rule of rhythm, the sovereign master of their bodies; in this black face, so mysterious to whites, the artist would discover tones so shifting and expressions so fleeting as to make either his joy or his despair; the cinema, the theatre, the music hall opened their doors to the conquering blacks.

All these reasons – from the most important to the most futile – must be taken into account to explain the birth among Negroes of a race spirit. Henceforth there would be some interest, some originality, some pride in being Negro, in turning back toward Africa, the cradle of Negroes, in remembering a common origin. The Negro would perhaps have his part to play in the concert of races, where until now, weak and intimidated, he has kept quiet.

From these new ideas, new words, whence the creative significance of the terms: Afro-American, Afro-Latin. They confirm our thesis while casting new meaning on the nature of this Black Internationalism. If the Negro wants to know himself, assert his personality, and not be the copy of this or that type from another race (which often earns him contempt and mockery), it does not follow from that, however, that he becomes resolutely hostile to all contributions made by another race. On the contrary, he must learn to profit from others' acquired experience and intellectual wealth, but in order to know himself better and to assert his personality. To be Afro-American, to be Afro-Latin, means to be an encouragement, a consolation, an example for the blacks of Africa by showing them that certain benefits of white civilization do not necessarily lead to a rejection of one's race.

Africans, on the other hand, could profit from this example by reconciling these teachings with the millennial traditions of which they are justly proud. For it no longer comes into the head of the cultivated man to treat them en masse as savages. The work of sociologists has made known to the white world the centers of African civilization, their religious systems, their forms of government, their artistic wealth. Hence the bitterness they feel for having been despoiled is understandable and can be attenuated by that peculiar effect of the colonization: that of linking together, or unifying in racial solidarity, and, in spite of the feuds between conquering peoples, tribes who hadn't the slightest idea in this regard.

Along this barely trodden path, American blacks have been the pioneers, I believe. To convince oneself of this, it suffices to read *The New Negro* by Alain Locke, which is slated to appear in French translation by Payot.

The obstacles they encountered (late emancipation, economic slavery still existing in the South, humiliations, lynchings) were so many incentives. And in business and industry, as well as in the fine arts and literature, their successes are impressive, and above all – what interests us here – the prejudices of whites who surround them have produced in them an unparalleled solidarity and race consciousness.

The Afro-Latins, in contact with a race less hostile to the man of color than the Anglo-Saxon race, have been for that reason retarded in this path. Their hesitation, what's more, is a credit to the country that understood it should try its best to assimilate them. Even though their loyalty is reassuring, their love of the Latin country, the adoptive land, and their love of Africa, land of their ancestors, are not incompatible. The Negro spirit, so supple, so capable of assimilation, so discerning, will easily surmount this apparent difficulty. And already, helped, encouraged by black American intellectuals, the young Afro-Latins, distinguishing themselves from the preceding generation, hastening to catch the masses up with those who are evolving in that effect, will go beyond them in order the better to guide them. In tending to this task, formed in European methods, they will take advantage of these methods in order to study the spirit of their race, the past of their race with all the necessary critical verve. That black youth are already taking on the study of slavery, facing up to, with detachment, a past that is quite palpable and so painful – isn't that the greatest proof that there does finally exist a black race, a race spirit on the path to maturity? Those who know how, among black people, certain subjects have recently been taboo can appraise the progress represented by these recent facts.

Dorothy Macardle

The Irish Republic (1937)

By January, 1916, when conscription was made law for Great Britain, the Government's dilemma in Ireland was complete. To force men into active service with an army which they regarded as that of their hereditary enemy was at all times a course full of danger; it was doubly precarious when the men were trained, armed, and resolute to resist. On the other hand, these men, if permitted to remain in Ireland, would give trouble. They were openly preparing for an Insurrection, of which only the date remained in doubt, and James Connolly was asking in *The Irish Worker*, "Are we not waiting too long?"

These Volunteers were holding recruiting meetings of their own; during every week-end the towns and countryside were filled with marching men, some in their green uniforms, others wearing the belts and soft hats which had come to be distinctive of their army; large numbers carried arms. One day they carried out a sham attack on the General Post Office; on St. Patrick's Day they held reviews in all the principal towns in Ireland; on March 28th their Executive published a warning that any attempt to deprive the Volunteers of their arms would be resisted by force. The Dublin Castle authorities knew that this was no empty boast and, while the Chief Commissioner of Police urged suppression, the Chief Secretary and the Under Secretary hesitated to act. They could not, without evidence of hostile association, intern the Revolutionary leaders for any length of time, and such evidence they had not so far been able to obtain.

Undoubtedly there was a section of the British Cabinet – the Ulster Covenanter element – which desired few things more than an outbreak in Ireland that would give the requisite pretext for ruthless suppression of the Irish Volunteers, and there was another section which opposed this attitude, while to avert bloodshed, if possible, was the Dublin authorities' immediate concern.[41]

---

[41] *Royal Commission* 1916 p. 30, paragraph 691.

204

Birrell and his colleagues in Dublin castle resorted to a policy of small legal measures and secret service work by which they defeated their own ends. The suppression of papers continued, a policeman trained as a printer helping to dismantle the machines; raids for arms were carried out until the threat of resistance caused them to be abandoned. Men were charged with "sedition" and imprisoned. Nearly five hundred prosecutions under the Defence of the Realm Act took place in Ireland between November, 1914, and April 15th, 1916. Immense protest meetings were held in Dublin. Speaking at one of these in the Mansion House on March 30th, Eóin Mac Néill said that the Government were attempting to provoke the Volunteers into an outbreak, but that until the Government sent its forces against them the Volunteers would go on with their preparations as before.

The British Administration in Ireland placed its chief reliance, and rightly, on the almost flawless system of espionage carried out by the R.I.C. There was scarcely a square ten miles of Ireland without its Constabulary Barracks at this time, there were over nine thousand officers and men of this semi-military force in the country, armed and trained to shoot and possessing the most intimate knowledge of the daily lives of their fellow countrymen in the districts where they were stationed. They acted as a great Intelligence Service; from almost every part of Ireland they sent to the Castle daily reports recounting even the political sentiments of individuals considered influential or "potentially dangerous." "Disaffected" men and women were closely watched: "I have them under the microscope," Mr. Birrell declared.[42] The police observations were regularly placed at the disposal of the Military Authorities.[43]

The Dublin Castle officials, not unnaturally, supposed that a Rising could not be attempted without a warning reaching them in time. Moreover, there was a large military garrison still in the country; it would be possible to summon five thousand troops to Dublin at a few hours' notice and more could be conveyed from England in one day, should any unexpected outbreak occur.

Birrell relied on these resources and on the fact that the Volunteers were insufficiently armed. Police reports, at the end of March, assured him that in Dublin the Volunteers and the Army between them possessed only about nine hundred rifles and that the total number of arms of all sorts held by the Volunteers in the provinces amounted to 4,466.[44]

---

[42] *Royal Commission* 1916 p. 22, paragraph 539.
[43] *Royal Commission* 1916 p. 15, paragraph 220.
[44] *Royal Commission* 1916, Appendix, p. 123 and paragraph 1259. This estimate proved to be less than the actual number.

This system of spying, benetting the whole Volunteer organization, and of arrests and prosecutions, had become a factor in the counsels of the I.R.B. None of the contingencies which, in 1914, they had envisaged as a signal for a Rising had occurred, but this urgent consideration had arisen meanwhile: if they delayed much their secret preparations would be disclosed, all the leaders imprisoned, the whole organisation destroyed and the greatest opportunity in centuries to achieve Ireland's liberation would be irretrievably lost. Not again, they believed, for many generations, would such an opportunity recur, nor could an organisation such as theirs, if it disintegrated now without action, ever be re-created again. Unless a blow was struck soon, if only as a protest, the Irish people would sink beyond redemption into despair, or worse, into contentment with servitude.

By their writings, many of the leaders were trying to prepare the minds of the people for an attempt. Pearse wrote poems and articles in *The Irish Volunteer* and pamphlets – *Ghosts*, *The Separatist Idea*, *The Spiritual Nation*, and *The Sovereign People* – of which the note was a trumpet call. "There has been nothing more terrible in Irish History," he wrote in *Ghosts*, "than the failure of the last generation. Other generations have failed in Ireland, but they failed nobly; or failing ignobly, some man among them has redeemed them from infamy by the splendour of his protest. But the failure of the last generation has been mean and shameful, and no man has arisen from it to say or do a splendid thing by virtue of which it shall be forgiven."

He questioned whether, by their ingratitude to Parnell, the people had not brought this punishment on themselves.

The leaders realised with complete clarity that the majority of the Irish people were almost lost to all sense of the rights of Ireland as a nation, had learned to rely on the vague optimism of the Parliamentarians and were ready to give thanks for a petty instalment of Home Rule. The Independence movement was the movement of a minority still and those who were ready to give and take life in armed insurrection were a minority in that movement.

They believed, however, that the inherent native passion for freedom was dormant not extinguished, and that only bold action was needed to arouse the people to a sense of their rights, their needs, and the strength that still lay within them unused.

Of the few who proceeded to act by the light of this conviction there was none more persuasive than Pearse or more vehement than Connolly or more unflinchingly determined than Thomas Clarke. Connolly was making delay impossible, declaring that if no one else acted he would go out with a few dozen of the Citizen Army men himself. He and the

Citizen Army were pledged to a Rising. But he hoped for success: he believed if the Volunteers rose throughout Ireland the people would awake to the significance of what was happening and rally to their support.

In January the Supreme Council of the I.R.B. decided on the date when the Rising was to begin. Easter Sunday, April 23rd, was the date they chose. This decision and the intensive preparations which followed were made by the few men who had been working together since 1914 with the help of Thomas MacDonagh, Commandant of the Dublin Brigade of the Irish Volunteers. To the members of the I.R.B., who regarded secrecy as the first necessity of their preparations, James Connolly's open methods and his tendency to precipitate the crisis seemed dangerous – so dangerous that they took the extreme action of arresting him and keeping him under guard until, a few days later, threats from the Citizen Army and Countess Markievicz procured his release. Meanwhile, he had won the leaders over to his own view of the urgency of the situation, and after this he was included in the counsels of the I.R.B., the only person outside its own oath-bound membership taken into its confidence and the only person outside their group to realise that the time of action was so near.

The I.R.B. leaders did not confide their plans to Arthur Griffith, knowing that he would oppose them, nor to Bulmer Hobson, the Secretary of the Volunteers, nor to The O'Rahilly, their Treasurer, nor to Commandant J. J. O'Connell, head of their Military sub-committee, nor even to Eóin Mac Néill, Chairman of the Volunteer Executive and Chief of Staff. All these were known to be in favour of defensive action if the Government should attempt to enforce conscription or to arrest or disarm the Volunteers but to be still against taking the initiative in attack.[45] Thus, while Mac Néill and his intimates on the Executive still supposed that only defensive action was contemplated, to be taken only when the Executive should determine, the secret preparations for Easter went on.

Early in February the I.R.B. Council communicated its project to the heads of the American Clan na Gael, to which they looked for a supply of arms. A message was sent secretly to Devoy. He has recorded his recollection of its terms as follows:

---

[45] See Le Roux, *Patrick H. Pearse*, for details of the relations between Eóin Mac Néill's group and the I.R.B. group on the Volunteer Executive during March and April, 1916, pp. 329 *et seq.*

"The message in a few preliminary sentences described the British military strength in Ireland, and stated that they could not expect the British Government to remain inactive much longer; so they had 'decided to strike on Easter Sunday, April 23.' Then it proceeded to state that they wanted us to 'send a shipload of arms to Limerick Quay' *between April 20 and 23*."[46]

At a meeting at the Old Irish American Club in Philadelphia that message was considered by the heads of the Clan na Gael. They realized now, for the first time, that it would not be possible to send the necessary arms to Ireland from the United States.

"It transpired," John T. Ryan, one of those present, wrote, "that a certain South Atlantic port, through which it had previously been expected shipment could be made, was no longer available for that purpose ... The only possible solution of the problem was to induce the German Military authorities to furnish the arms requested by the Republican leaders in Ireland."[47]

That request was transmitted through the German Embassy to Berlin, and the German reply came to Washington in the first week of March:

"Between 20th and 23rd April, in the evening, two or three steam trawlers could land 20,000 rifles and 10 machine guns, with ammunition and explosives at Fenit Pier in Tralee Bay. Irish pilot boat to await the trawlers at dusk, north of the Island of Inishtooskert, at the entrance of Tralee Bay, and show two green lights close to each other at short intervals. Please wire whether the necessary arrangements in Ireland can be made secretly through Devoy. Success can only be assured by the most vigorous efforts."

The Irish leaders were informed, and agreed to the proposition; through the same American agency further details were arranged with Berlin; these included code-words to be wirelessed from the German ship on approaching the Irish coast: if all were going well *Fionn*; if there appeared to be danger, *Bran*.

Meanwhile John Devoy, with Judge Cohalan, Judge Goff, Joseph McGarrity, T. St. John Gaffney and other leaders of the Clan na Gael proceeded to create an open organisation in the United States. To the Irish Race Convention which assembled at the Hotel Astor in New York on March 4th there came about twenty-three hundred delegates. "The Clan," the Ancient Order of Hibernians and every active organization of Ireland's friends in America took part. The Chairman of the Committee was Judge Goff. This Convention created the "Friends of Irish Freedom

---

[46] Devoy, p. 458. See, also, Casement's Diaries. Another version, apparently erroneous, appeared in *Documents Relative to the Sinn Fein Movement* and the error has been repeated in other writings, including earlier editions of *The Irish Republic*.

[47] *Irish World* (New York), April 11th, 1931.

Organisation" whose objects were "to encourage and assist any movement that will tend to bring about the national independence of Ireland". Its declared aim was to appeal to the Powers after the war on behalf of Irish independence. In order to be listened to at the Peace Conference, John Devoy declared at this meeting, Ireland would have to take action as a belligerent – establish a national government and hold military posts.

The Assembly launched a fund for Irish purposes known as the "Victory Fund." Robert Ford, in his paper *The Irish World* and Devoy and Cohalan in *The Gaelic American*, furthered the fund for all the purposes of the "F.O.I.F."

The question whether the United States could continue to remain neutral in the European War was becoming acute. The German threat to merchant shipping, made officially in February, and British interference at sea with American mails, were creating sharp divisions of feeling and President Wilson was visualizing the possibility of intervention.

On this question the Irish issue was destined to have its effect.

In Ireland the I.R.B. Military Council was completing its plans. The Council appointed Pearse Commander-in-Chief – an appointment which was kept secret for the time, his recognized position as Director of Organisation giving him all the control required. A few more officers were taken into the confidence of the leaders. Thomas MacDonagh approached his Adjutant, Éamon de Valéra, asking him to become a member of the I.R.B. and promising him that he would be required to do nothing more than he had already undertaken, as a Volunteer officer, to do. De Valéra, who disliked association with secret societies, consented only on the condition that he should simply be given his orders when the time came. He was never included in the I.R.B. Councils and his association with the Brotherhood soon after came to an end. Like most of the Volunteer commandants he carried out orders, guessing very little about dissension at Headquarters, but knowing that any day, at any hour's notice or with no notice, the Volunteers might find themselves in action.

Easter Sunday had been decided upon as a day on which the Rising was to begin. On April 3rd Pearse gave public orders for a three days' march and field manoeuvres to be held throughout Ireland on Easter Sunday. This was accepted without question by all except Eóin Mac Néill, Bulmer Hobson and their immediate associates. These had already become suspicious. Mac Néill summoned the Headquarters Staff and demanded a promise from Pearse, Kent and MacDonagh, who were present, that they would give no order, outside routine, to the Volunteers, without his endorsement. This undertaking they gave. They realized that Mac Néill had it in his power to wreck their enterprise at the last moment by issuing a countermand.

The knowledge that the Volunteers' Chief of Staff and Secretary and the majority of the members of the Volunteers' Executive were opposed to a Rising was one source of anxiety to the Military Council; another was the question of arms.

Sir Roger Casement was still in Germany, anxious and very ill. His project of forming an Irish Brigade amongst the prisoners of war met with no great success; only fifty-two men had joined and the German promises to give these instruction in the use of machine guns had not been kept. He had hoped, moreover, for a great German expedition to Ireland with German officers, with submarines, with at least two hundred thousand rifles and with machine guns for the use of his brigade. The knowledge that only a cargo of twenty thousand rifles and ammunition was to be sent reduced him to despair. He never realized that the Clan na Gael, on behalf of the I.R.B., had accepted this offer and counted on nothing more, or that a landing of Germans, other than a few officers, was not asked for or desired by the leaders at home.

Una Marson

From "To Joe and Ben" (1937)

(Brutally murdered in April 1937 at Addis Ababa by the Italians)

As David and Jonathan
So you seemed to me
In your love and devotion
One for the other.

They sent you forth
From "England's pleasant land",
Home of your fond adoption,
Of early boyhood's years –
They sent you forth
To the battle's front
To fight for a country
Yours, and yet not yours
By unfamiliarity.

I wept for you
As you two gallant sons
Went forth
From the brightness
Of an English summer
To die
On the mountain heights of Ethiopia.
I saw the tears
In your bright eyes
As you stood
Side by side
As ever you had stood –
I felt the swell of your throat
As bravely smiling
You bade farewell.

Forth you went
To your homeland

Gallant sons
Of Ethiopia
So young
And so beautiful
In your
Youthful splendour.
There were not enough
Of Ethiopia's youth
To dye her fields
Blood red
So you went forth;
But Nature cherished you,
Her darlings,
Grown in another clime,
Nurtured in her tongue,
Bred in her customs;
You were too young
And brave
And gentle
And so death
Passed you by.
Bombs rained
From hell's corsairs
Upon you
But you were still
Unscathed.
Conquered your land
But still
With the unconquered
Band of gallant warriors
You stood
Side by side,
In danger undivided.

One more gallant task,
One more desperate rush
To free the land
That gave you birth
From savagery's dark reign
And then –
Death met you,
Called you by name,
Not in the midst of battle,
Not hewn down
In heated blood
But after hellish tortures
You were murdered
In cold blood

As traitors
To the land
For which you died.
Jonathan and Benjamin
Two gallant sons
Of Ethiopia
Tender and young
And fair as women
Lay cold and dead
Side by side.
As they had lived
In love together
Even in death
They were undivided,
Even the death
Of traitors.

God, I know
That these thine own
And thousands more
Cut down in youth
And beauty
Are not dead,
They live forever
In our hearts
And their spirits
To earth will come
Again in other form
That they may live
For that high destiny
Which brought them
Earthwards.

God in heaven,
This hate and greed
That brings forth war –
When shall it cease?
Dost thou unmoved
Watch the destinies
Of man
Thy own creation?

Nancy Cunard

From *White Man's Duty* (1942)

Autumn 1942 – the third anniversary of the declaration of War has come and gone and at this time the thoughts of men and statesmen, particularly in Great Britain and the USA, are focussed not only on the struggle, and on victory over Nazi-Fascism, but on after-the-war reconstruction and a new policy of life for humanity – for the whole of humanity.

Never before in history has so much been said and insisted on for a total remaking of existence in the different countries of the earth. At the cost of this, the Second World War, what transformation of the social and economic world situation is being envisaged? Are the white peoples to be the sole beneficiaries?

British and the United States leaders in clear terms tell us: "No. This is to be for *all* peoples, for *all* races."

Worlds pronounced by President Roosevelt contain a hope: "A planet unvexed by wars, untroubled by hunger or fear, and undivided by senseless distinctions of race, colour or theory."

Roosevelt has voiced the "Four Freedoms:"

> "Freedom of Speech, Freedom of Religion,
> Freedom from Want, Freedom from Fear."

They are closely inter-related, inherent in Democracy, non-existent in Fascism, and an obvious necessity to all mankind. If these be won, and maintained, it is worth while being alive.

There are pledges, such as Cordell Hull's on July 24th, when he broadcast to the world that the American people are fighting that all peoples, without distinction of race, colour or religion, should be free, on condition that these people fight to safeguard their liberty.

There are also the findings of science to back up these sentiments on the material plane: the earth contains enough resources and man has attained knowledge sufficient to produce enough food and other matters of material welfare to bring every living being into a state of comfort, and even more, in one generation alone.

For Great Britain this immense new vision of the future is bound up with the question of her Empire and the 500 million subjects in it. Our politicians and prominent leaders in various fields, and of different political opinion, have made public statements: –

"We have already condemned and rejected the old inequalities between ourselves and the so-called subject races." (Sir Stafford Cripps.)

"We must make the Colonial peoples feel it is their Empire as well as ours ... we have got to make the Empire a people's Empire." (Captain Gammans, Conservative M.P. for Hornsey.)

"It is obvious that the pre-war epoch of British Imperialism in the East is over for good and all ... . The sooner we make up our minds to the realisation that the destiny of the East is no longer a part of the White Man's Burden the sooner we shall discover the foundations of an enduring peace there." (Professor Laski.)

A great case can be made out of the multiplicity of words, speeches, articles, sentiments voiced in Press and Parliament, of this kind – a case for hope.

Yet many of us, white as well as coloured, are in doubt as to whether or no[t] these sentiments and promises will materialise. We do not want to be cynical; but we remember. And to-day (this has to be said) the coloured soldier of the U.S.A. over here in very large numbers, records, that although he may be the same as a white American soldier in democracy when democracy is a battlefield, he is not to be the same in daily relations with the people of Great Britain, because some of his chiefs have requested that this not be so. What can he conclude, if he knows the pledges of Mr. Cordell Hull: "without distinction of race, of colour ...?"

Many of us feel that sincerity of purpose motivated the promises and pledges, as did perhaps in no less measure the realisation that such is the only policy which will maintain peace when it is won. Yet we know that between the promises and their realisation there is an immense No Man's Land.

What does it contain? Will the British "evolve" terms that can be accepted by the coloured "subject?" Will grudging "reforms" be arrived at in some sort of "appeasement of native unrest"? Or will they be real, necessary, sterling 100 per cent, democracy?

With the enemy at the gates of India, no solution has been reached, and we are told that one of the reasons is that Indians cannot agree among themselves. To this Nehru answers: "The people of England feel that this is their war and they have a job to do. But this feeling is lacking in India." Is that the truth or just the view of an "embittered man" as Nehru has sometimes been called by those who prefer anything to looking truth in the face?

Events moved very fast in the beginning and spring of 1942 in the Far East, and in the comments here which followed, British politicians and coloured leaders were of the same mind, for the facts were historically irrefutable.

In a debate on Colonial Policy in the House of Lords (May 21ˢᵗ), Lord Listowel asked if we had a policy which would rally the Colonial peoples in their own defence. In Burma, he said, local inhabitants had taken up arms against the British when the Japanese advanced; in Malaya there had been numerous fifth-columnists. Lord Wedgewood, in the same debate, said that natives of the Colonies should be given commissions in the army and become officials in the administration.

George Padmore, co-author with me of this pamphlet, pointed out in "The Crisis" (July, New York): –

"The Singapore natives, like those on the mainland, had no voice in their own affairs. Surely it is not really surprising that when the crisis came, the Governor, Sir Shenton Thomas, was unable to mobilise the common people – Malayan, Chinese, Indian – to withstand the Japanese onslaught. How could a people, whose existence has been entirely ignored, presumably because they were considered unfit to participate in the government of the country, suddenly resuscitate themselves, as it were, and assume responsibility in defence of the system which had until then failed to recognise their existence?"

What do Africa and its descendants feel about the all-in fight against Nazism and Fascism?

Rudolph Dunbar, the Negro journalist and composer from British Guiana, puts it very clearly: –

"You will not gain the full confidence and co-operation of coloured men and women by telling them they would be worse off under Fascist rule. You will only do that by convincing them that they will be better off in free association with you."

The crux of it all is: In war – to defend what is one's own. In peace – equal rights.

★ ★ ★

The logical feeling exists among coloured peoples: "Now Britain is in trouble she needs us, but when it is all over we shall be as before." This could be removed – but to do so would call for a change of heart, and of policy, toward coloured peoples on the part of many of the authorities and officials *particularly in the Colonies*.

In the United States the 13 million Negroes see the Call to the Colours translated for their race into a matter of segregated regiments and Army Service groups. One of their 400 newspapers, commenting on a proposal made here in London during the worst air-raids to create separate shelters for coloured people, wrote: "If this is all that Britain is fighting for, the *status quo*, then to ask American Negroes to fight and die for Britain is like asking them to fight and die for Mississippi" (land of lynchings).

True, civilians and soldiers of Great Britain are against treating the American coloured soldiers differently to the white, as they are requested to do. Yet is it possible to say that colour prejudice and colour bar are on the decline?

We salute the forceful article by our Minister of Information, Mr. Bracken, "Colour Bar Must Go" (*Sunday Express* September 20th), but we firmly believe that an Act of Parliament making all Colour Bar manifestations an offence (as was the case, for instance, in France before Hitler) would be an efficacious and sensible basis for its eradication. Race prejudice (of Jew, Negro, or any people) belongs to Nazi-Fascism and not to Democracy.

If the British Government intends colour prejudice to end, as Mr. Bracken states it does, it will have gone a long way in initiating "the second freeing" of all coloured peoples in the world, over 100 years, as this would be, after our abolition of slavery itself. The gratitude of those of colour and of those who understand the effects of race prejudice will be acquired in fullest measure.

What is said in this article of Brendon Bracken is to-day's parallel and continuation of the speeches of the great Abolitionists during the 20-year struggle in Parliament at the end of the 18th century. Let me quote some passages:

"The barriers still standing in the way of the social equality of coloured people must be withdrawn." "This is a process which will take time, but responsible people in Britain are determined that it shall be carried through, and the sooner the better." "I should like to emphasise that the theory of equal rights is not a mere high-sounding phrase." "I wish to emphasise here only that we in Britain do not intend to stand fast upon theories of political equality and economic freedom without seeing to it that the victory for which we are striving will be as much theirs as ours."

Colour Bar, (*legally* non-existent in Great Britain, as says Mr. Bracken) all too often does exist in hotels, lodging-houses, restaurants, bars, public-houses and the minds of landlords. A new clause added to the legal regulations to which these places conform, punishing Colour Bar, as, say, disorderliness is punished, would be excellent.

This outspoken article deals mainly with Colour Bar in our own country. It is Lord Samuel who throws a revealing light on the Colonial situation. In a letter to *The Times* (August 8th), Lord Samuel says that several recent articles on the Colonial Empire "all stress the need for a forward Colonial policy," and quotes from one: "Until an end is put to public indifference there is no hope of a truly dynamic policy for the Empire ... The key is in the hands of the people at home." Lord Samuel then writes: "The fact is that, while Parliament and public are becoming more and more uneasy about the Crown Colonies, they are still hardly alive to their own responsibilities." Further he states that the House of Commons "devotes *one day a year* (emphasis mine) to the Colonial estimates ... There are useful discussions from time to time in the House of Lords. *But there is no normal agency, continuously at work* (emphasis mine), *which will link the democratic forces of the nation with the processes of Colonial administration*, which will diffuse the spirit of British policy throughout the Colonial Empire."

What are the "democratic forces of the nation"?

Coloured people translate this, and logically enough, into those who understand and who will back up our pleas for "Equal Rights."

A year ago when I was in the British West Indies, black workers said to me constantly: – "In England the Government and the people talk a great deal now about 'Democracy for all after the war'. Do they include *us* in this?" But back in England I was unable to find the slightest increase of interest, concern or knowledge of our coloured subjects' lamentable conditions, although there was, and continues to be an immense amount of talk and writing and of hope about the future instauration of "the better life for all". Democracy is not a difficult idea, or theory, or concept, or state of being to understand, and the colonised peoples have a very clear sense of what it means. *It is exactly what they are asking for:* equal opportunities as the white people in all fields of life.

Full equal rights are of course freedom, and freedom has been set down last of all in the words of Clause 3 of the Atlantic Charter: "The right of all peoples to choose the form of government under which they live."

"To-day constant efforts are being made in India to end the terrible deadlock there, and the two facts contained in one phrase of Mr. P. N. Sapru's speech in the Council of State at New Delhi (Sept. 22nd), are the heart-cry of the totalitarian administration of India ..."

* * *

What is to be concluded from the sentiments and promises I have quoted here as examples of a very great many more of the same progressive kind? Are they to be casually dismissed: "Oh, this is just talk; nothing is meant to come of it!" (frequently the feeling of "the man in the street") – or are we to believe that they spring from a true determination to put an end to all the worst abuses and conditions of to-day? If Colonies are a national heartache to those who know them and who know also that coloured peoples are as human as ourselves and deserve the kind of life we ourselves desire, they could become the *real* British "Commonwealth" which, to-day, is a term on paper, and not more, as far as the native population of the Colonies is concerned.

With all of this in mind I went to talk to George Padmore, the young leader of colour, who was born in Trinidad, British West Indies. Author of several books and innumerable articles on the Negro, Padmore has travelled much, absorbing political experience in many lands. Our premise was: –

"We will take the statesmen who have made these promises at their word."

And so in several talks we examined the situation in the Colonies, and I asked Padmore to give me his analysis and solution of the problem; it will be found in the following pages. My questions and Padmore's answers were taken down in shorthand and only very slightly edited for clarity and sequence later on.

Simone Weil

From "The Colonial Question and the Destiny of the French People" (1943)

We cannot say that colonization is a part of the French tradition. It is a process that had taken place outside of the life of the French people. The Algerian venture was on the one hand a matter of dynastic prestige; on the other, a part of Mediterranean security policy; as often happens, defense is transformed into conquest. Later, the acquisition of Tunisia and Morocco was – as one of those who played a great part in the latter remarked – largely the reflex of the peasant enlarging his patch of land. The conquest of Indochina was a reaction of revenge against the humiliation of 1870. Having been unable to resist the Germans, and taking advantage of temporary unrest, we compensated by depriving of its fatherland a people with an age-old tradition, peaceful and well organized. But Jules Ferry's government carried out that act by an abuse of its powers and in open defiance of French public opinion; other aspects of the conquest were carried out by ambitious and amateurish officers who were disobeying the strict orders of their leaders.

The islands of Oceania were taken through the chance happenings of navigation, on the initiative of one officer or another, and delivered up to a handful of policemen, missionaries, and merchants, without the country having the slightest interest in them.

It is pretty well only colonization in Black Africa that has provoked public interest. It was also the most justifiable of France's colonizing ventures, given the state of this unhappy continent, whose history we are almost entirely ignorant of, but where the white man had in any case caused the greatest possible havoc over four centuries, with his firearms and his traffic in slaves. But colonization has not prevented Black Africa from remaining problematic.

It cannot be said that the *status quo* is an answer to the problems of the French Empire. And there is another thing that one can neither say nor think. That is that the problem concerns only the French people. Such a claim would be just as legitimate as Hitler's similar declarations regarding central Europe. The problem concerns, as well as the French people, the whole world, and first and foremost the subject populations.

The force upon which a colonial empire rests is a naval fleet. France has almost entirely lost hers. It cannot be said that she sacrificed it; she lost it to the enemy, who would have seized it if it had not been destroyed. Henceforth, after the victory, France will depend, for her relationships with her empire, on countries that have a fleet. How could those countries not have a say in any major problem concerning the empire? If it is force that decides, France has lost hers; if it is a question of rights, France never had the right to determine the destiny of non-French peoples. In no sense, either in terms of rights or of fact can one say that the territories inhabited by these peoples are France's property.

The greatest mistake that free France could make at present would be to maintain this claim as an absolute in its relations with the United States. There can be nothing worse than an attitude that is radically opposed at one and the same time to the ideal and to reality. An attitude opposed to one but in keeping with the other already has great disadvantages; the other attitude has nothing but.

The colonial problem has to be looked on as a new one. Two main ideas can throw a little light on it.

The first is that Hitlerism consists in the application by Germany to the European continent, and more generally to the countries belonging to the white race, colonial methods of conquest and domination. The Czechs were the first to note this analogy when, protesting about the protectorate of Bohemia, they said: "No European people has ever been subjected to such a regime." If the methods of colonial conquest are examined in detail, the analogy with Hitlerian methods is obvious. An example can be found in the letters written by Lyautey from Madagascar. The extreme horror which for some while now has seemed to distinguish Hitlerian domination from all others can be explained perhaps by the fear of defeat. It should not make us forget the essential analogy of methods – derived, moreover, in both cases from the Roman model.

This analogy provides a ready-made reply to all the arguments in favour of the colonial system. For *all* these arguments, the good, the less good and the bad, are used by Germany, with the same degree of legitimacy, in her propaganda concerning the unification of Europe.

The harm that Germany would have done to Europe if Britain had not prevented the German victory is the harm that colonization does, in that it uproots people. It would have deprived people of their past. The loss of the past is the descent into colonial enslavement.

This harm which Germany tried in vain to do to us, we did to others. Through our fault, little Polynesians recite in school: "Our ancestors the Gauls had blond hair and blue eyes ..." Alain Gerbault has described, in books that have been widely read but have had no influence, how we make these populations literally die of sadness, by forbidding their customs, their traditions, their celebrations, their whole enjoyment of life.

Through our fault, Annamite students and intellectuals can only exceptionally have access to the library that contains all the documentation relating to the history of their country. The conception they have of their country before the conquest is derived from their fathers. Whether accurate or not, this conception is that of a peaceful state, wisely administered, where the surplus of rice was stored in depots to be distributed in times of famine, contrary to the more recent practice of exporting rice from the south while famine ravages the population in the north.

By depriving peoples of their tradition, of their past, and thus of their soul, colonization reduces them to the state of matter, but matter that is human. The populations of occupied countries are just this in the eyes of the Germans. But it cannot be denied that the majority of colonials have the same attitude toward the natives. Forced labor has been extremely deadly in French Black Africa, and the method of massive deportations has been used there to populate the land enclosed by the bend of the Niger. In Indochina, forced labor, thinly disguised, exists in the plantations, exposed to red ants; a Frenchman, an engineer in one of these plantations, said on the subject of the beatings that are the commonest punishment: "Even if you look at it from a humanitarian point of view, it's the best method, since, as they're at the extreme limit of exhaustion and hunger, any other punishment would be more cruel." A Cambodian, servant to a French policeman, said "I'd like to be the policeman's dog; they give him food and he is not beaten."

In our fight against Germany, we can have two attitudes. Whatever the necessity of unity, we simply have to choose, make that choice public, and express it in acts. We can regret that Germany has accomplished what we would have liked to see France accomplish. This is the attitude of some of the young French people who say that they are behind General De Gaulle for the same motives that would line them up behind Hitler if they were German. Or we can be horrified, not at the person or the nationality of the enemy, but at his spirit, his methods, and his ambitions. We can hardly choose other than the second option. Otherwise it is useless to talk about the French Revolution or Christianity. If we make this choice, we must demonstrate it by all our attitudes.

Fighting against the Germans is not sufficient proof that we love freedom. For the Germans have not only taken away our freedom. They have taken away in addition our power, our prestige, our tobacco, our wine, and our bread. Mixed motives sustain our fight. The decisive proof would be to support an arrangement guaranteeing at least partial freedom to those from whom we in our turn have taken it away. We could thus persuade not only others, but ourselves, that we are truly inspired by an ideal.

The analogy between Hitlerism and colonial expansion, by dictating to us from a moral point of view the attitude to take, provides us also with the practical solution that is the least bad. The experience of the last few years demonstrates that a Europe made up of nations great and small, all sovereign, is impossible. Nationality is an undefined phenomenon in a great part of Europe. Even in a country like France, national unity has suffered quite a severe blow; people from Brittany, Lorraine, Paris, Provence, have a much sharper sense than before the war of being different one from another. In spite of several disadvantages, that is far from being a bad thing. In Germany, the victors will try and weaken to the maximum the feeling of national unity. Very probably part of the social life of Europe will be broken up into units much smaller than the nation; another part will be unified on a much larger scale; the nation will be only one possible context for collective life, instead of being practically everything, as it has been over the past twenty years.

Suzanne Roussy Césaire

From "Le grand camouflage" (1945)

There are, layered up against the islands, the beautiful green waves of water and silence. There is the purity of salt in and about the Antilles. There is before my eyes the pretty Place de Pétionville, planted with pines and hibiscus. There is my island, Martinique, and its fresh necklace of clouds puffed up by Mount Pelée. There are the highest plateaus of Haiti, where a horse dies, lightning-struck by the secularly murderous storm at Hinche. Nearby, his master contemplates the country he thought to be solid and expansive. He doesn't yet know that he is participating in the islands' lack of equilibrium. But this stroke of terrestrial insanity enlightens his heart: he begins to think about the other Antilles, about their volcanoes, their earthquakes, their hurricanes.

At this moment off the coast of Puerto Rico a great cyclone begins to turn amid seas of clouds, with its beautiful tail that rhythmically sweeps the half circle of the Caribbean isles. The Atlantic flees toward Europe in great oceanic waves. Our little tropical observatories begin to crackle with the news. The wireless goes haywire. Boats flee, flee where? The sea swells, here and there an exertion, a delectable surge, the water slackens its limbs to get a wider consciousness of its watery power, sailors with clenched teeth and a streaming face, and we learn that the southeast coast of Haiti is under the cyclone that passes at twenty-five miles per hour, heading toward Florida. Consternation takes hold of the objects and beings spared from the wind by being at its fringe. Don't move. Let it pass ...

In the heart of the cyclone, everything crackles, everything crumbles with the ripping sound of great displays. Then the radios fall silent. The great tail of palms of cool wind is unfurled somewhere in the stratosphere, there where no one will follow the crazy iridescences and violet lightwaves.

After the rain, then sun.

Haitian cicadas think about grinding love. When there is not a single drop left in the burnt grass, they sing furiously that life is beautiful, they burst out in a cry that is too vibrant for an insect body. Their thin pellicle of dried silk stretched to the extreme, they die suffusing the least moist cry of pleasure in the world.

Haiti remains, wrapped in the embers of the sun that are sweet to the eyes of the cicadas, to the scales of the *mabouyas,* to the metal face of the sea which is no longer made of water but of mercury.[48]

Now is the time to lean out the window of the aluminum clipper with its great turns.

The airplanes of the Pan American Airways System pass through once again the no-longer-virgin sea of clouds. If there is a harvest ripening, that is the time to try to get a glimpse of it [Haiti], but in the closed-off military zones, the windows are closed.

They bring out disinfectants, or ozone, it doesn't matter, you will see nothing. Nothing but the sea and the dim form of lands. We can only guess about the easy love of fish. They make the water move, which amicably winks at the clipper's porthole. Viewed from very high up, our islands take on their true dimension as shells. And as for the humming-bird-women, the tropical flower-women, the women of four races and dozens of bloodlines, they are no longer there. Neither the canna, nor the plumeria and the flame trees, neither the palms by moonlight, nor the sunsets unlike any other in the world ...

Nevertheless, they are there.

Nevertheless, fifteen years ago, the Antilles were revealed to me from the flank of Mount Pelée. From here I discovered, though still very young, that Martinique was sensual, coiled up, extended, distended into the Caribbean Sea, and I thought about the other islands that are so beautiful.

Once again in Haiti, during the summer mornings of 1944, I experienced the presence of the Antilles, more perceptible in places from which, like at Kenscoff, the mountain views are of an unbearable beauty.

And now, total lucidity. Beyond these perfect colors and forms, my gaze detects the innermost torments in the Antilles' most beautiful face.

For the plot of unsatisfied desires has ensnared the Antilles and America. Since the arrival of conquistadors and the maturation of their technology (beginning with that of firearms), the ultra-Atlantic lands have not only changed face, but also fear. Fear of being outpaced by

---

[48] *Mabouyas* is Creole for a type of small lizard.

those who remained in Europe, already armed and appointed, the fear of being in competition with peoples of color that were hurriedly pronounced inferior so as the better to torment them. It was necessary at first and at all costs, be it the cost of the slave trade's infamy, to create an American society richer, more powerful, and better organized than the European society left behind – and desired. It was necessary to take this revenge upon the nostalgic hell that belched forth its adventurous demons, its convicts, its penitents, and its utopians upon the New World and its islands. After three centuries, the colonial adventure continues – the wars of independence are but an episode – the peoples of the Americas, whose behavior toward the peoples of Europe remains often infantile and romantic, are still not free of the old continent's ascendancy. Naturally, the blacks in America are those who suffer the most, in a day-by-day humiliation, from the degeneracies, injustices, and pettiness of colonial society.

If we are proud to note our extraordinary vitality everywhere in the Americas, if that vitality seems definitively to promise our salvation, nonetheless it must dare be said that refined forms of slavery continue to be rife. Here, in the French islands, they debase thousands of blacks for whom the great Schoelcher [sic] sought, a century ago, along with freedom and dignity, the title of citizen. It must dare be shown, on the face of France, lit by the implacable light of events, the Antillean stain, since there are also indeed many among the French who seem determined to tolerate no shadow upon that face.

The degrading forms of modern wage labor still find among us a ground upon which to flourish without constraint.

Who will throw out, along with the antiquated material of their factories, these few thousand submanufacturers and shopkeepers, that caste of false colonizers responsible for the human deprivation of the Antilles?

When they are left off on the streets of their capitals, an insurmountable timidity fills them with fear among their European brethren. Ashamed of their drawling accent, of their unsure French, they sigh after the tranquil warmth of Antillean dwellings and the patois of the black "nanny" of their childhood.

Ready to betray any and all in order to defend themselves against the rising tide of blacks, they would sell themselves to America were it not that the Americans claim that the purity of their blood is highly suspect,[49] just as in the 1940s they devoted themselves to the Admiral of Vichy:

---

[49] The allusion is to the infamous "one-drop" rule that defines racial differences as absolute in the United States alone.

Pétain being for them the altar of France, Robert necessarily became the "tabernacle of the Antilles."

In the meantime, the Antillean serf lives with misery and abjection on the grounds of the "Factory," and the mediocre state of our cities-towns is a nauseating spectacle. In the meantime, the Antilles continue to be like paradise and that sweet sound of palms …

That day the irony was that, a shiny garment full of sparkles, each of our muscles expressed in a personal manner one parcel of the desire scattered among the blossoming mango trees.

I listened very attentively without being able to hear your voices lost in the Caribbean symphony that would hurl waterspouts against the islands. We were just like thoroughbreds, held back, impatiently pawing the ground, at the edge of that salt savanna.

On the beach, there were several "metropolitan officials." They were installed there, without conviction, and ready to take off at the first signal. The newcomers can scarcely adapt to our "old French lands." When they look into the maleficent mirror of the Caribbean, they see a delirious image of themselves. They dare not recognize themselves in that ambiguous being: the Antillean. They know that the métis share some of their blood, that they are also, like them, part of Western civilization. It is well understood that the "metropolitans" don't know racial prejudice. But their colored descendants fill them with dread, despite the exchange of smiles. They did not expect that strange burgeoning of their blood.

Perhaps they didn't want to answer the Antillean heir who does and does not cry out "my father." However, these unexpected sons, these charming daughters must be reckoned with. These turbulent folks must be governed.

Here is an Antillean, the great-grandson of a colonist and a black slave woman. Here he is on his island, seeing to its "running" in deploying all the energies once necessary for the greedy colonists, for whom other people's blood was the natural price of gold, and all the courage necessary for African warriors who forever gained their life through death.

Here he is with his double force and double ferociousness, in a dangerous equilibrium: he cannot accept his Negritude, yet he cannot make himself become white. Listlessness overtakes this heart divided in two, and with it comes the habit of rusing, the taste for "schemes." So blossoms in the Antilles that flower of human baseness, the colored bourgeoisie.

Along the roads bordered with glyciridia, pretty little Negro children ecstatically digesting their roots cooked either with or without salt smile at the luxury automobile passing by. They suddenly feel, planted in their navel, the need to be, one day, masters of an equally supple, shiny, and powerful beast. Years later you see them, sullied with the fat of happiness, miraculously give the tremor of life to junkyard carcasses, sold for a low price. Instinctively, the hands of thousands of young Antilleans have felt the weight of steel, have located joints, unscrewed bolts. Thousands of images of brightly lit factories, virgin steel, of liberating machines, have swollen the hearts of our young laborers. In hundreds of sordid sheds where scrap metal rusts away, there is an invisible vegetation of desire. The impatient fruits of the Revolution will inevitably spring forth from this.

Here among the bluffs polished by the wind, the free-person's estate. A peasant who himself has not been swept up by the uproar of mechanical adventure leans up against the big *mapou* that gives shade to an entire flank of the bluff, and he feels grow in him, through his naked toes sunken in the mud, a slow vegetal growth.[50] He has turned toward the sunset to know what the weather will be like tomorrow – the orange reds show him that planting time is near – not only is his gaze the peaceful reflection of the light, but he grows heavy with impatience, the very impatience that uplifts the land of Martinique – his land that does not belong to him and is nonetheless his land. He knows that it is the workers with whom he has common cause, and not with the béké or the métis. And when, suddenly, in the middle of the Caribbean night all decked out with love and silence, a drum call bursts out, the blacks get ready to answer the desire of the earth and of the dance, but the owners lock themselves up in their beautiful houses, and behind their wire gauze, beneath the electrical light, they are just like pale butterflies caught in a snare.

All around them, the tropical night swells with rhythms, the hips of Bergilde have taken their cataclysmic allure from the swells pushed up from the depths to the sides of volcanoes. And it is Africa itself which, across the Atlantic and across the centuries before slave ships, dedicates to its Antillean children the lustfully solar glances exchanged between dancers. With a raw and wide voice, their cry exclaims that there, present, that she waits, immensely virginal despite the colonization, turbulent, devourer of whites. And upon these faces bathed by the marine exhalations close to the islands, upon these and tiny lands surrounded by water like so many great moats, there passes an enormous wind come from Africa. Antilles-Africa, thanks to the drums, the nostalgia for terrestrial spaces, lives in these hearts of the insular. Who will fulfill that nostalgia?

---

[50] *Mapou* is Creole for silk-cotton tree.

Meanwhile, the cannas of Absalom bleed over chasms, and the beauty of the tropical landscape goes to the head of the poets who pass by. Across the shifting networks of palms they see the Antillean conflagration roll onto the Caribbean, which is a peaceful sea of lava. Here, life is lit by a vegetal fire. Here, on these hot lands that keep geological species alive, is found the fixed plant, passion and blood, in its primitive architecture, the anxious ringing emerging from the chaotic backs of the dancers. Here, the creepers swinging vertiginously take on airy allures to charm the precipices; with their trembling hands they hook on to the ungraspable cosmic tremor that rises all through the nights inhabited by drums. Here, the poets feel their heads overturn, and inhaling the fresh scents of the ravines, they take hold of the islands in their spread, they listen to the noise of the water around the islands, they see the tropical flames flare up no longer on account of cannas, gerberas, hibiscuses, bougainvilleas, or flame trees, but on account of the hungers, fears, hatreds, and ferocity that burn in the hollows of hills.

So it is that the conflagration of the Caribbean puffs out its silent vapors, blinding for the only eyes able to see, and suddenly the blues of the Haitian bluffs grow dim, suddenly the most dazzling reds grow pale, and the sun is no longer a crystal that plays, and if the public places have chosen Jerusalem thorns as their deluxe fans against the heat of the sky, if the flowers have found the right colors to make one thunderstruck, if the tree ferns have secreted a golden sap from their crook, all coiled up like a sex organ, if my Antilles are so beautiful, then it's because the great game of hide-and-seek has succeeded, and certainly that day would be too enchanting for us to see.

Eslanda Robeson

From *African Journey* **(1946)**

June 10. We have run into the "Cape Rollers" and believe me they are most uncomfortable. They are said to be caused by the meeting of the Indian Ocean with the South Atlantic, and the great difference in their temperatures causes currents and swells. Often it is very, very rough around the cape and far up on both sides as well. Thank heaven the ship is steady, and I can manage, although I took to my bed when we first ran into the rollers yesterday.

Mrs. G. was telling me about Julius, her Native servant ("boy" as they are called) who has been with her for years. He drives her car and is general houseman, I gather. It seems he fell in love with one of her maids, Native of course, and Mrs. G. became interested in the romance. "I gave her a lovely wedding dress, and they were married right in my own parlour. And Julius said a white bride could not have looked as lovely as his black one did." I could almost feel I was at home again, listening to a white Southerner from our own Deep South. I think it will be easy for me to understand the South Africans: Their attitudes, especially their patriarchal attitudes, are entirely familiar.

I have been asking the passengers, discreetly I hope, about the Cape Coloured people. Everyone seems a bit interested in the Cape Coloured, but very worried and shy about the Natives. I gather they feel rather safer with the Coloured, because they are "more like the Europeans," and their ideal is to become European. They are given just enough encouragement to make them feel themselves "above" the Native and "different" from him. Then too, their numbers are comparatively few: They are less than half of the number of the European population. The Natives are so much stronger numerically than the Europeans, and so entirely different, that they are frightening. And they have no desire whatever to become European, which makes them more frightening. (Natives are more than three times greater in number, in South Africa, than

Europeans. Hailey gives the number for all of Africa: Europeans 4,014,424, as against the total population of roughly 150,000,000.)

I find myself recognizing the tone of voice, the inflection of these South Africans. "Native" is their word for our "nigger"; "non-European" for our Negro; "European" means white; and "South African" surprisingly enough does not mean the millions of original black people there, but the white residents born there, as distinguished from the white residents born in Europe who are called "colonials" or "settlers".

Claudia Jones

From "The Caribbean Community in Britain" (1964)

Over a quarter of a million West Indians, the overwhelming majority of them from Jamaica, have now settled in Britain in less than a decade. Britain has become, in the mid-1960's, the center of the largest overseas population of West Indians; numerically relegating to second place, the once superior community of West Indians in the United States. This new situation in Britain, has been inimitably described in the discerning verse of Louise Bennett, noted Jamaican folklorist, as, "Colonization in Reverse." Immigration statistics, which are approximate estimates compiled by the one time functional West Indian Federation office (Migrant Services Division) in Britain, placed the total number of West Indians entering the United Kingdom as 238,000 persons by the year 1961. Of these, 125,000 were men; 93,000 women; 13,200 were children; and 6,300, unclassified. A breakdown of the islands from which these people came, showed that during the period of 1955–1961, a total of 142,825 were from Jamaica; from Barbadoes, 5,036; from Trinidad and Tobago, 2,282; from British Guiana, 3,470; from Leeward Islands, 3,524; from the Windward Islands, 8,202; and from all other territories, the sum total of 8,732. Distribution of the West Indian population in the United Kingdom indicates that by mid-1962, over 300,000 West Indians were settled in Britain. The yearly immigration and the growth of community settlement illustrates the rate of growth of the West Indian settlement. For example, the emigration of West Indians to the United Kingdom in mid-1955 totalled 24,473 and by 1961, this figure soared to 61,749. Corresponding to the latter, was the fear of family separation due to the then impending Commonwealth Immigrants Act. In the industrial city of Birmingham, by mid-1955, 8,000 West Indians formed the community there, while in mid-1962, this figure stood at 67,000. Similarly in London, where in Brixton the largest settlement of West Indians exist [sic]; the mid-1955 figure of 85,000 had by 1961 grown to 135,000.

West Indians were also to be found in the North of England (Manchester, Nottingham, Wolverhampton, Derby and Leeds) and in such cities as Cardiff, Liverpool, Leicester, Bath, Oxford, Cambridge and in other provinces. What constitutes the chief features of this unprecedented migration to Britain? To what factors may we ascribe this growth of overseas West Indians away from their original homelands?

Emigration from the West Indies has served for over two generations as a palliative, a stop-gap measure to ease the growing economic frustrations in a largely impoverished agricultural economy; in which under colonial-capitalist-imperialist relations, the wealth of these islands is dominated by the few, with the vast majority of the people living under unbearable conditions.

It was the outstanding Cuban poet, Nicholas Guillen, who noting a situation (also observed by other West Indian writers) in which the young generation, most of it out of work, "chafing at the bit," seeing as their only hope a swift opportunity to leave their islands, lamented thus: "*Scant, sea-girt land, Oh, tight-squeezed land ...*"

Indeed, as with all migrant populations here is mirrored in extension the existing problems of the nations and territories from which the migrants originally spring. West Indian emigration to the United Kingdom is no exception to this phenomenon. Furthermore, this emigration, as with many other Afro-Asian peoples, has occurred almost immediately prior to the achievement of political independence in two of the largest of the West Indies islands. It is because prospects have not yet qualitatively improved for the vast majority of the West Indian workers and people, inhibited by the tenaciousness of continued Anglo-American imperialist dominance over West Indian economic life, that this emigratory movement of people from the West Indies continues. History will undoubtedly evaluate this development as, in part, attributable to the demise of the West Indian Federation and the consequent smashing of wide hopes for the establishment of a united West Indian nation in which freedom of movement would have absorbed some of our disinherited, disillusioned, and unfilled people who were compelled to leave their homelands in order to survive.

Up to a decade ago, West Indian immigration was directed to America rather than to Britain. But this was sharply modified when, in 1952 the United States Federal Government enacted the racially based McCarran–Walter Immigration Law, which unequivocally was designed to protect the white "races' purity," and to insure the supremacy of Anglo-Saxon stock; limited to 100 per year, persons allowed to emigrate to the United States from each individual Caribbean territory. Henceforth all eyes reverted to Britain. This is not to imply that West

Indian immigration to Britain was wholly nonreciprocal. Another influence, was that post-war Britain, experiencing a brief economic boom, and full employment, needed overseas and cheap labor to staff the semi-skilled and non-skilled vacancies, the results of temporary postwar economic incline. Britain sought West Indian immigration as an indispensable aid to the British economy; indeed, encouraged it!

The presence of West Indian immigrants (who together with other Afro-Asian peoples total nearly a half million people) represent less than one per cent in an overall Anglo-populous [sic] of 52 million. But even this small minority has given rise to a plethora of new sociological and analytical works such as *"Newcomers"*; *"Colored Immigrants in Britain"*; *"The Economic and Social Position of Negro Immigrants in Britain"*; *"Black and White in Harmony"*; *"Colored Minorities in Britain"*; *"Colonial Students"*; *"Report on West Indian Accommodation Problems in the United Kingdom"*; *"Race and Racism"*; *"Dark Strangers"*; *"They Seek a Living, and the Like."*

Extreme manifestations of the racialism which underlies the present status of West Indians in Britain were graphically witnessed in late 1958, when racial riots occurred in Notting Hill and Nottingham. These events, which followed the as yet unsolved murder of a St. Vincentian, Mr. Kelso Cochrane, claimed world headlines. Clashes even occurred between West Indian and other Afro-Asian migrants with white Britons. The firm handling of the provocateurs by the authorities, following the wide protests of immigrants, labor, Communist and progressive forces, and the intervention of the West Indian Federal leaders, for a time quelled the overt racialists, and the "keep Britain white, fascist-propagandists." But the canker of racialism was now nakedly revealed. It exposed also the smugness of official Britain, who hitherto pointed to racial manifestations in "Little Rock" and Johannesburg, South Africa, but continued to deny its existence in Britain.

Today, new problems, underscored by the Tory Government's enactment, and recent renewal of the 1962 Commonwealth Immigration Act (one which ostensibly restricts Commonwealth immigration as a whole, but in fact, discriminates heavily against colored Commonwealth citizens) has established a second class citizenship status for West Indians and other Afro-Asian peoples in Britain. Accompanying the general social problems confronting all new migrant workers, West Indians, stemming as they do in large measure from African origins, are experiencing sharper color-bar practices. In common with other workers, the West Indians take part in the struggle for defense and improvement of their working and living standards. But the growing intensity of racialism forces them, as it does other Afro-Asians, to join and found their own organizations. In fact, their status, is more and more a barometer of British intentions and claims of a so-called "Multi-racial Commonwealth." As put in one of the recent sociological studies of the absorption of a West Indian migrant group in Brixton, financed by the Institute of Race Relations and the Nuffield Foundation:

Now that the whole equilibrium of world power is changing, and the Commonwealth is, by virtue of conscious British policy, being transformed from a family based on kinship, to a wider multiracial familia, *the presence of colored immigrants in Britain, presents a moral and a practical challenge. The people of these islands face the need not only to reformulate their views of Britain's role and status in such a Commonwealth, but also to apply the new relationships in their dealings with colored Commonwealth migrants here at home. And not only the color-conscious migrants themselves, but the newly-independent Afro-Asian countries and the outside world as a whole, show an inclination to judge Britain's good faith in international relations by her ability to put her own house in order.* from *Dark Strangers*, by Sheila Patterson.

The commonwealth immigrants act

Far from heeding the advice even of sociologists whose studies themselves show a neo-colonialist bias in its precepts (the study is full of pragmatic assertions that xenophobia is the "norm" of British life, and hence, by implication "natural," etc.) the Tory Government has shown utter disdain for putting its own house in order.

Faced with the coming general elections in October, having suffered from local government defeats, mounting criticism rises towards its ruinous domestic and foreign policies. Internally, these range from housing shortages and a Rent Act which has removed ceilings on rentals to the failures of providing new houses; high interest rates on loans to the rail and shipbuilding closures, mergers and the effects of automation.

The external policies of the present British Conservative Government also suffer similar criticism. As a junior partner it supports the United States imperialist NATO nuclear strategy, continuing huge expenditures for colonial wars in Malaysia, North Borneo and Aden. Its subservience to U.S. imperialism is also demonstrated in the case of its denial of long over-due independence to British Guiana, on whom it is imposing the undemocratic system of Proportional Representation which aims further to polarize and divide the political life in British Guiana in order to depose the left-wing, thrice-elected People's Progressive Party under Dr. Cheddi Jagan. As an experienced colonizer, shopping around for a scapegoat for its own sins, the British Tory Government enacted in 1962, the Commonwealth Immigrants Act. The Act sets up a voucher system allowing entry only to those who have a job to come to. Some of its sections carry deportation penalties for migrants from the West Indies, Asia and Africa, whom it especially circumscribes. Its passage was accompanied by the most foul racialist propaganda perpetrated against West Indians and other Afro-Asians by Tory and fascist elements. Thus, it coincided with the futile efforts then engaged in by the British Government to join the European Common Market. It was widely interpreted that these twin events demonstrated the dispensability in Britain's eyes of both the needs of the traditional market of the newly independent West Indian territories for their primary products, and the labor supply of West Indians and other Afro-Asian Commonwealth citizens. On the other hand, the doors would close on colored Commonwealth citizens, while open wide to white European workers.

The pious and hypocritical sentimentality accompanying the "bills" passage was further exposed when the Tory legislators removed the non-Commonwealth Irish Republic from the provisions of the Act, revealing its naked color-bar bias. The result, following a year of its operation, showed that eighty to ninety per cent of all Indian and Pakistani applicants were refused entry permits; and West Indian immigration dropped to a little over 4,000, qualifying for entry. The latter occasioned cautious queries, whether the West Indians had either turned their backs on Britain or had become bitter with the Act's passage.

What the figures showed, of course, was that the main blow fell as intended, most heavily on the *colored* Commonwealth citizens. So much for the facile promises of the then Home Secretary, now Britain's Foreign Minister, Mr. R. A. Butler, that *"we shall try to find a solution as friendly to these people as we can, and not on the basis of color alone."* (my emphasis: C. J.)

All Tory claims that the Act would benefit either Britain or the immigrants are, of course, easily refuted. The most widely prevalent Tory argument was that colored immigrants were "flooding Britain." At the time of the Act's passage, the 1961 British population census showed a two and a half million increase, during the very period of the growth of the immigration of West Indians and Afro-Asians, and this increase was easily absorbed by the British economy. The colored migrant is less than one in every hundred people. Yearly emigration of Britons shows that for every single person entering Britain, three leave its shores.

The shibboleth that "immigrants take away houses and jobs," when viewed in light of Tory responsibility for high interest property rates and the Rent Act makes this claim likewise ludicrous. As for new houses, there is no evidence that West Indians or other colored immigrants have taken away any houses. Allowed largely only to purchase old, dilapidated short-lease houses, it is the West Indian building worker, who helps to construct new houses, he makes an invaluable contribution to the building of new homes.

Even the usual last retort of the racial ideologists that West Indians and other colored citizens "lower moral stands" also fails to stand up. The world knows of the exploits of Christine Keeler and the British Ministers of State, an event which occasioned a calypso in the widely read West Indian Gazette. There has been no notable increase in jobs as a result of this Act. In fact, rail and shipbuilding closures, mergers and automation, continue apace. It is widely admitted that withdrawal of colored workers from transport, foundries and hospital services would cause a major economic dislocation in Britain, and that they continue to make a contribution to the British economy. Vic Feather, leading trade union official reiterated strongly, this view at an all-day conference recently in Smethwick, a Birmingham suburb, where a local election campaign slogan was that to elect Labor meant "*having a nigger for a neighbor.*" One finally observes regarding the asserted economic social burden of the migrant, that a "tidy" profit has been made by the Ministry of National Insurance from contributions of the surrendered cards of thousands of immigrants who returned home after a few years in Britain.

In the eyes of the world, the Tory record does not stand any better when it is known that nine times they have blocked the Bill to Outlaw Racial Discrimination by the Labor member for Parliament from Slough, Mr. Fenner Brockway. The main provisions of this bill would be to outlaw discrimination in public places, lodgings, inns, dance halls, and other leases; and also put penalties on incitement to racialism. The Bill has now gained the support of the Labor leadership who promised if they achieve office to introduce such a measure (although there are some indications that it may be watered down), as well as from leading Liberal M.P.'s and even from some Tory M.P.'s. Thus, there has been witnessed a reversal of the former open-door policy to Commonwealth citizens, and speciously to colored Commonwealth citizens. The result of all this has been a new degrading status and sufferance accorded to colored immigrants who are likewise saddled with the responsibility for Britain's social evils.

There is a reluctance on the part of virtually all sections of British public opinion to assess the fundamental reasons for the existence of racial prejudice. The citizens of the "Mother of Democracies" do not yet recognize that the roots of racialism in Britain are deep and were laid in the eighteenth and nineteenth centuries through British conquests of India, Africa, and great parts of Asia as well as the British Caribbean. All the resources of official propaganda and education, the superstructure of British imperialism, were permeated with projecting the oppressed colonial peoples as "lesser breeds," as "inferior colored peoples," "natives," "savages," and the like – in short, "the white man's burden." These rationalizations all served to build a justification for wholesale exploitation, extermination, and looting of the islands by British imperialism. The great wealth of present-day British monopoly-capital was built on the robbery of colored peoples by such firms as Unilever and the East Africa company to Tate and Llye [sic] and Booker Brothers in the Caribbean.

These artificial divisions and antagonisms between British and colonial workers, already costly in toll of generations of colonial wars and ever-recurrent crises, have delayed fundamental social change in Britain, and form the very basis of color prejudice. The small top section of the working class, bribed and corrupted, and benefiting from this colonial robbery have been imbued with this racialist "white superiority" poison. On the other hand progressive opinion rallied with the migrants' protests at the Commonwealth Immigrants Act, for the Labour Party leadership had voted in opposition to its enactment; yet allowing its subsequent renewal to go unchallenged, for fear of losing votes in the coming general elections. Labour offered the government an unopposed passage on the condition that it agree to place the Act with new and improved legislation drawn up "in consultation" with the Commonwealth countries.

The government, which had itself tried this tactic before, to the negative response of West Indian and other affected Commonwealth Governments, refused to give these assurances. The Labour M.P.'s voted against its renewal, but not before they made clear, to the dismay of the overwhelming majority of immigrants, that they too, stood for "quotas" and "controls." In essence, this stand does not differ in principle from the attitude of the Tory Government and the provisions of the Commonwealth Immigrants Act. With the sole exception of the British Communists, who completely oppose the system of "quotas" and "controls" for Commonwealth immigration, all other political parties have capitulated in one or another way to this racialist immigration measure. A recent statement of the Executive Committee of the British Communist Party declared its opposition to all forms of restrictions on colored immigration; declared its readiness to contest every case of discrimination; urged repeal of the Commonwealth Immigrants Act; and called for equality of access for employment, rates of wages, promotion to skilled jobs, and opportunities for apprenticeship and vocational training. It gave full support to the Bill to Outlaw Racial Discrimination and pledged its readiness to support every progressive measure to combat discrimination in Britain. It also projected the launching of an ideological campaign to combat racialism, which it noted, infects wide sections of the British working class.

[...]

Some issues facing colored immigrants

That the Tory color-bar Commonwealth Immigrants Bill has been enacted at the time when apartheid and racialism is under attack throughout the world from the African Heads of State, at Addis Ababa, to the half million Civil Rights March on Washington; from the United Nations, and world criticism of South Africa and the demand for application of economic sanctions, to the condemnation of apartheid and Jim Crow racialist practices in the U.S.; bespeak the fantastic blindness of Britain's Tory rulers even to Britain's own national interests. But as with every exploiting class, as the example of Hitlerism shows, faced with a radical movement of the masses against their rule, they seek to split and divert this anger onto a false "enemy."

Added to the second-class citizenship status foisted by such a measure, West Indians and other Afro-Asians are confronted in their daily lives with many social and economic problems. Forming several settlements in various cities, the overwhelming majority are workers, with a scattering of professionals. There are 3,000 students.

Throughout Britain, the West Indian contribution to its economy is undoubted. As building workers, carpenters, as nurses, doctors and on hospital staffs, in factories, on the transportation system and railway depots and stations, West Indians are easily evidenced. Lest the younger generation be omitted (without commenting here on the social mores "guiding" the cultural orientation of today's youth) one of the most popular current pop singers is a 16 year old girl from rural Jamaica.

Indicative of their bid to participate in the political life of the nation was the recent success of a West Indian doctor on the Labour ticket as London County Councillor for the second time in an area composed, though not solely, of West Indian migrants. For the first time many thousands of West Indian and Afro-Asian voters have registered and will be eligible to vote. It is not accidental therefore as reflected in an article entitled "The Color of Their Votes" in a leading Sunday periodical, that speculation is growing as to how they will use their vote. One such article entitled "The Color of Their Votes" concluded that they would vote "according to color" but in consonance with their class interests. But this observation is only a half-truth. For the common experience of all Afro-Asian-Caribbean peoples in Britain is leading to a growing unison among these communities as they increasingly identify an injury to one as being an injury to all. When added to this, one marks their pride in the growth of national-liberation achievements from the lands of their origin and among other nationally-oppressed peoples, they are likely to be influenced by this bond as much as by their particular mode of production. Most pre-election polls have indicated their leaning, if critical, towards Labour and other Independents.

[...]

Future perspectives

Conscious therefore of the need for alleviation of their second-class citizenship, determined to live and work in human dignity as is their natural right, the resourceful West Indian migrant, in common with all peoples involved (either consciously or not) in anti-imperialist struggles, are also thinking about their ultimate direction. That they are only now at the stage of tentatively formulating their views may be ascribed to three main factors: 1) to the constant pressure and concern with daily problems of survival, 2) to the groping in their own minds for the fundamental significance of their national identity and, 3) to the lack of an organized perspective for a progressive, united West Indies at home. Linked to the first factor is the urgent necessity to organize and unite the West Indian community in Britain around their fundamental demands. The level of organization in Britain is not yet commensurate to fulfill this urgent need. The West Indian worker, in common with all workers, is confronted with the necessity to engage in struggles, supported by their allies, for his own survival in a new environment. This also means engaging in the general struggle for peace, trade unionism, democracy and social change. While clinging strongly to his own roots, he is mindful of the conditions at home and the reasons for his emigration, and mindful too, of the disabilities which face him there. But his economic situation is relatively better and he views as a practicality that his children will grow up in England. If to this is added the recognition that as with all migrations, this too, will form a permanent community, it is only natural that steps should be taken to implement the recognition: that with permanency comes the growth of new institutions with all its accompanying aspects.

It is true, of course, that some measure of organization exists. West Indians are organized largely in social and welfare groups in the United Kingdom, established originally to meet the needs of incoming migrants. Only a smattering have thus far joined political movements or play an active role politically. This is undoubtedly attributable to the false twin ideas that they should only become politically active with their "return home," or the apolitical view that they should eschew politics. More fundamentally it is traceable also to the lack of previous political activity at home and the fact that for most West Indians their political baptism is occurring in their new environment. There exists [sic] such organizations as the Standing Conference of West Indian Organizations, a council composed of fifteen social and welfare groups in London boroughs, as well as Freemason Lodges in areas of large West Indian settlements. There are also similar organizations existing in the Midlands, all of which have close supervision by the Migrant Services Division of the Jamaica, Trinidad and Tobago, Barbados, Leeward and Windward Islands government offices in Britain. In addition there are a growing number of inter-racial committees and groups engaged in dealing with the problems of West Indians and other migrants, besides the student's organizations.

There are also special organizations based on island origins beginning to develop. The Church forms a center for many religious West Indian groups, choirs and the like. Yet questions are now arising as to whether these organizations fully meet the present needs of this community. This is evidenced in the concern being expressed by West Indians, as to whether integration in British life should be the sole aim in Britain or whether the self-organization of West Indian [sic] should not likewise be emphasized. Questions are being posed too, as to how to harness the national identity of West Indians towards this end.

A major effort designed to stimulate political and social thinking has been the launching, six years ago, of the progressive news-monthly, the West Indian Gazette. This newspaper has served as a catalyst, quickening the awareness, socially and politically, of West Indians, Afro-Asians and their friends. Its editorial stand is for a united independent West Indies, full economic social and political equality and respect for human dignity for West Indians and Afro-Asians in Britain, for peace and friendship between all Commonwealth and world peoples. It has campaigned vigorously on issues facing West Indians and other colored peoples. Whether against numerous police frameups, to which West Indians and other colored migrants are frequently subject, to opposing discrimination and to advocating support for trade unionism and unity of colored and white workers, W.I. news publications have attempted to emulate the path of progressive 'Negro' (Afro-Asian, Latin-American and Afro-American) journals who uncompromisingly and fearlessly fight against imperialist outrages and indignities to our peoples. The West Indian Gazette and Afro-Asian-Caribbean News has served to launch solidarity campaigns with the nationals who advance with their liberation struggles in Africa and in Asia. The present circulation and readership of the W.I. publication, would be larger, but for the usual welter of problems faced by most progressive journals. A campaign of support for financial aid among its readers and friends has recently been launched to help its expansion to a weekly and to establish its own printing plant. It counts among its contributors and supporters, many West Indian writers, who live in England, trade-unionists, and members of Parliament.

[...]

Underlying what may be termed "the search for a national identity," is the concern of West Indians to understand their historical and cultural heritage. This concern which arose with establishment of the now defunct West Indian Federation has become more widespread. The consequent polarization of West Indians into Jamaicans, Trinidadians, Barbadians, Grenadians, etc., has certain unrealities in England where existing problems among West Indians are shared in common. A consequence of emigration to England, has been that Afro-Asians and West Indians have come to know one another as they might not have previously, separated by the distance of their homelands.

Here, reference is not to some psuedo-intellectuals [sic] who, ignorant or unaware of a scientific definition of nationhood, deny the lack of a national identity on the spurious grounds of lack of a separate (not common) language. But rather to the leadership need to acquaint West Indians with their own history, and by a social interpretation of that history, better to arm them for future struggles by imparting a pride in their origins, struggles and future. This lack of historical perspective is at root, as Dr. Eric Williams correctly noted, from a society which eulogized the colonialist, and whose knowledge of West Indian history was limited to that of Anglo-Saxon conquests, Sir Walter Raleigh, Captain Morgan, and the feats of royalty. The task remains to enhance the knowledge of the true history: of the Morant Bay anti-slavery rebellion, the glorious Maroons, the early anticolonial struggles of Captain Cipriani, or of Chritchlows [sic] trade unionism, or of the significance of the movement towards closer West Indian federation, all of which early struggles created the preconditions leading to the contemporary struggle for nationhood, which thus is something less than that for which West Indian patriots fought and dreamed. Such an understanding would likewise help to create awareness of the need for support and aid to the bitter struggle being waged for British Guianese independence against U.S. imperialist intervention which fears social change along Socialist lines.

Related finally to the continued lack of an organized perspective for an advancing West Indies, is the indication of floundering in West Indian political life since the Federation [sic] demise. The present political parties in the Caribbean advocating a Socialist alternative, the only ultimate course for the West Indies, are still small and ineffective. But they represent the hope of the future, if only because they challenge the perspective of the present bourgeois-nationalist leaders, who heading a titularly independent West Indies continue to proclaim their reliance on the West, not only geographically, but in political and social aims even to the shame of all West Indians, and Jamaicans in particular, of the unprecedented offer of Jamaica's soil for a U.S. nuclear base.

Such advocacy may ultimately inspire West Indians at home and abroad to leap the shoals of struggle necessary to transform the economy of the West Indies, and consequently to establish a socialist West Indian nation that will play its role in the community of nations.

Such a perspective would win inspiring participation among West Indians in Britain, who adjure the gradualist view voiced by many of their Ministers that the pace of West Indian advancement will be "slow" and that the West Indian immigrant would do well to consider themselves primarily citizens of Britain and to cease to worry about their national identity. This idea is likewise based on the view held towards immigration by many bourgeois nationalist West Indian politicians who encourage migration as a "safety-valve," fearing the growth of militancy for social change, at home, more than they do the loss of their most valuable citizens.

A special importance attaches itself to the Caribbean, where there is evidenced the two paths to national liberation: either the path of obsequiousness to U.S. imperialism and neo-colonialism or the high road to Socialist advance as exemplified by Socialist Cuba. Particularly in the Caribbean, where United States imperialism threatens socialist Cuba; infringes on the national sovereignty of all Latin American peoples; intervenes in the internal affairs of British Guiana and Panama; and whose pretensions of a "free America in a free world" stands [sic] exposed before the massive hammer blows of the mounting Negro liberation struggle, which, as shown in our merged protests, Afro-Asians, and Caribbean peoples, held a Solidarity March to the U.S. London Embassy, in support of the Negro peoples' demands, the struggle for national liberation proceeds with singular emphasis.

5

International Law and International Organization
Introduction by Katharina Rietzler

"[E]verything which concerns sovereignty concerns international law."[1] These words were written in 1920 by Sarah Wambaugh, who, as the world-leading expert on international plebiscites, became perhaps the most recognized woman international lawyer of the interwar period. Self-determination as the sole legitimate mechanism for conferring sovereignty emerged as a paradigm in the era of the First World War. However, the self-determination that was on offer in the context of the League of Nations, the world's first global international organization, was largely shorn of its radical potential, racially differentiated, and institutionalizing empire. Sovereign equality remained aspiration more than reality despite the international establishment of the principle of self-determination, first in the 1945 Charter of the United Nations, and then in the 1960 Declaration on Decolonization (General Assembly Resolution 1514). Attempts to link self-determination with global economic redistribution faltered in the 1970s. The aspirations of self-determination in a world structured by hierarchy and domination thus run through twentieth-century histories of international law and international organization.[2]

Because it was predicated on the recognition of independent personhood, the principle of self-determination was inflected by both race and gender.[3] Processes for the transfer of sovereignty were intertwined with the fight for women's legal equality with men, for instance in the context of the global movement for female suffrage.[4] In very concrete ways,

---

[1] Sarah Wambaugh, *A Monograph on Plebiscites* (Washington, DC: Carnegie Endowment for International Peace, 1920), 30.

[2] Adom Getachew, *Worldmaking after Empire: The Rise and Fall of Self-Determination* (Princeton, NJ: Princeton University Press, 2019).

[3] Glenda Sluga, *The Nation, Psychology, and International Politics 1870–1919* (Basingstoke: Palgrave Macmillan, 2006), 7.

[4] For a history of female suffrage as a global issue see Mona L. Siegel, *Peace on Our Terms: The Global Battle for Women's Rights after the First World War* (New York: Columbia University Press, 2020).

sovereignty as a spatial structure was linked to women's political emancipation in post-First World War Europe, as the international plebiscites that were negotiated in the peace treaties to determine the sovereignty of disputed border territories gave votes to women at a time when female suffrage was the exception, not the norm. The question of whether unenfranchised women should be able to vote in international plebiscites impacted on definitions of nationality, sovereignty, the making and reach of international law, and who constituted the community of nations that was governed by it. In other words, the woman question was at the heart of questions around sovereignty in the aftermath of the First World War, and these were ones of international, not solely domestic, order.[5]

The thinkers excerpted in this section recognized that the actions taken by individuals and groups to attain self-determination necessarily impacted on relationships between peoples, states, and empires, as well as the organizational structures of international institutions. Few of them analyzed race and empire as structures of domination that shaped both the international state system and international organizations. They acknowledged the problem of equality in international law and international organization, sometimes but not always including the representation of oppressed groups, and how to deal with differences in national character, mentality, culture, and class. Their views on international organizations also diverged, ranging from conceiving of them as fora in which conflicts of interest among sovereign equals were articulated to analyses of international organizations as institutions that were prone to capture by powerful states and the interests of professional communities of statesmen and diplomats. Taken together, these excerpts express varying degrees of skepticism about the ordering potential of international law and organization, but they all reflect on how international norms and institutions should deal with the fact of human diversity.

The section begins with Mary Parker Follett (1868–1933), an American management theorist who deployed her insights into group psychology to critique traditional conceptions of sovereignty. Follett studied at the Harvard Annex (later Radcliffe College) and Newnham College, Cambridge, before publishing her undergraduate dissertation on the American House of Representatives in 1896 to wide acclaim. Finding it difficult to gain a foothold in academe, she then became a

---

[5] Sluga, *The Nation, Psychology, and International Politics*, chapters 4 and 5; Karen Knop, *Diversity and Self-Determination in International Law* (Cambridge: Cambridge University Press, 2002), chapters 6–8. On the invisibility of women in international legal history see Ignacio de la Rasilla, "Concepción Arenal and the Place of Women in Modern International Law," *Legal History Review*, 88:1–2 (2020), 211–253.

social worker in a poor Boston neighborhood. This formative period in a feminized profession shaped her ideas about group dynamics, which she further developed in two subsequent books. Never finding much resonance among political scientists, Follett became an authority in management and organizational studies, but remained deeply interested in questions of international organization. Follett, who was friends with F. Melian Stawell, a thinker discussed in the section on Field and Discipline, spent extended periods of time in Britain and conducted fieldwork at the League of Nations in Geneva, an institution that she regarded as the potential harbinger of a true community of nations.[6]

Follett has already been recognized in some disciplinary histories of IR.[7] The extract chosen here is from Follett's book *The New State*, written during the First World War and mapping out the future of international law and international organization. Both needed reforming: the international law of the future would be based on group psychology and serve an international society. This would not comprise independent sovereign states but would be a whole larger than the sum of its parts and held together by an "international will" (260). On the basis of Follett's observations of group dynamics, she argued that groups had the power to integrate interests, which gave them political authority. Against the traditional view that any international organization required states to cede some of their sovereignty, Follett contended that sovereignty could not be parceled up and redistributed as "bits of power" but that the way in which human beings related to one another had to be reconfigured to forge the "power of a larger whole" (258). This, she claimed, would unshackle nations from toxic competition and enmity. Yet, typically for her time, Follett principally meant the imperial powers when she imagined the creation of a community of nations, those who had "control of the regions which possess the raw materials" (258). The specter of decolonization, of the inhabitants of those regions claiming sovereignty over their own natural resources, was, for Follett, far in the future.

The international lawyer Sarah Wambaugh (1882–1955), writing around the same time, retained a more traditional view of sovereignty.

---

[6] Joan C. Tonn, *Mary P. Follett: Creating Democracy, Transforming Management* (New Haven, CT: Yale University Press, 2003); Mary Parker Follett, *The Speaker of the House of Representatives*. Radcliffe College Monographs, No. 5 (New York: Longmans, 1896); Mary Parker Follett, *Creative Experience* (New York: Longmans, Green and Company, 1924).

[7] Lucian Ashworth, *A History of International Thought: From the Origins of the Modern State to Academic International Relations* (London: Routledge, 2014), 222; Brian C. Schmidt, *The Political Discourse of Anarchy: A Disciplinary History of International Relations* (New York: SUNY Press, 1998), 168–171.

Wambaugh was the daughter of a Harvard law professor and also an alumna of Radcliffe College. Wambaugh's cutting-edge research on plebiscites, supported by the Carnegie Endowment for International Peace, made her a sought-after expert. The recipient of many academic honors and the first woman to lecture at the elite Hague Academy of International Law, Wambaugh was an exceptional woman in a predominantly male profession. She advised multiple international plebiscite commissions both in the interwar period and in the post-1945 period, and published several monographs.[8] She was also a member of the Women's International League for Peace and Freedom, an organization of mostly white European and American women that had formed during the First World War to press the cause of women's rights and a negotiated peace.[9] Wambaugh's work excerpted here should be cross-read with Margaret Lambert's piece on the 1935 Saar plebiscite in the section on Diplomacy and Foreign Policy. While Lambert's was an empirical case study, Wambaugh's legal analysis highlights the theoretical problems raised by international referenda.

The doctrine of self-determination was at the heart of demands for international referenda before transfer of a territory's sovereignty could take place. It was international law's way of responding to the challenge of democracy after the First World War. But who could make claims to self-determination?[10] The answer, Wambaugh suggested, extended from states to groups, to individuals. Self-determination as a principle had universal scope and even the smallest group could have "its day in court" (266). Wambaugh may not have foreseen the logical consequences of this assertion in the aftermath of US President Wilson's declarations, and she might not have welcomed the demands of anticolonial nationalists, but her rethinking of sovereignty had liberatory potential.

Buried in a footnote on the Confederate secession from the United States, Wambaugh criticized racism and slavery: "A vote from which a whole class is excluded, however, even if that class be unenfranchised slaves, cannot, by hypothesis, be considered as self-determination in the eyes of the twentieth century" (262 n33). If all humans living in a territory

---

[8] "Dr. Sarah Wambaugh, Plebiscite Expert Who Advised League and U.N., Is Dead," *New York Times*, November 13, 1955; Sarah Wambaugh, "La pratique des plébiscites internationaux," *Recueil des Cours*, 18 (1927): 149–258; Sarah Wambaugh, *Plebiscites since the World War*, 2 vols. (Washington, DC: Carnegie Endowment for International Peace, 1933); Sarah Wambaugh, *The Saar Plebiscite* (Cambridge, MA: Harvard University Press, 1940).

[9] Sluga, *The Nation, Psychology, and International Politics*, 108.

[10] For a discussion of this problem in international law see James Crawford, *The Creation of States in International Law*, 2nd ed. (Oxford: Clarendon Press, 2006).

had to be consulted on the transfer of that territory's sovereignty, was any restriction of voting rights legitimate? Wambaugh answered this obvious question somewhat timidly when she later suggested that women ought to have a vote in plebiscites, if not for a more "comprehensive expression" of public opinion then because these women could represent the views of their dead husbands, brothers, fathers, and sons (267).

While Wambaugh was clear that transfers of sovereignty were essentially processes that happened within international law and could not be decided by force of arms or politics, she side-stepped the question of whether international law was produced by sovereign consent in the first place. If sovereignty was latent within human groups that were not necessarily congruent with territorial nation states, do states make international law? Or does international law's existence necessarily precede the existence of sovereign states?

This question, which had wide-ranging implications in an age of decolonization, was addressed elegantly in a highly original book by Krystyna Marek (1914–1993). Although she was not located in the Anglo-American centers of IR, we include Marek because of the influence of her analysis and her association with the Graduate Institute of International Studies in Geneva (today the Graduate Institute of International and Development Studies), an institution that was created with American philanthropic funding and became an important node in transatlantic intellectual networks of IR and neoliberal economic and political thought.[11] Marek was born in Cracow, Poland, where she studied and practiced law. Her doctoral work was interrupted by the German invasion in 1939, when she fled her native country, never to return. After working for the Polish government-in-exile in London during the Second World War, Marek settled in Switzerland, where she returned to her intellectual work at the Graduate Institute. The resulting dissertation established her scholarly reputation as a brilliant and original mind, and eventually led to a professorship in Geneva.[12]

Contrary to Wambaugh, Marek was concerned not with transfers of sovereignty but with its emergence and extinction. Writing in the

---

[11] On this connection see, for instance, Quinn Slobodian, *Globalists* (Cambridge, MA: Harvard University Press, 2018); Katharina Rietzler, "Experts for Peace: Structures and Motivations of Philanthropic Internationalism in the United States and Europe," in Daniel Laqua (ed.), *Internationalism Reconfigured: Transnational Ideas and Movements between the World Wars* (London: I. B. Tauris, 2011), 45–65.

[12] Natasha Wheatley, "What Can We (She) Know about Sovereignty? Krystyna Marek and the Worldedness of International Law," in Patricia Owens and Katharina Rietzler (eds.), *Women's International Thought: A New History* (Cambridge: Cambridge University Press, 2021), 327–344.

tradition of continental legal positivism, Marek reflected on the birth and death of states. This enabled her to construct international law as an intellectual vantage point that made possible the legal appraisal of processes that preceded or followed a state's life span. Such a move was necessary, she argued. "Since they break the framework of municipal law, the birth, extinction and transformation of States can be made the subject of legal enquiry only by reference to a legal order which is both higher than State law and yet belongs to the same system of norms, on the basis of monism and the primacy of international law" (279). International law was thus not produced by sovereign consent, a position which ran contrary to traditional views on the emergence of the international system and its norms.

Such a more conventional approach may be exemplified by M. (Mary) Margaret Ball (1909–1999), a prolific academic, with a long teaching career spanning several decades. Born in California, Ball completed her education at Stanford but also earned a doctorate in law from the University of Cologne, Germany. In 1936 she became an instructor and later a professor of political science at Wellesley College in New England, where she also acted as faculty adviser to students participating in the Carnegie Endowment's International Relations Clubs. She moved to Duke University as Dean of Women in 1962.[13]

Ball's research publications range from a contemporary history of the political movement that paved the way for Nazi Germany's annexation of Austria in 1938 to books and path-breaking articles on international bodies such as the UN, NATO, and the Organization of American States.[14] Ball's trajectory is also relevant in terms of IR's disciplinary formation. Fellow scholars regarded her output as well-researched and authoritative, if technical, and grouped her together with well-known scholars in mid-century American IR that paved the way for the emergence of the field of International Organization.[15] The co-authored

---

[13] "Women's Dean Is Named at Duke," *New York Times*, October 21, 1962; "Forum Sends Messengers to Peace Conference," *Wellesley College News*, December 8, 1938.

[14] M. Margaret Ball, *Post-War German–Austrian Relations: The Anschluss Movement, 1918–1936* (Stanford, CT: Stanford University Press, 1937); M. Margaret Ball, *The Problem of Inter-American Organization* (Stanford, CT: Stanford University Press, 1944); M. Margaret Ball, "Bloc Voting in the General Assembly," *International Organization*, 5 (February 1951): 3–31; M. Margaret Ball, *N.A.T.O. and the European Union Movement* (London: Stevens & Sons, 1959); M. Margaret Ball, *The OAS in Transition* (Durham, NC: Duke University Press, 1969).

[15] John Rydjord, "Review of *The Problem of Inter-American Organization*," *Pacific Historical Review*, 14:2 (1945): 263; Ann Van Wynen Thomas, "Review of *The OAS in Transition*," *American Political Science Review*, 66:2 (1972): 670–671; J. Martin Rochester, "The Rise and Fall of International Organization as a Field of Study," *International Organization*, 40:4 (1986): 777–813.

extract included here represents Ball's attempt to branch out from her specialist studies. In it, she provides a panoptic overview of the historical emergence of the modern state system and nineteenth-century notions of a family of sovereign nations, brought about by socio-economic processes in emerging nation states. In Ball's narrative, sovereignty was made by states, and not decided over by individuals – a very different take than Wambaugh's emphasis on self-determination.

Louise W. Holborn's (1898–1975) work also falls within the field of International Organization. Holborn, whose books remain standard histories of international refugee organizations, analyzed the minutiae of the international negotiations preceding the formation of the United Nations High Commissioner for Refugees (UNHCR) in the aftermath of the Second World War.[16] Holborn also identified sovereignty as the bone of contention in the making of international refugee organizations, as evidenced in the East–West division over whether refugees from Eastern Europe should be repatriated or allowed to settle according to their preference. The Soviet Union demanded that all refugees had to be repatriated, precisely because it would violate the sovereignty of the state of origin if this were not to occur. Holborn's work itself provides a good example of how difficult it is to produce critical narratives of international organizations (IOs). There is evidence from her papers that she was pressured by UNHCR staff to tone down passages of her book to avoid embarrassment, and once it was published she faced allegations that her work was too deferential to IOs and governments.[17]

Holborn knew war and exile herself. Born in Wilhelmine Germany and originally trained as a social worker – a professional pathway not unusual for women international thinkers such as Mary Parker Follett or Jane Addams[18] – Holborn went on to study at one of the centers for IR research in Germany, the Deutsche Hochschule für Politik in Berlin, before leaving Nazi Germany in 1933. After a stint at the LSE in London, Holborn settled in the United States, gaining an MA and a PhD from Radcliffe College. A fellowship from the Harvard/Radcliffe Bureau for International Research and a job at the American Office of Strategic Services in the Second World War preceded her academic career, which led to a professorship at Connecticut College for

---

[16] See e.g. Peter Gatrell, *The Making of the Modern Refugee* (Oxford: Oxford University Press, 2013), *passim*.

[17] Emily A. Copeland, "Louise W. Holborn Archives, Schlesinger Library, Radcliffe College," *Journal of Refugee Studies*, 10:4 (1997): 503–506.

[18] See above as well as Valeska Huber, Tamson Pietsch, and Katharina Rietzler, "Women's International Thought and the New Professions, 1900–1940," *Modern Intellectual History*, 18:1 (2021): 121–145.

Women.[19] Holborn dedicated her scholarly life to the study of refugee organizations but also to friendships with women academics whom she met through the Radcliffe network, for instance Gwendolen M. Carter, her erstwhile fellow student and in the 1970s Director of African Studies at Northwestern University. Like all the US-based thinkers included in this section, with the notable exception of Pauli Murray, Holborn was shaped by the homosocial intellectual life of elite New England women's colleges.

French-born Lucie Zimmern (1875–1963) underwent a more unconventional formation as an international thinker. Zimmern, known as Lucie Barbier before her second marriage to the British internationalist and political scientist Alfred Zimmern, was a pianist and singer. Zimmern met Alfred in Aberystwyth, Wales, where she had founded the University College of Wales Musical Club in 1909 and promoted musical traditions as a concrete path towards international understanding.[20] In 1921 Zimmern left Aberystwyth with her husband, who was forced out of his job as the first professor of International Relations in the world because of their liaison. The pair co-founded the Geneva School of International Studies in 1925, a summer school that attracted students from all over the world, but especially the United States. At the "Zimmern School," women gave authoritative lectures, served on the advisory committee along with presidents of US women's colleges, and made up a large part of the student body.[21] It was one of the most successful internationalist education projects of the interwar years, and Zimmern became a well-known presence at conferences in the new field of International Relations.

In her 1932 book, her only published monograph, Zimmern sought to explain the League of Nations from her privileged vantage point in Geneva, analyzing self-fashioning in an international organization as well as the potential for reform at a critical time for the League. Zimmern, who must have encountered a fair share of British snobbery, included many jokes squarely aimed at her adopted countrymen and women in her writing. "Why is a Foreign Office a great office? Not because it deals with

[19] Schlesinger Library, Radcliffe Institute, "Additional Papers of Louise W. Holborn, 1898–1975," https://hollisarchives.lib.harvard.edu/repositories/8/resources/6107 (accessed January 10, 2020).

[20] Lucie Barbier papers, National Library of Wales, https://archives.library.wales/index .php/lucie-barbier-papers (accessed January 10, 2020).

[21] "The Geneva School of International Studies," pamphlet, 1927, Alfred Zimmern Papers, Bodleian Library, Oxford, box 87. Much of Lucie's personal papers and correspondence is contained in the Alfred Zimmern papers at Oxford, which is, however, not apparent from the finding aid.

foreigners, but because of the tone in which it talks to them" (269). In polemical fashion, Zimmern divided the delegates to the League Assembly into "insiders" and "outsiders," the traditional diplomats wedded to outdated practices such as war-making, and the naïve neophytes who populated the corridors of power on Lac Léman, either too shy to speak or taken in by "*megalomania internationalis*" (268, 271). In the end, Zimmern argued, the insiders managed to "capture Geneva" (270), not abandoning the old diplomacy but, on the contrary, extending its range of instruments, all the while posing as good internationalists. That such a cynical analysis should come from someone sharing a life and professional vocation with Alfred Zimmern, a thinker whom the IR scholar E. H. Carr labeled the archetypical idealist, should not surprise disciplinary historians long inured to Carr's distortion of the interwar conversation within IR.[22] But Lucie Zimmern's account is also a reminder of the extent to which the League of Nations as the world's first experiment in international governance actually preserved existing international power structures, inequalities, and hierarchies rather than challenging them.

The final two extracts deal with alternatives to both national sovereignty and international organization and feature the American lawyer and activist Pauli Murray and the British social scientist Barbara Wootton.

Pauli Murray (1910–1985) was born in the Jim Crow American South into a prominent family of mixed racial heritage. After graduating with a BA from Hunter College, a women's college in New York City, Murray unsuccessfully applied to the University of North Carolina, which, in 1938, did not admit African Americans but had counted Murray's white maternal great-grandfather among its trustees. Murray's case became a *cause célèbre* for civil rights activists. After graduating from Howard University in 1944, she again unsuccessfully sought entry to a bastion of privilege, this time Harvard Law School, which admitted only males. Murray persevered and completed a doctorate at Yale in 1965, the first African American to do so. During a professional life that combined civil and women's rights activism, legal practice, university teaching, and a call to the Episcopalian ministry, as well as publishing poetry and a family history, this versatile thinker made many notable contributions, not least to Title VII of the 1964 Civil Rights Act, which, on Murray's

---

[22] For a deconstruction of the "idealism paradigm" in the discipline of IR see Lucian M. Ashworth, "Where Are the Idealists in Interwar International Relations?," *Review of International Studies*, 32:2 (2006): 291–308.

recommendation, included a prohibition of workplace sex discrimination.[23] Recent historical writing has focused on Murray's theorizing of intersectionality, gender-nonconformity and sexual attraction to women.[24] What remains underexplored, however, is Murray's role as an international legal thinker, one which characteristically combined activism and scholarship.

It was Murray's sense of mission that brought her to newly independent Ghana as a law professor in 1959, meeting fellow expatriate Shirley Graham DuBois, whose work is included in the section on Population, Nation, Immigration. Murray's experiences in Ghana, where her association with members of the opposition put her in danger, reinforced both her conviction that white Americans had to show more respect for African Americans' cultural heritage *and* a commitment to the principles of American legalism and constitutionalism. Disturbed by Prime Minister and later president-for-life Kwame Nkrumah's autocratic tendencies and having criticized the arrests of dissidents, Murray left Ghana in 1961, but not before drafting a book on the 1960 Ghanaian constitution with her law school colleague Leslie Rubin, a Jewish South African former senator who had to leave South Africa because he opposed apartheid.[25]

While written as a textbook on African constitutionalism, *The Constitution and Government of Ghana* highlights the familiar problem of overlapping sovereignties in international law. The selection included here elucidates the tension between postcolonial sovereignty and regional solidarity in the form of the African Union as well as the post-imperial structures of the British Commonwealth of Nations. Remarkably for a nation that had only recently achieved sovereignty, Article 2 of the Constitution imbued the Ghanaian Parliament with the power "to provide for the surrender of the whole or any part of the sovereignty of Ghana" on behalf of the Ghanaian people, with the overarching aim of achieving political integration in Africa. Historians of political thought in the Black Atlantic have reconstructed a "federal moment" which sought to protect the sovereignty of African states from neo-colonial domination

---

[23] For a useful biographical note see Davison M. Douglas, "Foreword," in Pauli Murray, *States' Laws on Race and Colour*, reprint (Athens, GA: University of Georgia Press, 1997), xiii–xxvii.

[24] Brittney C. Cooper, *Beyond Respectability: The Intellectual Thought of Race Women* (Urbana, IL: University of Illinois Press, 2017), chapter 3; Rosalind Rosenberg, *Jane Crow: The Life of Pauli Murray* (New York: Oxford University Press, 2017); Simon D. Elin Fisher, "Challenging Dissemblance in Pauli Murray Historiography, Sketching a History of the Trans New Negro," *Journal of African American History*, 104:2 (2019): 176–200.

[25] Rosenberg, *Jane Crow*, 219–235.

by "creating new political and economic linkages between postcolonial states." Nkrumah himself deployed the federal model of the United States as a blueprint for regional federation.[26] Murray's analysis is thus an example of the transnational development of federal models in the context of postcolonial sovereignty, an issue that remained neglected among white European thinkers of federalism.

One of these was Barbara Wootton (1897–1988). The child of two Cambridge academics, Wootton took the academic route herself, and, after studying at Cambridge and the LSE, secured various academic posts and dedicated herself to workers' education. She took a professorship at Bedford College London and became an important public figure in post-1945 British debates on social and economic inequality and criminality. She was a member of Federal Union, founded as a pro-European integration discussion and pressure group in 1938.[27] Her international thought is marked by a fusion of liberal and socialist analyses and her preoccupation with Britain's place in the world, which, according to Wootton, should undergo a severing of imperial ties in favor of a "turn to Europe." However, Wootton rarely reflected on how self-determination for Britain's colonial possessions could be achieved.[28]

In the 1941 article included here, Wootton explored federalism as a workable alternative to international organizations in the midst of the Second World War. Citing the example of the International Labor Organization, and its inability to pressure member states into ratifying conventions on labor standards during the interwar years, Wootton argued that a federal government "does not tolerate thirty percent observance of the law!" (276). While the analogy between international conventions and domestic law seems flawed, Wootton nonetheless argued that federalism successfully combined territoriality ("its own territory," 276) with national self-determination as a federal government would never have an exclusive power of legislation. Exhibiting lofty thinking not uncommon in times of international turmoil, Wootton reasoned that federalism might even bridge the ideological gaps between socialist and non-socialist countries, and went so far as to imagine a post-war repurposing of Hitler's imposed unification of Nazi-occupied Europe. But Wootton's main argument, that federalism had the potential to fix the flaws of international law and international organization in a

---

[26] Getachew, *Worldmaking after Empire*, 11.
[27] Ann Oakley, *A Critical Woman: Barbara Wootton, Social Science and Public Policy in the Twentieth Century* (London: Bloomsbury Academic, 2011).
[28] Or Rosenboim, "A Plan for Plenty: The International Thought of Barbara Wootton," in Patricia Owens and Katharina Rietzler (eds.), *Women's International Thought: A New History* (Cambridge: Cambridge University Press, 2021), 286–305.

system in which states are reluctant to give up sovereignty, remains worth pondering. Wootton's analysis, however, did not stretch to the European and American colonial empires, and she retreated from international thought in the post-1945 period.

Returning to Wambaugh's quote at the beginning, all of the thinkers in this section claimed for themselves a vantage point which allowed them to make arguments about the changing nature of sovereignty within international legal and institutional frameworks, whether that was from the position of understanding groups and group dynamics (Follett, Wambaugh), the emergence of a system of states (Ball, Marek), the politics of international organizations (Holborn, Zimmern) or ways in which sovereignty could be repurposed (Murray, Wootton, but also Follett). If the woman question was indeed at the heart of twentieth-century international law, it matters that these arguments were made by women who witnessed profound changes to women's civic status and the ways in which the self could become an actor in the realm of international politics.

Katharina Rietzler

Mary Parker Follett

From *The New State* (1919)

The great lesson of the group process, in which all others are involved, is that particularism, however magnified, is no longer possible. There is no magic by which selfishness becomes patriotism the moment we can invoke the nation. The change must be this: as we see now that a nation cannot be healthy and virile if it is merely protecting the rights of its members, so we must see that we can have no sound condition of world affairs merely by the protection of each individual nation – that is the old theory of individual rights. Each nation must play its part in some larger whole. Nations have fought for national rights. These are as obsolete as the individual rights of the last century. What raises this war to a place never reached by any war before is that the Allies are not fighting for national rights. As long as history is read the contribution of America to the Great War will be told as America's taking her stand squarely and responsibly on the position that national particularism was in 1917 dead.

And as we are no longer to talk of the "rights" of nations, so no longer must "independent" nations be the basis of union. In our present international law a sovereign nation is one that is independent of other nations – surely a complete legal fiction. And when stress is laid on independence in external relations as the nature of sovereignty, it is but a step to the German idea that independence of others can develop into authority over others. This tendency is avoided when we think of sovereignty: (1) as *looking in*, as authority over its own members, as the independence which is the result of the complete interdependence of those members; and when we at the same time (2) think of this independence as *looking out* to other independences to form through a larger interdependence the larger sovereignty of a larger whole. Interdependence is the keynote of the relations of individuals within a nation. As no man can be entirely free except through his perfected relation to his group, so no nation can be truly independent until a genuine union has brought about interdependence. As we no longer think that every individual has a final purpose of his own independent of any community, so we no longer think that each nation has a "destiny" independent of the "destiny" of other nations.

The error of our old political philosophy was that the state always looks in: it has obligations to its members, it has none to other states; it merely enters into agreements with them for mutual benefit thereby obtained. International law of the future must be based not on nations as "sovereigns" dealing with one another, but on nations as members of a society dealing with one another. The difference in these conceptions is enormous. We are told that cessions of sovereignty must be the basis of an international government. We cannot have a lasting international union until we entirely reform such notions of sovereignty: that the power of the larger unit is produced mechanically by taking away bits of power from all the separate units. Sovereignty is got by giving to every unit its fullest value and thereby giving birth to a new power – the power of a larger whole. We must give up "sovereign" nations in the old sense, but with our present definition of sovereignty we may keep all the real sovereignty we have and then unite to evolve together a larger sovereignty.

The idea must be carefully worked out: we can take each so-called "sovereign power" which we are thinking of "delegating" to a League of Nations and we can see that that delegating does not make us individual nations less "sovereign" and less "free" but more so – it is the Great Paradox of our time. The object of every proper "cession" of sovereignty is to make us freer than ever before. Is it to be "sovereign" and "free" for nations suspiciously and fearfully to keep sleepless watch on one another while they build ship for ship, plane for plane? Have England and Germany been proudly conscious of their "freedom" when thinking of Central Africa? When the individual nations give up their separate sovereignty – as regards their armaments, as regards the control of the regions which possess the raw materials, as regards the greater waterways of the world, as regards, in fact, all which affects their joint lives – the falling chains of a real slavery will reverberate through the world. For unrelated sovereignty, with world conditions as they are to-day, is slavery.

The idea of "sovereign" nations must go as completely as is disappearing the idea of sovereign individuals. The isolation of sovereign nations is so utterly complete that they cannot really (and I mean this literally) even see each other. The International League is the one solution for the relation of nations. Whenever we say we can have a "moral" international law on any other basis, we write ourselves down pure sentimentalists.

There are many corollaries to this project. We do not need, for instance, a more vigorous protection of neutrals, but the abolition of neutrals. The invasion of the rights of neutrals in this war by both sides shows that we can no longer have neutrals in our scheme of union; all must come within the bond.

Further, diplomatic relations will be entirely changed. "Honor among thieves" means loyalty to your group: while to lie or to try to get the better of your own particular group is an unpardonable offence, you may deceive an outsider. We now see the psychological reason for this. Diplomatic lying will not go until diplomatists instead of treating with one another as members of alien groups consider themselves all as members of one larger group – the League of Nations.

Moreover, one nation cannot injure another merely; the injury will be against the community, and the community of nations will look upon it as such. Under our present international system the attack of one nation on another is the same as the attack of one outlaw on another. But under a civilized international system, the attack of one individual on another is an attack on society and the whole society must punish it. The punishment, however, will not consist in keeping the offender out of the alliance. If the Allies win, Germany should not be punished by keeping her out of a European league; she must be shown how to take her place within it. And it must be remembered that we do not join a league of nations solely to work out our relations to one another, but to learn to work for the larger whole, for international values. Until this lesson is learned no league of nations can be successful.

[...]

Organized cooperation is in the future to be the basis of international relations. We are international in our interests. We do not want an American education, an English education, a French education. "Movements" seek always an international society. We have international finance. Our standards of living are becoming internationalized. Socially, economically, in the world of thought, national barriers are being broken down. It is only in politics that we are national. This must soon change: with all these *rapprochements* we cannot be told much longer of fundamental differences between us which can be settled only by murdering each other.

People thought that Italy could not be united, that the duchies of Germany would never join. Cavour and Bismarck had no easy part. But if one hundred millions of people in Central Europe can be made to see the evils of separation, cannot others? With our greater facilities of communication, with our increased commercial intercourse and our increased realization of the interdependence of nations (a manufacturing nation cannot get along without the food producing nations, etc.), this ought not now to be impossible. Or has the single state exhausted our political ability? Are we willing to acknowledge this? We have had very little idea yet of a community of nations. The great fault of Germany is not that she overestimates her own power of achievement, which is indeed marvellous, but that she has never yet had any conception of a community of nations. Let her apply all her own theory of the subordination of the individual to the whole to the subordination of Germany to an allied Europe, and she would be a most valuable member of a European league.

The group process thus shows us that a genuine community of nations means the correlation of interests, the development of an international ethics, the creation of an international will, the self-evolving of a higher loyalty, and above all and including all, the full responsibility of every nation for the welfare of every other.

With such an aim before us courts of arbitration seem a sorry makeshift. We are told that as individuals no longer fight duels but take their disputes into the courts, so nations must now arbitrate, that is, take their dispute to some court. But what has really ousted duels has not been the courts but a different conception of the relation between men; so what will do away with war will not be courts of arbitration, but a different conception of the relations between nations. We need machinery not merely for settling disputes but for preventing disputes from arising; not merely for interpreting past relations, but for giving expression to new relations; not merely to administer international law, but to make international law – not a Hague court but an international legislature.

A community of nations needs a constitution, not treaties. Treaties are of the same nature as contract. Just as in internal law contract is giving way to the truer theory of community, so the same change must take place in international law. It is true that the first step must be more progressive treaties before we can hope for a closer union, but let us keep clearly before us the goal in order that in making these treaties they shall be such that they will open the way in time to a real federation, to an international law based not on "sovereign" nations.

We have already seen that it is the *creation* of a collective will which we need most in our social and political life, not the enforcing of it; it is the same with a league of nations – we must create an international will. We want neither concession nor compromise. And a vague "brotherhood" is certainly not enough. As we have seen the group as the workshop for the making of the collective will, so we see that we cannot have an international will without creating a community of nations.

Sarah Wambaugh

From *A Monograph on Plebiscites* (1920)

The arguments for and against the doctrine of national self-determination may be summarized as follows. The opponents of the doctrine agree that to legitimatize a title gained by conquest the express consent of the two contracting powers and the tacit assent of the inhabitants are sufficient. Against the method of the plebiscite they advance arguments attacking both the validity of its underlying theory and the expediency of leaving to a vote by universal suffrage a question of such importance as sovereignty. Their first argument is that the cession of sovereignty is outside the domain of international law and is of merely political importance, concerning only the two States involved. This position appears to result from a failure to analyze the threefold aspect of a cession of sovereignty, namely, alienation, transfer and integration. It is true that these three phases are of unequal interest in international law. The first phase, alienation, corresponding to "divesting of title," is obviously a matter largely of constitutional law, but a matter certainly open to regulation by international law, as it involves national debt, police and, if done during war, questions of neutrality and blockade. The second stage, that of transfer, clearly concerns international law, for it has to do with the relations of two States at least. The third stage, that of integration, is of a mixed character, concerning the municipal or constitutional law of the annexing State and, as it involves a question of title, concerning international law also. The subject of validity of title has long occupied the attention of writers on international law, for, as is well known, discussion of title by conquest, discovery, preemption, occupation and treaty occupy a place in the treatises, and the doctrines have broadened and developed to meet geographical and political exigencies.

The opponents next assert that the doctrine that a part of a State may resist a cession desired by the whole State is wholly subversive of the true doctrine of sovereignty, and that it defeats its own proposed object of securing the rule of the majority, since it allows that will to be thwarted by a minority.[29]

Such a result, they say, is like allowing a tenant to decide whether he will pay rent to his landlord or to another.[30] They also point out that a use of self-determination might well obstruct peace, for it might happen that only by a cession could a defeated State negotiate peace, as in the case of France in 1871. It might also defeat the ends of justice by preventing the victorious State, the victim of aggressive war, from enjoying the just fruits of victory.[31] The supporters answer that the punishment of guilt for starting a war should be arranged by indemnities or payment by other means involving property loss only, but that it should not be made by means of change of sovereignty over people. They assert, moreover, that although a State may with right separate a part of itself for its own interest or safety, with that separation sovereignty ceases, the part so abandoned having the right to dispose of itself. The proposition that the right of transfer does not exist, in which practically all the supporters of the doctrine agree, appears to be based on the presence of a latent sovereignty in each group, whether artificial or natural – a latent sovereignty which asserts itself when the former sovereignty ceases through separation. It is this conception of latent sovereignty as well as that of the right of a people to resist separation, which arouses that fear of secession which is so vividly felt by the opponents of the doctrine.[32] The supporters assert, however, that the right of secession is not an inevitable corollary, for to say that the people have the right to oppose separation or transfer is far from saying that they have the right to initiate it.

Indeed on this point it might well be said that the right of successful secession is already recognized by international law, and that to introduce the requirement of a popular vote in such cases would be to cast on the party of secession the burden of proving the extent of its strength not only by force of arms but also by the ballot. It might well be that by such insistence secession would be discouraged and the State protected.[33]

---

[29] Cf. *Lieber*, also *Bonfils* (1st ed.), § 571.

[30] *Fusinato*, p. 144, quotes Paul Laband, *Das Staatsrecht des Deutschen Reich*, vol. 1, p. 184, to this effect.

[31] Geffcken, *Heffter*, p. 438.

[32] Padelletti, Lieber, Bonfils, Rivier, Holtzendorff, Despagnet.

[33] In the case of the Southern Confederacy although no referendum was taken on the question of secession, except in Texas, especially elected State conventions in the States of the far south did indeed vote for secession, before the attack on Sumter. A vote from which a whole class is excluded, however, even if that class be unenfranchised slaves, cannot, by hypothesis, be considered as self-determination in the eyes of the twentieth century, whatever standing it may have had in the nineteenth. It is noteworthy that it was

The opponents' objection to the practical value of the plebiscite may be summarized under three heads. The first is the reluctance to allow the fate of the territory to be settled by a bare majority, swayed, in their apprehension, not by reason but by sentiment of a possibly evanescent sort. The answer is made that it is better to have the majority rule rather than the minority, and that the most important of all matters is precisely sentiment, which is the force most important to enlist for the purpose of stable order.[34] The second objection is that the plebiscite presents opportunity for pressure and fraud, exemplified particularly in Savoy and Nice.[35] The citation of the votes of Savoy and Nice against the doctrine is of no value according to Fusinato, who says that all the accusations brought, and fairly brought, against these plebiscites, especially on account of faulty execution, can not detract from the theoretical importance of the affirmation of the principle itself.[36] The third objection to the plebiscites of the past is that they have merely been an unnecessary ratification of a *fait accompli*. As to this argument Fusinato adds that it has even here a juridical value by showing that the right was bound up with the force used, because to force was added the will of the people, and that by resort to the plebiscite all occasion for doubt, dispute or recrimination is removed and the State is given that formal juridical title which is invaluable.[37] He points out that the practical objections raised are largely those always raised against universal suffrage, and that, with proper care, opportunities for fraud should be rendered negligible.

To avoid the several dangers enumerated, the opponents of the doctrine assert that the rights of the individual are sufficiently safeguarded by the doctrine of individual option. To this Fusinato answers at length that however relatively great may be the use made of option it always remains quite trivial as regards the mass of the inhabitants, for the great mass in its entirety, even after the exercise of individual option and the effective change of domicile by some, remains as it was before. Moreover, to say that the act of the man who remains inactive should be interpreted as an

---

only after the call for federal troops, after Sumter, that Virginia and the other border slave States changed their votes from union to secession.

[34] *Fusinato*, p. 41.

[35] Lieber was perhaps the first writer on international law to attack the Savoy vote. His attack has been repeated by practically every writer in opposition.

[36] "Tutte le accuse di cui fu oggetto questo plebiscito, specialmente, come diremo, per i vizii della sua esecuzione, non possono evidentemente togliere nulla alla importanza teorica dell'affermazione del principio in se medesimo." *Fusinato*, p. 104.

[37] "Il valore giuridico della pacifica manifestazione nei plebisciti, la quale segue la violenza della rivoluzione, consiste appunto in questo, che essi purificano l'opera della forza, dimostrando che con essa stava collegato il diritto, perocchè ad essa si aggiungeva l'elemento della volunta del popolo." *Fusinato*, p. 134.

act of spontaneous submission and of preference is often a sad irony. How little individual option favors the liberty of the people, he continues, is shown easily by the fact that the most liberal treaties in regard to the right of option were precisely those that settled the partition of Poland.[38] He might have added that the option clause [sic] in the treaties of Prague and of Frankfort were far from sufficient.

The war has rescued the principle of self-determination from its academic retirement. It comes to the fore again without the prestige of its past, for that has been forgotten with the passing of the generation of statesmen who supported it. Now, as then, it is turned to as a doctrine promising a practical solution for those difficulties which were certainly not solved successfully by the ephemeral experiments made in the Congresses of Vienna and of Berlin and in the Treaty of Frankfort. One hears no longer that it is a doctrine which does not concern international law; for it grows obvious to the world that everything which concerns sovereignty concerns international law. The question whether or not the doctrine of self-determination has standing in international law has yielded to the question of its fitness for the purposes of our generation. Thus to-day it becomes worthwhile to re-state the reasons which have been urged heretofore, and which will now inevitably be urged again in answer to its opponents. These reasons will now be summarized.

Title rests for its final sanction on public opinion. History would seem to prove that, in questions of territorial sovereignty, public opinion bases its judgment on an unexpressed major premise, namely, that no title acquired either through treaty, conquest or occupation, or based on economic, racial or historical arguments, or arguments of military necessity, is valid, no matter how many centuries it has run, unless it has behind it the consent of the majority of the inhabitants of the territory. Of this fact Ireland, Poland, Italy, Bohemia and Alsace-Lorraine are sufficient proof.

The doctrine of national self-determination was born of the chief contribution of the eighteenth century to political thought, the assertion of the right of the individual to freedom from despotic control. It is an axiom of the twentieth century that the individual's right to self-government must yield to the welfare of society as a whole. One must, therefore, ask how far the doctrine is consistent with our present philosophy. It is often asked whether or not the national aspirations of one group should outweigh the economic desires of another, if it should appear that satisfaction of those desires is for the good of society. The answer is that

---

[38] *Fusinato*, p. 156.

the main requisite of society is order, to which validity of title and territorial sovereignty is essential. If this is so, then it appears that the interest of the world and that of the group are one, and that only by basing title on the principle of national self-determination can there be a presumption of stability for the State or for the world-wide society of States.

The principle of national self-determination once accepted, there are practical reasons why the plebiscite should be resorted to in order that the will of the majority may be ascertained in a definite statistical fashion. The purpose might be thought to be served either by mere imagination or by indirect consultation through an international commission collecting evidence of the desire of the inhabitants by a survey of history, literature, economic ties and interests, statistics as to race, language and religion, and by receiving deputations and petitions. Even were it possible by these means to hear from unorganized masses and interests, it can be easily shown that the criteria of racial and geographic determination are not sufficient guides for judgment regarding national sentiment. This was particularly true in Alsace-Lorraine in 1870, when many believers in determination through language and race thought that language and race required the return of the provinces to Germany;[39] and it is true to-day in the case of Schleswig. It is a method subjective, not objective, too likely to be based upon inadequate generalization.

Further, even though the inadequate generalization may happen to reach the right result, there has been no proof that the result is right or desired. Inevitably there will be disaffection in the territory in question and in the State from which it is separated, or the State whose claim is not satisfied. The real problem is not only to ascertain the existence of a majority, but also to establish the incontrovertible fact of that majority in order to devitalize potential sources of agitation.

Again, the advantage to be acquired by the annexing State through enlisting that loyalty to the State which is the normal psychological result of participation in the processes of selection is another consideration and a strong one.[40]

That these advantages will accrue from an actual vote, if charges of fraud are not too serious, is shown by the Italian votes of 1860, '66 and '70, which effectually silenced the claims of Austria, the petty princes, the republicans and the Pope. It is shown by the votes of Savoy and Nice themselves, for whatever the pressure, it was obvious that it could not

---

[39] The Germans adduced common origin of races, similarity of language and customs, geographical configuration and historical rights to support their conquest. *Fusinato*, p. 1.

[40] Cf. *Fusinato*, p. 135.

account for the overwhelming majority cast for cession. The result of the votes made the protests of Great Britain, Switzerland and the other Powers appear as weak as they were futile. It is significant, too, that a disaffected party has not survived in those territories or in Italy. Yet it may be asserted that in each case there were other factors which accounted for the permanence of the solution. This is undoubtedly true, but here is an instance where the cumulative force of the invariable condition of stability following the votes can not be ignored, and where, consequently, one can not fairly accuse the argument of being an example of "*post hoc, ergo propter hoc.*"

Doubtless to be suited to the use of the twentieth century, the plebiscite must be modernized. The old methods of partisan administration would not satisfy the more sophisticated political standards of to-day. The plebiscite must be under international and obviously impartial auspices. The accumulated political experience of a century of representative government must be applied to commissions which should oversee and police the registration, and guarantee the secrecy of the ballot.

The real problems are, however, of a more general nature, and involve, among other questions, delimitation of the territory in which the vote shall be taken, electoral qualifications, and the drawing of the frontier line after the vote. It is obvious that a rigid plan to fit all cases is impossible. Special conditions necessitate special provisions. The conditions must be studied with infinite care, and the solutions must bear promise of justice to all parties, including both the majority and the minority. In cases of a mixed population and an indistinctly indicated frontier line, the international commission will be forced to follow the proposal made by La Tour d'Auvergne in the Conference of London and draw a line based on the vote, in the way that shall most nearly satisfy the obvious desires of the inhabitants of the region. Here is the proper place for the clause of option, a place first accorded it in the Treaty of Mulhausen of 1798. It is properly a measure to protect the dissatisfied minority.

The chief theoretical opposition to the doctrine comes now from the apprehension that, once admitted, small units, even so small as cities, may demand self-determination. Although this difficulty has so far been an academic one it has now become one of importance. No rule is, of course, possible. The question is one primarily of proportion, of geographic position and economic relation; in a word, it must be settled according to the specific case. No group, however small, should be without its day in court. The court should be an international commission to whose judgment the matter must be left. With the resources of customs zones and internationalization of rivers, ports and the like, the desires of the several parties in interest, even in the case of a single city, should be capable of being harmonized and the will of the majority satisfied.

The chief practical opposition to the doctrine comes at present from those who fear, and with reason, that application in various regions where the conqueror has bent every effort to denationalize the people and has resorted to restrictions on language, to deportation and to massacre, would sanction the former conquest. It is obviously necessary that such methods should fail of their object and that their results should be neutralized. To arrive at a just solution in such a case is not easy. There are, however, means of solution which suggest themselves. It might be well to let only those vote who are native-born, or who were domiciled in the region before the conquest, and even to let those children of emigrants or optants vote who will give pledge to live in the territory if the vote goes in their favor. Finally, by letting the women vote, not only would there be a more comprehensive expression of opinion but there would also be secured representation for the men who have been killed in war or have perished through deportation.

Lucie A. Zimmern

From *Must the League Fail?* (1932)

Thus the delegates, taken as a whole, tend to fall into two groups – the insiders and the outsiders. The psychology of these two groups is very different and they must be looked at separately.

The insider has been brought up in the old diplomacy. Usually his training dates from before the war, when the great game was being played with all the zest and skill which we can read about in the memoirs of its old actors. But, if not, he has entered into the tradition, which is none the less a tradition if his particular Foreign Office, belonging to a newly created State, has only come into existence since the war: for naturally every new Foreign Office must draw its methods and as much as possible of its personnel from those already existing. It is not only across the Atlantic that traditions can be manufactured.

The insider dislikes Geneva. He dislikes it for several reasons. Firstly, because it represents a challenge to his profession. Of course he knows very well that his profession is in no real danger because the world could never get on without diplomats. But if the existence of his profession is not at stake its authority, he feels, decidedly is. Promotion, no doubt, will not be endangered by the fact that a certain amount of international business is being transacted at Geneva: for there is no difficulty in ensuring that the total amount of Foreign Office business as represented by files and letters and reports, shall not be diminished; and a little more duplication can do no harm. Every Foreign Office is a Circumlocution Office and the existence of a Super-Circumlocution Office at Geneva, though a nuisance in some ways, may turn out to be rather a good joke. But what he cannot stomach is the prospect of his profession as such being overshadowed by the rise of a new bureaucracy. He is quite prepared to acquiesce in Geneva as a fifth wheel in the old diplomatic coach; but what he will on no account agree to is to be relegated to playing second fiddle to this latest addition to the orchestra of internationalism. The older branch of the profession must at all costs remain pre-eminent.

He also dislikes Geneva because he objects to its diplomacy and all the rest of it. He believes them to be dangerous, even revolutionary. International business, he considers, should not be carried on under such amateur and slap-dash conditions. Diplomacy deals with issues of the gravest importance and it is indecent that, instead of being dealt with discreetly in private conversations between negotiators, they should be discussed at public sessions with the representatives of all the other countries sitting by. What chance is there of striking a decent bargain under such circumstances? It is unfair to the diplomat, and especially to the diplomat of a Great Power, to expose him to such an ordeal.

[...]

The masters of the old diplomatic school would never have dreamt of trying to pull off their triumphs in a place infested with journalists, and with their opposite numbers, against whom their combinations are directed, actually on the spot in an adjoining hotel. No wonder the insider, eager to exercise his diplomatic craft, hankers after the old-fashioned solitude of a fashionable watering place or a royal yacht. But most of all the insider dislikes Geneva because it threatens to destroy his pre-eminence among the servants of the state by abolishing war. Why is a Foreign Office a great office? Not because it deals with foreigners, but because of the tone in which it talks to them. Dealing with foreigners is a ticklish and unpleasant business at best and no one in his senses would choose a Foreign Office in preference to ordinary Civil Service work, except for its one redeeming characteristic – that the Foreign Office holds the keys of war and peace. An official in an ordinary Home Department has the normal satisfactions of officialdom. He sits in his office signing papers and these papers are commands. They are obeyed. Or, if they are not obeyed, the courts and the police will hear of it sooner or later. The Foreign Office official cannot issue commands. He is not a centurion who can say do this or do that. He is a negotiator. But, if he is negotiating on behalf of a Great Power, he has the intimate and abiding satisfaction of knowing that at a certain stage of the argument he can raise his voice, or maybe only his expressive eyebrow, and indicate that there is more behind his argument than an appeal to pure reason. He too, though he may not look it, is a centurion – much more than a centurion indeed, for at the stamping of his feet legions will arise out of the ground. This secret satisfaction is the true reason for the superiority complex which the world has always rightly associated with diplomats. And it is precisely this hidden source of power of which Geneva proposes to deprive them. If, as the crazy notion now is, resort to war by one country in order to impose its will on another is to be declared illegal and even forcibly prevented by some general combination, the game will no longer be worth playing: for the stakes which gave it its chief interest will have been abolished. This, of course, is unthinkable; but it is worth guarding against all the same. And that is why the insider is very much on his guard at Geneva.

Under these circumstances there was only one course open for the insiders, and they would need to be very much less intelligent than most of them are not to have seen it and acted upon it. It was to capture Geneva and so bring it into the orbit of their own system. This was not only necessary in order to save the old diplomacy, with all that it means to the world in the way of social brilliance and intellectual distinction. It also presented a positive advantage which the insider, as he came to know Geneva better, could not fail to appreciate. It provided the old diplomacy with a field for manoeuvre – a bigger and better chessboard. Geneva the centre for the working out of a new international policy might be dangerous. But Geneva as the annex of the Foreign Offices, a sort of licensed diplomatic playground, presented incalculable possibilities. No doubt they needed to be carefully watched. But it was to the interest of the Foreign Office in general, whatever their policy on particular issues, to ensure that these possibilities should be wisely developed and not imprudently abused. There is honour among diplomats to maintain the rules of the good old game and to revise them according to new circumstances. Thus it was that as soon as the Foreign Offices discovered Geneva and began to take it seriously, which was about 1925, they embarked together on a systematic attempt, which does infinite credit to their zeal for international co-operation, in order to conquer it for the Old Diplomacy. The task was a difficult and delicate one, as it had to be performed largely in the public eye. They could never have carried it through successfully without the help of the Geneva Secretariat, as will be explained later. Nevertheless the main credit for the operation, one of the most brilliant in the eventful annals of the Foreign Offices of the Great Powers, rests with the insiders who conceived and inspired it.

[...]

But it is time to turn to the outsiders. These, so far as the Assembly Delegations are concerned, consist of the Civil Servants of Departments other than the Foreign Office, the Members of Parliament, the miscellaneous experts and Secretaries and the women delegates. But they include also the bulk of the members of the numerous other Committees and Sub-Committees which meet at Geneva during the year, with the exception of full-dress diplomatic affairs like the Disarmament Conference.

The outsider is generally quite new to international meetings. He has had little or no experience of them in the work on which he is engaged at home. Geneva he only knows by hearsay: and he therefore looks forward with particular interest and not a little pleasurable apprehension to his first appearance on the international scene. In England it is an unwritten rule that a member freshly elected to a Committee should not make himself too prominent at the first meeting: he must learn the ropes before he puts forward views. This natural and very proper bashfulness is considerably accentuated in the atmosphere of Geneva, where the neophyte is quickly made to feel that there is a whole world of custom and precedent against which it is treason to offend. So that he naturally leans upon the older members of his Delegation or Committee and, above all, upon its secretary, whether a Foreign Office man or a League official. Since the Assembly and most of the other Committees only meet once a year the outsider cannot hope to distinguish himself for a considerable time. It takes months to learn the work of a Committee at home. But what is measured by months at home is measured by years at Geneva. The outsider will be well on in his second year before he opens his mouth with assurance. By that time, it is highly probable that one of two things will have happened to him. He will either have been roped in by the insiders, or he will be a victim of that most characteristic Geneva disease, *megalomania internationalis*.

Of the outsider once assimilated there is little to be said except that he is likely to be imbued with the fervour of the neophyte and so to overdo his part. He is, therefore, a little dangerous to use in public, because he may make mistakes, what the insiders call *gaffes*, through lack of adequate training. But he is extremely useful in private for knocking sense into the heads of the suspicious and critical because, as an outsider, his judgment is highly considered. Some of the finest exploits of the old diplomacy at Geneva have been obtained with the co-operation, sometimes conscious, sometimes unconscious, more often sub-conscious, of the assimilated outsider. Like a new boy at school under the eye of the prefect, the outsider is extremely susceptible to professional praise: and if there is one art in which the professional diplomat has specialized it is the rationalization of flattery. He measures his words as the scientific manager measures movements: but each word counts. The outsider is an easy target: but the diplomat knows how to hit the bull's-eye with every shot.

The most conspicuous symptom of *megalomania internationalis* is an arrogant attitude towards the vulgar herd who have not crossed the sacred portals of Geneva. The patient differs from the assimilated outsider in that he is either unintelligent or too well-meaning to have been admitted into the free-masonry of diplomacy. But he resembles him in that he cut himself adrift from the normal life of his own country with its opinions and standards. The atmosphere of Geneva with its cease-less variety and stimulus has gone to his head like strong wine. It has unbalanced him and crippled his normal faculties, that he is not quite himself at Geneva and incapable of coming back to himself when he returns home. Thus he becomes what is known as an 'international figure,' which means that he leads an ineffective existence in both spheres, both at home and abroad. He resembles the farmer-statesman of whom it was said that Westminster admired him for his farming and his country neighbours for his politics. 'Abroad' in his case comes to mean far more than Geneva: for as a Geneva habitué he will be in demand on many platforms in many countries. There he will preach the gospel of Geneva as a representative of his country to audiences who little suspect that his name is not a household word among his fellow-citizens. Indeed one of the great advantages of Geneva for the outsider and for some insiders too is that it provides them with a secure and stately pedestal. An 'international reputation' has always, in modern times, been a much sought-after commodity and it has never been very easy to obtain. Einstein and Marconi, of course, secure one on their own merits; but when you except the absolutely and undeniably first class you come upon a miscellaneous crowd of politicians, magnates, dignitaries and other 'experts' of various kinds, all of them enjoying a certain fame in a limited area but none of them singled out as figures of world-wide distinction. Every country has its own road to national glory. Geneva has, for the first time, constructed what looks like a safe and assured road to international glory.

[...]

THE foregoing chapters have not been written with a light heart or without a strong sense of responsibility. It is one thing to wield the easy pen of the destructive critic, it is another to analyze the defects of an institution round which have gathered the hopes and longings of millions for the welfare of humanity. What has been set down in these pages has not been inspired by a spirit of factiousness or of idle fault-finding. The sole motive has been to explain to those who, in every part of the world, are interested in the League, how it actually works and why it has not produced better results. The Manchurian crisis has thrown a sudden searchlight on the methods into which Geneva has been drifting for the last ten years. It will prove a blessing in disguise if its lesson is fully understood and made the starting-point for a thorough-going process of overhauling. There is nothing wrong with the machine as such. Purely as an institution, the League in action is a remarkable testimony to the wisdom and foresight of its founders. All that is needed is to ensure that it should be worked in the spirit of those who constructed it.

After all, it would have been astonishing if the League had been made to work satisfactorily at the first attempt. It was a totally new experiment, set on foot under the most unfavourable conditions. Hardly anybody in any country in 1914 was thinking on lines of international organization, and though a certain amount of enquiry was carried on in this field during the course of the war, conditions were not exactly propitious for it: nor did they improve after the armistice. Thus the venture was launched without any public opinion, in the true sense of the term, to back it up. There was indeed a vast amount of aspiration. There was a *desire* for a League of Nations. There was a very widespread feeling – possibly among the majority of the civilized world, that, if it could be established and be made to work, it would provide mankind with just the institution which it needed and for the lack of which it was suffering. But as to what sort of a thing the League was to be and *how* it was to work, ideas were in general of the vaguest. And since another machine, the Old Diplomacy, extremely efficient in its own way, whatever one may think of it, was already in existence doing part of the work for which the League was intended, a struggle of some kind was inevitable. It has taken place behind the scenes and the public has known very little about it, though it is now witnessing the results. But the experience gained in the clash of forces and contrast of methods can be turned to invaluable use in the necessary readjustment. It is not a question of blame but simply of re-orientation.

The first thing that is needed is to adjust the relations between the two machines. The League machine was not constructed to do the work of the Foreign Offices and the Foreign Offices are equally incapable of doing the work of the League. If they try to do so, they are bound to make a mess of it: first, because they do not understand the job; secondly because they do not like it; and thirdly because in spite of a certain amount of professional free-masonry, they are not really a team that can be trained to work together but a number of competitive, even violently competitive, groups. Thus Foreign Office influence at Geneva is bad for the League because it perverts its normal working, and bad for the Foreign Offices because it not only encourages some of their worst habits but also involves the danger of more frequent and more violent clashes. Any international organization which brings together the incompatible and hostile elements without adequate precautions is playing with fire.

How can the League and the Foreign Offices each be put in their proper place? What are their respective functions? Let us look first at the League. The League has two functions, and two only. They are quite distinct and should be kept apart. The first is the prevention of war.

The second is the promotion of international cooperation. Nothing which does not come under one of these two headings belongs to Geneva. If one thinks out clearly what these two headings cover, one finds that a very large sphere of action is left to the Foreign Offices.

What is the prevention of war? It means intervention by the League when war has broken out, or when there is imminent risk of its breaking out, in order to keep the guns from going off. That is all that the League is concerned with. It has nothing, as such, to do with the situation out of which the war, or the threat of war, has arisen. It is not a negotiating body. All this side of things belongs to the Foreign Offices. It is true that the Covenant provides that *when there is a risk of a rupture* the League should intervene and make a report. But this is only part of its intervention *in order to prevent war*. What the League exists for is not to engage in diplomatic activities, for which the Foreign Offices are much better equipped, but, simply and solely, to prevent the parties from coming to blows. The prevention of war is one thing and the conduct of Foreign Policy is another. The two do not belong together. They no more belong together than the work of the Bench and the work of the Bar. People have only got into the habit of associating them together in their minds because, in the absence of a Bench armed with the necessary authority, the Bar and the parties have been accustomed to taking the law into their own hands. Under pre-war diplomacy, the parties began by arguing, went on to threaten and eventually either achieved a result by intimidation or came to blows. This is the system which the League exists to bring to an end.

Barbara Wootton

From "Socialism and Federation" (1941)

The fact that social progress is contingent upon international order is the primary reason for socialist interest in Federation; but it is by no means the only one. There are more positive grounds also. Conscious and planned direction of economic life over a wide area, is essential, in the opinion of socialists, in order to achieve the equality and prosperity for which they hunger. They have, therefore, a particular concern with the economic aspects and possibilities of Federation.

For the scale of plans is hardly less important than their content. Common sense suggests that the appropriate scale must vary enormously according to what you are dealing with. Common sense also suggests that it is extremely unlikely that the nation-state is the largest unit in this shrinking modern world of which constructive economic planning should ever take account. To take only two examples, the planning of transport and the planning of power on a purely national scale is quite out of keeping with reality. Western Europe at the very least is, or rather ought to be, a single power-cum-transport unit. Some years ago the socialist Labour Party in this country produced a scheme for a publicly-owned and publicly-operated combined coal and power industry. Within its own limits it may have been a wise enough plan; but it would have been far more effective, had it been able to link up British coal and power production with that of states across the water (some of which had played their part in bringing the British mines and miners to their sorry plight). A European Federation would be thinking in terms of such things as a publicly-owned European grid and (most decidedly) European airlines. Only under the settled and ordered government of a Federation is it possible to create interstate public utilities that are operated for the common welfare. In the Soviet Union the economic unit ranges from the All-Union enterprise to the village co-operative. In the (much smaller) area of non-Soviet Europe international anarchy condemns us always to stop short at the intermediate stage.

Other economic problems now also require a larger canvas. The socialist state is a social service state. Hitherto, tentative efforts have been made to raise international social standards through the activities of the International Labour Organisation. Like the League of Nations, the I.L.O. has no authority and no sanction behind its decisions. Its history is a pitiful record of work begun, but left undone for lack of power of enforcement. During the first (and most successful) ten years of its history only about one-third of the possible total ratifications of twenty-six agreed conventions had been secured. Twenty-five countries had ignored every single convention, and the majority had ratified less than half of the total. In other words the I.L.O. method of "legislation" has been, at best, less than thirty percent effective.

A government with authority behind it does not tolerate thirty per cent observance of the law! What the International Labour Organisation *tried* to do for Labour standards, a Federal government *could* do, within its own territory. It is not necessary that the Federation should have exclusive power of legislation in this field. In view of the great variety of local conditions and possibilities, it is not even desirable that it should. What is wanted is a federal constitution which gives concurrent powers to both state and federal governments to legislate on labour matters, provided only that in cases of conflict the latter must prevail. In this way a system of federal minima can be combined with higher standards in states where socialist practice is more advanced; and the citizens of the latter can be relieved of their perpetual fear of the low-standard neighbour across the frontier.

Finally, Federation smooths the path for that great ally of international socialism, an international Trade Union movement. Experience has shown that it is possible to build Trade Unions that are capable of concerted action over vast geographical areas, provided that they do not extend beyond the boundaries of independent states. Only in the case of the (unfortified) Canadian border has this limitation been overcome; and that only in certain industries. But over the great territories of the United States the Railway Workers, the Mine Workers, the Garment Workers, to mention only a few, have built powerful nationwide societies; whereas in Europe the international Trade Union movement has suffered exactly the same disasters as have the socialist internationals. It, too, cracked in 1914, under the stress of patriotic loyalty, when the German Trade Unions "accorded the most loyal support to the civil and military authorities"; and the British and French followed suit in their respective countries. And it cracked again in the stormy nineteen-thirties. Even during the intervals of comparative peace, its activities have been confined to consultation and conference (always without power to act) and to occasional mutual financial assistance in a modest way. Its conferences were conferences, not of fellow citizens, but of foreigners. Even in cases of the gravest social injustice, in Europe continental solidarity of the workers, even in a single industry, has remained always a dream. Yet from the Atlantic to the Pacific coast continental solidarity is both practicable and practised.

The foregoing arguments are not affected by the immediate events of the present war. They would have equal force even if the independence of Poland, Belgium, Holland, Norway, Denmark and France, and all who went before or may come after, had never been lost. But, paradoxically enough; the tragic plight of Europe actually adds point to the socialist-federalist case. For to-day (November 1940) the European peoples from the Baltic to the Atlantic on one side, and to the Mediterranean and the Black Sea on the other live under what is substantially one rule. The continent has indeed been unified – unified by conquest and under tyranny. Sooner or later, we who reject that tyranny hope to be in a position to decide what is to be done about that unity. One course is simply to break it up: to restore the pre-war European chess-board and to re-establish the independence of as many of the old jealous, frightened states as possible. (Frontiers might perhaps be drawn with a little more regard to professed principles of national self-determination and a little less strategic cynicism. But these are details.) We can, if we wish, forget both the logic of twentieth-century technique and the wider horizons of twentieth-century citizenship, and set to work to break the Nazi Empire into at least as many pieces as went to its making – *if* we wish. But is it conceivable that any socialist really does wish to take this line? To do so means to re-establish at least eight separate tariffs; at least eight different currencies; and at least eight different rules for excluding the workers of one state from entry into the territory jealously reserved for their comrades in another – all within an area which measures only three-fifths of that of the United States and less than one-third of that of the Soviet Union. It means also to re-open the door to all the old quarrels between the so-called haves and have-nots, as well as to the shameful system under which exploited colonial peoples are bandied about as the prize in the hideous game of European power politics. It is hard to believe that a movement which was launched with an exhortation to the workers of the world to unite, and which has consistently condemned the political tutelage and economic servitude of the black man, can put its influence behind a programme so narrow and so exclusive.

Krystyna Marek

From *The Identity and Continuity of States in Public International Law* (1954)

The problem of the identity and continuity of a State is the problem of its very existence. This is so because it merely represents another aspect of the problem of State extinction. To ask whether a State is identical with a State which has preceded it in time and with which it has enough common features for the question to be asked at all, is to enquire whether one State has died and another has been born in its place, or whether the old State continues its unchanged legal personality.

The practical importance of the question is obvious. The rights and duties of a new State will initially be derived exclusively from customary international law. The new State will not be internationally responsible for what has taken place on its territory prior to its birth. Its population and its frontiers will be undefined and doubtful, pending a final delimitation by way of international agreements. On the other hand, an old State will naturally enough continue to bear its international rights and duties both customary and conventional. It will enjoy the same international status, defined by both customary and conventional international law. Its territory and population will remain the same, except in the case of changes which, relating precisely to territory and population, leave the personality of the State unaffected. It will be subject to all legal duties and it will be entitled to claim all legal rights rising out of agreements to which it has been a party. It may be held internationally responsible for what has occurred in its territory. Thus, the question of the identity and continuity of a State raises the whole issue of its international status.[41]

---

[41] It is therefore incorrect to reduce the practical aspect of the problem chiefly to the question of debts and the survival of treaties in case of revolutions and territorial changes, as is done by Herz, *Beiträge zum Problem der Identität des Staates, Zeitschrift für öffentliches Recht*, XV, 1935, p. 241.

The problem is therefore intimately connected with that of the birth and death of States which traditional doctrine considered as metajuridical facts, incapable of legal appraisal.[42] This would indeed be the case if the problem of the birth and death of States were approached from the point of view of municipal law.[43] But it is clear that this problem can be investigated only from "outside" States themselves since the norms of municipal law are valid only "within" the State and cannot serve as a legal criterion of external happenings. Moreover, the creation of municipal norms does not precede the birth of a State, but coincides with it, – just as the end of their validity coincides with the State's extinction. Hence the time factor alone prevents the application of municipal norms to the question of the birth and death of States. For those who regard State law as the summit of the legal pyramid, the birth, extinction and transformation of the States are thus metajuridical matters, not capable of legal appraisal. Any attempt to solve these problems within the framework of municipal law fully deserves Kelsen's picturesque analogy with Baron Münchhausen's efforts to drag himself out of the mud by his own hair.[44] Nor is a legal explanation possible on the dualist basis which introduces an artificial cleavage between international and municipal law.[45]

When, however, the problem is seen in its proper perspective, all such artificial difficulties disappear. Since they break the framework of municipal law, the birth, extinction and transformation of States can be made the subject of legal enquiry only by reference to a legal order which is both higher than State law and yet belongs to the same system of norms, in other words, on the basis of monism and the primacy of international law.

On this clearly correct assumption, a legal evaluation of the birth, death and transformation of States can easily be undertaken from "without" and from "above", by means of a higher legal system whose norms have existed before the formation, and continue to exist after the extinction, of the State in question. Moreover, such an evaluation becomes not only possible, but indeed indispensable. A legal system which does not itself determine the character and existence of its subjects is unthinkable.[46] International law

---

[42] Jellinek speaks of the "Unhaltbarkeit aller Versuche … die Entstehung der Staaten juristisch zu konstruieren". *Allgemeine Staatslehre*, pp. 263–264.

[43] "… das Staatsrecht ist unfähig, den Staatenbildungsprozess zu erklären". Jellinek, *op. cit.*, p. 266.

[44] *Das Problem der Souveränität und die Theorie des Völkerrechts*, p. 236.

[45] Jellinek, *op. cit.*, p. 266

[46] « De même que tout ordre juridique détermine quels sont ses sujets, de même il détermine aussi le moment où ils commencent à exister, » Anzilotti, *Cours de Droit International*, p. 160. „… aus jedem Normensystem selbst beantwortet werden muss, welches die Subjekte seiner Pflichten und Rechte sind." Kelsen, *Souveränität*, p. 230.

does not "create" States, just as State law does not "create" individuals. But it is international law and international law alone which provides the legal evaluation of the process, determines whether an entity is in fact a State, delimits its competences and decides when it ceases to exist.[47]

The acceptance of international law as the highest and all-embracing legal order leaves no legal vacuum in which "bare facts" could exist and not be subject to legal appraisal.[48] Thus, a legal enquiry into the problem of State identity and continuity presupposes a definite attitude towards fundamental issues of legal theory. A repudiation of what is submitted to be the only correct view of the relations between international and State law, namely: monism based upon the primacy of the former, would necessarily result in the abandonment of this study. It could possibly be undertaken as a historical or sociological, but never as a juridical enquiry.[49]

The problem of State identity and continuity can, consequently, arise only within the international legal order and only on the basis of a co-existence within this order of a number of co-ordinated subjects, between which such rights and obligations can exist. However legitimate a purely theoretical and abstract enquiry into the problem of the "internal identity and continuity" of States, it is submitted that the problem is an artificial one and that in practice it does not exist.

This submission may be illustrated by an imaginary example of a State, existing like a collective Robinson Crusoe, in complete isolation from the outside world. The question of its continued rights and obligations could

---

[47] The following remark of Jellinek thus loses the meaning which he intended to give it: „Das Völkerrecht knüpft ... an das Faktum der staatlichen Existenz an, vermag dieses Faktum aber nicht zu schaffen". *Op. cit.*, p. 266.

[48] Kelsen, *Souveränität*, pp. 235–236; *Allg. Staatlehre*, p.127; *La naissance de l'Etat et la formation de sa nationalité*, p. 613; Verdross, *Die Verfassung der Völkerrechtsgemeinschaft*, pp. 125–131. Incorrectly, the Report of the Committee of Jurists on the question ot [sic] the Aaland Islands: "From the point of view of both domestic and international law, the formation, transformation and dismemberment of States as a result of revolutions and wars create situations of fact which, to a large extent, cannot be met by the application of normal rules of positive law". *LNOJ*, Special Supplement, No. 3, p. 6. Similarly Scelle, *Manuel de Droit International Public*, p. 125.

[49] The problem thus stands and falls within the acceptance of the primacy of international law. But it is submitted that *no* international legal problem can be correctly solved on any other basis. Thus, correctly, the Swiss Federal Council, in its Memorandum of 1934 to the League of Nations, in the dispute between Switzerland and other States concerning reparations for damage suffered by Swiss citizens as a result of the First World War: "The questions which Switzerland desires to bring before the Permanent Court of International Justice deal with some of the most delicate problems of the law of nations, including the central basic problem of all international law – namely, the origin of the rules of international law. There can be no correct solution of these problems which is not based on the postulate of the primacy of international law". *LNOJ*, 1934, p. 1485.

simply not arise, failing any party to such rights and obligations and failing a higher legal order which could decide the question. There would be no practical reason or inducement for the State organs to affirm or to deny its continuity. The population of the State would similarly lack any such incentive. The whole problem would be utterly unreal.[50]

---

[50] An entirely opposite view is put forward by Merkl in his *Das Problem der Rechtskontinuität und die Forderung des einheitlichen Weltbildes*, *Zeitschrift für öffentliches Recht*, V. 1926; see below, p. 28, f-n. 2.

M. Margaret Ball

From *International Relations* (co-written with Hugh B. Killough) (1956)

Economy and the Diplomacy of Developing States

The terms "modern state system" and "national state system" apply more accurately to the period after the French Revolution (1789) than to the political system of western Europe evolving in the general direction of modern states during the preceding centuries. During a period of about three centuries (roughly, from 1500 or before to 1750 or 1800), systems of political economy contributing to state development, from time to time and in various areas of Western Europe, had so much in common that they are frequently referred to by economists as the mercantile system or mercantilism. Each of the developing states needed precious metals to serve as reserves for war, to finance the king and his court, and to establish generalized money economies, central tax systems, and other national institutions. For this reason types of economic policy that developed in a number of states were designed to encourage an excess of merchandise exports, to be paid for in specie. This kind of policy was advocated, for example, by Thomas Mun and Sir Joseph Child, British economists of the early seventeenth century. Policy to achieve the foregoing ends took the form of complicated trade restrictive systems involving import tariffs, export bounties, and related regulations.

Mercantile patriotism was fashioned to promote the interests of a strong centralized state. State welfare took precedence over individual welfare. Increase in population and maximization of aggregate production were mercantile objectives. High per capita production and improvement of the living standards of the common folk were secondary considerations, if considered at all. The function of the common man was conceived by mercantile theorists to be that of promoting the independence, welfare, and dignity of the state, not the other way around. Prices of goods and wages of labor were regulated by justices of the peace in a manner deemed to promote the wealth, the power, and the glory of the state. The complicated system of economic controls favoured export goods at the expense of goods for home consumption. Much of the trade of the time – particularly the external trade – was controlled by crown-grant monopolies: Merchants of the Staple, British East India Company, Merchant Adventurers, and the Netherlands Company of the East Indies, for example. Only Merchants of the Staple might export raw wool from England. Only Merchant Adventurers might trade in English wool manufactures on the Continent. Merchant princes owned the weaving machines, assembled raw textile materials, had them made into cloth by peasants working at home on a piece basis, and assembled the finished product for sale to consumers. Much of the domestic buying and selling was carried on at periodic fairs by licensed traders.

The sixteenth and seventeenth centuries were periods of exploration, exploitation of native peoples in the Americas and Asia, and colonization. Treasure-seeking adventurers were required to share their loot with the Crown. Colonial trade was regulated in the interest of the mother country. All roads led to the Crown, which enforced a primary claim upon the fruits of all human endeavour.

Political Revolution

The mercantile countries were monarchies. In the course of national development churchmen retained a substantial amount of political influence; merchants and financiers gained political influence; and common folk threw off the yoke of serfdom.

Popular revolt against tyranny was a stage in the evolution of many of the Western states. The civil liberties of twentieth-century democracies were not easily won; the struggle was long and the paths of progress devious. The history of events resulting in less tyranny and more self-government unfolds neither in neat chronological order nor in uniform patterns. The Magna Charta (1215) was a stepping stone to civil liberty as was the Bill of Rights (1689), the American Revolution (1776), the French Revolution (1789), and a myriad other events, some striking, others less so. The Bill of Rights (enacted in December, 1689) and based on the Declaration of Rights delivered by lords and commons to the Prince and Princess of Orange, afterwards William III and Mary, was a landmark in the establishment of individual freedom in English-speaking countries. The Bill of Rights declared illegal the suspension or execution of laws by regal authority without consent of Parliament; the levying of money for use by the Crown without grant of Parliament; the fining of persons before conviction; and various other regal actions that impinged upon prerogatives and rights of individuals.

In some countries on the Continent – Sweden, Norway, Denmark, for instance – as in England, absolute monarchies gave way to more or less limited monarchies without violent, mass upheaval such as that which occurred in France in 1789, when the monarchy was overthrown and a republic established through bloody revolution.

The areas that were to become the national states of Holland and Belgium went through various stages of political evolution from loose confederation to independent national states. The separation of "Belgium" and Holland was recognized by the Peace of Westphalia in 1648. "Belgium" and Holland were united by the Congress of Vienna in 1815 as a buffer against France. The name "Belgium" came into general use only with the founding of the modern kingdom in 1830 when the United Kingdom of the Netherlands collapsed. As in other areas of Western Europe, the political, religious, economic, and cultural environment in Holland and Belgium did not favor absolute monarchies.

Like Holland, Switzerland began as a confederation. At the present time Switzerland is made up of twenty-two small federated states with populations differing in language, religion, and in other characteristics. The federation was formed initially around a nucleus of German districts that came together in a defensive alliance (1291) to resist Hapsburg rule. Around this nucleus gathered other German districts. French-speaking and Italian-speaking districts were also added to the alliance, but the Frenchmen and the Italians did not gain political equality with the Germans until early in the nineteenth century.

In the Spanish part of the Iberian Peninsula the developing state assumed the form of an absolute monarchy. Religious, political, cultural, and economic conditions in Spain seem to have been less well suited to liberal parliamentary government than was the case in France and England, although general assemblies did make their influence felt in Spain from time to time.

Italy was not united nationally and stabilized politically until after the middle of the nineteenth century. The government of Italy was a limited monarchy prior to the time Mussolini assumed dictatorial power after World War I.

In the large German-speaking area of Europe several hundred principalities had come into existence prior to the Franco-Prussian War of 1870–71. Bavaria, Saxony, and Hanover are examples. The *Zollverein* (a tariff union) had begun to unite the German states economically as early as 1830. The German Empire was formed late in the nineteenth century largely as a result of Bismarck's policy of maneuvering to bring the Germans together for mutual defense against the French. As in the German Empire, so also in the area that comprised the

Austro-Hungarian Empire, political union was a result of war, threats of war, and astute political maneuvering. In both the German and Austro-Hungarian Empires the common people had made some progress toward self-rule by the beginning of the twentieth century. In neither of these political juggernauts, however, had progress toward democratic rule equaled that of Great Britain.

[...]

Revolution

In the eighteenth century, scientific discovery and technological innovation thrust forward into new areas of accomplishment. Religious opposition to scientific heresy was weakened by the Reformation. The renaissance in art, literature, and other nonscientific fields of learning and the Enlightenment helped to create an atmosphere favorable to progress. In the early part of the modern period, industrial techniques in Europe were not very different from those of ancient Egypt, Greece, and Rome. Beginning in the eighteenth century, technological improvements profoundly modified Western methods of production; workers were released from agriculture for manufacture and trade, and hand-operated machinery gave way to power machinery.

As a result of foregoing changes and others, ordinarily thought of as phases of the Industrial Revolution, centers of great wealth and military power developed in the Western world. Western civilization thrust outward to penetrate and encompass older civilizations in Africa and elsewhere. Technical progress has been the most striking characteristic of the Western state system during the last century and a half. Technical and economic developments during this period may eventually prove to have been a prelude to a regrouping of national states into larger political units, a political change as significant historically as the transition from medieval feudalism to the modern state system.

Nineteenth-Century Family of Nations

When one stops to realize that for centuries political boundaries and the nature of political rule have been changing almost continuously, he may begin to wonder what the term "modern state system" signifies. The least it implies is coexistence of many independent states in the modern world. The term has more specific connotation when used to describe national political organizations and their international political relations existing at some particular period, as for example the decades of comparative peace prior to World War I or the period between World Wars I and II.

The political units that came into prominence in Western Europe after the Middle Ages were smaller and more homogeneous than the Ottoman Empire or the Mongolian Empire. They were larger than city states such as Venice or Genoa. As early as 1500, monarchies had been formed in the areas corresponding roughly to those we, in the twentieth century, ordinarily think of as England, France, Spain, Portugal, Denmark, Norway, and Sweden. During the period from the early 1600's to the late 1900's other states emerged in Europe; the Americas were colonized and most of these colonies were freed from mother country rule; and Japan emerged from a shell of isolation to become an active participant in world affairs. The term "family of nations" initially referred to those states that maintained diplomatic relations with one another. Historically, it was limited, at first, to European monarchies. In the course of time it included both monarchies and republics and was extended geographically to embrace non-European as well as European states. The terms "family of nations" and "modern state system" sometimes are used interchangeably in current literature.

[...]

Twentieth-Century Community of Nations

The peace treaties following World War I established a greater number of sovereign nations in Europe than had existed when the war broke out. Poland was recreated. The Austro-Hungarian Empire was divided, Hungary and a truncated Austria appearing as independent states. New nations were created, among them: Yugoslavia, Czechoslovakia, Lithuania, Latvia, Estonia, and Finland. The League of Nations was established to promote international cooperation and peace, but it failed to achieve its peace objectives. The world once again was overwhelmed by international conflict in which all of the greater powers and a large majority of the lesser powers were involved.

At the end of World War II other peace treaties were negotiated. Many of the familiar national names remained, but power relationships in the community of nations had undergone profound changes. The USSR and the United States emerged from the war as the two most powerful nations.

[...]

Another world organization was established after World War II for the purpose of promoting international cooperation and international peace. The United Nations is a voluntary organization of sovereign states. Ideological, political, and economic conflicts among the members of the United Nations are numerous and serious. To date there is no assurance that the United Nations will be able to find solutions for enough of these conflicting national interests to prevent World War III. When the interests of sovereign states clash in such a manner that compromise is not possible, there is danger of international warfare. No member state of the United Nations has relinquished – even theoretically – the long recognized prerogative of a sovereign state to resort to war in self-defense. What is a sovereign state? What is sovereignty?

Sovereignty The term "sovereignty" is modern; the idea which the term implies is ancient. It goes back to Aristotle, who spoke of the "supreme power" of the state, and to civilizations that antedate the ancient Grecian city states. The words "sovereign" and "sovereignty," however, are believed to have been first used by French jurists in the fifteenth century.[51]

Origins of the Concept

The rise of the modern state system – like that of ancient city states and empires – involved the development of a central authority in each nation. The administrative head of the state – customarily a monarch – strove both for absolute authority in the enforcement of law within his country's boundaries and for freedom from outside interference.

The rise of monarchs in Europe was paralleled by the development of theories justifying a concentration of power in the crown. The king was the sovereign. His actions were justified morally and legally by doctrines of sovereignty. According to these doctrines, a king was above man-made or king-made law. His power was limited only by divine law as interpreted by his own conscience and as manifested to other reasoning beings who were capable of interpreting the natural order of things and of recognizing natural law (the law of "right reason"). Moreover, since the king was subject to no higher earthly authority, each king was believed to be the equal of every other king.

[...]

Nature of the State

A modern state is a community of persons – very large or comparatively small, as the case may be. It occupies a definite territory. It has an organized government to which all or a large part of its inhabitants render

[51] James Wilford Garner, *Political Science and Government* (New York: American Book Co., 1935), p. 157.

habitual obedience. Its claims to independence are recognized by a sufficient number of other states to enable it to enter into international engagements. The sovereignty of such a state is exercised in two directions: internally and externally.

Internal Sovereignty

The degree of internal authority which the ruler or rulers of a state exercise over its inhabitants varies from state to state with the type of internal political organization. In democratic states an electorate – defined in various ways – selects its rulers, having already determined by constitutional ratification and amendment, or otherwise, the powers these rulers may exercise. The United States is an example. In states such as Great Britain, where democratic or parliamentary procedures have been superimposed upon ancient monarchical systems, kingship may survive. Nevertheless, ultimate authority is vested largely in some form of parliamentary organization that is responsible to an electorate. In nondemocratic states, on the other hand, rulers seize power in sundry ways and exercise authority over their peoples in varying degrees of absolutism.

[...]

External Sovereignty

While the term "external sovereignty" is frequently used in reference to the relations of states to each other, the word "independence" probably conveys a more precise meaning. Independence means exclusive domestic jurisdiction; absence of subjection to the authority of another state; freedom to manage the state's internal affairs; and freedom to manage its external affairs within the limits of treaty obligations and customary international law. An independent state has the right to establish its own constitution, to choose its own system of administration, and to enact its own laws, regardless of their effect upon its citizens. Independence implies freedom from unwanted external interference in management of internal affairs. External sovereignty conceived of in absolute terms implies an unlimited degree of freedom in the arrangement of a state's external affairs, affairs that impinge upon the interests of other states. Such unlimited freedom does not exist. In a world of many independent states, the external authority of each must be – and is, in fact – subject to limitations in the interest of all. Application of an absolutist concept of sovereignty in external affairs would tend to result in perpetual anarchy. Perpetual anarchy has been avoided, however, because states have voluntarily entered into long-term treaties and have tacitly consented to a recognition of international law within certain areas of international relations. These voluntary relinquishments of external authority have not jeopardized the sovereign character of states because, in the absence of an extranational enforcement authority, each state reserves ultimate freedom of action to protect its national interests by force of arms or otherwise.

So long as a state retains the authority and ability to enact and enforce laws that are not in violation of obligations under international law, it retains its freedom and a large part of the substance of sovereignty as traditionally conceived. In actuality sovereignty has never meant equality of power in international relations or freedom from restraints in international relations. The more interdependent modern states become – economically and politically – the more need there is for cooperation and for the exercise of restraint on the part of each in the interests of all.

[...]

Attempts to improve the present arrangements for collective security raise a variety of serious questions: What kind of agency is capable of negotiating or enforcing compromises among states to insure the greatest good for all? By what criteria is the greatest good for a world community of many diverse elements to be judged? What agency can develop the power and prestige necessary to enforcement of its decisions if individual states chose war in place of concessions necessary to preserve the peace? Sacrifice of national sovereignty or independence of action in greater or lesser degree is but one of many considerations necessary to the solution of these problems.

Personal greed, individual inequalities, and varying conceptions of good and bad, right and wrong, in a world of dissimilar nations inhabited by people of many racial origins and diverse traditions, are deeply involved not only in this specific problem but in the other problems of international relations to which the bulk of this volume is devoted. The federalist approach to the problem of collective security and general welfare implies the creation of a central government that can maintain its position in the face of conflicting group interests organized along contradictory ideological lines, competing economic lines, and disharmonious racial, religious, and other lines. The reasoning that would pattern a world federation after the United States raises many unanswered questions. Can these diverse groups be brought into a unified political system without war? Could such a world-wide political organization be maintained, at the present stage of cultural evolution, without the exercise of military force by a dominant power or group of dominant powers to an extent that would rebuff a majority of the world's population? How significant are conflicts in group interests in a world of many nations, inhabited by peoples of different ethnic origins, who are conditioned to different traditions and who live at very different economic levels in spite of the fact that they are economically interdependent?

Pauli Murray

From *The Constitution and Government of Ghana*
(co-written with Leslie Rubin) (1961)

Preface

GHANA has a special interest for students of constitutional development. The Gold Coast saw the beginning – in somewhat dramatic circumstances – of the process by which Britain has since undertaken the liquidation of her colonial empire in Africa. The first Leader of Government Business (head of the elected Legislature) was Kwame Nkrumah, a man released some fourteen days earlier from imprisonment for a political offence under the laws of the colonial régime. These circumstances were bound to endow Kwame Nkrumah and the Gold Coast with a special significance for other African territories looking forward to their own independence.

Thus, while this book is intended to be a description of the constitution and government of Ghana, it may well come to be regarded, also, as a study of African constitutional ideas. The Republican constitution enacted by the people of Ghana in July 1960 may not be accepted as a model for African countries achieving independence in the future; but it is bound to influence them. There are ideas firmly embedded in the constitutional fabric of Ghana – some original, others derivative – which are not likely to go unnoticed by emerging African states now planning their future. Among these are: provision for the surrender of sovereignty in the interest of African unity; the vesting of wide powers in a President who is both titular Head of State and the exclusive source of the executive power of the State; the special recognition of, and the vesting of special powers in, the first President; provision for the assimilation of customary law as part of the law of the land.

Ghana suffers from a serious shortage of legal works. This, as far as we are aware, is not only the first book on the constitution and government of Ghana, but also the first book devoted to a branch of the law of the country as a whole.

[...]

In the course of an address broadcast on March 6, 1960 Nkrumah said: "The Convention People's Party and the Government believe also that the people of Africa will never be truly great, happy and prosperous while they remain divided into a number of small states. In the new Constitution we advocate strongly the principle of African unity. So deep is our faith in African unity that we have declared our preparedness to surrender the sovereignty of Ghana in whole or in part, in the interest of a Union of African States and Territories as soon as ever such a union becomes practicable. The keynote of the Constitution we are putting before you is: One Man – One vote and Unity of Africa, namely, the political union of African countries."[52]

The White Paper states: "Apart from facilitating the entry of Ghana into a union of African states and territories, the draft Constitution is also designed to enable peoples who are at present outside Ghana but who are linked by racial, family and historical connections with Ghanaian peoples to join them in one integrated state."

Constitutional provisions. The contemplation of ultimate African unity is emphasised in the Constitution. In the Preamble the people of Ghana declare that they enact their Constitution "in sympathy with and loyalty to our fellow-countrymen in Africa" and "in the hope that we may by our actions this day help to further the development of a Union of African States."[53] Article 2 provides: "In the confident expectation of an early surrender of sovereignty to a union of African states and territories, the People now confer on Parliament the power to provide for the surrender of the whole or any part of the sovereignty of Ghana."[54] Article 13 includes the following two fundamental principles: "that the union of Africa should be striven for by every lawful means and, when attained, should be faithfully preserved; that the Independence of Ghana should not be surrendered or diminished on any grounds other than the further-ance of African unity."

---

[52] In April 1958, the first conference of independent African states, called on the intiative of Dr. Nkrumah, was held in Accra. The participants were Ghana, Ethiopia, Libya, Liberia, Morocco, Sudan, Tunisia and the United Arab Republic.

[53] *Cf.* Preamble to the Constitution of the Republic of Guinea: « Il affirme sa volonté de tout mettre en eouvre [sic] pour réaliser et consolider l'union dans l'Independence de la Patrie Africaine. »

[54] *Cf.* Art. 34 of the Constitution of the Republic of Guinea: « La Republique [sic] peut conclure avec tout Etat Africain les accords d'association ou de communauté, comprenant abandon partiel ou total de Souveraineté en vue de réaliser l'Unité Africaine. »

Ghana–Guinea declaration. What was, no doubt, intended to be a step in the direction of African unity, had already been taken on November 23, 1958, when Dr. Nkrumah and Sekou Touré, President of the Republic of Guinea, issued a joint statement, which was duly ratified by the National Assembly of Ghana during the following month.[55] The joint statement declared: "... we have agreed to constitute our two states as a nucleus of a Union of West African states ... we appeal to the Governments of independent African states and peoples of territories still under foreign rule to support us in our action. In the same spirit we would welcome the adherence to this Union of other West African states.

Ghana–Guinea–Mali communiqué. In November 1960 it was announced that Ghana and Mali had agreed to have a common Parliament, but no information was furnished indicating how this agreement was intended to be implemented. On December 23–24, 1960, talks took place in Conakry, the Capital of Guinea, between President Nkrumah, President Modibo Keita of Mali, and President Sekou Touré. A joint communiqué issued at the conclusion of their discussions announced that they had decided to establish a union of the three States, with common diplomatic representation and a common economic and monetary policy. Two special committees had been set up to examine practical methods of achieving the objectives of union and a common economic policy, and the three Presidents would meet four times a year – twice in Accra, once in Conakry, and once in Bamako in the capital of Mali.

Ghana–Guinea–Mali charter. On April 29, 1961, the three heads of state, after several days of secret talks in Accra, issued a joint communiqué that they had signed a charter which will be submitted to their parliaments for ratification. The charter provides for the establishment of the Union of African States. It also provides for later entry of other African states or federation into the union.[56]

[...]

25. Sovereignty

ARTICLE 4 (1) of the Constitution declares that "Ghana is a sovereign unitary Republic."

---

[55] Parliamentary Debates, Dec. 12, 1958, col. 392.
[56] See *New York Times*, April 30, 1961, p. 9, col. 1; *Africa Report*, June 1961, p. 5.

The declaration of sovereignty is, in truth, reaffirmation of an existing status. As we have seen,[57] Ghana achieved sovereignty when she became an independent state in 1957; thereupon, like all the other self-governing members of the Commonwealth she became "master of her fate". Although executive power was vested in the Queen, represented by a Governor-General, it was the chosen representatives of the people of Ghana in the National Assembly not the Queen or the Governor-General – who formulated her policies and made her laws.

Ghana did, however, under the 1957 Constitution, pursuant to the provisions of the Statute of Westminster, join with her fellow-members of the Commonwealth in owing a common allegiance to the British Crown. Now, as a republic, Ghana ceases to owe such allegiance; but she continues, like all her fellow-members to recognise the Queen as Head of the Commonwealth.

Our comment on the declaration of sovereignty, applies equally to the description of the Republic as "unitary". Although there had been pressure in some quarters for a federal form of government, the Bourne Commission recommended against federation, and the recommendation was acted on in formulating the 1957 Constitution.[58] Ghana has had a unitary constitution since 1957.

26. Surrender of Sovereignty

As we have already seen, the Constitution empowers Parliament to surrender the whole or any part, of the sovereignty of Ghana, in the process of achieving a union of African states and territories.[59] In so surrendering the sovereignty of Ghana, wholly or in part, Parliament is also empowered to provide a form of government which is not republican or unitary. Where, however, it is desired to provide a non-republican or non-unitary form of government, otherwise than in the process of achieving a union of African states and territories, the change in the existing

---

[57] Chap. 1, § 8. A *republic* is a government by representatives chosen by the people, as distinguished from the monarchy in which the office of the Head of the State is hereditary. A *unitary* state is a state in which the supreme authority rests in one central government. A *federal* state is a state in which two or more independent states form a union delegating the exercise of certain powers to a superior body or federal government, and surrendering their independent sovereignty to such federal government. The federal power operates directly both upon the states and the people of the states as citizens of one nation. A *federation* is an association of states who agree to limit the exercise of their sovereignty in order to attain a common objective, but each state remains fully sovereign and independent, although yielding to the central authority for a few limited purposes. See Earl Jowitt, *The Dictionary of English Law*; Black's *Law Dictionary*, 4th ed.

[58] Chap. 1, §§ 7, 8.   [59] Art. 2. See Chap. 2, § 21.

constitutional status of Ghana requires a decision of the electors in a referendum ordered by the President.[60]

[...]

151. Ghana: Inter-state Relations

In considering Ghana's relations with other states, it will be found that they fall naturally into three categories. First, Ghana is, like other independent states, a member of the community with the recognised right to enter into relations with other member-states, and to participate in international organisations. Second, she is a member of the association of sovereign independent states which go to make up the Commonwealth. Third, she is an African state committed to the idea of African unity.

We have already drawn attention to the emphasis in the Constitution on the desire for a union of African states, and have described the steps which Ghana has taken, in conjunction with Guinea and Mali, as an advance towards that ideal.[61] It is safe to assume that her dedication will play an important part in her future relations with other African states.

In relations with other states (as also, in some cases, with African States) her membership of the Commonwealth and of United Nations, are important factors.

152. The Commonwealth

The Commonwealth is an association of sovereign independent states. It came into existence in the course of the gradual process of evolution by which Britain granted independence to the countries which comprised her colonial empire. Both the status of the Commonwealth, and the mutual relationship of the member nations, are not susceptible of precise definition in legal terms. The first attempt to recognize the Commonwealth in formal terms is to be found in the statement at the Imperial Conference of 1926, which defined the member nations as: "autonomous communities within the British Empire, equal in status, in no way subordinate one to another in any aspect of their domestic or external affairs, though united by a common allegiance to the Crown, and freely associated as the British Commonwealth of Nations".[62] The United Kingdom retained certain powers in relation to legislation by the

---

[60] Art. 4 (2).   [61] § 21.

[62] Imperial Conference. Summary of Proceedings. Cmd. 3768; Bishop, op cit., p. 182. See also Amery, *Thoughts on the Commonwealth*, 2nd Ed., p. 105.

parliaments of the member nations, but these were removed by the Statue of Westminster, 1931.[63]

In 1949, India, while a member of the Commonwealth, decided to become a republic and expressed a desire to continue her membership. She was permitted to do so, but as a republic she could not owe allegiance to the Crown as required by the formula of the Imperial Conference of 1926. The new basis for her membership then formulated was that she accepted "the King as the symbol of the free association of its independent member nations and as such the Head of the Commonwealth".[64]

This formula has been recognized as a precedent for the basis of membership of other republics. The Commonwealth today comprises the United Kingdom, Canada, Australia, New Zealand, Ceylon, the Federation of Nigeria, Sierra Leone, India, Pakistan, the Federation of Malaya, Ghana and Cyprus.[65] Thus the first seven owe allegiance to the Crown; the remainder accept the Queen as the symbol of their free association as members of the Commonwealth, and as such, as the Head of the Commonwealth. From the date of her independence ("attainment of fully responsible status within the British Commonwealth of Nations")[66] in 1957, until she became a republic in 1960, Ghana owed allegiance to: "Elizabeth the Second, Queen of Ghana and Her other Realms and Territories, Head of Commonwealth."

[...]

154. United Nations

The Charter which brought the United Nations into existence was agreed to at San Francisco on 26, 1945, the original signatories being the Republic of China, France, the Union of Soviet Socialist Republics, the United Kingdom and the United States of America. The Charter provides that membership "is open to all other peace-loving states", declares that the purposes of the United Nations are *inter alia* (1) to maintain international peace and security; (2) to develop friendly relations among nations; and (3) "to achieve international co-operation in

---

[63] 22 and 23 Geo, 5 c, 4; Wade and Phillips, *op. cit.*, pp. 462–469.

[64] Communique issued by meeting of Commonwealth Prime Ministers in London, April 1949.

[65] At the Prime Ministers' Conference in March 1961, South Africa applied in advance for continued membership after she had become a republic, but withdrew the application after criticism of the policy of *apartheid*. South Africa became a republic outside the Commonwealth on May 31, 1961.

[66] § 8.

solving international problems of an economic, social, cultural or humanitarian character, and in promoting encouraging respect for human rights and for fundamental freedoms for all without distinction as to race, sex, language or religion".[67]

While the United Nations may not "intervene in matters which are essentially within the domestic jurisdiction of any state,"[68] this prohibition does not prevent appropriate action to deal with "any threat to the peace, breach of the peace, or act of aggression".[69] The Charter also provides that the United Nations "shall promote ... universal respect for, and observance of, human rights and fundamental freedoms for all without distinction as to race, sex, language or religion", and embodies a pledge by all members to take action for the achievement of this purpose.[70]

The principal organs of the United Nations are: the General Assembly, the Security Council, the Economic and Social Council, the Trusteeship Council, the International Court of Justice, and the Secretariat.[71]

The General Assembly consists of all the members of the United Nations, each member being limited to a maximum of five representatives.[72] The Security Council consists of permanent and non-permanent members. The Republic of China, France, the Union of Soviet Socialist Republics, the United Kingdom, and the United States of America are permanent members; six non-permanent members are elected by the General Assembly biennially.[73]

On March 7, 1957, – the day after she attained independence – Ghana's application for membership of the United Nations was unanimously approved by the Security Council. On March 8, 1957, Ghana became the eighty-first member of the United Nations, when the General Assembly unanimously approved a resolution sponsored by the United Kingdom, Australia, Canada, Ceylon, India, New Zealand and Pakistan. The South African delegation was absent, having previously walked out of the current session in protest against a decision to discuss South West Africa.

---

[67] Art. 1.   [68] Art. 2 (7).   [69] Art. 39.   [70] Arts. 55, 56.   [71] Art. 7.   [72] Art. 9.
[73] Art. 23.

Louise W. Holborn

From *Refugees: A Problem of Our Time* (1975)

Two major kinds of political issues marked the process which produced the UNHCR from the debates of ECOSOC and the GA during 1949 and 1950. The first was a product of the growing tensions between the West and the East and was linked with the second, the very basic issue of what the international community should do with refugees. This discontent had been a major factor in the debates that had created the IRO and had also been a factor of great importance in shaping the way in which the IRO had operated, and in determining its successes and failures. These tensions had reached much more serious proportions by early 1948 with the Communist takeover of Czechoslovakia and the Berlin blockade and airlift. It reached its height in 1949–50 with the dispute between the USSR and Yugoslavia, the appearance of the People's Republic of China and the beginning of the Korean conflict in 1950. In Europe, growing East–West tensions had brought about the declaration of the Truman Doctrine (12 March 1947), the initiation of the Marshall Plan economic aid program (June 1947), and the creation of the North Atlantic Treaty Organization (NATO) as the Western military shield against the threat of Soviet attack (April 1949). There was also the establishment of the Federal Republic of Germany out of Western-occupied Germany, and the setting up of the German Democratic Republic out of what had been Soviet-occupied Germany (May and October 1949). Moreover, the East in October 1947 had created the Cominform as the central organization for international communism. Thus Europe had become politically, economically and socially divided, and the opposition of each side to the other had gravely hardened.

This basic ideological division between East and West was reflected in their division at every level and on every issue before the organs of the UN, and it affected the debates on future action for refugees as well. The basic Soviet and Eastern position was that all refugees should be repatriated forthwith to their homelands; any other action in some manner constituted exploitation of the refugees and violated international law by infringing on the sovereignty of the refugees' states of origin. The basic position of the West, as we have seen, was that repatriation could only be carried out with the voluntary agreement of the refugees themselves, and that all other refugees had a right to be granted a home elsewhere. While it had been possible to reconcile these two views somewhat in 1946 when the IRO was created, by defining that organization's functions as first repatriation and secondly resettlement, the split between East and West by 1949 made any common effort between them for future action on refugees impossible during the period of the establishment of the UNHCR. The East opposed further international action unless it was repatriation; the West continued to favor international action for refugees of some kind, but was divided over what the nature of that action should be.

During and after WWII the US had played the foremost role in designing and bringing into being the UN and its functional agencies, and it envisaged the UN as an instrument for "harmonizing the actions of nations in the attainment of common ends" (UN Charter, Preamble). The US Government had committed itself to an active international role and to collective responsibility. But the hardening of the cold war had a deep impact on the foreign and domestic policies of the US and brought about a fundamental reorientation of US foreign policy. Moving from a predominant reliance on multilateral organizations, notably the UN, to a strengthening of bilateral and regional ties with its allies, the US less and less viewed the furtherance of the UN as a significant cornerstone of its foreign policy. In a similar development, many of the states of Western Europe were moving towards closer regional cooperation as contrasted with dependence on international organization.

The profound change in US foreign policy resulting from the changing international setting of 1949 and 1950 affected the government's policy in dealing with refugee problems. While the US Congress in 1946 had supported establishing a UN agency which included Soviet representation, by 1950 the East–West split had become so acute that Congress vetoed the use of American funds for any international organization which would include Iron Curtain countries. The US Government now preferred that its participation in UN organs be held constant or be diminished and it proposed that future action for refugees be handled through agencies created outside the UN where only the US and its allies would be directly involved. This was not an inflexible policy, it was recognized in the case of the Palestinian refugees and the Korean refugees that aid programs must be set up under UN auspices, and the US was a substantial instigator and supporter of the United Nations Relief and Works Administration (UNRWA) in 1949, and of the United Nations Korean Reconstruction Agency (UNKRA) after the Korean War. The US was also not unconcerned with refugees in Europe. Long after the issue of what the form of the UNHCR should be was settled, American contributions to the resettlement of refugees from Eastern European countries who were fleeing Soviet domination continued through the creation and support of ICEM and USEP (United States Escapee Program). But whenever possible, the US sought to find forums outside the UN for such refugee activities and to restrict the role of the UN in handling such problems. In planning for European economic recovery, Will Clayton, Assistant Secretary of State, in a State Department memorandum wrote that other nations might help with surplus food and raw materials, "but we must avoid getting into another UNRRA. The United States must run this show."[74]

There was another change in US policy in the period between 1946 and 1949–50 that directly affected refugees; this concerned the view of the need for continued large-scale financial contributions.

A very large number of refugees had been resettled, several years had passed since the end of the war, and there was no longer the same willingness to accept refugee immigrants, especially those who were more costly or less useful to the host country. A great deal of money had been donated by the US to the IRO, and there was strong feeling that the time had come to terminate that support. Furthermore, the US had now turned decisively to the economic assistance of the European countries through the Marshall Plan. Such aid, it was felt, would make it easier for these countries to absorb the remaining refugees, who were after all basically "their" problem. The US believed it had done its share, and that in any case all that remained was to "clean up" the remaining, comparatively small problem by absorbing the refugees into the countries of asylum. In short, there were both political and economic reasons for the change in US refugee policy. Although the humanitarian aspect remained unchanged – concerned Americans did want to see the problem of the refugees solved – the question was how that was to be done in the light of the new US attitude toward resettlement and toward making heavy contributions.

Meanwhile, the problem of refugees continued to plague the countries of first asylum in Europe. They had, of course, a great deal of assistance in diminishing the number of refugees who were on their soil, but the

---

[74] Quoted from Dean Acheson, *Present at the Creation, My Years in the State Department* (New York: W. W. Norton & Company, 1969), 231.

refugees remaining were in general those who seemed more a burden upon their host countries than an asset. A truth about refugee resettlement is that countries are most willing to accept refugees when they can see an economic benefit to themselves in so doing and least willing when only the humanitarian consideration is involved.

The Western European countries realized that, given the new US policy, there was no realistic hope of the IRO continuing to handle the problem of refugees by relieving the countries of first asylum of their presence. Everyone, both in Europe and overseas, realized that the major burden of the remaining refugees would now have to be carried by the countries of first asylum, and the issue to be decided was what if any assistance the international community was going to provide to those countries and the remaining refugees, within that context. The governments which carried the brunt of refugee influx as countries of first asylum wanted both material assistance and assurance that the possibility of overseas resettlement remained open. The US and the other countries of overseas resettlement sought to minimize international action, because they wanted to reduce their financial contribution and because they felt the problem was essentially solved, the remnants being in fact someone else's responsibility. Within that context, they were more than willing to support the creation of a successor to the IRO – if the term "successor" is an appropriate one for such a different kind of organization.

In 1949 and 1950 then, two lines of international action for refugees were being simultaneously pursued. The IRO was working desperately to complete as much of its mission as possible before its time ran out. The member states, having established and contributed to the IRO, were anxious for the job to be completed. The deadline for its termination was extended and extended again, more funds were provided by its members, and other funds were sought in order to get the greatest possible number of refugees resettled. But at the same time, the existence of the so-called "residual problem" became clearer, along with the need for a long-term, albeit different, approach to that problem. Such was the setting in which debate was initiated on a future agency to handle the residual problem. The Director-General in his report on residual problems stressed that

the whole nature of the refugee problem had undergone a radical change since IRO was established. Large numbers of displaced persons who were uprooted during the war and immediately afterwards, turned out in fact to be political refugees. This determines the essential nature of the IRO's plans and programs, dictating a shift in emphasis from repatriation to resettlement. As political tension increased, the displaced persons who became refugees because they refused to return home, were joined in the swelling numbers by those who fled from the same homelands and arrived as refugees in the areas of IRO operations. This exodus continues, and will continue as long as its causes persist.[75]

The East–West dispute, while the overriding issue of the period, did not affect appreciably the form of the action to be agreed upon within the UN. While the substance of the mandate was affected very considerably by the fact that the West was anxious to get along if it could with the East, by 1948 the Cold War was such that there was virtually no possibility for cooperation. The UN existed as a shell in which the two factions talked at rather than to each other. The East was full of recriminations for the way in which the IRO had, in its view, been used as a tool for the purposes of the West, in violation of the resolutions which had created it, and of its own Constitution. Charges were regularly hurled back and forth concerning the treatment of unspecified refugee groups and specific individual refugees during this period. The East objected at every step of the process that created the UNHCR; but its draft resolutions received little support, and when the time came for action, the West had more than enough votes to support its view. The question of what kind of action the Western states did desire was the more important issue in determining the form of the UNHCR and its powers.

In one major regard there was general agreement among the states of the West: the primary function of a new international refugee organization should be to provide international protection to refugees. This task, aimed at safeguarding the rights and legitimate interests of refugees and at overcoming any disabilities arising from their status as refugees, had been the major purpose of the refugee agencies set up under the auspices of the LON and was one of the functions of the IRO as well. It was fully accepted by Western states that this protective function should continue to be exercised by some international body. There was such general agreement on this point that international protection was little discussed in the debates at the UN, although it was a most important factor in shaping the views of each delegation concerning the form and substance of the agency to be created. But while they agreed that international protection should be the agency's principal purpose, they did not agree on the implications that followed from that decision. Accordingly, the deliberations that went on within the organs of the UN for two years were centered around the two very different views held by the countries of overseas asylum on the one hand and the European states of first asylum on the other. The delegates debated the refugee problem itself; what

---

[75] IRO, GC (VIII), 22–27 Oct. 1951.

international action beyond protection, if any, was needed; and what sort of international organization was therefore appropriate for the task.

The US, as the dominant spokesman for the states of overseas resettlement, sought a strictly defined agency with narrow authority and limited function which would be temporary (lasting three years), require a small staff and little financing, and which would seek to achieve very limited objectives, notably the protection of the remaining IRO refugees until they were permanently settled and assimilated. Specifically, the US favored the establishment of a refugee service within the UN Secretariat rather than the appointment of a HC or the creation of a new specialized agency. If there must be a HC, then he should be appointed by the Secretary-General rather than elected by the GA (because, it was felt, he should serve under the Secretary-General and not exercise some independent authority where he might exert influence on public opinion or on governments while in office). The US favored a very narrow definition of refugee in order to limit the new agency to the protection of refugees, as set forth in the Constitution of the IRO. It opposed at first any broadening of the definition which might extend the lifetime of the agency and perhaps, in time, again require the expenditure of sizable funds because of the appearance of new refugee groups. The US also sought a very narrow purpose for the new organization – merely the provision of international protection – and tried to rule out the possibility of the new agency extending material assistance to refugees.

As has been noted, elements within the country were not without sympathy for refugees and their problems; many Americans were deeply concerned and undertook very substantial efforts in the hope of alleviating refugee problems. The US had been a substantial contributor to, and instigator of, UNRWA and UNKRA and had not been unconcerned in regard to the European refugees. But there was considerably less public interest in the US in the problems of the residual refugees than there had been in the heat of 1946–47, and government desire to minimize involvement and cost was correspondingly greater.

One can summarize the views of the Western European states toward the nature and purposes of the new refugee organization as being in most cases the opposite of the US view. There were, of course, differences of opinion among them as there were among the countries of overseas settlement. France, for example, was a leader of the view that the UNHCR should be a strong, permanent, multipurpose organization with an independent HC, and most importantly, with the power to raise funds and disburse them to refugees. France also sought throughout 1949 to broaden as much as possible the definition of the term refugee and therefore the scope of the agency's authority. There was a certain realism in seeking a broader definition for a newly established organization, so that it could be influenced by the Western European states to provide assistance when and if the residual problem was swollen by new groups of refugees. (Refugees from Eastern Europe were already appearing in increasing numbers.) France's approach was also realistic in that it sought to secure some action through the creation of an agency and to assure that controversy did not result in a stalemate. In several crucial matters France gave way (as did the US) in order to achieve a compromise position, while other states, most notably Belgium and the UK, then demanded broader and longer lasting powers than were urged by either the US or France.

6

Diplomacy and Foreign Policy
Introduction by Katharina Rietzler

Work on foreign policy and diplomacy forms one of the core subject matters of International Relations today and has done so from the early twentieth century. How foreign policy is made and implemented, why diplomatic practice changes over time, which *forces profondes* shape a state's diplomatic decisions, and to what extent it is possible to foresee the unintended outcomes of these policies are questions which remain the stock-in-trade of international affairs think tanks and university IR departments.

Women formulated these and other questions throughout the twentieth century, even if they were marginalized from the world of high politics and the diplomatic service in Western democracies.[1] Some elite women built on their family connections, for instance Margaret Lambert, and elsewhere in this volume Sibyl Crowe and Agnes Headlam-Morley, all daughters of influential British statesmen. Others took influential positions in foreign policy think tanks, for instance Vera Micheles Dean, the head of the Research Department of the US-based Foreign Policy Association, an organization dedicated to narrowing the space between diplomats and "the people." Coral Bell and Adda Bozeman moved between the worlds of think tanks and university IR departments. For some women writing on diplomacy and foreign policy, historical research offered a suitable array of intellectual tools, especially in England, where International Relations was considered a branch of History. Scholars such as Elizabeth Wiskemann, Merze Tate, and Agatha Ramm trained as diplomatic historians in interwar Cambridge, Oxford, and London.[2] But even then, traditional diplomatic history did

---

[1] Glenda Sluga and Carolyn James (eds.), *Women, Diplomacy and International Politics since 1500* (London: Routledge, 2016); Helen McCarthy, *Women of the World: The Rise of the Female Diplomat* (London: Bloomsbury, 2015); Edward Crapol (ed.), *Women and American Foreign Policy: Lobbyists, Critics, and Insiders* (Wilmington, DE: Scholarly Resources, 1992).

[2] Other women international thinkers who trained as historians include Mary Macdonald Proudfoot, Sibyl Crowe, Agnes Headlam-Morley, Elizabeth Monroe, Lillian M. Penson, and Eileen Power, all included in this volume.

not privilege events and historical contingency at the expense of the influence of culture and *mentalités*. By the 1960s, the analysis of foreign policy and diplomacy had become influenced by the anti-legalist shift within IR to realism and social scientific models such as game theory, a development that is critiqued here by political theorist Judith Shklar.

The selections in this section address three questions. Who makes foreign policy? What are the structures and norms (if not pathologies) that shape a nation's foreign policy? And, on an epistemological level, how should one write about foreign policy and diplomacy? The selections by Lambert, Bell, Bozeman, and Tate form part of contemporary foreign policy analyses, often in the form of commentary on current affairs. The selections by Wiskemann and Ramm are taken from works of diplomatic history. Dean and Shklar, both naturalized American citizens born in the lands of the Russian Empire, reflect on the possibility of dispassionate analysis in the context of American Cold War liberalism, a concern that is also visible in the work of Bozeman, a fellow immigrant.

Although not mentioned explicitly by the authors in this section, the question of analytical standpoint raises the issue of gendered subjectivity. It is hard to ascertain how exactly the gendered and racialized exclusions that shut women out of the formal practice of diplomacy until at least the 1940s influenced their writings. And yet, to a remarkable extent, women writing on foreign policy and diplomacy demonstrated an awareness that modern diplomacy could not remain cloistered away from the demands of electorates and, more broadly, the world's peoples. There is a debunking quality in tone and analysis of these extracts, sporting the occasional snide joke, sarcasm and skepticism, pitting high politics against low politics, and illuminating the stark disconnect between the highfalutin language of diplomatic protocol and real-world outcomes, even in those writings that valorize the work of statesmen.

Whether the current trend, certainly in the United States and some other Western democracies, of appointing women to the offices of Secretary of State, Secretary of Defense, or senior ambassadorial positions will influence practices of foreign policy analysis written by women is a matter for careful examination of gendered subjectivities in intellectual production, both historically and in the present moment.

In the aftermath of the First World War, women intellectuals engaged with aspects of the New Diplomacy and the use of policy innovations such as the international plebiscite. One of them was Margaret Lambert (1906–1995), the daughter of Viscount Lambert, a British parliamentarian and Civil Lord of the Admiralty. Lambert studied history at Oxford. She then embarked on a PhD at the London School of Economics (LSE), researching the run-up to the international plebiscite in the

Saar, a border region between Germany and France that was governed under a League of Nations mandate between 1920 and 1935. After working for the BBC in the Second World War, Lambert accepted positions editing British and captured German diplomatic documents but also taught at the Universities of Exeter and St Andrews. Her female life partner was the well-known designer Enid Marx, with whom Lambert co-authored two books on English folk art.[3]

Lambert's 1934 dissertation-turned-book on the Saar betrays the ease with which its urbane author navigated international travel. Written in a breezy style, it is a report from the frontlines of interwar diplomatic innovation that should be read together with the work of *the* specialist on international plebiscites, the international lawyer Sarah Wambaugh, included in the section on International Law and International Organization. But while Lambert's account is far from legalistic, it does not shy away from the complex theoretical problems that the proposed transfer of a territory's sovereignty via referendum brought up. Economically and strategically, it would have made sense to incorporate the Saar into France. This, however, had been impossible to achieve at the Paris Peace Conference due to the principle of self-determination. And by "race and tradition" (319), the Saar was quintessentially German, with "trim little houses and stocky thick-set people" (317). Lambert suggests that all manners of international theoretical problems could be analyzed in the microcosm that was the Saar. The plebiscite – which returned the region to Nazi Germany by over 90 percent of the vote in 1935 – was an "experiment" (322), an empirical test case for interwar assumptions about international governance, self-determination, nationality, and demography.

Questions of "national identity and purpose" (351) also concerned Coral Bell (1923–2012), an Australian expert on alliance diplomacy. Bell served in the Australian diplomatic service but in 1951 moved to the LSE, where she obtained a doctorate and, intellectually, became close to Martin Wight, the famous anti-theoretical theorist of International Relations who had also researched colonial administration for Margery Perham at Oxford. After a stint as a researcher at the Royal Institute of International Affairs think tank, Bell accepted a professorship at the University of Sussex in England and later at the Australian National University.[4] Bell has been characterized as a "conservative realist," who

---

[3] Eleanore Breuning, "Margaret Lambert," *Independent* (London, England), February 1, 1995, 16; Fay Sweet, "Enid Marx," *Independent* (London, England), May 19, 1998, 21.

[4] Desmond Ball and Sheryn Lee, "Introduction," in Desmond Ball and Sheryn Lee (eds.), *Power and International Relations: Essays in Honour of Coral Bell* (Canberra: ANU Press, 2014), 1–8.

subscribed to an "agent-centered interpretive theory of international relations," which accounted for shifts in the practice of international society by studying beliefs and conventions.[5]

In her 1964 book on Anglo-American relations, Bell seeks to provide explanations for a "special" relationship not grounded on formal treaties. Shared history and institutions did not suffice to understand the nature of an alliance that was "the hardest of all alliances for America to make" (353–354). According to Bell, pre-1945 American isolationism was a product of anti-imperialist Anglophobia but also ethnic loyalties. It was only a deep-rooted opposition to the Soviet Union, reviled by religious Irish-Americans, German-Americans, and Americans of Eastern European descent alike, that made the Anglo-American special relationship possible. Although Bell's analysis has its flaws, not least her conceit that she was above partisan politics, it forms an interesting contrast to more recent scholarship that locates the emergence of American anti-isolationism during the Second World War at the heart of the foreign policy establishment in Washington, DC, far removed from mentalities and group interests.[6] In that sense, Bell's account is more dedicated to uncovering what "ordinary" Americans thought than some of the self-consciously critical scholarship today.

This point is also of concern in Merze Tate's extract, written for the *Journal of Negro Education* in 1943. Founded to combat racial segregation in the United States and to provide a forum for political discussion among African Americans, the journal was published by the historically Black Howard University, Tate's employer. Here, the conditions of publication are directly linked to a thinker's positionality and analysis. While Lambert's and Bell's accounts take stock of ways in which the inhabitants of border regions and ethnic minorities brought about shifts in foreign policy, Tate highlights the absent voices of those who had no way of shaping policies that directly impacted them, not least disenfranchised African Americans during the Second World War. At the time of writing, Tate had recently completed her doctorate in government at Harvard, the first African American woman to do so.[7] She was trained as

---

[5] Ian Hall, "The Interpretation of Power Politics: Coral Bell's International Thought," in Desmond Ball and Sheryn Lee (eds.), *Power and International Relations: Essays in Honour of Coral Bell* (Canberra: ANU Press, 2014), 45–56, quotes at 46; See also Coral Bell's first major monograph, *Negotiation from Strength: A Study in the Politics of Power* (London: Chatto & Windus, 1962).

[6] Stephen Wertheim, "Instrumental Internationalism: The American Origins of the United Nations, 1940–3," *Journal of Contemporary History*, 54:2 (2019): 265–283.

[7] For more biographical information on Tate see the section on Public Opinion and Education.

a diplomatic historian at Oxford, where she studied with Alfred Zimmern and Agnes Headlam-Morley, and, fittingly, begins her analysis of great power peace-making with a quote from a Prussian diplomat at the end of the Napoleonic Wars: peace-making ultimately came down to dividing "amongst the conquerors the spoils taken from the vanquished" (323).

But, Tate asks, what about those who fought on the side of the British Empire and the United States, but were treated as inferiors? In the United States, it was African Americans who were most concerned over the professed war aims, along with the rest of the "colored world" (327). Offering a withering dissection of both the Atlantic Charter and the Roosevelt Administration's Four Freedoms, Tate's text is an excellent example of a kind of foreign policy analysis that cannot be found in more conventional outlets. It analyzes the contradictions of wartime policy proclamations within internally hierarchical polities, especially those that make grand claims to international democracy and human rights.

The foreign policy analysis from Adda Bozeman (1908–1994) adopts a similarly contrarian tone but takes a very different political stance. Written for the scholarly journal *World Politics*, it seeks to contextualize the deteriorating diplomatic relations between India and the United States during the Eisenhower Administration but aims the blame squarely at India's leader Jawaharlal Nehru.[8] In Bozeman's reading, Nehru, whom she considers an excessively "emotional" (344) statesman, found in Marxism-Leninism a convenient rationalization of his anti-Western beliefs, even though he owed key concepts in his thinking to the modern history of international organization as developed in the Western world. As a consequence, Nehru praised the Soviet Union's foreign policy, despite being fully aware of communism's shortcomings.

Bozeman's unwavering opposition to the Soviet Union can partly be explained by her biography. Adda (von Bruemmer) Bozeman was born in what would become Latvia, into a Baltic German family which had to leave Riga in the tumultuous period after the First World War. As a teenager and young woman, Bozeman experienced displacement and considerable hardship but nonetheless managed to earn qualifications in Germany, France, the Netherlands, Britain, and the United States while also working for an international law firm in Berlin. She emigrated permanently to the United States in the late 1930s, where she conducted research at the Hoover Library at Stanford. The result of her research was her first book, a specialist study on Article 435 of the Versailles Treaty. As Bozeman's legal career stalled, she turned to college teaching.

[8] Ramachandra Guha, *India after Gandhi: The History of the World's Largest Democracy* (Basingstoke: Macmillan, 2007), 155–161.

After being offered a professorship in 1947, Bozeman – now a divorcee – taught for thirty years at Sarah Lawrence College, a reform-minded women's college which became co-educational during her tenure. After leaving college teaching, Bozeman joined the Committee on the Present Danger, a foreign policy pressure group that advocated a muscular US foreign policy and would produce many officials in the Reagan Administration, among them Jeane Kirkpatrick.[9]

Bozeman was a prolific scholar, publishing numerous well-received books and articles in the course of five decades. Her specialty was the influence of culture on international politics. Her biographer suggests that Samuel P. Huntington lifted without acknowledgement Bozeman's ideas to formulate his hypothesis on the "clash of civilizations," although she herself characterized his claims as too simplistic.[10] Bozeman argued that effective statecraft necessitated the objective understanding of cultural sources of foreign policy and that culture was a key explanatory variable. She first developed these ideas in *Politics and Culture in International History*, covering international relations over 5,000 years, and comparing cultures and civilizations across time. This monograph was followed by several studies, many on non-Western societies.[11]

The condescending stance Bozeman took towards India and its leaders – after all, she suggests that Indian statesmen had failed to develop a foreign policy that would accommodate "those traditions that are found to have an enduring hold on the Indian mind" (338) – does not imply that she was an uncritical cheerleader for the United States. On the contrary, many features of her adopted homeland's foreign policy incurred her objection. She thought that Americans too easily jettisoned the past and assumed that everyone was like them. She remained wary of the promotion of democracy and human rights, arguing that such policies were the product of Western culture and not necessarily applicable elsewhere.[12] Yet, at the same time, she remained wedded to the idea that

---

[9] Wolfgang Saxon, "Adda Bozeman Barkhuus 85, Expert in International Relations," *New York Times*, December 10, 1994, 52; Carol Keim, *An Affair of Flutes: The Life of Adda Von Bruemmer Bozeman*, PhD Dissertation, University of Cincinnati, 2003, 12–14, chapter 1, 99–100, 109, 124. Kirkpatrick is notable as a neglected theorist of totalitarianism and wrote one of the most influential foreign policy treatises in US conservatism, "Dictatorship and Double Standards," *Commentary Magazine*, 68:5 (1979): 34–45.

[10] Keim, *An Affair of Flutes*, preface.

[11] Adda B. Bozeman, *Politics and Culture in International History* (New Brunswick, NJ: Princeton University Press, 1960); Adda B. Bozeman, *The Future of Law in a Multicultural World* (Princeton, NJ: Princeton University Press, 1971); Adda B. Bozeman, *Conflict in Africa: Concepts and Realities* (Princeton, NJ: Princeton University Press, 1976).

[12] Keim, *An Affair of Flutes*, 7–12.

a successful foreign policy had to be in tune with a nation's values and identity, sometimes to the extent that the protection of this identity became synonymous with the national interest.[13]

If foreign policy could not be abstracted from democratic demands, individual decision-making still hinged on the contingent behavior of diplomats. In the middle of the twentieth century, several British women intellectuals produced foreign policy analyses that used historical methods to examine the decisions of statesmen and their political contexts. The authors included here are Elizabeth Wiskemann (1899–1971) and Agatha Ramm (1914–2004), both of whom had Anglo-German backgrounds, trained as historians, and tried to explain the doomed rise to power of the German Reich from the 1880s to the 1940s.

Wiskemann became a well-regarded foreign affairs journalist and spent much of the 1930s in Germany. Her first book, *Czechs and Germans*, was commissioned by the Royal Institute of International Affairs and appeared in 1938. After the Second World War, Wiskemann began to write more academically, which eventually led to appointments at the universities of Edinburgh, where she took the Montague Burton chair in International Relations, and Sussex. Her scholarly reputation was bolstered by her 1949 study on the relations between Hitler and Mussolini, excerpted here.[14]

In contrast to Tate, Bell, and Lambert, Wiskemann focuses on the pathological personalities of dictators to explain the course of international politics. She suggests that what she termed the Rome–Berlin Axis was entirely held together by Hitler's Nietzschean "will to power" which "subjugated Mussolini" (331), who was, she claims, merely "an ordinary human being in doubt" (329). Writing a mere four years after the end of the Second World War, Wiskemann resorts to psychological speculation, which sits uneasily with her usually more empiricist analysis. Nonetheless, her book became a standard account and was positively reviewed by academic luminaries such as Hugh Trevor-Roper and Martin Wight. Wiskemann's attention to Nietzsche's philosophy as a key to understanding fascism was not uncommon at the time, and further

---

[13] Adda B. Bozeman, "U.S. Foreign Policy and the Prospects for Democracy, National Security, and World Peace," *Comparative Strategy*, 5:3 (1985): 223–267.

[14] James Joll, "Wiskemann, Elizabeth Meta (1899–1971), Historian and Journalist," *Oxford Dictionary of National Biography*, September 23, 2004, www.oxforddnb.com/view/10.1093/ref:odnb/9780198614128.001.0001/odnb-9780198614128-e-31848 (accessed November 20, 2019); Elizabeth Wiskemann, *Czechs and Germans: A Study of the Struggle in the Historic Provinces of Bohemia and Moravia* (London: Oxford University Press, 1938); Elizabeth Wiskemann, *Italy* (London: Oxford University Press, 1947).

developed by historians who sought to explain fascism's rise by focusing on its animating ideas and personalities, such as Ernst Nolte.[15]

Nietzsche and his theories of the *Übermensch* also appear in Agatha Ramm's 1967 account of the origins of the First World War. However, Ramm's approach contrasts with Wiskemann's, which, despite being aimed at an academic audience, engages in sensationalism (for instance, when discussing Hitler's sexual proclivities). While Ramm concedes that Nietzschean thought impelled German statesmen to prepare for war in the years leading up to 1914, she emphasizes structural reasons: the Franco-Prussian War of 1870–1871 and the subsequent alliance system bequeathed a habit of operational planning for war, bolstered by a German federalism in which military conflict became the central expenditure of the German state. Ramm modifies Lenin's thesis of economic concentration and competition as the cause of international conflict by highlighting political concentration, an elimination of the power of small and medium states within the German Empire that used to enable small adjustments in the overall system. In her reading, statesmen failed to perceive how choices in nation-building could propel a state towards international conflict, thus failing to control the systemic causes of war.

Statesmen and their decisions were a central focus in Ramm's work, and her restrained manner of writing formed part of a certain scholarly habitus. Her best-known work was a multi-volume edition of Gladstone's correspondence with Lord Granville, but she also published monographs on German and diplomatic history. Born to an English father and a German mother, Ramm read History at Bedford College, a women's college in London, where she came under the influence of the diplomatic historian Lillian M. Penson, whose work appears elsewhere in this anthology. Ramm secured posts first at Bedford and, in 1952, at Somerville College, Oxford, where she modeled the typical English college woman: old-fashioned, severe, private, but utterly committed to the education of her female students (and, more unusually, a convert to Catholicism).[16]

---

[15] Geoffrey Field, "Elizabeth Wiskemann, Scholar-Journalist, and the Study of International Relations," in Patricia Owens and Katharina Rietzler (eds.), *Women's International Thought: A New History* (Cambridge: Cambridge University Press, 2021), 198–222; Ernst Nolte, *The Three Faces of Fascism* (London: Weidenfeld and Nicolson, 1965).

[16] "Agatha Ramm," *The Times*, July 16, 2004, 34; Agatha Ramm (ed.), *The Political Correspondence of Mr. Gladstone and Lord Granville, 1876–1886* (Oxford: Clarendon Press, 1962); Agatha Ramm, *Germany, 1789–1919: A Political History* (London: Methuen, 1967); Agatha Ramm, *Sir Robert Morier: Envoy and Ambassador in the Age of Imperialism, 1876–1893* (Oxford: Clarendon Press, 1973).

Even if it is not immediately obvious, these historical accounts were very much written in the shadow of the present. Wiskemann and Ramm engaged in the post-1945 historiographical battles over the origins of Nazi Germany's foreign policy, punctuated by the controversies around the British historian A. J. P. Taylor's publication of *The Origins of the Second World War* in 1961. Ramm's thesis seemed to contradict Taylor's assertion that the German Empire was inherently aggressive even before Hitler's rise to power, while Wiskemann, in a letter to the *Times Literary Supplement*, criticized what she regarded as Taylor's exculpation of Hitler as an "ordinary" statesman, which, she implied, strengthened neo-Nazis in 1960s West Germany. Taylor, Britain's first popular television historian, delighted in his role as dispassionate provocateur, and bluntly rebuffed attempts to make him responsible for the lamentable political consequences of his historical enquiries.[17] But such a carefree pose would have been harder to assume for a woman in the public eye.

The career of Vera Micheles Dean (1903–1972) highlights the dangers of foreign policy analysis for a woman who was ideologically suspect. Perhaps more than any other mid-century woman in the United States, Dean was a public authority on foreign affairs, present in the mass media, in civil society organizations, and on university campuses. Born in imperial Russia, she moved to the United States as a university student, and, after a Radcliffe PhD on international law and international relations, joined the liberal-internationalist Foreign Policy Association in 1928. She started out as a researcher but directed its Research Department from 1936, before moving to the University of Rochester to lead its Non-Western Civilization Program in 1954, and to New York University in 1962. She continued her association with the Foreign Policy Association until 1961, directing its Publications Department. Combining serious scholarship with the ability to speak to ordinary Americans, Dean managed to sell hundreds of thousands of copies of her books, which were also used in college classes.[18]

In the late 1940s, Dean moved into the crosshairs of the ascendant American right. Since her earliest days as a foreign policy analyst, Dean had consistently argued that the Soviet Union did not necessarily pose a threat to the United States. She sought to elicit Americans' understanding for the economic needs of the Russian people and highlighted the

[17] Kathleen Burk, *Troublemaker: The Life and History of A. J. P. Taylor* (London: Yale University Press, 2000), 291–294.
[18] Andrew Jewett, "Collective Security for Common Men and Women: Vera Micheles Dean and U.S. Foreign Relations," in Patricia Owens and Katharina Rietzler (eds.), *Women's International Thought: A New History* (Cambridge: Cambridge University Press, 2021), 308.

extent to which the Soviet Union provided a model for rapid industrialization to those who were not the beneficiaries of an American-style consumer economy. Dean's claim that even Stalinism was capable of democratic reform now appears as a misjudgment, and it made her the target of anti-communist attacks that lasted until the early 1960s. These attacks were sometimes formulated by conservative women activists who accused Dean of co-opting women's organizations and presenting her vision of an anti-isolationist and anticolonialist US foreign policy as one shared by all American women.[19] It is likely that these accusations were fomented by Dean's public visibility and status as a foreign-born American.

In the foreword to her 1953 book *Foreign Policy without Fear*, written at the height of McCarthyism, Dean examines the objectivity question as it poses itself to scholars of current affairs. She maintains that they should try to strive for objectivity, be prepared to be proved wrong, but still speak their mind according to their conscience, even if their conclusions are unpopular. Clearly rattled by the accusations leveled at her, Dean concedes that such a stance could make one "an object of public abuse such as once reserved for hardened criminals" (334). A democratic society such as the United States provided no protection, as "myths can be created even in a society which offers opportunities for free discussion" (336). This was a partial admission of failure, as Dean had dedicated the better part of three decades to fostering what she regarded as free discussion. Nonetheless, she continued to address a broad audience, putting forward her vision of the Cold War as a conflict that could be overcome with sufficient good will on both sides. She chose to be candid about her politics, a move that distinguishes her from the anti-politics of so much foreign policy analysis that became common in the American academy of the 1950s and 1960s.

This is the world that is analyzed in the extract written by Judith Shklar (1928–1992), the famous political theorist of liberalism. Shklar's general stance was one of "reasoned skepticism," committed to speaking the truth based on experience and history.[20] An émigré, Shklar was born in Latvia to a Jewish family and left her country of birth in 1939, prior to the Soviet occupation. After stations in Sweden, Japan, and Canada, Shklar settled in the United States and graduated from Harvard's Government

[19] Jewett, "Collective Security for Common Men and Women"; Lucille Cardin Crain and Anne Burrows Hamilton, "Packaged Thinking for Women," *American Affairs*, Supplement to Autumn 1948 issue.

[20] Giunia Gatta, *Rethinking Liberalism for the 21st Century: The Skeptical Radicalism of Judith Shklar* (New York: Routledge, 2018), 28.

Department in 1955, where she spent the rest of her working life as a scholar. Like several of the thinkers in this volume, Shklar was wary of associating herself with any academic camp, whether that of legalists in law schools or IR realists in political science departments.[21]

Her 1964 essay on decisionism dissects the style of foreign policy analysis that was established in the American discipline of International Relations at the time. Privileging "power and power manipulation as *the* essential concepts of politics," realism represents a rejection of what Shklar terms "legalism," the idea that in international politics there are rules that should be followed. Yet this rejection rests not so much on a logically coherent argument but a temper, the general feeling that looking for rules is itself a foolish enterprise. Decisionists thus become obsessed with individual decision-making, which represents a "technical rationality" to them (349).

According to Shklar, decisionism held sway in the form of realism in American academe and sustained a sense of self-importance by denying its own ideological nature. Shklar sets out to debunk the realist debunkers, whose critiques of liberal internationalism focus on Woodrow Wilson as the "villain of the modern world" but let Hitler and Stalin off the hook (346). American realism in its search for "men with orderly minds," cold-blooded, de-ideologized decision-makers, constructs an alternative, masculine rationality, which is nothing but "an artifact" (346, 347). This imagined rationality might explain realism's affinity with highly abstract mathematical models, a phenomenon that intellectual historians have remarked upon recently but one that Shklar already outlines in this piece.[22] In her view, game theory applies only to a tiny number of situations and appears thus to be of limited use in the analysis of everyday diplomacy. Once every conceivable variable of political behaviour is added, one arrives back at "old-fashioned narrative history," a model of writing that European and American IR scholars spent considerable energy on denigrating in the first half of the twentieth century (348).

It is interesting to read Shklar's eloquent put-down of fashionable analytic models together with the traditional historical narratives of diplomacy produced by other women in this period. None of them, with the possible exception of Agnes Headlam-Morley, discussed elsewhere in

---

[21] Judith N. Shklar, *Legalism: Law, Morals, and Political Trials* (Cambridge, MA: Harvard University Press, 1964).

[22] Nicolas Guilhot, "Cyborg Pantocrator: International Relations Theory from Decisionism to Rational Choice," *Journal of the History of the Behavioral Sciences*, 47:3 (2011): 279–301.

this anthology, endeavored to produce a "mirror of princes," heroic accounts and templates that men could gaze into to admire their likeness (347). Although separated by politics, race, age, nationality, ethnicity, religion, and disciplinary formation, most of the authors in this section infuse their careful analyses with a spirit of gentle mockery.

Katharina Rietzler

Margaret Lambert

From *The Saar* (1934)

As you travel through the Saar district on the way from Berlin to Paris, it is difficult to realize that these lovely wooded hills are part of one of the densest industrial areas of Western Europe. Further on, as the railway runs through a chain of large industrial villages, tall chimneys and the smoke of blast furnaces appear, but even here there is enough woodland visible to make the Saar valley look quite different from any vista in England's Black Country. 'This', the affable German gentleman sitting opposite will tell you, for no German is averse to giving information with perhaps a dash of propaganda thrown in, 'is because the coal mines have always been government property, and so have the forests, and one is not allowed to spoil the other. See how German the country looks,' he adds eagerly, 'there can be no doubt of how the people will vote when the plebiscite is held.' Certainly the country looks very German, with the trim little houses and stocky thick-set people. There are even plenty of the new German flags to be seen hanging from the windows, black, white and red, with here and there a swastika. All this is German enough but (if you have just left Germany) there seems to be something missing. Where are all the brown uniforms? 'Forbidden by the Governing Commission,' you will be answered gloomily, if you voice your question aloud. Whereupon it will be explained to you that here the Government is not German at all, it is run by the League of Nations.

Nowadays it has become fashionable in some quarters to put the blame for all our political troubles on the peace settlements after the war, and particularly on the League of Nations. In considering this view, however, we ought to take into account that a good many unpleasant labours, which no one nation could or would undertake, have been thrust upon the League. One such thorny task was the provision of a temporary but impartial neutral government for the Saar Territory. In the words of a recent French writer: 'For the government of the Saar, if there had been no League of Nations it would have been necessary to create one.' At the

Peace Conference the fate of the Saar Territory provided one of those awkward gaps between principle and practice which have to be bridged somehow. So the infant League was called upon to provide a temporary stop-gap. Now, however, the arrangement is coming to an end, and something more permanent will have to be put in its place.

The Saar Territory, a little country not quite as big as Westmorland, but supporting one of the densest populations in Europe, has been living since 1920 under international rule. The League of Nations acts as its trustee, and appoints a Commission of five members – one might almost call them a board of guardians – to govern the country. On January 13th, 1935, however, the people of the Saar will have to take a hand in deciding their own future. They will have to choose between joining either Germany or France, or else remaining what they are, a little neutral district under the League.

To English minds there is nothing strikingly original in the proposal that a country should choose its own government. The plebiscite through which the Saarlanders will express their choice seems not unlike a magnified form of General Election, with three candidates in the field. The issues involved, however, will be very different from any that we have ever had to face. The notion of a whole country having to change its nationality (shall it be French, German or just Saar) is something quite outside our experience. Our own nationality has always seemed so secure that the bitter passions which such things can arouse amongst borderland peoples are almost unintelligible to us.

Yet plebiscites involving changes of nationality have been held quite often. Several of them were included in the Treaty of Versailles, and, incidentally, they shed some fresh light on this curious question of nationality – whether it is just a matter of use and wont, or whether it really is a deep-rooted feeling that will survive through the centuries. There have even been a couple of plebiscites held before in this Saar district, a little more than a century ago. They were held when the armies of the French Revolution were sweeping over half Europe, bringing with them the twin novelties of liberty and the guillotine, and calling upon the inhabitants of invaded provinces to burst their chains, and join free France. The Saarlanders voted for France on both these occasions. Still, as they were under the influence both of the Terror and an inspiring new gospel of government, their votes can hardly be assumed to provide a reliable index to their present feelings, as so many French writers managed to persuade themselves when the peace treaty was being made. It is curious to reflect that to-day the leading roles are reversed; Germany holds out the new gospel, and is accused of using terrorism.

Compared with the general run of plebiscites, however, the present one in the Saar is unusual. For one thing there are three alternatives, so that cautiously minded Saarlanders, if there be any such, can cry: 'A plague on both your houses!' and choose a middle way. Then there has been the long delay of fifteen years before holding it. France and Germany have both had plenty of time to put their case. The Saar has been a cockpit for a war of propaganda, increasing or lessening in bitterness according as Franco-German relations in other spheres have been more or less strained.

If we ask why a little country like the Saar should cause two great nations so much trouble, the answer is twofold. In the economic sphere it is very simple, and can be expressed in the two words Coal and Iron. Lying next to what is now French Lorraine, the Saar covers one of the richest coalfields in Western continental Europe. It is only second to the Ruhr Westphalian field. In the last year before the war, the Saar field produced over 13,000,000 tons of coal. Compared with other countries, this is about 7 per cent of all the coal produced by the rest of Germany that year, about 33 per cent of France's coal, and about 5 per cent of Great Britain's. But since the Saar coal mines are only about forty miles away from the iron ore fields in Lorraine, a big iron and steel industry has grown up in the Saar Territory, using native coal and Lorraine iron ore. Before the war, most of Lorraine belonged to Germany, so there were no customs to interfere with this trade, and Lorraine and the Saar grew up together as part of the same country. Naturally, when France got Lorraine back after the war, she wanted the Saar as well, so as to have the coal for the iron ores. This was also in the economic interests of the Saar people; without the iron ores from Lorraine their industry would have been ruined.

But by race and tradition the Saar people are unmistakably German and, if their inclinations were to be consulted, they would obviously hate to go with France. Not even the most persuasive of French statesmen at the Peace Conference would induce President Wilson to believe that by transferring three-quarters of a million passionate Germans to France he was sticking to his principles of self-determination of peoples. It seems an irony of nature that has placed these rich mineral deposits so near together on the borderline between two peoples. Which ought to be put first, the reasonable use of minerals which will, after all, create trade and employment, or the happiness of the population which chances to live above them? Here we have one of those impossibly difficult situations where economic interests and national feelings are pulling in opposite directions. Which ought to give way? The question proved too difficult for the Peace Conference to settle there and then, so a temporary arrangement was made, and time left to bring wisdom. For fifteen years the Saar was placed under League of Nations rule; France was given the coal mines, and control of the Saar customs to help her exploit them. If, at the end of this period, the people still wanted to return to Germany, then the German government was to buy the mines back from France in gold, at a price to be fixed by the arbitration.

There is another much less tangible, but at the same time far older reason why both France and Germany want the Saar. It goes back to the days before coal and iron became part of politics, when the Saar land was just sparsely populated forest, but was none the less part of the border region which has caused trouble between France and Germany for over a thousand years. Their quarrel dates back to the almost legendary days of Charlemagne, and his three grandsons, who divided his Empire between them. The middle kingdom between France and Germany went to Lothair, the eldest grandson, but his two brothers combined to oust him from it, only to start quarrelling over it themselves. It has been an intermittent source of strife ever since. As France grew stronger under a centralized monarchy, and Germany weaker under a loosely knit empire, the French government managed to encroach further and further into this territory. Thus at various times quite a large slice of the present Saar Territory came into their hands. Although, when Prussia replaced the feeble empire as dominant power in Germany, this slice was gradually lost again, French patriots have never ceased to hanker after it. Their feelings are part of that urge towards a better eastern frontier, and chronic fear of invasion, that have become part of the psychological make-up of so many Frenchmen. However much we may ridicule these fears, we cannot allay them. The thought of sixty odd millions of Germans balanced against only forty million French, has increasingly haunted French statesmen ever since the humiliation of 1870. The Saar Territory, with its fifteen years' pause from German rule, gave France a chance to transmute at least three-quarters of a million Germans into Frenchmen; for to a French mind who could resist the attractions of French civilization, when given such an excellent opportunity of sampling it? Germany, however much she may pooh-pooh this sort of alchemy, has been rather uneasy. To her it looks like French imperialism, though to neutral observers it is really that old French fetish of security.

Nowadays France would be content if the Saar were to become what pre-war Luxemburg and Belgium used to be: little neutral buffer states along her treacherous eastern frontier, guaranteed by other powers. This arrangement, however, would probably be less palatable for the Saarlanders. If they stay under the League, France is still economically dominant in their country, for although France had declared herself willing to dispose of the mines to the Saar on reasonable terms, should it vote for the League, so small a country could scarcely remain outside either the German or French Customs Union. We can scarcely suppose that the Saar would be included in the German Customs Union, should it reject German sovereignty.

Indeed, all three proposals for their country's future present difficulties to the unfortunate Saarlanders. Up to now they have derived a good deal of benefit from the doubt about it. They have been the pampered children of two countries, each trying to win them with favours. Under the Treaty, they were given free trade with France; Germany, not to be outdone, has given them special quota arrangements which virtually amount to free trade too. So they have a double outlet for their goods, and the home markets of two countries are open to them. Once however they have thrown in their lot with either side these favours will cease. France would probably continue her concessions if they chose to stay under the League; she would retain her economic importance, and also a certain strategic advantage. Germany certainly would not. [...]

Until recently, the stubborn Germanic character of the Saarlanders proved impervious both to economic arguments and to all such blandishments as France was prepared to offer. Indeed French public opinion had begun to accept an overwhelming majority for Germany as a foregone conclusion. Now, however, the economic crisis and the rise of Hitlerism have somewhat altered the complexion of things, at least in French eyes. Knowing that the economic and therefore political development of the Saar has inevitably taken a different course from the rest of Germany, and that a predominantly working-class and Catholic population is inclined to distrust movements which owe their appeal to middle-class ideals, French hopes have begun to revive. Even if the Saar as a whole may not be ready to turn its back on its German fatherland, as the voting is to be by districts, some of the villages on the French border may be tempted to secede. [...]

Colour is lent to these reviving French hopes by the activities of the Social Democrats, Communists and other elements in the Saar, whose brethren have been 'liquidated' by the Nazis in the Third Reich. It would be surprising if the patriotism of these people consisted in voting themselves straight into the concentration camps which they believe to await them if the Saar returns to Germany. How many Saarlanders still belong to these parties there is no knowing; the Nazis have admittedly made great inroads on their numbers, but amongst an industrial population these elements are usually strong. For such people the chance of remaining as they are will be the best bait; before the rise of the Nazis they were among France's bitterest opponents, so a vote for the League will strain their patriotism less. The relations between the Third Reich and the Catholic Church will also play a very considerable part in determining the Saar's future. The population is predominantly Catholic.

Should Germany have even a small minority against her, this will mean a severe loss of prestige. For as the Saarlanders have always been very faithful to their native land, this would virtually amount to a vote of censure on the Third Reich. Perhaps this affords a clue to the German eagerness to avoid the plebiscite, and France's persistent championing of the rights of the inhabitants to record their opinions. In any case, feelings on both sides are likely to run very high before the actual voting takes place. There will be the worst possible atmosphere for negotiating a reasonable settlement of the outstanding economic questions; yet without some such agreement Saar industries will be in a very bad way.

As we consider the various aspects of the Saar problem, we naturally wonder how far they have grown better or worse under this curious arrangement of a postponed settlement. How has international government fared in this important test? The Saar presents a case where economic interests and patriotic ties seem to be pulling in diametrically opposite directions. Similar situations are common enough today; they are one of the banes of contemporary Europe, the rock on which so many peace pacts and disarmament conferences split. Indeed this very Saar question almost broke up the Peace Conference, to plunge Europe back into chaos and send President Wilson home to America, shaking the dust of the Old World from his feet. No part of the Treaty of Versailles has come in for such severe criticism as the Saar scheme. Was it a mere hypocritical pandering to French imperialism, or was it a genuine attempt to ease an intolerable situation? Has it really tided Franco-German relations over a period of strain, and if so, is it a system that might be profitably applied elsewhere? Or has it simply managed to provide an incessant irritation that will come to a head in the excitement over the plebiscite? These and many other questions require an answer before we can decide whether the experiment in the Saar has succeeded or failed. We know that it was an innovation in international politics; nothing quite like it has ever been tried before. Perhaps now, when it has almost come to an end, is as good a time as any for taking stock impartially of the whole situation.

Merze Tate

From "The War Aims of World War I and World War II and Their Relation to the Darker Peoples of the World" (1943)

"Universal expectation has perhaps never been raised to such a pitch," wrote the Prussian statesman, Frederick von Gentz, of the Congress of Vienna assembled one hundred and twenty-eight years ago to bring peace to a Europe overrun by Napoleon Bonaparte. War-weary peoples looked forward to an "all-embracing reform of the political system of Europe," to "guarantees of universal peace"; in a word, to "the return of the golden age." But the "real purpose of the Congress was to divide amongst the conquerors the spoils taken from the vanquished." Well might these words describe the deep longings of the peoples and the objectives of most statesmen one hundred years later at Paris. And again, today, there is universal expectation of an all-embracing reform of the political system, not of Europe alone but of the entire world, which will herald a just and durable peace. Will the hopes of the peoples, especially of the darker peoples, be realized or will the Peace Congress convened at the end of this global war have as its ulterior purpose the division of the spoils of the vanquished and a return as near as possible to the *status quo ante bellum*?

What is meant when one refers to the darker peoples of the world? Such a reference is not confined to the nearly thirteen million Negroes in the United States, who so far as war aims are concerned are hardly taken into consideration, nor to the millions of colored in the Caribbean and in Central and South America. Rather, in addition to these groups, the term must comprehend most of the inhabitants of Africa, including those Islamic peoples of the Mediterranean littoral and those natives south of the Sahara Desert; the 400,000,000 or more of India and Burma; the Malaysians who inhabit the Malay peninsula and archipelago, including the former Netherlands East Indies; the Chinese; the Japanese; and, finally, the Polynesians of Oceania and the Melanesians, those Negroid inhabitants of the islands of the Central and Western Pacific, including the Solomon Islands.

All over the world the peoples of color are aroused, although in varying degrees, to the *Imperium* of the white nations. They are no longer willing to accept the white man's exalted view of trusteeship; they no longer quake at the teachings of the white man's missionaries, who bring them the white man's God but a God in whom the white man does not believe; no longer are glass beads and trinkets marvelous to them; they are much more interested in the marvels of the white man's guns. Once the colored races feared the white man; today that fear has turned to secret contempt. Once they were filled with terror at the white man's power; today they know that they themselves are power. Their past weakness has not been due to their lack of numbers nor to inferior physical stamina but to the fact that the white man had guns, cared little for God and much for his guns. Today the yellow, brown, black peoples know that the whites are in a minority with no special "capacities" which mean "innate superiority"; moreover, that minority is divided and is slaughtering itself. The white man's culture has gradually become familiar to the man of color, who is capable of analyzing and evaluating it according to the limits of its efficiency. He has participated in the wars and revolutions of the ruling nations and perforce has been initiated into the former dark mysteries of their armaments, economics and diplomacy, and has thus come to question the reality of the white man's superiority and to contemplate the possibilities of attack and victories for himself. Oswald Spengler observes: "It was not Germany that lost the World War; the West lost it when it lost the respect of the coloured races."[23]

How did the darker peoples figure in the aims of World War I and what gains did they make as a result of that war? Woodrow Wilson proclaimed that we were fighting the World War to "make not only the liberties of America secure but the liberties of every other people as well."[24] "Peoples and provinces are not to be bartered about from sovereignty to sovereignty as if they were mere chattels and pawns in a game. ... Every territorial settlement involved in this war must be made in the interest of the populations concerned."[25]

Yet, in the final settlement the wishes of colonial peoples were not consulted; the colonies and possessions of the victorious states remained in the same status, and those of the defeated powers were not, as Wilson proposed, declared the common property of the League of Nations to be administered in the interest of the peoples concerned by smaller nations,

[23] Oswald Spengler, *The Hour of Decision* (New York: Alfred A. Knopf, 1934), 209.
[24] Address of July 4, 1918.   [25] Address of February 11, 1918.

but were parcelled out for the benefit of the mandatory powers – Great Britain, France, Japan, the Union of South Africa, Australia and New Zealand. The mandate system and its idea of trusteeship, which represented a compromise between the new and old colonial ideas, soon became an "obvious sham and hollow pretense." At the outbreak of the present war there was no outward evidence of any intention on the part of Great Britain, France and Holland to permit their black and brown wards to share in the responsibilities of government. Throughout native Africa, Indonesia and Malaya the imperialist mentality was that of master and subject peoples. The forces of government had come to serve primarily as a repressive agency holding back the progressive development of peoples whom it had introduced to Western civilization. Thus, "imperialism appears always to be committed to perpetuating its own rule unless it is challenged by a force which makes it necessary or expedient for it to withdraw."[26]

At the Paris Peace Conference the Japanese and Chinese demands for international recognition of the principle of racial equality challenged the theory of white superiority, and the refusal of the British Empire delegation to accept a revised and innocuous clause endorsing the "principle of equality of nations and just treatment of their nationals" embittered the Japanese. Will the white man and the colored man now find a basis for co-operation as equals? The answer to this question will determine the future of civilization; it will determine whether this war will result in a just and durable peace or in only a truce in preparation for a race war. The white man is a century behind the colored man in his thinking on civilization. Long years of imperialism have very nearly deprived him of vision. He still reasons in terms of colonies, colonial development, economic exploitation of "backward regions," and even the most liberal cannot divorce from their minds the idea of "trusteeship" and "international mandate." An example of this latter type of temporizing is the Phelps–Stokes Fund's Committee on Africa, the War, and Peace Aims, which in 1942 produced a study entitled *The Atlantic Charter and Africa from an American Standpoint*. Those Englishmen and Americans who envision plans for and approach the problems of lasting peace have an egocentric view of the world and think primarily in terms of Europe, the Western World, the balance of power in Asia, and appear to take for granted a return to something akin to the pre-war African and Asiatic status quo. They think and write entirely too much in terms of saving European civilization, ignoring the fact that that civilization is a partial

[26] Rupert Emerson, *Malaya: A Study in Direct and Indirect Rule* (New York: The Macmillan Co., 1937), 519.

and secondary culture serving a minority of the peoples of the world. Examples of well-meaning but completely inadequate approaches to the problems of a global peace are Edward Hallett Carr, *Conditions of Peace*, Herbert Hoover and Hugh Gibson, *The Problems of Lasting Peace*, Harold Butler, *The Lost Peace*, and J. B. Condliffe, *Agenda for a Post-War World*. World War II, when considered realistically, is not fought for the Four Freedoms everywhere. It is a militarist and imperialist struggle for freedom and power – power for some at the expense of others. The Eight Points of the Atlantic Charter and the Four Freedoms may have been intended to serve as idealistic platitudes for Europe but we cannot foresee their voluntary application to areas outside that continent.

[...]

What is the alternative to the white man's refusal to assume the responsibilities for a global peace, for his refusal to abandon the old policy of putting limits on freedom for others? That alternative is sounded specifically in Krishnalal Shridharani's *Warning To The West*, stated clearly by Pearl Buck in her speeches and articles, and predicted in the writings of Oswald Spengler – that alternative is an inter-continental war between the East and West, the greatest war the human race has ever seen, a war between whites and non-whites. That war will come as a result of the white man's unwillingness to give up his superiority and the colored man's unwillingness to endure his inferiority. "Such a titanic struggle," Shridharani warns, "would be a hundred years war, far graver and more horrible [sic] than the one we are fighting now."[27] In the words of Miss Buck: "At home and abroad the white race has the choice to make – whether it will follow the totalitarian principle of ruler and subject races, even to the inevitable end of rebellion and the worst of wars, or whether peoples of all colors will decide to work out ways of living in mutual harmony and freedom." The crisis between white and colored, she maintains, "is not two steps off – it is close, inextricably mingled with this war, because the war against nazism carries race equality or inequality as one of its main issues. It does no good that we ourselves keep the issue hushed and hidden apart from the thinking mass of the white people. The crisis approaches, whether white people are willing to know it or not. It approaches in the world, and with that inexorable march our own people are keeping step."

Oswald Spengler, a twentieth century German philosopher, in his realistic books, *The Decline of the West*, *Man and Technics* and *The Hour of Decision*, repeatedly emphasized that each of the past great cultures had

[27] K. Shridharani, op. cit., p. 273.

been confronted by the hopeless downtrodden races of the outer ring –
"savages or barbarians" who were exploited without means of redress by
the unassailable superiority of nations which had reached maturity in
their political, military, economic and intellectual forms and methods.
Rome fell to the "barbarians" within and on her borders. The position of
the twentieth century Imperium of the white nations, which embraces the
whole globe and includes the colored races, is far more difficult than that
of the Roman Empire because that empire was an enclosed area that
could be guarded. Today the Yellow–Brown–Black–Red menace lurks
within the field of the white power. Dark peoples have participated in the
military agreements of the white peoples; they have seen white peoples
humiliated by each other; they have been summoned to take part in
imperialist wars. Would it be unusual if the colored world were to act
on its own initiative and for its own interests? Spengler adds to the
possibility of a struggle between East and West the question of greatest
concern to occidental civilization, the danger of the class war and the race
war joining forces.

Thus the peace that follows World War II may prove only an inter-
lude – a breathing spell before the race and class war – unless Great
Britain and the United States act to implement their professed aims. In
the coming global order there must be freedom for all or freedom for
none. Hearken to the words of Wendell Willkie: "The day is gone when
men and women of whatever color or creed can consider themselves the
superiors of other creeds and colors. The day of vast empire is past. The
day of equal peoples is at hand."

Elizabeth Wiskemann

From *The Rome–Berlin Axis* (1949)

At Christmas 1888, in Turin, Nietzsche wrote the preface to his main fulmination against Wagner[28] which he called – as well he might – 'an essay for psychologists, not for Germans'. Crispi was Premier of Italy at the time and was leading the country into quarrels with France and closer friendship with Germany. It was four months before Hitler's birth. 'I would have a word to whisper in the ears of the Italians, whom I love ... an intelligent people will never make anything but a *mésalliance* with the Reich.' We have seen how the Axis which Hitler created and to which Mussolini gave its name fulfilled Nietzsche's warning.

Each of these dictators was like a malicious caricature of his own people. Mussolini was theatrical, vain, hypersensitive, and sceptical; he never really stepped outside traditional continuity. Hitler was hysterical, fanatical, romantic, and cruel. In their satisfaction in inflicting pain on other human creatures the cruelty and romanticism of Germans like Hitler and Himmler met; in sadism their split personalities were integrated. They were barbaric without the excuse of being primitive.

For many years Mussolini had rolled his eyes and brandished his chin, he had shouted cruel phrases with Romagnol violence, but his goal had never become clear to him: after years of delay, he had committed certain vague aspirations to paper, but without ever thinking out a method by which they might be realized. The aspirations in fact served chiefly as a Sorel 'myth' or as the stimulus to the political speculation so dear to Italians. In practice Mussolini was an opportunist and, far from destroying the ideas and institutions which he found in existence, he generally sought a compromise with them. Hitler made himself President as well as Chancellor of Germany and immediately started a preliminary campaign against the Christian Churches, but Mussolini came to terms with both the King and the Pope. The fact

---

[28] *Nietzsche contra Wagner* (Vorwort).

that the Fascist Grand Council, which the Duce created, could instigate his downfall, was a piece of 'conservatism' which seemed ludicrous to Hitler: it helped to convince him that Mussolini was no 'world-wide revolutionary'. By and large Mussolini remained an ordinary human being in doubt. Perhaps it is doubt which distinguishes the sane and the civilized from the mad and the barbarous.

Mussolini, partly owing to physical weaknesses, doubted excessively. [...] Sometimes he liked to play the hero enthroned in solitude, above all he had been potent – except in Germany – as an orator addressing the masses; but Mussolini was dependent upon personal relationships. How different from Hitler who was never in doubt and who was never amused!

The metal with which the Rome–Berlin Axis was forged, so that it seems to have been warped from being a straight line into becoming a vicious circle, was Nietzsche, inspirer of Mussolini's words and of Hitler's deeds. Nietzsche was a German who longed to be a Pole; he admired France and he loved Italy. The medical records of his madness[29] show that he identified himself either with God or with the first King of modern Italy. He feared the Germans as Mussolini did, and he despised them as Hitler despised them when he found them unappreciative. Out of his fear of the commonplaceness of the German middle class and of the mentality of anti-Semitism, Nietzsche formulated the doctrines which then nourished Hitler; [...]

Nietzsche's was not the only thought which influenced Hitler; it has been seen that there were strong currents of the old Pan-German Austrian state of mind in him and of Wagnerian mythology which intermingled with them. The influence of Nietzsche, however, remained pre-dominant, of Nietzsche who was shocked by the 'vulgarity' of John Stuart Mill.[30] It is almost incredible to find how exactly Nietzsche formulated Hitler's egocentric obsessions. 'I teach that there are higher and lower men,' he wrote, 'and that a single individual may in certain circumstances justify whole millennia of existence – that is to say, a wealthier, more gifted, greater and more complete man, as compared with innumerable imperfect and fragmentary men ...'; '... the "higher nature" of the great man manifests itself precisely in being different, in being unable to communicate with others ...'; and, again, he defines mighty men as those with a passion for dominion and a love of change and deception. Nor does Nietzsche fail to insist upon the forcible prevention of the reproduction of lower beings. All this is to be

[29] See E. F. Podach, *The Madness of Nietzsche* (1931).
[30] This because Mill could claim that 'what is right for one man is right for another'.

found in *Der Wille zur Macht*. As for *Zarathustra*, it echoes through the events of Hitler's life; [...]

It has been said that Hitler's ascendancy over the Germans has never been explained. The Communist formula which equates National Socialism with Fascism as a camouflaged 'come-back' of the propertied classes at the price of bread and circuses is misleading. It is true that the most powerful industrialists in Italy used Fascism as their instrument. In Germany the majority of the big employers and landowners favoured Hitler's rise to power. Rearmament and the policy of Schacht suited them very well, and the *Führerprinzip* in the organization of industry satisfied their most conservative dreams. On the other hand, it is certain that Hitler went to war against their wishes, and it is probable that they would have liked to be rid of him long before material destruction in Germany reached the point at which it had arrived in April 1945. Hitler was the ally, while it suited him, of the German industrialists, but never their tool. Like Mussolini, they were forced to be part of the dream of this subnormal adolescent who, with all his consistency in action, might well have ended in a humbler madhouse than the Berlin bunker of the Führer.

It seems monotonous to refer to Nietzsche again, but it is he who illuminates most brightly the irrational nature of the power of Adolf Hitler. In one of his outbursts against Wagner[31] Nietzsche speaks of that *hysterical-erotic* quality which so much pleased Wagner in women. 'Only look at our women when they are "wagnetisiert": *welche "Unfreiheit des Willens"! ... Welches Geschehen-lassen, Über-sich-ergehen-lassen.*[32] Perhaps they guess that they are more attractive to some men in this state ... reason the more to worship their Cagliostro and magician!' Anyone who has lived in Germany will recognize what Nietzsche meant – Shirer described it in his *Berlin Diary* when he spoke of the audience at Hitler's *Winterhilfe* meeting on 4 September 1940.[33] [...]

With the madman's knowledge of how to excite, Hitler combined the madman's – or the superman's – inability to communicate normally with others as individuals: he either mesmerized or frightened them or perhaps did both these things.

The women of Germany, it has been seen, were peculiarly susceptible to his approach, nor were the men very different. Though Hitler, like Nietzsche, was probably impotent[34] and not a pervert, the masculine

---

[31] *Aufzeichnungen zu einer Schrift über Wagner* (*Werke*, Bd. vii, Leipzig, 1931).

[32] Impossible to render in English – it indicates an hysterical passivity.

[33] See Chapter XIV.

[34] Both of them were thought to be syphilitic, but either of them might have imagined the symptoms; nor is it certain that an impotent man is immune from sexual infection.

homage he received was often passionate, whether it came from members of the Stefan George circle or from groups of *Wandervögel*. Negatively it was of importance that 'he had the gift of inspiring in those who resisted him a feeling of isolation',[35] a gift which had helped him to conceive the system of the Nazi concentration camp.

Another factor in Hitler's success was his skill in concealing his true objectives except from an inner *élite*. The majority of professing National Socialists held only Fascist views; they were willing to sacrifice liberty to efficiency and they were racially arrogant, but they did not wish for the destruction of 1,500 years of civilization nor for the inversion of accepted morality. By the time that they began to feel that Hitlerism spelt the end of Christianity and humanism in favour of biological mechanism, there was very little they could do by way of protest. The scepticism and gloom in Germany, and especially in Berlin, during most of the Axis period, may be attributed to the hysterical and the esoteric nature of Hitlerism. Between the injections of hysteria, enthusiasm flagged, and doubts grew as to what it was to which one was committed.

Mussolini was neither perverse nor hysterical. To charm Italian crowds he had had to be theatrical. It was by stimulating his lust for power and the fear of isolation that Hitler had subjugated Mussolini; from the day in 1936 when he felt cut off from France he had been won by the Führer. There was never any personal intimacy between Hitler and Mussolini, quite apart from the formal second person plural to which their sense of their importance kept the dictators. When Hitler wrote to Mussolini in 1942 that he perhaps better than any other human being could share the Duce's feelings at the Acropolis[36] he was writing in terms of 'greatness', not in terms of friendship. While Mussolini was perplexed by Hitler, for Hitler Mussolini was simply a symbolic figure in Hitler's world of fantasy until September 1943. [...]

It has been seen that the New Order can most nearly be explained as Hitler's interpretation of the aspirations of Nietzsche, and it has been seen that the Italians had sabotaged this New Order with growing effect, both before Mussolini's dismissal in July 1943 and after his supposed rehabilitation in the north of Italy. Between the collapse of Fascism and the end of the war, the biggest shock to Hitler's New Europe came in August 1944 with the liberation of France and the defection of Rumania. When De Gaulle arrived in Paris to witness the damaged Fifth Column of the Hotel Crillon it was felt that Europe was freed. But this was a dangerous anticipation. Though the Russians joined up with the Partisans and freed

---

[35] Gafencu, op. cit.   [36] Hitler to Mussolini, 4 Aug. 1942.

Belgrade in October 1944, and the British were in Athens in November, it was May 1945 before the Germans in Croatia surrendered. Between summer 1944 and spring 1945 Hitler worked much evil, an enormous amount of pointless destruction, until suddenly the Germans collapsed and the concentration camps gave up their living and their dead. One of the finest performances of this time was the prevention by the Italian Partisans of the destruction of their factories as Hitler had planned it; by their skillful preparation they saved the major part of Italian industrial plant from the fate of the factories in many other parts of Europe.

With masochistic German method the *Götterdämmerung* was prepared. Since 1941 plans for the case of defeat had been begun, and it appears that Hitler communicated some of this programme to Mussolini at Rastenburg on 14 September 1943.[37] The earth was to be scorched so that the Allies should be blamed for famine and unemployment. One must go on fighting a hopeless struggle partly because the Allies and Russia might fall apart before they had won, but for other reasons too. The fighting must go on in order to gain every possible hour for the preparation of the Nazi Redoubt in the mountains of Styria, Bavaria, and the Tyrol. There it might be possible to resist actively for some time, Hitler thought, and this would not only give scope for the nihilistic joys of self-destruction after the will to power had been temporarily satiated, but would have great importance for the Nazi myth. For two or three years now the Nazi leaders had been willing to admit that Germany might lose the second great war in the Nazi century, only to triumph more tremendously in the third. And she would never have been beaten. In 1918, as the legend ran, she was 'stabbed in the back', but now she would fight till she could fight no more, only to rise again. Sometimes there was talk of an Italian sector in the 'Redoubt' to which the Neo-Fascists should retire, but it has been seen that they and Mussolini were without any steady enthusiasm for the plan.

When on 20 July 1944, at the Hitler–Mussolini tea-party at the Führer's headquarters, someone mentioned the massacre of 30 June 1934, Hitler leapt to his feet with foam on his lips; he ranted for half an hour about the revenge he would take against women and children after Stauffenberg's attempt upon his life. But the intensified S.S. terror which closed in upon Germany after this was not merely a matter of revenge, for it was more deliberate. Mass arrests of all possibly oppositional personalities were intended also to prevent any group from negotiating with the Allies to accept surrender.

---

[37] See *Il Momento* (Rome), 3 Nov. 1945, and other (earlier) sources.

Preparations were made to provision and fortify the 'Redoubt' and Hitler was to go to Bavaria on his last birthday, 20 April 1945, to direct the fighting from there. He decided, however, that events had overtaken that part of his plan. The rest of it held good. The Führer himself was to leave no trace behind him so that some kind of Barbarossa legend should arise – he would not have feared refutations by witty Oxford dons. The tenacious Martin Bormann, in whose hands the organization of clandestine Nazi activity for the future was concentrated, was to disappear; of the major War Criminals he was the only one who could not be found. Lastly, the initiated were to become Communists in the Russian area of occupation and whatever facilitated their work in the Allied zones, in order to foment discord between the U.S.S.R. and the English-speaking Powers. [...]

It is a terrifying reflection that a sick man like Nietzsche, who knew that he would lose his reason and who was written off years ago as a *fin de siècle* failure, should have projected and facilitated the agony of Europe forty years after his death. The fact is not altered by dismissing Nietzsche as an early symptom of decay. Where Nietzsche gloried in the cruelty of nature, half a century later Hitler gloried in the cruelty of machines. It seems strange that Nietzsche has been classified with the philosophers; his place is perhaps with the poets and certainly with the prophets. [...]

Europe revolted against Axis rule, human decency rose up against *Furchtbarkeit*. But both the New Order and the struggle against it were so costly that we do not know yet whether the price paid was not civilization itself. That would be the fulfilment of Hitler's suicidal dream.

Vera Micheles Dean

From *Foreign Policy without Fear* (1953)

A period of tumultuous flux like the one in which we are living poses grave problems for the government officials who must make policy decisions. For if the American people are led to feel that the officials have failed, as on the question of policy toward China, the verdict will be: "Off with their head" – figuratively, at least.

This period also poses soul-searching problems for the contemporary historian whose diagnosis of the situation, however indirectly, may influence public opinion and thus be reflected in policy. For obviously the wrong diagnosis could in this age of atomic warfare bring about incalculable catastrophe.

The historian finds himself in a practically untenable position. At best, he sees only the tip of the iceberg of events, the bulk of which is concealed below the surface of documents classified as secret. The best the expert can do is to work like an impressionist painter, putting down on paper the impressions he has of world affairs in his own times. But no matter how much he strives, with utmost integrity, to describe events as they appear to him, the same events appear quite different to others, onlookers or participants, who do not hesitate to accuse him of bias or myopia. The role of the expert is curiously ill defined in the United States. He is apparently expected not merely to report what he sees, to the best of his ability, but also to act as prophet – and then if changing events over which he has no control do not conform to the views he expressed ten or twenty years before, he becomes an object of public abuse such as was once reserved for hardened criminals.

An interpreter of the past may face many predicaments comparable in kind – obviously there is more than one interpretation of the fall of Rome, the Napoleonic conquests, or the effects of the French Revolution – but not in the immediacy of his own existence. For contemporaries who passionately differ with him concerning events which they, too, have an opportunity to observe may, as we have seen in our own time, traduce him publicly and deprive him of livelihood on charges of subversion or treason. Yet the historian who, out of anxiety about his personal interests, capitulates to public clamor and becomes a mere recorder of the most popular interpretation placed on current events is the one really guilty of betrayal. He betrays the trust placed in him as the appraiser – not wholly dispassionate, since man can never be a mere calculating machine, but striving for dispassionateness – of events analyzed in the perspective of history.

But in the life-and-death struggle of empires and ideas the historian is summoned by his fellow men to take sides, to pronounce himself, not merely to record. Yet the moment he does so he properly loses his claim to Olympian detachment; he becomes, and is praised or denounced, as partisan. He is urged to depict "reality." He is warned against cherishing "illusions" – illusions about democracy, or communism, or international cooperation, or isolationism, as the case may be. He becomes engulfed in somewhat the same controversy as has been rending the world of art and the world of science – the controversy between the "realists" and the "abstractionists." What is the truth in contemporary events? Are all those who differ from us in our views of the world mistaken individuals whom we must endeavor to enlighten – or are they scoundrels beyond our power to reform whom we should verbally destroy? Do all heretics genuinely see things differently from us – or are they willfully spreading lies about their concepts of the universe?

The exchange of views in August 1951 between Viscount Samuel of Britain and Dr. Albert Einstein about contemporary physics has a poignant relevance for the historian. To Viscount Samuel's charge that "contemporary physics are based on concepts somewhat analogous to the 'smile' of the absent cat," Dr. Einstein replied: "The real is in no way immediately given to us. Given to us are merely the data of our consciousness ... There is only one way from the data of consciousness to 'reality,' to wit, the way of conscious or unconscious intellectual construction, which proceeds completely free and arbitrarily ... . One is in danger of being misled by the illusion that the real of our daily experience 'exists really' and that certain concepts of physics are 'mere ideas' separated from the 'real' by an unbridgeable gulf." Dr. Einstein places more trust in the "real" which is arrived at as a result of intellectual construction than in that which appears "real" because it stands in a correspondence with our sensations. "These facts could be expressed in a paradox," he holds, "namely that 'reality' as we know it is exclusively composed of 'fancies.'" Speaking of scientists, he says: "We are free to choose which elements we wish to apply in our construction of physical reality. The justification of our choice lies exclusively in our success."

Like the scientist, the historian, too, must make a choice of those elements of reality in contemporary events which to him seem particularly significant, and must place them in the relation to each other which, in his judgment, appears most accurate.

The making of these choices is a grave, an onerous, responsibility. Unlike the scientist, the historian is not in a position to subject his conclusions to the concrete test of laboratory experiments. His success or failure cannot be measured with exactitude in charts or statistical tables. Only the actual trend of public affairs can demonstrate whether or not his choices were justified; and by the very nature of things such justification may not be forthcoming in his lifetime. To an even greater extent than the scientist, therefore, the historian must be willing to take full responsibility for his interpretation of the contemporary world – for such distinctions as he draws between realities and myths.

This task is particularly harrowing in a period of profound upheavals, when the contenders for material power and ideological influence understandably seek to bolster their own claims with impassioned assertions on behalf of their own beliefs and achievements and equally impassioned denigrations of the beliefs and achievements of their opponents. As has been discovered by all those who are engaged in forming public opinion, there is hardly any situation or idea, no matter how unrelated to reality, which cannot be made to appear real in people's minds by sufficient reiteration. This is true not only in countries like nazi Germany or communist Russia, where a totalitarian state controls all channels of communication; but, as we have learned from our own experience here in the past few years, myths can be created even in a society which offers opportunities for free discussion. Even the historian, either through deference to public opinion or out of the sheer fatigue of resisting popularly accepted slogans, is apt to succumb to the reiterative process and stop trying to ascertain whether there may be another side to the official picture or possible alternatives to current policies.

But the historian who abdicates his capacity to diagnose events really surrenders his function both as a student and as a citizen in a free society. If he wants to live at peace with his conscience, he must continue to speak his mind as long as the opportunity to do so exists. For his role is not merely to list events, but to try and interpret them – let the chips fall where they may.

Adda B. Bozeman

From "India's Foreign Policy Today" (1958)

The foreign policy of any modern state devolves from implied or explicit references to strategic, economic, and ideological considerations, and aims at the preservation and furtherance of the national interest. But the conceptual sources and political definitions of the national interest vary from country to country, as do the meanings and emphases given to the factors that influence its determination. The Indian government has been less outspoken than most other governments in defining the national interest in strategic terms, but even a cursory glance at India's northern boundary will convince an observer that considerations of military security must be a primary concern in New Delhi. This impression is borne out by the actual measures that have been taken in order to repress the revolts of the Naga Hostiles and to keep the peace in Bhutan, Sikkim, and Assam, and by the obvious and understandable, but not openly admitted, Indian interest in controlling the strategically vital valley of Kashmir.

That India's national interest is wound up inextricably with its economic development goes without saying. Although this connection has not been made explicit whenever the government has explained its foreign policies to the public, it has been stressed by the Prime Minister when he has had occasion to theorize about the essence of all foreign policy. A speech he delivered on December 4, 1947, at the Constituent Assembly in New Delhi, contains the following passage: "Ultimately, foreign policy is the outcome of economic policy, and until India has properly evolved her economic policy, her foreign policy will be rather vague, rather inchoate, and will be groping."

Most foreign policy statements since 1947 have been presented in deliberately political and ideological terms. It seems justifiable, therefore, to focus this inquiry upon the intellectual sources of India's present foreign policy.

A survey of India's long history leads to the conclusion that contemporary political thought is caught in a welter of different and

337

contradictory intellectual references that have been derived in successive stages from Hinduism, Buddhism, Islam, Western liberalism, and Marxism-Leninism. It is the predicament of the present generation of political theorists and statesmen that they must identify and evaluate each of these references in terms of its political content, and reconcile conflicting intellectual positions, before they can hope to find an overall orientation that would both meet the practical problems of the twentieth century and still accord with those traditions that are found to have an enduring hold on the Indian mind. This predicament has not yet been recognized in India. A stimulating lecture which K. M. Panikkar delivered on July 22, 1955, before the Harold Laski Institute of Political Science at Ahmedabad, illustrates some aspects of this problem. "The melancholy fact about India today," Mr. Panikkar said, "is that political science is the most neglected course of study in our universities, one on which there has been little or no original contribution made by our thinkers," "that there has been no systematic thinking in modern India outside the academic life on the foundations of politics," and "that our leaders of thought have never considered it worth while to examine the relation of the individual to the state. No political leader among us has tried to formulate any theory of social order, inquire into the principles on which we have reared our political institutions, examine the validity of the many assumptions of our public life. Indeed, this is a strange and melancholy situation."

This state of affairs, Mr. Panikkar holds, is due to the impact which Western political thought has had on India: "The textbooks which are taught in our universities and the doctrines that are expounded by our teachers and studied by our students are unrelated to our social order, and are generally speaking foreign to our experience, [so] that I have often wondered whether as at present constituted these studies serve any purpose at all. To study Aristotle, Bodin, Hobbes, Rousseau, Green and others may be an intellectual discipline, to be familiar with their views may be a part of liberal education, to be concerned with such imprecise terms as democracy, dictatorship, will of the people and social contract, may not be less useful than being engaged in perpetual discussions on metaphysical problems, but no one could pretend that they touch the hard core of power in society."

Now there was a time, Mr. Panikkar stated, when India was the home, as it were, of political science, and it is the political doctrine that was then taught, studied, and practiced which should be reinstated in the minds of Indians today in order to promote the development of "independent political thinking related to our social order and institutional structure, [which] is the basic need of India today."

Mr. Panikkar's reference here is to the *Mahabharata*, which he explained as "that encyclopaedia of Indian thinking, which has long been the one instrument of the education of the Indian mind, and to which, in spite of all our familiarity with Western literature and thought, we still return for the solution of our problems," and to the *Arthasastra*, that central text of Indian political science, which "enables Hindu thinkers to evolve a purely secular theory of state of which the sole basis is power."

The idea of the state which had been evolved in this context by Kautilya and his successors went, in Mr. Panikkar's opinion, "far beyond the limited imagination of Machiavelli," for the author of the *Arthasastra* "thought of the state as an organization which took within the range of its interests every sphere of human activity – in fact it was the prototype of the modern omnipotent administering state," against which the individual could advance few, if any, rights.

The conception of international relations that is embodied in the political tradition evoked here derives from a philosophy of power and success which permits of no ethical or moral considerations. For international politics as conceived in the *Arthasastra* is an enterprise of battle in which all forms of trickery and deceit are permissible, and in which each neighboring state is presumed to be unfriendly, jealous, and aggressive, biding its hour of surprise and treacherous assault. In these circumstances a formula was evolved for attaining success and power which became known as the "science of the mandala." This science stipulated that each king was to regard his realm as located at the center of a kind of target, surrounded by "rings" (mandalas) which represented, alternately, his natural enemies and his natural allies.

So much for the Hindu theory of government and foreign relations which a leading and influential Indian intellectual would like to resurrect as a living frame of reference in contemporary Indian politics.

But while Mr. Panikkar may well be right in his assumption that this intellectual inheritance, while not always openly avowed, is yet firmly lodged in the unconscious mind of India, it is not possible to conclude from the record that Indian foreign policy actually reflects the kind of statecraft that the *Mahabharata* and *Arthasastra* recommend. For not only are policies rarely, if ever, explained and analyzed by the government in the context of a national interest or of strategic thinking generally, but certain policies, notably those toward Russia and China, actually deviate from Kautilya's precepts of political geometry, in that they seem to disregard the presence of aggressive tendencies among strong neighboring states.

The question, then, is, to what intellectual context does the government refer its policies? The policy statements that were reviewed earlier point rather obviously to Buddhist ethics, citing as the principal platform of India's present foreign policy the so-called *panca sila*. It is important, therefore, for the purposes of this discussion, to examine the relationship of Buddhist ethics to Indian foreign policy.

[...]

Without entering into the merits of the question whether Buddhism can ever be transformed into a political ideology governing the conduct of states and still retain its character as a religion of individual salvation, let us see what is actually involved in the evocation of Buddhist ethics in twentieth-century Asian, especially Indian and Chinese, politics.

Firstly, it must be remembered that Buddhism has long ceased to be a frame of reference for individual conduct in both India and China, the two nations that discovered the *panca sila* as the governing principle in their foreign relations.

Secondly, it is obvious from the biographies of the two leading statesmen – Nehru and Chou En-lai – that both are far removed in their thoughts and actions not only from Buddhism but also from any other religion.

And, thirdly, it is difficult indeed to find any relationship whatsoever between the *panca sila* as formulated by Nehru and Chou En-lai, and the *panca sila* of the Buddhist religion. In other words, the reference to Buddhist ethics in the context of Indian foreign policy is spurious.

The true provenance of the concepts contained in Mr. Nehru's *panca sila* – namely, mutual respect for each other's territory, nonaggression, noninterference in each other's internal affairs, equality and mutual advantage, and peaceful coexistence and economic cooperation – is the modern history of international organization as developed in the Western world. For each and all of these principles of international conduct are not only embodied in the Charter of the United Nations, but may be found also in many documents that preceded this international constitution. Such an acknowledgment could not be expected in the prevailing climate of opinion; and even if it had been forthcoming, it would have been unreasonable to assume that India's interpretation of the concepts would have been in accord with Western traditions. But what is disconcerting here is the realization that few Indians today actually perceive the parallel between their "new" statement of policy on the one hand, and the old political tradition of the West on the other.

Now, this was different in the less self-conscious days of India's movement toward independence, when the nation's intellectual leadership frankly acknowledged the validity, for India's foreign policy, of the cultural context in which such preferred values as national independence, self-government, and sovereignty had been developed – witness the resolutions of the Congress in 1920 and 1927, discussed earlier. Indeed, it was Gandhi's imaginative and original reading and use of the literary, philosophical, and religious traditions of the West which accounts, to a considerable extent, for the apt formulation of the concept of nonviolence in international relations. It is true that this policy was actually applied only to India's relations with the British, and its singular success is therefore no proof of its intrinsic value or wisdom. Nevertheless, a significant new reference for the conduct of international relations had been found, and it is proper to ask, therefore, whether the principle of non-violence has been accommodated in post Gandhian India and, if so, in what form.

Few aspects of the intellectual history of the independence movement are as interesting and significant as the relationship between Gandhi and Nehru. In fact, it is possible to read this history as a continuous dialogue between two outstanding personalities who viewed the great problems of life in general, and of their nation in particular, in very different ways. Their biographies make it clear that Nehru could not accede to a philosophy that glorified the nation's poverty and stressed the importance of nonpolitical activities, and that he could not understand or appreciate the older man's insistence on nonviolence as a cardinal principle of political behavior. The choice between violence and nonviolence was to be determined in Nehru's view by practical, not by moral, considerations. In 1929 he condoned the tactic of nonviolence on the ground that resort to violence, far from promising substantial results in the struggle for freedom, would have been conducive to the disruption of the nation. After 1947 Mr. Nehru saw the problem differently, for his government did not hesitate to resort to armed force in Hyderabad and Kashmir. One must thus agree with Moraes when he writes that India has no doctrinaire attachment to the concept of nonviolence.

If India's present foreign policy is not anchored in Indian systems of thought, where are its ideological roots? The answer, derived from a study of recorded political pronouncements and actions, points clearly to the Marxist-Leninist theory of history and economics as it was expounded at the London School of Economics in the 1920's and 1930's, and as it was understood by Nehru personally. This body of references, which was not accepted by Motilal Nehru, Gandhi, and other older leaders of the Congress, impressed Jawaharlal Nehru as a dynamic set of principles and as a call to action. It illumined his reading of world history, his interpretation of India's experiences under British rule, his pessimistic analysis of Europe's problems, and his optimistic view of all developments in the Soviet Union. The principal theoretical propositions appropriated by Mr. Nehru from this source are: that the European concept of democracy is a shell cloaking great inequalities and that it is apt to become perverted in terms of fascism; that capitalism provides its own grave diggers; that capitalism is the head and fount of the vicious sin of colonialism; that its spawn, imperialism, nurtures within itself the seeds of conflict and decay; and that socialism as implemented in the Soviet Union holds out the greatest hope in this dismal age. [...]

And in his book *Toward Freedom*, Nehru expounds this thesis in the following terms:

"Two rival economic and political systems faced each other in the world, and, though they tolerated each other for a while, there was an inherent antagonism between them, and they played for mastery on the stage of the world. One of them was the capitalist order, which had *inevitably* developed into vast imperialisms, which, having swallowed the colonial world, were intent on eating each other up. Powerful still and fearful of war, which might endanger their possessions, yet they came into *inevitable* conflict with each other and prepared feverishly for war. They were quite unable to solve the problems that threatened them, and helplessly they submitted to slow decay. The other was the new socialist order of the U.S.S.R., which went from progress to progress, though often at terrible cost, and where the problems of the capitalist world had ceased to exist. Capitalism, in its difficulties, took to fascism with all its brutal suppression of what Western civilization had apparently stood for; it became, even in some of its homelands, what its imperialist counterpart had long been in the subject colonial countries. Fascism and imperialism thus stood out as the two faces of the now decaying capitalism ... they represented the same forces of reaction and supported each other, and at the same time came into conflict with each other, for such conflict was inherent in their very nature. Socialism in the West and rising nationalisms of the Eastern and other dependent countries opposed this combination of fascism and imperialism. Nationalism in the East, it must be remembered, was essentially different from the new and terribly narrow nationalism of the fascist countries; the former was the historical urge to freedom, the latter the last refuge to reaction."

To the question where India should stand, Nehru answered that "Inevitably we take our stand with the progressive forces of the world which are ranged against fascism and imperialism."

The affinities between Mr. Nehru's application of the Leninist formula of Marxism to world politics and that expounded by Harold Laski in the 1930's and 1940's are striking. For Laski, too, was convinced that the capitalist democracies would "inevitably" degenerate into fascism. Indeed, he maintained that the Fascist state is, "nakedly and without shame, what the state, covertly and apologetically is, in capitalist democracies like Great Britain or the United States," and that the distinction between the judicial systems of capitalist democracies and of Fascist dictatorships is one of degree rather than of kind. The only possibilities,

Laski concluded, are therefore the opposite alternatives of fascism and revolutionary socialism. Like Nehru, Laski pointed continuously to the sharp contrast between the spirit of exhilaration and optimism found in the Soviet Union and the general sense of insecurity and anxiety found in capitalist countries. Both men were convinced that the Soviet Union held out the highest hope for a regeneration of mankind, and both were immensely impressed with the capacity of communism to arouse mass enthusiasm. But neither has ever wanted to identify himself completely with the cause of communism. Their writings indicate that they were irritated by the methods which the Communists employed in the further- ance of their aims and that they preferred the means of effecting change that had been perfected in the Western democracies. But while Laski dropped this preference gradually, Nehru has continued to insist that Marxist blueprints can be executed by democratic means. [...]

That India is still a democracy – however hollow this form of govern- ment is made to appear in Mr. Nehru's theories – is, as a matter of fact, largely due to the Prime Minister's insistence on maintaining democratic processes at home.

The contradiction between Mr. Nehru's approach to government and his interpretation of international relations has never been resolved. It is nowhere more apparent than in his attitude toward the Communist Party. For while he approves of what the Party stands for in the context of world politics, he evidently does not like it as a political phenomenon. Indeed, he goes out of his way in trying to separate the Party and its international activities from the policies which Communist nations pursue.

These assumptions, implicit in Mr. Nehru's mode of thinking, seem to have become immovable fixtures in the official Indian system of political references. No one in authority has questioned their intrinsic validity in the light of the many political and economic changes that have occurred in the Western democracies and the Soviet orbit during the last twenty years. Nothing in the development of the United States seems to have shaken the thesis that America is a capitalist country in the doctrinaire sense of the word, and therefore imperialistic by definition. Nothing in the evolution of Russian communism seems to have suggested to Mr. Nehru close analogies to Fascist totalitarianism, and nothing in the expansion of the Soviet Union seems to have reminded him of the phenomenon of imperialism as he had defined it in his younger days.

The survival of this stereotyped set of intellectual references in world affairs, which stands in marked contrast to the resourceful and imagina- tive use of ideas in Indian domestic politics, is due primarily to the fact that foreign policy matters are generally regarded in India as falling within the exclusive competence of the Prime Minister, whereas domestic issues are constantly reviewed and reappraised by India's numerous democratic institutions. In these circumstances it is only Mr. Nehru personally who could have scrutinized the basic assumption of his approach to international relations. Such a scrutiny has not been forthcoming, for reasons that appear clearly in Mr. Nehru's written and oral pronouncements. These biographical records reveal that the Prime Minister is a man of very strong feelings, and that two emotions in particular have dominated his thoughts about foreign affairs: a deep hostility to the West and an unshakeable faith in everything Asian. And these emotional commitments became irrevocable when it was found that they could be vindicated by certain rational propositions implicit in the dogma of Marxism-Leninism. In other words, it was the seeming concurrence of emotionally and rationally held truths which provided the Prime Minister with a formula for the analysis of international relations. And it is this Indian formula which supplies the key to an understanding of the inconsistencies that the non-Indian non-Marxist observer finds so puzzling in India's approach to foreign affairs.

[...]

To conclude: the principal source of Indian thinking on the subject of foreign affairs is neither Hinduism, Buddhism, Gandhianism, the Western European tradition, nor a rational analysis of reality in terms of India's long-range national interest, but the complex biography of the Prime Minister. One does not have to go as far as one of Mr. Nehru's fiercest critics D. F. Karaka, when he writes that "Our attitude to the powers of the West has been conditioned by the personal complexes of Pandit Nehru," and "the translation of these complexes into action has become our foreign policy," in order to be impressed with the highly emotional content of Indian foreign policy, the omnipotent influence of the Prime Minister personally on the conduct of his country's foreign policy, and the immense popular support that is given to his enunciations on this subject.

Judith Shklar

From "Decisionism" (1964)

The most prevalent form of decisionism today is not concerned with domestic politics. It is rather centered on the all-important realm of foreign policy. The realism of the moment is no longer legal, but political. This realism has as its main theme the notion that power is, or at any rate ought to be, the central concept of politics, especially of international politics. Without this notion, it is argued, intellectual disorder and practical failure are bound to occur.[38] Considering the vagueness of such favorite realist conceptions as "power" and the "national interest," the great professional and popular appeal of this neo-Machiavellian doctrine might seem astonishing. It is only when its negative impulses are understood that realism, as an ideological reaction, becomes comprehensible. For power as the central concept of political thought makes sense, even as an ordering device, only if it is understood as a negation. Power politics is the antithesis of legalistic and moralistic politics.

Political realism is saved from utter vagueness only by its opposition to that still-lingering legalism, the "Hague fantasy," that regards international adjudication as both a substitute for foreign policy and a means to end conflict. Even more noxious, in realist eyes, is the tendency to ideology, especially in America, where it takes the form of treating international rivals as if they were criminals upon whom the righteous are executing a judgment.

The argument is not just that, *in fact*, politics is a series of power calculations made by governments. Realism is not a descriptive approach to international relations. It is extremely didactic. Politics should be a matter of decisions, taken by those who have the power to make them stick. The greatest danger to success in politics is not just indecisiveness, but a faith in legalism, in the belief that rules of international law, or of

---

[38] For the best brief statement of the position, see H. J. Morgenthau, *Dilemmas of Politics* (1958), pp. 54–87.

personal morality, have any application to power relations. In some cases it appears that the sheer hypocrisy, not only the impracticality, of using moral and legal arguments in foreign affairs is what the realist finds intolerable. This is, I think, very evident in the writings of George Kennan. In truth, however, it is far from clear that hypocrisy does not work. Quite the contrary, one would think. More to the point is that political realism is a rejection of a certain kind of hypocrisy, that is, that of the great "isms" which, it is argued, prevent power-manipulators from coming to a rational, calculated decision which would enhance their power. Especially the traditional moralistic and legalist ideology of America has led to delusion, hysteria, and collective bungling. This, too, is a response to frustration, to feelings that America's traditional institutions and attitudes have become a liability in its relations with other world powers and that the old rules are deceiving us, as indeed *all* rules that limit our faculty for making calculated power decisions must.[39] Here too the note of compensatory megalomania enters. For all realists persist in blaming every setback or failure on Americans, and on the liberals especially. The villain of the modern world is less Hitler or Stalin than Woodrow Wilson. The assumptions, of course, are that America is omnipotent and that, if its leaders followed the advice of these artists in the use of power, we would have it our own way all the time. Like the individual of romantic morality, this nation is alone in the world, completely free to decide and succeed in its own interests. This, too, is an outsider's view, not that of the actual politician, who is apt to be more aware of his limitations. It is also a sum of frustrations put forth as an explanation. As such, it is in some respects a comforting theory. In the past, democratic thinkers dreaded "secret covenants" and diplomatic negotiations carried on by professionals as conspiratorial enterprises in which the destinies of entire peoples were ruthlessly manipulated. Today, on the contrary, people are frightened by the absence of caretakers, of individual figures in corporate, bureaucratically structured governments where no one appears to be in control of an intolerably complex international scene. Realism at least holds out the hope that statesmanship, as de-ideologized power-planning, may yet bring to government men with orderly minds, who will succeed in reestablishing the international world of the nineteenth century, which in retrospect has acquired all the attractions of reasonable, comprehensible dimensions.

Unlike romanticism and legal realism, political realism is radical only in its rebellion against American traditions. In European terms it is

---

[39] G. Kennan, *American Diplomacy: 1900–1950* (1952), especially pp. 49–50, 65, 82–89.

conservative and backward-looking. Far from looking to such typically American social saviors as the experts, the social engineers, and adventurous experimenters, it looks to a vaguely Metternich like image. When we are told that what is needed is true statesmanship, not law, a very traditional sort of politician is resurrected. The man who has a grasp of the "eternal verities of politics" has no use for scientific gimmicks.[40] His knowledge of the proper rules of the "political art" is drawn from history, where lessons are still to be learned. That too, of course, is a comforting thought. To the question, who exactly today corresponds to this kind of statesman, who is prudent in the sense of Machiavellian rationalism, there are few clear answers. One author of the realist persuasion suggests the British official classes as a model of traditional wisdom in the conduct of diplomacy.[41] To a student of international affairs in the decade preceding the Second World War this model may not be quite convincing. The only conclusion to be drawn is that this modern, like the oldest, "mirror of princes" is just a piece of polished glass. The new decider is only an artifact, the sum of all the virtues that contemporary politicians appear to lack. It is evident enough what he is *not*; it is not clear what he, in fact, does.

A theory of statesmen pursuing something as vague as the national interest has not proven acceptable to theorists of a more systematic turn of mind. Decisionism, however, has a vast appeal, precisely because the vision of a limited number of political actors engaged in making calculated choices among clearly conceived alternatives is an essential basis for any theory that wishes to reduce international complexities to systematic, diagrammatic form. This impulse may be the same as that which inspires neo-Machiavellian statecraft, but it is certainly a rejection of the intuitive, historically oriented, "unscientific" character of the latter. Instead, we are offered highly abstract paradigms of game-playing by actors who make rational decisions according to rules that both sides observe. Others, most notably Professor Richard Snyder and his associates, have devised very elaborate models for decision-making which do not exclude any conceivable element in the process of politics. As such, they escape the artificial pseudorationality of game theory, but many observers have found them too cumbersome.[42] If every possible factor leading to an

---

[40] H. J. Morgenthau, *op. cit.*, pp. 1–2, and *Scientific Man vs. Power Politics* (1946), pp. 108–121 *et passim*.

[41] K. W. Thompson, *Political Realism* (1960), pp. 113–127.

[42] H. McCloskey, "Concerning Strategies for a Science of International Politics," in *Foreign Policy Decision-Making*, ed. R. C. Snyder *et al.* (1962), pp. 186–205, for this criticism of R. C. Snyder *et al.*, "Decision Making as an Approach to the Study of International Politics," *ibid.*, pp. 14–185.

action by a government is taken into account, then the word "decision" means only that at a given time certain actions were performed. To understand what led up to this action, everything relevant that preceded it must be investigated. If this be the object of decision-making models, old-fashioned narrative history has been at it for a long time, without the benefit of a new vocabulary. This, however, does not appear to be the aim of those who have devised decision-making models. Their general belief is that "the acts of nation states result from more or less deliberate and conscious choices by someone at some time."[43] The emphasis thus is upon decisiveness, upon choosing. This impression is reinforced by the one example offered to illustrate the uses of the decision making model, President Truman's decision to enter the Korean War. Here we do, in fact, have an occasion on which a great deal of decisiveness was displayed by a limited and identifiable number of persons. It was also a highly exceptional event. Declarations of war are, after all, relatively rare incidents in international relations. A model of international relations based on such examples could hardly cover the routine conduct of foreign affairs, least of all that part which concerns the relations between allied states or states that do not have the remotest expectation of engaging in war with each other. Indeed, a model, whether structured in terms of game theory or decision-making "boxes," that assimilates foreign policy to strategic calculations is apt to have little relevance to situations which are not crises, in which no spectacular acts of choice are expected, and which are characterized by the slow, grinding routine processes of politics-as-accommodation. That, however, is not the purpose of decisionism in international affairs. It too, is a surrogate rationalism. Its main end is to impose a pattern of calculable and predictable moves upon an international scene that looks chaotic. If the moral and legal rationalism of the past, that suited an age when Americans could afford to ignore foreign affairs totally or to think of them in domestic, familiar ideological terms, is gone, it has been replaced by the technical rationalism of those who want to reduce sudden complexity to manageable proportions and to a formal vocabulary.

The demand that prudent decision-makers remove themselves from the hurly-burly of democratic political processes and ideology in order to conduct foreign policy in a statesmanlike manner or to make rational strategic choices has an elitist air about it. This should not be taken too seriously, however. Traditional elitism was an ideology with a specific content. The decisionist is out to de-ideologize politics entirely. Who is

---

[43] R. C. Snyder et al., "U.S. Decision to Resist Aggression in Korea," op. cit., p. 211.

to make the decisions is not really determined. If there is explicitly or implicitly a call for decisiveness, there is no concern with finding a new group to bring it to government, nor is the content of decisions pre-scribed. To do so would, at once, lead to an ideological stance, which decisionism, as a method or a program, is designed to avoid. This is especially clear in those instances when "decision-makers" is a phrase used in evident preference to the older word "elites." In the highly technical literature on decisions, this is not the case, but there is a relatively simple, descriptive approach to decision-making and -makers that is recognized as the methodological heir of the old elite theories. Since these theories are not normatively elitist, the use of "decision-makers" is to provide a neutral, antiseptic, and ideology-free substitute for the comparatively controversial word "elites." The intention here is to pay due attention to those who happen to occupy the seats of power. As such it is a conscious reaction against the group-interest approach to domestic politics. It is meant to examine the behavior of the most active and professional participants in politics, who are often neglected by those who concern themselves exclusively with the social groups whose inter-ests the politicians are said to represent.[44] This is surely a needed corrective, as long as one does not go on to attribute too high a degree of conscious power-manipulation and premeditated choice to the agents of government. This, however, is something that seems likely to occur in decision-oriented studies of domestic politics no less than of inter-national affairs. There is simply an ideological; though not logical, affin-ity between the notions of "politics as power operations" and "politics as decision-making."[45]

Both cling to a rather simple faith in the technical rationality of polit-ical actors. Concentrating on those who are conspicuously in the seats of power appears to involve the view that power is an entity that is managed purposefully. Whether this is really the way the professional officials of modern governments behave is, nevertheless, an open question. Do they really choose policies, or is it a more complex series of minute inter-actions? Thus, an academic study of the British Treasury asserted that its highest permanent officials wield great power because they can get their decisions accepted by other agencies of government. To this an insider replied that one does not make decisions out of the blue in Whitehall.

---

[44] For an example of all these trends, see D. Marvick, "Introduction: Political Decision-Makers in Contrasting Milieus" in the collaborative volume, *Political Decision Makers, International Yearbook of Political Behavior Research* (1961), II, 13–28.

[45] B. Leoni, "The Meaning of 'Political' in Political Decisions," *Political Studies*, V (1957), 225–239.

One accepts *idées reçus* [sic], being surrounded by the opinions of other men, inside and outside. Far from imposing decisions, the official spends his day listening to others.[46] In short, the decision-makers are not decisive and the crisis view of government as perpetual choice and change is artificial. Its attractions may lie precisely in the emotionally intolerable realities of big government as an undirected, faceless, infinitely complex series of numberless little human actions and reactions.

This brief review of some types of decision-oriented political thinking is by no means exhaustive. It is merely intended to illuminate some of the attitudes which appear to condition it. It seems to be a way of thinking congenial to people who, having rejected the substantive moral and legal rationalism of the past, try to reconstruct for themselves new images of a world upon which they can impose their own order. Since, however, his personal rationality is so deeply identified with the rejection of any of the conventional ideologies, be they radical or conservative "isms," it is difficult for the decisionist to establish anything but a formal framework for his ideal of rational deciding. He is clear as to what it is not, he is clear about the *conditions* under which choice is made, and clear too as to the necessity of making decisions, but nothing is said about the content, the purpose, or the validity of these choices. One rebels in order to rebel, one decides in order to decide, one chooses because one simply ought. It is an ideology without any substance, the resort of those who are perennially on the periphery. It is the outsider's view of moral unity, the political patient's view of social health, and the academic's tidy little picture of the corridors of power. It epitomizes every sort of malaise in an overinstitutionalized social world.

In view of the many doubts about decisionism raised so far, one might well suppose that the purpose of this paper has been simply to criticize. This is not, in fact, the case. If decisionism is not a self-evident necessity in morals and politics, it is at least an effort to cope with the most difficult issues. At least it is better than its alternatives, the conventional lament and call to a return to the ancestral pieties and academic systems, and the total apathy of those who are crushed entirely by the difficulties of not being able to live either with, or without, ideological sustenance.

---

[46] C. H. Sisson, *The Spirit of British Administration* (1959), pp. 129–130.

Coral Bell

From *The Debatable Alliance: An Essay
in Anglo-American Relations* (1964)

Evidence enough that the Anglo-American relationship is a debatable one may be found in the fact that it is debated, even at tedious length. Evidence that it is an alliance in any specific or bilateral sense might be harder to establish. All fifteen of the member-states of NATO, to be sure, are formally allies, and it is no doubt true, though not an officially defensible proposition, that some allies are more allied than others. But the claim that the relationship between Britain and America is of more significance, or better worth examining than, say, that between Norway and Turkey would have to look to other evidence than the formal words of treaties.

It might look to the debate itself. 'Debatable' has, of course, overtones that convey more than the existence of debate. 'Dubious', suggests the dictionary, 'questionable, uncertain, ambiguous, contested between two parties'. In the last fifteen years most of the sentiment that might seem to justify these adjectives has been felt on the British side of the relationship, and practically all the debate has been in Britain. This is not surprising: since the war America has in the nature of things loomed enormously larger on the British horizon than Britain has on the American horizon. Indeed one would perhaps have to go back to the pre-revolutionary period to find a time when Britain was as vital a factor in American destinies as America has been in British destinies since 1940. The intensity of the debate in Britain is an index of the real importance of the interests involved.

But one need not retreat to the eighteenth century to find a time when the relationship with Britain seemed to many Americans to raise the issues of national identity and purpose that some people in Britain have seen in the relation with America in the post-war period. There is a direct parallel between the pre-1917 debate over the U.S. entry into the first world war and the contemporary debate in Britain, which is essentially over the British role in the present power conflict. The progressive-pacifist movement in Woodrow Wilson's America and the CND New Left group now in Britain have shared not only the repudiation of power as an instrument of diplomacy, and a tendency to see industrialists with markets to win as the sponsors of conflict, a preoccupation with social and economic reform and a belief that more weapons meant fewer benefits at home, but a kind of provincialism in a sense of the unique importance of their own nation's international role, as an example to the world both domestically and in foreign policy, a natural standard bearer to lead the powers towards its own righteousness.[47] It has been ironical but inevitable that the sector of British opinion for whom, throughout the nineteenth century, America seemed most unqualifiedly the good society, the young radical intelligentsia, should now be its most ardent critics. Once they saw America as the society that had rejected both the class hierarchy and power politics, the last best hope of earth. Now they tend to see it not only as the very fount and origin of power politics, but (swallowing Vance Packer's [sic] ingenuous conclusions), as domestically a rat-race for status-seekers. Isolationism is not solely an American tradition: it is in a sense every plain man's reaction to foreign politics, so it is natural that Tom Paine's latter-day English disciples should urge that diplomatic independence of America would enable Britain to cut herself off from America's wars (interpreted to mean the cold war and a possible third world war) just as Paine in his time argued a similar case for American independence.

Of course not all the left in Britain feels this way. Transferring to it Professor Schlesinger's classification of the American left between the Utopians and the pragmatists we may say that the pragmatists (much the larger section) tend rather to be admirers of America as 'the efficiently producing society', not marred by the class stratification of England, and are inclined to regard central heating and a good supply of frozen orange juice as more reasonable objects of endeavour than the new Jerusalem – a substitution that endears neither them nor America to the Utopians. Similarly, to the modernist right, the brisk young business man element in the Conservative Party, America represents not merely a diplomatic bastion against revolution but 'the successful capitalist society', the proof that the system can really work, producing goods and freedom, and bestowing power, rewards, and prestige according to ability and success

---

[47] Cf. Aneurin Bevan's remark: 'There is only one hope for mankind, and that hope still remains in this little island.' Bevan did not of course share most CND positions. For the American side of this parallel see Arthur Link, *Woodrow Wilson and the Progressive Era 1910–17* (1954).

rather than inherited privilege. Only the traditionalist right, clinging to a value-system still paternalist and patrician, reacts with an antipathy equal to that of the radical left to a society where standards are set by majority taste. The political values of *The Loved One* and *The Quiet American* may be at opposite ends of the spectrum, but the reactions to America that they enshrine are closely akin.

In this fashion, the diplomatic alignment between the two powers, itself complex enough, is overlaid and given a sharp emotional edge by another relationship so broad that it is difficult to find an adequate name for it: one might call it the intellectual exchange. It is an outcome of the accessibility of life and thought in each of the two countries to the inspection of the other, and this of course is chiefly a matter of language, though the relative familiarity of institutions such as the law and the political system is also important. The sense of *terra incognita* with which most people approach lives lived in other languages than their own, and which usefully restrains judgement and comparison, does not operate between English speaking countries. They suffer from what might be called 'instant comparability'. America is, and historically has long been for many Englishmen, 'the alternative society', the measuring-rod for their own way of life in a way no other country could be. For each sector of political opinion it may represent either what could be constructed or what is being constructed at home, either shining example or awful warning. And one obsessively discovers in the other country evidence about what one hopes or fears for one's own. The highly developed American and British literatures of national introspection are very important to this process. Feiffer's subtly wounding blows at President Kennedy, Wright Mills's nightmares of the power elite, the popular notion of the 'warfare state' sustained only by its arms budgets, Professor Galbraith's elegant demonstration of the seamy side of affluence – all these strands of American self-examination, enormously valuable and instructive when digested against a knowledge of the country itself, make rather heady wine for foreigners when taken without this balancer. The CND-supporting student, far better versed than the average American in how many ex-admirals are on the board of General Dynamics, is one typical product of this intellectual cross-fertilization, though there are more reassuring ones.

For Americans the alliance with Britain has lost in the post-war period the emotional charge that it had earlier in this century, because the disparate sectors of political opinion usually lumped together in Europe as 'isolationists' have for various reasons assumed new foreign policy stances. The particular kind of alliance with Britain which was at issue in the period before the first and second world wars was in some ways the hardest of all alliances for America to make. That is to say, the elements in American society which most resisted American involvement in Europe's affairs were resisting, as much as anything, the identification of Britain's enemies as America's: Irish Americans with inherited hostilities, German Americans unwilling to see their country at war with their fathers' country, those whose ethnic ties were with Scandinavia or Eastern Europe, tending to see Britain's ally, Russia, as hereditary enemy or Germany as hereditary friend. The reason why isolationism was strong in the Middle West was not, as Europeans assumed, because this part of the country was geographically remote from the outside world, but because these ethnic groups were strongly represented there. There were other kinds of American isolationism than that based on ethnic origin, but these also tended to be isolationist 'against' Britain. The left-idealist sector, somewhat akin to the radical element in the British Labour Party, and assuming American innocence of the wickedness of power politics, tended to identify the forces making for American war participation with international imperialist interests whose home base was inevitably Britain. On the other hand, the right-nationalist isolationism, strong even now in the rank and file of the Republican Party, which has tended to prefer a go-it-alone position and xenophobically to spurn allies as mere burdens, tended also to be especially suspicious of Britain as a pre-eminently Machiavellian 'free-loader' on American effort. So one may say that all three main varieties of American isolationism – ethnic, left idealist, and right nationalist – contained a large element of distrust of Britain and that therefore a straight alliance with Britain would probably have been the most likely of all arrangements to raise what remained of isolationist hackles, even in the post-war period.

However, precisely those sectors of U.S. opinion which were most prone to isolationism were also (with one exception) prone to an ardent anti-Communism. Irish Catholic Americans reacting to the persecutor of the Church, German Americans reacting to the power that divided the fatherland and occupied half of it, East Europeans reacting to the oppressor of their relatives in the old country – for all these the anti-Communist alliance was the easiest of all alliances to accept. Only the left-idealist sector of the old isolationist cohorts remained unreconciled, and survives, much diminished, in the American peace movement, though no longer with an anti-British bias, since Britain is ambiguously blessed with the strongest of such post-war movements. All that remained in general American policy of the once-formidable tradition of isolationism after 1949 was the sense that the new policy was a regrettable though a necessary deviation from a happier past. Robert Sherwood in pre-Pearl Harbour days called the Anglo-American relationship a 'common law alliance', less in the sense of one between countries adhering to the English common law, than on the analogy of 'common-law marriage', a *de facto* arrangement with a touch of sin about it, a hint of America's being seduced from her proper diplomatic celibacy to a mildly unfortunate entanglement. That tradition is not dead. And even now the choice of involvement to America's present degree in world politics is not automatically continued from administration to administration. It has to some extent to be renewed by every President. Since 1947 it has never appeared likely, assuming a prudent regard to the national interest, that any American President could conceive the world balance to be of such a nature that he had the option of reducing America's commitment to it. But the possibility of such a balance appearing to emerge within the foreseeable future cannot, in 1964, be dismissed.

The transformation in Britain's relation to the central power-balance, comparing the inter-war and the post-war years, was in some respects more profound and radical, and perhaps harder to take than the equivalent process for America. One can cast Britain as the Hamlet of the inter-war tragedy, her hesitations and ambivalences, her tendency to 'think too precisely on the event' as the mainspring of the drama. But for the post-war period the country has been obliged to say, in the words, appropriately enough, of that most notable exemplar of the intellectual exchange, Mr T. S. Eliot,

> ... am not Prince Hamlet, nor was meant to be;
> Am an attendant lord: one that will do
> To swell a progress, start a scene or two.

To be demoted from protagonist to 'attendant lord', (or at best to 'Horatio, his friend'), that is to find that the central decisions must be taken elsewhere, and that the cultivation of influence must replace the exercise of power would have been a hard enough adjustment to make in the best of circumstances, quite aside from the other adjustments that Britain has had to make. But it was an inescapable one, since the war had destroyed the old European balance, and had left only the possibility of a world balance, in which the main Western weight would inevitably be America. In the event it was taken with surprising speed and lack of hesitation. The year 1939 was the last year of decay of the old balance: less than ten years later the new one was almost articulated.

Agatha Ramm

From *Germany 1789–1919: A Political History* (1967)

Even before the beginning of the new century a general European war, as an expected event, had been much in men's minds. The novelist, Theodor Fontane, in 1896 foresaw a war between Germany and England 'with such great certainty, that it does not matter if it happens now or in a year's or in ten years' time. Whose fault it will be', he wrote, 'is neither here nor there: it is a matter of historical necessity.' An English naval officer summed up the mood of the years before 1914: 'We prepared for war in our professional hours, we talked war, thought war, and hoped for war. For war would be our opportunity, and it was what we had been trained for.' Universal military service in Germany made this kind of expectancy more widespread there than in England. Young men beginning careers in the public service fitted in a period of service as army officers and valued their association with the army then and subsequently through the reserve or militia, not least because of the high respect accorded in Germany to the army officer. Germany, as other countries, had her stories and novels prompted by popular Darwinism and notions of the survival of the fittest, written to the theme that 'war with all its evils, calls out and puts to the proof some of the highest and best qualities of men'. In Germany their influence was heightened by the fashionable cult of the 'great man'. The Emperor himself had avowed his adherence to the doctrine that God revealed Himself in great men and included William I – together with Hamurrabi, Moses, Shakespeare and Goethe – in a list of such men. The cult was stimulated by the harsh doctrine of Friedrich Nietzsche (1844–1900) that humanity must work unceasingly for the production of the solitary great man – 'this and nothing else is its task' – as well as by the liberal writings of the Swiss, Jakob Burkhardt, or even of Fontane.

Nietzsche's influence was one thing; what he had to say was quite another. His philosophy was a constant questioning – an education of the mind. Every conclusion, even the last supposing there could be one, was the formulation of another problem. This abyss of uncertainty was not understood. But doctrines of dogmatic certainty were culled from Nietzsche and often erroneously interpreted. The doctrine of the will to power as the impulse to all human activity was proclaimed in *Thus Spake Zarathustra* (written 1883–85, published 1892). It was *taken* as the endorsement of a political programme. It was *meant* as an invitation to think of the individual striving constantly to transcend himself. The will to power meant self-overcoming. Nietzsche argued that it is only sensible to speak of one force overcoming another force, not of its overcoming itself. The will to power, therefore, must express itself both in a man's impulses and in his reason. The battle between those two. When reason gained the victory it reduced the chaos of a man's impulses to order, that is it fulfilled them or both cancelled them and raised them, in a word sublimated them. Nietzsche's doctrine of the superman – the *Übermensch* – also made its most famous appearance in *Zarathustra*. Correctly interpreted it is linked with self-overcoming. The superman was the man who had overcome himself: had transcended his impulses and acquired value in himself: become great by what he was and not by what he did. Nietzsche did not see the human story as a steady movement forward until perfection was attained, but as a constant recurrence, relieved here and there by the apparently accidental existence of a single great man. The doctrine of the superman was interpreted as an invitation to the individual to think of *himself* (not of others) – potentially at least – as greater than other men with a right to claim power over *others* (not himself). The doctrine of constant recurrence was interpreted not as an acceptance of life as it was, but as an invitation to strive that the kind of supremacy that suited oneself constantly recurred. To Nietzsche the nation state was the arch-enemy of self-realisation, of the single man's striving to remake his own nature, and doctrines of racial purity were anathema. Rather, believing in the capacity of men to transmit both inherited and acquired characteristics and believing in their capacity, by a mixture of races, to combine the best qualities of several, he contemplated the possibility of the great man of the future who might be the highest possible specimen of a European. Yet it was precisely to national and racial self-glorification that Germans turned Nietzsche's teaching. The doctrine was used to endorse the superiority of one nation, not to induce men to treat all their fellow-men with equal respect lest any one of them should turn out to be the one truly great man. Finally the chapter on 'War and Warriors' in *Zarathustra* led to the glorification of war being ascribed to Nietzsche. What he had in mind was that the individual in his self-exertion after truth and knowledge might find that there were greater virtues than squeamishness in competing or disagreeing with others.

Nietzsche's philosophy was a sustained celebration of creativity as, indeed, Herder's very different philosophy also was. But Nietzsche was not read that way.

In Germany there were special reasons why war should be held in prospect: the success, overwhelming but not easily won, of 1870–71 had gained it a place among those things for which the new nation stood; the tradition of operational planning, which Moltke had bequeathed to the army's General Staff and Schlieffen taken over, and the diplomatic planning for war, which the Bismarckian alliance system implanted as a habit in the foreign office, encouraged it; the great expenditure on armaments was more noticeable to Germans than to others in so far as it was the only *great* expenditure nationally incurred – other expenditure was borne piecemeal by the states. Yet the tension produced by the armaments race and this expectancy of war was offset by the sense of security derived from the doctrine, if you wish for peace prepare for war. In any event the war that was expected was not associated with civilian starvation, unprecedented casualties and political and social revolution.

Lenin showed in 1916 that the concentration of economic power had caused a struggle among the great powers to redivide the world. Each great power sought to gain a balance of economic strength more favourable to itself. The War of 1914–18 was the outcome. What Lenin does not tell us is that what was true of economic power was also true of every other kind of power. By 1914 seven great powers divided between themselves all the military and naval strength of the world. They also monopolised all the capacity (in, for example, railways and administrative techniques) to bring resources to bear on a particular place at a particular time. Gone was that multiplicity of small states – one can bring the count up to forty-nine – which had enabled Metternich or Canning to adjust the balance of power with a margin for manoeuvre. Apart from Portugal and Spain, the modern continental middle-sized state did not exist and the new Balkan states, small states, it is true, did nothing to relax the tension. The concentration of economic and political power, like the armaments race, created the circumstances in which statesmen had to work. They were not much different, except in having existed longer in 1914, from what they were in 1912, or 1908 or, for that matter 1898. Yet Bethmann-Hollweg on 30 July 1914 was not alone in thinking 'that a war that nobody wanted was being unleashed as it were by elemental forces and by the long state of exacerbation of one Cabinet against another'. Why did the statesmen in 1914 fail to control these general causes of war?

7

World Peace
Introduction by Sarah C. Dunstan

Within histories of international thought, war has received much attention as a frame through which to understand state actors and human nature. Inextricable from reflections on war is the question of peace: the conditions necessary to create peace, the relationship between decisions made in war to the peacetime that follows and the tension between the imperative of social change and the desire to end suffering. The thinkers excerpted in this section were born between 1843 and 1898 and, with the exception of Bertha von Suttner (1843–1914) and Jane Addams (1860–1935), lived to see both the First and the Second World War. Their writings, which range chronologically from Suttner's speech at the 1899 Hague Peace Conference through to Edith Sampson's 1952 Address at Washington University, engage with one or both of these cataclysmic conflicts. Their solutions to the problem of "peace" run the gamut from international institution building and collective security to more individualized approaches rooted in civic rights. Three of these women, Bertha von Suttner, Jane Addams, and Emily Greene Balch (1867–1961), won Nobel Peace Prizes for their efforts.

Our first piece is the 1899 speech, "Universal Peace – From A Woman's Standpoint," delivered by the Austrian-Bohemian pacifist Bertha von Suttner at the first of two pre-war international peace conferences held at The Hague. Von Suttner had first become a key figure in the Austrian peace movement with the publication of her 1889 novel *Die Waffen nieder!*, a sweeping condemnation of war, as well as a critique of women's position in Austrian society. The book was translated into English in 1892 as *Lay Down Your Arms!* and reached huge audiences across Europe. Von Suttner capitalized upon the book's success to become the editor of the international pacifist journal *Die Waffen nieder!*, named after her book, from 1892 to 1899. She was a staunch advocate of disarmament and had been a key organiser of the 1899 Hague Conference, hoping that it would result in multilateral agreements for peace. Both the first and the second of these conferences resulted in the Hague Conventions of 1889 and 1907: these were amongst the first documents to outline an international law of war and of war crimes. Von Suttner was recognized for this work when, in 1905, she became the first woman to win the Nobel Peace Prize.[1]

Despite the explicit link between women and peace in the title of her speech, von Suttner opened by declaring that she did not believe it necessary to "treat the problem of peace and war exclusively, or even principally, in its relations to the feelings and lives of women".[2] Decrying the notion that women should care about war because they were likely to suffer most from it, she urged her listeners instead to adopt a rational approach to war that was not contingent upon identities of characteristics such as sex. War, she believed, "represents a check to the development of culture, and that from every standpoint – the moral and the economical, the religious and the philosophical – it is to be condemned." Rather presciently, she warned that a war between all the states in Europe would "surpass all horrors that have hitherto taken place" because human progress made techniques of death more sophisticated.[3] The only natural course of human progress, then, was towards peace. Implicit in her argument was the idea that history unfolded in a teleological and Eurocentric fashion whereby human civilization constantly advanced. For von Suttner, this meant that "disputes should be settled hencefor-ward by arbitration instead of by force" (373). She proposed "the estab-lishment of international justice" in the form of "inter-parliamentary" tribunes (374). The inter-governmental conference at The Hague was a potential model.

Whilst von Suttner had been at pains to separate her identity as a woman from her thinking on peace, a large number of women thinkers concerned with peace found the vantage point of their sex central to their elaborations of peace on the international stage. Indeed, many of the women included here were also deeply involved in suffragette move-ments in their own countries and connected peace with women's eman-cipation and increased participation in the public sphere.[4] Suttner died before women won the vote in Austria in 1918. The end of the First World War coincided with a number of victories for the suffrage

---

[1] For an account of Suttner's reception in IR, and a fuller account of her international thought, see Kimberly Hutchings and Patricia Owens, "Women Thinkers and the Canon of International Thought: Recovery, Rejection, and Reconstruction," *American Political Science Review*, 115:2 (2021): 347–59.

[2] Bertha von Suttner, "Universal Peace – From a Woman's Standpoint," *The North American Review* 169:512 (1899): 50.

[3] Suttner, "Universal Peace," 51; 54.

[4] For a study of this in the case of the United States and the United Kingdom see J. Vellacott, *Pacifists, Patriots and the Vote* (Houndmills: Palgrave Macmillan, 2007).

movement. That same year, the Representation of the People Act gave British women over thirty who resided in the constituency or occupied land or premises worth above £5, or whose husbands did, the right to vote. In 1920, the passage of the 19th Amendment gave women suffrage in the United States, although for women of color it was not until the civil rights legislation of 1964 that they had this right in any great numbers.

Women's suffrage activists Jane Addams, Emily Greene Balch (1867–1961), Helene Stöcker (1869–1943), Helena Swanwick (1864–1939), and Mary Church Terrell (1863–1954) were major figures in the peace movements of their respective national contexts and were all part of the congresses that led to the foundation of the Women's International League for Peace and Freedom (WILPF). In an effort to stop the war, the International Congress of Women held its first congress in The Hague in 1915, and the second, the Second International Congress for Peace and Freedom, was held in Zurich in 1919 in connection with the peace treaties that ended the First World War. This overlap between the peace and suffrage movements is important to note, but it was not without controversy. The decision to meet at The Hague in 1915 was a response in part to the cancellation of the International Women's Suffrage Alliance's meeting that was to take place in Berlin in 1915. In Britain the National Union of Women's Suffrage Societies (NUWSS) was split over the decision to attend the 1915 Congress. Many believed that combining the movement for suffrage with the movement for peace was strategically risky. Ultimately the NUWSS President Millicent Fawcett declined the invitation to The Hague, but half of the twenty-four members of the NUWSS's Executive Committee resigned over the decision.[5]

Amongst those who resigned over this issue was Helena Swanwick. For Swanwick, at least, the transition from the suffragette movement to pacifist organizing was natural. In her 1935 memoir, *I Have Been Young*, she reflected "I felt that in working for the emancipation of women, I was contributing to the cause of peace."[6] Educated at Girton College, Cambridge, Swanwick had worked as a journalist for the *Manchester Guardian* and, from 1909, as the editor of the NUWSS's journal, *The Common Cause*. In 1913 she published a book, *The Future of the Women's*

---

[5] Anne Wiltsher, *Most Dangerous Women: Feminist Peace Campaigners of the Great War* (London: Pandora Press, 1985), 77–78.

[6] Helena Swanwick, *I Have Been Young* (London: Gollancz, 1935), 264. See also Lucian Ashworth, "Women of the Twenty Years' Crisis: The Women's International League for Peace and Freedom and the Problem of Collective Security," in Patricia Owens and Katharina Rietzler (eds.), *Women's International Thought: A New History* (Cambridge: Cambridge University Press, 2021), 136–157.

Movement, which sketched out her position on gender roles in politics. When war broke out, she became a key force in the Congresses that led to the WILPF, becoming the Chair of the British Section of the WILPF, known as the WIL, as well as a key advisor to Emily Greene Balch and Catherine Marshall in their advocacy work for the WILPF at the League of Nations in Geneva. Swanwick's official contacts were very important to the WILPF's international advocacy as well as their lobbying of national officials in the British government. Aside from her work with the WILPF, she was a founding member of the Union of Democratic Control (UDC), an anti-war organization whose co-founders included E. D. Morel, Charles Trevelyan, Ramsay MacDonald, Arthur Ponsonby, and Norman Angell. The UDC was not necessarily a pacifist organization but instead sought to give British citizens greater control over foreign policy. Swanwick edited the house journal at the UDC, *Foreign Affairs: A Journal of International Understanding*, from its launch in 1919.[7] Her 1924 book on the Union, *Builders of Peace, Being Ten Years History of the Union of Democratic Control*, remains a key work on the organization.

The extract included here is from a pamphlet Swanwick wrote for the UDC, "Women and War," in which she connected the emancipation of (white) women to the conditions of peace. Although women had long been "more opposed to war than men ... they have been subjected, ignorant, inarticulate, disorganised" (388). With their full integration into society as citizens, they would be able to study "the causes of war and set themselves against them" (388). Swanwick asserted that sex distinction delineated different roles for men and women within the framework of the "human family." Women were "the life-givers and the home-makers" and as such war, as the destroyer of the children of women and of their homes, was also the destroyer of the "woman's place" or role in society. This meant that women were "eternal non-combatants" (388), a position always "distinct from men" that gave them "a prima facie right to be heard" (389). In states which prized war and conquest over peace, women would always occupy subservient positions. Disputes between nations, then, needed to be resolved by means other than resorting to armed conflict. Swanwick advocated instead for the development of international tribunals for the mediation of such disputes.

Swanwick's maternalist critique of war went hand in hand with a belief in the intellectual equivalence of men and women. Whilst she saw women as more naturally inclined towards peace due to their

---

[7] Marvin Swartz, *The Union of Democratic Control in British Politics during the First World War* (New York: Oxford University Press, 1971), 220.

biological role in reproduction and their historical position within society, she nonetheless also believed opposition to war could be justified on rational grounds and was thus a position that could be shared by men and women.[8] She was particularly frustrated when, in 1924, she served as a British delegate to the League of Nations Assembly and found her role curtailed to topics deemed best suited to her gender.[9] It is important to note, however, that Swanwick's work on peace more broadly was considered to be a significant contribution to early international thought. It is only latterly that she has been elided from international intellectual histories.[10]

Jane Addams, too, was recognized as a serious international thinker, social reformer, and political theorist in her own time. Indeed, the book we have excerpted here, *Peace and Bread in Times of War* (1922), was reissued in 1945, leading the *Journal of Philosophy* to publish a discussion of "the theory of international relations contained therein."[11] In terms of her social reform work, Addams is perhaps most famous for founding the Chicago Hull House settlement alongside Ellen Gates Starr in 1889. Their aim was to provide social and educational opportunities to the impoverished, primarily immigrant, communities in the surrounding neighborhood. As shown in the excerpts of her work in "Religion and Ethics," Addams's time working with these communities deeply shaped her thinking on the importance of tolerance. The piece we have included in this section gives insight into her belief in the link between internationalist feeling and long-lasting peace, modeled on the behavior she witnessed in the settlement. Writing in 1922, Addams noted that "although it may take years to popularize the principles of international cooperation, it is fair to remember that citizens of all nations have already received much instruction in world-religions" (394). So although the "national grievances and animosities so paramount when the League of Nations was organized in Paris" (394) might still play a role in deciding

---

[8]   Lucian M. Ashworth, "Feminism, War and the Prospects for International Government: Helena Swanwick (1864–1939) and the Lost Feminists of Interwar International Relations," *International Feminist Journal of Politics*, 13:1 (2011): 31; Beryl Haslam, *From Suffrage to Internationalism* (New York: Peter Lang, 1999), 60.

[9]   Swanwick, *I Have Been Young*, 385. See also Helena Swanwick, *Labour's Foreign Policy: What Has Been and What Might Be* (London: Fabian, 1929); Helena Swanwick, *The Roots of Peace: A Sequel to Collective Insecurity, Being an Essay on Some of the Uses, Conditions and Limitations of Compulsive Force in the Prevention of War* (London: Cape, 1938).

[10] For a recent work that points to Swanwick's significance see Lucian M. Ashworth, *A History of International Thought: From the Origins of the Modern State to Academic International Relations* (New York: Routledge, 2014), 126, 128.

[11] On Jane Addams's international thought see Molly Cochran, "Jane Addams und ihre internationale Ethik eines sozialen Radikalismus: Globale Gerechtigkeit als realistische Utopie," *Deutsche Zeitschrift für Philosophie*, 64:5 (2016): 740–756.

international relations, deeper motivations and needs would lead to solidarity. She hoped that a world-wide religious revival would be key to fusing "together hostile nations" (395). In such thinking she believed a genuine society of nations would need to be grounded in the lives of "earth's humblest toilers" for whom the concerns of everyday existence were a driving imperative.

Addams combined this thinking about peace with an understanding of gender binaries that equated men with warmongering and military force and women with a disposition towards care-taking functions in society. In relegating women and their socialized strengths to subservient positions, societal norms had allowed the creation of an imbalance between these roles that would ultimately lead to war. In her first work on peace, the 1907 book *Newer Ideals of Peace*, Addams had pushed for a civic household model of societal organization that elevated "civic housekeeping" above the male and "traditional type of government, which had to do with enemies and outsiders."[12] In this regard Addams had much in common with Swanwick's position and that of the African American suffragette, journalist, and teacher, Mary Church Terrell, who believed that mothers in particular would play a special role in guaranteeing peace in the aftermath of the First World War.

One of the few women of color involved in the WILPF, Terrell is also a key figure in the history of civil rights. In the American domestic sphere, she had been one of the founding members of the National Association of Colored Women (1896) and the National Association for the Advancement of Colored People (1909). She studied Classics at Oberlin College, the first US college to accept both women and African American students. When she graduated with her first degree in 1884, she was one of the first African American women to gain a bachelor's degree, alongside her contemporaries Ida Gibbs Hunt and Anna Julia Cooper, who appears elsewhere in this volume. Terrell gained a Masters' degree in education at Oberlin, graduating from that program in 1888. She began her career teaching modern languages at the historically Black college of Wilberforce in Ohio before working at the first African American public school – M Street High School in Washington, DC – and becoming the first African American woman to be appointed to the school board in the District of Columbia.

Terrell begins the speech extracted here, originally delivered in German and French at the 1919 Zurich conference, with the comment that "as the sole woman in attendance with a drop of African blood in my

---

[12] Jane Addams, *Newer Ideals of Peace* (Champaign, IL: University of Illinois Press, 2007 [1907]).

veins it falls to me not just to represent black American women but the women of Africa and other black races" (392). It seemed impossible to Terrell that there would ever be a "permanent peace" so long as the color of a man's skin made him the victim of prejudice and injustice (393). Her speech roundly criticized US race relations as well as the tendency of European powers to refuse "colored nations" an equal seat at the table in international affairs despite their willingness to deploy troops of color during the war. She called upon white mothers "to teach their children to accord by the sublime principles of justice and liberty and equality" and "to teach them to judge men and women by their intrinsic merits rather than their race, color or religion".[13] In this way, mothers could take the lead in embedding the values necessary for peace in the next generation. Many in the audience shared Terrell's view of the role of mothers in ensuring peace, but none was prepared to specifically address the relationship between racial discrimination and the war.

It is worth clarifying that the invocation of motherhood in Terrell's thought and in the thought of contemporaries such as Addams was not a default to a biological understanding of women's role in society. To the contrary, these peace women saw their sex as the product of a social conditioning. They argued for the inclusion of women into the public sphere precisely because this conditioning led them to think about issues such as peace in very different ways than men.[14] For Terrell, her socialization as both a woman and a woman of color meant that she could offer a position that reflected both positionalities.

Aside from her speech, Terrell also took the lead in drafting and presenting to the Congress a resolution titled "Nationality, Race and Colour," which set the agenda for the WILPF's official anti-racist position. She was also elected to the organization's board in 1919, but she remained an outlier within the WILPF and was not re-elected in 1923. Many of Terrell's fellow members considered her race-based advocacy as a hindrance to their goal of peace.[15] Despite her own criticism of eugenicist thinking and its links to imperialism, Emily Greene Balch was amongst those who were critical of Terrell's approach to international peace activism. In earlier publications, Balch had in fact made a very similar argument to Terrell, suggesting a firm link between racial and

---

[13] Mary Church Terrell, "Speech and Resolution Presented at International Women's Congress, Zurich" (1919), 16.

[14] Linda Schott, *Women against War: Pacifism, Feminism, and Social Justice in the United States, 1915–1941*, PhD Dissertation submitted to the Department of History, Stanford University, August 1985.

[15] Melinda Plastas, *A Band of Noble Women: Racial Politics in the Women's Peace Movement* (Syracuse, NY: Syracuse University Press, 2011), 20–25.

national prejudices and the outbreak of war.[16] In a 1915 article, for example, Balch had taken aim at ethnic nationalism, writing that "the pseudo-science of race," had no grounding in fact. Moreover, it had led directly to the "the war cries of the jingo and the imperialist," encouraging the need to dominate.[17] As far as she was concerned, the origins of the contemporary conflict lay in this "dogma of the white man's burden" and the "colony-grabbing" it veiled.[18] In many ways Balch was ahead of her time: much of her work criticized the eugenicist beliefs of her contemporaries and argued for a cultural understanding of the concept of race. Nonetheless Balch's criticism of race-based imperialism went hand in hand with her belief that different peoples occupied different "stages of development."[19] Moreover, in 1919, she felt her vision of the dynamics of international peace activism was incompatible with Terrell's assertion of racial equality and critique of race relations in the United States.

Balch was both academic and activist, combining a career at Wellesley, the private women's liberal arts college, with activism on poverty, child labor, and the peace movement. Yet, in 1918, she was dismissed from Wellesley for her leading role in the WILPF, work that in 1946 earned her the Nobel Peace Prize. Balch's piece here is drawn from a book she co-wrote with Addams and another US delegate, Alice Hamilton, about the earlier, 1915 Congress, *Women at The Hague: The International Congress of Women and Its Results*.[20] Therein Balch argues that "the question of peace is a question of terms," inextricable from movements for national independence, minority rights, and geopolitical borders. She understood the world conflict as a manifestation of the irreconcilability of the national policies of imperialism and democracy, two approaches to be found in differing degrees in every nation involved in the war.

The final three pieces in this section were written in a later context, after most white women had gained the vote in Britain, the United States, and Germany. Questions of women's positionality vis-à-vis peace and

---

[16] Emily Greene Balch, "Racial Contacts and Cohesions: As Factors in the Unconstrained Fabric of a World at Peace," *The Survey*, March 6, 1915, 611.

[17] Balch, "Racial Contacts and Cohesions," 611.

[18] Balch, "Racial Contacts and Cohesions," 611. See also Catia Confortini, "Race, Gender, Empire, and War in the International Thought of Emily Greene Balch," in Patricia Owens and Katharina Rietzler (eds.), *Women's International Thought: A New History* (Cambridge: Cambridge University Press, 2021), 244–265; Glenda Sluga, "From F. Melian Stawell to E. Greene Balch: International and *Internationalist* Thinking at the Gender Margins, 1919–1947," in Patricia Owens and Katharina Rietzler (eds.), *Women's International Thought: A New History* (Cambridge: Cambridge University Press, 2021), 223–243.

[19] See Confortini, "Race, Gender, Empire and War," 255–256.

[20] Jane Addams, Emily Greene Balch, and Alice Hamilton (eds.), *Women at The Hague: The International Congress of Women and Its Results* (New York: Macmillan, 1915).

war remained in flux and these extracts were written long after any hopes for peace through the League of Nations had been dashed. The first of these is a 1935 piece by the British writer and pacifist Vera Brittain (1893–1970) written in the lead up to the Second World War, as faith in the League of Nations crumbled. The second, a 1940 review of E. H. Carr's *The Twenty Years' Crisis* by Helene Stöcker, was composed after war had already broken out and reflected upon the failures of the League. The third, a 1951 speech by the African American diplomat and lawyer Edith Sampson (1898–1979), was delivered as the United States urged international intervention into a different conflict, the Korean War of 1950–1953. In all three cases, these thinkers looked to international co-operation and collective security as mechanisms for peace.

Brittain, who had worked as a nurse in the First World War before returning to Oxford to read History, is perhaps best known for her 1933 memoir *Testament of Youth*.[21] That book traced the impact of the war on her life and her struggles to establish herself as a writer in a literary landscape dominated by men. It has been read alternatively as a condemnation of war and a feminist rallying cry. The piece we have included here, from "Peace and the Public Mind," is a continuation of both aims and an effort to establish the extent to which the general public supported the peace movement. As far as Brittain was concerned, there was only one answer for peace that would not automatically result in another war: "collective security and … the maintenance and improvement of that machinery which, for all its imperfections, represents our sole defence against anarchy" (397). Brittain had been a supporter of the League of Nations in the 1920s and a regular speaker for the League of Nations Union, an organization set up in 1918 to promote international justice and permanent peace on the basis of collective security.[22] However, by the mid-1930s when this piece was written, Brittain professed very little faith that the League of Nations could be an effective enforcer. Her doubts were prescient. In the year following the publication of her piece, the League failed to respond decisively to two international crises, the 1935 Italian invasion of Ethiopia and the outbreak of the Spanish Civil War.

Helene Stöcker would have had both these events in mind when reviewing E. H. Carr's *The Twenty Years' Crisis, 1919–1939*, one of the most influential books in twentieth-century international thought, to

---

[21] See Paul Berry and Mark Bostridge, *Vera Brittain: A Life* (London: Virago, 1995). For the context to this extract in particular see pp. 351–359.

[22] For more on the reception of the League of Nations in Britain see Helen McCarthy, *The British People and the League of Nations: Democracy, Citizenship and Internationalism, c. 1918–45* (Manchester: Manchester University Press, 2011).

parse her own thoughts on peace-making. Written in 1940, the review praised Carr's book for approaching the question of international relations with an "unprejudiced attitude." It seemed to her that the basics of this science of international relations should "be the property of every responsible human being" (403). She made the case that a deep knowledge of "the political history of the past century and the last twenty years" would allow peacemakers to design a peace that compelled states to abide by their treaty commitments (403). She went so far as to suggest that if the architects of the League of Nations had read even Carr's "short chapter on peaceful change" then they might well have been able to "prevent the disaster of this deep destruction of Europe" (404).

Stöcker had also been one of the delegates alongside Addams at the 1915 International Congress of Women and was heavily involved in the international women's suffrage movement. Initially trained as a teacher, she studied in Berlin and Glasgow before earning a doctoral degree in Bern, Switzerland, in 1901.[23] The following year, when she returned to Berlin to teach, Stöcker became involved in the women's suffrage movement, co-founding the League for Women's Suffrage with German activists Anita Augspurg and Lida Gustava Heymann.[24] In 1905, she also founded the League for the Protection of Mothers and its journal *Die neue Generation*. The outbreak of war forced her to reflect upon the relationship between women's suffrage and peace. Although she was a staunch advocate of both, she understood suffrage as only one among many necessary social reforms to improve the lot of humanity. Suffrage alone, she argued, would "not protect us from the outbreak of war," and peace needed to be the priority.[25]

Writing during the First World War, in *Die neue Generation*, Stöcker described war as a space in which life is reduced to a "struggle for bare existence, of self-preservation for both the individual and the state." Stöcker lamented the outbreak of war because she believed that the divisions it encouraged weakened white Europe and threatened the European civilizational mandate.[26] A proponent of eugenicist birth policies as a means of improving populations, she worried that the war

---

[23] For a biography of Stöcker see Christl Wickert, *Helene Stöcker, 1869–1943: Frauenrechtlerin, Sexualreformerin, Pazifistin* (Bonn: Dietz, 1991).

[24] Regina Braker, "Bertha von Suttner's Spiritual Daughters: The Feminist Pacifism of Anita Augspurg, Lida Gustava Heymann, and Helene Stöcker at the International Congress of Women at The Hague, 1915," *Women's Studies International Forum*, 18:2 (1995): 105.

[25] Helene Stöcker as cited in Braker, "Bertha von Suttner's Spiritual Daughters," 107.

[26] John M. Hobson, *The Eurocentric Conception of World Politics: Western International Theory, 1760–2010* (Cambridge: Cambridge University Press, 2012), 147.

threatened "the domination of the white race in relation to the yellow and black races."[27] She argued that the war needed to be understood in terms of the peace that would follow and those who were not soldiers had to fight to preserve the kind of "national community" on behalf of which they were fighting the war. In these circumstances, women had a responsibility not to give in to "war mentality" and to instead practice a "morality of humanity" that included treating "enemies" as "fellow human beings."[28] By the time her 1940 review was written, Stöcker was less dogmatic in her support of pacifism. She argued that it was now "difficult to think that it is always and under all circumstances wrong to start a war" (404). By no means pro-war, this stance nonetheless reflected her belief that in some instances justice required changes that could only be wrought by war or rebellion.

Writing in 1952 amidst a flurry of international institution building intended to ensure peace, Edith Sampson shared Stöcker's conviction that some wars were just, as well as Brittain's belief that peace required collective security and an effective international enforcer. Emphasizing that, for some, the *raison d'être* of the United Nations was "to save succeeding generations from the scourge of war," Sampson argued that the idea of collective security was the best means of ensuring peace.[29] Peace, for Sampson, meant the enjoyment of democracy in each of the respective member states. Using the war in Korea as her case study, she suggested that imperialist tendencies of communist nations such as North Korea and the Soviet Union were the cause of war. She praised the United Nations for taking action to save South Korea from the fate of those already under communist rule. Those uncertain as to what living "under the heel of the Kremlin" meant should "ask the millions of helpless souls dying today in soviet slave labor camps." She placed the United Nations in opposition to "Communist Imperialism," thereby equating world peace with the spread of democratic liberalism, and making repeated comparisons between Soviet leaders and Hitler. In such a framing, the United States, and to a lesser extent Britain and France, became the champions of peace at the UN General Assembly.

When Edith Sampson became the first Black woman appointed to the permanent US delegation to the United Nations, the sociologist and activist St Clair Drake dismissed her appointment as an act of

---

[27] Helene Stöcker, "Rassenhygiene und Mutterschutz," *Die neue Generation*, 13 (1917): 138–142.

[28] Helene Stöcker, "Der Krieg und die Frauen," *Die neue Generation*, 10 (August 1914): 422–427.

[29] Cf. Hobson, *The Eurocentric Conception of World Politics*, 84–105.

propaganda on the part of the US State Department, an effort "to offset communism" by painting the nation as racially progressive.[30] The arguments Sampson makes here are certainly indicative of her anti-communist stance. Sampson and other African Americans who believed in the potential of American democracy were commonly labeled "the left wing of McCarthyism," and contemporaries such as St Clair Drake, W. E. B. Du Bois, and Claudia Jones refused to take their political work and thought seriously, accusing them of selling out in exchange for career advancement.[31]

Sampson was hardly an apologist for American racism nor unqualified for the posts that she held. Although she had certainly had a scant presence in the male-dominated civil rights organizations of her local Chicago, her experience fighting for civil rights and racial justice was far from inconsequential. Born to a launderer in Pittsburgh, she had become a social worker before retraining as a lawyer. After graduating, she established a successful private practice and by 1934 had been admitted to practice law before the US Supreme Court. That same year, Sampson had been one of the founding members of the National Council of Negro Women (NCNW). An organization dedicated to "the complete integration of Negro women into the American commonwealth, with all normal rights and privileges," the NCNW was active on both a domestic and an international scale.[32] From its inception, the NCNW's founders and leaders – women such as Sampson and Mary McLeod Bethune – had grounded the organization's domestic political goals in terms of the international struggle against racism. They, like Mary Church Terrell had done before them, argued that race-based thinking was key to the ensuring peace. Despite this, the criticism Sampson faced from many of her contemporaries was reflected in her treatment in the historiography. It is only recently that she has been treated as a serious thinker in her own right and only now that she appears in histories of international thought.

All of the figures in this section were influential thinkers and activists in their own time. For many, their thought and influence on the question of peace in the international context was inextricable from their fight for

---

[30] St Clair Drake, "The International Implications of Race and Race Relations," *Journal of Negro Education*, 20:3 (1951): 267.

[31] Gerald Horne, "Who Lost the Cold War? Africans and African Americans," *Diplomatic History*, 20 (1996): 613, 623. For commentary on the way "mainstream" African Americans were characterized see Manning Marable, *Race, Reform, and Rebellion: The Second Reconstruction in Black America, 1945–1982* (London: Macmillan, 1984), 33; Helen Laville Scott Lucas, "The American Way: Edith Sampson, the NAACP, and African American Identity in the Cold War," *Diplomatic History*, 20:4 (1996): 565–590.

[32] Edith Sampson, *Council History 1*, Edith Sampson Papers, Box 9, Folder 188.

suffrage. The interlinked nature of their thinking on these topics and the specifically women-centered spheres in which they moved account in part for their marginalization in histories of international thought. The radical nature of their positions often attracted virulent challenges to their authority. As we have already noted, Balch lost her position at Wellesley on account of her work for the peace movement. Both Balch and Addams were also targeted for their support of labor reform and civil liberties protection in the post-war anti-communist Red Scare that engulfed the United States. Others, such as Bertha von Suttner and Helena Swanwick, occupied spaces primarily dominated by men but were recognized by their peers as key thinkers on the subject of peace. It is only latterly that their thought has been elided from histories of international relations. This anthology is an effort to rectify their exclusion.

Sarah C. Dunstan

Bertha von Suttner

From "Universal Peace – From A Woman's Standpoint" (1899)

The value of life rises with the embellishments and alleviations afforded by daily advancing progress; and lastly, as regards the advantages of the final victory, a strip of land or a heap of fortress stones, or the absolutely illusory "Fame" – these things, powerless to enrich or to make happy, sink in an ever greater disparity to those sacrifices, increasing to the uttermost, which they render necessary.

  – So much for the approaching (or, it is to be hoped, not approaching) war. As regards universal peace, which may now not be so remote – for at the present time a conference is assembled in this name, called together by the most powerful military ruler in the world – people are by no means clear as to its foundations and aims. Most persons believe that members of Peace Societies imagine under the name of universal peace a condition of general harmony, a world without fighting or divisions, with undisputed frontiers settled for all time, and inhabited by angelic beings, overflowing with gentleness and love. It is an old custom of the enemies of any movement to represent it in a false light, to attribute absurdities to it which it has never asserted, and then to attack them with cheap sarcasm and obvious refutations. So also here. The friends of peace do not desire to found their kingdom on impossibilities, nor on conditions that might perhaps prevail thousands of years hence, but on the living present and living humanity. The avoidance of all disputes is not demanded – for that is impossible – but that the disputes should be settled henceforward by arbitration instead of by force, as was hitherto the case. This level of culture has already been attained by the individuals of organized states: that it should be attained also by the states themselves in their relations to each other, is the aim and object of the whole peace movement. Thereby one right would certainly be lost – a right which, although it bears the proud name of sovereignty, is in truth a great wrong; the right of one state to attack another. But if ten persons agree among themselves to desist from mutual attack, each exchanges one-tenth of his lost chance of plunder for nine-tenths of assured safety. Immutability of existing frontiers and social arrangements is demanded as little as the avoidance of disputes. For this, too, would be contrary to nature. Obstinacy, bearing the proud title of Conservatism, which opposes all natural alterations and displacements, is itself the cause of all forcible revolt. Just as in private life, the individual's possessions are protected from robbery by a civilized commonwealth, but the possessor is not guaranteed for all time, and the poor are not prevented from gaining possessions. Rich and poor families grow or die out, increase or decrease in fortune; new groups are formed, drawn together by natural selection; a growing population must overflow the frontiers; forms of state belonging to a lower level of culture must be supplanted by the civilization of those culturally superior. *Elasticity* is the only quality which ensures peaceful duration or painless and imperceptible transition from one form to another. The world should remember this, now that it has learned the law of evolution, and knows that all life and development is the work of adaptation.

But to contemplate peace and war from a general standpoint is what philosophers and politicians have done from the earliest times. To work out plans and propositions, by which the ruling state of war may be replaced by the establishment of international justice, is a labor which has been carried on systematically for the last ten years by the various groups of the League of Peace, and the inter-parliamentary union. An entire literature already exists on this subject, and by consulting Dr. Evan Darby's "International Tribunal" and Dr. Benjamin Trueblood's lately published work, "The Federation of the World," a complete knowledge of the ideal and practical aims may be gained, as also of the results already acquired. [...]

But now, at the present moment, when the work of peace is placed in the hands of an inter-governmental conference at the Hague, furnished with powers to realize the resolutions passed, it is no longer fitting to draw up theories of the abstract idea of universal peace: now everyone sympathizing with the great cause, and especially such as are in immediate proximity to the conference, are compelled to concentrate all their interest upon it. And, therefore, I will close these lines with a few thoughts, which, quite apart from the "woman's standpoint," might bear the title: "Universal Peace and the Conference at the Hague."

It appears to me that in the criticism and discussion of this unique phenomenon, this unprecedented historical event, the importance of the fact that such a Conference is sitting is too much forgotten. One either loses oneself in the question: "What will be discussed?" and subjects every item of the programme to a minute technical criticism, or one enquires: "What will be the result?" and indulges in more or less hopeful, or more or less sceptical, conjectures and prophecies. One forgets to contemplate the overwhelming fact that such a Conference has been called together by an autocrat in our ultra-military times, and in which every State takes part.

Apart from all that will be achieved by speeches, propositions and resolutions, the significance and the effect of the event itself must be of the greatest influence, and the first official Peace Conference appears like a miracle in the history of the world.

Among the many arguments brought against peace movements on the part of sceptics, the most powerful used to be: "What is the use of private exertions?" Rulers will never agree to restrict militarism, which is the support of the throne, or to abolish war, which is the *raison d'être* of militarism. Autocratic Russia itself presented the most serious menace of war. "Suppose you attempt," was the scornful remark, "to get the Tsar upon the list of your societies; then you might speak!" Now, the Tsar stands at the head of all peace movements, but the opponents set aside the circumstance that the most obvious of their ten ordinary arguments has been refuted, and, undismayed, employ the nine remaining ones against the Tsar himself.

People do not only forget to observe the magnitude of such an event as the meeting of an inter-governmental Conference; they also forget, in speaking of the subjects under discussion, to open their eyes to the importance of them. They know what the point in question is, but they do not realize it. Like a person ignorant of music before a symphony of Beethoven, like a three-year-old child before a picture by Raphael, so do people stand before the chronicle of the Conference. They hear and see, but the awe of comprehension does not thrill through them. "Universal Peace!" How few can comprehend the harmony and the glory that lie in these words. How few reflect, while discussing the problems lying before the Conference, *what* is really at stake: the happiness or ruin of themselves and their children! For, that the *regime of* international justice would shower an undreamed-of abundance of moral and material benefits upon the civilized world, and on the other hand, that continued military equipments and the eventual employment of the increasingly deadly weapons of war *must* lead to ruin and annihilation, can be denied by none. Thus it is nothing less than our highest happiness or deepest misery which is being discussed in the *Huis ten Bosch*. But the world looks on as though it were a question of customs duties or weights and measures; many boast of "being indifferent to the matter." They think thus to prove their superiority, and only show that they do not understand. Not only without but within the Conference is there an uncomprehending majority. Among the delegates, as well as among the

Governments that sent them, most are as indifferent, in some cases as hostile, as unintelligent, generally speaking, as the ordinary public towards the idea of universal peace. But that matters nothing: the fact remains that an international parliament is now assembled in the name of this idea; the spirit abiding in the idea, and inspiring the originator as well as a number of the delegates, will exert its power upon the indifferent, the hostile, and the uncomprehending, and will penetrate the world.

The true significance of the Conference is contained in the following words, addressed by the President, von Staal, to the delegates at the opening of the first sitting:

"To seek the most effective means of ensuring to all nations the benefits of a real and lasting peace, that is the chief aim of our deliberations according to the text of the circular of August. The name 'Peace Conference,' which the instinct of the nations, anticipating the resolution of the Governments, has given to our Assembly, this name well describes the principal object of our labors; the Peace Conference must not be faithless to the mission laid upon it; it must bring forth a tangible result from these deliberations, which is awaited in confidence by all mankind."

All mankind? Not yet. A great portion of it, that which still holds fast to the thousand-year-old institution of war, be it through personal interest or the power of imparted prejudice, hopes that the Conference will produce no result which may endanger war; a still greater portion, the dull masses, expect nothing at all. But those who really have confidence in the progress of culture, who, in agreement with the originator of the Conference and his faithful fellow-workers, are convinced of the necessity of the present ruinous system giving place to another, these latter will note these words of the President of the Conference; and in case of disappointment, in case the Conference were faithless to its mission, would raise the demand for fulfilment so loudly and continuously that at length all mankind would be carried away by it. But such disappointment will not take place. That may be boldly said beforehand. The proposals already put before the Assembly vouch for the earnestness and sincerity of the work which has been begun. They are a proof that the following sentence from Staal's speech is no mere phrase, but the expression of noble resolve:

"Diplomacy, following a universal law, is no longer an art in which personal skill plays the principal part, but is striving to become a science, which must possess fixed rules for the settlement of international conflicts. That is to-day the ideal aim that it must bear in view, and great progress will indubitably be made, if diplomacy succeeds in laying down some of these rules at this Conference. We shall also particularly endeavor to codify the practice of arbitration and mediation. These ideas form, so to speak, the essence of our task, the chief aim of our exertions; 'to prevent conflicts by peaceful means.'"

These words faithfully echo the instructions given by the Tsar to his ambassador. And already much has been done in the specified direction. It is clear that other powers had come to the Conference with plans equally far-reaching if not more so, and the subject of an "International Permanent Tribunal of Arbitration" – this wildest dream of the Utopians – has already been discussed and even in many points unanimously accepted.

The propositions offered by the representatives of Russia, England, Italy and the United States are known through the newspapers. To the opponents of the peace movement that have lately pointed out with special satisfaction that America, that stronghold of efforts for peace, has lately entered military channels, to these the plan sent by the American Government must have caused remarkable stupefaction. With these proposals, with this energetic and open participation in the work of peace, the American will again fill that position in the history of civilization with which the friends of peace in the whole world have always credited him: the Pioneer of peace and freedom.

A tangible result will be produced by the Conference, something newly created, constituted, permanent, that can be developed and expanded. And besides this, a direct result, how many indirect ones? The whole world must now take part in the question, and the various branches of the social organism, the Church, Art, Literature, the Press, are drawn into the service of propagandism. Gifted men like Stead and Bloch, now resident at the Hague, have an opportunity of a field worthy of their labors. Stead has prevailed upon a Dutch daily paper to publish an article on "War against War," which plays the same part towards the Conference as the weekly paper for the English, "Crusade of Peace." Bloch is giving lectures, illustrated by views, offering a *resumé* [sic] of the great six-volume work in which, supported by dates and facts, he proves that the war of the future is a technical impossibility, an "Utopia." Even if the general public has not comprehended the marvelous significance of the meeting of the Conference, perhaps it will be capable of perceiving the significance of positive results. Facts and successes are always more powerful than the most glorious theories, however irrefutable. And the positive results will be of various kinds. One brings another with it. The question of neutralizing the States, the question of the coalition of neutrals, and lastly the question of disarmament, although the two former are not upon the programme, and the latter seems to have been momentarily put aside will come to the front. Disarmament and a check to military equipment, these were the chief motives of the Tsar's manifesto. To avert the ruin and misfortune brought upon nations by "armed Peace," was mentioned as the object for which remedies were to be found. When once these remedies – international justice, etc. – have been found, the object can no longer be evaded.

I believe that the decision of the Conference upon the question of disarmament will offer a startling resolution, or at least a declaration of principle, which will be binding in the future. One need not fear to be confounded when prophesying agreeable surprises. Truly, I venture to assert with confidence, the progress from the first of the past eight Peace Congresses in 1889 to the Hague Congress of 1899 has been far longer and more difficult than that leading from this Conference to a complete attainment of its aims; i.e., to the abolition on principle of the institution of war. In the midst of our endeavors for universal peace the Tsar's initiative fell like a bombshell; but now, even were it in the near future, the inauguration of lawfully guaranteed peace would appear to those qualified to judge no longer as a surprise, but as a fulfilment.

Emily Greene Balch

From "The Time for Making Peace" (1915)

There is a widespread feeling that this is not the moment to talk of a European peace. On the contrary, if we look into the matter more deeply, there are good reasons to believe that the psychological moment is very close. If, in the wisdom that comes upon us, after the event, we see that the United States was dilatory when it might have helped to open the way to end bloodshed and to make a fair and lasting settlement, we shall have cause for deep self-reproach.

The question of peace is a question of terms. Every country desires peace at the earliest possible moment, if peace can be had on what it regards as satisfactory terms. Peace is possible whenever the moment comes when each side would accept what the other side would grant, but from the international or human point of view a satisfactory peace is possible only when these claims and concessions are such as to forward, not to hinder, human progress.

If Germany's terms are the annexation of Belgium and part of France and a military hegemony over the rest of Europe, or if the terms of France or England include "wiping Germany off the map of Europe," then there is no possibility of peace at this time or at any time that can be foreseen, nor does the world desire peace on these terms.

In each country there are those that want to continue the fight until military supremacy is achieved, in each there are powerful forces that seek a settlement of the opposite type, one which instead of containing within itself the threats to international stability that are involved in annexation, humiliation of the enemy, and competition between armaments, shall secure national independence all round, protect the rights of minorities and foster international co-operation.

In one sense the present war is a war between the two great sets of belligerent powers. In another and more significant sense, it is a struggle between two conceptions of national policy. The catchwords imperialism and democracy indicate briefly the two opposing ideas.

In every country both are represented, though in varying proportions, and in every country there is a strife between them.

The overriding of the regular civil government by the military authorities in all the warring countries is one of the too little understood effects of the war. The forms of constitutionalism may be undisturbed but as *inter arma leges silent* [sic] so military power tends to control the representatives of the people none the less really because unobtrusively. Von Tirpitz, Kitchener, Joffre, the Grand Duke Nicholas have tended to overshadow their nominal rulers.

Another effect of war is that as between the two contending voices, one is presented with a megaphone and the other is muffled if not gagged. Papers and platforms are open to "patriotic" utterances as patriotism is understood by the jingoes; the moderate is silenced not alone by the censor, not alone by social pressure, but by his own sense of the effect abroad of all that gives an impression of internal division and a readiness to quit the fight.

In our own country during the tension with Germany, loyal Americans who believe that the case of the United States is not a strong one (and a hundred million people cannot all think alike on such an issue), those who loathe the idea of going to war cannot and will not seek any commensurate expression of their views for fear this may make it harder for our Government to induce Germany to render her naval warfare less inhuman.

Thus everywhere war gives an exaggerated influence to militaristic and jingo forces and creates a false impression of the pressure for extreme terms as a basis of settlement. Each side, of course, would like to make peace when the struggle, which is in a rough general sense a stalemate, is marked by some incident favorable to itself. Germany would like to make peace from the crest of the wave of her invasion of Russia; Russia and England from a conquered Constantinople. If the disinterested neutrals, who alone are free to act for peace, wait for the moment when neither side has any advantage, they will wait long indeed. The minor ups and downs of the war are shifting and unpredictable, but their importance is much less than it appears. The gains that either makes are as nothing to its losses. The grim unquestioned permanent fact, which affects both sides and which is to the changing fortunes of battle as the miles of immovable ocean depths are to the waves on its surface, this all-outweighing fact is the intolerable burden of continued war.

This fact is that which makes a momentary advantage comparatively unimportant. All the belligerents want peace; though they none of them want it enough to cry "I surrender."

The making of peace involves not only the questions of the character of the terms, of demands more or less extreme – it also involves the question of the principle according to which settlements are to be made. Here too there are two conflicting conceptions.

On the one hand there is the assumption that military advantage must be represented *quid pro quo* in the terms, – so much victory, so much corresponding advantage in the terms. There is even the commercial conception of war as an investment and the idea that the fighter has a right to indemnity for what he has spent.

On the other hand, starting from the fact that the war has thrown certain international adjustments into the melting pot, the problem is to create a new adjustment such as on the whole shall be as generally satisfactory and contain as much promise of stability as possible.

The gains won by force have no claims that any one is bound to respect. The expenditure of blood and treasure is no basis for a demand for reimbursement, no one has contracted to render any return for it, and it is to the general interest that such expenditure, undertaken on speculation, should never prove a good investment. Admitting these things, yet since the arbitrament of war is an arbitrament of force, this fact is bound to tell in the resulting adjustment. But a fact that it is important to understand is that with a given balance of relative strength as between the two sides, an equilibrium may be reached in more than one way, as there are equations which admit of more than one solution. The equilibrium of peace might be secured by balancing unjust acquisition against unjust acquisition or by balancing magnanimous concession against magnanimous concession.

A mediator or mediating group, without throwing any weight into the scale of one or the other side, can help to find the equilibrium on the higher rather than the lower level. We find a parallel in the economic sphere when there is a choice between a balance based on low wages and low efficiency and one based on high wages and high efficiency and when the state, not interfering with the economic balance, yet helps to secure that balance by the socially desirable method.

On the basis of military advantage or on the basis of military costs the neutrals have no claim to be heard in the settlement. The soldier is genuinely aggrieved and outraged that they should mix in the matter at all. Yet, even on the plane of fighting power, unexhausted neutrals are capable of throwing a sword into the scale and on the plea of costs suffered they have good claim to a voice. It is however as representatives of civilization and the true interests of all sides alike, that those who have not been in the thick of the conflict can and should be of use in the settlement and help to fix it on the higher plane.

The settlement of a war by outsiders – not their mere friendly cooperation in finding acceptable terms – is something that has often occurred, exhibiting that curious mixture of the crassest brute force with the most ambitious idealism which frequently characterizes the conduct of international dealings. The fruits of victory were refused to Russia by the Congress of Berlin in 1878, Europe recently denied to Japan the spoils of her war with China, the results of the Balkan wars were largely determined by those who had done none of the fighting. While mere physical might played a large part in such interferences from the outside, there is something besides hypocrisy in the claim of the statesmen of countries which had taken no part in a war to speak on behalf of freedom, progress, and peace.

A peace involving annexation of unwilling peoples could never be a lasting one. The widespread sense of irritation at all talk of peace at present seems to be due to a feeling that a settlement now would be a settlement which would leave Belgium, if not part of France, in German hands. Such a settlement would be as disastrous to Germany as to any nation. It might put an end to military operations, but it certainly would not bring peace, if we give any moral content to that much-abused word. Europe was not at peace before August, 1914, nor Poland for long before, nor Ireland, nor Alsace, nor Finland. Any community which, if it could, would fight to change its political status may be quiet under coercion, but it is not at peace. Neither would Europe be at peace with Germany in Belgium.

The question is, then, what sort of peace may we hope for now – on what terms, on what principles?

We may be sure that each side is ready to concede more and to demand less than appears on the surface or than it is ready to advertise. The summer campaign, in which marked advantages are most likely, once over, the belligerents are faced with a winter in the trenches which will cost on all sides, in money and in suffering, out of all proportion to the gains that can be hoped for.

It must be remembered, too, that the advantages hitherto won are not all on one side, but that each side has something to concede. The British annexations of Egypt and Cyprus may be formal rather than substantial changes, but the conquest of Germany's colonies, large and small, Southwest Africa, Togo Land, Samoa, Neu-Pommern, Kaiser Wilhelm's Land, the Solomon, Caroline, and Marshall islands, to say nothing of Kiao-Chao – and probably Russian gains at the expense of Turkey in the East, give bargaining power to the allies. So, even without success in the Dardanelles, does their ability to thwart or forward German enterprise in Asia Minor and Mesopotamia or possibly in purchasable parts of Africa or elsewhere. Friends of Finland and of Poland must see to it that the debatable lands of the Eastern as well as of the Western front are kept in mind. From the point of view of Poland the main thing to be desired is the union of the three dismembered parts – Russian, German, and Austrian Poland and their fusion in some sort of a buffer state, independent or at least essentially autonomous. Something like this appears to be the purpose of both Germany and Russia, with the difference that this Polish state would be in the one case under Teutonic, in the other under Russian auspices. No one knows, as between the two, which would be the choice of the majority of the Poles concerned. Concessions to Germany in Finland and in Poland, especially if coupled with adequate security from nationalistic oppression, might prove to be in the ultimate interest of European peace, and would render it easier for Germany to make the concession on her side of complete withdrawal in the West. Very important too are the concessions in regard to naval control of the seas that Great Britain ought to be willing to make if the safety of her commerce and her intercolonial communications could be secured otherwise, and this would seem to be the natural counterpart of substantial steps toward disarmament on land.

But all this is speculation. The fact, obvious to those who look below the surface, is that every belligerent power is carrying on a war deadly to itself, that bankruptcy looms ahead, that industrial revolt threatens, not at the moment but in a none too distant future, that racial stocks are being irreparably depleted. The prestige of Europe, of the Christian Church, of the white race, is lowered inch by inch with the progress of the struggle which is continually closer to the *débâcle* of a civilization.

Each power would best like peace on its own terms, although our common civilization would suffer by the imposition of extreme terms by any power. Each power would be thankful indeed to secure an early peace without humiliation on terms a long way short of its extreme demands. There is every reason to believe that a vigorous initiative by representatives of the neutral powers of the world could at this moment begin a move towards negotiations, and lead the way to a settlement which, please God, shall be a step toward a nobler and more intelligent civilization than we have yet enjoyed.

Helena Swanwick

From "Women and War" (1915)

"We do not war upon women and children!" This is a commonplace of British rhetoric at the present moment. But it is not true. War is waged by men only, but it is not possible to wage it upon men only. All wars are and must be waged upon women and children as well as upon men. When aviators drop bombs, when guns bombard fortified towns, it is not possible to avoid the women and children who may chance to be in the way. Women have to make good the economic disasters of war; they go short, they work double tides, they pay war taxes and war prices, like men, and out of smaller incomes.

There are in this country seven millions of "gainfully occupied" women and girls, and yet it is curious how officialism generally overlooks this large body of wage and salary earners and assumes that all is well if there is not extensive unemployment of men. The sea and land forces draw off a million men and thus a shortage of male labour is created and (what we are very apt to forget) a shortage of the useful things which that male labour would have created for the benefit of the country; but men and women so largely still do different work that this withdrawal of men does not create any considerable demand for female labour, and the curtailment of men's work often causes the dismissal of the women whose labour dovetails with men's. To take only the clerks and typists, we have seen how the reduction of business by the withdrawal of men has hit the women. Again, the effect of war upon all the luxury trades, in which so many women are employed, is sudden and disastrous, throwing out thousands of dressmakers, milliners, embroidresses, and so forth, while teachers, artists, and many classes of professional women suffer terribly also. One half of these earning women have relatives dependent on them, making the strain and the suffering heavier. And, if we take the other half of the working women of the country – those who are humorously reckoned as not being "employed persons," the working housewives – it does not take much imagination to realise what a rise in the prices of necessaries amounting to 25 per cent, means of pinching and penury to the woman who is trying to housekeep on a sum which is round about a pound a week in the towns and far less in the rural districts.

But, far more heavy than the burden which they share with men, is the burden more particularly their own, which war lays upon women. Two pieces of work for the human family are peculiarly the work of women: they are the life-givers and the home-makers. War kills or maims the children born of woman and tended by her; war destroys "woman's place" – the home. Every man killed or mangled in war has been carried for months in his mother's body and has been tended and nourished for years of his life by women. He is the work of women: they have rights in him and in what he does with the life they have given and sustained. Here is a true description of what war does to men's bodies: – "The primary object of this war and of all wars is to lacerate human flesh, to break bones, to inflict torture, to paralyse, and to kill. Every army in the field to-day is out for maiming and homicide, and for nothing else … . This is war. This is the confessed first aim of Prussia and all militarists, for no ulterior military aim can be achieved until this aim is achieved. This is what is going on daily just now in many different parts of Europe, against the outraged conscience of the world. This is the basis of military glory, and of all those other fustian things that overlords rant about. This is what overlords wish to perpetuate among the usages of mankind. Let us never forget that war is first and last the tearing of human flesh, the shattering of human bones, and the greatest source of human agony, both physical and mental."[33]

And the homes of the women? Within the zone of war, what is left to the women? The best that can be done for them is to round them up with the children, like cattle, sick and old, the nursing mothers and the women with child, and turn them into concentration camps, to rot and go mad and die. And the worst – Ask Belgium and East Prussia and Serbia.

These are notorious facts, which no rhetoric can abolish. Another obvious fact is that a constant state of preparedness for war requires a tremendous yearly sacrifice of the fruits of toil; wealth, which might be used to nourish and enlarge and make beautiful the life which is women's charge, is wasted in the competive [sic] increase of armaments, yearly scrapped and replaced by fresh inventions of destruction. Men cannot afford to protect motherhood adequately and to start their children well in life, because they must expend so much wealth in making engines to destroy the children of foreign nations. Again, homicidal wars tend

---

[33] *The Daily News and Leader*, March 24, 1915. Article by Arnold Bennett.

greatly to reduce the proportion of young men to young women, and this disproportion must result either in polygamy or in the establishment of a very large class of celibate women, or of a combination of both, such as we are at present familiar with. There are, besides, all the deep injuries to women created by the barrack system and the corrupting effect of the breaking up of homes. Moreover, when men are called upon to waste their lives in war, women are called upon to spend (and frequently to give up) their lives in child-bearing to make good the waste; the greater the waste of life the greater the waste of women in repairing life. Militarist states always tend to degrade women to the position of breeders and slaves.

In all these ways the possibility of war, the preparation for war, the militarist basis of States (whether "civilised" or "uncivilised") affect the position of women and affect it altogether evilly.

When Might Is Right

There are, however, other less obvious ways in which women, and through women the causes of civilisation and democracy, suffer from militarism. The fact that so many people do not clearly apprehend these injuries makes them particularly insidious. They are, however, the inevitable result of a barbarous conception of the foundations of government. In militarist states, women must always, to a greater or less degree, be deprived of liberty, security, scope, and initiative. For militarism is the enthronement of physical force as the arbiter of nations, and under such an arbitrament women must always go under. Women, whose physical force is specialised for the giving and nurture of life, will never be able to oppose men with destructive force. If destructive force is to continue to dominate the world, then man must continue to dominate woman, to his and her lasting injury. The sanction of brute force by which a strong nation "hacks its way" through a weak one is precisely the same as that by which the stronger male dictates to the weaker female. Not till the idea of public right has been accepted by the great nations will there be freedom and security for small nations; not till the idea of moral law has been accepted by the majority of men will there be freedom and security for women.

We all do lip-service, of course, to these ethical principles, and no one would deny that they do inspire most private and much public conduct; but they are not yet embodied in political institutions; they are still held on a very precarious tenure, they are at the mercy of greedy, or ambitious, or truculent individuals and classes. In his speech (Sep. 26th, 1914) in Dublin, Mr. Asquith quoted Mr. Gladstone's declaration:

"The greatest triumph of our time will be the enthronement of the idea of public right as the governing idea of European politics." How is this enthronement to be accomplished? On another occasion, the Prime Minister spoke of the necessity of adequately securing France from aggression and of placing the rights of the smaller nationalities of Europe "upon an unassailable foundation." These objects are certainly good, but they do not go far enough. Not France alone, but all countries must be secured from aggression before we can flatter ourselves that public right rules in Europe. And the Prime Minister has not yet shown that he intends to lay the one unassailable foundation for the rights of the weak. That foundation is a true democracy, free and informed. No politician speaking to the common people but finds he must appeal to the principle of public right; this alone really and permanently moves the people – "not thrones and crowns, but men" – and anyone honestly desiring the enthronement of public right would recognise that by the democratic control of policy, at home and abroad, by the enfranchise-ment and enlightenment of the people, women as well as men, by making real the sovereignty of the people, so largely still a sham, we should be establishing public right in the only way humanly possible. It is not the abolition of physical force that is required by civilisation. It is the control of it by moral and intellectual force. As things are now, each belligerent nation appeals to the god of battles to defend the right. This, when it is honest, is honest barbarism. It is not honest in the Europe of the twenti-eth century. We know that the god of battles defends the best fighting machine. We know that it is only the God of love who defends the right, and He does not defend it with machine guns.

Prussianism in Great Britain

We British have invented the name of "Prussianism" for a doctrine which we are finding very ugly and hateful. But we should not forget that it is the doctrine with which our British Anti-Suffragists have made us very familiar during the past ten years and which has been enunciated even by the Prime Minister. Suffragists call it "the Physical Force Argument." It runs: – Political power (which alone gives freedom) must always be in the hands of those who can enforce their will; women can never enforce their will as against men; therefore women can never have political power (which alone gives freedom). Once you admit the validity of the major premise, you have proved much more than the necessity for the eternal subjection of women to men; you have proved the necessity for the eternal subjection of small nations and the necessity for the eternal strife of nations, to determine which is the stronger, and the eternal necessity for competitive armaments and shifting alliances and the eternal necessity of wars like this one. It is time that British men realised that anti-suffragism is "Prussianism"; it is time that women suffragists realised what their denial of the major premise of the anti-suffragist entails. People who desire the enfranchisement of women will only be effective workers if they work for pacifism, or the control of physical by moral force. Pacifists will only be effective if they admit that woman's claim to freedom is based on the same principle as the claim of small nations. The anti-suffragist's major premise of force as the basis of political power is not argument; it is man's knock-out blow. We have no right to assume that what has been always will be; that men are incapable of development; that they must always worship the god of brute force. There is no reason whatever why men should not gradually learn that they get no good, but much evil, from the uncontrolled domination of force. They have shown already in countless ways that they are learning the lesson. They will learn it much faster when women have studied the causes of war and set themselves against them; when women cease to idealise pugnacity in men and see it in its true light as fretful egotism; when, finally, women who demand citizenship join with democratic men and thus show that they understand the very foundation of their own claim and can teach men to understand better the democratic creed which they profess.

Women will then be more effective peace-makers than, with all their good will, they have been in the past. On the whole, no one can doubt that they have been more opposed to war than men, because they have had nothing to gain and all to lose in war. But they have been subjected, ignorant, inarticulate, disorganised. Those who have kept them so should be the last to blame them. British women are rapidly emerging from subjection and are catching up with men in respect of knowledge, power of organisation, and expression. The lesson of this war for women is that the causes of war will result in war, and it is too late, when men have launched their ultimatum, to talk of a "women's crusade" or a "down-tools" policy for women, as was done last August. Catastrophic reforms do not happen. Reforms must be prepared for in the human heart. Things are what they are and their consequences will be what they will be. We must deal with causes.

[...]

Democratic Control

There is no argument for the democratic control of foreign policy which should exclude women. As eternal non-combatants, women have a prima facie right to be heard, as distinct from men. The chief arguments for secret diplomacy and autocratic control are that popular control would be full of indiscretions and ignorances, and it is a favourite theme of some people that women are even more ignorant and indiscreet than men. They forget that, when there is no secrecy, there is little scope for indiscretion, and there need be no ignorance. One thing women will never be so ignorant about as men, and that is – how a woman feels.

No one supposes that the man in the street will be called upon to decide highly complex and specialised details of foreign policy, nor will the woman in the home. Effective Parliamentary machinery and a reformed diplomatic service, together with an accurately and regularly-informed Press, would give the elector the kind and degree of control for which the common people is fitted. If debates in Parliament and discussions in daily and weekly papers were based upon unimpeachable facts, we should not have the absurd spectacle of a Foreign Minister, who has for eight years shrouded himself in impenetrable mystery, coming down to the People's House and declaring within forty-eight hours of his ultimatum that the issue of peace and war is in the hands of the people and subsequently hurling at the bewildered public a justificatory white book, whose diplomatic jargon is so remote from the language of common life that it is only with difficulty that the plain man can discover from it that his country has for years been committed to a policy which he – the plain man – thought had been categorically and repeatedly repudiated by the Cabinet. When the war had been declared, the Government revealed itself as extremely anxious that the people should understand the British Cause. It would have been better understood if the people had been kept informed of what was going on during all these years.

It is not ignorance which is the real danger, and if it were, the Government could remove it. The real danger lies in the factious nature of our party system. This is the real danger which politicians will not face, because so few of them are free from the factious spirit. Granted that there are different parties: in the State with different ideals, it is quite clear how greatly it might be in the power of an unscrupulous opposition to wreck all and any negotiations if they became aware of them. The doctrine that it is the duty of an opposition to oppose has been carried so far that many politicians seem to think it their duty to prevent the majority from governing at all. This very real difficulty would, however, be more completely met by the boldest and extremest frankness than by the present system of prevarication, in which dangerous half-truths get abroad and a state of twittering nervousness is chronic in the Chancelleries of Europe. The candid and the bold course of diplomacy would in the end be the safest, although, of course, there can be no security where there is not good will. At present, the good will of the great mass of the common people has no chance of penetrating the dense fog of diplomacy; when, by chance, the fog lifts for a moment, and common men and women are allowed to see the mysteries, they are more apt to be shocked at their squalor and futility than impressed by their subtlety.

It is sometimes suggested that only a very few can form right judgments, because only a very few can have studied all the precedents and know all the various ways in which human nature has failed. One does not want to depreciate the study of history, but anyone who knows how extraordinarily difficult it is to form an accurate estimate of contemporary events and persons will feel healthily sceptical of dogmatic inductions from what we are pleased to call history. We shall do well to remember that, even if conditions seem to be repeated, the human soul is always individual, and to the discouraging historian who tells us that "It is no use trying to do that; it was tried before and was a failure," the proper answer of a living person is, "If it seems good, I must try it again. Who knows why it failed before?" And women, more particularly, must feel this, because, whoever has tried to control diplomacy in the interests of peace, it has not been the women. They must take up this great new struggle with their old courage and faith –

> To go on for ever and fail and go on again,
> And be mauled to the earth and arise,

And contend for the shade of a word and a thing not seen with the eyes:

> With the half of a broken hope for a pillow at night,
> That somehow the right is the right
> And the smooth shall bloom from the rough.

Men and Women Together

It has been the object of these pages to show that women have a point of view distinct from the point of view of men towards this matter of peace and war; because so much more even than men women suffer from militarism, which excludes and enslaves them; because they win from it none of the things which make it attractive to men; and because the whole course of their life's work gives to women a standard of values different from that of men in important particulars. Some people seem to think that women ought not to have an outlook or a standard of values different from those of men because their interests are one: This is an odd method of reasoning. No one maintains that the bodies of women are the same as those of men; everyone admits that their lives are very different; most people will admit that their characters tend to differ somewhat. Yet those who are most insistent upon these differences would impoverish life and experience by refusing their fruits. Emphatically men's and women's interests are one, and therefore men cannot afford to overlook the women's point of view, and no one can describe it so well as the women themselves. War is bad business for men in the mass, always and all the time; it is not less bad for men because it is even worse for women.

It is sometimes assumed that a "Woman's Party" is necessary. If by a woman's party is meant a party consisting only of women, this, as a permanence, does not seem desirable. Yet it will infallibly arise unless women are accepted freely as coworkers with men. It has been found necessary in the past for women to organise separately, partly because men would not have them and partly in order to attain that self-direction of thought and act, without which women become merely weak echoes of men and all the precious variations of sex are lost to public life. But this has been a temporary necessity, due to the subjection of women, and though it may continue for some time to come, progressive people should work for its extinction. But, above all else, the nature of the work which has to be done for the abolition of militarism demands the co-operation of men and women.

Now at last, when a democratic movement has got down to the basis of right government; when democracy is held to be the rule of the whole people, women, as well as men, on the only foundation upon which this is possible – the foundation of public right and moral law; when it is seen how all the things which women care for and give their lives for are at the mercy of secret diplomacy, about which none of the people have the slightest knowledge and over which none of them have the slightest control; now is the great opportunity for the whole people, women as well as men, to work together for an object which women, if only they understood it, would desire more ardently even than men. And women, knowing that men do not and probably cannot escape from feminine influence, will hold that it is for the common good that that influence should not be purely personal. Hecuba had her opinion of Helen and the siege of Troy.

Mary Church Terrell

From "Speech and Resolution Presented at International Women's Congress, Zurich" (1919)[34]

It is right that, in a congress called upon to pronounce on peace, there should be at least one representative of black women. Since I am the only person present with a single drop of African blood in my veins, it is up to me to represent not only the women of color from the United States, but also the women of Africa and other black races.

I would first like to thank the white women of the United States, those of broad mind and generous heart, because it is thanks to their kindness and consideration that I have been invited to this conference. There would be no race problem in the world if people everywhere followed the example shown by these women.

No woman abhors war and desires peace more than the woman of color, whether she lives in Africa, in the United States, or in the Caribbean. In everything that may have been true in the past, in the wars started and fought today by white men, men of color were inevitably conscripted and made to play an active part.

It is not my intention to discuss or comment on the cause of the recent war or to make observations on the way in which it has been conducted. But to demonstrate the fact that I have just stated, let me draw your attention to the large number of men of color who have actively participated in it. Among the Allies there are at least five nations: China, Japan, Siam, Liberia, and Haiti which do not have a notable white population.

A large majority of the people of the British Empire live in the Indies: certainly white men, but also natives and non-Europeans. Taking France and its colonies as a whole, it contains almost as many blacks as whites, and French Indochina contributes a large number of men of the yellow race (*hommes de race jaune*) to increase the total. Italy, Belgium, Portugal,

[34] Translated from the French by Sarah C. Dunstan. Terrell delivered her speech in both French and German.

Brazil, Cuba, and other Allies have a large number of non-white subjects and citizens. The United States, with its ten million negroes and *métis*, its Indian tribes, its colonies in the Pacific, cannot claim to be homogeneous from the point of view of races.[35] If we add up all the people who fought against Germany, we would find that at least three out of four were *indigènes*, that is to say non-descendants of European races. It goes without saying that the white race is the most represented on the current battle front, but since the army is only the delegate of a people, we should think of the war that it is like a League of all the races of humanity against the common enemy of all humanity.

[...]

If we think of the large number of men of color who took an active part in the terrible war which has just ended, it is quite obvious that in the future there could not be a war between white men which does not also affect men of color; just as there could be no peace for the white man which the black man would not enjoy.

Peace does not draw the color line, nor does peace take account of the race to which human beings might belong. Nothing, therefore, could more vividly interest or appeal more directly to the hearts of women of color from around the world than a congress convened by white women to address the issue of permanent peace.

But as long as men are victims of prejudice and injustice because of the color of their skin, there can be no lasting peace in the world. As long as one can, anywhere in the world, bar people of color from devoting themselves to certain careers or from reaching the highest position in the various fields of human activity – positions that their natural skill, their energy or their perseverance would otherwise enable them to attain – there will be no justice and permanent peace in the world.

[...]

Many black women hoped that the situation of their peoples world-wide would be greatly improved by the victory of the Allied forces. In my own country women of color were told that we must let our men go with joy, so that they can fight for freedom – so that they can save the world for democracy.

This is how women of color, together with their white sisters, sent their husbands and sons 3,000 leagues across the ocean to fight for a freedom that they did not have, in some cases, themselves.

---

[35] The word *métis* has multiple connotations in the French- and English-language contexts. It is likely Terrell used it here as the French equivalent of "mixed-race."

Jane Addams

From *Peace and Bread in Time of War* (1922)

Dr. Fridjoff Nansen, appointed high commissioner at the Red Cross meeting in August, after a survey of the Russian Famine regions returned to Geneva for the opening of the Assembly on September 5th, in which he represented Norway, with a preliminary report of Russian conditions. He made a noble plea, which I was privileged to hear, that the delegates of the Assembly should urge upon their governments national loans which should be adequate to furnish the gigantic sums necessary to relieve twenty-five million starving people.

I believed that, although it may take years to popularize the principles of international cooperation, it is fair to remember that citizens of all nations have already received much instruction in world-religions. To feed the hungry on an international scale might result not only in saving the League but in that world-wide religious revival which, in spite of many predictions during and since the war, had as yet failed to come. It was evident in the meeting of the Assembly that Dr. Nansen had the powerful backing of the British delegates as well as others, and it was therefore a matter for unexpected as well as for bitter disappointment when his plea was finally denied. This denial was made at the very moment when the Russian peasants, in the center of the famine district, although starving, piously abstained from eating the seed grain and said to each other as they scattered it over the ground for their crop of winter wheat; "We must sow the grain although we shall not live to see it sprout."

Did the delegates in the Assembly still retain the national grievances and animosities so paramount when the League of Nations was organized in Paris or where they dominated by a fear and hatred of Bolshevism and a panic lest the feeding of Russian peasants should in some wise [sic] aid the purposes of Lenine's [sic] government? Again I reflected that these men of the Assembly, as other men, were still held apart by suspicion and fear, which could only be quenched by motives lying deeper than those responsible for their sense of estrangement.

This sense of human solidarity for the moment seemed most readily obtained by men leading lives of humble toil and self-denial, as if they might teach a war-weary world that the religious revival which alone would be able to fuse together hostile nations, could never occur unless there were first a conviction of sin, a repentance for the war itself! As long as men contended that the war was "necessary" or "inevitable" the world could not hope for a manifestation of that religious impulse which feeds men solely and only because they are hungry.

A genuine Society of Nations may finally be evolved by millions of the earth's humblest toilers, whose lives are consumed in securing the daily needs of existence for themselves and their families. They go stumbling towards the light of better international relations, driven forward because "Man is constantly seeking a new and finer adjustment between his inner emotional demands and the practical arrangements of the world in which he lives."

Vera Brittain

From "Peace and the Public Mind" (1935)

When we talk of "the public" we really mean the persons who compose it. The so-called "public" is merely an illusion, a will o' the wisp, a vanishing spectre. Mr. Walter Lippmann has called it a "phantom". Professor Dewey describes it as "not only a ghost, but a ghost which walks and talks and obscures, confuses and misleads governmental action in a disastrous way."

On the analogy of Voltaire's famous epigram that the Holy Roman Empire was neither Holy, nor Roman, nor an Empire, it might well be stated that average public opinion "is neither average, nor public, nor an opinion." A "nation, a government, a populace" cannot, as entities, have ideas; it is the men and women constituting these units who do the thinking and make the decisions. The "average mentality" so often discussed in the Press or on platforms can be dismissed as a loose though convenient generalisation for the use of writers and speakers.

The public mind may be roughly described as the sum total of opinions produced by a conglomeration of groups, each composed of like-minded persons. Even between the largest of such groups – men, women, the rich, the poor, the old, the young – the dividing line is often purely artificial. Party political divisions, in spite of their convenient labels, are also notoriously difficult to assess. If we could in fact assess them, we should know beforehand the result of every general election. As it is, elections are largely determined by "floating voters" – those individuals who constantly change their allegiance and are, apparently, permanently open to conviction; who must have voted one way in 1924, another in 1929, and yet another in 1931.

Probably the most trustworthy divisions between groups are those based upon character and intellect; it is possible with reasonable accuracy to describe some people as idealists and others as cynics, some as intelligent and others as stupid. But since idealists, cynics, cowards, heroes, philosophers and dunces are drawn from all ages, all classes and both sexes, we cannot precisely estimate their influence; we have no evidence of the number of persons who share a given quality, and hence cannot base our political assumptions upon so incalculable a factor. Unsatisfactory as are the familiar divisions of men, women, and the rest, we can roughly assume that the members of these groups will to some extent resemble one another because certain traditions and experiences have moulded them which have had less influence, or a different influence, upon others.

We can, for instance, calculate that many women be more deeply affected by such questions as maternal mortality or nursery school education – and therefore by the destructive economies in these fields which follow increased military expenditure – than men who do not experience childbirth or play an intimate part in the rearing of infants. Again, we know that the old are liable to be imprisoned within certain prejudices which, owing to new opportunities or a different educational system, have never operated upon the young. Although it is dangerous to apply generalisations too rigidly and to forget that in any group the individual exceptions are likely to constitute a large minority, practical experience in political work has gone to prove that certain attitudes towards war and peace are on the whole characteristic of certain groups, and that very considerable group differences do exist which must be taken into account when calculating the amount of support that a given project is likely to obtain.

With this tedious but necessary preamble, we can proceed to discuss, first the evidence of support or non-support for a peace policy from the public in general, and secondly, the evidence of support or non-support from certain groups.

To what extent is the general public, in so far as it is articulate at all, behind the peace movement to-day? In seeking the answer to this question, I propose to disregard the various divisions within the movement itself. It has been truly said that the most tragic conflicts in life arise, not between good and evil, but between one good and another. The fact, however, that methods of destruction or reaction are usually simple and obvious, while construction and revolution are faced with a bewildering variety of alternative procedures, is a fundamental difficulty which every progressive movement has had to face. In spite of it, the emancipators of slaves and of women achieved their objects, and the strong civilising impulses which carried them through their controversies to ultimate success are on the side of reason and sanity to-day.

The authors of this book stand for collective security and for the maintenance and improvement of that machinery which, for all its imperfections, represents our sole defence against anarchy. They visualise, as an intermediate step without which it is impossible to proceed to that rational Utopia which all desire, the collective ownership of armaments and the collective enforcement, in the last resort, of sanctions against an aggressor. But every advocate of peace who may differ from them with regard to the application of sanctions or the value of existing international machinery shares their view that a return to competitive armaments and the so-called balance of power could not maintain peace, but would prove, as in the past, an inevitable prelude to war. Beneath all external differences, the peace movement is united by its determination to find some workable alternative to the old destructive system. I shall now try to estimate what support exists for that fundamental endeavour.

Pessimists have pointed within recent years to the declining membership of peace organisations as evidence that the enthusiasm of even "the converted" is waning. Too much attention need not be paid to any such diminution of "paper" supporters. In times of economic depression, subscriptions to voluntary organisations are one of the first avoidable expenses to be cut down, particularly when the process of conversion has been achieved, and propaganda, owing to its very success, no longer provides the same personal stimulus. Some organisations are compensating for a setback in orthodox progress by development in other directions; the League of Nations Union Youth Groups, for example, are likely to prove a more than sufficient substitute for a further increase of mature disciples.

A more accurate estimate of the public attitude may be made from the direction taken by popular reading; from the reactions of audiences, as shown especially by the type of their questions, at public meetings; response made to questionnaires and enquiry campaigns and from the subjects discussed in the letters and conversations of thoughtful persons. To the customary objection that only a small proportion of the population read books, go to meetings and answer questionnaires one can but reply that the world has always been altered by minorities, who drag behind them the large apathetic majorities which are only able to visualise change when it has already been accomplished. This is likely to remain true of even the most democratic societies until that purely hypothetical day when the equalisation of human ability has followed the equalisation of social opportunity.

The four lines of enquiry just indicated suggest that between the two extremes of the politically constructive persons who are consciously trying to build civilisation upon a rational basis, and the obdurate, rigid-minded jingoes whose blindly nationalistic propaganda is hastening the advent of another war, lies a vast middle section of puzzled individuals, conscientious, benevolent, eager to do "right," but genuinely uncertain what course to pursue. Their anxious, bewildered preoccupation with current problems, their hope of finding in books some explanation or panacea for the distressing mysteries of contemporary life, account for the popularity of such informative volumes as *What Would Be The Character of a New War?*, *The Intelligent Man's Way To Prevent War*, and the comprehensive sociological excursions of those modern encyclopædists, Mr. and Mrs. G. D. H. Cole. It also explains the success of some recent publications which have gone over "big," not by appealing to obvious passions and curiosities, or by the grotesque pictures of hysterical sadism characteristic of certain best-selling war-books five or six years ago, but because they have touched some emotion or expressed some anxiety lying latent in individual minds on a large but hitherto unrecognised scale.

Public meetings offer the most direct opportunity of demonstrating anxiety and resolving doubts. At Sir Oswald Mosley's Olympia beargarden, a change from restlessness to quiet attention on the part of the silent section of the audience was noticeable as soon as the speaker began to discuss Fascist proposals for keeping this country at peace. Quite obviously the hope of hearing some new creed, of finding some new inspiration for living, brought many of those quiet, depressed-looking men and women to Olympia, but Sir Oswald's notion of maintaining order "by arming this country to such a point of mail-clad efficiency that at every international council it could dictate to the foreigner" (who apparently is meekly to accept this heaven-born right of the British race to superiority without opposing its claim by anything so heinous as competitive arming), roused no one to enthusiasm but his own obedient Blackshirts.

At less spectacular but more politically effective meetings, public apprehensions appear to run in two or three well-defined directions.

"Recently, the Far Eastern crisis has aroused the gravest doubts and misgivings," writes a peace speaker. "Comparatively few people," he adds, "use it as a peg for destructive criticism of the League system. In fact the simpler audiences seem almost pathetically eager to be assured that this failure will not necessarily mean the end of the post-war efforts to abolish war. Since the withdrawal of Germany from the Disarmament Conference last October, there has been a remarkable increase of interest at meetings. My impression is that large numbers of people, who hitherto have been apathetic about international affairs, have been realising that profoundly significant events are taking place. They come to meetings frankly to find out what is happening and what are the chances of avoiding being dragged into war in the future."

My own experience, at approximately a hundred public meetings in different parts of the country during the past twelve months, has been very similar. Almost without exception the audiences have been larger, more responsive, and more keenly alive to current political problems than they were at similar gatherings in 1923 and 1924. Even when the subjects have been literary rather than political, the discussion following the address has often reflected the universal anxiety about war and peace.

A meeting seldom closes without questions on the Far Eastern crisis, the situation in Germany, our national defence, and the traffic in armaments being raised and debated. An appeal for the abolition of the private manufacture of arms usually arouses applause, and would be supported even more enthusiastically if it were not popularly associated with the unemployment problem. "I do not find any fear or many questions about poison gases," testifies a woman speaker, "but I do find uppermost in everyone's mind and colouring everything the question of unemployment. Armament firms employ many, under ideal conditions as a rule."

Discussions of national defence reveal a widespread conviction – amounting, in certain minds, to a frenzied faith – that our own country is the only one which has disarmed or made any constructive proposals for disarmament. References to the still unfulfilled disarmament clauses of the Treaty of Versailles, or to the comparative record of England, France and Italy at the Disarmament Conference – which very few persons have followed in detail – make little impression upon the popular view of ourselves as a virtuous and peace-loving nation and "the foreigner" as disorderly, aggressive and dangerous. The inaccurate aphorism that "human nature never changes" also presents itself with unfailing regularity, accompanied by a secret reservation that the human nature thus aspersed may be German, or French, or Russian but never British.

The following twelve questions, some or all of which crop up in various forms at every meeting where discussion is held, probably represent the chief sources of anxiety now troubling the conscientious but bewildered section of the public:–

1. Isn't it human nature to fight?
2. What effect would disarmament have on unemployment?
3. How can we safely disarm any more, when we have done all we can and other countries have not followed?
4. Oughtn't we to arm to protect ourselves against attack by Germany (or Russia, or Japan, or France, or whoever is the "guilty nation" of the moment)?
5. Ought we to have kept out of the Great War, and would it ever have happened if England had been properly prepared?
6. Could the League ever really enforce its authority against a Great Power?

7. What's the use of working to make this country back the League when we can't affect what foreigners do?
8. What ought the League to have done to stop Japan going into Manchuria?
9. What does the League cost?
10. Why aren't Russia and America in the League?
11. Is German youth being trained for war?
12. Will England go Fascist like Germany and Italy?

The only reply which satisfies the universal apprehensions embodied by the first eight of these questions is one indicating the possibility of an international police force capable of putting direct pressure upon an aggressor. In the present state of public opinion in England and most certainly elsewhere, any demand for complete disarmament which does not visualise this intermediate stage is likely to play directly into the hands of those who advocate an increase of armaments. So far as the public mind is concerned to-day, the practical alternative does not lie between national war and unilateral disarmament, but between national and international control over the means of defence. An international police force may not appear a very direct route to the Kingdom of Heaven – for some distinguished pacifists it is certainly not direct enough – but many peace-workers closely in touch with public opinion accept it as the only effective method of arresting a new race in armaments which, unless directly challenged, will certainly prevent the Kingdom of Heaven from ever arriving at all.

Helene Stöcker

From "Review of *The Twenty Years' Crisis, 1919–1939* by E. H. Carr" (1940)[36]

If, in a time of blindly burning political passions the quiet but clear voice of a thinker and psychologist were heard, then I would wish it were from the spirit of this book, which is no more necessary than now. This book is dedicated to the creators of the coming peace. But especially after reading with inner approval and satisfaction, thankful for the unfortunately so rare psychological insight and objectivity free from political passions, it is barely possible to hope that the book will have the conserving and preserving effect it should have in the interest of a humanity confused by war and its passions.

The book's publication had been planned for 1937; it went into print in July 1939 and could only appear in late September 1939, by which time the war had broken out. The author did not let this publication date tempt him to hastily insert comments that would create the appearance of a work written after the outbreak of the war.

This reflects a responsible thinker who sees the coming calamity and who, with all the clarity available to him, seeks to temper the violence of blind passions. Will he be heard? The reader who makes an attentive effort to absorb the more than three hundred pages will be grateful for the patience with which Professor Carr attempts to disentangle the convoluted problems evolving around politics, power, and morality; and for the unprejudiced attitude with which he draws his conclusions. One might be tempted to think that it is possible to achieve a more fruitful configuration of world affairs if this spirit were applied in analyzing political science in our schools and universities, in our press, and in our diplomatic offices.

---

[36] Translated from the German by Vanessa Ogle. In Stöcker's papers at the Swarthmore College Peace Collection, there are two versions of the text. This translation combines them by using most of the first version and including crucial passages from the second, revised version.

For centuries, philosophers, great thinkers, researchers, and sociologists have dealt with the problem of state and society and the relationship among states, and the relationship of the individual to the state and society as a science. If we are talking seriously about 'democracy', then the basic traits of this science ought to be the property of every responsible human being. Yet it seems as if this science is only in its infancy. Professor Carr seeks to clarify the two opposed views, which in some ways can only further the progress of mankind through a reconciliation. In general, there is a perpetual struggle between those who imagine they can make the world follow their politics and those who arrange their politics according to the reality of the world. Surrounded by the noise of belligerent explosions, tanks, and bombers perhaps only a few might be inclined to even listen to such a calm voice.

Professor Carr's presentation distinguishes itself by steering clear of any vague utopianism while at the same time it is filled with a deep desire to further the ethical progress of mankind. Carr is entirely aware how difficult it is to realize this. He knows that those who walk around with moral demands without knowing or exploring the conditions under which they can be realized, are not the ones most likely to help bring about the progress of the world.

Only an expert on the political history of the past century and the last twenty years, such as Pofessor Carr, is able to detoxify the atmosphere and to show how similar situations in different countries, with different nations, have always led to similar reactions. He realizes how states only abide by their treaties when they believe that they have to. In the moment where they feel strong enough to rise above the law they will do so with deadly certainty. For example, in 1848, France declared void the treaties that had been imposed in 1815. Russia did the same in 1871 regarding the Straits convention imposed at the end of the Crimean War. Every treaty carries meaning only as long as the specific position and commitment that led to it lasts.

Theodore Roosevelt declared: 'Every nation has the right to dissolve a contract if it considers this to be just, just as it has the right to declare war'. Regarding the violation of Belgian neutrality, Permanent Undersecretary for Foreign Affairs Lord Hardinge declared in 1908, 'If France were to violate Belgian neutrality in a war with Germany, then it appears dubious to me under the current circumstances that we in England would do even so much as lift a finger in order to preserve Belgian neutrality, whereas if Belgian neutrality were violated by Germany it would likely be completely different'.

As long as the sovereignty of individual states is valid, every state will reserve for itself the right to place its vital interests beyond the formal law.

In order to limit the unilateral dissolution of treaties by force to a minimum, which so easily leads to belligerent embroilments, 'peaceful change' would have to be exercised to a much greater degree. This was meant to happen at the League of Nations. It is the allied powers' great and fateful sin of omission in 1918/19 that they hardly made any use of this means to prevent war. For example, if the short chapter on peaceful change alone had entered the conscience of political leaders of all countries and the press outlets sponsored by them a little more clearly, it might have indeed been possible to prevent the disaster of this deep destruction of Europe.

Carr reminds us that in his *Reflections on the Revolution in France* even such a conservative thinker as Burke claimed that, 'A state without the means for change is simultaneously also without means for preservation'. And Marx wrote in 1853 with regard to the Eastern Question: 'It is powerlessness that expresses itself in the only proposition: the maintenance of the status quo. This general conviction, that a state of affairs which arose from coincidence and special circumstances, is maintained doggedly, is proof of bankruptcy, an admission by leading powers that they are entirely unable to advance the cause of progress and civilization'. The English historian Gilbert Murray says the same in slightly different words: 'War does not always emerge from mere malice or foolishness. It often simply stems from growth and movement, as mankind cannot stand still'.

The distinction between war of aggression and war of self-defense is therefore misleading, according to Carr. If change is necessary and desirable, then the use of violence or the threat of violence for the maintenance of the status quo can be more culpable than the use of violence for the purpose of changing the current state.

Few people today think that the actions of the American colonists that in 1776 attacked the status quo with violence, or the Irish who sought to change the status quo with violence between 1916 and 1920, were less moral than those of the British who defended the status quo with violence. Morally, the telltale sign is not whether violence is aggressive or defensive but in the nature of the changes sought or resisted. 'Without rebellion, mankind would stagnate and the injustice would be irreparable', stated Bertrand Russell.

Few serious thinkers today are of the opinion that it is always and under all conditions wrong to start a revolution, and it is equally difficult to think that it is always and under all circumstances wrong to start a war. War and revolution are undesirable in and of themselves. It is precisely the challenge of peaceful change to bring about desirable transformation in national politics without revolution and in international politics without war.

In a wealth of examples especially from the history of the past century, Professor Carr shows us the actions that have characterized politics. The task is to find that narrow path between fruitless utopianism on the one side and reckless realism on the other, leading to a higher form of international relations.

In light of Carr's superior clarity, the reader experiences great regret at the fact that the occupations of politician and statesman – those responsible for the fate of the majority of people – are often filled with people whose historical knowledge and philosophical–psychological insight is no match for the enormous task that they have to meet.

[...]

In and of itself it is to be welcomed that in some countries in their despair over the present, many well-known personalities are preoccupied with the question of how to build a better world after the end of the war.

Professor Carr's work shies away from all exuberance, from any all too lofty design for the future. But he does something that might be much more fruitful and necessary: through a thorough and sober investigation that nevertheless is sustained by a deep love for a humane and dignified design of our international relations, he tries to lay the foundations that can truly carry weight, and on which a better and more harmonious design of international relations between peoples can be built.

I believe that nobody in these months of blind, hate-filled passions obscuring our vision can engage with this book without being deeply grateful to the author for his research, his insights, and his comforting sense of justice.

'Tell me, where is that justice which is love with open eyes?' says Nietzsche. A hint of this justice and love for mankind pervades this book.

Edith Sampson

From "Address by the Hon. Mrs. Edith Sampson" (1952)

[...] I am, as you see, an enthusiastic believer in the United Nations. I believe in its objectives. I believe in what it has done and is doing. I believe in what it *can* do.

My talk today has been entitled *A Record of Performance*.

Well, I like that title. I like action. I like seeing things *done*.

Some of you have heard, no doubt, the United Nations accused of being too windy. "Talk, talk, talk, that is all you do" some people grumble.

Well, we do talk. I will have to admit that. In fact, I have never been in a place where such a volume of words poured out so continuously in so many languages. We talk in the assembly. We talk in committee meetings. We talk, among ourselves, in the corridors, on the streets, in the dining halls. And then we go back to our hotels and talk some more.

But the United Nations does not stop there. And that talk has meaning. It is the prelude which leads to action. So I am going to talk tonight about what the United Nations has *done ... Its record of performance.*

It is a record of which I am proud. It is one of which you, all Americans, can be proud. All of us have had a part in it. The United Nations, as my fellow-delegate, Mrs. Franklin Roosevelt, said recently, is not and can not be any greater than the nations of which it is composed. And those nations can be great only if their people are great. I think Americans have been great.

Whatever the United Nations has done *you* have done. You have had a part in it.

And what has it done?

Let us go back to the *reason* for the United Nations. What was, and is, its *first objective?*

The Charter states that objective very clearly.

"... to save succeeding generations from the scourge of war."

Most of the men and women who wrote those words had, twice in their lifetimes, seen world war bring "untold sorrow" to mankind. They were determined to prevent a repetition of that tragedy.

The United Nations was established not just to *talk* about preventing war but to *do* it.

And on this the United Nations had today a clear record of performance.

Let us look at that record.

Fighting has been stopped in Palestine, in Indonesia, in India, peaceful settlements have been attained in Syria, Lebanon, and Iran.

The nations, in each of these cases, are settling their differences by peaceful means. The disputes have *not* exploded into general war.

Each was a test case. The United Nations met the test.

The greatest challenge of the United Nations, of course, has been the aggression launched against the Republic of South Korea.

Secretary of State Acheson, talking last week before the Assembly, put it this way:

"It is in Korea that the whole structure of collective security is meeting its supreme test. It will stand or fall upon what we do there."

Let us make no mistake here. Korea is important. Just how important can be judged from a report picked up by American intelligence in North Korea after the trouble started. The report has to do with a speech made by a "red" army officer to his troops several months before the attack. He said:

"In order to successfully undertake the long awaited world revolution we must first unify Asia ... Java, Indochina, Malaya, India, Tibet, Thailand, The Philippines and Japan are our ultimate targets."

Another North Korean officer said:

"Our forces are scheduled to attack South Korea ... The attack marks the first step toward the liberation of Asia."

Note the communist double talk. Liberate, indeed. Ask the peoples of the unhappy nations *now* under the heel of the Kremlin what their liberation by the communists has meant. Ask the millions of helpless souls dying today in Soviet slave labor camps.

But the United Nations acted, and as a result that "first step" failed.

My own conviction is that Korea marked a turning point in world history. No one can say with certainty, of course, but I believe by the action taken ... promptly, decisively ... the United Nations prevented a whole series of similar aggressions, the other steps of which that "red"

officer spoke. Those steps would *inevitably* have led to world war ...
World War III with all its sure horrors.

Having failed to win their objective by force, the communist imperialists turned to negotiation. It is 15 months since the truce talks started.
Those talks have dragged on, wearily, tediously.

It has become increasingly obvious during the talks, first at Kaesong
and later at Panmunjom, that the communists hope to salvage victory
through trickery. They have assumed that the United Nations would
make almost any concession to bring the fighting to an end.

It has required patience and firmness to carry on the struggle for peace
against the determination of those "would be" world conquerors. But it
is, we believe, and I think you will agree, worth anything it takes. The
goal we seek, as the late President Roosevelt said, is freedom from fear.
Until that goal is attained there can be *no* security in the world for any
nation or any people.

The record of the United Nations in maintaining peace and dealing with
aggression is not perfect. But it *is* good. If it had not acted at the danger
points I have mentioned the fires of disputes and local conflicts might have
spread. I can almost say that they *would* have spread. Experience ... bitter
experience ... has taught the world that the time to stop general war is in
the *early* stages. Not when it has burst into flame throughout the world.

Military adventurers have always enjoyed certain advantages in dealing
with truly peace-loving peoples. They play upon the deep-seated yearn-
ings of those peoples to avoid war at all ... almost all ... costs. They
exploit the conviction that war, and everything pertaining to war, is a
wicked waste of human and material resources.

Hitler followed that pattern. With what results you know.

Today the wish-thought of many people to escape the hard necessity of
building their defences and uniting for security is being again exploited in
the name of "peace". But we know from bitter experience that weakness
and division invite war. We know that they encourage aggressors to
believe that they can succeed. That their victims love peace and comfort
so much that they will bow even to slavery rather than resist.

Said Secretary Acheson:

"Korea is a test, not only of our courage at the initial moment of decision, but
even more of the firmness of our will, the *endurance* of our courage. The
aggressor, having defied the United Nations and lost, having found himself
pushed back behind his initial line of attack, now counts for victory upon those
of faint heart who grow weary of the struggle."

Well, we, the peace-loving people, are *not* faint hearted. We are not
growing weary.

Mr. Acheson, as you know, was followed in the Assembly a few days later by the Soviet delegate, Mr. Vishinsky.

I sat through that talk. It was some 70-odd minutes long and little more than a rehash of everything the communists have been saying the past three or four years. The statements were fantastic. Incredible. Hitler made great use of the technique of the "big lie" but the Soviets are improving on him.

We are, Mr. Vishinsky says, imperialist warmongers. *We* started the trouble in Korea! Yes, he did say that. Imagine. *We* have bungled the negotiations at Panmunjom! We ... well, it was the same old theme song.

Mr. Vishinsky went through his routine. He said the same things. He made the same old gestures, in the same old places. Later I talked to a number of the delegates. The reaction was "Oh well, he has to say those things. He has his orders."

In a totalitarian system one *does* obey orders. It is that, or else.

Our danger, and this Mr. Vishinsky indicated he knew very well, is that we might grow weary of the struggle. Mind you, I don't believe we will but the danger is *there*.

We have to guard against it.

This year, in the Assembly, the *will* to peace of the peace-loving nations had been made sharply manifest. The United States, separately and in conjunction with the United Kingdom and France, has again offered the United Nations a realistic disarmament proposal by which the possibility of aggression can be reduced and ultimately erased.

It may sound impractical to talk of disarmament at this time.

But that talk *is* important. It builds a foundation for the peace we seek.

It prepares the *blueprints* of the type of peaceful world we want.

And, by presenting this proposal, we and our colleagues, have forced the aggressor minded nations to play *their* hand. They have had to come forward with a program.

The soviet program is phony. Make no mistake about *that*. It is designed to deceive and mislead. It hopes, again, to play upon the sincere yearning of the peace-loving peoples.

The Soviets, for example, lay great stress upon piece-meal pledges not to use this weapon or that weapon. Their idea, it seems, is that we should regulate how wars should be fought. Not stop them.

The regulations, of course, are all to the advantage of the Soviets.

In answer the United States has reminded the Assembly that all members of the United Nations, in signing the Charter, pledged themselves to refrain from aggression in any form and with any weapons.

Last week Secretary Acheson, speaking for the United States, reaffirmed that pledge. He said:

"We make the pledge absolutely specific. We will not commit aggression with rifles or machine guns or tanks. We will not commit aggression with atomic bombs or any other kind of bombs. We will not commit aggression with chemical weapons or bacteriological weapons ... we will not commit aggression with *any* weapons or by any means.

"We reaffirm *for all the world to hear* that pursuant to our solemn commitment under the charter, we pledge ... not just that we will avoid the use of one weapon or another ... but that we will not use any form of force contrary to the charter."

I wish you, all of you, could have been in the assembly hall when he made that statement. It was an impressive moment. I personally, thrilled with pride ... pride in being an American and a member of the U.S. Delegation. It was a grand sensation.

We, in the United States, do not insist that this is the only road to peace.

We offer it only for consideration by other genuine peace-loving peoples. Some day, I solemnly believe, some such proposal will be accepted.

The great danger lies in the fact that the Soviets have a wish-thought too. They *want* to believe that we, the hard-pressed peace-loving peoples of the world, will become weak and confused. They look for dissension and weariness. That is the background of their phony "peace" campaigns. They seek to weaken us by neutralizing the power of the people. A democratic policy, remember, *must* have the understanding support of the masses. The whole effort of the United Nations to build a system of collective security and from there on to work for disarmament depends upon the clear thinking and determination of *all* the free peoples. [...]

8

World Economy
Introduction by Patricia Owens

In *International Political Economy: An Intellectual History*, Benjamin J. Cohen argued that a "magnificent seven" individuals shaped the modern discipline of "IPE" when, in reaction to the turmoil of the Oil Crisis of 1973, it was founded as a separate academic subfield of International Relations (IR) within Political Science.[1] On this account, IPE was a necessary and belated unification of political–economic thought after the historical separation between the academic disciplines of Political Science and Economics. But as with the omissions and erasures that characterize IR's more general disciplinary history so with IPE. In dating its beginning to the 1970s, numerous women inter-national economic thinkers are easily erased from the history of thought on the world economy. International economy is a field so fundamental to understanding international relations that it ought to be thought ludicrous that the earliest woman to be reckoned with is Susan Strange, one of the "magnificent seven," who both founded IPE in Britain and co-founded the British International Studies Association.

With one exception, most of the works selected here can be under-stood as examples of "white women's" international economic thought, and all are drawn largely from thinkers with advanced academic training, most often at the London School of Economics. Most figures were middle or upper class and were activist intellectuals or academics; some primarily working inside academe, others beginning their career inside the academy and re-joining after diplomatic or other public service; one began her career as a journalist and another, the first woman to be hired to an IR department, left academe to follow her husband and never returned. These thinkers encompass the ideological range from Marxist analyses of imperialism to liberal and "realist" readings of the relation between states and markets, from development economics to one of the earliest formulations for a "developing economy" of what is now referred

---

[1] Benjamin J. Cohen, *International Political Economy: An Intellectual History* (Princeton, NJ: Princeton University Press, 2008).

to as "neoliberalism." Selections address subjects ranging across the economic origins of imperialism, the colonial organization of Chinese indentured labor, international labor legislation, international banking, multinational corporations, the "coming serfdom" in India, and the economic consequences of Britain's imperial decline.

We begin with the only historical woman other than Susan Strange afforded partial recognition in histories of international thought. Rosa Luxemburg (1871–1919) was born into an assimilated Polish-Jewish family in the Russian Empire, living in exile in Switzerland from the age of eighteen, then in Germany. She split from the Social Democratic Party over its support for the First World War, forming the Spartacist League and later becoming a founding member of the German Communist Party. A revolutionary and activist intellectual, Luxemburg developed and disseminated her ideas in the service of the working class as the universal class, opposing national self-determination, including Zionism, even as a stepping-stone to socialism. Though she earned a doctorate from the University of Zurich, she worked without the security of an academic position. She was imprisoned multiple times and murdered by members of the rightwing paramilitary Freikorps during Germany's post-First World War revolution that toppled the German Empire and established the Weimar Republic. She was forty-seven.[2]

Luxemburg is recognized as a leading Marxist theoretician at the forefront of thinking on the intersection between capitalism and international relations. Her original analysis of capitalism's fundamental and violent dependency on non-capitalist territories and modes of labor underpinned her analysis of early capitalism, the late-nineteenth-century scramble for Africa, the causes of the First World War, and ultimately capitalism's "final phase ... as a period of catastrophes" (425). Without doubt, Luxemburg is a canonical thinker.[3] Yet, her reception in Marxist circles, including within international theory, has been muted despite the originality and significance of her work. This is due partly to sexism but also to intra-ideological factionalism within Marxism itself.

---

[2] For contextual and biographical analysis see J. P. Nettl, *Rosa Luxemburg* (Oxford: Oxford University Press, 1969); Elżbieta Ettinger, *Rosa Luxemburg: A Life* (London: George G. Harrap & Co., 1987). For a collection of substantial excerpts from the widest range of Luxemburg's writings, including on political economy, imperialism, and non-Western societies, see Peter Hudis and Kevin B. Anderson (eds.), *The Rosa Luxemburg Reader* (London: Monthly Review, 2004).

[3] Kimberly Hutchings, "Revolutionary Thinking: Luxemburg's Socialist International Theory," in Patricia Owens and Katharina Rietzler (eds.), *Women's International Thought: A New History* (Cambridge: Cambridge University Press, 2021), 52–71.

We have chosen a selection from Luxemburg's 1913 masterwork, *The Accumulation of Capital*, in which she described late-nineteenth-century imperialism as a product of leading capitalist states competing over the remaining non-capitalist spheres. For neo-mercantilists, such as Lilian Knowles, late-nineteenth-century imperialism emerged from the competition between national-imperial states. For Luxemburg, deeper economic structures explained the rush to imperialism: the antagonistic and competitive struggle for markets and investments in non-capitalist territories only commenced once capitalism was securely established in the major European states, when the owners of the means of production had fully appropriated property and extracted surplus value; "protective tariffs" were the "basis for, and supplement to, the imperialist military system" (429).

Luxemburg insisted that the period of free trade in the 1860s and 1870s was "a fleeting episode in the history of capital accumulation," but one which nonetheless became the basis for the liberal ideological trope of the "harmony of interests" (427). The period of so-called "free trade" was one of enormous violence; markets were brutally forced open in China, Egypt, and south, southwest, and north Africa. Luxemburg refused to assimilate "capital's thunderous shows of force" into "more or less contingent expressions of 'foreign policy'" (429). She thus provided the basis for a distinctly Marxist analysis of the unity between the capitalist economy and the states system, where "violence, fraud, oppression, and plunder are displayed quite openly" (429). Where so-called "realist" approaches isolate international relations as a sphere of "foreign policy" from the economic processes internal to capitalism (class domination masked by the language of freedom and rights), Luxemburg argued that spheres of interest, war, and colonial policy were intimately related to class exploitation on a global level.

It is possible to read our second selection, an analysis of the foreign competition over indentured Chinese "coolie" emigrant labor in the middle of the nineteenth century, as empirical evidence for Luxemburg's claims about the violence of early capitalist global economy. Though surprisingly absent in most histories of the field, immigration was a central international economic question in the late nineteenth and early twentieth centuries and features later in this volume. As in the previous discussion of geopolitics, the international economy of labor was analyzed in a context dominated by racial anxieties about non-white immigration. This is the context for Persia Campbell's (1898–1974) *Chinese Coolie Emigration to Countries within the British Empire*, published in 1923. The research for the book was carried out at the LSE under the supervision of Lilian Knowles, Britain's first full-time lecturer in Economic History and, with Eileen Power, prefigures the field of global economic history by almost a century. Both Knowles and Power appear elsewhere in this volume.[4]

Born to a middle-class family in Australia, Campbell was educated at the University of Sydney, moving to the United States, via postgraduate work at the LSE and Columbia. Campbell's politics were Fabian socialist and feminist, but not so radical as to prevent her combining an academic career with involvement in some of the leading international governmental and non-governmental organizations of her day. She received a Rockefeller fellowship for a study of immigration to the United States and was a member of the Rockefeller-funded Institute for Pacific Relations. She was active in the American Association of University Women, an advisor at the American delegation to the Food and Agricultural Organization at the UN, and served on President Lyndon Johnson's national advisory committee on international trade negotiations. In the late 1960s, she wrote for *International Development Review*, a United Nations journal, and in the early 1970s she was a delegate to the UN Conference on the Human Environment.

Campbell's first book analyzed debt-bondage, effectively the debt-slavery system that brought Chinese indentured labor to the British West Indies, a process referred to as "the buying and selling of pigs" (434). The emancipation of slaves in 1833 led to labor shortages on the West Indies sugar plantations; and the Sugar Act of 1846, which equalized duties on foreign and colonial sugar, caused further economic crisis. After the loss of their (human) "property," colonial planters not only insisted on "economic justice" (for themselves); they demanded more labor which, if necessary, should be introduced to the colony by force. Campbell was sympathetic toward Edward Stanley, Secretary of State to the Colonies. In contrast to most planters, he expressed concern for the welfare of Chinese laborers. Yet, British administrators and firms at the treaty ports licensed and oversaw a system that was comparable to slavery. Campbell described in some detail the process of recruitment, in which brokers received money for each individual delivered to the port, who was then restrained before they could flee. "A promise of lucrative work to the half-starved coolies was usually sufficient to get

---

[4] Kirsten Madden and Robert W. Dimond (eds.), *The Routledge Handbook of the History of Women's Economic Thought* (London: Routledge, 2018) does not exclusively focus on world economy questions but contains essays on historical women working on thinking about empire, development finance, and international development.

them … onto the receiving ships, from which it was difficult to escape … The 'pigs', recruited by debt, deceit, or argument, were conveyed by the brokers to 'pig-pens'" (434). The British government outlawed the "coolie" trade in 1916, given its dependence on the support and manual labor of over 100,000 Chinese workers during the First World War.

At the end of the First World War, the internationalization of labor legislation was forced onto the peace-making agenda by the increasing power of organized labour. "Revolution," as Lilian Friedländer put it, "was in the air, and the statesmen feared that any day the tide of Bolshevism might sweep in from the east" (437). Friedländer was the first woman to teach in a university department of International Politics, from 1924, three years before Lucy Philip Mair began teaching at the LSE, as discussed in the first section of this anthology. Indeed, for the academic year preceding E. H. Carr's arrival to the Woodrow Wilson Chair in 1936, Friedländer was in sole charge of lecturing on International Politics in Aberystwyth, University of Wales.[5] Born in London to a Jewish family from Königsberg, East Prussia, she received her BSc in Political Science at London; became a research fellow and assistant lecturer in Aberystywth in 1924; and was awarded fellowships from the Carnegie Endowment and Rockefeller Foundation. When Friedländer returned to Aberystwyth, she worked under her married name, Lilian Vránek, alongside her husband Jiří, who attended the British Coordinating Committee of the second International Studies Conference in 1932. In 1935, Jiří resigned to take up a post at the International Institute of Intellectual Cooperation in Paris. The following year, Lilian left Aberystwyth to join her husband and did not return to academe. She worked for the British Embassy in Rome, for which she received an MBE in 1968.[6] The Department in Aberystwyth awards the Lilian Friedländer Prize for postgraduate Masters' work.

Friedländer researched both the admission of "new states" to the League and technical cooperation in the field of labor regulation. Here we have selected her writing on the internationalization of labor legislation in response to the success of labor movements in forcing "industrial

---

[5] There is a brief discussion of Friedländer in Brian Porter, "E. H. Carr – the Aberystwyth Years, 1936–47," in Michael Cox (ed.), *E. H. Carr: A Critical Appraisal* (London: Palgrave, 2000), 36–67. With their brother, the philanthropists Gwendoline and Margaret Davis used their inherited wealth to co-fund IR's first Professorship, the Woodrow Wilson Chair at Aberystwyth.

[6] In Britain, membership of the "Most Excellent Order of the British Empire" (MBE) is an award within the "honours system."

questions" onto the international agenda.[7] The newly formed International Labour Organization (ILO) dealt with, among other matters, minimum standards concerning child and immigrant labor, the length of the working day, unemployment, accidents, and social insurance. The United States joined the ILO, but not the League. Yet agreeing and enforcing minimum standards at the Commission on International Labour Legislation was a difficult task, made more so by the federal character of the United States. Friedländer compared the problem of regulating labor standards in the US and the ILO itself, where in both the "relics of the theory of sovereignty have strayed from the realms of pure political science into an economic field where they are more than ever meaningless and cumbersome" (441). Friedländer's article was published the year of the Wall Street Crash and the onset of the Great Depression, after which the political theory of sovereignty seemed less a relic than a useful political fiction.

Eleanor Lansing Dulles's (1895–1989) first book, written in the wake of the 1929 Wall Street Crash, and based on her Radcliffe College PhD, was a study of the runaway inflation of the French Franc in the 1920s, a work John Maynard Keynes called "the best book on monetary inflation that I know."[8] Eleanor was a so-called "dowager of one of America's best-known political families"; her grandfather, uncle, and brother were secretaries of state; another brother directed the CIA.[9] Eleanor was clearly born into the US governing elite, but her own intellectual credentials were excellent. Before the Radcliffe PhD in 1926, she studied at Bryn Mawr, the Sorbonne, and the LSE, where she worked "under Beveridge" and "took tea with Sydney and Beatrice Webb."[10] She taught economics at Bryn Mawr and the University of Pennsylvania and was a leading member of the US delegation to Bretton Woods. Her most celebrated government service was overseeing Germany's economic reconstruction after the Second World War. As a Dulles, she benefited from her name and connections, but she was also culled from the State

---

[7] International and industrial relations were closely linked. Montague Burton had endowed professorships in both these fields. The Montague Burton Professorship in Industrial Relations was endowed at the universities of Cambridge and Leeds in 1930, the same year that the Montague Burton Professorship in International Relations was endowed at Oxford.

[8] Leonard Mosley, *Dulles: A Biography of Eleanor, Allen and John Foster Dulles and Their Family Network* (New York: The Dial Press/James Wade, 1978), 84.

[9] Jacqueline Trescott, "A Most Determined Eleanor Lansing Dulles," *The Washington Post*, April 24, 1980. Dulles published her memoir in 1980. Eleanor Lansing Dulles, *Eleanor Lansing Dulles, Chances of a Lifetime: A Memoir* (Upper Saddle River, NJ: Prentice Hall, 1980).

[10] Mosley, *Dulles*, 69.

Department when her brother, Allen Foster, mishandled the covert invasion of Cuba at the Bay of Pigs in 1962. Leaving government service, Dulles taught international economics at Duke and Georgetown and wrote numerous works on Cold War international relations.[11]

Here we include a selection from Dulles's first book, *The Bank for International Settlements at Work*, which was published in 1932 under the auspices of the Harvard-Radcliffe Bureau of International Research, discussed in the first section of this anthology. Analyzing its history, origins, and economic and legal structure, as well as the wider international financial context in which it was established, Dulles identified the Bank for International Settlements (BIS) as a revolutionary institution. New economic theory was required to understand and structure the Bank's operations. The BIS, established in 1930 and still in operation, was initially created by financiers as a "bankers club," a bank joining together central bankers to coordinate reparations payments and oversee emergency aid. But following the end of the gold standard after 1931, the BIS became a different type of organization, seeking to ensure the financial and monetary stability of the global capitalist economy itself. While recognizing the limits of the Bank's influence on "interest rates, credit, foreign exchange rates, and gold movements," Dulles defended the Bank against accusations of being "weak and selfish"; such critiques were based on the "exaggerated hopes" of the Paris Peace Conference (444). She identified the central role international economic institutions would play in twentieth-century world politics.

Like Campbell and Dulles, Ursula K. Webb's (1896–1985) interest in economics led her to enrol at the LSE, where she received her doctorate in 1935. Born in Dublin to a prominent Quaker family, she was privately educated in England, studied History at Somerville College, Oxford, and for a time taught at the Workers' Educational Association, which was founded in 1903 as the education arm of the labor movement. After marrying John Hicks, Ursula K. Hicks resigned her lectureship at the LSE to follow her husband to a fellowship at Cambridge, and then to Manchester and finally Oxford. John Hicks's entry in the *Dictionary of National Biography* makes no mention of Ursula's work; only that "she protected him and organized their lives."[12] Yet, she was a prolific writer

---

[11] J. R. Hicks, U. K. Hicks, and L. Rostas, *The Taxation of War Wealth* (Oxford: Clarendon Press, 1941); Ursula Kathleen Hicks, *Development from Below: Local Government and Finance in Developing Countries of the Commonwealth* (Oxford: Clarendon Press, 1961); Ursula Kathleen Hicks, *Development Finance: Planning and Control* (Oxford: Clarendon Press, 1965).

[12] R. C. O. Matthews, "Hicks, Sir John Richard," *Oxford Dictionary of National Biography*, September 23, 2004.

and advisor to governments on economic and fiscal policy, holding a University Lectureship in Public Finance in Oxford for eighteen years and visiting positions in Chicago, Harvard, Delhi, Osaka, Buenos Aires, Northwestern, Purdue, and the Australian National University. Her 1947 *Public Finance* was seminal and published in several editions. Here we include a selection of Hicks's writing on "development economics," that branch of colonial administration and later IPE that sought to understand and intervene in the colonized and later postcolonial and neo-colonial economies.

Hicks's interest in development began in the 1950s with lectures in New Delhi, followed by advisory work in Nigeria, Malaysia, the Caribbean, Iran, and the World Bank, and involvement in what has been described as "the rather unique husband-and-wife Commission on Taxation in Jamaica."[13] In 1961, she published *Development from Below*, focused on the role of local government, followed by *Development Finance: Planning and Control* in 1965. In the 1957 essay we excerpt, "Learning about Economic Development," Hicks argues that the unprecedented interest in this new field was the result of a "desire to raise the standard of the economically and socially backward countries" (447); an "interest ... aroused largely on humanitarian grounds. It is the same sort of instinct which sent [young people's] fathers and mothers slumming or out on missionary work" (448). As with Elizabeth Monroe, discussed in the section on Geopolitics and War, imperial and postcolonial hierarchy and interests are sublimated, with the emphasis on the good intentions of development economists themselves. The academic organization of colonial economic knowledge is indicated by Hicks's association with Oxford's Institute of Commonwealth Studies, which was formerly the Institute of Colonial Studies led by Margery Perham, and subsequently amalgamated with the Institute for Agricultural Economics and the International Development Centre to become the Oxford Department of International Development.

Hicks's major intellectual influences were John Maynard Keynes and her husband, John Hicks, who won the 1972 Nobel Prize for Economics. But, of course, the other main strand of economic thinking that dominated the early- to mid-twentieth-century LSE is associated with the so-called "Austrian School," promulgated by, among others, Friedrich von

---

[13] Wilfred L. David, "Introduction," in Wilfred L. David (ed.), *Public Finance, Planning and Economic Development: Essays in Honour of Ursula Hicks* (London: Macmillan, 1973), xiii; also see Lucy Brilliant, "Ursula Hicks' and Vera Lutz's Contributions to Development Finance," in Kirsten Madden and Robert W. Dimond (eds.), *The Routledge Handbook of the History of Women's Economic Thought* (London: Routledge, 2018), 341–357.

Hayek, winner of the 1974 Nobel Prize in Economics, who taught at the LSE from 1931 to 1950. Opposing any form of planned economy as an unjustified and dangerous infringement on the spontaneous economic order generated by individual economic action and innovation, the Austrian School is one of the intellectual progenitors of what is now commonly referred to as neoliberalism. Despite the scale of interest in this "ism," including work on the global intellectual history of neoliberalism, this work has all but ignored Sudha Shenoy (1943–2008). Yet she claimed "the longest connection to the Austrian movement of anybody ever," she attended the 1974 conference in South Royalton, Vermont, where the contemporary historical resurgence of the Austrian School is said to have begun, and her intellectual work prefigured the contemporary neoliberal transformation of India.[14] Born in India, Shenoy received her PhD at the LSE, where her father, B. R. Shenoy (1905–1978), a member of the Mont Pelerin Society, also studied with Hayek. Though her research focused primarily on India, Shenoy also contributed to the history of economic thought, compiling and introducing a selection of Hayek's writings, *A Tiger by the Tail: The Keynesian Legacy of Inflation*, a work described as "as much Shenoy's book as it is Hayek's."[15] She worked at the Ludwig von Mises Institute, was a Research Assistant at Oxford's Institute of Commonwealth Studies, and in the early 1970s became a Lecturer in Economics at the University of Newcastle in New South Wales.

Here we excerpt Shenoy's 1966 essay "The Coming Serfdom in India," the title a play on Hayek's 1944 *The Road to Serfdom*. It was published in *The Freeman*, a libertarian magazine of the Foundation for Economic Education published between 1950 and 2016. The essay draws a distinction between two types of liberals, "advocates of liberty" and "statists." The former are the "true" liberals because they understand that freedom is indivisible. It is not enough to have free elections if the conditions of economic freedom are strangled by the political

---

[14] "The Global Perspective: An Interview with Sudha Shenoy," *Austrian Economics Newsletter*, 23:4 (2003), 1. Cf. Quinn Slobodian, *Globalists: The End of Empire and the Birth of Neoliberalism* (Princeton, NJ: Princeton University Press, 2018); David Harvey, *A Brief History of Neoliberalism* (Oxford: Oxford University Press, 2005). For a discussion see Giandomenica Becchio, "Austrian School Women Economists," in Kirsten Madden and Robert W. Dimond (eds.), *The Routledge Handbook of the History of Women's Economic Thought* (London: Routledge, 2018), 309–324.

[15] Joseph T. Salerno, "Introduction to the Third Edition," in *A Tiger by the Tail: A 40-Years' Running Commentary on Keynesianism by Hayek*, 3rd ed. (London: The Institute of Economic Affairs, 2009 [1972]), xiii. See Sudha Shenoy, "The Debate, 1931–1971," in *A Tiger by the Tail: A 40-Years' Running Commentary on Keynesianism by Hayek*, 3rd ed. (London: The Institute of Economic Affairs, 2009 [1972]), 1–14.

intervention of the state. The concentration of economic power in the hands of state administrators is a form of political exploitation, "the politically strong exploiting the politically weak" (453).[16] In India, Shenoy argued, state-led economic planning, particularly preferential treatment for the industrial sector, consolidated the oligarchic power of ruling-party officials, civil servants, and favored businessmen. Government-sanctioned industrial production enriched those able to reap the rewards of private monopolies or protected internal markets at the expense of "the starving, ill-clothed, and unsheltered Indian masses" (453). The consolidation of economic power in the hands of the government, and government-dependent businesses, hindered the development of political opposition. Foreign aid from the industrialized West only made things worse. "Given in order to 'feed starving orphans in Orissa' ... or to 'keep India from going communist' ..., it is in fact one major cause why orphans in Orissa are starving and why India is now so firmly set down the road to serfdom" (455).

International economic development, emerging out of colonial economic administration, was included among the fields encompassed within the British International Studies Association established in 1975. Edith Penrose (1914–1996) was instrumental in establishing development studies at the LSE and SOAS and was one of the six speakers at the 1975 inaugural British International Studies Conference held at Oxford. Penrose was born in Los Angeles, studying at UC-Berkeley, then Johns Hopkins, where she received her PhD and later taught and researched.[17] She crossed academe and policy worlds with ease, from assisting Eleanor Roosevelt at the UN Human Rights Commission to advising international tribunals on the oil industry. Appalled by the McCarthyite treatment of her colleague and friend Owen Lattimore – accused of spying for the Soviets and complicity in the so-called "loss of China" – Penrose and her husband quit the United States. They pursued academic careers first in Australia, then in Iraq, but were expelled after the 1958 Iraqi Revolution, eventually settling in Britain. Her most influential work was *The Theory of the Growth of the Firm*, considered one of the most influential works of economics in the second half of the twentieth century. She co-edited *New Orientations: Essays in International Relations* (1970) and co-wrote *Iraq: International Relations and National Development* (1978).[18]

---

[16] The essay appears online at https://fee.org/articles/the-coming-serfdom-in-india/.

[17] For contextual and biographical information see Angela Penrose, *No Ordinary Woman: The Life of Edith Penrose* (Oxford: Oxford University Press, 2018).

[18] Edith Penrose, Ernest Penrose, and Peter Lyon (eds.), *New Orientations: Essays in International Relations* (London: Cass, 1970). Her other works include Edith Penrose, *The Economics of the International Patent System* (Baltimore, MD: Johns Hopkins

Here we excerpt a passage from Edith Penrose's *The Large International Firm in Developing Countries: The International Petroleum Industry*, published in 1968, a synthesis of economics, politics, and history. At the end of the Second World War, the world's crude-oil reserves were under the control of seven international corporations colluding to ensure high prices. However, by the 1950s, there was a new story to tell of major structural transformation in the global economy: the increasing power of the crude-oil-producing countries themselves. In telling the story of the international petroleum industry in historical and comparative detail, Penrose offered what one reviewer described as "the raw material and direction for a new theoretical approach to international economic relations ... Few books in the currently arid field of international economics can claim as much."[19] Penrose showed the confluence of international political and economic forces shaping oil prices and the prospects for international regulation of the industry. "The deeper root of the problem," she argued, "is simply that international firms, including the oil Companies, have not yet found a way of operating in the modern world which would make them generally acceptable as truly international institutions."[20]

We conclude this section with easily the most influential figure in late-twentieth-century British IR, not just international political economy, and perhaps the only academic figure in this volume who has received their due recognition as an international thinker. Susan Strange achieved this standing while raising six children and only publishing her first book, excerpted here, at the age of forty-eight. Indeed, had she not entered academe, taken up acting, comedy or painting – "and had no children" – she claimed, "I would also have dearly liked to be an independent newspaper columnist."[21] Like Elizabeth Wiskemann, she began her professional career as a journalist. She was editorial assistant at *The Economist*, where she worked with foreign editor Barbara Ward, and then White House correspondent for *The Observer*, at the time one of the most

University Press, 1951); Edith Penrose and Ernest Penrose, *Iraq: International Relations and National Development* (London: E. Benn Publishers, 1978).

[19] Robin Murray, "Review of *The Large International Firm in Developing Countries: The International Petroleum Industry* by Edith T. Penrose," *International Affairs*, 45:3 (1969): 517.

[20] Edith Penrose, *The Large International Firm in Developing Countries: The International Petroleum Industry* (London: Allen & Unwin, 1968), 263.

[21] Susan Strange, "I Never Meant to Be an Academic," in Joseph Kruzel and James N. Rosenau (eds.), *Journeys through World Politics: Autobiographical Reflections of Thirty-Four Academic Travelers* (New York: Lexington Books, 1989), 429; also see Susan Strange, "1995 Presidential Address ISA as a Microcosm," *International Studies Quarterly*, 39:3 (1995): 289–295.

exciting and radical of British newspapers. Strange took her first academic post in 1949 at University College London (UCL). Pregnancies and maternity leaves made her vulnerable to what she called the "bullying ways" of the senior IR professor, Georg Schwarzenberger. "But the feminist case in the professions," she later reflected, "still had to be made, and with four young children at home I didn't relish the fight." Susan Strange was effectively forced out of UCL for having children.

Already during the evacuation of the LSE to Cambridge during the Second World War, Susan Strange had developed a strong distaste for those male professors compelled to cultivate cliques and surround themselves with devotees. On leaving UCL, she became a full-time researcher at Chatham House between 1965 and 1976, where she developed her powerful analyses of global political economy and her critique of formal modelling and the pretensions of contemporary international theory, and planned the interdisciplinary academic field of international political economy, "the key to the perennial political question, who gets what?" Inter-state relations were a subfield of the organization of the global economy. She took the Montague Burton Chair in IR at the LSE in 1978. According to one disciplinary historian, Susan Strange "was well aware of the heritage she was entering, and had scant respect for it. Not only did she have something like contempt for [Charles] Manning's ingenious word-play and subtle philosophising, but was not much impressed with the subject as it had hitherto been taught in the Department ... [S]he remained dismissive of its intellectual heritage."[22] But conventional IR's vice could also be turned into a virtue. "International relations," she observed, "stands as the one social science with barriers to entry so low that anyone can jump them. It has been and will remain the richer for keeping those barriers low."[23]

Like Penrose, Susan Strange was an institution-builder, establishing Britain's first graduate program in IPE and founding the British International Studies Association in 1975. She viewed the latter as an antidote to the conferences organized by the male "barons" who had dominated British IR to date – "the dreadfully constipated and hierarchical Bailey conferences that Charles Manning used to run at the LSE."[24] Here we have selected the concluding passages from *Sterling and British Policy: A Political Study of an International Currency in Decline*, published

---

[22] Brian Porter, "A Brief History Continued, 1972–2002," in Harry Bauer and Elisabetta Brighi (eds.), *International Relations at LSE: A History of 75 Years* (London: Millennium Publishing Group, 2003), 36–37.

[23] Strange, "I Never Meant to Be an Academic," 435.

[24] Strange, "I Never Meant to Be an Academic," 435.

in 1971, and written on the research staff of Chatham House.[25] Aimed at a broad readership, the book is a political and economic account of the history and decline of sterling, the dominant world currency until the Second World War. It is a story of national elites in denial about the international economic consequences of the loss of empire. Britain's "Top Currency Syndrome," born of imperial and multilateralist ideology, led a series of British governments to pursue a futile monetary policy intended to keep sterling as an international currency. This effort, along with accompanying military spending and foreign aid, negatively affected Britain's domestic economy, Strange argued, and was largely unnecessary. Charles Kindleberger accused Strange of enthroning "neo-mercantilism" because she advocated for some controls on capital exports and food imports, and a tax on foreign finance.[26] For Strange, Britain had much more room to maneuver to "deviate from the policy standards set by the United States – or by multilateral associations such as GATT" (464).

Some readers may have noticed that none of the selections included here focus on the gendered nature of the global economy. But, of course, the recovery and retrieval of these earlier writers, whether explicitly feminist or not, is a feminist project and part of the gendered intellectual history of international political economy. It constitutes a significant part of what Elias and Roberts in their *Handbook on the International Political Economy of Gender* conceive of as the "multiple and diverse roots and influences" on feminist IPE.[27] Yet the absence of earlier women thinkers in the *Handbook* reflects a more general tendency to assume that, barring the exceptional figures of Luxemburg and Strange, there were no important historical women thinkers on the world economy before the emergence of feminist IPE or they are not precursors to contemporary approaches to the IPE of gender. But enquiring into the conditions and reception of historical women's work – who is recognized when and by

---

[25] Her later other major works include Susan Strange, *Paths to International Political Economy* (London: Allen & Unwin, 1984); Susan Strange, *Casino Capitalism* (Oxford: Wiley-Blackwell, 1986); Susan Strange, *States and Markets* (London: Pinter, 1988); Susan Strange, *The Retreat of the State: The Diffusion of Power in the World Economy* (Cambridge: Cambridge University Press, 1996); Susan Strange, *Mad Money: When Markets Outgrow Governments* (Ann Arbor, MI: University of Michigan Press, 1998). For a collection of Susan Strange's most important essays, edited by her literary executor and former students, see Roger Tooze and Christopher May (eds.), *Authority and Markets: Susan Strange's Writings on International Political Economy* (Basingstoke: Palgrave, 2002).

[26] C. P. Kindleberger, "Review: *Sterling and British Policy: A Political Study of an International Currency in Decline,*" *International Journal*, 27:4 (1972): 621.

[27] Juanita Elias and Adrienne Roberts, "Introduction: Situating Gender Scholarship in IPE," in Juanita Elias and Adrienne Roberts (eds.), *Handbook on the International Political Economy of Gender* (Cheltenham: Edward Elgar, 2018), 1.

whom, who is not recognized by whom and how – might reveal something quite important about the conditions of this subfield's intellectual reproduction. After all, that just Susan Strange, as an exceptional founding figure, is the only thinker in this volume to receive the recognition they deserve, was itself gendered, and is surely part of the context for the later production and reception of feminist IPE. As economic history enjoys a "global" turn, both feminist IPE and women's and gender history are thriving, and IR is renewing itself, in part, through investigating its intellectual and disciplinary history, now is a good time for these fields to start speaking with and learning from one another.

Patricia Owens

Rosa Luxemburg

From *The Accumulation of Capital* (1913)

Imperialism is the political expression of the process of the accumulation of capital in its competitive struggle over the unspoiled remainder of the non-capitalist world environment. Geographically, this still comprises huge areas of the earth's surface. However, this remaining field for the expansion of capital appears as an ever-diminishing residue taking into account both the enormous mass of already accumulated capital in the old capitalist countries, which is vying for markets for its surplus product as well as for opportunities to capitalize its surplus value, and the rate at which areas of precapitalist civilization are transformed into capitalist ones – in other words, given the high level of development of the productive forces of capital that has already been achieved. The international behavior of capital on the world stage is shaped accordingly. Imperialism's force and the violence exerted by it – both in its aggressive action toward the noncapitalist world and in the sharpening antagonisms between the competing capitalist countries – are heightened in tandem with the development of the capitalist countries and the increasingly fierce competition between them to acquire noncapitalist areas. Yet the more violently, forcefully, and thoroughly imperialism brings about the decline of noncapitalist civilizations, the more rapidly it removes the very basis for the accumulation of capital. As much as imperialism is a historical method to prolong the existence of capital, objectively it is at the same time the surest way to bring this existence to the swiftest conclusion. This does not mean that this endpoint has literally to be reached. The tendency toward this terminal point of capitalist development manifests itself in forms that configure the final phase of capitalism as a period of catastrophes.

Hopes for a peaceful development of capital accumulation, for "trade and industry, which can only flourish in peace," and the whole semi-official Manchester ideology of a harmony of interests between the trading nations of the world – the other side of the harmony of interests between capital and labor – derive from the *Sturm und Drang* period of classical economics; such hopes seemed to be validated in practice during the brief era of free trade in Europe in the 1860s and 1870s. The foundation on which these hopes are based is the false doctrine of the British free trade school that commodity exchange is the only pre-supposition of, and condition for, the accumulation of capital, and that the latter is identical with the commodity economy. As has been shown, the whole Ricardian school identified the accumulation of capital and the conditions for its reproduction with simple commodity production and the conditions for simple circulation. This was subsequently to become even more evident in the practice of the free trader *vulgaris*. [...]

This gospel never constituted the true expression of the interests of capital accumulation as a whole. In the U.K. itself, it had already been given the lie in the 1840s, when the harmony of interests of trading nations was proclaimed to the thunder of cannons in the Opium Wars in the Far East; with the annexation of Hong Kong, this doctrine turned into its opposite, that of the system of "spheres of interest." On the European continent, the free trade of the 1860s did not represent the interests of industrial capital, because the leading free trade nations there were still at that time predominantly agrarian countries, in which the development of large-scale industry was still relatively feeble. The free trade system was instead implemented as a measure to facilitate the political constitution of the central European states. Under the policy of [Otto Theodor von] Manteuffel and [Otto von] Bismarck in Germany, it represented a specifically Prussian means in order to force Austria out of the German Confederation and the Customs Union, and to constitute the new German Empire under Prussian leadership. From an economic point of view, free trade here was only in the interests of commercial capital, especially that of the Hanseatic cities, oriented as they were toward international trade, and in those of agrarian consumers; as far as German states' own industry was concerned, the iron industry was only won over with great difficulty to the idea of conceding the abolition of the Rhine tolls for the sake of free trade, whereas the southern German cotton industry remained resolutely opposed, and demanded the reten-tion of protective tariffs. In France, the most favored nation treaties, which laid the foundations for the free trade system in the whole of Europe, were concluded by Napoleon III without the consent, and even against the will, of the firm majority in parliament, which was composed of industrialists and landowners, and was in favor of retaining protective tariffs. The government of the [French] Second Empire only resorted to the free trade treaties themselves as an expedient, with the acquiescence of the U.K., in order to circumvent the opposition of the French parliament and to impose free trade behind the back of the legislature via the international route. [...]

Between 1853 and 1862, the previous system of protective tariffs was dismantled by 32 separate imperial decrees, which were then rubber-stamped en masse by the legislature in 1863, with scant regard for the formal process. In Italy, the dependence of [Camillo Benso] Cavour's policy on French backing dictated the adoption of a free trade agenda. In 1870, an inquiry opened under the pressure of public opinion revealed the lack of support for the free trade policy among interested groups. Finally, in Russia, the trend toward free trade in the 1860s was initially a mere preliminary to the creation of a broad foundation for the commodity economy and for large-scale industry; it was only during this period that serfdom was abolished and a railway network established.

It was clear from the very outset, then, that the international system of free trade would constitute no more than a fleeting episode in the history of capital accumulation. For this reason alone, it is perverse to attempt to explain the general reversion to protective tariffs since the end of the 1870s as merely a defensive reaction to British free trade.

Several facts speak against such an explanation: in Germany, as well as in France and Italy, the leading role in the reversion to protective tariffs was played by agrarian interests, which were in competition not with the U.K., but with the U.S.; furthermore, it was not so much against the U.K. that the emerging home-grown industry in Russia and Italy needed to be protected, for example, but rather against Germany and France, respectively. Nor was the protracted general depression on the world market since the crisis of the 1870s, which engendered a readiness to embrace protective tariffs, bound up with the U.K.'s monopoly to any great extent. The general cause of the *volte-face* on the question of protective tariffs thus lay deeper than this. The pure standpoint of commodity exchange, which was the origin of the illusions of a harmony of interests on the world market harbored by the adherents of the free trade doctrine, was abandoned as soon as large-scale industrial capital had gained enough of a foothold in the most important countries in continental Europe to gain an awareness of the conditions of its accumulation. That which now came to the foreground was the antagonistic character of these conditions, and the competitive struggle over the noncapitalist milieu, both of which ran counter to the reciprocity of interests of the capitalist states.

At the very inception of the free trade era, the Far East was opened up by the Opium Wars in China, and European capital began to gain ground in Egypt. Throughout the 1880s, in parallel with the return to protective tariffs, the policy of expansion was pursued with increasing force in an uninterrupted sequence of events: the British occupation of Egypt [in 1882], the German colonial conquests in Africa, the French occupation of Tunisia [in 1881] and expedition to Tonkin [from 1883 to 1885], Italy's advances into Assab and Massawa, the Abyssinian War and the formation of Eritrea and the British conquests in South Africa [...] The conflict between Italy and France over the sphere of interest in Tunisia [...] represented the characteristic prelude to the Franco-Italian customs war seven years later [in 1888 to 1889], which formed a dramatic epilogue to the end of the free trade harmony of interests on the European continent. For capital, the solution was now to monopolize noncapitalist areas for its expansion, both within the old capitalist states as well as overseas, while free trade (the "open door" policy) became a specific form of the defenselessness of noncapitalist countries in the face of international capital and its competitive equilibrium, and constituted a preliminary stage of their partial or total occupation as colonies or as spheres of interest. If the U.K. alone has remained true to free trade, this is first and foremost bound up with its status as the oldest colonial empire and its possession of vast noncapitalist areas; these provided it from the outset with an operational basis offering the prospect of virtually unconfined capital accumulation, and in practice placed it beyond competition from other countries, at least until very recently. This is the reason for the universal drive toward protective tariffs, as capitalist countries seek to close themselves off from each other, even as international trade between them is constantly increasing and they are becoming ever more dependent upon each other for the material conditions of reproduction, and even though protective tariffs have now become utterly redundant from the standpoint of the technical development of the productive forces, even leading in many instances to the artificial preservation of antiquated forms of production. The internal contradiction within the international policy of protective tariffs, like the contradictory character of the international credit system, is a mere reflection of the historical contradiction that has arisen between the interests of accumulation – i.e. those of the realization and capitalization of surplus value, of expansion – and the pure standpoint of commodity exchange.

A palpable expression of this is the fact that the modern system of high protective tariffs was essentially introduced as the basis on which capitalist states could strengthen their military capabilities in line with colonial expansion and the intensifying antagonisms within the capitalist milieu. In Germany, as in France, Italy, and Russia, the reversion to protective tariffs went hand-in-hand with the expansion of the armed forces, and was implemented for this purpose, constituting the basis for the European system of competitive armament that started at that time, as states increased the military capabilities first of their armies, and then of their navies. The continental military system, whose main focus was the army, corresponded to the European system of free trade; this has now given way to the protective tariff as the basis for, and supplement to, the imperialist military system, which increasingly revolves around naval power.

As a concrete, historical process, capitalist accumulation as a whole thus has two different facets. The first of these consists in the process that occurs at the point of production of surplus value – in the factories, the mines, the farms – and on the commodity market. Viewed from this aspect alone, accumulation is an economic process whose most important phase is played out between the capitalist and the wage laborer, but it is one that moves exclusively within the confines of commodity exchange – the exchange of equivalents – in *both* phases (i.e. both within the sphere of production and that of circulation). Here, on the level of form, it is peace, property, and equality that prevail, and it required the acute dialectic of a scientific analysis to expose the way in which, during the process of accumulation, the right of property turns into the appropriation of alien property, commodity exchange turns into exploitation, and equality turns into class domination.

The other dimension of capital accumulation consists in a process that takes place between capital and noncapitalist forms of production. Its setting is the world stage. In this case, the dominant methods are those of colonial policy, the system of international credit, the policy of spheres of interest, and war. Here violence, fraud, oppression, and plunder are displayed quite openly, without any attempt to disguise them, and it requires a lot of effort to uncover the strict laws governing the economic process beneath this turmoil of political violence and trials of strength.

Bourgeois liberal theory only takes one side of this process into consideration, namely the sphere of "peaceful competition," the marvels of technology, and pure commodity exchange; it thus separates off the other dimension of capitalist accumulation, the realm of capital's thunderous shows of force, which it holds to be more or less contingent expressions of "foreign policy," from the economic domain of capital.

In reality, political violence is nothing but a vehicle for the economic process; both sides of capital accumulation are organically bound up with each other through the very conditions of the reproduction of capital, and it is only together that they result in the historical trajectory of capital. Capital does not merely come into the world "dripping from head to toe, from every pore, with blood and dirt," […] it also imposes itself on the world step by step in the same way, thus preparing its own demise amid ever more violent convulsions.

Persia Campbell

From *Chinese Coolie Emigration to Countries within the British Empire* (1923)

"When I came to the investigation of this traffic, I had no adequate conception of its enormity."

(Mr. Parker, U.S.A. Minister in China Jan. 14, 1856.)

The Act of Emancipation, 1833, was the expression of a determined public opinion in Great Britain. Petition followed petition from the people to the Parliament. Their argument was perhaps exaggerated, but its demand was plain. Liberty! – And the rights of man must be recognized in a slave as in a free society. Fraternity! – And the cruelties of the slave system must be terminated by its abolition.

On the other hand, the West India planters insisted on economic justice. They must be compensated for the loss of slaves recognized as property by British law. It was agreed by Parliament that compensation should be paid by voting a sum of money and by securing the services of the freedmen to their masters for a period of years. A system of apprenticeship was to be substituted for slavery [...] In this manner for a period of six years a temporary labour force was to be secured for the planters and in the meantime the negroes were to be trained to the responsibilities of freedom. The system was instituted. When it became known that cruelties were practised by the employers against the indentured labourers, the British people demanded that it be brought to a premature end. [...]

The abundance of fertile land in British Guiana, Trinidad and Jamaica made it possible for the emancipated negroes to win an easy livelihood without the necessity of regular work on the plantations, and their continued withdrawal into the interior left the planters with a steadily diminishing labour force. Various schemes for the importation of labour had been put into operation when the system of apprenticeship was terminated, but they had proved more or less abortive. In 1838, the West India planters had agreed to follow the successful example of

430

Mauritius by importing Indian coolies. But the alleged abuses of Indian emigration led the Government of India in 1839 to prohibit further recruitment of its subjects. Africans had been introduced from the smaller and more populated West India islands, but they had at once associated themselves with the emancipated negroes. [...]

No adequate constructive policy had accompanied the overthrow of the social order founded on slavery. The sugar industry, already burdened by the debts of an artificial past, remained dependent on the irregular and unwilling labour of the freedmen. By 1842 the financial position of the West India planters was admittedly critical. Lord Stanley's select Committee on July 26, 1842, emphasized the need of compensating for this diminished supply by promoting "the immigration of a fresh labouring population to such an extent as to create competition for employment."

The West India Committee had already realized this necessity and had forwarded on July 11, 1843, a memorial [...] to the Secretary of State in which they pointed out the serious position of the planters and requested that immigration from Africa should be more actively encouraged and that the right recently accorded to Mauritius of reopening Indian immigration should be extended to them. This request was given careful consideration by Lord Stanley, Secretary of State for the Colonies. The financial position of the West India estates was unsound even under the slave system, but the effect on the labouring population of the Act of Emancipation and the subsequent abolition of apprenticeship had undoubtedly precipitated the crisis. Hence the abrupt refusal with which he had replied [...] to the squatters of New South Wales when they asked permission to introduce Indian coolies at the public expense, was unsuited to the West India occasion. But though the economic position of the planters demanded his sympathetic consideration, Lord Stanley was determined to prevent the institution of any order approximating to slavery. He would not remove the safeguards from the African recruitment. Nor would he disregard the welfare of the Indian coolies. [...]

The application followed the receipt of letters [...] from a British Guiana proprietor who had been visiting the British possessions in the East. He had witnessed the heavy annual movement of Chinese immigrants into the labour markets of the Straits Settlements and did not doubt that they could meet the requirements of the West India planters. [...] On the other hand, the proprietor warned the West India Committee that there were certain disadvantages in the Chinese character as compared with that of the Indian. The Chinese were not so likely to subject themselves to the discipline of the estate; they would probably demand higher wages; they would cause trouble if an attempt was made to keep their wages lower than those current at the time. "They would no more bear ill-usage than an English labourer." Nevertheless, on the whole, he considered them far superior to the Indian coolies. [...] Vessels were easily chartered, freight was low, and rice and salt fish could be had at Singapore at cheap rates. [...]

Lord Stanley gave close attention to the proposed system of Chinese contract labour. The subject was "under constant discussion at the Colonial Office." [...] Lord Stanley in his reply to the West India Committee, September 4, 1843, [...] admitted that the introduction of Chinese coolies would probably have a better effect on the emancipated negroes than the introduction of any other race. They would set them an "example of continuous and industrious application." From the information he had been able to obtain he was led to believe that the Chinese were fully competent to stipulate for what would be most to their own advantage.

Present political considerations in China made it necessary to limit the ports of embarkation to the Straits Settlements. Therefore any Chinese coolies engaged for the West India Colonies would have already found their way to the Straits ports – a fact which gave some guarantee that they would understand the nature of the proposals made to them. A serious difficulty in the way of sanctioning a bounty upon their introduction into British colonies was the purely male character of their immigration. It was said that tradition bound the women to the ancestral village. However, since it was the habit of the Chinese to return to China after a temporary engagement abroad, Lord Stanley did not consider the difficulty insuperable. He agreed with the West India Committee that a contract would be necessary to induce the Chinese coolie to engage for the West Indies, but he limited its period to five years and insisted that the coolie must have power to rescind it after arrival in the colony. This was to be his security against terms which might seem unjust when compared with those under which free labourers were engaged. The West India Committee objected to a power of immediate termination. Their desire was to secure the supply of steady labour which a contract system promised. [...] Lord Stanley accepted a compromise. The contract was to be obligatory on the labourer for six months after his arrival. Then and at the end of every subsequent year, he was to have the option of continuing or rescinding it. Lord Stanley agreed also to the bounty system, [...] but although a maximum rate of bounty was to be fixed ($65), only the actual amount spent was to be reclaimed. [...] After the first six months a graduated scale of bounty was to come into operation, one-fifth being deducted for every subsequent six months served. [...] The planters were determined to secure a labour-force. Lord Stanley, while admitting their necessity, was determined to safeguard the welfare of the immigrants. On December 1, 1843, he curtly refused any further discussion on the subject. [...]

The subject of Chinese importation was not reopened until the "Free Trade" crisis 1846–9 had swept away the old proprietary and "transmuted colonial agriculture into a business entirely commercial and speculative."

The second crisis was even more serious than the first. The Order in Council, September 1838, had prevented any contract with the Indian and Portuguese immigrants other than an agreement for one month. Their ranks were swept by discontentment and disease. At the end of the first month many of them wandered away into the interior to die. Both Indian and Portuguese immigrations were discontinued. The planters insisted and the Home Government agreed that the only satisfactory solution was to legalize contracts to labour for not less than three years (Ord. 3, 1848). But before any system of free labour had been satisfactorily established on the ruins of slavery – before an immigrant population had been introduced to take the place of the emancipated negroes who continued to withdraw from the plantations, the colonies were plunged into the crisis which ended in temporary collapse. The Sugar Act of 1846 had equalized duties on foreign and colonial sugar. Free Trade had followed hard on Emancipation. The result was inevitable to a system of sugar cultivation pushed under Slavery and Protection far beyond the limit warranted by its real resources. [...] In these circumstances the necessity of introducing both Chinese and Indian immigration was again discussed. [...]

These various official and semi-official reports and memoranda were considered by the Colonial Office and the West India authorities 1849–52. They described the impoverishment of Southern China and the annual emigration of large numbers of coolies under the pressure of want. Such emigration was nominally illegal – Chinese law forbidding a Chinese subject to emigrate without a special permit. But the local authorities did not interfere. The facts were too much for them. The result was the annual outflow of "hungry able-bodied men," part of which the planters and squatters of the new world were already diverting into the channel of a peculiar contract system of labour.

The first shipment of coolies under contract to foreigners was made in 1845 in a French vessel from Amoy to the Isle of Bourbon [...] It was estimated that by July, 1852, agents had entered into contracts for the shipment to Havana of coolies to the number of from 8,000–15,000. By August 25, 1852, 2,025 coolies had left China for South America, many of them destined for the guano works of the Chincha Islands. [...]

Large shipments [...] had been effected in the Canton waters by 1852; contract coolies had also been embarked at Hong Kong, though the latter port was the centre of the "credit-ticket" movement. It was Amoy, however, that was fast becoming the chief port of the early contract-trade. In August, 1852, Dr. Winchester estimated [...] that 6,255 coolies had been shipped under foreign contract from Amoy while some 10,756 tons had been employed.

Whatever the destination of the coolies under contract the method of their recruitment was essentially the same. "A trifle advanced to give their hungriness food, a suit of clothes to cover their nudity, a dollar or two for their families, and candidates in abundance are found for transportation to any foreign land." The common designation of the system was "the buying and selling of pigs." It centred in the payment of head money. British firms at the treaty ports were engaged either by the would-be employer or associations of employers (as in New South Wales), or by merchants speculating on the profit of a sale of contracts to employers (as in Cuba). These firms employed Chinese recruiters or coolie brokers, men of questionable reputation who were paid per head for the number of coolies brought to the barracoons. A promise of lucrative work to the half-starved coolies was usually sufficient to get them into the land barracoons or on to the receiving ships, from which it was difficult to escape. Moreover, peculiar laws in China as to debt bondage made it an easy method for obtaining possession of the persons of the coolies either by way of the gaming tables or by a small advance in money or goods. The sudden and competing labour-demands of 1852 having forced up the price of coolies, the cupidity of the Chinese brokers was stimulated by the foreign gold and during 1852 resorts to fraud in recruitment were not infrequent, the brokers having the support of their European employers. The "pigs," recruited by debt, deceit, or argument, were conveyed by the brokers to "pig-pens." The "pig-pens" were the emigrant depots. At Amoy the firm of Messrs. Syme, Muir & Co. had erected a special barracoon in front of their hong. [...] The coolies were detained in the barraccons under restraint until their shipment, the exercise of restraint increasing with the irregularities of the system. The argument advanced for its necessity was that some coolies offered to emigrate, entered the depots, received food, and even perhaps the advance given before embarkation – and then made their escape, as they had from the first intended. Obviously the temptation was great. The force of the argument, however, was generally invalidated by questionable methods of recruitment.

Prior to signing the contracts a medical examination was held. Coolies found physically defective were rejected. Their fate was pitiful. Their native village being often at some distance from the port, and they without means of returning to it, they died in the streets. [...]

Coolies medically fit signed the contracts. [...] Once the contracts were signed, final advances were made to the coolies, who were frequently indebted to the brokers for the full amount of the money received. Embarkation was then effected.

Lilian M. Friedländer

From "Labour Problems in Two Worlds" (1929)

For historical purposes the nineteenth century may be said to have ended in 1914 with the outbreak of the Great War. The New World came into the fight to "redress the balance of the Old," and at the close of that vast struggle between highly industrialised modern States, a Peace Conference met in Paris to settle the political and economic problems of half a world, much as Vienna of 1815 had settled the affairs of Europe alone.

No need for a twentieth-century Robert Owen to plead the cause of the factory workers before the assembled diplomats at Paris. A century of machine production, and a world struggle for markets; the inevitable and growing technical co-operation between governments – evidenced, for example, in the Universal Postal Union or the International Telegraphic Federation; the rise of organised labour, grouped by craft, trade or locality, consolidated into national associations of great strength, and forming its own international unions, whether Trade Union, Socialist, or Communist – all these were powerful factors in the world of 1919 which the Peace Conference set out to rebuild.

Even before the war, there had been a handful of international labour conferences, varying in tone from the purely voluntary to the semi-official and diplomatic. Governments had met for the discussion of labour problems for the first time in 1890 in Berlin, and had voted for many fine-sounding resolutions that led to no practical reforms. The International Association for Labour Legislation, founded in 1900 and with its central statistical office in Basle, had even been able to organise periodic conferences, technical and diplomatic, upon the more urgent questions in the international labour field. [...] During the war, labour movements in all countries, whether belligerent or neutral, had expressed their determination to achieve both representation at the peace confer-ence and a treaty which should include international action on industrial questions. The International Federation of Trade Unions – to which the

436

organised labour movement in the United States had never affiliated – held a meeting in January, 1919, and the charter of minimum rights which it drew up served both as a warning and a guide to the Peace Conference. Revolution was in the air, and the statesmen feared that any day the tide of Bolshevism might sweep in from the east.

It is, therefore, not surprising that at its first plenary meeting the Peace Conference should have set up a Commission on International Labour Legislation, "to enquire into the conditions of employment from the international aspect, and to consider the international means necessary to secure common action on matters affecting conditions of employment."[28] On the Commission sat delegates from the five Big Powers and from four small States; and its chairman, strangely enough, was Mr. Samuel Gompers, president of the American Federation of Labor.

The impact of the United States of America – or, to be correct, of the mind of Woodrow Wilson – on post-war European politics is marked. It is engraved in Part I of the various peace treaties, and embodied in the Palais des Nations at Geneva. The impact of America on the Commission on International Labour Legislation, in legal and economic thought, can be clearly traced [...] In this study we are chiefly interested in the problems created for the Commission by the complexities of American government, and their reactions on the shape of the organisation in which America finally declined to take a part.

The Constitution of the U.S.A. is a political document which was elaborated in the eighteenth century and is to-day proving itself increasingly inadequate for the government of some 110 millions of people inhabiting an immense continent. In addition to the Federal Constitution, there are now forty-eight separate states, each having its own constitution, "self-governing" within fixed limits, but clearly, since the Civil War, not possessing full "sovereignty." There is a national government of three departments, and power is divided between the nation and the several states. [...] The police power is expressly reserved to the separate states, and this includes power to regulate industrial conditions. As a result there is "not one Labour Code in the United States but forty-eight Labour Codes, framed on no common or uniform plan."[29]

This was the situation which the American delegates on the Paris Commission tried to make clear to their European colleagues, who desired quite definitely to build an organisation which should have the form of an international labour parliament. Government delegates,

[28] *Official Bulletin of the International Labour Office*, Geneva, vol. i, p. 1.
[29] H. B. Butler: "Industrial Relations in the United States," p. 10. [...]

together with representatives of employers and workers, would meet annually to discuss labour problems, and they would draft Conventions tending to set world standards in the conditions of employment. The British, in opposition to many continental delegates, held to the necessity of giving the government the legal right of refusal to ratify such conventions.

But, asked the Americans, what is the position of a Federal State, which for purposes of international action and the signature of treaties is a unity (although power in the U.S. is divided, in this respect, between president and senate) and for purposes of labour legislation is not an entity at all, but a congeries of forty-eight "self-governing" states? The government of the United States, if a member of the international labour organisation, would be represented by officials from the federal Department of Labour; it could clearly not send forty-eight separate delegates. Yet these federal officials would have no power by their approval, recommendation or action, to bind the separate states of the Union. The federal government might be held responsible for the non-enforcement of an international convention which it had ratified, because a number of states refused to take the necessary measures.[30] And always there loomed up the shadow of possible action by the Courts, declaring unconstitutional such federal or state labour legislation. [...]

The Commission spent many hours, in plenary session and in the negotiations of a sub-committee, trying to steer a way out of the impasse created by American legal difficulties. The situation was often distinctly humorous. Mr. Robinson frequently had to read to the Commission a comprehensive study on the constitutional structure of the United States. [...] The American delegates proposed that the international labour conferences should work not only by means of conventions, but also by recommendations, "which would have results because of the moral force which they would be bound to possess." This, said M. Fontaine, was a return to the system of 1890, and was unthinkable in Europe.[31]

Finally, the Americans suggested, and the Commission accepted, a compromise which would allow the United States, and other federal states where a similar constitutional situation might exist, to treat a draft convention of the labour organisation as though it were merely a recommendation. This represented, of course, a "serious change in the substance of the scheme," but the exception extended only to federal states which are subject to limitations in respect of their treaty-making powers on labour matters, and only in so far as these limitations applied.[32] [...]

---

[30] *Official Bulletin*, vol. i, pp. 92, 178.   [31] *Ibid.*, pp. 153–4.
[32] H. B. Butler, op. cit., pp. 15–16.

The International Labour Organisation held its first Conference at Washington, D.C., in November, 1919, at a time when President Wilson was ill and the debates in the Senate were showing how strong was the opposition in America to the Treaty of Versailles. The United States Secretary for Labour presided over the Conference, but no American delegates took part in its deliberations. Among the practical results of the Conference was a Convention which fixed the age of fourteen as the minimum age for the employment of children in industry – a principle which was extended to shipping and agriculture in the Conferences of 1920 and 1921. These Conventions have now been ratified by a dozen or more of the chief industrial countries of the world, and the problem of child labour, which had just come into the international forum before the war, is now to some extent removed from the field of low competitive standards. The Senate of the United States, however, rejected the Treaty of Versailles, and the nation refused to co-operate officially in the League of Nations and the International Labour Organisation. The "world in miniature" and the world at large went their separate ways, and watched with interested and sympathetic eyes the problems which each of them encountered. [...]

While the International Labour Organisation works by means of annual conferences and draft international conventions, which try to set a world standard in some of the more urgent labour problems, the United States of America must use all possible constitutional devices to deal with an economic problem which in a unitary state could be solved by one act of the national legislature, enforced by national inspectors. [...] State frontiers in the United States do not mean tariff barriers, as they do in Europe, but they remain political lines cutting across an economic world.[33] We have seen that in 1825 Massachusetts had thought of a child labour law. A little less than a century later the federal government of the United States passed its first Child Labour Law [...]

The necessity for such action might be stated in words from the Preamble to Part XIII of the Treaty of Versailles, "the failure of any nation to adopt humane conditions of labour is an obstacle in the way of other nations which desire to improve the conditions in their own countries." Child workers in America cross state lines and thereby create problems analogous to the problems in international law which the Labour Organisation tries to solve. Investigations made by the Children's Bureau of the federal Department of Labour have proved how the conditions of child labour, the laws and their effectiveness, differ

---

[33] Cf. Walter Thompson: *Federal Centralisation.*

from state to state; children migrate, with their families, for seasonal occupations, or sometimes even live in one state and work in another.[34] It is difficult for any one state to improve its legislation and inspection, when its industries and its agriculture are competing in the home market with those of states where lower standards obtain. [...]

This Child Labour Act of 1916 was declared unconstitutional by a 5–4 decision of the Supreme Court in 1918, because, in the opinion of the majority, "to sustain this statute would sanction an invasion by the federal power of the control of a matter purely local in its character and over which no authority has been delegated to Congress."[35] [...] Once again, problems of constitutional law cut across the path of social progress, and the second federal Child Labour Law was annulled.

It was left for the federal government to enlarge its powers by an amendment to the Constitution. Accordingly, in June, 1924, large majorities in the House of Representatives and in the Senate passed an amendment giving Congress the power "to limit, regulate and prohibit the labour of persons under eighteen years of age." [...]

The amendment was put before the forty-eight states of the Union, and its acceptance by two-thirds of them is necessary before it can come into force. It has so far been ratified by the legislatures of five states, and rejected or postponed in most of the others; some states have taken no action at all. Rejection of the amendment, however, in no sense implies low standards of child protection in a state. The old jealousy of "states' rights" has been aroused [...] We are reminded of horror-struck speeches in the Assemblies of the League of Nations, or in the Conferences or Governing Body meetings of the International Labour Organisation, whenever the mere idea of a "super-state" is breathed, and a heretic is thought to have attacked the sacred rights of sovereignty.

There is, therefore, no likelihood in the near future of Congress obtaining the power to lay down national minimum standards for the protection of the children in the United States. [...] There is no half-way stage in the United States between the entire freedom now given to the separate states, and the enactment and enforcement of one federal law for the whole continent.

Meanwhile, the International Labour Organisation has held ten Conferences, to which its half a hundred Member-States regularly send their four delegates apiece – two representing the government, one for the employers and one for the workers. More than twenty international

---

[34] *Industrial and Labour Information*, xiv, 83, xvi, 93–4, xviii, 316. Cf. Julia E. Johnsen: *Child Labour*, especially pp. 284–5.

[35] *Hammer v. Dagenhart*, 247 U.S. 251, quoted Gorham Rice, op. cit., p. 629.

conventions have been passed, dealing with maritime, agricultural and industrial matters, ranging from social insurance to accident prevention, from hours of labour and the use of white lead in painting to unemployment and the inspection of emigrants. [...]

By every means at its disposal – debate, publication, convention – the Organisation endeavours to raise the labour standards in the backward countries, to encourage progressive legislation in the more highly industrialised countries. The Organisation has been the champion of the child workers in the rug-workshops of Persia; it has done all it could, without encroaching upon national sovereignty, to persuade China to protect by law the children in her factories, and it has watched with sympathy the efforts made in this same direction in the International Settlement in Shanghai;[36] it has set standards for the employment of children which the government of India has now very largely enforced. Among the European countries its conventions, and the annual reports on their application which must be sent in by every State which ratifies them, guarantee at least an international minimum of protection to the children.

This analogy between the problems of the United States and the International Labour Organisation is interesting both for the contrasts and the comparisons it affords. Into the solution of those problems enter diverse factors, political, economic, juridical. In both cases, legal conceptions which are clearly out of date hinder or check social progress; it has, indeed, been said that "law to-day rests on the political philosophy of yesterday and the legal philosophy of the day before yesterday."[37] In both cases, relics of the theory of sovereignty have strayed from the realms of pure political science into an economic field where they are more than ever meaningless and cumbersome. Professor Laski says: "It would be of lasting benefit to political science if the whole concept of sovereignty were surrendered."[38] The American states, and the States-Members of the League of Nations, each gave up a portion of their so-called sovereignty when they joined in the federal or the international association respectively. In political matters the American states have clearly only a limited authority; in matters of economic and industrial law they still play with the idea of a sovereignty which in the world at large has already begun to give way before the pressure of post-war facts and ideology. Washington and Geneva both stand for a process of levelling *up*.

[36] See *Humanity and Labour in China*, by Adelaide Anderson.
[37] J. S. Reeves: *La Communauté Internationale*, p. 39.
[38] Laski: *Grammar of Politics*, p. 44.

It is being slowly recognised in the United States, as it has been recognised in Europe, that competition in the conditions of labour – between the states of the Union or between the nations which are members of the Labour Organisation – will, if unchecked, mean the triumph of the lowest standards; it is as undesirable, and as potentially dangerous, as the competition in armaments.

The methods in constitutional law which the United States can use are paralleled by, but different from, the technique in international law evolved for the Labour Organisation. The question of child labour in the States shows most clearly the limitations of a constitution which was drawn up on the very eve of immense changes in the methods of production. These changes have created problems altogether outside the scope of eighteenth-century political thought, that to-day urgently need treatment on a national scale. The difficulties of amending written constitutions are proverbial; in a vast federal state or an international association of states they often seem insuperable. Radical minds in Washington and Geneva can have sympathy with one another on this point! The International Labour Organisation is more fortunate in that its "charter" was drawn up in recent times. Though its machinery may need adjusting to unforeseen developments in the economic world, the general principles which it seeks to enforce are stated – in the Preamble to Part XIII and in Article 427 of the Treaty of Versailles – in such excellently broad terms that its scope of action would seem to be sufficiently wide, and its efficacy to depend on the use of its machinery by men of goodwill and of *twentieth-century* political ideas.

Eleanor Lansing Dulles

From *The Bank for International Settlements*
at Work **(1932)**

Recent events have made it more evident than ever before that there are grave dangers in the lack of regulation and coordination in international finance. The outstanding new development, aimed to assist financial co-operation, is the Bank for International Settlements. Although it originated in the special problems connected with Reparation, it soon extended its work over a wide field and attacked many urgent questions of money and credit. In fact, it is because the work of the Bank in its early years sheds light on the larger problems of finance that this study has been undertaken.

In describing the nature of the new institution the subject matter, quite naturally, takes two forms. There is, first, a review of the laws, decisions, committees, and transactions relating to the Bank, and, second, a theoretical appraisal of its aims and policies, with suggestions of the probable lines of development in the years to come.

The source material is varied and, in some cases, unique in character. There are, for instance, those documents which determine the general nature of the Bank and the published statements of its acts and financial condition. There are in addition numerous critical and descriptive studies written when the plan was first outlined or during the first weeks of the Bank's existence. Finally there is the less formal body of material which consists of confidential documents, letters, and interviews.

It is evident that a considerable part of this source material is not readily available to the reader. [...] Because of this fact special care has been taken to assure the accuracy [...]

The Bank for International Settlements came into existence in May 1930. This unique organization created under the Young Plan grew rapidly and survived the depression years which destroyed many institutions.

The new Bank commands attention everywhere as one of the most important forward steps in economic life of recent years. The results cannot be appraised accurately until some time has elapsed but the past achievements and future programs deserve careful attention. It is because these early steps are important in conditioning future development and because the Bank's history will be momentous to economic institutions that this study has been undertaken.

It is an international clearing house and trustee founded under certain treaties and granted a charter by the Swiss government. Seven of the more important banking systems of the world were concerned in its organization; the Central Banks of Belgium, England, France, Germany and Italy participated directly, while the United States and Japan shared in the undertaking through consortiums of private banks. The occasion for the creation of this new and revolutionary institution was the need for some agency which would take over certain responsibilities in connection with reparation payments. The financiers who created the Bank, however, added many ambitious plans to the limited functions growing out of political debts.

In fact, great hopes had led bankers and statesmen to suggest a very wide field of activity. It was expected by some that the Bank would become a powerful link between all the more important financial systems of the world. Even those who looked for a slower development expected that it would perform a much needed service in coordinating the policies of Central Banks. They often worked for divergent aims, and there was confusion and uncertainty as to the meaning of discount policies and capital movements. The widespread use of the gold exchange standard involved grave dangers. There was a fear of a gold shortage. The plan for the new Bank was greeted with enthusiasm in many quarters. Unfortunately, critical events in the next three years and the nature of the Bank's own structure and resources, prevented it from taking an aggressive part in the distressing period of world depression. Many criticized the Bank for what they considered to be weak or selfish policy. This comment was natural in view of the exaggerated hopes held in some quarters after the first announcement of the plan in 1929.

These criticisms were in the main superficial or occasioned by the lack of knowledge of what the Bank could and did do. It is true that it had not performed miracles. It had not even become at once a dominating factor in the development of monetary policies in the principal countries of the world. On the other hand, it had served in times of terrific stress and had accomplished very real services for a number of Central Banks.

It is possible to indicate very briefly at this point work done in the first two years. Later discussion will show both the exact nature of its operations and the significance of its accomplishments to the financial world. An appraisal of the first years shows that from the beginning the Bank had carried out loyally and efficiently all the functions assigned to it under the Trust Agreements. [...] It had received and transferred reparation payments; it had handled the financial operations involved in deliveries in kind; it had floated the Young loan and discharged various obligations in connection with the Young, Dawes and Austrian bonds. Later, in 1931, it had called together the Special Advisory Committee under the Young Plan and had materially facilitated its work.

More important than these functions, however, was its assistance to various Central Banks and the fact that it was a regular assembly place for the governors who came to the Directors' Meetings. Thus it became at once the "bankers' club" which had been so much desired. The prompt establishment of these regular contacts made it possible for the Bank to fulfill the role of Central Bank for Central Banks in furnishing emergency aid in the summer of 1931. This rescue work was not generally appreciated, for the help rendered at this time and in the months directly preceding could not be heralded abroad – such publicity would have disturbed many delicate financial relationships, and increased general distrust.

There is no doubt that credits granted to distressed banks at this time were very important. In addition the Bank was constantly working on plans and policies which would aid individual Central Banks and which would be of general service in reestablishing some coordinated system of value when the gold standard difficulties should have passed their acute stage.

Three things can be done in analyzing the first two years of the Bank's existence. It is possible to trace the history of the Bank from the day when it was first suggested in Paris to the second annual meeting in May, 1932. This narrative of events shows a varied and interesting series of acts modified by changing circumstances in the financial world. Then, it is possible to demonstrate how the intervention of the Bank affected different countries, and changed the course of affairs during this period. For instance, the role of the Bank in the reparation problem, in the gold standard crisis, and in the credit panic are all significant to the economic world. Finally, it is possible, even at this early stage, to indicate its theoretical powers and also the limits of its influence on basic economic factors such as interest rates, credit, foreign exchange rates, and gold movements. In a general way the region of its future work is already marked out and procedures in the first months will have an important bearing on its functions in later years.

The accomplishments of the early period, however, are no measure of the future power and influence of the Bank. These will grow with time and experience. Decades must pass before all the potentialities now evident will be fully realized. The intervening years will undoubtedly show many changes, but the Bank's continued existence and growing authority seem assured.

Ursula K. Hicks

From "Learning about Economic Development" (1957)

Since 1945 the problems surrounding development or growth have aroused far more interest in the economic world than any other subject, perhaps than all other subjects put together. We need not explore the genesis of this enthusiasm, but it is evident that it has two quite separate roots: on the one hand the desire to raise the standard of the economically and socially backward countries, on the other the anxiety to secure that the economically forward countries go on going forward and do not slip back into the apparent stagnation of the 1930's. The economic analysis springing from these two roots have certain aspects in common (especially the emphasis placed on the need to secure a higher rate of investment and saving); but the economic and institutional background in the two types of country are so different as really to constitute them different spheres of discussion. It is convenient to refer to the problems of the developed countries as concerned with *growth*, most of their resources being already known and largely developed, apart from certain minerals for which uses have only recently been discovered. The problems of the backward countries can then be regarded as those of *development* of hitherto unused sources whose uses in general are, however, well known. We are here concerned only with the study of development in this sense.

The number of books which daily flow from the publishers is an indication of the widespread interest in development, so also is the fact that (or so it seems) most universities in the U.S.A. and a good many in this country as well as in the other 'metropolitan' countries of Europe (France, Belgium, Holland, and Portugal) have established special departments for the study of the problems of backward countries, and often for the training of administrators for, and from, them. The interests of the people who read these books, listen to the lectures, and go to the conferences are varied. If their several needs in learning about development are to be catered for adequately a variety of approaches is necessary.

447

In the first place there are the large number of young men and women in the advanced countries whose interest in the backward countries has been aroused largely on humanitarian grounds. It is the same sort of instinct which sent their fathers and mothers slumming or out on missionary work. Some of these may want to train to work in backward countries; others with no such definite intention are still worth attention because they include the voters and leaders of tomorrow on whose interest will largely depend the continuance of aid from the advanced countries. Most of these young people (especially in a country like the U.S.A. with little tradition of overseas service) are, to start with, completely ignorant of conditions in the backward countries and need to have their basic characteristics and difficulties set out clearly and simply.

Next come the actual administrators and planners in the backward countries, whether 'expatriate' or locally recruited, and virtually in the same class are those whose responsibility it is to train them – quickly and in large numbers – for their jobs. Their need is first for a good understanding of the principles of smooth development and of the standard difficulties which are likely to be encountered; and secondly for detailed knowledge (especially statistical knowledge) of the particular countries with which they are likely to be concerned. Thirdly comes the need, perhaps most fundamental of all, of the growing educated classes in the backward countries, for a good non-technical analysis of the process of development, in order that they may understand the potentialities of their own countries and appreciate what the administrators and planners are trying to do, without losing patience at the inevitable slowness of achievement. [...]

It is useful to distinguish between background knowledge of the data and understanding of the development process itself. In the first category would come the essential characteristics of the backward countries and the lessons of history. In spite of striking differences between the backward countries in one part of the world and another, it is possible to single out five elements which seem to be present everywhere to a greater or less degree.

Of first importance is the low average standard of living, often extreme poverty, in places to the point of serious undernourishment, of large sections of the population. Very commonly this is accompanied by some very large concentrations of wealth or income. These, however, will probably not be functional to the development process; they will probably be in the hands of traditional authorities such as tribal chiefs, churches, temples, or possibly of the unrestrained profiteers of the development process. Whatever the average level of incomes the existence of extreme poverty poses an awkward dilemma as to how much consumption can be restrained in order to divert funds from unproductive hoarding to play an active part in the development process. This is one of the key problems everywhere.

Secondly there is the problem posed by the shortage of available resources for development. In many cases this is not primarily due to their absolute shortage, but rather to their inavailability, and in order to remedy this it is not necessarily implied that large investments are needed. [...] Thirdly, almost everywhere, a major obstacle to rapid development is the underdeveloped state of the entrepreneurial instinct, that is, the absence of willingness to lock up funds in a continuing process of production as contrasted with frequently a great eagerness to undertake short-term trading ventures. The absence of true entrepreneurship is one (but perhaps the most important) aspect of a more general absence of a desire to operate in an economic manner at all [...]. The lack of spontaneous entrepreneurship is an important, although by no means the only, cause of the small volume of savings and investment relative to resources. In spite of all its efforts, for instance, India has not yet succeeded in boosting its rate of investment above 5 per cent. of the national income, a depressing contrast to the 10–15 per cent. currently being invested by the more advanced countries and still more to the 25–30 per cent. achieved by a number of countries at the period of their most rapid advancement. A caution is necessary here, however; by no means all investment is really functional – or functional to the same degree – to the development process [...]

The low rate of saving and of entrepreneurial ability implies that in practically all backward countries there is a need for the State to undertake a good deal of investment, not only in social and economic overheads, but also, directly or indirectly, in manufacturing industry. Messrs. Buchanan and Ellis are reluctant to admit this; but the facts are against them, even in respect of the early stages of development in the U.S. and U.K. The basic obstacle here for the present batch of developing countries is the small size of the public sector, due frequently to the presence of a large inert 'subsistence economy' sector, and nearly everywhere to want of expertise in tax administration. Thus in India current revenue is no more than about 8 per cent. of the national product, in Trinidad 16 per cent., and in Uganda 17 per cent., as compared with over 29 per cent. and 37 per cent. in the U.S. and U.K. respectively.

Finally there exists a whole complex of problems concerned with the availability of the labour force for development. Although these exist in every backward country, they take such substantially different forms from country to country that they call for special consideration every time. Many developing countries are already suffering severely from population pressure, as is well understood (especially India, Egypt, and some of the Caribbean islands). [...]

Against this fantastically rapid reduction in death rates must be set, in order to appreciate the gravity of the problem, the chronically high birth rates of the tropics, and the virtual absence so far of any adjustment in them to the changed expectation of life. This is no doubt largely due to the swiftness of the change. This situation implies an abnormally large section of the population which is below working age. Low ratio of working to total population on this account is further aggravated nearly everywhere by taboos on employment of particular sectors, or taboos operating to prevent mobility between occupations. In addition existing methods of production entail a good deal of underfunctioning of the working population. The economic policy which will deal effectively with this complex of labour problems is by no means straightforward, although once the entrepreneurial instinct has been aroused many of them wither away spontaneously. It is, however, a gross over-simplification to view policy in terms either of merely drawing away surplus labour from farms, or of establishing labour-intense industries. It is much more important to make additional food supplies available, both by increasing the cultivable area and by improving methods of agriculture. It is not too much to say that every underdeveloped country in the tropics has a problem of population pressure waiting for it round the corner, if it is not experiencing it today. [...]

In the nineteenth century the development process was so long drawn out that adjustments took place gradually and on the whole smoothly, not only in respect of the birth rate. Again, several of the quickest developing countries already possessed at the beginning of the process of industrialization a large educated sector with well-established habits of business enterprise and saving, as well as considerable capital accumulation. Thus eighteenth-century England had the past profits of the East India trade to draw on, nineteenth-century Japan of the silk industry, which had established an almost monopoly position ahead of other developments. This initial provision in the two countries supplied just that pump priming which is so very helpful in enabling the wheels to start turning of themselves. It is again noteworthy both of England and Japan that in the first vital stages of advancement it was acceptable to pay little more than subsistence wages to industrial labour. Ideas of the Welfare State and the rapid spread of trade unionism almost ahead of development, alike make this impossible now, except by the use of compulsion.

It has often been remarked that the slow progress of the earlier developing countries was largely due to the necessity to make technical inventions as they went along, and it is claimed that this cause need no longer slow down development. The difference, however, can easily be exaggerated. On the one hand not a few of the key inventions (such as iron puddling in seventeenth-century England) were made many decades before any general application was possible, so that technical factors were seldom a bottle-neck; on the other the inventions as they were made were in terms that were appropriate for the climate, degree of capital accumulation and labour expertise available. Today the extent to which other people's inventions are inappropriate without substantial adjustment is only gradually being realized, so that much further research and experimentation (Prof. Lewis puts it at 1 per cent. of the national product) is in fact still required.

Of all the countries that have 'got on', the experience of Japan and Russia seem to be the most relevant to the present developing countries. One factor in this is that, developing later than western Europe or the U.S.A., they have been able to draw on other people's technical advances. Russian experience is especially interesting, not least for the degree of compulsion which seems to have been necessary (in spite of magnificent resources), in order to produce the unique achievement of developing heavy industry before light, and without reliance on exports. Russia is interesting too for the relative failure of its food policy (bound up with the compulsory nature of the programme), and in spite of exceptionally good opportunities of importing from the satellites.

Although not authoritarian, it seems clear that the Japanese regime in the early stages of development was tougher than most developers today. It was able also to draw on a unique tradition of self-discipline and national loyalty. Of special relevance today for Asian countries, and above all for India, is the account given in Buchanan and Ellis of the supersession of the feudal landlords and their compensation by State bonds; it seems that from this position they slipped more easily into enterprise than if they had received a sum of money. Further relevant was the Japanese use of an efficient and up-to-date land tax to ensure that extra food produced by farms was not all consumed on them. Although the Indian abolition of the Zamindari has been a very parallel operation to the supersession of the Japanese landed nobility, it seems unfortunately clear that economically it has been much less successful.

[...]

Those who have spent much of their time in recent years in trying to push and pull the backward countries forward are often in danger of losing heart and patience. This is really not right: in spite of ups and downs, disappointments and frustrations, much solid progress has been made in virtually every backward country since 1946.

Sudha R. Shenoy

From "The Coming Serfdom in India" (1966)

The major issue that divides liberals (advocates of liberty) from "liberals" (statists) is the question of the importance of economic freedom. As the statist sees it, economic freedom is the "freedom" of the few to exploit the many. The right to vote, on the other hand, is common to all men. Hence, for statists, the dividing line between democracies and dictatorships is drawn in answer to the question: Are elections free or not? But it will be noticed that totalitarianism is the implicit criterion here: any situation which is not yet totalitarian would be described as "free" by the statist.

As the true liberal sees it, freedom is indivisible. Hence, measures ostensibly aimed at the weak political minority of businessmen will in fact only prevent the market process from functioning as well as it might have done, and will confer on some people – i.e., politicians and administrators – a power over their fellow men otherwise exercised by no one; a power deriving from this group's ability to determine, *de facto* though not *de jure*, the uses to which resources may be put. This power, the liberal affirms, is of entirely another nature from the "power" alleged to be exercised by businessmen operating in a market context. Control over resources by businessmen is not only scattered among a much larger group of individuals; these businessmen themselves are in effect simply the agents of their fellow men in determining the use of these resources, via the market process of profit and loss. But where economic power is concentrated in the hands of a *politically* selected group, the chances for the emergence and establishment of a political opposition are precarious, to say the least. The statist overlooks the necessity for independent sources of material support for a political opposition; even though *some* opposition may seem to be present, the real criterion is the range of different views that would have emerged if economic power had not been so concentrated. In other words, freedom is more than one value among others; it is rather the foundation for a whole social order. Intervention embodies a principle that is diametrically opposed and must lead to the destruction of this social order (where it exists) and the establishment of an order founded on the principle of political exploitation: the politically strong exploiting the politically weak. In short, intervention leads to the suppression of *potential* political opposition and thus ends in totalitarianism.

India as an Oligarchy

This abstract and theoretical argument is vividly illustrated by the experience of India. Most statists regard India as an excellent example of economic planning combined with democracy. It would perhaps be more accurate to describe India as an oligarchy – in the Aristotelian sense of government of, for, and by the rich. These rich, however, unlike those who earn high incomes in a free market by supplying their fellow men's needs, have obtained their wealth via the very instruments of planning – permits, licenses, quotas, concessions, and contracts. In the first place, virtually all investible resources – i.e., savings and foreign aid – are forcibly drawn (via capital controls and taxation) into the preferred "industrial" sectors, both private and public. The industrial output thus artificially produced adds nothing to the flow of goods and services for the starving, ill-clothed, and unsheltered Indian masses – but those businessmen, civil servants, and others sharing in this forced expansion obtain high incomes (legal and illegal). Hence, we see that the output of coarse cotton bought by the masses has expanded the least, while the output of rayon – a luxury in India – has multiplied by *twenty-one* times over the last 15 years and three five-year plans [...]

In the second place, even this private industrial sector is very closely controlled by a minutely detailed network of regulations: government sanction is required to start, expand, or close down an undertaking; permits are required for virtually all raw materials and certainly all imported machinery and components. Government regulations extend to such points as the manner of conducting board meetings and the width of *sari* borders in the case of mill-made *saris*. In effect all these controls and regulations have created and protected private monopolies in virtually all fields of nonagricultural production.

Thirdly, there is import and exchange control. No imports of any kind are permitted without a license, and imports of a wide range of commodities are banned altogether. Prohibitive tariffs have been imposed on a large number of other goods. All this means that Indian producers of import substitutes have a highly-protected sellers' market. To reinforce import control, all exchange earnings have to be surrendered to the

Reserve Bank at the official price – which is well below the true market price. It is, of course, forbidden to send exchange or rupees out of the country in any form.

Fourthly, the government sector has continually expanded over the last 15 years – even though this sector provides the least employment and adds nothing to the real national income. The driving force here is public contracts; the larger the public sector, the larger are its contracts, and the larger, therefore, the rake-offs for the contractors and civil servants involved. (Where 100 rupees are accounted to be spent on a project, they never are. Some say 60 rupees are spent and 40 distributed; others would reverse the proportions – but no Indian would agree that the full amount was spent.)

Fifthly, there are innumerable other controls over the internal economic life of the country, ranging from controls over the movement of food grains between states, to those over the establishment of bus routes. All of these serve to increase the powers of officials over their fellow men. [...]

A Limited Private Sector

From all this, it will be clear how small is the sector of the Indian economy from which a political opposition can draw material support, and how minute a portion of even this sector is independent of the government. [...] The industrial sector in India owes its establishment and continued existence to the government. In the absence of the forced draft of resources into it, and of exchange and import controls and tariffs, this sector's artificiality and unviability would be quickly and unmistakably revealed. It follows that though Indian businessmen technically may be independent of government and even complain of some types of intervention, in fact they must be included as part of the government sector.

It is, therefore, hardly surprising that the opposition in India should be so small and that opposition parties should complain of a dearth of funds while the ruling party has no complaint in this regard. Naturally, virtually all businessmen are ardent supporters of the government. Again, a leading South Indian newspaper charged that government had used Journalists' Wages Boards and newsprint controls to penalize papers consistently opposing it; charges have also been heard that government departments have threatened to withhold valuable advertising from the opposition press. [...] And more recently, opposition M.P.'s have protested in Parliament against Criminal Investigation Department harassment – their telephones, they say, are tapped, their letters (even letters from their wives) are censored, and they are shadowed by C.I.D. plain-clothesmen. [...] When M.P.'s are treated thus, the ordinary citizen can hardly feel aggrieved when he finds that letters abroad – even registered letters – are opened in order to ferret out violations of the Exchange Control Regulations.

Finally, the Essential Commodities (Amendment) Bill of 1966 is yet another straw showing the direction in which the political wind in India is blowing. As mentioned, food grains movement is controlled. Hitherto, the government could only impound food grains suspected of being moved illegally. But now the government can summarily confiscate both food grains and vehicles suspected of being involved in illegal movements; it is up to the poor merchant to prove his innocence. [...]

Perhaps the most ironic element in this whole situation is the role of foreign aid. Given in order to "feed starving orphans in Orissa" (as Milton Mayer would have it) or to "keep India from going communist" (as many Americans believe), it is in fact one major cause why orphans in Orissa are starving and why India is now so firmly set down the road to serfdom. This is because in India foreign aid provides the major portion of the finance for the Plans: for every rupee of internal resources, almost 2 rupees worth of resources comes from foreign aid. If aid is calculated at the official exchange rate for the rupee, its economic value is understated – even allowing for the recent devaluation. It is only if aid is calculated at the free market exchange rate that its true significance emerges. Planning in India, as has already been pointed out, involves essentially a forced transfer of resources out of the uses where they would benefit the masses – i.e., the agricultural sector – into an artificially created and propped up "industrial" sector. It follows that agricultural output has lagged far behind all industrial outputs; consequently, the Indian people are hungrier after three Plans than they were before. Per capita availability of food grains has fluctuated downward over the last 15 years, and stands today at about 14 ounces per day. Meanwhile, since planning implies the concentration of economic and political power in the hands of the ruling clique, it has effectively smothered a wide range of potential political opposition. It would not be too much to describe India as a one-party state.

Democratic forms in themselves are meaningless. The right to vote can be effective only in the context of a whole network of other freedoms. Elections can be free only in the framework of a free market and the Rule of Law.

Edith Penrose

From *The Large International Firm in Developing Countries* (1968)

Throughout the history of the modern industry, governments have intervened in a variety of ways to protect or advance what they conceived to be their national economic interests. In the late 1950s and in the 1960s, government policies became of increasing significance for the oil industry in almost all countries. In addition to taxation, governments in the developing countries became more concerned about international prices, foreign exchange receipts and payments, currencies of payment, security of supply, foreign investment, and the location, ownership or control of producing and refining facilities. Most countries can be classed as either primarily consumers of crude oil (and products) or primarily producers of crude oil. [...]

The US became a net importer of crude and products toward the end of the 1940s. All during the 1950s mounting imports, with the consequent greater dependence on foreign supplies, raised fears of a danger to the country's economic security from a military standpoint. This, plus political pressure from domestic producers of coal as well as oil, led to the imposition of voluntary and then mandatory import controls in spite of the fact that US companies had acquired ownership of large reserves of crude oil in many parts of the world. [...]

In the less developed consuming countries, governments became increasingly less willing to accept without scrutiny the operations and plans of the international Companies. [...] India conducted a full-scale inquiry into the price of oil in 1961 in which the dissatisfaction of the Committee of Enquiry was plainly expressed. Subsequently the Government restricted the freedom of action of the refining affiliates of the international majors, forced a discount in the price of crude oil, and began actively to encourage the entry of other refiners willing to act in co-operation with the Government. In Pakistan, too, the Government undertook directly to participate in the industry. Both India and

456

Pakistan promoted domestic exploration for oil by domestic and foreign Companies and by partnerships between them, with some favourable results in India and considerable supplies of natural gas in Pakistan. Ceylon set up a state oil company to market oil and eventually expropriated the facilities of the existing distributors, who were affiliates of international majors, for the use of the State company. Cuba similarly expropriated the international oil Companies. In Africa, the governments went little further than occasionally to obtain shares in refining facilities, although the offers by ENI of State participation were usually accepted.

Political pressures from governments have also been partly responsible for the establishment of refineries in numerous countries the markets of which would ordinarily have been considered too small to support a refinery. [...] But also important, especially in developing countries, were government policies demanding the establishment of local refineries either to save foreign exchange through the import of crude oil instead of products or to promote national industrialization. [...]

It was among the crude-oil producing countries where the governments were most insistent on their right to an extensive voice in the conduct of the industry. In Burma the State took over the industry in 1963 (along with other foreign enterprises), but without a head-on collision with the Companies. Indonesia and Argentina permitted foreign Companies to work largely as contractors on behalf of the government; other countries insisted on considerable State participation in producing operations; in still others the State maintains an extensive supervisory and regulatory system, for example, in Venezuela. In almost all producing countries State-owned national oil companies have been created.

Of great concern to the crude-producing countries, of course, is the revenue the government receives from the industry's operations, and it was a threatened reduction in revenue through a reduction in the prices on which profits were calculated that brought the formation of the Organization of Petroleum Exporting Countries in 1960. There can be little doubt that the establishment of OPEC increased the bargaining power of the crude-oil producing countries, and most observers give OPEC credit for the fact that after its formation posted prices were not reduced as 'market' prices continued to slide, but rather became a subject for negotiation with the oil-producing countries along with other proposals designed to increase their revenues.

OPEC was established at a conference of the five major petroleum exporting countries (Iran, Iraq, Kuwait, Saudi Arabia and Venezuela) at a conference held in Baghdad in September 1960 on the invitation of the Government of Iraq. Much of the initiative that led to the establishment of OPEC had come from Venezuela who, as the producer with the highest average costs of all the major exporters, had the strongest interest in the prevention of competition which would bear heavily on prices. She had early recognized that stronger control over the rate of supply would be essential if the pressure on prices was to be relieved and had endeavoured to adapt her domestic policies accordingly. Since no other producing country followed suit, Venezuela's policy was doomed to failure. At the ninth OPEC conference in 1965 Venezuela was still attempting to persuade the exporting countries to co-operate to restrict production, and a voluntary programme to regulate supply was agreed upon. By then, however, the problem was even more difficult than it had been in 1960 in view of the clear success of the newer producers, particularly Libya, Nigeria and Abu Dhabi [...].

In addition to resolutions establishing the Organization and providing for a common front of the exporting countries vis-a-vis the oil Companies, the first OPEC conference agreed to attempt to get posted prices restored to their previous level. In subsequent conferences the arrangements for the constitution and financing of the Organization were completed, provisions for various studies made, new members admitted (Qatar, Indonesia, Libya), and the aims of the member countries were stated together with the demand that negotiations should be entered into by the Companies to achieve these aims. It became clearer as time went on that restoration of the cuts in posted prices was not practicable and the issue was not actively pursued, but a number of other ways of effectively raising the revenues of the producing countries were successfully negotiated. In 1964, agreement was achieved on the expensing of royalties, and the elimination of marketing allowances. [...]

That the world's crude oil reserves outside the US and the Communist countries ended up after the Second World War almost entirely in the hands of seven large Companies capable as a group of developing them rapidly, yet at the same time refining most of the output and selling it as products within their own marketing organizations, was not entirely due to perseverence [sic] in exploration crowned with the luck of discovery; it was brought about quite deliberately by the creation of associations among the major groups in the ownership of crude-oil producing affiliates and marketing companies, and by the negotiation of long-term contracts. In the Middle East, until the formation of the Iranian Consortium, only Anglo-Iranian held in splendid isolation sole ownership of the reserves it had discovered and developed.

It was no coincidence that the Companies, which together obtained control of Middle East oil by the 1950s, also dominated refining and marketing in Europe and Asia. Jersey Standard and Shell had begun their international operations with markets and distribution networks and had sought crude oil to keep them supplied, building refineries as the oil became available; during the 1950s Jersey refined more crude oil in or near Venezuela than in the Eastern Hemisphere, and shipped products all over the world. Socony Mobil, as the successor to the old Standard Oil of New York, which had been charged with foreign marketing in the original Standard Oil Trust before the First World War, had long experience in distribution in Asia and Africa as well as in some countries of Europe. Texaco had been selling in foreign markets since the beginning of the century. Only Gulf and Standard of California, like British Petroleum earlier, owed their entry on the international scene largely to the fact that they had been fortunate in the gamble of exploration and astute in the struggle for control in the Middle East, but they had to make arrangements with others who could use the oil they discovered. [...]

It may well be argued that the result thrown up by history could hardly be expected to have been other than it was, at least in its broad outlines: Western enterprise and Western capital were required if the oil of Venezuela, the Middle East and South-east Asia was to be developed, and the Companies with the greatest interest in the matter were the existing marketers. These could afford to outbid all others in most matters, they could supply capital that others lacked, take the oil that others could not use, and purchase those lesser companies that were weak, or faint-hearted, or merely useful to them. Thus, it was, as has often been noted, 'logical' that the great Companies should prevail – not necessarily all of those that in fact did so, but certainly those that had acquired extensive Eastern Hemisphere markets. It was logical in the sense that the result seemed a thoroughly natural and reasonable outcome of the economic circumstances and needs of the time, and is therefore explicable without the aid of special hypotheses resting on the existence of deep-laid imperialistic plots, conspiracies between governments and Companies, abnormal subversion through bribery or violence, etc.

Nevertheless, the dominance of the industry by a few large firms was also the result of government policies that permitted the growth of monopolistic business organizations. The evolution of the petroleum industry within the US was characterized by the emergence of vertically integrated firms. This was by no means a technical or economic 'necessity', but historically was largely a by-product of the early position and competitive tactics of Standard Oil of New Jersey, which made integration by its rivals a competitive necessity in practice. [...] When US firms reached abroad – and again particularly Jersey standard – similar competitive relationships were established. If we add to this the terms on which concessions were obtainable in the Middle East, the size of the financial resources of the firms in the international industry, and the policies of governments, we have sufficient conditions for the emergence of vertically integrated oligopoly in the production, refining and marketing of crude oil from the Eastern Hemisphere.

By the 1960s the international petroleum industry had been thoroughly stirred up: rapid changes were taking place in the location of activity, in the organization of the industry, and in the relative position of the governmental and private groups involved in it. The industry was still largely in the hands of the seven international majors, however, for the changes occurring were changes at the margin. Nevertheless, the policies of the majors no longer had a decisive influence on the course of events since their freedom of action was in many ways very much more restricted both by their competitive position and by governments. The Companies were often on the defensive, fighting rear-guard actions, which could only retard changes that seemed inevitable. In the Middle East political tensions were often high, but the most severe crisis began in May 1967 and provoked an attack by Israel on her Arab neighbours. Oil exports to the US, Britain and Western Germany were for a while banned by the major Arab producers in view of the generally pro-Israel position of these powers during the Arab–Israel war, and pressures for nationalization increased in some of the countries.

The Arab ban on exports, which was serious for Britain and British Companies, apparently actually benefited the US balance of payments and some US Companies. The export ban was short-lived, however, and demands for nationalization quickly died down to 'normal' levels. The most important economic consequence of the Israeli war for the international oil industry was the closing of the Suez Canal, which, again, hurt Britain without much affecting the US since the latter does not significantly depend on Middle East Oil, and indeed could increase its own exports to the countries affected by the difficulties.

The crisis had not been resolved at the time of writing nor the Canal re-opened. The long-run consequences for the oil Companies were thus not clear. The attitudes of the ruling régime in Iraq toward the IPC hardened further, but the political position of the Companies in other producing countries was unaffected. [...]

Political disturbances apart, the disturbance of the old order was fundamentally brought about by the increased competition among suppliers of crude oil, which was in part the consequence of the desire of those in control of ever-increasing reserves in the Middle East to secure or enlarge their position in rapidly growing markets, and in part the result of the entry of newcomers into world markets. The spreading effects of increased supplies and sharper competition were also partly responsible for the more active interest of some governments in the operations of the industry, although other factors such as concern for the security of supply, nationalism, 'anti-imperialism' etc., played a significant role. The governments of a number of countries importing crude oil began more clearly to understand the nature of the industry's price structure, and in particular to understand the significance for their economies of the vertical integration of the major firms, and especially of their control of local refinery capacity.

Susan Strange

From *Sterling and British Policy* (1971)

There are and always have been just two basic objectives of all national governments: to secure the defence of the realm and the value of the currency. The kind and form of domestic order and justice is a matter of choice and therefore of wide variety. The standard of welfare which the government feels able and willing to provide for its citizens is a matter of individual choice within the state. But where foreign and economic policies are concerned, only military security and monetary stability are universally sought and pursued by states above all other aims. The wider international goals about which political speeches are endlessly written – the establishment of peace, the reduction of armaments, the increase of economic development, the pursuit of human rights and a fair deal for the poor, the black, the religious and racial minorities, the under-regarded of all kinds – are so far beyond the reach of individual governments and their policies that they are, by comparison with the two basic aims, mostly either rhetoric or dreams. We enact, as Conor Cruise O'Brien says, our sacred dramas on the international stage but they amount to a ritual and a prayer. They express our deepest longings; they do not necessarily bear very much upon our realistic ambitions in the world of everyday politics.

This may seem to convey too cynical and defeatist an attitude to world problems. Others will find it only realistic. But both idealists and realists will perhaps still agree that for most national governments the two basic targets of policy I have mentioned must in practice take precedence over all other more distant hopes and aspirations.

They now require, however, more precise definition before we can go on to consider the policy steps that, in Britain, might be needed to achieve them – so far as this is practically possible.

Securing the defence of the realm, I interpret as relating primarily to the security of the British Isles. But this may be attainable in our time only so long as a major war in Europe is averted. The security of Britain

462

may therefore require a British government to contribute materially in some form or another to the security of the European mainland as well as of these islands. This is not the place to discuss more precisely what form this contribution could or should take, nor what methods are best for the organization of our collective European defence. It is only necessary for present purposes to point out that it follows from the general proposition that Britain will have in future to choose more carefully than she has done in the past the priorities of her military strategy. Thus, if it is necessary to post British forces in Germany – and no amount of tough negotiation will persuade the Germans wholly or partly to hire them from us – then that would clearly be an acceptable charge on the British balance of payments. On the other hand, protecting British investments abroad, whether in India or in Latin America, securing cheap oil supplies and 'contributing to stability' in the Persian Gulf or for that matter in the neighbourhood of Singapore would not, because its relevance to the security of this country is much too distant. Similarly, the British military concern with the affairs of Africa cannot now, in a post-imperial period, be any greater than that of other members of the United Nations Security Council.

This is not to say that Britain should cease to make a contribution to world peace – as indeed to international economic stability or economic development and trade. It does not mean that she should wantonly go about flouting international standards. Only that these misty and distant objectives should never take precedence or be sought regardless of cost. We have a duty to pull our weight but not more than our weight in comparison with other leading countries in the western world. Therefore all considerations of status, prestige, sentiment, Auld Lang Syne, or good form should be considered secondary to our two prime purposes.

The second basic target of securing the stability of the national currency does not necessarily require that the domestic economy it serves should achieve any particular rate of growth or attain any specific standard of affluence or consumption. That, again is a matter of domestic political choice. However, in this day and world, no national currency can ever be quite divorced from the general state of the economy. Inflation or any propensity to import or invest abroad more heavily than is warranted by the capacity of exports or services to pay for them, have both to be avoided if the currency is to be secure.

Whether, therefore, you want more government intervention, planning, and ownership within the state, or whether you wish for less, whether you start from the broadly conservative private enterprise point of view or a broadly socialist and anti-capitalist one, it is still incumbent on any national government, in order to secure the currency from collapse and depreciation, to secure also that the domestic economy is as viable, healthy, and stable as possible. In other words, the pursuit of the basic economic target of national policy cannot be conducted by monetary means alone and without reference to its broader economic foundations.

Looking back, it seems clear that part of the failure of British policies – diplomatic and economic – in the last ten or fifteen years has been in misjudging where these confining barriers or parameters really lay. A great deal of effort, of official and political time and public funds were repeatedly given to the pursuit of policy goals lying outside the parameter of feasibility. For example, all recent British Prime Ministers – especially Mr Harold Wilson but also 'Supermac' Macmillan and Sir Alec Douglas-Home – shared the fatal illusion that Britain still enjoyed a measure of initiative in international affairs that in reality had long since vanished. The real lesson of Suez was never properly learnt. Whether dashing to Moscow to mediate between the Americans and Russians, convening the Commonwealth to solve the riddle of Vietnam, posturing over Rhodesia, or pretending to intervene between Nigeria and Biafra, the emptiness of British diplomatic influence without the capacity to intervene with decisive force has been demonstrated again and again. A reluctance to abandon the familiar 'policeman' and 'broker' roles of Britain's past has been yet another part of the failure to adjust to change. In fact, it was a predictable consequence of Britain's altered status in international politics and in the international economy that the feasibility parameter would become more inhibiting. But a parallel consequence of this change, to which British policy-makers seemed no less blind, was that it also made the acceptability parameter rather *less* inhibiting. By this I mean simply that the loss of imperial power made it no longer necessary to reconcile the imperial and the metropolitan interest. And with the loss of Top Currency status it was no longer so necessary to reconcile the international commercial welfare with the domestic commercial welfare. In both respects, Britain was in reality freer to look after her own national interest than she had been for a very long time. The trouble was that the habits of mind which I have called the Top Currency Syndrome prevented her from taking advantage of this greater freedom and caused British governments to underestimate repeatedly their freedom to deviate from the policy standards set by the United States – or by multilateral associations such as GATT dominated by the US. Meanwhile, the Commonwealth Myth substituting for the imperial role, imposed other limits on British policy in the hope of pleasing her Commonwealth associates.

The result was a common tendency in official explanations of policy to confuse and blur the two parameters. It was often hard to know whether the British government rejected a policy measure on principle, out of consideration for national interest, or out of fear of displeasing associated governments – in the UN, the Commonwealth, GATT, or simply the United States. 'Not only would it be immoral to act so,' the official explanation of policy has often gone, 'we should not be allowed to do so.'

This was the essence of the explanations given for not devaluing sterling in 1964 and afterwards (until forced to do so by speculative pressures); for not applying import controls to improve the current balance; for not offering tax incentives to exporters for the same purpose; for not budging from a 'cheap' food policy, and for a good many other aspects of economic policy. The 'morality' in question usually derived from the multilateralist ideology of the Top Currency Syndrome or from the instinctive sense of responsibility of a former imperial power towards the Commonwealth, or from a combination of both.

The latter was the case with the over-long attachment to the $2-80 exchange rate for sterling. It was clung to partly as a matter of preserving the 'status of sterling' as an international transactions currency, and also as a reserve currency which would stiffen the wilting bonds of Commonwealth policy. It was because they were reluctant to abandon an outworn section of the acceptability parameter that British official minds tended to exaggerate the inhibiting effects of the Anglo-American and Anglo-Commonwealth associations.

If, in the future, British policy is to be more realistic and more successfully self-regarding, both parameters will have to be more accurately defined and plotted. The feasibility parameter will need to be better understood – both where it is hard and cannot be over-stepped and where it may be soft and likely to give under pressure. The acceptability parameter will need to be redrawn in the light of a much cooler assessment of vital national interest and orders of priority than was possible so long as officials clung to either the Top Currency Syndrome or the Commonwealth Myth.

Looking forward, it seems clear that if we keep the two basic targets constantly in mind and give them consistent and unwavering priority over all else, our policy towards the balance of payments must be bent towards attempting to reinforce (so far as we can) all those encouraging trends I noted earlier. I then qualified my optimism by saying that these expectations could be thought reasonable 'given a reasonable degree of prudence and determination.' I had in mind that these qualities would be particularly needed to guard the points of potential weakness in the balance of payments. These points are the outflow of British capital for overseas investment; defence policies; the aid programme; the debts to foreign creditors; and the potential dangers through leads and lags and through the operation of international money markets centred in London. These are the key problems which, together with the policies that might help to deal with them, perhaps require a little further consideration.

9

Men, Women, and Gender
Introduction by Kimberly Hutchings

Gender has always formed a part of international thinking, but in a male as norm context, the entry of women into the conversation makes gender visible, both in terms of the objects of knowledge (militaries, foreign policymakers, "men" in a state of nature) and in terms of the producers of knowledge (scholars, journalists, soldiers, politicians, revolutionaries). In histories of international thought, recognition of work on the significance of gender for international relations and vice versa has been limited. Most accounts associate such work with the revival of feminist thinking in IR in the late 1980s.[1] Certain figures, such as Emily Greene Balch (1867–1961) and Virginia Woolf (1882–1941), are acknowledged as part of the history of liberal internationalism, and the categories of women and gender are widely understood as central to the history of pacifism.[2] Nevertheless, accounts of historical thinking on gender and international relations are predominantly confined to references to a small number of particularly well-known thinkers, most of whom focus on the idea of a women–peace connection and are assumed to work with fixed, binary conceptions of sex and gender. In this section, we will show

---

[1] See Patricia Owens, "Women and the History of International Thought," *International Studies Quarterly*, 62:3 (2018): 467–481; Fred Halliday, "Hidden from International Relations: Women and the International Arena," *Millennium: Journal of International Studies*, 17:3 (1988): 419–428; Fred Halliday, "Gender and IR: Progress, Backlash and Prospect," *Millennium: Journal of International Studies*, 27:4 (1998): 833–846. For early contributions to the revival of work focusing on gender in international thought see Jean Bethke Elshtain, *Women and War* (Chicago, IL: Chicago University Press, 1987); Cynthia Enloe, *Bananas, Beaches and Bases: Making Feminist Sense of International Politics* (Berkeley, CA: University of California Press, 1990); V. Spike Peterson (ed.), *Gendered States: Feminist (Re)Visions of International Theory* (Boulder, CO: Lynne Rienner, 1992); Christine Sylvester, *Feminist Theory and International Relations in a Postmodern Era* (Cambridge: Cambridge University Press, 1994).

[2] See for example Judy D. Phipps, "The Feminist Pacifism of Emily Greene Balch," *NWSA Journal*, 18:3 (2006): 122-132; Peter Wilson, "Attacking Hitler in England: Patriarchy, Class and War in Virginia Woolf's Three Guineas," in Henrik Bliddal, Casper Sylvest, and Peter Wilson (eds.), *Classics in International Relations: Essays in Criticism and Appreciation* (London: Routledge, 2013): 36–47.

that this picture vastly underestimates the range and sophistication of women's thinking about gender and international relations in the first half of the twentieth century.

The women thinkers excerpted in this section were born between 1856 and 1908, and their writings range chronologically from Anna Julia Cooper's 1892 *A Voice from the South* to Jane Vialle's 1951 essay *Femmes africaines*. Within the texts, even though the category of gender is not necessarily named (terms such as sex, men, women, masculine, and feminine are more common), the authors offer distinct understandings of the meaning of gender and processes of gendering, and of the work that gender/gendering does in the theory and practice of international relations. Across these works we can trace themes, arguments, and questions. What is gender? Is it natural or constructed, essential or optional? How does it cross cut with categories of race and class? Is it culturally specific or transcultural? How can gender norms be contested? What roles do gender structures play in constituting world politics? How does gender relate to peace and war? What are the gendered effects of transnational and international processes of imperialism, militarism, and capitalism?

At the end of the nineteenth century and beginning of the twentieth century, the "woman question" became a huge focus of attention in public debate, as well as in fiction, throughout Europe and America. This followed the rise of women's visibility in the public sphere in their campaigns for women's suffrage, for abolitionism and social reform, and for access to higher education and professional work. For Cooper, Semple, Lee, and Balch, all born in the middle of the nineteenth century, this intellectual and political context was crucial. They all started their lives in a context in which women were legally subordinated to men, they all participated in campaigning or arguing for change, and to some extent benefited from the opening up of opportunities for women. For Anna Julia Cooper (1858–1964), however, this was not as straightforward as for the other thinkers. Cooper was born a slave, growing up during Reconstruction in the American South. She had to deal with multiple axes of subordination in relation to race and class as well as gender and her access to education, work, and publication of her writings was consequently far more difficult than for her white middle-class peers. She was a teacher and a leader in improving educational opportunities for African Americans. She was involved in promoting the cause of civil rights and was part of an international network of pan-Africanist scholars and activists, including W. E. B. Du Bois. Later in her long life she gained her PhD, on the relation between the French and Haitian revolutions, from the Sorbonne (see the section on Imperialism in this volume).

A century before intersectionality became a buzzword in the academy, Anna Julia Cooper's long neglected book *A Voice from the South* (1892) developed a thoroughly intersectional and international analysis of gender.[3] The book ranges over a series of issues concerning black women's position within the US state, and their position within struggles for greater freedom and representation waged by feminist, anti-racist, and labour movements. Cooper's book carefully dissects the complex politics of gender, race, and class of her time. In doing this, she demonstrated how this politics was embedded in transnational material and ideational economies of imperialism and slavery that enabled the building and maintaining of the US state from the seventeenth century onwards. In this respect, Cooper prefigures much contemporary feminist and decolonial work that challenges IR's "realist" picture of the international as comprised solely of states interacting with each other.[4] In the extract below, Cooper gently mocks those American feminists who urged the freedom of women at the expense of the freedom of Black or Native American men.[5] She emphasizes the significance of positionality for knowledge and for political judgment.

For Cooper, gender was always refracted through race and class, and Black women's standpoint was a source of insight and a resource for political change. In contrast, her contemporary, the white American Ellen Churchill Semple (1863–1932) essentialized gender, but also instrumentalized it, drawing on her own experience to argue that women (like her) were particularly well suited to produce certain kinds of international knowledge. Semple was unusual for her time in that she was a woman who successfully followed an academic career and became a respected scholar in the US and Europe. Her major work, *Influences of Geographic Environment on the Basis of Ratzel's System of Anthropo-Geography* (1911) was highly influential (see the section on Geopolitics and War). Semple rarely addressed gender in her academic work. The extract below comes from a 1915 speech she made at the Fiftieth Anniversary of the founding of Vassar College, where she had gained her BA in 1882. Here there is a strong suggestion that although racial and

---

[3] See Vivian M. May, *Anna Julia Cooper: Visionary Black Feminist* (London: Routledge, 2012); Vivian M. May, "Anna Julia Cooper on Slavery's Afterlife: Can International Thought 'Hear' Her 'Muffled' Voice?," in Patricia Owens and Katharina Rietzler (eds.), *Women's International Thought: A New History* (Cambridge: Cambridge University Press, 2021), 29–51.

[4] See Kimberly Hutchings and Patricia Owens, "Women Thinkers and the Canon of International Thought: Recovery, Rejection, and Reconstruction," *American Political Science Review*, 115:2 (2021): 347–359.

[5] Allison L. Sneider, *Suffragists in an Imperial Age: U.S. Expansion and the Woman Question, 1870–1929* (New York: Oxford University Press, 2008).

cultural difference may be explained by the effects of the interplay between heredity and environment, gender is a fixed, biological fact. Women have certain innate characteristics. They are observant, do detailed work, are patient, have intellectual humility and imagination. Semple's list of characteristics speaks to a racialized (white) ideal of feminine qualities.[6] In spite of her universalist language, in her own research in colonial Japan, it was her positionality as an elite white woman that enabled her to pursue her inquiries, and commend the Japanese for their colonization of Korea.[7]

Amongst all the debates about women's nature and place in society that came under the heading of the "woman question," one strand that emerged was the idea of a link between women and peace (see the section on World Peace).[8] Many women involved in campaigns for women's rights were prominent in peace movements from the 1890s onwards. These included the Americans Jane Addams (1860–1935; see the sections on World Peace and Religion and Ethics) and long term fellow-campaigner Emily Greene Balch (1867–61, discussed below and in the section on World Peace). In this context, Vernon Lee (aka Violet Paget 1856–1935) is an odd woman out. She does not fit neatly with the profile of Addams or Balch. She did not get involved in internationalist, pacifist movements until relatively late in her career. And she claims that she had not really been interested in the "woman question" prior to encountering Charlotte Perkins Gilman's book *Women and Economics* in the text included here, which was first published in 1902.[9]

Lee was a white British cultural historian, literary critic, and fiction writer. She came from an affluent, cosmopolitan, and literary family, who lived in continental Europe, and was, unusually for her time, educated by her mother to be a writer.[10] She was multi-lingual and fascinated by the

---

[6] bell hooks, *Ain't I a Woman: Black Women and Feminism* (London: Routledge, 2015 [1981]).

[7] Ellen Churchill Semple, "Japanese Colonial Methods," *Bulletin of the American Geographical Society*, 45:4 (1913): 255–275.

[8] See Heloise Brown, *The Truest Form of Patriotism: Pacifist Feminism in Britain 1870–1902* (Manchester: Manchester University Press, 2003).

[9] Charlotte Perkins Gilman published the book under her married name of Stetson, *Women and Economics: A Study of the Relation between Men and Women as a Factor in Social Evolution* (Gutenberg e-book: www.gutenberg.org/ebooks/57913, first published 1898). Lee's review essay of Gilman's book was later published in Lee's *Gospels of Anarchy* under the title "The Economic Parasitism of Women," see Vernon Lee, "The Economic Parasitism of Women," in *Gospels of Anarchy and Other Contemporary Studies* (London and Leipzig: T. Fisher & Unwin, 1908, reprinted Whitefish, MT: Kessinger Publishing, 2004) (www.kessinger.net).

[10] Vineta Colby, *Vernon Lee: A Literary Biography* (Charlottesville, VA and London: University of Virginia Press, 2003); Christa Zorn, *Vernon Lee: Aesthetics, History, and*

contrasts between different national/cultural contexts across Europe. She chose to publish her work under the name of Vernon Lee, because she thought that no one would take seriously work known to have been written by a woman. Vernon Lee was not simply a pseudonym; she used the name in her private as well as public life, and identified with the masculine persona of an intellectual, and as part of the late nineteenth-century aesthetic movement, with which she shared a strong interest in sexual ambivalence.

In her fictional writings and essays Lee questions the ways in which particular characteristics become associated with either sex, as well as arguing that there are significant differences in what sexual difference means in different national contexts. She frequently extolled the superiority of Greek civilization, and the fact that we cannot tell the difference between which statues "to give the name of Apollo, or that of Athena" (487). She also points to the connection between the gendered basis of the contemporary economic order, social inequality, and investment in war.[11] Lee's criticism of a fixed binary difference between men and women echoes her broader skepticism about boundaries, whether between genres or nations. For her, the experience of traveling in other countries illuminated the arbitrariness of the laws and norms at home and enabled connections with different ways of thinking and feeling.[12] She became a committed pacifist in response to the First World War. In her anti-war allegory, published in 1920, she notes: "there comes to be for each group of combatants a perfectly innocent victim, namely itself, and an entirely guilty monster, namely the adversary; and there is only black and white."[13]

Balch does not complicate ideas of sexual difference in the same way as Lee (see also the discussion of Murray in the section on International Law and International Organization). Although Balch insists that gender is a cultural construction and, like Lee, argues for the ontological unity of humanity,[14] she

the *Victorian Female Intellectual* (Athens, OH: Ohio University Press, 2003); Catherine Maxwell and Patricia Pulham (eds.), *Vernon Lee: Decadence, Ethics and Aesthetics* (Basingstoke and New York: Palgrave Macmillan, 2006).

11 Lee, "The Economic Parasitism of Women," 152, 154.

12 Vernon Lee, *The Sentimental Traveller: Notes on Places* (London and New York: John Lane, Bodley Head, 1908).

13 Vernon Lee, *Satan the Waster: A Philosophic War Trilogy with Notes and Introduction* (London and New York: John Lane, Bodley Head, 1920), xxiii–xxiv.

14 See Catia Confortini, "Race, Gender, Empire, and War in the International Thought of Emily Greene Balch," in Patricia Owens and Katharina Rietzler (eds.), *Women's International Thought: A New History* (Cambridge: Cambridge University Press, 2021), 244–265; Glenda Sluga, "From F. Melian Stawell to E. Greene Balch: International and *Internationalist* Thinking at the Gender Margins, 1919–1947," in Patricia Owens and Katharina Rietzler (eds.), *Women's International Thought: A New History* (Cambridge: Cambridge University Press, 2021), 223–243.

still tends to treat gender as a binary category mapped onto particular characteristics and values. Balch, along with Jane Addams, participated in the Hague 1915 Women's International Congress and played a leading role in the Women's International League for Peace and Freedom (WILPF) (see the section on World Peace). She was from a middle-class background, and was able to pursue an academic career, as well as being involved in reformist movements, later embracing socialism. Balch worked full-time for the WILPF after she was dismissed from her academic post at Wellesley due to her political activities, including support for the Russian Revolution and defense of conscientious objectors.[15] She was a regular commentator on international affairs, a critic of imperial and racial hierarchies, and produced many reports for the WILPF on cases of international tension such as Manchuria and Spain in the 1930s. Balch was awarded the Nobel Peace Prize in 1946.

For Balch, men behave as men and women as women because of norms of masculinity and femininity. These norms are deeply embedded in the institutionalization of war in the international system. In her text, Balch points out that traditionally women have been just as likely to support war as men. She argues that exclusion of women from participation in war and from public life can render many of them overly susceptible to state propaganda, passive and unwilling to take a stand on any political issue. Nevertheless: "it is natural that the half of mankind which has never done the fighting and which has always had the main responsibility for children and the suffering and the weak should be especially ready to make sacrifices on behalf of peace" (496). Women are therefore a crucial constituency for mobilization against the "competing imperialisms" structuring world order in the wake of the Versailles settlement, and, once mobilized, they will transform gender norms by practicing gender differently.

Woolf represents a later generation to that of the women so far considered. Like Lee, she worked predominantly as a novelist and essayist. She was neither an academic nor a political activist but was married to a figure hailed as one of the leading international thinkers of his generation, Leonard Woolf. She was, however, sympathetic with some of the strands of thought we find in Lee and Balch. She shares their view that gendered norms and practices, learned in the home, are central to nationalism and militarism. She differs, however, from Balch in that she does not see the feminine qualities traditionally nurtured within the private sphere as offering a resource for better, more internationalist foreign policy. Rather, in common with Lee, she links the undermining

---

[15] Confortini, "Race, Gender, Empire, and War," 252.

of war as a social institution to a more profound unsettling of the gender binary.

The text of *Three Guineas* was written in 1938 as another European war became more certain. Woolf outright refuses to join the game of national and international politics. She makes perhaps the most famous claim ever about gender and international relations: "in fact, as a woman, I have no country. As a woman I want no country. As a woman my country is the whole world."[16] Whereas Balch looks for reform, Woolf gestures towards an alternative "outsider society" premised on the refusal to participate in anything to do with exclusive national identities (her hostility to nationalism rivals that of Luxemburg, see the section on Population, Nation, Immigration). Woolf's argument, echoing points raised by Balch and prefiguring the argument famously made by Jean Bethke Elshtain, is that it is not enough to use the feminine as a corrective to the masculine. The complementarity of the feminine "beautiful soul" and the masculine "just warrior" is part of the problem.[17] Both of these tropes sustain the imagination and practice of war. Women must neither support nor condemn their brothers' fighting, but rather cultivate an attitude of indifference. In this respect, like Lee, Woolf may be seen as aspiring to get beyond the gender binary. She refuses to identify either with women's complementarity to men or with their identification with men. For her, neither femininity nor masculinity can be a resource for progress.

Woolf is a white British woman from the imperial core of the international order, writing as the high point in feminist internationalist movements dominated by white women (not entirely exclusively, see Terrell in the section on World Peace) was coming to an end. The same period saw the development of Black internationalisms, of which Cooper is an early representative, which continued to flower after the Second World War in the context of the beginnings of decolonization and the Cold War (see the section on Anticolonialism). Pearl S. Buck (1892–1973) and Eslanda Robeson (1895–1965) met each other in the 1930s and worked collaboratively on various political, anticolonial, anti-racist, and socialist causes in the 1930s and 1940s. Although both women were born in the United States, the contexts for their thinking were, from the beginning, thoroughly transnational. Buck, a white American, was brought up in China. She was a prolific novelist and won the Nobel Prize for literature in 1961. She was highly critical of the failure of the Allied powers in the Second World War to embrace a properly anti-imperialist position. After 1945, she developed a gendered

---

[16] Virginia Woolf, *Three Guineas* (London: Hogarth Press, 1938), 99.
[17] Elshtain, *Women and War.*

critique of the Cold War.[18] Eslanda Robeson was a chemist, anthropologist, journalist, and political activist. For a long time, her association with her famous husband, Paul, blocked appreciation of the independent importance of her thought. She was a communist and long-time supporter of the Soviet Union, deeply interested in Pan-Africanism as well as in African culture, civil rights, feminism, and anticolonial and labor movements at home and abroad.[19] Robeson and Buck shared a lot of ground in their attitudes towards imperialism, racism, sexism, and militarism. They disagreed profoundly on the questions of revolutionary violence and Soviet communism.

Internationally, the United States had emerged from the Second World War as a pre-eminent world power. Domestically, in an era of increasing affluence, millions of Black Americans were denied civil rights and women, having expanded their involvement in all sectors of the economy during the war, were being cast back into a domestic role. *American Argument* (1949)[20] is the record of a discussion between Buck and Robeson on a range of questions about contemporary America at the opening stages of the Cold War. In the text they return to issues considered by Balch a generation before about the implications of women's work and the gendered public/private divide for the support for militarism and war. In this case, they are considerably more pessimistic than Balch, arguing that the confinement of American women to the domestic sphere restricts their understanding of public issues and makes them more likely to support national service for men and a bellicose foreign policy. Both also follow earlier thinkers in making a direct connection between the gendered norms of the household and matters of state.

American Argument was published in the same year as Simone de Beauvoir's (1908–1986) *The Second Sex*.[21] Unlike some of the other thinkers discussed in this section, Beauvoir's name is famous as a philosopher, novelist, and one of the founding figures in what has come to be called "second wave" feminism. In a similar way to Goldman,

---

[18] See Peter Conn, *Pearl S. Buck: A Cultural Biography* (Cambridge: Cambridge University Press, 1996); Robert Schaffer, "Women and International Relations: Pearl S. Buck's Critique of the Cold War," *Journal of Women's History*, 11:3 (1999): 151–175.

[19] See Barbara Ransby, *Eslanda: The Large and Unconventional Life of Mrs Paul Robeson* (New Haven, CT and London: Yale University Press, 2013); Imaobong Umoren, "'Ideas in Action: Eslanda Robeson's International Thought after 1945," in Patricia Owens and Katharina Rietzler (eds.), *Women's International Thought: A New History* (Cambridge: Cambridge University Press, 2021), 93–114.

[20] Pearl S. Buck and Eslanda Goode Robeson, *American Argument* (London: Methuen and Co, 1950).

[21] Simone de Beauvoir, *The Second Sex*, trans. H. M. Parshley (London: Jonathan Cape, 1953).

Luxemburg, and Arendt (discussed elsewhere in this volume), she is also famous for her life, and almost as much attention has been paid to it as to her work. *The Second Sex* explores the reasons for women's subordination. As we see in the extract below, she makes the claim that the normative structure of gender treats men as the norm and women as "other." Famously, she draws a parallel between mechanisms of gendered and racial subordination, though she argues that women's placement as not being able to fight makes it even more difficult for them to challenge their oppression. For Beauvoir, gender in the sense of a normative structure of dominance and subordination with direct material consequences is universal. This has specific analytical and political implications which are taken up in the IR literature of the late 1980s and 1990s. Analytically, gender provides a tool for interrogating transnational and international phenomena and is assumed to carry the same significance across contexts. Politically, Beauvoir's argument is linked to feminism as an international project premised on the sameness of women's structural position across borders. France was still a major imperial power when Beauvoir published *The Second Sex*. In the context of later anticolonial struggles, she was passionately critical about the actions of the French state and army in Algeria, helping to draw attention to the case of a woman victim of torture, Djamila Boupacha.[22] Nevertheless, critics have pointed to elements of orientalism in Beauvoir's representation of Djamila, which are not fully consistent either with her (Beauvoir's) universalist account of gender or with her feminism.[23]

During the Second World War, at a time when the French metropole was completely under occupation, there was successful resistance against the Nazi regime in Africa. Jane Vialle (1906–1953) was a contemporary and compatriot of Beauvoir but from a very different background. She was the daughter of a French man and a Congolese woman, a journalist, a resistance fighter who was imprisoned by the Vichy regime. Later she became a politician, representing constituencies in the Central African Republic in the French Senate in 1948–1949, and a member of the UN ad hoc Committee on Slavery (1950–1951).[24] She had an untimely death

---

[22] Simone de Beauvoir, Preface to *Djamila Boupacha*, trans. Marybeth Timmerman, extracted in Simone de Beauvoir, *Political Writings*, ed. Margaret A. Simons, Marybeth Timmerman, and Sylvie le Bon Beauvoir (Urbana, IL: University of Illinois Press, 2012 [1962]), 272–281.

[23] For a good discussion see Judith Surkis, "Ethics and Violence: Simone de Beauvoir, Djamila Boupacha, and the Algerian War," *French Politics, Culture & Society*, 28:2 (2010): 38–55.

[24] Sarah C. Dunstan, "'Une Nègre de drame': Jane Vialle and the Politics of Representation in Colonial Reform, 1945–1953," *Journal of Contemporary History*, 55:3 (2020): 645–665.

in an aeroplane crash in 1953. Eslanda Robeson met her in Africa in 1946 and recorded in her diary her impressions of Vialle ("very keen, alert and dynamic") and their wide-ranging conversation.[25] Vialle understood her own gendered subjectivity as encompassing more than one identity, French and African, white and Black. Although she shared with Beauvoir assumptions about modernity, she departs from Beauvoir's universal account of the meaning of gender, and focuses attention on how transnational processes of modernization, globalization, and decolonization affect women differently from men, and different women differently. In her work for the UN Committee on Slavery, she was particularly concerned with how modernization processes produced new ways in which women were vulnerable to exploitation. However, she also thought that there were ways to embrace modernization while holding on to traditional African culture: "African girls have their faces turned towards a future in which the forms of Western civilization have outlined new horizons mingling with the old ... At the same time, faithful to their traditions, they hesitate when confronted with the new ways of life ... This must indeed go forward not by destroying, but by safeguarding and giving full opportunity for orderly development to the fine human qualities which African women have inherited from a long and hard past" (515–516).

In 1988, when attention to questions about gender and international relations was revived within IR, gender questions were treated as mapping out a new, critical terrain. What this section shows is that these questions were integral to an earlier history of thinking about gender and world politics. This points not only to the ongoing analytical and normative significance of gender/gendering in international relations, but also to the fact that teleological accounts of gender scholarship within the IR discipline are open to question. These texts demonstrate relations between gender, imperialism, capitalism, nationalism, and internationalism. They also demonstrate the ever-present imbrication of gender with race, class, and heteronormativity. They raise questions not only about how norms of gender identity underpin international political and economic relations, but also about how masculinity and femininity mean different things in different contexts, and relate to different political agendas.

Kimberly Hutchings

---

[25] Lorelle Semley, "Women Citizens of the French Union Unite: Jane Vialle's Post-War Crusade," in *Gender and Citizenship in Historical and Transnational Perspective: Agency, Space, Borders* (London: Palgrave Macmillan, 2017), 186–187.

Anna Julia Cooper

From "Woman versus Indian" (1892)

It cannot seem less than a blunder, whenever the exponents of a great reform or the harbingers of a noble advance in thought and effort allow themselves to seem distorted by a narrow view of their own aims and principles. All prejudices, whether of race, sect or sex, class pride and caste distinctions are the belittling inheritance and badge of snobs and prigs.

[...]

The cause of freedom is not the cause of a race or a sect, a party or a class, – it is the cause of human kind, the very birthright of humanity. Now unless we are greatly mistaken the Reform of our day, known as the Woman's Movement, is essentially such an Embodiment, if its pioneers could only realize it, of the universal good. And specially important is it that there be no confusion of ideas among its leaders as to its scope and universality. All mists must be cleared from the eyes of woman if she is to be a teacher of morals and manners: the former strikes its roots in the individual and its training and pruning may be accomplished by classes; but the latter is to lubricate the joints and minimize the friction of society, and it is important and fundamental that there be no chromatic or other aberration when the teacher is settling the point, "Who is my neighbor?"

It is not the intelligent woman vs. the ignorant woman; nor the white woman vs. the black, the brown, and the red, – it is not even the cause of woman vs. man. Nay, 'tis woman's strongest vindication for speaking that *the world needs to hear her voice*. It would be subversive of every human interest that the cry of one-half the human family be stifled. Woman in stepping from the pedestal of statue-like inactivity in the domestic shrine, and daring to think and move and speak, – to undertake to help shape, mold, and direct the thought of her age, is merely completing the circle of the world's vision. Hers is every interest that has lacked an interpreter and a defender. Her cause is linked with that of every agony that has been dumb – every wrong that needs a voice.

It is no fault of man's that he has not been able to see truth from her standpoint. It does credit both to his head and heart that no greater mistakes have been committed or even wrongs perpetrated while she sat making tatting and snipping paper flowers. Man's own innate chivalry and the mutual interdependence of their interests have insured his treating her cause, in the main at least, as his own. And he is pardonably surprised and even a little chagrined, perhaps, to find his legislation not considered "perfectly lovely" in every respect. But in any case his work is only impoverished by her remaining dumb. The world has had to limp along with the wobbling gait and one-sided hesitancy of a man with one eye. Suddenly the bandage is removed from the other eye and the whole body is filled with light. It sees a circle where before it saw a segment. The darkened eye restored, every member rejoices with it.

What a travesty of its case for this eye to become plaintiff in a suit, *Eye vs. Foot.* "There is that dull clod, the foot, allowed to roam at will, free and untrammelled; while I, the source and medium of light, brilliant and beautiful, am fettered in darkness and doomed to desuetude." The great burly black man, ignorant and gross and depraved, is allowed to vote; while the franchise is withheld from the intelligent and refined, the pure-minded and lofty souled white woman. Even the untamed and untamable Indian of the prairie, who can answer nothing but 'ugh' to great economic and civic questions is thought by some worthy to wield the ballot which is still denied the Puritan maid and the first lady of Virginia.

Is not this hitching our wagon to something much lower than a star? Is not woman's cause broader, and deeper, and grander, than a blue stocking debate or an aristocratic pink tea? Why should woman become plaintiff in a suit versus the Indian, or the Negro or any other race or class who have been crushed under the iron heel of Anglo-Saxon power and selfishness? If the Indian has been wronged and cheated by the puissance of this American government, it is woman's mission to plead with her country to cease to do evil and to pay its honest debts. If the Negro has been deceitfully cajoled or inhumanly cuffed according to selfish expediency or capricious antipathy, let it be woman's mission to plead that he be met as a man and honestly given half the road. If woman's own happiness has been ignored or misunderstood in our country's legislating for bread winners, for rum sellers, for property holders, for the family relations, for any, or all the interests that touch her vitally, let her rest her plea, not on Indian inferiority, nor on Negro depravity, but on the obligation of legislators to do for her as they would have others do for them were relations reversed. Let her try to teach her country that every interest in this world is entitled at least to a respectful hearing, that every sentiency is worthy of its own gratification, that a helpless cause should

not be trampled down, nor a bruised reed broken; and when the right of
the individual is made sacred, when the image of God in human form,
whether in marble or in clay, whether in alabaster or in ebony, is conse-
crated and inviolable, when men have been taught to look beneath the
rags and grime, the pomp and pageantry of mere circumstance and have
regard unto the celestial kernel uncontaminated at the core, – when race,
color, sex, condition, are realized to be the accidents, not the substance
of life, and consequently as not obscuring or modifying the inalienable
title to life, liberty, and pursuit of happiness, – then is mastered the
science of politeness, the art of courteous contact, which is naught but
the practical application of the principal [sic] of benevolence, the back
bone and marrow of all religion; then woman's lesson is taught and
woman's cause is won – not the white woman nor the black woman
nor the red woman, but the cause of every man or woman who has
writhed silently under a mighty wrong.

Vernon Lee

From "The Economic Parasitism of Women" (1902)

[...] My conversion to the importance of the Woman Question was, as I have said, the work of "Women and Economics"; and I was thus converted by Mrs. Stetson's unpretending little book, because in it the rights and wrongs of *Femina, das Weib,* were not merely opposed to the rights and wrongs of *Vir, der Mann,* but subordinated to those of what is, after all, a bigger item of creation: *Homo, der Mensch.*

There was nothing new in connecting the Woman Question with Economics. [...] Indeed, I much suspect that, as in my case, many thinking persons shelve the question of women's abilities and disabilities exactly because it seems to depend almost completely upon the far more important question of the redistribution of wealth; to demand only a minor act of social justice and social practicality (bringing much waste energy under cultivation) inevitably involved in the greater act of social justice and social practicality which, through revolution or evolution, must needs take place some day or other.

The originality, the scientific soundness and moral efficacy of "Women and Economics," appear to me to lie in its partially reversing this fact; and in its substituting a moral and psychological reason for the rather miraculous mechanicalness which mars every form of the "historical materialism" of the Marxian school. In other words, this book shows that the present condition of women – their state of dependence, tutelage, and semi-idleness; their sequestration from the discipline of competition and social selection, in fact their economic parasitism – is in itself a most important factor in the wrongness of all our economic arrangements, in the insufficient production, the wasteful expenditure, the degrading mal-distribution of wealth.

This main thesis of the book can be summed up as follows:

In consequence of the immense benefit which a prolonged stage of infancy, that is to say of intellectual and moral plasticity, obtained for the human race, all other advantages tended, during the beginnings of civilisation, and have tended ever since, to be sacrificed to the rearing of children; and, first and foremost there has been sacrificed to it that equality in the power of obtaining sustenance, and that consequent mutual independence in such matters, which we find existing between the male and female half of almost every other race of animal. The human race [...] has obtained much of its superiority through the partial replacing of instinct by individual experiment and conscious tradition; but this has meant that the human infant has been born into the world far less mature, far less typically developed, and far less near to independence than the young sheep which can walk within half an hour of its birth, let alone of the chick which can find the right seed almost as soon as it has broken out of the shell. In proportion as the human adult has become rich in individual powers, has the human infant required a longer and longer period of tutelage; with the result of requiring of the human mother a longer and longer devotion of her strength, her mind, and, even more, of her time, to the rearing of offspring. [...]

This all seems very simple; but the consequences are complex. The female *homo*, thus left to rear the children (and do what else she can), becomes, what the female of other animals is not, or only (in birds and certain lower creatures) for a very short time, the *dependent* of the male *homo*. The home which she inhabits is *his* home, the food she eats is *his* food, the children she rears become, whether father or only patriarch, *his* children; and, by a natural devolution, she herself, the woman thus dependent upon his activity and thus appropriated to his children's service, becomes part and parcel of the home, of the goods, of the children; becomes appropriated to the nursing, the cooking, the clothing, the keeping in repair; becomes, thus amalgamated with the man's property, a piece of property herself, body and soul, a slave (often originally a captive, stolen or bought), and what every slave naturally is, a chattel. [...]

Thus, in my opinion, Mrs. Stetson's truly valuable achievement consists in showing that the exclusion of women from the world's activity and their subordination to men, have ceased to be either beneficial or inevitable, however beneficial and inevitable they may have been towards securing the lengthened infancy and greater educability of human beings, and also the storage and increase of inventions and laws, thanks to a rigidly organised home. Mrs. Stetson has satisfactorily demonstrated (to me at least) that one particular automatic arrangement of social evolution has done its work: like slavery, like serfage, like feudalism, like monasticism, like centralisation (according to individualists), like capitalism (according to socialists), the subordination of women has served its purpose and now become an impediment to progress; an impediment which progress is therefore bound to sweep away. [...] Civilisation is being impoverished by the paying off of a debt. It is time that debt should be cancelled. The benefit has long been secured beyond all possibility of loss; but the price is still being paid. Now what is this price?

M. Durkheim and the sociologists of whom he is typical, have answered with complacent simplicity: "The stagnation and regression of the Female Mind." [...]

Philosophers and others of M. Durkheim's way of thinking will here interrupt in favour of those qualities thus developed; and insist that the distinctively feminine peculiarities are not a drawback, but a blessing. Of course some are. But even if we admit that chastity, maternal unselfishness, tenderness, gentleness, are due to woman's dependent position (a theory invalidated by the coyness in courtship and the passion for their young of she-animals, who are anything but dependent on their males), and if we add to these solid perfections, æsthetic graces which the æsthetic Greeks by no means viewed as especially feminine; even if we grant for argument's sake that all the good in women is due to their parasitic status, this gain must be added to the main advantage resulting from "feminine stagnation and regression," namely, the prolongation of childhood and the establishment of the family group, not deducted from the price at which it has been bought. And similarly, we must not let our Durkheim friends and adversaries argue as if these virtues would vanish off the earth if the position of women were changed. For, whatever their origin, they have become sufficiently common to both sexes for Buddhism and Christianity to have made chastity, mansuetude and unselfishness the basis of their ethical system, which means that even if women were to become spiritual facsimiles of men, they would still be exhorted to practise these virtues, or else that these virtues (as Nietzsche contends) are by no means so essential as M. Durkheim and other respectable sociologists take for granted. [...]

The woman, therefore, has worked; but – and here comes the subtle distinction on which the whole economic and sociological part of the subject reposes – she has worked not for the consumption of the world at large, and subject to the world's selection of good or bad, useful or useless, work; but for the consumption of one man and subject to that one man's preferences. The woman has worked without thereby developing those qualities which competition has developed among male workers. She has not become as efficient a human being as her brothers; whatever her individual inherited aptitudes [...], she has not been allowed to develop them in the struggle for life; but has been condemned, on the contrary, to atrophy them in forms of labour which can require only the most common gifts, since they are required equally of every woman in every family. [...]

But this is by no means the whole of the price which the human race has had to pay for the needful "division of labour" between its two halves. Negatively, the position of women has prevented their developing certain of their possibilities; positively, it has forced them to develop certain other of their possibilities. It has atrophied the merely human faculties, which they possess rudimentarily in common with men: it has, on the other hand, hypertrophied the peculiarity which distinguished them from man: hypertrophied their sex. There is one particular sentence in "Women and Economics" which converted me to the cause of female emancipation: "Women are over-sexed."

Women over-sexed! *Over-sexed*! [...] Let me try to explain the extreme importance of Mrs. Stetson's thought. *Over-sexed* does not mean over-much addicted to sexual indulgence; very far from it, for that is the case not with women, but with men, of whom we do not say that they are *over-sexed*. What we mean by *over-sexed* is that, while men are a great many things besides being males – soldiers and sailors, tinkers and tailors, and all the rest of the nursery rhyme – women are, first and foremost *females*, and then again females, and then – still more females. [...] That women are *over-sexed* means that, instead of depending upon their intelligence, their strength, endurance, and honesty, they depend mainly upon their sex; that they appeal to men, dominate men through the fact of their sex; that (if the foregoing seems an exaggeration) they are economically supported by men because they are wanted as wives and mothers of children – that is to say, wanted for their sex. And it means, therefore, by a fearful irony, that the half of humanity which is constitutionally (and by the bare fact of motherhood) more chaste, less dominated by sexual impulses and thoughts, has unconsciously, and all the more inevitably, acquired its power, secured its livelihood, by making the other half of humanity less chaste, by appealing through every means, material, æsthetic and imaginative, sensual or sentimental, to those already excessive impulses and thoughts of sex. The woman has appealed to the man, not as other men appeal to him, as a comrade, a competitor, a fellow-citizen, or an open enemy of different nationality, creed, or class; but as a possible wife, as a female.

This has been a cause of weakness and degradation to the man; a "fall," like that of Adam; and, in those countries where literature is thoroughly outspoken, man, like Adam, has thrown the blame on Eve, as the instrument of the Devil.

[...]

The old, old story is repeated with slight variations from Schopenhauer to Nietzsche, and from Michelet to Dumas *fils*. I think it may be studied best in the works of this really very humanitarian though exceedingly amusing dramatist.

"Well, then," asks Mme. Leverdet in his "Ami des Femmes," "what conclusion have you come to as a result of your studies of womankind? You needn't mind telling me, for I am a *femme d'esprit*."

"My conclusion," answers De Ryons, the "Ami des Femmes" – "my conclusion is that Woman, such as she exists at present, is a creature entirely illogical, inferior, and harmful – '*un être illogique, subalterne et malfaisant.*'"

[...]

All this is, you will answer, mere literary exaggeration. There have been an enormous number of most useful women in the world, Mrs. Fry, Queen Elizabeth, Joan of Arc, the mother of the Gracchi; and, as a fact, it is these selfsame Latin countries, with all their filthy talk about *La Femme*, her ailments and powers, who bore us Anglo-Saxons almost equally with their talk about the miraculous virtues of *La Mère*, who is, after all, only *La Femme* ... well, as the Latins would put it, when she is too old or too busy to be *La Femme*.

Doubtless. And it is not "Women and Economics," nor I, its converted expounder, who give so inordinate an importance to the influence of the over-sexed woman upon the moral cleanness, the chastity, of mankind; it is the very people, like Dumas, who believe, which we do not, in the universal existence and eternal duration of *La Femme*.

[...] Now the chief point made by the author of "Women and Economics," the point which, as it converted myself, ought to convert many others from indifference to the Woman Question, is concerned with the misapplication and waste of the productive energies and generous impulses of men, thanks to the necessity of providing not only for themselves and their offspring, but for a woman who has been brought up not as a citizen, but as a parasite, not as a comrade, but as a servant, or – well, consider the word even in its most sentimental and honourable sense – as a lover. The economic dependence of women (however inevitable and useful in the past) has not merely limited the amount of productive bodily and mental work at the disposal of the community, but it has very seriously increased the mal-distribution of that work and of its products by creating, within the community, a system of units of virtuous egoism, a network of virtuous rapacity which has made the supposed organic social whole a mere gigantic delusion. [...] A man has to be first a good father and husband, and only afterwards, with such honesty as remains over, a good citizen.

"Such honesty as remains over! Sacrifice of the community to the wife and children!" you exclaim. "Why, this accusation of yours against the modern man and the modern woman is far more really dreadful than any of that French rubbish about *La Femme* and her victims!" Exactly so; and a great deal more important, because it is a great deal truer and more sweeping. The very fact of its truth not being recognised merely goes to prove how extraordinarily our moral sense in economic matters has been perverted (or has failed to grow), owing to the fact of the man having to supply the material wants and satisfy the caprices not only of himself, but of that "better" – or worse – self who sees the world only through his eyes, and damages the world only through his hands. […] What cannot be punished (but is on the contrary praised and admired, when successful) is exactly the chronic and all-pervading preference of the interest of the individual as against the interest of the community, the debasing of the standard of work and the quality of products. Now, this kind of dishonesty triumphs not merely in commerce and industry (perhaps almost least there, where most visible), but in all the professions which are exercised, and in many cases (bureaucracies of all kinds, civil and ecclesiastic, and who shall say how large a portion of our supposed necessary military system?) are kept in useless existence merely because men have to make a living.

[…]

But the spirit of wastefulness is by no means the worst co-relative among women of the spirit of rapacity, of "getting wealth, not making it," as Mrs. Stetson luminously describes it, which the economic dependence of the wife develops (as a virtue, too!) in the husband. An enormous amount of the hardness in bargaining, the readiness to take advantage, the willingness to use debasing methods (such as our modern hypnotising advertisement system), the wholesale acceptance of intellectual and moral, if not material, adulteration of work and its products – corresponds in the husband to what is honoured as thrift, as *good management*, in the wife. It is more than probable that the time wasted, the bad covetousness excited, the futile ingenuity exercised by the women who crowd round the windows of our great shops and attend their odious "sales," are really the result of a perverted possibility of virtue.

For the man's virtue is to *make money*; the woman's virtue is to *make money go a long way*. And, between the two virtues, we are continually told that a business house cannot give better wages and shorter hours because it would be "crowded out of the market"; and we are told also, by more solemn moralists still, that nations cannot do without war, lest they lose their "commercial outlets," or fail to secure those they have not yet got.

Who can object? All these people are good husbands and good wives; the home is the pivot of our morality. And the most disheartening thing is, that all this is true.

How do you propose to remedy it? By what arrangements do you expect to make the wife the economic equal of her husband, the joint citizen of the community?

[…]

... the one thing certain about the future of women is, surely, that they ought to be given, by the removal of legal and professional disabilities, a chance, if not of becoming different from what they have been, at all events of showing what they really are. For one of the paradoxes of this most paradoxical question is precisely that, with all our literature about *La Femme*, and all our violent discussions, economical, physiological, psychological, sociological (each deciding according to some hypothesis of his immature science), as to what women must or must not be allowed to do, and what women must and must not succeed or fail in – we do not really know what women *are*. Women, so to speak, as a natural product, as distinguished from women as a creation of men; for women, hitherto, have been as much a creation of men as the grafted fruit tree, the milch cow, or the gelding who spends six hours in pulling a carriage, and the rest of the twenty-four standing in a stable.

[...]

One of the very great uses of Mrs. Stetson's most useful book is to accustom those who *can* think, to think in terms of change, of adaptation, of evolution; to free us from the superstition that the present is the type of the eternal, and that our preferences of to-day are what decide the fate of the universe. *Woman* – even letting alone *La Femme* – is, so to speak, the last scientific survival of the pre-Darwinian belief in the invariability of types; *Woman*, I may add, is almost a relic of the philosophy of the Middle Ages; for has not *Woman* an *Essence*, something quite apart from herself, an essence like the "*virtus dormitiva*" of opium (not always so tranquillising), an essential quality of being – well – being a woman?

One word more. There is a notion, founded in the main on the facts of a period of struggle, segregation of interests, and general uncomfortable transition, that if women attain legal and economic independence, if they get to live, bodily and intellectually and socially, a life more similar, I might say more symmetrical, to that of men, they will necessarily become – let us put it plainly, less attractive to possible husbands. Of course, if they have changed, they will no longer realise the ideal of gracefulness, beauty, and lovableness of the particular men who like them just as they are; but then those particular men will themselves probably no longer exist. Moreover, there is, undoubtedly, a certain co-relation between the qualities of the two sexes, due to the fact, which we are all of us [...] inclined to forget, namely, that the woman is, after all, not merely the *wife* (since that noble word must be put to such mean use) of the man, but also his daughter, his sister, and his companion; and that, as such, he requires her to be not *unlike*, but *like* himself. There is, if we watch for it, a family resemblance, after all, between the men and women of the same country. I was very much struck, while at Tangier, by the fact that the husbands of those veiled and painted Moorish women were themselves so oddly like women in men's clothes, those languid Moors lolling in their shops, with black beards which looked almost as if they had been gummed on to their delicate white faces: the ultra-feminine woman belonged, quite naturally, to the effeminate man. In a similar way, the "masculine" Englishwoman, fox-hunting, alp-climbing, boating, is the natural companion of the out-of-door, athletic, sporting, colonising Englishman; she has been taught by her big brothers during their holidays "*not to be a muff*"; she has learned to be ashamed of the things "the boys" would be ashamed of. And, living as I do equally among Latins and Anglo-Saxons, I have got to guess that, if the Latins see a "third sex" in a portion of Anglo-Saxon womankind, the Anglo-Saxons, on the other hand, have a vague but strong feeling that a corresponding category might be found among the Latin males morally emasculated by belief in *La Femme*. For if *manly* be an adjective denoting certain virtues, and *effeminate* an adjective denoting certain weaknesses, you may be sure that the same civilisation, the same habits and preferences, will produce more of the one than of the other in all the members of a race, just because they do belong to the same race. The man makes the woman, and the woman […] in her turn makes the man; woman in the image of man, man in the image of woman.

And since I have used the word *image*, and have alluded to the grace and beauty, or the gracelessness and ugliness, of the women of the future, let me remind Mrs. Stetson's readers that it is just the most æsthetic, but also the most athletic and the most intellectual, people of the past which has left us those statues of gods and goddesses in the presence of whose marvellous vigour and loveliness we are often in doubt whether to give the name of Apollo, or that of Athena.

Ellen Churchill Semple

From "Geographical Research as a Field for Women" (1916)

Mine own people, – mine in the common ideals which Vassar has bequeathed to her children; mine in the common training for life, no matter what its tasks may have proved to be; mine in the common purposes and hopes born of that good heritage and training: I should like to take you all into my arms, but unable to do that, I want to take you into the heart of my work. I invite you to green fields and pastures new, fields as broad as this great continent, stretching on across river and plain and mountain out to the wide Pacific; fields stretching on beyond the ocean and across the eastern hemisphere. This land is yours for the taking. Little of it has been pre-empted. Here you may stake out your claim and measure it by the square league, as the pioneers did on the colonial frontier of Argentine. Here you find a field rich and fertile, waiting for a labor force to develop it, promising an abundant harvest to the tiller.

[...]

There are several reasons for recommending geographical research as a field of work for women. In the first place, it is an uncrowded field; nay, it clamors for laborers. A few years ago – perhaps I should say a few days ago – when women began to push into the various domains of men's activities, a sense of crowding went through the world of production, like that which disturbed the nations of the Old World about thirty years ago, when Germany and Italy began to elbow their way into the colonial field.

For women, geography maintains "the open door," especially as the teaching of this subject in grade schools, high schools, and colleges is making insistent demands for more and better trained instructors. To investigators it offers a wide choice of themes in its many subdivisions. The field of physical geography or physiography, though fairly well worked, has still many neglected corners. There are numerous type districts in all parts of our country which need to be investigated,

488

scientifically described, and interpreted in terms of their long geographical and geological history. Economic and commercial geography, though well developed, are by no means exhausted. They still present interesting problems for the investigator. Plant geography, or the influence of geographic conditions upon vegetable life, is still in its early morn with the dew on its flowers. It offers an almost unlimited field of entrancing labor, and promises to the subject of botany a hitherto unsuspected development.

Finally, there is the field of anthropo-geography, or the influence of geographic environment upon human development. It deals with the geographic factors which have helped to shape history in all ages, in all parts of the world, and among all races. This is the phase of geography to which I have especially devoted myself, and for which in particular I wish to elicit your sympathy and interest to-day. The subject is new and vast. Moreover, it is big with possibilities. I should like to convert this whole audience into a seminar for anthropo-geography, and I would promise to keep you all busy at research for the rest of your lives.

This subject is particularly suited to women because of their natural endowment, – their power of observation, their capacity for detail work, their patient perseverance in the collection of material, their intellectual humility, which makes for cautious induction, and finally their imagination. This last qualification I would emphasize; because modern education, which seems to be a big mill especially designed for crushing the imagination, finds a more resistant element in the mind of woman, probably due to her strong emotional nature.

Women have another point in their favor in the study of anthropo-geography; that is their taste and their opportunity for travel, which is a valuable aid in general preparation and specific research in this field. Now women, and particularly American women, are ubiquitous travelers in the world to-day, leaving their men in the security of the home nest. If they are idle and rich, they travel to take on the semblance of work. If they are poor and hard-working, they scrape together their meagre funds for a summer of rest and travel in Europe. In all the continents I have met them, – on the border of the Gobi Desert, starting on a twelve days' caravan journey across the drifting sands to the frozen plains of Siberia; at the foot of the Himalayan glaciers, preparing to ascend the snow-capped heights; or tramping alone over Alpine passes, as the best way to see the country. There are few countries to-day in which they cannot safely travel, and none in which they do not wish to travel. Moreover, in the last few decades women have written many admirable books about the lands of their wanderings. These books might be more numerous, and certainly would be more valuable, if their authors had been trained geographers.

The scientific equipment which is necessary for research work in anthropo-geography embraces subjects which women students for the most part naturally select in their college course. These are geology, physiography, economics, sociology, and history, with an occasional excursion into the fields of anthropology, biology, and statistics. As mere preparation, this list may seem a large contract; but as the average college woman comes out equipped with the majority of the subjects and the most important, the supplementary ones to be later mastered represent an easy task.

The method of research, again, is well suited to feminine tastes and the feminine order of mind. It involves careful induction from a broad comparison of data. The collection of the data leads the student into wide and varied fields of reading, which forever charm by their novelty and by the lure of the chase to the hunter. Histories, books of travel and exploration, descriptions of lands and peoples, are the chief sources, varied occasionally by the duller material of census reports. The plan of procedure is to compare typical peoples of all races and all stages of cultural development, living under similar geographic conditions. If these peoples of different ethnic stocks but similar environments manifest similar or related social, economic, or historical development, then it is reasonable to infer that such similarities are due to environment and not to race. Thus the race factor in the historical problem is eliminated by wide comparison, and the geographic factor can be estimated. For instance, if the influences of an island environment be the subject of research, we investigate the history and cultural development of island peoples over the whole world, whether they be Malays, Mongolians, Papuans, Polynesians, American Indians, or the various branches of the white race; whether savage, barbarous, or civilized; whether ancient or modern; whether they dwell in an island continent like Australia, or a mere fragment of land like the Isle of Man. From this wide comparison of the manifold and varied slowly emerge the common social or historical traits, due to the common factor of insular environment.

Suppose we are investigating the natural transit regions of the world. These are small open districts, located between physical barriers of mountain, sea, or desert, and therefore offering a nature-made passway for migration, trade, and conquest. Such was the location of the Iroquois country in the low Mohawk depression between the Catskill Mountains on the south and the Adirondacks on the north; of the ancient Philistine plain between the rugged Judean highland on the east and the Mediterranean on the west; of mediaeval Austria or the East Mark at the Danube gate between the Little Carpathians on the north and the spurs of the Alps on the south; of the long Rhone trough, offering a valley highway from the Mediterranean northward between the western Alps and the rough Cevennes Plateau.

If we compare the history of all these transit districts, we find that they were small areas of correspondingly small populations, occupying a location that was at once dangerous but full of opportunity to acquire wealth, owing to the trade which passed through each. Recurrent danger came from the streams of migration and conquest deflected through these natural channels of movement. Attack was invited by the abundant opportunity of the position. Hence the inhabitants of such transit regions have developed courage and military power out of proportion to their number. They have developed also a talent for shrewd diplomacy, when their larger neighbors courted and conciliated them instead of attacking; and thus they gained a protector for a time, playing off one enemy against the other. But the inherent weakness of small numbers and an exposed location has always made desolating conquest their national lot, in whatever continent they were found.

Moreover, the history of one such transit region, if compared in its successive stages of civilization and in its distinctive periods, will show an almost monotonous recurrence of the same big historical events and the same type of national character, though the ethnic stock may have changed. The low plain of Flanders and Brabant forms a passway only fifty miles wide between the North Sea and the rugged Ardennes Plateau, which, from the western Alps to the heart of Belgium, raises a natural barrier between the Rhine valley and the smiling plains of France. From time immemorial this Belgian gateway has been assailed from the approaching highways on east and west. Its defenders first appear in history when Julius Caesar made his campaign in northern Gaul in 57 BC. He defeated them in the first battle of the Aisne, and won another costly victory from them between the Sambre River and the Scheldt; but he treated the conquered with the compassion due to a courageous people, and in his history he left a eulogy on their heroism. In the introduction to his "Commentaries," he enumerates the three divisions of Gauls, and then adds: "But the bravest of all these are the Belgians, because they fight almost daily battles with the Germans who live across the Rhine."

History has moved in a narrow groove across this Belgian plain. Hordes of Teutonic barbarians swept in from the east during the early Middle Ages. During the seventeenth and eighteenth centuries the invaders were the armies of expanding France. To-day the plain of Flanders and Brabant is one vast battle field. The Roman eagle is superseded by the Prussian eagle, the Roman legion by the German army corps. Only the compassion of the Roman general is lacking. And the larger world to-day, with a painstung conscience, feeling itself somehow an accomplice in the betrayal of the twentieth century civilization, cries with remorseful pity, "The bravest of all these are the Belgians."

[...]

When the research student has collected all the necessary material and has deduced from it the scientific principle, the problem is to put it all, both data and conclusion, into literary form. For anthropo-geography, having to do with mankind, is entitled to the same literary treatment as the best history. The scientist, barred from the easy-running narrative of the historian, must nevertheless make his style move as smoothly. As a scientist he must load up each sentence as if it were a pack-horse, and he must place each parcel of data accurately, lest it fall off. Higher and higher grows the load. He must compress the unwieldy mass, shape and model it to better balance and better form, but losing nothing. The heavy load is reduced, but it is all there. Its ugly shape is changed, but its content remains unaltered. The pack-horse carries his burden more easily; he scarcely perceives its weight. More smoothly, more swiftly, he moves. He spreads his wings! Your pack-horse has become Pegasus. Your book is literature but it is still science, Darwinian in method but Hellenic in form. Thus it seeks to establish two claims to immortality: Truth that is eternal, and Beauty that is eternal.

Such is the field of activity, such is the reward to which I would invite you all, – because I love you.

Emily Greene Balch

From "Women's Work for Peace" (1922)

Women have the same emotions as men and with them are inflamed by nationalism, intoxicated by the glories of war, embittered by old rancors. But as we look through history we realize that in the mass they have taken little part in the political life of their peoples and have been mainly immersed in private affairs, in the household and in personal relations. Psychologically they have a less powerful instinctive pugnacity than men; and furthermore, in war they have always stood to lose even more than men, as Europe knew. In-place of the excitement of the great adventure they had the heavy hours of suspense and bereavement; dishonor and slavery were a worse lot than wounds or death itself.

On the whole, then, throughout the ages, women must have counted, as far as they counted at all, rather against war than for it. But this was regarded by men, and by themselves as well, as a weakness to be hidden. It is only as war in its modern guise reveals itself as a menace to the race that it begins to occur to people's minds that women's oposition [sic] to war may be a precious asset of humanity.

The great war revealed facts which it would seem should have been clear to us long before. We have been made to realize that we are living on a thin crust barely concealing a substratum of explosive passions and interests which may break out in a disastrous eruption at any time. What can be done to prevent the calamity? The question is one of life and death; of more than that, if hell on earth is more than death.

Latzko and Rolland rebuked women in stinging and tonic words for their responsibility for the war that has devastated humanity and have called them to a positive role for the future.

In many ways they are as yet peculiarly unready for such a task. First, they are very suggestible. Practically every person is so by nature; but women are unconsciously, and even consciously, trained to be so, and they even less than men are protected by a discipline of the critical faculty against the effects of political propaganda. For the most part, also, they

493

are not only destitute of political power but they feel themselves apart from any responsibility for public affairs and are quite unused to organization. This is not true of American and English women, nor of women in Scandinavia and Holland, but it is true of the great mass of womankind.

Yet women have not been and are not inactive. Indeed already they more than pull their weight in peace movements and in pacifist organizations, working either side by side with men or by themselves. The fine work done by American women in connection with the Washington Conference a year ago is fresh in our minds. One of the most important aspects of this work was that it was very largely done by organizations not formed for peace work which none the less recognized the significance of the occasion. Not the least of the gains registered by that meeting was the fact that it opened a channel for the expression of a vast 'will to peace' long artificially held back and hidden.

This movement in connection with the Washington Conference was, in its elaborate organization for the education of public opinion and for pressure on the official representatives of the country, characteristic of America.

Not less characteristic of Italy was the opposition offered by women, who in co-operation with the socialists, actually succeeded in preventing the proposed attempt to conquer Albania. This adventure if successful would have added a new injustice to those that have stained the post-war period and would have created a permanently discontented subject people in the Balkan peninsula, constituting an ever present danger to European peace. The *non volumus* of thousands, among the plain people and in the first line of the soldiers themselves who mutinied in Valona, not only saved Albania but prevented a European calamity.

[...]

But the most unique of women's efforts for peace is an international organization, represented in almost every country and constituting as it were a world peace party. It includes women who in other respects have widely divergent views, church women and free thinkers, socialists and conservatives, all united in condemning war, in working for friendly co-operation between peoples and in recognizing the reciprocal facts that women have political duties and that they must be politically free in order to fulfil these duties. This organization is infinitely more significant in its essence, in its purpose, than in its accomplishment, but this is not to say that it has not already counted in practical action.

In 1915, when the war was some nine months old, women from twelve countries met at the Hague under the presidency of Jane Addams. Roosevelt sped the voyage of the fifty or so American women who sailed with her by stigmatizing the undertaking as "not so much silly as base."

Yet the international programme agreed on by the Hague congress was a precursor of Wilson's, and the organization there created has developed into the Women's International League for Peace and Freedom with its twenty national sections and its correspondents in Siam and Syria, Iceland and South Africa.

Its first practical effort (in 1915) was what I still believe to have been not only an extraordinarily courageous undertaking but one that held the possibility of enormous practical results. I refer to the effort (described in Miss Addams's "Women at the Hague" and in her "Peace and Bread in Time of War") to induce the neutral governments to initiate, and the warring governments to tolerate, "continuous mediation" by the neutral governments, according to a plan proposed by Julia Grace Wales, a Canadian.

The second notable act of the Women's International League was the pronouncement against the Versailles Treaty at its second congress at Zurich in 1919, when the first peace terms had just been made known. It already clearly foresaw and stated what kind of fruit a "Peace" of this sort was bound to produce. The protest was worded by women of the entente countries and the German and Austrial [sic] delegates abstained from voting. The Vienna congress of the league in 1921 represented a special effort to draw in women from the southeastern countries of Europe through which the Secretary made a tour in the previous spring.

Four international summer schools have carried the doctrines of peace and internationalism to many hitherto quite unreached by such ideas. The last, and perhaps the most successful of these, held in Lugano in August, was distinguished by the presence of Romain Rolland and was a most enthusiastic success. The next congress should regularly come next summer, but the present situation in Europe is so terribly threatening that it has been decided not to wait so long but to hold instead an emergency conference at the Hague in December to discuss treaty revision – " A New Peace." No one not on the spot can easily realize the sense of impending catastrophe throughout Europe. Women are determined at least to leave nothing in their power unattempted to bring the peoples to a better state of mind and to realize this in a new settlement.

The league maintains its headquarters at the seat of the League of Nations, and it is quite in character that its Geneva "Maison Internationale," with its quaint garden high above the street, is not only an office building but a homelike international social centre offering hospitality to men and women passing through the city.

If the most conspicuous efforts of the league are those connected with its congresses, the great bulk of its steady work for peace is done by the twenty national sections, each in its own way. For example, the British section was working to substitute for the Black and Tan regime in Ireland measures of constructive conciliation, while the German section was endeavoring to bring home to the German public the element of justice in the demands for reparation and working for improved feeling between

Germans and Poles in Upper Silesia; the Mexican group was actively petitioning the King of Spain to put an end to the bloody and futile war between Spain and Morocco, and the American section was doing all in its power for better relations with Mexico, Russia and Japan. The great success of the French section has been in arousing in France zeal to help famine stricken Russia. In fact almost all the league members have been teachers in the healing and constructive work of international relief in which Jane Addams has been so preeminent. No one will ever know how largely America's contribution of $20,000,000 to Russia was owing to her indefatigable efforts.

Happily this special organization has no monopoly of the field. Cooperating with it and quite apart is many another of women working for peace. The Ligue de Femmes contre la Guerre of Madeleine Vernet is one, the Women's Peace Association in Tokio [sic] is another, the Union Mondiale de Femmes, likewise with its office at Geneva, is a third comrade in the cause.

Women too are in all the peace and international movements – the Association of League of Nations Unions, the No More War movement, the Christian International and the Fellowship of Reconciliation, and especially in the Quaker missions which have carried the doctrine of love between peoples, in its most practical form, far and wide.

[...]

Behind all these visible and coordinated efforts, and more important, is the revolt of simple unspoiled human feeling which is already leading millions of mothers to bring up their children to abhor war and all its works and which, if political leaders are so mad as to attempt to mobilize their peoples for a fresh war, may reveal itself in quite unsuspected force.

What can be recorded so far is a beginning, a tendency, a body of symptoms suggesting the presence of a far-reaching transition of ideas.

Women and men are in the main moved by the same motives to the same ends, but it is natural that the half of mankind which has never done the fighting and which has always had the main responsibility for the children and the suffering and the weak should be especially ready to make sacrifices on behalf of peace. It is for the men to see that this often deeply touching readiness for sacrifice for the cause should not be an excuse for them to leave the burden on the women. Their work is essential but it is hopeless if men do not do their part.

It is hard to suggest through cold printed words the real meaning to ourselves and to our children's children of the choice between ordered international good will and competing imperialism which now confronts the world. It is the choice between love and life on the one hand and New York, London, Berlin and Paris perishing under poison-gas raids on the other.

Virginia Woolf

From *Three Guineas* (1938)

Now that we have tried to see how we can help you to prevent war by attempting to define what is meant by protecting culture and intellectual liberty let us consider your next and inevitable request: that we should subscribe to the funds of your society. For you, too, are an honorary treasurer, and like the other honorary treasurers in need of money. Since you, too, are asking for money it might be possible to ask you, also, to define your aims, and to bargain and to impose terms as with the other honorary treasurers. What then are the aims of your society? To prevent war, of course. And by what means? Broadly speaking, by protecting the rights of the individual; by opposing dictatorship; by ensuring the democratic ideals of equal opportunity for all. Those are the chief means by which as you say, "the lasting peace of the world can be assured." Then, Sir, there is no need to bargain or to haggle. If those are your aims, and if, as it is impossible to doubt, you mean to do all in your power to achieve them, the guinea is yours – would that it were a million! The guinea is yours; and the guinea is a free gift, given freely.

But the word "free" is used so often, and has come, like used words, to mean so little, that it may be well to explain exactly, even pedantically, what the word "free" means in this context. It means here that no right or privilege is asked in return. The giver is not asking you to admit her to the priesthood of the Church of England; or to the Stock Exchange; or to the Diplomatic Service. The giver has no wish to be "English" on the same terms that you yourself are "English." The giver does not claim in return for the gift admission to any profession; any honour, title, or medal; any professorship or lectureship; any seat upon any society, committee or board. The gift is free from all such conditions because the one right of paramount importance to all human beings is already won. You cannot take away her right to earn a living. Now then for the first time in English history an educated man's daughter can give her brother one guinea of her own making at his request for the purpose specified above without asking for anything in return. It is a free gift, given without fear, without flattery, and without conditions. That, Sir, is so momentous an occasion in the history of civilization that some celebration seems called for. But let us have done with the old ceremonies – the Lord Mayor, with turtles and sheriffs in attendance, tapping nine times with his mace upon a stone while the Archbishop of Canterbury in full canonicals invokes a blessing. Let us invent a new ceremony for this new occasion. What more fitting than to destroy an old word, a vicious and corrupt word that has done much harm in its day and is now obsolete? The word "feminist" is the word indicated. That word, according to the dictionary, means "one who champions the rights of women." Since the only right, the right to earn a living, has been won, the word no longer has a meaning. And a word without a meaning is a dead word, a corrupt word. Let us therefore celebrate this occasion by cremating the corpse. Let us write that word in large black letters on a sheet of foolscap; then solemnly apply a match to the paper. Look, how it burns! What a light dances over the world! Now let us bray the ashes in a mortar with a goose-feather pen, and declare in unison singing together that anyone who uses that word in future is a ring-the-bell-and-run-away man, a mischief maker, a groper among old bones, the proof of whose defilement is written in a smudge of dirty water upon his face. The smoke has died down; the word is destroyed. Observe, Sir, what has happened as the result of our celebration. The word "feminist" is destroyed; the air is cleared; and in that clearer air what do we see? Men and women working together for the same cause. The cloud has lifted from the past too. What were they working for in the nineteenth century – those queer dead women in their poke bonnets and shawls? The very same cause for which we are working now. "Our claim was no claim of women's rights only;" – it is Josephine Butler who speaks – "it was larger and deeper; it was a claim for the rights of all – all men and women – to the respect in their persons of the great principles of Justice and Equality and Liberty." The words are the same as yours; the claim is the same as yours. The daughters of educated men who were called, to their resentment, "feminists" were in fact the advance guard of your own movement. They were fighting the same enemy that you are fighting and for the same reasons. They were fighting the tyranny of the patriarchal state as you are fighting the tyranny of the Fascist state. Thus we are merely carrying on the same fight that our mothers and grand-mothers fought; their words prove it; your words prove it. But now with your letter before us we have your assurance that you are fighting with us, not against us. That fact is so inspiring that another celebration seems called for. What could be more fitting than to write more dead words, more corrupt words, upon more sheets of paper and burn them – the words, Tyrant, Dictator, for example? But, alas, those words are not yet obsolete. We can still shake out eggs from newspapers; still smell a peculiar and unmistakable odour in the region of Whitehall and Westminster. And abroad the monster has come more openly to the surface. There is no mistaking him there. He has widened his scope. He is interfering now with your liberty; he is dictating how you shall live; he is making distinctions not merely between the sexes, but between the races. You are feeling in your own persons what your mothers felt when they were shut out, when they were shut up, because they were women. Now you are being shut out, you are being shut up, because you are Jews, because you are democrats, because of race, because of religion. It is not a photograph that you look upon any longer; there you go, trapesing along in the procession yourselves. And that makes a difference. The whole iniquity of dictatorship, whether in Oxford or Cambridge, in Whitehall or Downing Street, against Jews or against women, in England, or in Germany, in Italy or in Spain is now apparent to you. But now we are fighting together. The daughters and sons of educated men are fighting side by side. That fact is so inspiring, even if no celebration is yet possible, that if this one guinea could be multiplied a million times all those guineas should be at your service without any other conditions than those that you have imposed upon yourself. Take this one guinea then and use it to assert "the rights of all – all men and women – to the respect in their persons of the great principles of Justice and Equality and Liberty." Put this penny candle in the window of your new society, and may we live to see the day when in the blaze of our common freedom the words tyrant and dictator shall be burnt to ashes, because the words tyrant and dictator shall be obsolete.

That request then for a guinea answered, and the cheque signed, only one further request of yours remains to be considered – it is that we should fill up a form and become members of your society. On the face of it that seems a simple request, easily granted. For what can be simpler than to join the society to which this guinea has just been contributed? On the face of it, how easy, how simple; but in the depths, how difficult, how complicated ... . What possible doubts, what possible hesitations can those dots stand for? What reason or what emotion can make us hesitate to become members of a society whose aims we approve, to whose funds we have contributed? It may be neither reason nor emotion, but something more profound and fundamental than either. It may be difference. Different we are, as facts have proved, both in sex and in education. And it is from that difference, as we have already said, that our help can come, if help we can, to protect liberty, to prevent war. But if we sign this form which implies a promise to become active members of your society, it would seem that we must lose that difference and therefore sacrifice that help. To explain why this is so is not easy, even though the gift of a guinea has made it possible (so we have boasted), to speak freely without fear or flattery. Let us then keep the form unsigned on the table before us while we discuss, so far as we are able, the reasons and the emotions which make us hesitate to sign it. For those reasons and emotions have their origin deep in the darkness of ancestral memory; they have grown together in some confusion; it is very difficult to untwist them in the light.

To begin with an elementary distinction: a society is a conglomeration of people joined together for certain aims; while you, who write in your own person with your own hand, are single. You the individual are a man whom we have reason to respect; a man of the brotherhood, to which, as biography proves, many brothers have belonged. Thus Anne Clough, describing her brother, says: "Arthur is my best friend and adviser ... . Arthur is the comfort and joy of my life; it is for him, and from him, that I am incited to seek after all that is lovely and of good report." To which William Wordsworth, speaking of his sister but answering the other as if one nightingale called to another in the forests of the past, replies: The Blessing of my later years Was with me when a Boy: She gave me eyes, she gave me ears; And humble cares, and delicate fears; A heart, the fountain of sweet tears; And love, and thought, and joy. Such was, such perhaps still is, the relationship of many brothers and sisters in private, as individuals. They respect each other and help each other and have aims in common. Why then, if such can be their private relationship, as biography and poetry prove, should their public relationship, as law and history prove, be so very different? And here, since you are a lawyer, with a lawyer's memory, it is not necessary to remind you of certain decrees of English law from its first records to the year 1919 by way of proving that the public, the society relationship of brother and sister has been very different from the private. The very word "society" sets tolling in memory the dismal bells of a harsh music: shall not, shall not, shall not. You shall not learn; you shall not earn; you shall not own; you shall not – such was the society relationship of brother to sister for many centuries. And though it is possible, and to the optimistic credible, that in time a new society may ring a carillon of splendid harmony, and your letter heralds it, that day is far distant. Inevitably we ask ourselves, is there not something in the conglomeration of people into societies that releases what is most selfish and violent, least rational and humane in the individuals themselves? Inevitably we look upon society, so kind to you, so harsh to us, as an ill-fitting form that distorts the truth; deforms the mind; fetters the will. Inevitably we look upon societies as conspiracies that sink the private brother, whom many of us have reason to respect, and inflate in his stead a monstrous male, loud of voice, hard of fist, childishly intent upon scoring the floor of the earth with chalk marks, within whose mystic boundaries human beings are penned, rigidly, separately, artificially; where, daubed red and gold, decorated like a savage with feathers he goes through mystic rites and enjoys the dubious pleasures of power and dominion while we, "his" women, are locked in the private house without share in the many societies of which his society is composed. For such reasons compact as they are of many memories and emotions – for who shall analyse the complexity of a mind that holds so deep a reservoir of time past within it? – it seems both wrong for us rationally and impossible for us emotionally to fill up your form and join your society. For by so doing we should merge our identity in yours; follow and repeat and score still deeper the old worn ruts in which society, like a gramophone whose needle has stuck, is grinding out with intolerable unanimity "Three hundred millions spent upon arms." We should not give effect to a view which our own experience of "society" should have helped us to envisage. Thus, Sir, while we respect you as a private person and prove it by giving you a guinea to spend as you choose, we believe that we can help you most effectively by refusing to join your society; by working for our common ends – justice and equality and liberty for all men and women – outside your society, not within.

But this, you will say, if it means anything, can only mean that you, the daughters of educated men, who have promised us your positive help, refuse to join our society in order that you may make another of your own. And what sort of society do you propose to found outside ours, but in co-operation with it, so that we may both work together for our common ends? That is a question which you have every right to ask, and which we must try to answer in order to justify our refusal to sign the form you send. Let us then draw rapidly in outline the kind of society which the daughters of educated men might found and join outside your society but in co-operation with its ends. In the first place, this new society, you will be relieved to learn, would have no honorary treasurer, for it would need no funds. It would have no office, no committee, no secretary; it would call no meetings; it would hold no conferences. If name it must have, it could be called the Outsiders' Society. That is not a resonant name, but it has the advantage that it squares with facts – the facts of history, of law, of biography; even, it may be, with the still hidden facts of our still unknown psychology. It would consist of educated men's daughters working in their own class – how indeed can they work in any other? – and by their own methods for liberty, equality and peace. Their first duty, to which they would bind themselves not by oath, for oaths and ceremonies have no part in a society which must be anonymous and elastic before everything, would be not to fight with arms. This is easy for them to observe, for in fact, as the papers inform us, "the Army Council have no intention of opening recruiting for any women's corps." The country ensures it. Next they would refuse in the event of war to make munitions or nurse the wounded. Since in the last war both these activities were mainly discharged by the daughters of working men, the pressure upon them here too would be slight, though probably disagreeable. On the other hand the next duty to which they would pledge themselves is one of considerable difficulty, and calls not only for courage and initiative, but for the special knowledge of the educated man's daughter. It is, briefly, not to incite their brothers to fight, or to dissuade them, but to maintain an attitude of complete indifference. But the attitude expressed by the word "indifference" is so complex and of such importance that it needs even here further definition. Indifference in the first place must be given a firm footing upon fact. As it is a fact that she cannot understand what instinct compels him, what glory, what interest, what manly satisfaction fighting provides for him – "without war there would be no outlet for the manly qualities which fighting develops" – as fighting thus is a sex characteristic which she cannot share, the counterpart some claim of the maternal instinct which he cannot share, so is it an instinct which she cannot judge. The outsider therefore must leave him free to deal with this instinct by himself, because liberty of opinion must be respected, especially when it is based upon an instinct which is as foreign to her as centuries of tradition and education can make it. This is a fundamental and instinctive distinction upon which indifference may be based. But the outsider will make it her duty not merely to base her indifference upon instinct, but upon reason. When he says, as history proves that he has said, and may say again, "I am fighting to protect our country" and thus seeks to rouse her patriotic emotion, she will ask herself, "What does 'our country' mean to me an outsider?" To decide this she will analyse the meaning of patriotism in her own case. She will inform herself of the position of her sex and her class in the past. She will inform herself of the amount of land, wealth and property in the possession of her own sex and class in the present – how much of "England" in fact belongs to her. From the same sources she will inform herself of the legal protection which the law has given her in the past and now gives her. And if he adds that he is fighting to protect her body, she will reflect upon the degree of physical protection that she now enjoys when the words "Air Raid Precaution" are written on blank walls.

Pearl S. Buck and Eslanda Robeson

From *American Argument* (1949)

I notice that the last war and the flood of veterans of marrying age have changed somewhat our own ruggedness toward marriage. To-day many married men are not supporting their families. The government pays them enough to marry on, and parents add small private subsidies. This is a good change, provided the young couples realize that they owe a debt to society and their parents which must be paid eventually. In China a young couple is sheltered but the old ones expect shelter in their time, also. It is a mutual family insurance. I am interested to see that these recent American marriages seem to be working out well enough.

There are plenty of divorces but the reasons given are not that the young veteran does not support his wife. The American marriage ought to be taken off the old economic basis.

I contemplated that young Eslanda. 'You had the housework, too!'

Most foreign women are appalled at the amount of work the American housewife does. And the American feels that she has a full-time job in the house. Are they both right? This matter of housework is very important to American civilization. The average woman drags through the day. I am not speaking of the few rich who have all the gadgets, and even perhaps servants, but the average woman who has an electric iron and maybe a washing machine and a sewing machine.

'We had no electric iron when I was young,' Eslanda was saying, 'and no washing machine. I will always remember Paul's shirts when we were first married. I will always remember that, because his shirts were so very big! I wash Saturday afternoons and iron Sundays.' With all our gadgets, housework in America remains an unsettled problem. Somebody has to stay home to run the gadgets. And even with gadgets, which have to be cleaned and taken care of, there remain the inescapable jobs. I myself am fortunate enough to enjoy housework and cooking.

There is no better way of resting after a hard morning at writing than to go into the kitchen and get a good meal or attack a closet that needs ordering. At such tasks brains can rest. But I shouldn't like to let my brains rest all the time. They would ferment.

As I say, I am lucky in my enjoyment of common tasks. But I know plenty of women who do not have such enjoyment and yet who must stay by home and children twenty-four hours a day because they cannot be left. Here is the chief reason for women's backwardness. Housework is the career of most American women, the doom of some, and the reason why our country, religion, and politics are run by men. It is the reason why our women, who have matchless opportunities for education and freedom, maintain their petty rounds while atomic war threatens. Most American women are imprisoned by housework. It accounts in large measure for the lack of important contributions from women to science, the arts, and government. Whether they can get the laundry done and what they will buy for dinner claim their attention more than the United Nations, international relations, or even immediate death and destruction by war.

Women cannot leave the boiling pot and the crying child. Men can and do, and the world is the worse for woman's absence. Not that I put the least faith in women as they are, I have learned better. When a woman's companions are a boiling pot and a crying child, and when four walls make her world, she has no mind left, and she only echoes what the man says when he comes home and tells her what the world is like. She doesn't even read the newspapers – why should she? What is going on has nothing to do with her.

I used to think that women wanted a different world. I think they will when they have thought of some way to cope with their housework. As it is, they are docile, although often irritable and petty. They vote with the conservatives and the militarists. Ah, but they do! I went to Washington one fine spring day, in the highest optimism as an American citizen, to tell a senatorial committee why I think universal military training is absolute folly. The president of a great industry was there, too, to tell the committee why he believed in complete militarism now and maybe always. I was still complacent when I saw him, for I knew that there were other women there beside me. One represented what she called 'two million home women', or in other words, women's clubs, and the other represented what might be called career women, the business and professional women. Among the three of us I thought we could outnumber the big fellow.

It was I who was outnumbered. The other two women spoke with the big fellow for complete militarization, mainly, from what I gather, because they thought boys of eighteen needed discipline and were a nuisance in the community and better off in the Army. This dazed me, for from what I had observed the boys were much more of a nuisance when they came back from the Army.

It did not matter very much. There were only four of the senatorial committee present during that afternoon. I was surprised at this, for there were thirteen on the committee. But I was told that an attendance of even four was large. When the big fellow and the three women finished there was one senator left. The people who stayed through were not on the committee, but three rather grim-looking military men in uniform, who sat near the senators and stared at each one of us as we came up to testify. I was the only one to testify against what they wanted and I felt their stares. But I am a reckless woman, and long ago I ceased to be afraid of uniforms. It is not uniforms I now fear but women, ignorant and under-standing nothing; women, who worship uniforms; women, who put Hitler into power in Germany; women, who blindly believe what they are told. Women, millions strong, who never think and never know; women, who breed sons and send them into the Army without protest.

I refuse to believe that the strong stand which American women have taken for militarization has reasons more sinister than ignorance. But there are dark moments when I fight against the possibility that our women want to hug their shelters and privileges. Perhaps they want to keep the sort of society that has made shelters and privileges possible for them and they are willing to breed sons and send them out to fight to keep safe what they have. God forgive me for even imagining such creatures of evil! But why do women so easily fall victims to the propagandists and militarists? Are their minds benumbed by the dull daily round? What is the cause of their dreadful apathy?

Simone de Beauvoir

From *The Second Sex* (1949)

From 44–45

These biological data are of extreme importance: they play an all-important role and are an essential element of woman's situation: we will be referring to them in all further accounts. Because the body is the instrument of our hold on the world, the world appears different to us depending on how it is grasped, which explains why we have studied these data so deeply; they are one of the keys that enable us to understand woman. But we refuse the idea that they form a fixed destiny for her. They do not suffice to constitute the basis for a sexual hierarchy; they do not explain why woman is the Other; they do not condemn her forever to this subjugated role.

It has often been claimed that physiology alone provides answers to these questions: Does individual success have the same chances in the two sexes? Which of the two in the species plays the greater role? But the first question does not apply to woman and other females in the same way, because animals constitute given species and it is possible to provide static descriptions of them: it is simply a question of collating observations to decide if the mare is as quick as the stallion, if male chimpanzees do as well on intelligence tests as their female counterparts; but humanity is constantly in the making. Materialist scholars have claimed to posit the problem in a purely static way; full of the theory of psychophysiological parallelism, they sought to make mathematical comparisons between male and female organisms: and they imagined that these measurements directly defined their functional abilities. I will mention one example of these senseless discussions that this method prompted. As it was supposed, in some mysterious way, that the brain secreted thinking, it seemed very important to decide if the average weight of the female brain was larger or smaller than that of the male.

From 46–48

But what removes much of the interest of these careful debates is that no relation has been established between brain weight and the development of intelligence. Nor could one give a psychic interpretation of chemical formulas defining male and female hormones. We categorically reject the idea of a psychophysiological parallelism; the bases of this doctrine have definitively and long been weakened. I mention it because although it is philosophically and scientifically ruined, it still haunts a large number of minds: it has already been shown here that some people are carrying around antique vestiges of it. We also repudiate any frame of reference that presupposes the existence of a natural hierarchy of values – for example, that of an evolutionary hierarchy; it is pointless to wonder if the female body is more infantile than the male, if it is closer to or further from that of the higher primates, and so forth. All these studies that confuse a vague naturalism with an even vaguer ethic or aesthetic are pure verbiage.

Only within a human perspective can the female and the male be compared in the human species. But the definition of man is that he is a being who is not given, who makes himself what he is. As Merleau-Ponty rightly said, man is not a natural species: he is a historical idea. Woman is not a fixed reality but a becoming; she has to be compared with man in her becoming; that is, her possibilities have to be defined: what skews the issues so much is that she is being reduced to what she was, to what she is today, while the question concerns her capacities; the fact is that her capacities manifest themselves clearly only when they have been realized: but the fact is also that when one considers a being who is transcendence and surpassing, it is never possible to close the books.

However, one might say, in the position I adopt – that of Heidegger, Sartre, and Merleau-Ponty – that if the body is not a thing, it is a situation: it is our grasp on the world and the outline for our projects. Woman is weaker than man; she has less muscular strength, fewer red blood cells, a lesser respiratory capacity; she runs less quickly, lifts less heavy weights – there is practically no sport in which she can compete with him; she cannot enter into a fight with the male. Added to that are the instability, lack of control, and fragility that have been discussed: these are facts. Her grasp of the world is thus more limited; she has less firmness and perseverance in projects that she is also less able to carry out. This means that her individual life is not as rich as man's.

In truth these facts cannot be denied: but they do not carry their meaning in themselves. As soon as we accept a human perspective, defining the body starting from existence, biology becomes an abstract science; when the physiological given (muscular inferiority) takes on meaning, this meaning immediately becomes dependent on a whole context; "weakness" is weakness only in light of the aims man sets for himself, the instruments at his disposal, and the laws he imposes. If he did not want to apprehend the world, the very idea of a grasp on things would have no meaning; when, in this apprehension, the full use of body force – above the usable minimum – is not required, the differences cancel each other out; where customs forbid violence, muscular energy cannot be the basis for domination: existential, economic, and moral reference points are necessary to define the notion of weakness concretely. It has been said that the human species was an anti-physis; the expression is not really exact, because man cannot possibly contradict the given; but it is in how he takes it on that he constitutes its truth; nature only has reality for him insofar as it is taken on by his action: his own nature is no exception.

It is not possible to measure in the abstract the burden of the generative function for woman, just as it is not possible to measure her grasp on the world: the relation of maternity to individual life is naturally regulated in animals by the cycle of heat and seasons; it is undefined for woman; only society can decide; woman's enslavement to the species is tighter or looser depending on how many births the society demands and the hygienic conditions in which pregnancy and birth occur. So if it can be said that among the higher animals individual existence is affirmed more imperiously in the male than in the female, in humanity individual "possibilities" depend on the economic and social situation.

In any case, it is not always true that the male's individual privileges confer upon him superiority in the species; the female regains another kind of autonomy in maternity. Sometimes he imposes his domination: this is the case in the monkeys studied by Zuckerman; but often the two halves of the couple lead separate lives; the lion and the lioness share the care of the habitat equally. Here again, the case of the human species cannot be reduced to any other; men do not define themselves first as individuals; men and women have never challenged each other in individual fights; the couple is an original Mitsein; and it is always a fixed or transitory element of a wider collectivity; within these societies, who, the male or the female, is the more necessary for the species? In terms of gametes, in terms of the biological functions of coitus and gestation, the male principle creates to maintain and the female principle maintains to create: What becomes of this division in social life? For species attached to foreign bodies or to the substrata, for those to whom nature grants food abundantly and effortlessly, the role of the male is limited to fertilization; when it is necessary to search, chase, or fight to provide food needed for offspring, the male often helps with their maintenance; this help becomes absolutely indispensable in a species where children remain incapable of taking care of their own needs for a long period after the mother stops nursing them: the male's work then takes on an extreme importance; the lives he brought forth could not maintain themselves without him. One male is enough to fertilize many females each year: but males are necessary for the survival of children after birth, to defend them against enemies, to extract from nature everything they need. The balance of productive and reproductive forces is different depending on the different economic moments of human history, and they condition the relation of the male and the female to children and later among them. But we are going beyond the field of biology: in purely biological terms, it would not be possible to posit the primacy of one sex concerning the role it plays in perpetuating the species.

But a society is not a species: the species realizes itself as existence in a society; it transcends itself toward the world and the future; its customs cannot be deduced from biology; individuals are never left to their nature; they obey this second nature, that is, customs in which the desires and fears that express their ontological attitude are reflected. It is not as a body but as a body subjected to taboos and laws that the subject gains consciousness of and accomplishes himself. He valorizes himself in the name of certain values. And once again, physiology cannot ground values: rather, biological data take on those values the existent confers on them. If the respect or fear woman inspires prohibits man from using violence against her, the male's muscular superiority is not a source of power. If customs desire – as in some Indian tribes – that girls choose husbands, or if it is the father who decides on marriages, the male's sexual aggressiveness does not grant him any initiative, any privilege. The mother's intimate link to the child will be a source of dignity or indignity for her, depending on the very variable value given to the child; this very link, as has already been said, will be recognized or not according to social biases.

From 73

This world has always belonged to males, and none of the reasons given for this have ever seemed sufficient. By reviewing prehistoric and ethnographic data in the light of existentialist philosophy, we can understand how the hierarchy of the sexes came to be. We have already posited that when two human categories find themselves face-to-face, each one wants to impose its sovereignty on the other; if both hold to this claim equally, a reciprocal relationship is created, either hostile or friendly, but always tense. If one of the two has an advantage over the other, that one prevails and works to maintain the relationship by oppression. It is thus understandable that man might have had the will to dominate woman: but what advantage enabled him to accomplish this will?

Ethnologists give extremely contradictory information about primitive forms of human society, even more so when they are well-informed and less systematic. It is especially difficult to formulate an idea about woman's situation in the preagricultural period. We do not even know if, in such different living conditions from today's, woman's musculature or her respiratory system was not as developed as man's. She was given hard work, and in particular it was she who carried heavy loads; yet this latter fact is ambiguous: probably if she was assigned this function, it is because within the convoy men kept their hands free to defend against possible aggressors, animals or humans; so their role was the more dangerous one and demanded more strength. But it seems that in many cases women were robust and resilient enough to participate in warrior expeditions. According to the accounts by Herodotus and the traditions of the Amazons from Dahomey as well as ancient and modern testimonies, women were known to take part in bloody wars or vendettas; they showed as much courage and cruelty as males: there are references to women who bit their teeth into their enemies' livers. In spite of this, it is likely that then as now men had the advantage of physical force; in the age of the clubs and wild animals, in the age when resistance to nature was at its greatest and tools were at their most rudimentary, this superiority must have been of extreme importance. In any case, as robust as women may have been at that time, the burdens of reproduction represented for them a severe handicap in the fight against a hostile world: Amazons were said to mutilate their breasts, which meant that at least during the period of their warrior lives they rejected maternity. As for ordinary women, pregnancy, giving birth, and menstruation diminished their work capacity and condemned them to long periods of impotence; to defend themselves against enemies or to take care of themselves and their children, they needed the protection of warriors and the catch from hunting and fishing provided by the males. As there obviously was no birth control, and as nature does not provide woman with sterile periods as it does for other female mammals, frequent pregnancies must have absorbed the greater part of their strength and their time; they were unable to provide for the lives of the children they brought into the world. This is a primary fact fraught with great consequence: the human species' beginnings were difficult; hunter, gatherer, and fishing peoples reaped meager bounty from the soil, and at great cost in effort; too many children were born for the group's resources; the woman's absurd fertility kept her from participating actively in the growth of these resources, while it was constantly creating new needs. Indispensable to the perpetuation of the species, she perpetuated it too abundantly: so it was man who controlled the balance between reproduction and production. Thus woman did not even have the privilege of maintaining life that the creator male had; she did not play the role of ovum to his spermatozoid or womb to his phallus; she played only one part in the human species' effort to persist in being, and it was thanks to man that this effort had a concrete result.

Nonetheless, as the production–reproduction balance always finds a way of stabilizing itself – even at the price of infanticide, sacrifices, or wars – men and women are equally indispensable from the point of view of group survival; it could even be supposed that at certain periods when food was plentiful, his protective and nourishing role might have subordinated the male to the wife-mother. There are female animals that derive total autonomy from motherhood; so why has woman not been able to make a pedestal for herself from it? Even in those moments when humanity most desperately needed births – since the need for manual labor prevailed over the need for raw materials to exploit – and even in those times when motherhood was the most venerated, maternity was not enough for women to conquer the highest rank. The reason for this is that humanity is not a simple natural species: it does not seek to survive as a species; its project is not stagnation: it seeks to surpass itself.

The primitive hordes were barely interested in their posterity. Connected to no territory, owning nothing, embodied in nothing stable, they could formulate no concrete idea of permanence; they were unconcerned with survival and did not recognise themselves in their descendants; they did not fear death and did not seek heirs; children were a burden and not of great value for them; the proof is that infanticide has always been frequent in nomadic peoples; and many newborns who are not massacred die for lack of hygiene in total indifference. So the woman who gives birth does not take pride in her creation; she feels like the passive plaything of obscure forces, and painful childbirth a useless and even bothersome accident.

Later, more value was attached to children. But in any case, to give birth and to breast-feed are not activities, but natural functions; they do not involve a project, which is why the woman finds no motive there to claim a higher meaning for her existence; she passively submits to her biological destiny.

Because housework alone is compatible with the duties of motherhood, she is condemned to domestic labor, which locks her into repetition and immanence; day after day it repeats itself in identical form from century to century; it produces nothing new. Man's case is radically different. He does not provide for the group in the way worker bees do, by a simple vital process, but rather by acts that transcend his animal condition. *Homo faber* has been an inventor since the beginning of time: even the stick or the club he armed himself with to knock down fruit from a tree or to slaughter animals is an instrument that expands his grasp of the world; bringing home freshly caught fish is not enough for him: he first has to conquer the seas by constructing dugout canoes; to appropriate the world's treasures, he annexes the world itself.

Through such actions he tests his own power; he posits ends and projects paths to them: he realizes himself as existent. To maintain himself, he creates; he spills over the present and opens up the future. This is the reason fishing and hunting expeditions have a sacred quality. Their success is greeted by celebration and triumph; man recognizes his humanity in them. This pride is still apparent today when he builds a dam, a skyscraper, or an atomic reactor.

Jeanne Vialle

From "Femmes africaines/African Women" (1951)[26]

The Oubangian capital sits on the shores of the river. Its houses nestle in clusters of greenery thrown into sharp relief by the red patches of laterite.

That day, there was a great commotion in front of one of the big Motor Transport Companies. The trucks were loading and the passengers, surrounded by companions, were waiting their turn to take their places in the convoy which was heading north.

The signal was given. Everyone hurried to their truck amid laughter, shouts and embraces of farewell. In this chaos, one passenger stood out; not young but small and slender, wrapped in a sombre loincloth and seated modestly upon a pile of cloths. She was silent but her eyes anxiously sought someone in the crowd. She found her. She made a small gesture with her hand, and smiled weakly to hide the tears falling from her eyes.

On the ground, the person arousing so much emotion was also a small scrap of a woman, younger than the passenger. She clasped a newborn child to her breast.

> – Who is this woman up there on the truck?
> – It is my mother who came for the birth of my child.
> – Why is she leaving?
> – She is going to her son who no longer has a wife.

The two women were still waving affectionately as the trucks moved out and a turn in the road obscured the mother's tears from view.

[...]

A line of women wrapped in long and colourful loincloths brings joy and light to a dusty construction site of the Djoué. Important electrification works are done there, and a large amount of manpower is required.

---

[26] Translated from the French by Sarah C. Dunstan.

The site directors decided to give the midday meal to all the workers and they advertised for suppliers for the canteens. Women, major cassava producers, were amongst the first to respond and now twice a week they bring the fruit of their harvest and their preparation: the chikouang, which is cassava made into a compact and tender dough that they wrap in bread in banana leaves.

The women came in large numbers that morning and waited, patient and cheerful, for their produce to be weighed and purchased. Viewed from the front, one thing in particular surprises and attracts the attention of the onlooker. On each side of their waist, two small white patches stand out clearly. A closer look reveals that the patches are little feet. The child is there, kept close to his mother's back by a cloth that, at the front, reveals only these white-soled little feet; and from behind a little head peeks out – often wearing a pretty, knitted woollen hat – and nodding sleepily or smiling as the child watches the surrounding spectacle.

Together these women and their children will return to their villages, often located about ten kilometres away.

Tomorrow, they will return to their plantations, hardworking, courageous, to bring home food and some resources: they sell what their household cannot consume. But it will always be with their child either in their arms or on their back, as if they wanted to pass on all the vitality and the accomplishments of their daily work to the child with them.

As they scrape the ground with their hoe, pound the cassava, as they prepare the meals, the child never leaves them. He is part of them, both before and after the birth.

[...]

She is 20 years old. She went to school, passed her primary school certificate several years ago. Now, after having continued her studies at the higher level, she is a teacher at a school in Poto-Poto, a large village close to Brazzaville. Marie-Thérèse is a magnificent young girl who can be described as an "evoluée". However, she remains strongly attached to the customs and traditions of her home.

Two years ago she was offered the opportunity to go and continue her studies in the metropolis, but this departure would have caused so much grief to her mother that she declined, not without regret but she had, before all, a duty to obey her mother.

Another opportunity has come this year for Marie-Thérèse to accept a scholarship that would allow her to study in France.

Will she have the courage, this time, to overcome the wishes of her mother? No, because her mother no longer opposes her daughter's departure from home but instead wants her to promise herself to the boy the mother has chosen for her. The mother claims that it would bring shame on the family if, in two or three years, when Marie-Thérèse returns at the age of 22 or 23, she is neither married nor at least engaged.

Marie-Thérèse, divided between her deep desire to go to the Metropole, to see something else, to come back with degrees that will develop and accredit her work, and the no less deep feeling of love and submission to the will of her mother, will not leave without giving the promise her mother asks.

[…]

These three rapid sketches of African women, drawn from my last trip to Equatorial Africa are often on my mind. They symbolize for me the African woman of yesterday, today and tomorrow.

Above all a mother, the African woman is capable of the greatest sacrifices. She has an instinctive love for her child nourished by this physical contact between her and her child who is an integral part of herself. The child grows up, calls for her, and she gives up everything to go to him, to give him her help, support and love.

The African woman is hardworking. It is she who takes responsibility for the family and food crops. If we don't see her in the industrial coffee or sisal plantations, it is working in the fields of cotton, cassava, corn or peanuts.

It is she who transforms the palm fruits into a beautiful orange oil which she then sells at the region's monthly market. It is she who takes care of the harvest. She is the one who, through patient, daily work, brings food home, and prepares it.

It is she who manages the family interests when the man brings the money he earned from the plantation, the factory or the port, using it for the purchase of imported clothing and small utensils.

As in so many other ancient civilizations, it is she who ensures the future by protecting and nourishing life, and by bringing up the new generation in the traditional surroundings.

African girls have their faces turned towards a future in which the forms of Western civilization have outlined new horizons mingling with the old. While moving towards the new, they retain the fundamental features of their character. Mothers first, they are strongly attracted by the possibility of better caring for and better protecting their children. As workers, they hope to make their work more productive and to become proficient in more delicate tasks – such as needlework for example.

At the same time, faithful to their traditions, they hesitate when confronted with the new ways of life. The responsibility is great both for them and for those who wish to hasten the process of evolution. This must indeed go forward not by destroying, but by safeguarding and giving full opportunity for orderly development to the fine human qualities which African women have inherited from a long and hard past.

10

Public Opinion and Education
Introduction by Katharina Rietzler

The history of twentieth-century international thought cannot be understood without an account of mass enfranchisement on the back of organized labor, and the ensuing debates on its consequences. One of these consequences was an analysis of the ways in which members of the public determined relations between peoples, empires, and states. The campaigns for women's suffrage intensified the widespread sense that henceforth international affairs would be shaped by mass public opinion. But the advent of the public as a crucial factor in international relations came with profound anxieties. Liberals sought the answer to the problem of public ignorance in educational reform. Socialists also emphasized education but argued that the material conditions of the working class had to change – a change that some labeled "industrial democracy."[1] Conservatives and realists were skeptical about the potential for improvement. This skepticism often mobilized negative stereotypes about the limited rationality of women. Harold Nicolson, for instance, argued in the early 1940s that giving women the vote had introduced "dangerous qualities" into international affairs, heralding a decline of the West.[2]

The exclusions that marked women's enfranchisement – which gave women in metropolitan Britain (1928) and the United States (1920) the vote on an equal basis with men, but excluded almost all African American women and many in British colonies – are an indication of the gap that existed between abstract concepts of "the public" and the profound transformations of existing imperial, racial, gender, and class orders that would have been required by a true people's diplomacy.[3]

---

[1] As suggested by socialist thinker and pacifist Jessie Hughan, covered in the section on Field and Discipline.

[2] Quoted in Christine Sylvester, *Feminist Theory and International Relations in a Postmodern Era* (Cambridge: Cambridge University Press, 1994), 82.

[3] Ian Christopher Fletcher, Philippa Levine, and Laura E. Nym Mayhall (eds.), *Women's Suffrage in the British Empire: Citizenship, Nation and Race* (Abingdon: Routledge, 2000); Rosalyn Terborg-Penn, *African American Women in the Struggle for the Vote, 1850–1920* (Bloomington, IN: Indiana University Press, 1998); Martha S. Jones, *Vanguard: How*

Across the political spectrum, Western international thought remained, for the most part, wedded to Eurocentric ideas about publicness. The idea that sophisticated publics with distinct forms of knowledge production on international politics existed outside the West was rarely explored by white Anglophone thinkers before the second half of the twentieth century. Even after the Second World War, modernization theory aimed at assimilating traditional societies into the discursive practices of Western democracies, for instance by promoting literacy programs. Few questioned the inherent paternalism in the educational systems of colonialist societies, even when they recognized the importance of education in the formation of political consciousness.

Education is relevant to analyses of women's international thought for multiple reasons. When asking the question "where are the women in international affairs?" in 1929, Florence Brewer Boeckel concluded that American and European women would provide different answers. While Europeans looked for "outstanding individual women," Americans focused on the key role women played in education as they were "the greatest present factor in educating public opinion for a new world order."[4] Yet both in Britain and in the United States, similar trends structured women's positions in educational institutions and are reflected in the attention paid to questions of pedagogy and popular education by women international thinkers. Primary and secondary education became feminized professions by the First World War. Academic women began to organize transnationally, for example in the International Federation of University Women.[5]

However, racial exclusions remained in place. Black women scholars in America mostly taught at historically Black colleges and universities (HBCUs) because often they could find no other employment. By the 1940s, the American Association of University Women (AAUW), the largest and best-funded national organization of women academics, contained only one branch that was racially integrated, even though African American scholars could become national AAUW members.[6] And, of

---

Black Women Broke Barriers, Won the Vote, and Insisted on Equality for All (New York: Basic Books, 2020).

[4] Florence Brewer Boeckel, "Women in International Affairs," Annals of the American Academy of Political and Social Science, 143, issue on Women in the Modern World (1929): 230–248, at 230.

[5] Christine von Oertzen, Science, Gender and Internationalism: Women's Academic Networks, 1917–1955 (New York: Palgrave Macmillan, 2014).

[6] Stephanie Y. Evans, Black Women in the Ivory Tower 1850–1954: An Intellectual History (Gainesville, FL: University Press of Florida, 2007); Susan Levine, Degrees of Equality: The American Association of University Women and the Challenge of Twentieth-Century Feminism (Philadelphia, PA: Temple University Press, 1995), 107.

course, the question of how African American students were taught went to the heart of the United States' racial order. Segregated education was one of the pillars of the Jim Crow system which relegated African Americans to vastly inferior facilities and put a bar on their economic advancement. White teachers rarely applied ideas of intercultural education that benefited the children of immigrants racialized as white to people of color. It fell to African American educators to inculcate "race pride," drawing on a long tradition of Black thought which includes Anna Julia Cooper's famous *A Voice from the South*, excerpted in the section on Men, Women, and Gender.[7]

Nannie Helen Burroughs (1879–1961) also belongs in this tradition. Like Cooper, she ran a Black school, the Christian National Training School for Women and Girls in the District of Columbia, which opened in 1909. Burroughs, the daughter of former slaves, belongs to a generation of southern-born African American club women such as Mary McLeod Bethune and Charlotte Hawkins Brown, educators and reformers who were invested in a discourse of Christian moralism, racial uplift, and female respectability.[8] After graduating from the prestigious M Street High School in Washington, DC, Burroughs worked for the Foreign Mission Board of the National Baptist Convention but also became active in civil rights and women's organizations such as the National Association for the Advancement of Colored People (NAACP) and the National Association of Colored Women (NACW). Burroughs's substantial corpus of published writings is of interest to scholars of religion, philosophy, political thought, education, and feminism.[9]

Burroughs's educational work was by no means focused on racial uplift in the United States alone. From the early 1900s, and while she worked for the National Baptist Convention, Burroughs became concerned with the uplift of people of color throughout the world. According to her, African American women occupied a special role as missionaries

---

[7] Zoë Burkholder, *Color in the Classroom* (New York: Oxford University Press, 2011), 34–38; Karen A. Johnson, *Uplifting the Women and the Race: The Educational Philosophies and Social Activism of Anna Julia Cooper and Nannie Helen Burroughs* (New York: Routledge, 2000).

[8] Opal Easter, *Nannie Helen Burroughs* (New York: Routledge, 1995); Audrey Thomas McCluskey, *A Forgotten Sisterhood: Pioneering Black Women Educators and Activists in the Jim Crow South* (Lanham, MD: Rowman and Littlefield, 2014).

[9] Kelisha B. Graves (ed.), *Nannie Helen Burroughs: A Documentary Portrait of an Early Civil Rights Pioneer, 1900–1959* (Notre Dame, IN: Notre Dame University Press, 2019); on Burroughs's place in African American religious life and thought see Barbara Savage, *Your Spirits Walk beside Us: The Politics of Black Religion* (Cambridge, MA: Belknap Press, 2008).

spreading the gospel in foreign lands, exemplifying women's leadership and self-sacrifice in the spirit of Christ. Burroughs regarded colonial oppression in Africa and racial oppression in the United States as intrinsically linked, referring to Africans as "our kinsmen." Her National Training School trained both African American and African women students. Some of the latter became civic and religious leaders in their countries of origin.[10]

Amidst the fierce early-twentieth-century debates on African American education that pitted proponents of industrial education against those who criticized the latter as entrenching socio-economic subordination, Burroughs occupied a middle ground. She crafted a "hybrid" curriculum that offered vocational training but also included a mandatory course on "Negro History."[11] The teaching of domestic science skills at her school conformed to definitions of female purity and domesticity in the respectability tradition. However, Burroughs's efforts to professionalize domestic service also furthered Black women's economic independence as wage earners in a time of economic boom and bust, and combated racist stereotypes. In the end, she offered her women students a carefully calibrated mix of respectability, racial uplift, and leadership.

The dilemmas of Black education are also present in the speech excerpted here, given when Burroughs was the Corresponding Secretary of the Women's Auxiliary to the National Baptist Convention. Burroughs admits that domestic service may not conform to the aspirations of educated Black women "but educated women without work and the wherewith to support themselves … are not worth an ounce more to the race than ignorant women" (534). Burroughs regarded the race problem as an international one, in which the forces of capitalism and the legacies of slavery pitted "white imported help" (533) against African American women seeking economic independence. The demands of the hour were those brought about by the radical transformations of the Progressive period, marked by urbanization, industrialization, and mass immigration. Burroughs's case for professionalizing domestic science is also a plea for racial solidarity among African Americans in the face of global white supremacy which ensured that "guilds and other organizations" (535) put white competitors at an

---

[10] Angela Hornsby-Gutting, "'Woman's Work': Race, Foreign Missions, and Respectability in the National Training School for Women and Girls," *Journal of Women's History*, 31:1 (2019): 37–61.

[11] Ibid., 41.

advantage in the marketplace. In Burroughs's speech, global labor movements and the global color line internationalize the question of industrial education and link it to gendered discourses of Christian morality.

For white American educators in the Progressive Era, a much more important discourse for internationalizing the question of education was "peace," often in ways that downplayed stark educational disparities and injustices in the age of Jim Crow segregation. Curriculum reformers sought to educate children in the spirit of an ever-expanding world community, which, as some historians have argued, makes the United States' tradition of peace education a neglected strain of US intellectual history.[12] One of the most important white peace educators was Fannie Fern Andrews, with her American School Peace League. Andrews (1867–1950) trained as a teacher at Salem Normal School (1884) and Radcliffe College (1902). A marriage to a wealthy man made it possible for her to abandon the classroom and become a campaigner, first for educational reform and then for peace. In 1908 Andrews co-founded the American School Peace League, one of whose major publications, co-authored by Andrews and first published in 1914, was a 400-page curriculum that instructed children in how to resolve conflicts by empathizing with others. Andrews went on extensive speaking tours to promote the aims and activities of her organization and influenced public policy as Special Collaborator of the United States Bureau of Education from 1912 to 1921.[13]

What is less well known is that, after the First World War, Andrews also sought to become an authority in the new academic field of International Relations (IR). Armed with a Harvard PhD, she presented her work on the League of Nations' mandates regime – a cutting-edge topic in the early 1920s – at scholarly conferences and unsuccessfully sought to get her dissertation published. Andrews was impeded by the gender conventions of academe and, while male IR scholars such as Quincy Wright and Raymond Leslie Buell reviewed her work, they dismissed it as unsystematic and lacking in scholarly rigor. Having been rebuffed from academic IR, Andrews, a good example for "academic

---

[12] Aline M. Stomfay-Stitz, *Peace Education in America, 1828–1990: Sourcebook for Education and Research* (Metuchen, NJ: Scarecrow, 1993).

[13] Hollis France, "Andrews, Fannie Fern Phillips," in Lynne E. Ford (ed.), *Encyclopedia of Women and American Politics* (New York: Facts on File, 2008), 32–33; Cristy Jo Snider, "Peace and Politics: Fannie Fern Andrews, Professional Politics and the American Peace Movement, 1900–1941," *Mid-America*, 79:1 (1997): 71–95; E. L. Cabot, F. F. Andrews, F. E. Coe, M. Hill, and M. McSkimmon (eds.), *A Course in Citizenship* (Boston, MA: Houghton Mifflin, 1914).

failure" among women international thinkers, returned to transnational educational reform, where she found international renown.[14]

The piece included here was published during Andrews's heyday as a teacher-campaigner. Emblematic of the triumphalist American internationalism of the pre-First World War period, it positioned the United States at the pinnacle of world trends in commerce and culture, brought about by ever more densely woven global interdependence. Andrews was also typical in her narrow conception of what "the world" was – it comprised what she would have called "civilized nations" only, in effect those nations that were represented at the Hague Peace Conferences of 1899 and 1907 and included under the conventions of Eurocentric international law. This new internationalism, Andrews claimed, would eliminate inter-state war: "An organized world means international peace" (536). Women, she argued, had a special responsibility in bringing about world organization, through women's civic associations and by co-operating with school authorities. Andrews's was, ultimately, a feminine claim to authority, an appeal that sought to mobilize the sentiment of the people against war-mongering governments.

For intellectuals who came of age in the era of the First World War, the League of Nations often formed the core of their thinking on public opinion, education, and international politics. The idea that the new intergovernmental machinery had to be supported not only by governments but by committed citizens in all member states became a truism. Yet how that pro-League, educated public opinion was to be forged was a more complicated question. One route lay, paradoxically, in the institutions of the nation state, especially its schools. International bodies investigated school curricula to root out content that was excessively nationalistic.[15] The other route towards world consciousness was collaboration among intellectual elites, embodied by two League-affiliated intergovernmental institutions, the International Commission for Intellectual Cooperation and the International Institute of Intellectual Cooperation.

In the early 1920s, Eileen Power (1889–1940) was one of a group of British women historians who confronted the question of teaching the aims of the League of Nations to the young. Her career took her, via Girton College, Cambridge, to a professorship in economic history at the

---

[14] Valeska Huber, Tamson Pietsch, and Katharina Rietzler, "Women's International Thought and the New Professions, 1900–1940," *Modern Intellectual History*, 18:1 (2021): 121–145.

[15] Tomás Irish, "Peace through History? The Carnegie Endowment for International Peace's Inquiry into European Schoolbooks, 1921–1924," *History of Education*, 45:1 (2016): 38–56.

London School of Economics (LSE), where she lectured on World History. As a scholar and public intellectual, she was best known for her work on women in the Middle Ages but also became involved in writing children's history books, schools broadcast services, and the Unity Schools run by the British League of Nations Union (LNU).[16] Power's commitment to school education centered on the teaching of history, especially comparative and world history and social and economic history. Her notion that a unified narrative of history, teaching commonalities not differences to schoolchildren, could avoid conflict was popular among British internationalist intellectuals of the time. They included H. G. Wells and his unacknowledged wife Jane Wells, who together developed the idea in *The Outline of History*, and F. Melian Stawell, the author of *The Growth of International Thought*, who also wrote internationalist books for the classroom.[17] Both influenced Power.

In Power's 1921 essay "The Teaching of History and World Peace" the impact of the First World War is palpable. Europe and Asia were still suffering from its "unspeakable miseries" (543) but the nascent institutions of the League of Nations represented a potential way out. Like many liberal internationalists of the time, Power believed that the League had to "be driven by an educated public opinion" (543). Schools, which had expanded their hold on young minds as Western industrial nations increased the resources that went into state-funded education, thus became cognitive and emotional "engine rooms in which power is created to drive the machinery of the League of Nations" (546). Power's suggestion to establish new rituals such as the annual celebration of a "Humanity Day" in schools parallels the establishment of International Good-Will Day by American educators, Fannie Fern Andrews among them, in 1923.[18]

Yet, the League's universalism privileged the interests of the great powers and the perpetuation of European colonialism.[19] The question of whether Power adopted a similarly Eurocentric vision in her treatment of world history has been answered ambivalently by scholars. Some have argued that in her writings on Asia she subverted colonialist ways of

---

[16] Maxine Berg, "The First Women Economic Historians," *The Economic History Review*, New Series, 45:2 (1992): 308–329.

[17] Helen McCarthy, *The British People and the League of Nations* (Manchester: Manchester University Press, 2011), 106; Maxine Berg, *A Woman in History: Eileen Power, 1889–1940* (Cambridge: Cambridge University Press, 1996), 225–226.

[18] Burkholder, *Color in the Classroom*, 26. On international education in the United States see also Katie Day Good, *Bring the World to the Child: Technologies of Global Citizenship in American Education* (Boston, MA: MIT Press, 2020).

[19] Susan Pedersen, *The Guardians* (Oxford: Oxford University Press, 2015).

knowing and questioned the narrative of just colonial rule dedicated to progress.[20] However, Power was not a fervent critic of colonialism, and her teleological tropes about a common world history that would unfold according to a preordained "march of civilization" (544) make her appear, in this sense at least, like other Eurocentric visionaries of world history familiar from recent histories of international thought. At the same time, Power advocated teaching a common history "of all races and of all classes" (544). Nonetheless, for her, European history held the key to world history in the classroom.

Writing a decade later, Virginia Crocheron Gildersleeve (1877–1965), the Dean of Barnard College, also probed the moral and intellectual basis of world peace. Gildersleeve's biography makes her an archetypical representative of Anglo-American women's educational internationalism in the interwar years. She led an elite women's college, co-founded both the American Association of University Women and the International Federation of University Women, and was the only woman delegate from the United States to the San Francisco United Nations Conference on International Organization in 1945.[21] The piece included here is from one of the speeches that she frequently gave, in 1932. By that time, Gildersleeve and other American liberal internationalists could look back on a decade of energetic capacity building both in popular education and in scholarly research in international affairs. Surveys of the field, most importantly that carried out by Edith Ware, portrayed shaping public opinion and academic research as two sides of the same coin, which was to rationalize foreign policy making.[22]

In her speech, Gildersleeve adopted a by then conventional differentiation between institutional structures such as the World Court or the Kellogg–Briand Pact and "public opinion – that is, the international mind among the peoples of the world, so that they will support this political machinery" (547), channeled through the League of Nations. As did Power, Gildersleeve marked out schools, colleges and universities for reform: "we must influence the choice of textbooks and the minds of the teachers" (548). But there is little sense of giving autonomy to

---

[20] Billie Melman, "Under the Western Historian's Eyes: Eileen Power and the Early Feminist Encounter with Colonialism," *History Workshop Journal*, 42 (1996), 147–168.

[21] Justus D. Doenecke, "Virginia Crocheron Gildersleeve," in Anne Commire and Deborah Klezmer (eds.), *Women in World History* (Waterford, CT: Yorkin Publications, 2000), 221–226; Virginia Gildersleeve, *Many a Good Crusade: Memoirs* (New York: Macmillan, 1954).

[22] Edith Ware, *The Study of International Relations in the United States: Survey for 1934* (New York: Columbia University Press, 1934).

teachers or students, which might be explained by the provenance of Gildersleeve's concept of the "International Mind."

The phrase had been coined in 1912 by American university president, foundation leader, and unofficial diplomat Nicholas Murray Butler, an unabashed elitist who imagined cultivated (male) opinion leaders inducting the populace into conduct fitting for a world power.[23] By the interwar period, international-mindedness had become a popular concept among American teachers, but it retained its moralistic hue. Gildersleeve spoke of the cultivated International Mind as one "which accepts as normal international cooperation rather than competition, friendly understanding rather than hostile suspicion" (547). In her analysis of international conflict, Gildersleeve pointed to innate "ancient instincts," rooted in "differing racial psychology" (548, 549). Her reduction of the First World War war debts dispute between the United States and European powers to "feelings" (549) betrays her class position as a woman who thought it vulgar to talk about money. But during the Great Depression, European governments were simply not able to persuade their voters to undergo hardship so as not to default on war debt payments to American creditors.

It was the absence of a political analysis of conflicts of interest that made liberal internationalists like Gildersleeve and Power seem out of touch in the 1940s. They became an easy target for the emerging realist paradigm of American IR, a paradigm that does accommodate women intellectuals such as Merze Tate (1905–1996) and Dorothy Fosdick (1913–1997). Neither of them would have been happy to be identified with what they might have regarded as "soft" topics. While feminist IR scholars such as J. Ann Tickner have argued that the masculinist nature of classic realist theorizing has produced reductionist theories of international relations that do not consider women's experiences, this – obviously – did not prevent women from espousing realist positions.[24] Yet, both Tate and Fosdick were exceptional women whose achievements belied early-twentieth-century expectations for their sex and, in Tate's case, also her race.

Tate's intellectual powers were visible at an early age and led her to the universities of Oxford and Harvard, where she was the first African

---

[23] Nicholas Murray Butler, *The International Mind: An Argument for the Judicial Settlement of International Disputes* (New York: Charles Scribner's Sons, 1919 [1912]).

[24] J. Ann Tickner, *Gender in International Relations: Feminist Perspectives on Achieving Global Security* (New York: Columbia University Press, 1992), 3–37; see also Marysia Zalewski and Jane Parpart, *The "Man" Question in International Relations* (Boulder, CO: Westview, 1998); Charlotte Hooper, *Manly States: Masculinities, International Relations, and Gender Politics* (New York: Columbia University Press, 2001).

American woman, respectively, to receive a graduate degree and to earn a PhD in government. Originally, though, she had trained as a high school teacher. Tate's background was highly unusual. Born not in the Jim Crow South but in rural Michigan, she hailed from a family of African American homesteaders who were proud of their "Old Settler" status. Tate's Mid-Western origins and relatively comfortable upbringing did not protect her from racial discrimination. In 1927, when she graduated as the first African American student from Western Michigan University, the state of Michigan did not employ African Americans at the high school level and she had to seek a teaching job in neighboring Indiana. An extended tour of Europe that included a stint at Lucie and Alfred Zimmern's Geneva School of International Studies convinced her to apply for a highly competitive three-year fellowship from the American Association of University Women to go to Oxford.[25]

Tate's British academic mentors Alfred Zimmern and Agnes Headlam-Morley both supported the League of Nations. They suggested the transnational disarmament movement as the topic for Tate's 1935 Oxford BLitt, which fed into Tate's 1941 PhD dissertation, completed at Harvard's Government Department. Tate's resulting first book, *The Disarmament Illusion: The Movement for a Limitation of Armaments to 1907*, adopted a power political analysis of armaments in international politics: armament build-ups represented states' attempts to upset the international political status quo, whereas arms limitation agreements sought to freeze power relations in time. Therefore, Tate argued in defiance of her liberal internationalist mentors, civil society-based movements for disarmament generally failed to receive a hearing among statesmen.[26]

However, Tate was a diligent pupil, and while she became a public opinion skeptic, she carefully applied mid-twentieth-century democratic theory to the history of the late-nineteenth-century disarmament movement. She analyzed the prevalence of disarmament topics in the press, scholarly journals, parliaments, labor unions, women's groups, and peace societies, concluding that an organized public opinion favoring

---

[25] Barbara Savage, "Professor Merze Tate: Diplomatic Historian, Cosmopolitan Woman," in Mia Bay, Farah J. Griffin, Martha S. Jones, and Barbara D. Savage (eds.), *Toward an Intellectual History of Black Women* (Chapel Hill, NC: University of North Carolina Press, 2015), 252–269. For more information on Tate see the sections on Field and Discipline and Diplomacy and Foreign Policy.

[26] Barbara Savage, "Beyond Illusions: Imperialism, Race and Technology in Merze Tate's International Thought," in Patricia Owens and Katharina Rietzler (eds.), *Women's International Thought: A New History* (Cambridge: Cambridge University Press, 2021), 266–285.

disarmament was "non-existent" in the late nineteenth century (555). Hans J. Morgenthau, probably the most famous realist of his generation, commended Tate's work and drew from it the conclusion that giving the public a say in the making of foreign policy was a blind alley for Western democracies.[27] But that was not necessarily Tate's assessment. Tate grounded and historicized Walter Lippmann's theory of the "phantom public" and left open the possibility that in other historical contexts public opinion would effectively influence foreign policy, "when the educative process has been worked out" (556).[28]

Fosdick also took education seriously. A PhD in political theory from Columbia and family connections to the highly networked world of US foreign policy think tanks and philanthropic foundations ensured that she was the only woman present at an influential 1954 Rockefeller Foundation conference on IR theory. In 1942, she joined the US State Department, where she eventually served on the Policy Planning Staff. From 1954 to 1983, she worked as foreign policy advisor to Henry M. "Scoop" Jackson, the hawkish Democratic Senator from Washington.[29]

A Christian realist in the mold of Reinhold Niebuhr, Fosdick adopted his disavowal of both pacifist utopianism and the "cynical excesses of the Machiavellian." She criticized mass democracy in America, where "politically active" ordinary people had adopted the "robber morality" of unscrupulous rulers. In her view, modern warfare waged by democratic states threatened to unleash unchecked violence on the world.[30] Nevertheless, her answer to the dilemmas of democratic diplomacy lay not in the insulation of the foreign policy making process. "Foreign policy is the business of every American," Fosdick declared in the preface to her popular 1955 treatise *Common Sense and World Affairs*, in which she presented twelve maxims for the wise and restrained projection of American power in the world. Peppered with references to classical

---

[27] Hans J. Morgenthau, "Review," *The Russian Review*, 2:2 (1943): 104–105, cited in Savage, "Beyond Illusions," 274.

[28] Walter Lippmann, *The Phantom Public* (New York: Harcourt, Brace, 1925).

[29] Nicolas Guilhot (ed.), *The Invention of International Relations Theory; Realism, the Rockefeller Foundation, and the 1954 Conference on Theory* (New York: Columbia University Press, 2011), 197–198, 239; Dorothy Fosdick obituary, *Washington Post*, February 8, 1997; Dorothy Fosdick, *What Is Liberty? A Study in Political Theory* (New York: Harper, 1939).

[30] Dorothy Fosdick, "Ethical Standards and Political Strategies," *Political Science Quarterly*, 57:2 (1942): 214–228, at 228 and 222. Fosdick highlights her intellectual debts to German-speaking social theorists such as Mannheim and Weber, which puts her in conversation with other democracy-skeptic realists. See Nicolas Guilhot, *After the Enlightenment: Political Realism and International Relations in the Mid-Twentieth Century* (Cambridge: Cambridge University Press, 2017).

writers yet written in a highly accessible style, this foreign policy self-help book for the common man and woman sought to reconcile its readers to the status quo of the Eisenhower years. It resolutely opposed Soviet Communism while offering a qualified commitment to multilateral institutions, American cultural diplomacy, and development programs.

While it is remarkable that education remained a relevant category for someone placed at the heart of American realism such as Fosdick, who employed a feminized form of intellectual labor, mass-market pedagogical writing, to implement its core theoretical demands, realism was not the only possible critique of liberal internationalist ideas on education, public opinion, and international politics.

Amy Ashwood Garvey's (1897–1969) extract from her unpublished autobiography provides a stark contrast to, for instance, Power's vision of a common, uplifting world history taught to British school children in the service of world peace. Reminiscing about her school days in the British colony of Jamaica, Garvey recounts the moment when, at the age of twelve, she learns from her white school principal's wife that she is descended from slaves brought to the island by English traders. Garvey "recoil[s] in horror" (570) and embarks on genealogical research into her family history, pressing first her businessman father and then her grandmother for information.

It transpires that Garvey's grandmother had been born in the land of the Ashanti in the colony of the Gold Coast in West Africa, before being sold into slavery at the age of sixteen. Britain only fought the last of four wars against the Ashanti in the year before Garvey's birth. In Garvey's recollections, it is this recent history that is quite literally a genealogy, delivered in letters and orally by her ancestors, which sensitizes a young Amy to the realities of international politics in the nineteenth and twentieth centuries: a history of colonial wars, slavery, forced migration, lost markers of identity. These momentous events are mediated through family and individual memory, and shape her political consciousness. Garvey returns to school "proud" and determined to "get back to Africa" (570, 571).

School education thus had little to offer Garvey in terms of political education. Her understanding of world citizenship questioned the liberal internationalist cultivation of friendship between nations, abstracted from bonds of kinship, culture, and language, and in no direct competition with institutions of the European imperial nation state. Garvey's emerging race consciousness would lead in due course to the creation of arguably the most important global organization for the liberation (and political education) of people of African descent in the twentieth century, the Universal Negro Improvement Association (UNIA). After co-founding it with her husband Marcus Garvey in Jamaica in 1914, both moved to New York City to build the American branch of the organization as well as the Black Star Line.[31]

In the decades that followed, Garvey became a thought-leader on Black liberation and decolonization. Active in West Africa, Europe, the Caribbean, and North America, Garvey continued her ethnographic investigations but also advocated educational schemes that reveal a complicated relationship with the gendered politics of respectability, for instance when she proposed a domestic science training program for Jamaican women in the 1940s.[32] While Garvey's liberatory politics may have been complex, her commitment to bottom-up transnational organizing and institution-building on the basis of racial solidarity among people of African descent mirrored and yet subverted liberal internationalist educational projects. Garvey's commitment to reaching the masses, by giving speeches on street corners or publicly reciting poetry, offers evidence for a capacious conception of education in her thought, one that did not necessarily depend on middle-class institutions such as schools and universities or scholarly and middle-brow publications.[33] In Jamaica, Garvey's place of birth, education became an important avenue for nation building. Black women educators such as Amy Bailey were crucial in formulating anti-imperialist critiques while harnessing the power of education.[34]

The British anthropologist Margaret Read (1889–1991) offers a very different perspective on education in the colonies. While recognizing the shortcomings of international education projects in the era of the League of Nations, and paying attention to the empowerment of colonial peoples through literacy campaigns, Read's account of the purpose of colonial

---

[31] For biographical information see Tony Martin, *Amy Ashwood Garvey: Pan-Africanist, Feminist, and Mrs. Marcus Garvey No. 1 or a Tale of Two Amies* (Dover, MA: Majority Press, 2007). While Martin rejects the idea that Amy Ashwood Garvey co-founded the UNIA, other scholars have disputed his account. Keisha N. Blain, *Set the World on Fire: Black Nationalist Women and the Global Struggle for Freedom* (Philadelphia, PA: University of Pennsylvania Press, 2019), 13–19; Lionel Yard, *Biography of Amy Ashwood, 1897–1969: Co-founder of the Universal Negro Improvement Association* (Washington, DC: Associated Publishers, 1990). Note also that Amy Jacques Garvey has been similarly side-lined as Marcus Garvey's helpmeet rather than an intellectual force in her own right.

[32] Robbie Shilliam, "Theorizing (with) Amy Ashwood Garvey," in Patricia Owens and Katharina Rietzler (eds.), *Women's International Thought: A New History* (Cambridge: Cambridge University Press, 2021), 175.

[33] Blain, *Set the World on Fire*, 18.

[34] Linnette Vassell, "Amy Bailey," in Colin A. Palmer (ed.), *Encyclopedia of African-American Culture and History*, 2nd ed. (Farmington Hills, MI: Gale, 2006), 171–172.

education remained paternalistic and wedded to the hierarchies inherent in mid-twentieth-century developmental discourse.

Read studied history at Newnham College, Cambridge, before turning her attention to anthropology at the LSE, where she began a doctorate in 1930 under the direction of Bronisław Malinowski. In the late 1930s, she conducted fieldwork in Nyasaland, which resulted in two books. Although Read's studies were well regarded at the time, anthropologists have subsequently criticized them for their inconsistent use of evidence and prejudices against African women in matrilineal societies. During the Second World War Read moved to the Institute of Education in London, where she eventually became a professor of colonial education, assuming a position of prominence in post-1945 British colonial education comparable to that of Lillian Penson, covered in the section on Imperialism. Read also began advising the British Colonial Office, a role that she maintained until the 1950s. Read represented Britain at the UNESCO general conferences in 1946 and 1947, which is when she published her pamphlet on mass education.[35]

Read's link to both UNESCO and the Colonial Office was far from unusual. Julian Huxley, UNESCO's first director-general, had also managed education in the British Empire, and knowledge derived from colonial administration fed into the educational programs of the new international organization.[36] UNESCO claimed to work for peace through cognitive transformation. Its focus, however, was on the masses, not on elite intellectuals, as had been the case with its predecessor, the League's international intellectual cooperation organization. Between 1946 and 1958, UNESCO implemented a program for what it termed "fundamental education."

There were obvious breaks with the interwar period. As Read recognized, under the UNESCO umbrella, non-Western powers such as the Soviet Union and China emerged as educational standard setters because of their achievements when it came to mass literacy. To Read, there was a direct link between illiteracy and international conflict: "while illiterate, poverty-stricken masses of people existed in different parts of the world, the possible exploitation of them by ambitious and

---

[35] Clive Whitehead, "Read, Margaret Helen (1889–1991), Social Anthropologist and Colonial Educationist," *Oxford Dictionary of National Biography*, September 23, 2004 (accessed October 14, 2019); Clive Whitehead, *Colonial Educators: The British Indian and Colonial Education Service 1858–1983* (London: I. B. Tauris, 2003); Cynthia Brantley, "Through Ngoni Eyes: Margaret Read's Matrilineal Interpretations from Nyasaland," *Critique of Anthropology*, 17:2 (1997): 147–169.

[36] Poul Duedahl (ed.), *A History of UNESCO: Global Actions and Impact* (Basingstoke: Palgrave Macmillan, 2016).

unscrupulous leaders would always threaten stability and peace, both within and among, the nations" (558). Framed in such terms, paternalist colonial education within the British Empire acquired a new justification and urgency under the avowedly anti-racist UNESCO, even in an age of decolonization. As Read put it: "let us see that we in Britain do our job in the colonies" (563).

That Read clung to a colonialist mindset which built on racist ideas of human hierarchy and the "civilizing mission" is strongly suggested by the way in which her argument was presented. In its original form, Read's pamphlet was illustrated with drawings that included crudely stereotypical and racialized depictions of Africans as cannibals reading a cookbook while preparing to boil a white male European, accompanied by the caption "Training in better living?" Intended to be humorous at a time when it could count on shared assumptions among readers, the cartoon reveals profound anxieties about how colonial subjects would turn mass literacy against their white masters, and suggests fears of a coming postcolonial reckoning.

There is a tension between Read's valorizing and mobilizing of the anthropologist's knowledge (for instance in the shape of an African proverb) and her insistence that the "time has gone" for traditional societies (559, 560). While analyses that argued for the retaining of some traditions were common in developmental thinking prior to the emergence of modernization theory, the dissonances in Read's writing may also result from the uneasy adaptation of a colonial educational paternalism to the new age of mass education for common men and women.[37] By the 1950s, the language of empowerment, a clear sense that international education was first and foremost for the people themselves and not for institutions of international governance such as the League of Nations, had become inescapable.

Katharina Rietzler

---

[37] Nils Gilman, *Mandarins of the Future: Modernization Theory in Cold War America* (Baltimore, MD: Johns Hopkins University Press, 2003), 9; on how the universities of Oxford and Cambridge reinvented their provision to Commonwealth elites in the context of decolonization see Sarah Stockwell, *The British End of the British Empire* (Cambridge: Cambridge University Press, 2018), chapter 3.

Nannie Helen Burroughs

From "The Colored Woman and Her Relation to the Domestic Problem" (1902)

You ask what is meant by the domestic problem. It is that peculiar condition under which women are living and laboring without the knowledge of the secrets of thrift, or of true scientific methods in which the mind has been awakened, and hands made capable thereby to give the most efficient services. It is a condition of indifference on the part of our working women as to their needs to how we may so dignify labor that our services may become indispensable on the one hand and Negro sentiment will cease to array itself against the "working girls" on the other hand. It is a question as to how we may receive for our services compensation commensurate with the work done. The solution of this problem will be the prime factor in the salvation of Negro womanhood, whose salvation must be attained before the so-called race problem can be solved.

The training of Negro women is absolutely necessary, not only for their own salvation and the salvation of the race, but because the hour in which we live demands it. If we lose sight of the demands of the hour we blight our hope of progress. The subject of domestic science has crowded itself upon us, and unless we receive it, master it and be wise, the next ten years will so revolutionize things that we will find our women without the wherewith to support themselves.

Untrained hands, however willing, will find themselves unwelcomed in the humblest homes. We may be careless about this matter of equipping our women for work in the homes, but if we are to judge from the wonderful progress that recent years has brought in the world of domestic labor we must admit that steps must be taken, and that at once, to train the hands of Negro women for better services and their hearts for purer living. All through the North white imported help is taking the place of Negro help. Where we once held forth without a thought of change we find our places filled by those of other races and climes.

The people who had to have servants declared that they wanted intelligent, refined, trained help, and in the majority of cases we were not ready to give them what they needed. Our intelligent Negroes, even though they may not have bread to eat, in many cases shun service work, when the fact is evident that ignorant help is not wanted by the best class of people in this country. The more thorough and intelligent the help the better.

What will this crowding from service mean to Negro women? It will mean their degradation. Our women will sink beneath the undermining influences of insidious sloth. Industry is one of the noblest virtues of any race. The people who scorn and frown upon her must die. While little heed may have been paid to the demand for better help and the supplanting of Negro servants by Irish, Dagoes and English may have been unnoticed by all of us, yet it is time for the leaders to sound the alarm, ere we are rooted from the places we have held for over two centuries. The time will come when we will stand as helpless as babes, as dependent as beggars, without the wherewith to sustain life, unless we meet the demands squarely.

Our women have worked as best they could without making any improvements and thus developing the service into a profession, and in that way make the calling more desirable from a standpoint of being lifted from a mere drudgery, as well as from the standpoint of compensation received.

The race whose women have not learned that industry and self-respect are the only guarantees of a true character will find itself bound by ignorance and violence or fettered with chains of poverty.

There is a growing tendency among us to almost abhor women who work at service for a living. If we hold in contempt women who are too honest, industrious and independent, women whose sense of pride is too exalted to be debased by idleness, we will find our women becoming more and more slothful in this matter of supporting themselves. Our "high-toned" notions as to the kind of positions educated people ought to fill have caused many women who cannot get anything to do after they come out of school to loaf rather than work for an honest living, declaring to themselves and acting it before others, that they were not educated to live among pots and pans. None of us may have been educated for that purpose, but educated women without work and the wherewith to support themselves and who have declared in their souls that they will not stoop to toil are not worth an ounce more to the race than ignorant women who have made the same declarations. Educated loafers will bear as much watching as ignorant ones. When the nobility of labor is magnified, and those who do labor respected more because of their real worth to the race, we will find a less number trying to escape the brand, "servant girl."

We are not less honorable if we are servants. Fidelity to duty rather than the grade of one's occupation is the true measure of character. Every gentle virtue will go down before a people and their endeavors come to naught when they forget that the foundation stone of prosperity is toil.

[...]

Young women from rural districts flock to great cities like New York, Chicago, Philadelphia, Boston, Baltimore and Washington in search of employment. Not only are they unprepared to serve but are woefully ignorant of the new social conditions into which they must be thrown. The white women in these large cities conduct guilds and other organizations that employ attendants to meet the trains and be on the alert for the white servant class that may be coming in seeking work or homes. Christian homes and churches are pointed out to the new-comers. The strong arms of Christian women are thrown about them, and while they are far from home and loved ones, they have the assurance that they have friends who will be ever mindful of them and their interests.

[...]

The solution of the servant girl problem, then, can only be accomplished first, by making it possible for these girls to overcome their ignorance, dishonesty and carelessness by establishing training classes and other moral agencies in these large cities and maintaining one or more first-class schools of domestic science. Second, by employers demanding the trained help from these classes or schools and paying wages in keeping with the ability of the servant to do the work. Third, by giving to women who work time for recreation and self improvement. This constant all-day "go" has made service a drudgery. If servants had hours for rest and improvement, like other laborers, they would come to their work with a freshness and intelligence that is now absent.

Emphasize the importance of preparation for service work. Let Negro women who are idle find work, stick to it and use it as a stepping stone to something better. Let us cease reaching over women who are servants and have character enough for queens to queens who haven't brains and character enough for servants. By becoming exponents of the blessed principles of honesty, cleanliness and industry, Negro women can bring dignity to service life, respect and trust to themselves and honor to the race. Then in deed and in truth we can mount up as with the wings of eagles, soar above the mountains of virtue and hide our heads among the stars. If anybody is to be scorned, scorn those women who will not honestly toil to raise themselves and are pulling us from the throne of honor and virtue.

Fannie Fern Andrews

From "The Relation of Teachers to the Peace Movement" (1908)

What surer indication of a new spirit among the nations than the world-wide interest in the limitation of armaments, and in the establishment of an international congress, in which the nations may consider any and all subjects which concern their common relations! The passage of such measures would produce results of far-reaching significance. It is only a logical inference from past procedure that eventually the international congresses will culminate in a world legislature, where the representatives from every government will legislate for the common welfare. The legislative department of a world government is distined [sic] to develop side by side with the judicial; and it also follows that an executive department, formed to carry out the provisions of the world legislature, will complete the rounding out of a world republic; each department is a necessary complement to the other two.

And what is the final result of all this? An organized world means international peace; and ultimate progress is dependent on harmonious, unrestricted, uninterrupted communication among the peoples of the earth, which will be possible only when the nations feel the security of permanent peace. To develop men and women, then, who can carry on the work of the world, the teacher must have a full appreciation of all these tendencies toward world unity. They have not gone on of themselves; for back of the intercourse among the peoples in industry, education, religion, science, literature, art, philanthropy and government, and the co-operative action of the nations toward an organized world, there has been a force, strong and impelling, which has organized and directed these natural and inevitable currents of progress. This specific, definite work for international peace began more than three centuries ago. The Great Design for the federation of Europe, formed by Henry IV, of France, in the sixteenth century, was a remarkable plea for unity, fraternity and co-operation; so, indeed, in his Rights of War and Peace, published in 1624, has Hugo Grotius inspired the thought of all ages with the hope of universal brotherhood. A contemporaneous expression of the same sentiment is shown in the founding of the Society of Friends, by George Fox, whose organization has preached the doctrine of non-resistance down to the present day. That remarkable Plan for the Permanent Peace of Europe, published by William Penn in 1693, Kant's essay on Eternal Peace, showing that war will not cease until the world is organized, and the later words of Channing, Sumner, Burritt, Cobden and Jean de Block express with unmistakable emphasis the fundamental principles of human brotherhood. These peace prophets have interpreted the meaning of history; with clear and true vision they have mapped out the course of progress, consistent with the universal laws of life.

One of the very first organizations to work for international peace was the American Peace Society, formed in 1815. This association originated the international peace congresses, and has seen develop more than five hundred peace societies throughout the world, which are now formed into a great international organization, having annual congresses and a permanent bureau at Berne, which conveys to the governments of the world the recommendations of the peace congresses. The peace movement, however, is not confined to peace societies; to-day, associations of almost every character, and individuals in every walk of life are pledging themselves to the cause of peace; never before in the history of the world were the active forces of mankind joined so unitedly in the achievement of a common purpose. Twenty-five hundred statesmen from the parliaments of the different nations are working out together a practical plan for an organized world. This body of men, called the Interparliamentary Union, is the symbol of interdependence; this voluntary association, formed in the interest of the world's political progress, has quickened among the governments a live consciousness of the necessity for common effort; has proclaimed an organized world the prerequisite for the fullest development of each nation. Of all the forces working directly for the peace of the world, this distinguished company of legislators holds first rank.

[...]

Coincident and co-operative are the efforts of the business men of the world, who are arraying themselves against war by the adoption of plans that will bring about world peace. The business men of England and France were a powerful influence in effecting the arbitration treaty between these two countries; and in the United States over a hundred business men's organizations have pledged themselves in favor of international arbitration. It is this great body of public benefactors who are urging the neutralization of the trade routes of the ocean, a condition consistent with an organized world.

Throwing also their weight into the scale in favor of international arbitration are the labor organizations of the world. At the Convention of the American Federation of Labor in November, 1906, a Resolution was passed, asking that the Convention go on record as favoring lasting peace among the nations, on the ground that constant peace contributes to the welfare of workingmen. The endorsement of this resolution by labor organizations in other countries and the recent resolutions adopted by the American Federation of Labor, show the great mass of people to be in favor of international unity.

So, too, are the churches preaching the gospel of peace in a practical way, not only by observing peace Sunday, and teaching the sentiments embodied in this idea, but in actual demonstration, concerning the movement for an organized world. A cablegram, creating much interest during the first Peace Congress, was that sent by thirty Baptist ministers in the state of Oregon, each paying one dollar for its delivery, asking the delegates at The Hague to adopt such measures as would tend toward international justice and unity. Last April Rt. Rev. William Croswell Doane, Bishop of the Episcopal Diocese at Albany, N. Y., sent a letter to his people, earnestly calling attention to the Peace Conference at The Hague, and beseeching them to pray that the members of the Conference may be of one mind, to the end that "God may give unto his people the blessing of peace."

The women's organizations have joined this progressive march. There is hardly a woman's club that has not considered this subject; and in many cases, the women of the United States have co-operated with school authorities in having the matter presented to the children in the schools. The Peace Department of the Women's Christian Temperance Union, having local organizations all over the world, the International Council of Women, with members in sixteen countries, are actively working for the promotion of peace. Both these organizations have given special attention to securing a universal peace demonstration on the eighteenth of May, the anniversary of the opening of the first Peace Congress, and especially the observance of the day in the public schools. The presentation to Mr. Carnegie of a peace flag, by the Daughters of the American Revolution, at one of the sessions of the National Peace Congress, which met in New York last April, is an evidence of the support which that association is giving to this great cause.

And what part has the teacher taken in this great movement? He, too, has joined the ranks in the cause of peace. At Lille, in 1905, the Association of French Public School Teachers, having fifteen thousand members, declared in its Resolutions that the teachers are energetic disciples of peace. Their watchword is, war against war. The same year, the International Congress of Teachers at Liege, represented by eighteen nations, devoted an entire day to the theme, "What can the schools do to spread the peace idea?" Among their recommendations was the special observance in schools of the eighteenth of May. Such celebration began in the United States through the initiative of the State Superintendents of Instruction in Massachusetts and Ohio in 1905. The next year, other states, Vermont, Rhode Island, Connecticut, New Jersey and Kansas, authorized the schools to hold special exercises on that day: and this year, Pennsylvania, Montana, Idaho, Colorado and California, recommended its observance. That the celebration of peace day will become general in the schools is practically assured by the action of the Department of Superintendence, meeting in Chicago last winter, when eight hundred superintendents passed a Resolution recommending suitable exercises in the schools on the eighteenth of May. In his first Annual Report, Hon. Elmer E. Brown, United States Commissioner of Education, says, concerning the day, "would accordingly recommend that, so far as consistent with state and local conditions, the eighteenth of May in each year be designated as a day of special observance in the schools." Consistent with all this, was the presidential address of Dr. Nathan C. Schaeffer, Superintendent of Public Instruction in Pennsylvania, who, at the opening of the National Educational Association in Los Angeles, last July, spoke on the topic, "What can the School do to Aid the Peace Movement?" "Teach history," said he, "in such a way, that the pupil will write the name of the poet, the orator, the artist, the inventor, the educator, the statesman, the philanthropist, in a place as conspicuous in the temple of fame as that occupied by the victorious general or the successful admiral. Lead the pupil to see that Pasteur, the scientist, has done more for humanity than Napoleon, the destroyer of thousands; that Carnegie, the philanthropist, has done more for civilization than the admiral who sinks a hostile fleet." Dr. Schaeffer urged that the eighteenth of May be regularly observed in all the schools of America to inculcate sentiments of peace and international fraternity.

[…]

Last Fourth of July two other educational gatherings in the United States sent cablegrams to The Hague. The American Institute of Instruction, meeting in Montreal, after devoting a whole session to the discussion of patriotism and internationalism, cabled an earnest request that the conference consider the full Interparliamentary Union program, especially the limitation of armaments. And at the Fourth of July celebration by the great summer school of the South, at Knoxville,

Tennessee, where three thousand teachers and citizens were in attendance, a most appropriate message was sent to our delegates at The Hague. This was inspired by the address of Edwin J. Mead, who had described an impressive scene on the Fourth of July, 1899, during the first Hague conference. By invitation of the American delegation, all the members of the conference had gathered in the old church at Delft, and Andrew D. White, the head of our delegation, after giving a stirring address, laid a silver wreath upon the tomb of Hugo Grotius, the father of international law, in the name of the American government and people. The message from the summer school reads as follows:

"America's representatives at the first Hague Conference on July 4 led the nations in honoring Grotius. We urge them to-day to lead in behalf of limiting armaments and of a regular international parliament."

These appeals from three of our largest educational gatherings give utterance to the solid support of the American teacher to the movement for international peace. And this spirit of the teacher finds a responsive chord in the child, as was manifested at the great young people's meeting during the National Peace Congress in New York last April, where four thousand young people voted unanimously to appoint a committee to organize the children of the United States into a League of Peace.

The educational organization for peace, however, is not confined to the public schools; the students in the colleges have taken up the work. As a part of the National Peace Congress, a most enthusiastic meeting, having representatives from several colleges, was held at Columbia University, where a committee of students was appointed to organize peace clubs in the colleges. Bright, indeed, seems the future of this plan, backed as it is by the Intercollegiate Peace Association, formed for the purpose of disseminating peace sentiments in the colleges, and already represented by over thirty universities and colleges in the United States. And now comes the announcement from President Reed, of Dickinson College, that a department of peace and public service will soon be opened as a memorial to William Penn. What finer tribute to the man who, in 1693, published that remarkable essay on the permanent peace of Europe!

The educational campaign for international peace has begun, and every teacher in the world is responsible for its progress.

Eileen Power

From "The Teaching of History and World Peace" (1921)

The teacher of history who is also a believer in what (for want of a better word) we call internationalism, must often have asked himself in despondency why it is that the teaching of history in the past has so often worked against peace and international good feeling. For certainly the devil can quote history to his purpose and Clio has too often been a *vivandière* in the army of politicians and militarists, instead of a grave and just muse, whose equal gaze surveys the world and whose hands weigh men's deeds in a balance. The historian is driven to demand of himself whether history is not indeed an unmitigated curse to humanity, keeping alive the memory of old enmities better dead, teaching that because a thing has been therefore it always shall be; a sort of malignant old man of the sea, clinging to our shoulders and preventing us from moving to new and better things. [...]

But we cannot destroy history, nor need we, for it is not history which is the enemy of mankind, but a mistaken and imperfect reading of history. Our task is not to reject in despair the most fascinating and most human of studies: it is to bring back truth and proportion into history and to ask ourselves, not vaguely but with precision, how it may be taught so as to widen instead of to narrow sympathies. The purpose of history teaching, as indeed of all teaching, is the disinterested study of truth. But the pursuit of truth in school teaching is a question of method rather than of subject matter. Besides this general search for truth what particular lesson has history to offer us? Surely the teacher, looking round upon a troubled world, is driven to see more and more clearly that the great aim of history teaching must be to show mankind its common heritage the past and its common hopes for the future.

Democracy sorely needs this lesson. Children to-day are born into a world in which two problems must be solved or the people perish. One is the problem of labour; the other is the problem of international relations. The internal and external peace of every country depends on a solution being found. How can a solution, other than international or class war, be found? only by understanding these problems in their origin and development, and by bringing to them a certain spirit, which will found upon understanding the knowledge of how to live in a community, that old knowledge which man began to seek even in the prehistoric cave.

The study of history, then, must explain his environment to the young citizen of the world; and at the same time must leave him with a sense of community which is confined neither to his own class nor to his own nation. It is with a regard for these ends that the teacher must select his subject-matter. But history as hitherto taught in the majority of schools has been ill-adapted to either purpose. It has dwelt almost exclusively upon the abnormal, the kings, the wars, the high politics, and it has dwelt almost exclusively upon the national; it is a sobering thought that to the majority of the children of Europe the people of other nations have appeared as 'the enemy' or 'the allies', in the long series of struggles which form so great a part of political history. Yet infinitely more time has been spent by infinitely more people in the pursuit of the normal, and the likenesses between different nations engaged in the pursuit of the normal are infinitely greater than their differences. If a child is to leave school with some understanding of the why and the wherefore of these matters, with which as a citizen he will be intimately concerned, we must teach him more social history and we must teach him more world history. No child ought to leave school without knowing something of the work of ordinary people and the history of every-day things in England; it is just as important that he should understand (for instance) the origin and development of the trade union movement as that he should understand the causes of the war of the Spanish Succession. And no child ought to leave school without knowing something of the history of the world: it is just as important that he should understand the place of his country within the larger whole of mankind, swept by great movements common at least to Europe, as that he should understand the place of Whigs and Tories in the politics of his country.

[...]

Consider the usual treatment of the seventeenth century. There is probably not one of them which does not mention that in 1649 King Charles I lost his head. There is probably not one of them which mentions that in 1645 Sir Richard Weston introduced the turnip into England. Yet the turnip has had more effect upon the history of England, political and economic, than King Charles's head, as we should understand if so many of our history books had not been written by Mr. Dick. The turnip, by providing a new winter crop, gave the country at once more bread and more meat, since the farmer who introduced it no longer had to leave a third of his land fallow every year, nor to kill off a large proportion of his cattle every autumn, because the hay crop and the scanty pasture were not sufficient to support them. The turnip gave an extra stimulus to the enclosure movement, which was an economic benefit, although the method by which it was carried out made it too often a social disaster. The turnip made possible that immensely increased production of food, which at the close of the eighteenth century enabled England to feed a population increasing by leaps and bounds, owing to the Industrial Revolution, at the very moment when the Napoleonic war was narrowing the source of supply by shutting out foreign markets. The turnip it was which enabled her to hold out during the struggle and from her agricultural and industrial wealth to finance her allies. If the armies of Russia marched against Napoleon under the leadership of General January and General February, the armies of England were headed by General Turnip. The battle of Waterloo was won upon the turnip fields of Townsend. Yet where in our history textbooks is the meed due to this distinguished warrior?

[...]

The teacher is not absolved from the necessity of teaching civil wars and Dutch wars and Thirty Years wars; if he left them out he would still be a yellow journalist. But he must set them side by side with turnips and the development of civilization; he must show that war means acquisitions and settlements – but also unspeakable miseries. And he must try to leave in his pupils' minds some sense of the proportions borne by these things to each other. For in this proportion lies truth.

It is perhaps possible for the teacher to do even more. If the League of Nations is ever to be a success it must be driven by an educated public opinion. An educated public opinion will recognize that in spite of national antagonisms and divergent interests mankind as a whole is what the League of Nations presupposes it to be: a community with common aims and a common history. 'There can be no common peace and prosperity', says Mr. H. G. Wells in the introduction to his gallant *Outline of History*, 'without common historical ideas.' It is unnecessary to labour the point that consciousness of a common history is one of the most potent of unifying agents. There is not a nationalist movement which has not buttressed itself by an appeal to national history, and of late years class solidarity has been promoted in precisely the same way, as every one is aware who has studied the influence of the Marxian interpretation of history upon the labour movement. Both national solidarity and class solidarity are good things, in so far as they promote cohesion, but they are good only up to a point; when they operate so as to prevent intercourse and understanding between nation and nation and between class and class they are bad. The only way to cure the evils which have arisen out of purely national history (and to a less extent out of purely class solidarity) is to promote a strong sense of the solidarity of mankind as such; and how can this be better begun than by the teaching of a common history, the heritage alike of all races and of all classes? Hitherto children have left school with some idea of the history of their nation. If the League of Nations is ever to be real they must leave it with some idea of the history of that other community to which they belong, mankind.

There are many ways in which this sense of mankind as a community may be fostered.

1. It may be done by the teaching of world history and more particularly of European history. A course of world history should at some time or other, find a place in the curriculum of every child. The longer school life of the secondary school pupil has always made such a course possible in the secondary schools and in some schools it already has a place. With the extension of school life secured by the Education Act of 1018, no child need leave without an outline knowledge of world history.

In dealing with any course as wide as world history, or even of European history, the most which the teacher can do is to bring out the great movements and the really important events. [...] [T]he child who has given some years to the study of world or of European history, will have, not a detailed knowledge of certain periods or countries (which is a matter for the specialist), but, what is better, some understanding of the value and significance of the march of civilization.

2. A sense of the solidarity of mankind is also stimulated by an insistence throughout upon social history, whether it be English or world history that is being taught. Social history necessarily lays more stress than does political history upon the likenesses of nations, upon their interdependence, upon the debts which the civilization of each owes to that of the others. The fundamental problem is, after all, the same for all men; it is to conquer nature. [...]

3. The same impression may be drawn from the study of English history, if the teacher treat England not as an isolated planet, moving through space and at intervals colliding disastrously with other planets; nor as the sun, round which the stars move; but as part of a whole in which other nations are also parts. The framework of European history ought to be insisted upon throughout the syllabus and whenever the events dealt with are part of general movements, affecting the rest of Europe, this should be made clear. [...] Everywhere his aim should be to show how England has been part and parcel of a common civilization. It is more important that a child should understand something of the

great mediaeval ideal of a world church and a world empire than that he should know the puzzling details of the quarrel between Anselm and Becket and the English kings, which is intelligible only as the backwash of a larger struggle. Indeed, throughout the Middle Ages all the most important forces in English life were European forces, which lose half their real meaning if presented in isolation.

4. The brevity of the period of time covered by history, as compared with the vast aeons of prehistory, in itself helps to emphasize the oneness of the community of mankind. After all nations are so much younger than man. [...]

5. There remains to consider one other method, which may find place as an adjunct to the history lesson, though not in the history lesson itself. This is the method of direct teaching in internationalism. We have, for example, our Empire Day. Why not also our Humanity Day, celebrating not merely the great soldiers and sailors, who have been the glory of our nation, but all the great men who have conquered nature or disease, created beauty, or won knowledge for the service of mankind? [...] Every boy and girl knows something of Julius Caesar, the Black Prince, Robert Bruce, Cardinal Wolsey, the Duke of Marlborough, and William Pitt, but who knows anything about Erasmus, Galileo, Grotius, Pasteur, Elizabeth Fry, Froebel, or Tolstoy? Every one can reel off a list of the wives of Henry VIII, but who can give a list of the disciples of St. Francis of Assisi? It is the heroes of peace, both English and foreign, who must be celebrated on Humanity Day; but they must be celebrated in a humane spirit, in the spirit which sets on Miss Cavell's statue 'For King and Country', when she (wiser and more heroic) said 'I see that patriotism is not enough.'

Again, many schools have already introduced into their curriculum some simple instruction in the duties of citizenship. It would not be difficult to widen their conception of citizenship and to teach them the links which bind all civilized men together. In continuation schools and in the upper classes of secondary schools a more reasoned study would be possible, approximating to the adult study circle or tutorial class. Already in some of these schools a weekly class is held for the discussion of current events, and much can be done in this way to form a life-long habit of taking an interest in international relations.[38]

---

[38] A good little book as a basis for such a class is Miss Melian Stawell's *Patriotism and the Fellowship of Nations* (Dent). For an interesting experiment in correlating history and politics see Gollancz and Somervell, *Political Education at a Public School* (Collins).

[...] We cannot doubt that such an understanding will do something to create in the child a feeling of community with his fellow men of all nationalities and a sense that a war, such as that from which we have emerged, is as truly a civil war as were the wars of king and parliament in the seventeenth century. The schools are the engine rooms in which power is created to drive the machinery of the League of Nations, which without it must stand motionless and rust away.

Virginia Gildersleeve

From "The Creation of the International Mind" (c. 1931/1932)

By the international mind I mean the mind which accepts as normal international cooperation rather than competition, friendly understanding rather than hostile suspicion. What I mean by the creation of the international mind has been called recently also "moral disarmament."

In the lifetime of many of us we have been able to see this new international mind born and grow. When I recall the attitude of mind of Barnard College students at the time of the Spanish–American War and compare it with that of students today, I can appreciate the enormous advance we have made. This is only typical of what has been going on among all thinking people.

In order to avoid the annihilation of civilization which would result from another world war, we must as quickly as possible build up the two things necessary to preserve peace and secure cooperation between nations. The first is political machinery, such as the World Court, the League and the Kellogg Pact. The second is public opinion – that is, the international mind among peoples of the world, so that they will support this political machinery. My own field of international work has been the creation of the international mind through educational institutions and organizations.

The central agency for all the work of this sort is the Committee on Intellectual Cooperation of the League of Nations, through which the multitudes of organizations busily engaged throughout the world in developing the international mind should connect with the League. Our American National Committee on Intellectual Cooperation, a subsidiary of the International Committee at Geneva, is just being reorganized under the chairmanship of Professor James T. Shotwell, who has succeeded Professor Robert Millikan. It can serve as a valuable clearing-house for all our American international work, especially now that it has included in its field the economic, social and political sciences. Its position is, however, a rather embarrassing one, because of the fact that America is not a member of the League of Nations, and our work therefore has not the same authoritative support from the government enjoyed by the National Committees in other nations.

It is enormously important to create the international mind in the pupils of our schools, as well as in the students in our normal schools, colleges and universities. To achieve results in the schools, we must influence the choice of textbooks and the minds of the teachers. Textbooks are vitally important. They should be written in the proper spirit of truth-seeking and openmindedness and not with prejudice and narrow nationalism. The minds of millions of Americans have probably been prejudiced against England by the stories of the "redcoats" in our textbooks of our Revolutionary history.

How are we going to see that our textbooks of history are properly international in their tone? The League Committee on Intellectual Cooperation has devised machinery by which one National Committee may appeal to another to have its textbooks corrected, but obviously any interference by any outside agency, such as the League, in American textbooks for American schools would cause tremendous trouble and bad feeling in this country. Our influence must come from within, as it is coming. The American Association of University Women has been working along these lines, and so have other groups. Most important of all, probably, is a special committee of the American Historical Association, which is about to report on the text book question.

So far as possible all our teachers must have knowledge of foreign nations and international affairs and personal contacts with other countries. Fellowships for foreign study are immensely important. International conferences give valuable experience. Travel with properly arranged contacts is very helpful, and in this connection such international centres for scholars as Crosby Hall in London and Reid Hall in Paris are peculiarly precious aids. Summer schools abroad, particularly the one conducted by the women's colleges of Oxford for American high school teachers and college graduates, contain interesting possibilities.

All these things, however, must be conducted with the utmost tact and intelligence, because contacts may produce not friendliness but friction.

In trying to create the international mind, we encounter many obstacles, mostly psychological. Some of them arise from ignorance of facts and misconceptions. Many are deep-rooted ancient instincts, such as contempt for people different from ourselves, suspicion of aliens, and most of all, fear.

Our difficulties are sometimes caused by the super-patriots, who have such a mistaken idea of patriotism that they think it conflicts with internationalism. We also have internationalists of the wrong sort, who despise patriotism. Real international understanding is fundamentally difficult because of differing racial psychology. Various peoples have different underlying ideas and traditions and sense of values. We cannot change these, but must try to understand them. As an example of the difficulty of securing the real international mind, take the present question of international debts. It is hard to even find the facts, which are differently stated on both sides of the Atlantic. Even after the facts can be agreed on by both sides, they appear different from the opposite shores of the Atlantic Ocean, partly because of a different emphasis. Both sides are largely right, and each must try to understand the other's point of view.

More difficult than an agreement on facts is the guiding of the very intense feelings on both sides. These include suspicion of the alien, sensitiveness to anything affecting one's own pocket, and, on our side, that American inferiority complex which makes us think that the foreigners are far cleverer than we are and are going to "pull the wool over our eyes."

The creation of the international mind is a very long task. As I see it, civilization is now involved in a great race between this international education on one side and the development of instruments of destruction on the other. If the "next war" is to mean annihilation, because of the perfection of these instruments of destruction, can we educate the peoples quickly enough to save them from this appalling catastrophe?

Mr Wells in his book, "Mr. Britling Sees It Through", wrote at the time of the Great War, "Is it conceivable that this mad monster of mankind can ever be caught and held in the thin-spun webs of thought?" This is what we are trying to do in all our efforts for the creation of the international mind. We are weaving webs of thought, – of understanding, of friendliness, of cooperation, that will save mankind from annihilation by war and enable the nations to work together for a better world. The invisible filaments of the mind and of the spirit – weaving them is harder than manufacturing bombs or poison gas. Shall we be too slow in the race?

Merze Tate

From *The Disarmament Illusion* (1942)

Public opinion is a new compelling political force which has come into the world since the Middle Ages. In fact, it is a development of the last century; before the French Revolution nothing of the kind was known or dreamed of in Europe. This new force in political life may be divided into two types. One is the popular belief in the fitness or rightness of something, a belief that certain lines of conduct should be followed or a certain opinion held by good citizens or right-thinking persons. This is what Mr. Balfour calls "climate." Such a belief does not impose any duty on anybody beyond outward conformity to the accepted standard. But public opinion in the true sense is a consensus among large bodies of persons which acts as a political force, imposing on those in authority certain enactments or certain lines of policy.[39]

This study is concerned with public opinion in the second meaning, and its influence, if any, upon the movement for a limitation of armaments.

Although it cannot be measured with a tape, public opinion in a modern constitutional state, we are all agreed, should prevail. But creating and formulating public opinion is the great problem. In the nineteenth century there were two accepted methods of expressing public opinion: by elections and by the use of the press. But the elections were held only at intervals, and they served only as a medium through which this force manifested itself in action. We must, therefore, turn to the press, which as an organ of public opinion not only expresses views and tendencies already in existence but is a factor in further developing and moulding the judgment of the people. According to Lord Bryce, newspapers are influential in three ways: "as narrators, as advocates, and as weather cocks. They report events, they advance agreements, they

---

[39] E. L. Godkin, "The Growth and Expression of Public Opinion," *The Atlantic Monthly*, LXXXI (January, 1898), 2.

indicate by their attitude what those who conduct them and are interested in their circulation take to be the prevailing opinion of their readers."[40] He continues:

It is chiefly in its third capacity, as an index and mirror of public opinion, that the press is looked to. This is the function it chiefly aims at discharging; and public men feel that in showing deference to it they are propitiating, and inviting the commands of public opinion itself.[41]

Although newspapers reflect and mould a general state of mind, the public mind must be ripe for moulding and directing. The moulding process may have been due to newspaper agitation over a period of time, but even then the public mind must have been receptive.[42] In order to build a strong structure of public opinion there must be unanimity of thought in the newspapers, and there is no such unanimity except in the state controlled and censored press. In the last half of the nineteenth century the press did not play an important part in the formation of a strong current of public opinion favoring disarmament. If all the newspapers and magazines, or a great majority of them, had said the same thing about the heavy armaments of the period or if they had all come out in favor of a limitation of armaments they would have wielded a powerful influence; but this they did not do.

On the subject of armaments, both the liberal and conservative journals of Great Britain showed a tendency to extreme caution. An occasional paper like the *Daily News* might call attention to the need for reducing standing armies. Another might offer advice. The *Manchester Times*, for example, called attention in 1848 to the fact that the London daily press was, on the whole, unfavorable to peace proceedings. It advised the friends of peace to concentrate on enlightening opinion at home, and to undertake the conversion of the *Times* and its satellites.[43] English papers and periodicals of the mid-century Christina Phelps divides according to their attitude to the peace movement into three classes: the eulogistic, the neutral, the hostile. In a case apart were the London *Times* and *Punch*, the former antagonistic, the latter friendly to the cause. The *Times*, most influential of the daily papers, was actively opposed to the early peace movement and its editorials alternately ridiculed and denounced the whole movement.[44] The *Year-Book* regularly

[40] James Bryce, *The American Commonwealth*, II (Macmillan, New York, 1911), 275 and 277.

[41] *Loc. cit.*   [42] R. D. Blumenfeld, *The Press in My Times*, 44–45.

[43] Christina Phelps, *The Anglo-American Movement in the Mid-Nineteenth Century* (New York, 1930), 184.

[44] *Ibid.*, 181.

mentioned the Peace Congresses; the *Annual Register* noticed briefly the London Convention of 1843 and made flippant comments on the Frankfort Convention of 1850.

The *Daily News* supported the peace movement in 1848, then gradually lost interest in it, ceasing in 1851 even to report the peace congresses. Twenty-two papers gave unqualified, though spasmodic support to the movement. Ten of these were provincial papers including the *Leeds' Mercury* and the *Manchester Examiner*. The sympathetic London papers were either liberal, free trade or religious, and they included the *Morning Advertiser* which had the second largest circulation in the kingdom.[45] Of the opponents of the peace movement, *Blackwood's Edinburgh Magazine* was the most consistently denunciatory, and the *Morning Chronicle* was the most intelligently hostile. They argued that the friends of peace were impracticable and unpatriotic, that arbitration was no guarantee against the use of force, and that disarmament would never be practicable so long as human nature remained unchanged.[46]

A survey of the articles on disarmament published in the newspapers and periodicals of the decade 1888–98 shows that the press was not moulding public opinion on the subject; nor was it, on the other hand, being noticeably influenced. True, more was published on the topic than at any other previous time in history; but the number of articles compared with those on wars, battles, armies, navies and soldiers was very small. Disarmament items in the *Times*, the *Daily News*, the *Daily Telegraph*, *Le Temps*, *Le Figaro*, the *New York Times*, and the *New York Herald* were tucked away in inconspicuous columns and probably read by only a few. Many British magazines which might have exerted a great influence upon public opinion completely ignored the existence of the problem. The *Athenaeum*, the *Edinburgh Review*, the *Fortnightly Review*, the *Quarterly Review* and the *Humanitarian* remained silent on the question of disarmament. In the August number of the *Nineteenth Century*, Henry Geffcken referred to the question briefly by stating that all attempts to limit armaments were futile; disarmament comes only when it imposes itself by exhaustion. The *Contemporary Review* for May and June, 1894, published articles on the limitation of armaments as did the *Spectator* and the *Standard* for March and April of the same year. But only the *Review of Reviews*, edited by W. T. Stead, took a definite stand on questions of peace and disarmament.

The American periodicals played no better part. The *International Journal of Ethics*, devoted to the advancement of ethical knowledge and

[45] *Ibid.*, 180.   [46] *Ibid.*, 181.

practice, did not treat the problem until after the Tsar's Rescript appeared. The *Atlantic Monthly, Harper's Monthly, Scribner's Magazine,* the *Century Magazine,* the *American Review of Reviews, Littell's Living Age* and the *Living Age* devoted ample space to the treatment of "The Benefits of War," "The Study of War," "Warlike Europe," "The Evolution of the Naval Officer," "The French Navy," "The Standing Army of Great Britain," "The Russian Army," "Austro-Hungarian Army," "The French Army," "The Italian Army," "The German Army," "Side Lights on the German Soldier," "The Problem of the Philippines" and "The Economic Basis of Imperialism," yet never once during the decade did these magazines touch the question of disarmament.

M. de Blowitz contributed an article entitled "The Peace of Europe" to *McClure's Magazine* for June, 1894, but that same periodical completely ignored the Tsar's Rescript. At the time it was engrossed in the Spanish American War and devoted its space to "The Cost of War," "The Fighting Leaders," "Theodore Roosevelt," "Dewey at Manila," etc.

If we agree with Mr. Walter Lippmann that public opinions, if they are to be sound, must be organized for the press not by the press; and if this organization is the "task of a political science that has won its proper place as a formulator in advance of a real decision, instead of apologist, critic, or reporter after the real decision has been made,"[47] then again, there was no organized opinion favoring disarmament in the decade before 1898. […] If we look elsewhere than in the press for disarmament agitation, we are forced to draw practically the same inference.

A. Lawrence Lowell maintains that the political community as a whole is capable of public opinion only when the great bulk of the citizens is united and agreed upon the ends and aims of government in regard to a particular problem.[48] In the nineteenth century there was not a body of men agreed upon the means whereby the action of governments on the limitation of armaments should be determined. "Public opinion," writes Charles W. Smith, "is composed of individual opinions that have been subjected 'to a process of consolidation and clarification' until they have attained unity of direction. If individual opinions are not similar enough to flow together, there cannot be a public opinion."[49] Individual opinions on disarmament had not arrived at unity. In the national parliaments there were isolated complaints by liberals, pacifists and radicals against armaments, and resolutions were proposed requesting the governments to consider the convoking of an International Congress to deal with the

[47] Walter Lippmann, *Public Opinion* (Macmillan, New York, 1921), 32.
[48] *Popular Government* (Longmans Green, New York, 1914), 9.
[49] Charles W. Smith, *Public Opinion in a Democracy* (Prentice Hall, New York, 1939), 19.

problem; but these were neither supported by the chambers in which they originated nor considered seriously by the governments. There was no concerted, simultaneous approach to the problem in the various parliaments. The Inter-Parliamentary Union, a practical organization which might have organized a unified international effort to bring about a limitation of armaments, carefully avoided taking a definite position on the problem at its conferences. International jurists in their official bodies – the Institute of International Law and the International Law Association – refrained from touching the question of disarmament.

If it is true that "only when a conflict imposes heavy sacrifices on us that an opinion makes itself felt in favor of preserving or cutting loose"; if "we develop opinions when called upon to act, to fight, or to pay";[50] then the laboring class and women should have been the leading agitators for a limitation of armaments. Although the burden of war and armed peace weighs heaviest upon the working classes, who have to support the largest part of the taxes and suffer the most from obligatory military service, labor, as a class did not, in the nineteenth century, take a firm and determined stand on the question of disarmament.[51] Neither did women. It is only natural that women should hate war – which breaks up their homes, robs them of their sons, husbands and support – but this hatred had done little by 1898 to assist in the struggle for a limitation of armaments. In the decade 1888–98 women took a greater interest in peace and Peace Societies than at any time before in history, and they occasionally uttered isolated complaints and warnings against war and heavy armaments; but a great international organization of women, supporting disarmament and opposing war because the members comprehended that it is an evil for the whole human race, did not exist. As early as 1868, Marie Georgg, the Treasurer of the Geneva League of Peace and Liberty, had urged the formation of an international league in "Les Etats-Unis de l'Europe"; but not until 1895 was an International Peace League of Women founded. In November, 1896, *La Ligue Internationale des Femmes pour les Desarmement General* called a Congress of international journalists to meet in Paris to examine the question of disarmament. The members hoped to find a practical method of approach to the problem. But no truly international Peace Congress of Women met in the nineteenth century. It took the cataclysm of a World

---

[50] L. B. Namier, "Public Opinion and Representative Government," in *Skyscrapers and Other Essays* (London, 1931), 37.

[51] Only the Socialist wing of the laboring class directed attention to the problem of armaments.

War to awaken women from their lethargy. At the few women's international meetings of the nineties disarmament was not touched. [...]

Only the national Peace Societies, the Universal Peace Congresses, and the Churches of Great Britain took a definite stand in favor of a limitation of armaments. But the churches, slow to participate in the peace movement, gave only a temporary and half-hearted support to the cause. Their agitation reached its zenith in the years 1894–97 and then declined so that by 1898 they were not actively engaged in promoting a disarmament policy. Consequently, we must conclude that a public opinion favoring a limitation of armaments, being "something always there – always being influenced and influencing – an invisible public meeting of the whole country in perpetual session, with the press a new and indispensable organ of government,"[52] was non-existent in the decade 1888–98.

If we go deeper into the question of public opinion and try to discover what moves large bodies or groups of people or parties to demand that their government take action along a certain line on any matter, we learn that by the latter part of the nineteenth century utilitarianism had become the primary motive.[53] Utilitarianism had fully taken possession of political discussion. A writer or speaker on a political subject had to show that his proposition would make people richer or more comfortable. Historical experience no longer influenced political affairs. Religious and moral authority which, from the Middle Ages down to the eighteenth century had been so powerful, had ceased to exert much influence on the affairs of the world. Any attempt to mould public opinion by its instrumentality was almost certain to prove ineffectual. Therefore, the disarmament resolutions of the Universal Peace Congresses and the National Memorial sponsored by the Churches and Arbitration Alliance were not destined to compel the governments to take action. For, as Dicey writes, "it is difficult to make emotion, however respectable, the basis of sound legislation."[54] This does not imply that Peace Societies and the Church can play no part in a movement for disarmament. Their field lies, however, not in petitioning governments but in educating the public to a sense of its responsibilities. Mr. Elihu Root once said: "The open public declaration of a principle in such a way as to carry evidence that it has the support of a great body of men entitled to respect has a wonderfully compelling effect

---

[52] A. D. Lindsay, *The Essentials of Democracy* (University of Pennsylvania Press, Philadelphia, 1929), 27.

[53] A. V. Dicey, *Lectures on the Relation between Law and Public Opinion in England during the Nineteenth Century* (Macmillan, London, 1914), 450; and E. L. Godkin, "The Growth and Expression of Public Opinion," The Atlantic Monthly, January, 1898, 2.

[54] A. V. Dicey, *loc. cit.*

upon mankind."[55] When the educative process has been worked out and the multitude of men have reached the point of genuine and not perfunctory acceptance of a new standard, they can, through their chosen representatives, bring pressure to bear on the governments which eventually must conform themselves to it.

Mr. Walter Lippmann is convinced that the public is not a fixed body of individuals; it is merely those persons who are interested in an affair and can effect it only by supporting or opposing the actors.[56] The group most actively interested in the problem of limiting armaments always has been the international armament ring, which in the nineteenth century as well as in the twentieth naturally used its influence and great resources to prevent a limitation. If we agree, with Professor E. H. Carr that propaganda is ineffective until it becomes linked with military and economic power – "that power over opinion cannot be dissociated from military and economic power"[57] – then we must recognize the fallacy of a belief in an international opinion on a limitation of armaments; for the military and naval experts, the high governmental officials and those who controlled the factors of production were all opposed to disarmament. In the nineteenth century movement for a limitation of armaments, numbers did not make public opinion; numbers did not give the directive for the particular decisions made; numbers were not consulted on the matter; numbers did not consider what road should be taken until the Tsar's decision was made. For the late nineteenth century disarmament movement at least, it appears that we must accept Lippmann's and Namier's conclusions that the public was a mere phantom, an abstraction,[58] that there was no public opinion with regard to a thing so delicate as the limitation policy to be pursued.[59]

[55] *Addresses on International Subjects* by Elihu Root (Harvard University Press, Cambridge, 1916), 134.
[56] Walter Lippmann, *The Phantom Public* (Macmillan, New York, 1925), 77.
[57] Edward Hallett Carr, *The Twenty Years' Crisis 1919–1939* (Macmillan, London, 1939), 17.
[58] Walter Lippmann, *op. cit.*, 77.   [59] L. B. Namier, *op. cit.*, 37.

Margaret Read

From *Problems of Mass Education* (1947)

When the Colonial Office in January, 1944, published the White Paper on "Mass Education in African Society," it was the first publication in which the experience of different countries was brought to bear on this world-wide problem. Although this report was written with the British Colonies definitely in mind, and in particular the African territories, it was in effect an attempt to consider Mass Education as a world problem in its broadest aspects.

[...]

The more precise situations and conditions dealt with in the report are common to all non-self-governing territories, and indeed to many independent nations who have to carry the burden of illiterate millions and poverty-stricken areas within their boundaries. Common too to all such "backward" areas are the stresses and strains which follow from accelerated social change, the pressure of economic planning and of new political developments.

[...]

Before we go on to discuss the nature of the problems involved in Mass Education in "backward" areas, let us see what prompted the British Government to compile and issue the Mass Education Report during the worst years of the war. It was partly due to a change in colonial policy – a new emphasis on progress towards self-government, in which development and welfare were two of the keynotes, and in which the Colonial Development and Welfare Act played a leading part. But the motives which moved the Advisory Committee on Education in the Colonies to take action resulting in this report were two more definite ones. One was the needs of the men and their families who had been drawn into industrial enterprises such as mines, factories, railways, harbour works, etc. These workers had the right to expect welfare services in housing, health, and feeding arrangements for themselves and their families. But they needed something more. If they were not to be the "plaything of impersonal forces," they needed education. The first step in this was the achievement of literacy. When they could read and write, they could become better technicians and benefit by further training to become skilled workmen. They could also improve their general knowledge and extend their interests through reading books and newspapers. They could, in fact, begin to understand the economic, social and political changes which were going on around them. They had been pitchforked into unfamiliar industrial conditions without preparation of any kind, and they needed to achieve through education the kind of knowledge of the industrial system, and self-discipline in their trade-unions and other societies, which adult education had given to the workers of this country.

The second leading motive was the inherent British belief in adult education in its widest sense as a dominant factor in the political development in a democratic country. Many of the larger African towns had municipal authorities, elected by varying forms of franchise. In the development of these forms of local authority, as well as in the evolution of the more traditional forms of local authority such as chiefs and tribal councils, literacy and general adult education was an essential element in real progress. As the African colonies were going to accelerate their movement towards self-government, it was vitally important that the masses of the people, and not only a literate élite should take a conscious and intelligent part in their own government. This could only be achieved through a rapid widening of educational opportunities, and to make up for lost time this would have to be at the adult level as well as in schools for children. In China it was an awakened national spirit which inspired the desire for mass education. That same sense of national unity and purpose between the literate élite and the mass of the people will have to be developed in Africa, and indeed in all "backward" areas.

We should now return to the UNESCO Preparatory Commission and to the interest shown by members in the field and in the problems of Mass Education. We have seen that it was the incipient menace to world peace which inspired some of the delegates to demand the abolition of illiteracy on a world-wide scale. Inherent in many of their statements was the belief that, while illiterate, poverty-stricken masses of people existed in different parts of the world, the possible exploitation of them by ambitious and unscrupulous leaders would always threaten stability and peace both within and among, the nations.

It was not, however, only the menace to peace which was the keynote of the discussions at this first meeting of UNESCO. Before all the delegates was the ideal of a One World outlook.

[...]

The interest shown by the Preparatory Commission was quickly translated into action. A report was prepared by several people who had worked at Mass Education, embodying the experience of different countries, and analysing the main problems to be dealt with in this field. This report will shortly be published under the title: "Fundamental Education: Common Ground for all Peoples." Now at last, on the international level, the attempts made by many countries to attack this world-wide problem are gathered together, and this strange, bold enterprise begins to take form. The best comment on this seems to be an African proverb: "A river is made great by its little streams." Thanks to the action of UNESCO the little streams of Mass Education, rising in many different countries, have reached the main river of world interest and action.

[...]

There is also considerable evidence to show that adults who have become literate are more ready to listen to new ideas and new ways of living. When they discover that they can master a new and difficult technique like reading, which has hitherto been quite outside their range of skill, they become interested in trying new things and confident that they can succeed. They are certainly more likely to maintain improvements if they can be fed with reading material, which reminds them of the new teaching and suggests still further advance. The Chinese, whose experiences with those of the Russians are most relevant here, are insistent that adult literacy must be given *the first priority* in Mass Education. But adult literacy campaigns must lead to better living – that is reading books and periodicals written for new literates must be about practical problems of daily life. They must bring home the lessons of the agricultural demonstrator about the value of manuring and irrigating or draining fields; they must give the women further hints on child care and household management; they must suggest how to build better homes and how to improve living conditions in them; they must deal with everyday affairs like marketing crops and livestocks, mending bicycles, keeping accounts, putting by money in the Post Office Savings Bank, and so on. This is a possible content for Mass Education in rural areas. It needs modification, of course, where the demand is for understanding new forms of economy and urban social life.

Bitter experience has brought home to us in this country today the essential lesson that raising the standard of living is a costly business and must ultimately be paid for by the people themselves, through increasing their productive capacity and so adding to the national wealth. This lesson is no less true in the undeveloped areas and among the underprivileged peoples, who are dependent on agriculture and are only now emerging from a subsistence economy. Its truth, however, is not so apparent to those whose horizons have been limited to their own farms and villages, and to a traditional and long-established low level of living.

Hence education, at the adult level, must be one of the main levers to increase production. Better health and better food will also help towards more production, but the main drive and the steadiest drive will come from understanding and enlightenment.

There was a time when through geographical isolation, or the protective policy of their governments, millions of people could live in their own traditional manner, with little or no outside contact. That time has gone. For good or for ill, war, air travel, industrialization, trade, missions, scientific studies have penetrated most of this earth's "backward" areas. The modern world, and that means the very modern world, complete with aeroplanes, hydro-electric works, bull-dozers, radio and cinema, has broken into remote places, and the people living in them must now be prepared for a new sort of life. In many cases it is a rude awakening, and the social tensions and psychological shocks are hard to take, as the quotations from the Mass Education Report showed clearly.

Nothing but education in its widest sense can help here. The Russians have proved that in a quarter of a century the most amazing progress can be made among illiterate and impoverished peoples. The alternative to such action on a wide scale is, as the UNESCO delegates pointed out in their speeches at the Preparatory Commission, the exploitation of the masses by unscrupulous individuals and groups, and ultimately a "disequilibrium incompatible with peace."

Among individuals who have been in close touch with "backward" peoples there is every range of opinion about their potential rate of progress, from the Russians, who point to their dramatic achievements, to the die-hards of every nation, who think that all progress is a matter of centuries of evolution. The only rational attitude is a sturdy refusal to accept defeatism and a determination to get on with the job. This attitude is at the core of Mass Education. Granted that belief, and it is in the nature of a faith, we have to take stock of this problem of bringing remote areas and their people into the modern world. We must do more, too, than just ease the shock by providing what education can offer. We must see to it that education makes it possible for these people to preserve what is best in their heritage among the social values and ideas and artistic achievements, which are theirs and no one else's. If the best in these cultures is preserved, the world will be the richer, and modern contacts, however, inevitable, will not have made these people lose all their links with their past.

If adult literacy and better living campaigns are going to succeed they must step off on the right foot. And it is very easy to step off on the wrong one. We cannot, for instance, go about labelling people as "ignorant." It is quite all right for the people of the United Nations to agree in the Constitution of UNESCO that "ignorance of each other's ways and lives has been a common cause of suspicion and mistrust."

[...]

The second step is to act on the assumption that he *wants* to learn these new skills – writing and reading, arithmetic, food values, use of manures, etc. He may have been persuaded to come for a lesson, or may have volunteered to come and learn. The important thing is that here he is, ready to be taught. He must be regarded, therefore, as an active co-operator in this learning business, and encouraged to find out for himself how he can learn best.

The third step is a leap in the dark. We have to impress on a man or woman that he or she can learn quickly. Time matters to an adult. He doesn't want to drone away happy idle hours in a classroom, chanting alphabets or multiplication tables. He wants to read now, this evening, this week; and to write a letter next week to his son who is away working; and next month to read the notices at the post offices; and the month after to read the local newspaper. That is why "targets" matter so much in adult education, and why the teacher should be just as eager as the learner to pull it off in a given time.

The fourth step is to have a wide and suitable range of reading material to make the effort worth persisting in. Most of this early reading material will be on practical everyday affairs, *written specially for adults*. But there will also be people who would like to read about politics and history and travel, as well as about bees and bicycles and housebuilding. So the wealth of the books ahead must always draw the learner on, and while some will stop at reading for information, others will go on and read eventually for pleasure as well as profit. Already in the British African territories there is a large output of books both in African languages and in English. African Literature Committees and Bureaux exist in many territories to stimulate the production of literature in the vernaculars, and African writers of promise have been given scholarships for special training on problems of orthography and language standardization at the School of Oriental and African Studies in London.

The fifth step is to make the most extensive and intelligent use of the modern techniques of films and radio. The drawback about using these techniques in remote areas is that they need mechanical appliances, whereas books and newspapers need none. But wherever a broadcasting system has been set up, and wherever mobile cinema vans have been in operation, the interest and imagination of remote villagers have been awakened, and a stimulus given to further study. [...]

Who is going to do all this Mass Education, and who is going to pay for it? So far there has been every kind of experiment among the nations concerned: State control and sponsoring, local initiative and control, and volunteer efforts. Two things seem clear from what has been done already. The first is that no state can afford, for the sake of its own reputation, to stand aside deliberately from this modern phase of adult education. Hence in independent countries with large illiterate populations, you find the government encouraging in one way or another adult literacy campaigns. And in most British colonial territories the colonial governments are prepared to assist campaigns, and in many cases are appointing Mass Education Officers. But though State aid is essential, the main drive must come from the peoples themselves. The bulk of the work done so far has been achieved by a combination of voluntary effort and State aid, and it is clear that most of the drive has come from the people's own organization and enthusiastic support. Where this popular support is lacking, the response is disappointing. As in many popular movements, adult education seems to prosper best under local control. A local committee or education authority is aware of difficulties and opportunities which no central body can easily understand. As more adults become literate, the handling of local education whether for adults or children is one of the first and best ways in which they can take a direct part in local government on democratic lines.

To say that the State must take part, that local initiative and local organization is most successful, and that voluntary effort is essential, is no complete answer to the question where to find workers and money. But they point the way. Yet another pointer comes from the English tradition of associating adult education with centres of higher learning and especially with the universities. True, in this country, adult education has today a very different content and aim from literacy campaigns in "backward" areas. Nevertheless, there is a strong case in those areas for associating centres of higher education and teacher training colleges with this desperately urgent work, since in such centres problems can be studied, workers trained and voluntary effort encouraged. [...]

There are at least two tasks which UNESCO can undertake in its headquarters in Paris. One is to continue to collect information on all aspects of Fundamental Education (as we must call it if we go to Paris; Mass Education goes down better as a name in London). The report "Fundamental Education" was a beginning, and already steps have been taken to collect further information. It is no easy job. If adult literacy work were carried on solely by governments, it would be easy. A questionnaire could be issued and a card index made of the answers. But how are we going to find out about the factory workers in West

China who are going to night classes, and the church congregations in Africa who are teaching reading to each other, and the work done during their vacations by boys from schools, and the thousands of efforts made by one individual to teach another? We can't, of course, but a beginning must be made of collecting information about experiments, and, as it comes in, it will be clear how to classify it, so that it can be put together and sent out to people who want ideas for their own experiments. So UNESCO will pool all this experience and send it out again – a formidable but a highly necessary job.

Then someone has got to sit down and worry out the statistical aspects of this job. We talk airily about illiterate millions, but can get no nearer accuracy until someone has devised literacy tests and how to apply them; and until someone else has inspired the taking of censuses on which literacy estimates can be based. Meantime, the people who don't like cooked statistics will show miserable figures about literacy, and less particular may show startling results. The sensible person remains sceptical about figures and what is based on them, merely acknowledging the size of the job to be done.

Dotted about the world are a few individuals who really know something about Mass Education. Some of these know a lot and might be called. UNESCO will bring them together in regional groups, to discuss the problems common to the countries in that region, and so to help devise methods of assisting in local campaigns. UNESCO is planning, too, to use these "experts" in other areas than the one to which they belong, partly to give advice in existing campaigns and partly to assist in launching new ones. In this way UNESCO will make use, not only of its own secretariat, but of people with first-hand knowledge which might be useful to others.

Perhaps the most useful job UNESCO can do, besides all these others, is to keep us all on our toes. Bound up with us in this country are 63 million people overseas in the colonies for whom Mass Education is a desperate and urgent need. We in the United Kingdom shall have to answer to UNESCO about Mass Education in those backward areas.

After World War I there was a committee of the League of Nations called the Committee on Intellectual Co-operation. Its members were very learned people, and they discussed whether illiterate people should learn to read and write. UNESCO is a child of the new age – what Henry Wallace called the "Age of the Common Man." Characteristically it has made the illiterate masses its first and chief job. Let us see that it gets a chance to do its job well and quickly, and let us see that we in Britain do our job in the colonies – also well and quickly.

Dorothy Fosdick

From *Common Sense and World Affairs* (1955)

Wanting to contribute to a sensible foreign policy, many of us are at a loss what to do about it. With big decisions made in Washington, D. C., what can a mere individual in Oshkosh achieve? Public opinion, we are continually told, plays a vital role in foreign policy. No people, it is said, gets any better foreign policy than it deserves. But what can any one person usefully accomplish?

What each American does, taken together with what others do, forms the context of will and opinion in which official American policy is made and shapes the image of America. This country will rise to the demands upon it only if its citizens rise to the demands that come to them individually. It is congenial to all the requirements of our time that each one of us does the little good he or she can, and lets it add up: "The kingdom of heaven is like unto leaven, which a woman took, and hid in three measures of meal, till the whole was leavened."

Each of us can refuse to be resigned to the worst. Granted the dangers are serious, to wash our hands of them is no help. Yet many young people today are doing just that. Traditionally American youth have been a critical and discontented lot, confident that they could do better than their forebears. In my father's college days optimism was apparently unmitigated. Assured by Tennyson that the battle flags would be furled

> In the Parliament of man,
> the Federation of the world,

his generation was confident that each succeeding one would move forward toward that earthly paradise. Even in my college generation, which knew the disillusionments of world war and depression, we were full of hope, believing that the troubles of the world were due chiefly to the mismanagement of problems, and that once we got our hands on them things would go better. My generation, too, had its illusions, but we could scarcely wait to get into the fray and take over the reins.

[...]

Many of us would be glad to have a sensible foreign policy if only we could accomplish this without altering our preference for "going it alone," without modifying our suspicions of Europe and its age-old troubles, and without relinquishing the idea of an American purity which is corrupted in contact with outsiders. We would approve of wise programs if we could get them without paying any additional taxes, without broadening our concept of the national interest, and without modifying our racial prejudices. We are in favor of common sense, when that requires no change in us.

Many of us have brought our *minds* up to date on these matters, only to fail to get our *feelings* under control. We can see the logic in resisting Communist encroachment on the free world. Our heads can accept the necessity both of allies and of cooperative agencies. But our emotions rebel. We get all upset at the risks involved, the losses of blood and treasure, the frustration, the inevitable compromises, and the defeats. With our feelings running riot, our one wish is for a respite from it all. We may *know* we have to stay up and about, but we *feel* like getting into bed and pulling the covers over our heads. Yearning for the good old times is wasted effort. History is moving toward the future, and there are no good old times to go back to. The advice of Jean Jaures is today apropos: "We should take from the past its fires and not its ashes."

Individual citizens can put themselves sympathetically into the situation of the responsible government official. When people outside the government argue that the President and Secretary of State made a bad decision, and then suggest what should have been done, they usually do not realize that the proposal they favor had occurred to officials but had been rejected. A basic difference between officials making policy and citizens stating their preferences is that official decisions commit the prestige, material resources, and manpower of America to a course of action, while the opinions of an individual citizen set off no such momentous train of events. Officials cannot write their private preferences into state papers.

If each of us, when favoring a certain policy, asked ourselves why government officials and experts might reject it, then public debate on foreign policy could be more fruitful. By thinking ourselves into the situation of the responsible government official, we are likely to come up with more responsible judgments ourselves. This does not mean, of course, that we will concur in the wisdom of all official decisions!

We can refrain from substituting vituperation for debate, denunciation for evidence. Important as it is to identify and examine both past and current mistakes we should be able to do this without wholesale condemnation of either the patriotism or the integrity of the officials concerned.

Thucydides described the deep trouble in Athens after its long ordeal of war: "Society became divided into camps in which no man trusted his fellow." Too many of us have reached the stage where we can no longer rationally communicate with one another. Instead of talking about the facts, sharing our different points of view, and reasoning together, we are apt to consume our energy in calling each other names, making charges, and striking out at someone. Many of us are like the senator in the cartoon saying: "This speech you whipped out for me, Sneedby, deals with facts! Surely we're not that devoid of issues!"

For the conduct of foreign policy, we have to rely on the President and his advisers, working with the advice and consent of the Senate. But the public has its part to play also – above all, to discuss and debate policies on their merits. Official assumptions and estimates are never above reproach and so beyond criticism. Officials may propose unwise policies, act imprudently, or fail to act when they should act. It is appropriate and necessary for citizens to ask questions, raise doubts, and, where they believe it is needed, urge reappraisal, thereby encouraging officials to follow the truth of matters. No one of us can perform this function, however, if instead of following the truth ourselves, we are engaged in recrimination.

Each of us can grow in *understanding*. Not simply our officials, but any of us may be in error about affairs of state. Firm believers in democracy as we are, we have enough experience to know that the voice of the people is not necessarily the voice of God. The wisdom of a policy bears no direct relation to the number of people favoring it. The great majority of Americans wanted to "bring the boys home" after World War II, but as things turned out this move was unwise. Shortly we were rushing the boys back to Europe to bulwark the common defense. While many Americans want to withdraw from the United Nations should the Communist Chinese government be seated over our protests, it does not follow that such a move would be sensible. To leave the United Nations without the rallying point of American leadership might well change that organization from being sometimes a nuisance into being continually a menace – a United Nations in which Peking had the veto and Washington not even a voice. Should a *majority* of Americans favor cutting our commitments abroad and attempting to retire to a fortress in this hemisphere, such a policy would not thereby be sound. Even if 95% of the people favor a given line, still it may not be the best available one.

Some of us are tempted to argue that without access to "classified information" we cannot be expected to reach adequate decisions – that it is all right to plead for understanding, but that since the layman lacks sufficient facts wise judgments are precluded. If each of us read the *New York Times* regularly we would have enough information to go on. Persons who have once worked with classified materials, and then leave the government, almost invariably testify that they have no trouble keeping abreast of the facts. Information is less the problem than the inherently difficult dilemmas involved in so many foreign policy decisions, together with a human reluctance to think hard and to overcome biases and prejudices. One recalls the man who said: "Don't confuse me with the facts. My mind already is made up."

We can do the little good close at hand. What each of us accomplishes in just ordinary situations may have important repercussions on foreign policy. The restaurant operator in South Carolina who threw a dark-skinned customer and his family out of his restaurant one night did not realize how disastrous the results would be. He did not anticipate that by humiliating this man and his children, he was preparing his conversion to communism. Returning to his South American homeland that man is now a leader of the Communist party, and he attributes his new faith to the night in South Carolina.

The American professor who befriended a lonely and disillusioned Japanese student visiting in this country did not foresee what was in store. He had no idea that out of that friendship would grow an abiding faith in the best of this country, so that when that Japanese student became president of a great Japanese university he would devote himself to cultivating the common interests of Japan and America.

The full consequences of modest activities may be long delayed. West German Chancellor Konrad Adenauer has pointed out that the men of the Middle Ages who built Germany's famed free cities did not anticipate what important work they were doing. They simply did the job at hand. Yet now it is their traditions of liberal self-government which are the model for the free German Republic – and their example has outlasted kaisers and dictators.

What any one of us does in his own small corner of the world, joined with the accomplishments of others, can have unexpected, weighty effects. If we wait until we can have some perceptible, decisive influence on national policy in Washington, D.C., innumerable, worthwhile opportunities right near at home will slip by us.

While doing good works ourselves, we can also uphold our statesmen who have to do the less pleasing things required in the national interest.

There is no limit to the CARE packages we can personally send abroad, except our private inclinations and the limits of our own resources. Statesmen, however, must make the wisest use of public assets in the light of all the demands upon the nation, and they have responsibilities not only to this generation but to coming generations.

We personally can develop friendships with nationals of other countries, opening our hearts and our homes. But our officials still must see that the hydrogen bomb goes forward and that money is appropriated for the development of new weapons, until a satisfactory system of international control and reduction of armaments is implemented.

[...]

Because each of us individually can do some good, it does not follow that we can ask our statesmen in their official capacity always to do the same sort of good. It is up to us to pay the price of sustaining them in their stewardship of our national interests. We can exercise our political influence, by voice and vote, against antidemocratic forces from any quarter. Abraham Lincoln warned in a speech entitled "The Perpetuation of Our Political Institutions" in 1837:

> Is it unreasonable, then, to expect that some man possessed of the loftiest genius, coupled with ambition sufficient to push it to its utmost stretch, will at some time spring up amongst us? And when such a one does, it will require the people to be united with each other, attached to the government and laws, and generally intelligent, to successfully frustrate his designs.

Just as our officials keep an eye on minority parties and nascent groups in other nations, our friends and allies are reading the signs here, and calculating the significance of political trends. They question today whether our leadership at home will successfully resist challenges to constitutional restraints and other depredations of demagogues. What our allies are hoping from us in this respect is what we should be demanding of ourselves.

If Western Civilization is to continue, and with it our American democracy, we have to demonstrate that we understand what our tradition is all about. We can content ourselves with nothing less than resolute leadership in safeguarding civil and religious liberties, in coping effectively and by due process of law with the problem of Communist infiltration and internal security, in maintaining political traditions of fair play, and in guarding a civil and foreign service from both the "spoils system" and the "vigilante." If there ever was a time to use our individual voice and vote selectively and wisely, this is it.

Amy Ashwood Garvey

From "The Birth of the Universal Negro Improvement Association" (*c.* 1960s)

When the glowing recital ended, I remained silent for a while. I wanted to be reassured that my feet were still on terra firma – solidly placed on the earth. I had heard so much in a short time that it had acted like heady wine. Such a deluge of dreams was overwhelming. I was disturbed, too, because Marcus was assuming that I, just as much as himself, was prepared to shoulder the herculean responsibilities of working for the uplifting of our race with all the implications of that formidable challenge.

As I sat in reverie, I saw the stern face of my mother uttering words of solemn maternal warnings. My mother was imbued with a strong sense of realism; the responsibilities of a family left her little time for flights of fancy, even had she been temperamentally so inclined. As for Marcus and his vision, they would have received scant sympathy from her. My doubts and hesitations did not deter the Black Moses. He must have read my mind, for he then addressed me in a much quieter voice and invited me to speak about my life and ambitions.

Before long I was relating how a sense of racial consciousness had been awakened in my own breast at the age of 12. It went back to an incident in my school days at Westwood. My school had been collecting money for a mission fund, the Dorcas Society. Later I had visited Mrs. Webb, the wife of Rev. William Webb, the founder of our school. I told her the amount we had collected. Her reply somewhat nettled and startled me. She said that it was a pity it was not going to "your people". I explained to Marcus that I had thought Mrs. Webb meant my own parents. The good lady, however, had noticed my confusion and then added that by "my people" she meant the people of Africa. When I asked her to explain she replied that the people of far-away Africa were living in heathen darkness and needed help from Christian missionaries. No one before had told me that I was of African descent. Being so young I was very puzzled by this bit of news and naturally I asked the lady many more questions about Africa.

At first her story of Africa intrigued me; but when I was told that my forebears had been brought from Africa as slaves and sold to white plantation owners in the West Indies, I was horrified and frightened. I heard about slave ships and slave markets and cruel practices. I asked Mrs. Webb who had brought my ancestors from their land. I remember how she replied in a low voice that English traders had done this many years before. She then explained more fully what a great and thriving business the slave trade had been. By that time I was unable to listen further. I recoiled in horror as if from the presence of a newly-discovered enemy, and rushed out of the room.

It was this incident, I explained to Garvey, that had caused the birth of racial consciousness within me. Marcus, of course, was eager to learn what happened after that. Immediately I told him that I had written a long letter to my father. In it I had asked "Who are you? What is your name?" In his answer to my anguished queries my father seemed very puzzled as to what was troubling me. I did not find the reply satisfactory, despite the fact that he related the story of how an African King had proposed to Queen Victoria after the death of Albert. In my youthful agitation I hurriedly sent off another letter beseeching my father, "I want to know something about myself immediately! I am told that my ancestors were slaves right here in Jamaica!"

This time my father really was worried; so much so that he hurried back from Panama to Jamaica. His remedy for me was to take me to see my very old Grandmother. This old matriarch told me a very strange story. She had been born many years before in Jaubin the land of Ashanti, then Gold Coast, now Ghana. When she had been still a girl of about sixteen, she had been kidnapped by a warring tribe along with her two sisters and sold into slavery. Along with many others she had been brought in a great ship across the ocean and sold again to a white master. In Ashanti her family name was Dabas, meaning iron or strong will: her first name was Boahimaa. The old lady was very proud of her lineage. She was very emphatic about the virility of her people and their prowess in war, producing the highest type of Ashanti. (In 1946 when the Asantehene, Sir Asi Agyeman Prempeh II, King of Ashanti, Custodian of Akan custom and culture, confirmed me an Ashanti and returned me to my family, I then learned that Amporte, one of Ashanti's greatest military generals, was my great, great-uncle).

Marcus still urged me to continue with my story. So I had to tell him that after the meeting with Grannie Dabas, I returned to school proud of my family and my people. I told him how this pride increased and how

I often used to ask myself, "How shall I get back to Africa?" I explained how I felt impelled to be of use and service to my race in some positive way. I even told him that I had thought of becoming a missionary, but yet felt that this was not the right road for me: I had yet to discover by what means my ambition to help Africa and all her sons and daughters could be realised. Thus deep in my own heart I was in full sympathy with what Marcus had said concerning the future welfare of the African race.

In a short space of time, Marcus had already revealed his heart's secret to me. In response I had made my own confession of faith to him. Throughout my outpouring, he listened intently. He only rose when I had finished speaking, once again to astonish me with a sweeping and completely self-confident statement.

"Together" he said "We can conquer the world; together we can help to educate our people; together we can help to awaken the Negro to his sense of racial insecurity! When I met you last night our fate was sealed. We are neither of us able to resist the other in this hour of need ..." I was all the more astonished and thrilled because of the sincerity and old-world courtesy with which he addressed me.

This meeting of ours on a July morning a few days before the outbreak of the Great War was a wonderful event. It was a memorable occasion, not only for the two of us, but also, as later events proved, for the whole or our race. Neither Marcus, nor I, fully realised what had taken place, nevertheless we sensed that events of far-reaching consequences had been set afoot. As far as we were personally concerned, both of us felt that our private dreams were beginning to take tangible form. Hitherto, we had been groping in the dark. Now there was light and a way ahead. Each had helped the other to understand how better to serve the cause of Africa and her peoples.

Our joint love for Africa and our concern for the welfare of our race urged us on to immediate action. Together we talked over the possibility of founding an organisation to serve the needs of the peoples of African Origin. We spent many hours deliberating what exactly our aims should be and what means we should employ to achieve those aims. Out of this lengthy tête-à-tête we finally improvised a policy and formulated a pro-gramme for our infant "organisation." In fact the two member move-ment was christened the Universal Negro Improvement Association and African Communities Imperial League. (The imperial was dropped later.)

The birth of what was to grow into a world-wide mass movement could not have been simpler or less pretentious. It began with a mem-bership of two, but grew eventually, like a grain of mustard seed, into an organic whole of several millions. Doubtless, anyone who might have witnessed the foundation of the U.N.I.A., would have hooted with scorn and derision, dismissing its two founders as vague starry-eyed idealists. Certainly the vast majority of Afro-Americans at that time would have laughed loudly at our seemingly crazy notions.

Before the lengthy conference finally broke up for that day, it ended upon a most solemn note. Marcus Garvey stood before me and said in a very earnest voice, "Amy Ashwood, I appoint you secretary of the Universal Negro Improvement Association." I replied with an equal earnestness, "And Marcus Garvey, I appoint you president."

11

Population, Nation, Immigration
Introduction by Sarah C. Dunstan

The field of international relations has long been occupied with questions around the form and composition of the nation-state and its relation to international orders. The works contained in this section reflect the ways in which the categories of population and nation, and the movement of populations across national borders, were highly contested in international thought throughout the twentieth century. Many are demonstrative of the extent to which earlier generations of thinkers understood the relationship between individual responsibilities and the actions of states in the international arena. These questions were never just academic but grounded in the desire to directly engage with and shape some of the pressing challenges facing the international order in the first half of the twentieth century: problems of racial tensions and discrimination, immigration and perceived population over-crowding, nationalist fervor and conflict.[1]

Such challenges were deeply entwined with racist anxieties about threats to an imagined (white) European or Western civilization. As Robert Vitalis has shown in the case of the United States, "international relations meant race relations" in the first few decades of the twentieth century.[2] The same can be said to be true in Britain, albeit in different ways. The First World War, for example, was widely understood in both contexts to be the result of the tensions produced by heterogeneous populations with competing interests residing in the same political state. Those who took such a view also often criticized immigration on grounds that it threatened the sanctity of each nation by adulterating homogeneous populations. In the United States, the 1924 Immigration Act was chiefly designed to curb the influx of people of color into the country. African American intellectuals such as W. E. B. Du Bois and Alain Locke

---

[1] Glenda Sluga, *Internationalism in the Age of Nationalism* (Philadelphia, PA: University of Pennsylvania Press, 2013), 21.
[2] Robert Vitalis, *White World Order, Black Power Politics: The Birth of American International Relations* (Ithaca, NY: Cornell University Press, 2015), 1.

had been at the forefront of public debates in the 1920s with eugenicist thinkers such as Lothrop Stoddard, arguing vehemently against the racialized hierarchies such immigration policies engendered.[3] The selections that follow indicate the diverse variety of thinking that emerged in response to these issues, from those who sought to defend racial hierarchies through to those who sought to imagine new world orders.

Our first selection is the 1907 work "The Right of Nations to Self-Determination" by the Marxist revolutionary thinker Rosa Luxemburg (1871–1919). The work explicitly addressed the question of the reconcilability of national identity and political solidarity. At the turn of the twentieth century, tensions between national (and local) identities and international solidarity provoked great debate amongst Marxist thinkers. For many socialists in Central and Eastern Europe national identity was not only a reality but a crucial aspect of worker's movements, despite Marx's rejection of nationalism.[4] Luxemburg sought to resolve the national question through international socialism.

Luxemburg's essay begins with the declaration that the 1905 Russian Revolution has made "the need to solve the nationality question … a matter of practical politics" (587). The logical conclusion of the professed right of each nation to self-determination is the condemnation of "every attempt to place one nation over another, or for one nation to force upon another any form of national existence" (592). She addresses in particular the program of the Social Democratic Labor Party of Russia (RSDLP), pointing to how demands for equal citizenship – regardless of differences of race, class, gender, and nationality – come into direct conflict with the concept of the right to self-determination of each nationality. Luxemburg would later expand this thinking to argue that this conflict manifested itself on the international stage through aggressive imperialism, which we include in our section on World Economy. The solution Luxemburg proposed here was that the Polish proletariat unite with their Russian class brothers in revolutionary struggle rather than to fight for national independence. This position reflected her own peripatetic life, in which her acts of solidarity reflected political rather than national affiliations. Returning to Luxemburg's life also gives us a sense of the conditions in which theorizing around the state and its relation to the international took place at the turn of the twentieth century.[5]

---

[3] Vitalis, *White World Order, Black Power Politics*, 60–67.

[4] On Marx's conceptualization of nationalism see Ephraim Nimni, *Marxism and Nationalism: Theoretical Origins of a Political Crisis* (London: Pluto Press, 1991).

[5] Kimberly Hutchings, "Revolutionary Thinking: Luxemburg's Socialist International Theory," in Patricia Owens and Katharina Rietzler (eds.), *Women's International Thought: A New History* (Cambridge: Cambridge University Press, 2021), 52.

Born in a Russian-controlled section of Poland to a Jewish family, Luxemburg's involvement in proletarian politics began at fifteen when she joined the first Polish socialist party – the First Proletariat – in 1886. Within months of her joining, the party leaders were imprisoned and executed for taking strike action. Luxemburg remained politically active, however, and, following her graduation from high school in 1887, she was forced to flee to Switzerland to avoid imprisonment. At the University of Zurich, she studied history, politics, and philosophy, ultimately becoming one of the very few women to be awarded a Doctor of Law for her dissertation on industrial development in Poland. She remained active in socialist politics in Zurich, moving in cosmopolitan Marxist circles that emphasized the importance of internationalist rather than nationalist solidarity. In 1893, she helped to launch a newspaper, *The Worker's Cause* (*Sprawa Robotnicza*), dedicated to this agenda. Despite remaining outside Poland, that same year she co-founded the Social Democracy of the Kingdom of Poland and Lithuania (SDKPiL) party. She moved permanently to Berlin in 1898, where she became an active member of the Social Democratic Party of Germany (SPD).[6] Her politics were to the left in the SPD, arguing that the emancipation of workers and minorities would occur only through revolution and the renunciation of national loyalties. Luxemburg's commitment to internationalism reflected her own experience of community formation on the basis of political commitment and class status rather than nationality.

The experience of statelessness or exposure to the realities of being an "alien" within a nation state was also crucial in shaping the thought of Caroline Elizabeth Playne (1857–1948). In Playne's case, this manifested itself in a sharp critique of anti-alien sentiment. Her mother was a Dutch immigrant, and this dual-nationality identity was integral to Playne's sense of self. When the First World War began, she joined the Executive Committee of the Society of Friends' Emergency Committee for the Assistance of Germans, Austrians and Hungarians in Distress and witnessed first-hand the deprivations suffered by those dubbed "enemy aliens" in England. As a result, she lobbied for the rights and material comforts of these communities.[7] Playne saw anti-alien sentiment as the antithesis of the unity required for world peace. In the work extracted

---

[6] For more on the German communist landscape see Eric D. Weitz, *Creating German Communism, 1890–1990: From Popular Protests to Socialist State* (Princeton, NJ: Princeton University Press, 1997).

[7] On this committee see R. Fry, *A Quaker Adventure: The Story of Nine Years' Relief and Reconstruction* (London: Nisbet, 1926).

here, from her 1925 book *Neuroses of the Nations*, Playne uses mental illness as a metaphor for the experience of war and its impact upon society. She describes the "nationalistic crazes of the great mass" as a fundamental impetus of the First World War (603). Drawing on contemporary scientific writing to understand this in terms of "neuroses," she argued that these neuroses led nation-state communities to forget prior experiences of rapprochement with individuals and groups from other nations (in this case the Germans) and to understand these nations in terms of stereotyped behaviors. Whilst Playne's equation of neuroses with conflict between different nation states set her apart from her contemporaries, the notion that differences in national character needed to be accounted for in international relations was a thread running throughout international thought in this period. Playne prefigured early work on psychology and international relations by scholars such as Karl Mannheim.[8]

We know very little of Playne's early life or education, although she was elected in 1908 as an associated Member of the University Women's Club, which welcomed "graduate and professional women." By 1904, she had been one of the founding members of the British National Peace Council, and was a committee member of several peace groups, including the Church of England Peace League, the National Peace Council, and the Union for Democratic Control of Foreign Policy (UDC). Drawing on this activist experience as well as meticulous research, Playne wrote three further works of history: *The Pre-War Mind in Britain* (1928), *Society and War, 1914–16* (1931), and *Britain Holds on, 1917, 1918* (1933).[9] In 1936, she published a biography of the pacifist and first woman recipient of the Nobel Peace Prize Bertha von Suttner, whose work features in our section on World Peace. Before her death, Playne arranged for her papers to be held at the Senate House library in the hope that they would be of use to those taking up her own life's work of "studying the psychological causes of the decline and fall of European civilization in our times."[10]

The threat of European or Anglo civilizational decline also preoccupied the birth control activist Margaret Sanger (1879–1966). In contrast

---

[8] Karl Mannheim, "The Psychological Aspect," in Charles Manning (ed.), *Peaceful Change: An International Problem* (New York: Macmillan Co., 1937). Lucy Philip Mair, who appears later in this section, also had an essay on colonial administration in this edited volume.

[9] Caroline Elizabeth Playne, *The Pre-War Mind in Britain* (London: Allen and Unwin, 1928); Caroline Elizabeth Playne, *Society and War, 1914–16* (London: Allen and Unwin, 1931); Caroline Elizabeth Playne, *Britain Holds on, 1917, 1918* (London: Allen and Unwin, 1933).

[10] University of London Archive, Senate House Library, UoL/UL/4/18/54.

to Playne, however, she argued for changes to state and international organization that specifically reflected the socio-biological function of its citizens. Sanger's personal history explains a great deal about her positions.[11] Originally trained as a nurse at the White Plains Hospital in New York, Sanger had worked in slums in New York's lower East Side, witnessing at first hand the impact of self-induced abortions and multiple pregnancies. Closer to home, her own mother had eighteen pregnancies with eleven live births and, perhaps unsurprisingly, died at the age of fifty, when Sanger was seventeen.[12] She became a vocal proponent of contraception, writing a sex education column for a socialist magazine, the *New York Call*.[13]

Initially, Sanger articulated the need for access to information about contraception as an issue of free speech but expanded her thinking to national and international politics, of female emancipation, civic citizenship, and war.[14] In the extract that follows Sanger describes the "motherhood [of] ... blind chance" as the "greatest crime of modern civilization" (594). Contraception was a means of curbing national poverty and unemployment and thus creating better conditions within the democratic nation state. On an international level, Sanger saw a clear link between family planning and war, arguing that contraception would prevent over-population and competition for dwindling resources, thus reducing the impetus for conflict.[15] Writing around the same time, the sociologist Anne Marion MacLean (1869–1934) made similar remarks in her work on immigration, arguing that over-population could be addressed only by "the adoption of new methods of extracting a livelihood, and in a rational control of fecundity". In this framework, efforts to postpone such measures through unrestricted migration were only postponing an inevitable reckoning.

[11] See Margaret Sanger, *Margaret Sanger: An Autobiography* (Oxford: Pergamon Press, 1938).

[12] See Jean H. Baker, *Margaret Sanger: A Life of Passion* (New York: Hill and Wang, 2011); Ellen Chesler, *Woman of Valor: Margaret Sanger and the Birth Control Movement in America* (New York: Simon & Schuster, 2007).

[13] Margaret Blanchard, *Revolutionary Sparks: Freedom of Expression in Modern America* (New York: Oxford University Press, 1992), 50.

[14] Carole McCann, "Women as Leaders in the Contraceptive Movement," in Karen O'Connor (ed.), *Gender and Women's Leadership: A Reference Handbook* (Thousand Oaks, CA: Sage, 2010), 749–762.

[15] For some of these positions see Esther Katz, Cathy Moran Hajo, and Peter C. Engelman (eds.), *The Selected Papers of Margaret Sanger, vol. 1: The Woman Rebel, 1900–1928* (Champaign, IL: University of Illinois Press, 2002); Esther Katz, Cathy Moran Hajo, and Peter C. Engelman (eds.), *The Selected Papers of Margaret Sanger, vol. 2: Birth Control Comes of Age, 1928–1939* (Champaign, IL: University of Illinois Press, 2007).

In many of Sanger's speeches and writings she advocated the selection of the "torchbearers of civilization" for reproduction and endorsed the forced sterilization of "unfit" individuals. When taken in tandem with Sanger's critique of immigration, this thinking has to be read as both racist and classist.[16] In this extract, for example, she warns against a future in which "the parents whose earnings are the lowest ... create the race of the future" (595). In so doing, she links poverty with moral "unfitness" and "degeneracy." Whilst Sanger never explicitly associated "unfitness for reproduction" with a particular race – to the contrary, she emphasised that "intelligence and other inherited traits vary by individual, not by group" – her arguments overlapped considerably with her eugenicist contemporaries.[17] So, for example, whilst Sanger worked hard to set up a Birth Control clinic in Harlem that would improve Black women's bodily and economic health, many have read her efforts there as a move towards curbing Black reproduction.[18] Sanger's work is indicative of the extent to which the organization of the family and the regulation of population growth (or lack thereof) were fundamental issues in conceptualizations of the problems of establishing and maintaining state borders in the face of immigration, and constituted a core international relations question in this period.

Sanger's contributions, like most in this section, sat at the interstices of thought and praxis, rooted in an activism intended to realize visions of world order. Lucy Philip Mair (1901–1986) and Anne Marion Maclean are unusual amongst the figures here for pursuing primarily academic careers. Mair, who graduated with a first-class degree at Newnham College, Cambridge in 1923, combined her career as an academic at the London School of Economics with policy work.[19] In the 1920s, she spent five years at Gilbert Murray's League of Nations Union, representing the organization at the Assembly of the League in Geneva. During the Second World War, she returned to this policy work, at Chatham House in the British Empire section of the Foreign Research and Press Service. There is more information on Mair in the section on Field and Discipline.

---

[16] On criticisms of her thinking see G. Grant, *Grand Illusions: The Legacy of Planned Parenthood* (Brentwood, TN: Wolgemuth & Hyatt, 1988), 87–101.

[17] Chesler, *Woman of Valor*, 215.

[18] J. M. Rodrique, "The Black Community and the Birth-Control Movement," in K. Peiss and C. Simmons (eds.), *Passion and Power: Sexuality in History* (Philadelphia, PA: Temple University Press, 1989).

[19] Patricia Owens, "Women and the History of International Thought," *International Studies Quarterly*, 62:3 (2018): 468.

MacLean began her career several decades earlier than Mair, becoming the first woman at the University of Chicago to earn a Masters degree in Sociology in 1897 and then a doctorate in 1900.[20] Between 1903 and 1934 she worked in various roles as an adjunct at Chicago and, amongst other work, published six textbooks and nine articles in the *American Journal of Sociology*. MacLean still understood her work to have a practical application. This is evident in the piece extracted here from *Modern Immigration*, a book explicitly designed to confront contemporary problems of population movement. In this selection, MacLean conveys an understanding of each nation as constituted by a particular "character." Immigration threatened the deterioration of that character "by the further admixture of unassimilable groups" given their "divergent physical, economic and religious standards" (598). In MacLean's assessment, the First World War was evidence of how undesirable such a "mixing" was, "a polyglot people" made for "structural weakness" in a nation. Her understanding of the international order was premised upon difference conceived in racialized terms. Relations between nations were the manifestation of competition, a Darwinist "survival of the fittest." MacLean's contemporary moment, she believed, was "the hour of the white man's triumph," but she understood history in terms of "each race in turn ... ris[ing] to supremacy" (599). Nevertheless, she believed that "in all nations, the problems connected with assimilation would be less disturbing if there were a more generous recognition than there is of the worth that exists in all racial strains" (602).

Lucy Philip Mair's 1928 book *The Protection of Minorities* was similarly occupied with the question of racial and national difference. The first chapter opens with the declaration that "[o]ne of the most difficult problems of present-day Europe is" the problem of "heterogeneous populations within the borders of a single State" (610). She showed how minority populations within nations could legally be citizens but still "feel like aliens in a country which is not theirs" because they were subject to a host of discriminations ranging from violence and expulsion through to restrictions on the language they spoke. This question of the relationship between national belonging and political borders was one of the defining issues of the twentieth century. As one reviewer of Mair's book put it, "the great output of recent literature in many languages on

[20] Silvia García Dauder, "Annie Marion MacLean: 'Madre de la etnografía contemporánea' y pionera en la Sociología por correspondencia," *Athenea Digital: Revista de pensamiento e investigación social*, 13 (May 2008): 237–246.

this subject is … a disquieting little cloud on the international horizon."[21] This was an understatement, as the nationalist fervours that had led to the First World War remained central in its aftermath.

Whilst the problem of heterogeneous populations within states predated the First World War, as we have seen, the peace treaties of 1919–1923 placed the question of "minorities" (and thus, of race) center stage given the break-up of the Ottoman and Austro-Hungarian empires. The US President Wilson is often credited with framing this agenda in the language of "self-determination" through his speech to Congress on February 11, 1918. Therein he offered a vision of a new world order organized around nation-states and predicated upon the right of self-determination for white populations within them understood as the right of enfranchised peoples to be governed by their own consent. Likewise, British Prime Minister Lloyd George updated British war aims to include the principle that territorial settlements must be based on "the right of self-determination or the consent of the governed," if they reached the appropriate level of civilization. Thus, in a world of states and empires comprised of multiple ethnic, religious, and linguistic groups, two questions quickly emerged: what constituted "a people or nation" and which national groups had the right to self-determination?[22] In the sections on Anticolonialism, and Diplomacy and Foreign Policy, we can see Simone Weil and Merze Tate questioning how these issues would relate to "the colored people of the world." Whilst the peace treaties at Versailles redrew the geopolitical boundaries of Europe and European colonies the world over, they did not result in an international order of nation states comprised of homogeneous populations. As a result, the protection of minority and self-determining populations became one of the key questions of the newly formed League of Nations. This innovation, however, placed international law into direct conflict with state sovereignty, a right many nation-states put above the need to protect minority populations.

Like Wilson and Lloyd George, Mair was primarily thinking about these tensions in relation to eastern European states. The issues she raised, however, were equally applicable to those peoples under European colonial rule as well as, for example, the African American community in the United States, which neither Wilson nor Lloyd George believed possessed the right to self-determination. Although

---

[21] Blanche E. C. Dugdale, "Review: *The Protection of Minorities. The Working Scope of the Minorities Treaties under the League of Nations*," *Journal of the Royal Institute of International Affairs*, 7:3 (May 1928): 224.

[22] Erez Manela, *The Wilsonian Moment: Self-Determination and the International Originals of Anticolonial Nationalism* (New York: Oxford University Press, 2007), 21–22.

the United States had ultimately refused to join the League of Nations, the question of self-determination remained a contentious political issue in the United States. Certain strands of leadership within the African American community – including those associated with W. E. B. Du Bois's brand of Pan-Africanism and Marcus Garvey's "Back to Africa" movement – saw the League's petition system as a potential mechanism for remedying the United States' "race problem."[23] Indeed, in 1928, the Communist International recognized the Southern Black Belt of the United States as a separate nation with the right to self-determination.[24] Such official recognition from the Comintern is indicative of the contested nature of the relationship between states and nationalities in this period.

Questions around minority status remained central to African American political and international thought throughout the first half of the twentieth century. It is a theme that emerges here in Shirley Graham Du Bois's 1961 essay "Minority Peoples in China," a portrait of the People's Republic of China (PRC). She claimed that this new state, established in 1949, had dealt with the question of minority populations by self-identifying as a "multi-national state" comprised of "fifty-one … nationalities" (624). Prior to the creation of the Republic, "the one common denominator between all these minorities was fear and hatred towards other peoples" (625). However, after 1949, national difference was transcended by political unity. Such unity was created by the equal redistribution of land, the provision of food, access to health care and, most crucially, through the education of "young people of differing national backgrounds … for leadership" (629).

Graham's portrait of this relationship between nationality and state formation in the PRC said more about her utopian vision of statehood than reality. In 1958, China's Great Leap Forward, the second of its five-year economic plans, had faltered badly, leading to the death of more than eighteen million people.[25] The principle of political community

---

[23] See Sarah C. Dunstan, "Conflicts of Interest: The 1919 Pan-African Congress and the Wilsonian Moment," *Callaloo*, 39:1 (Winter 2016): 133–150.

[24] See Hakim Adi, "The Negro Question: The Communist International and Black Liberation in the Interwar Years," in Michael O. West, William G. Martin, and Fanon Che Wilkins (eds.), *From Toussaint to Tupac: The Black International since the Age of Revolution* (Chapel Hill, NC: University of North Carolina Press, 2009), 162–165. Claudia Jones, whose writing appears in our sections on Anticolonialism and Geopolitics and War, also wrote on this question in "On the Right to Self-Determination for the Negro People on the Black Belt," *Political Affairs*, 25:1 (1946), 67.

[25] David Levering Lewis, *W. E. B. Du Bois: A Biography 1868–1963* (New York: Henry Holt, 2008), 563.

over national and ethnic difference was little more than theory. Moreover, those "young people being trained for national leadership" were not representative of the population at large, many of whom had little to no education. Nevertheless, the China Du Bois described was the model of state organization that she herself believed would overcome the problems presented by diverse populations and the entwined problem of racial discrimination. Implicit in her portrait of a multi-national Chinese state tolerant of difference was a critique of the United States' system of Jim Crow segregation. "Minority Peoples in China" was first published in *Freedomways*, a progressive journal Shirley Graham Du Bois had co-founded in 1961 with fellow African American radical thinkers Louis Burnham, Edward Strong, and W. E. B. Du Bois. The journal became one of the leading Black Arts Movement magazines until the 1980s, publishing authors such as James Baldwin and Alice Walker. In the first few years of its run, however, *Freedomways* had a particularly international coverage. Articles on the American civil rights movement appeared alongside reporting on decolonization. Its aim was to encourage racial equality through acceptance of difference within nation-states and respect for newly liberated African countries.

Other minority groups within the United States with even less formal legal status than African Americans took a different approach. One such thinker is the Guatemalan-born Luisa Moreno (1907–1992), who spent much of her life in the United States as a labor activist, emigrating there in 1927 after spending several years in Mexico. Despite being well-educated and fluent in English, French, and Spanish, Moreno was only able to find work as a seamstress in Spanish Harlem. Dissatisfied with her working conditions, she became involved in trade union activism. Throughout the 1930s she worked to improve the conditions of immigrant workers with the Communist Party of the USA, the American Federation of Labor (AFL), the Congress of Industrial Organizations, and the United Cannery, Agricultural, Packing, and Allied Workers of America (UCAPAWA-CIO). She was especially attracted to the latter's commitment to inclusion across race, nationality, and gender.[26]

Like Luxemburg, Moreno believed that national identity should have little bearing upon the guarantee of rights for workers and minorities,

---

[26] For more on cannery as a particular space of Mexican women's work see Vicki L. Ruiz, *Cannery Women, Cannery Lives: Mexican Women, Unionization and the California Food Processing Industry, 1930–1950* (Albuquerque, NM: University of New Mexico Press, 1987).

although she did not understand this in terms of the overthrow of capitalism. In the 1940 speech extracted here and delivered to the American Committee for the Protection of the Foreign Born, Moreno articulated her ideas in the context of the contemporary forced repatriations of Latin American migrant workers from the United States to their native countries. The title of Moreno's speech, "Caravans of Sorrow: Noncitizen Americans of the Southwest," set the tone for Moreno's scathing indictment of these repatriations. She argued that migration for work was a natural part of the relations between capitalist states. By privileging state sovereignty over the guarantee of rights for these workers, the US administration was betraying the principles of liberal democracy. As far as Moreno was concerned, migrant workers had earned the same rights as citizens because "they have contributed their endurance, sacrifices, youth, and labor to the Southwest" and thus played a crucial part in developing the US economy (615). As normative notions of citizenship were based on a contract between the state and the individual, these workers had more than held up their side of the bargain. For Moreno, by repudiating this relationship the United States had begun a slippery slide towards the corruption of the rights of those who officially held citizenship status.

Such an analysis did not mean that Moreno understood naturalization, as the process then stood, as a viable option for most Latin American workers. The sheer cost of application was prohibitive, and the realities of workers' lives meant that it was unlikely they would ever meet the requisite educational requirements of language and national history. Instead, Moreno proposed the overhaul of the system of naturalization, lobbying for "legislation that would encourage naturalization of" the United States' worker communities, its "Latin American, West Indian and Canadian residents." Doing so would encourage a view of the state that emphasized contribution to political community rather than idealizing the unrealistic equation of a political unit with a homogeneous population. This step would be in the interests of western "hemispheric unity," a notion that would remain "an empty phrase" whilst prohibitive naturalization requirements fostered a climate of "anti-alien sentiment" (616). Moreno's criticism of the homogeneous nation state clashed with longstanding efforts within the United States to prevent non-white immigration. We can read Moreno in terms of this activist tradition of critiquing prevailing, and racist, approaches to immigration and state organization.

Immigration was not just a problem of interwar international relations. Post-war immigration of Commonwealth subjects to Britain forced a confrontation with race in an unprecedented fashion. As the final essay in this section, written by the British social anthropologist and childcare campaigner Sheila Kitzinger (1929–2015), indicates, the issue of immigration – and what became referred to as "race relations" – was also deeply entangled with questions around decolonization and the empire "coming home" in the decades after the Second World War. Kitzinger is, like Sanger, best known for her activism and writing around pregnancy, childbirth, and parenting, for which she received an MBE in 1982. Unlike Sanger, Kitzinger advocated education around pregnancy and birth for the empowerment of mothers rather than the selective so-called bettering of the population. She championed better rights for those she believed had been marginalized within society. Prior to her activism in this area, however, she studied social anthropology at Ruskin and St Hugh's College, Oxford, in the late 1940s. Of course, interest in race relations research was not limited to academic settings: both the Colonial Office and the then-Conservative British government engaged extensively in this kind of research as they sought to redefine Britain at the latter stages of the formal empire.

Kitzinger's article appeared in *Phylon*, an academic journal founded by W. E. B. Du Bois in 1940 at the historically Black university in Georgia, Atlanta (now Atlanta Clark). Conceived as part of Du Bois's ongoing struggle against racism, the journal's first issue explicitly indicated that it sought to "emphasize that view of race which regards it as cultural and historical in essence, rather than primarily biological and physiological."[27] This aligned with Kitzinger's analysis of race relations in the privileged locations of the universities of Oxford and Cambridge, where several figures in this volume were educated and worked. Kitzinger's experiences at Oxford influenced her to pursue work on race relations and, in 1951, she accepted a post at the University of Edinburgh to study race relations in London. At the time, the Anthropology Department at Edinburgh was the center of race relations work in Britain. Scholars such as Kenneth Little, Sydney Collins, Eyo Bassey Ndem, Sheila Patterson, and Michael Banton were conducting research into Black–white relations in urban sites across Britain.[28]

For Kitzinger, "[t]he problem of race relations confronting the educated and liberal-minded British today" was that they see "the relation between Britain and the underdeveloped countries as one between leader and led, teacher and taught" (623). Drawing on the arguments

---

[27] "Apology," *Phylon*, 1:1 (1940): 3.
[28] Robbie Shilliam, "Behind the Rhodes Statue: Black Competency and the Imperial Academy," *History of the Human Sciences*, 32:5 (2019): 14.

of the French existentialist philosopher Jean-Paul Sartre, Kitzinger examined the ways in which racism manifested itself in the Oxbridge system where the "more obvious problems of race prejudice" were less common but more subtle and insidious. African or West Indian peoples were relegated to the position of "a 'thing.'"[29] Even well-intentioned peoples treated anyone of color not "as a person" but as part of an anonymous national group defined by skin color. Religious groups on campus saw people of color as "souls to be saved" rather than individuals in their own right. Other students regarded their Commonwealth colleagues as potential instruments of Communism and thus took "great pains to enlist colored people" as "an effective bulwark against militant Communism" (619, 620). Commonwealth students were regarded as a novelty and invited to social gatherings as part of the entertainment or as sponsored by a political party to make that "organization look more successful." Yet white women undergraduates were not permitted to join "on the grounds that it would be 'unsuitable' for them to get to know colored men." As we see in our Imperialism section, this anxiety around the "mixing" of men of color with white women was a common motif in post-war work on "race relations," a core international relations subject that was later marginalized during the relatively late establishment of a separate disciplinary identity for International Relations in Britain.

The fluctuating and complex categories of nation and state had a tangible impact upon the lived realities of populations the world over throughout the twentieth century. The thinkers included in this section were, in different ways, part of the effort to resolve some of the problems arising in this context. Their writings show the extent to which state organization and nationality were not necessarily coterminous. So too do they emphasise the extent to which race and class lay at the heart of discussions over national belonging and immigration. While thinkers such as Luisa Moreno and Shirley Graham sought to define the political state in ways that appreciated and capitalized upon difference, others, such as Lucy Philip Mair, understood minority populations as problems to be solved. The eugenicist implications of Margaret Sanger's work also indicate the extent to which impoverished and vulnerable people were viewed as burdens upon the state and impediments to progress. Sheila Kitzinger's insight into the dynamics of racism in late-imperial Britain illustrates how deeply embedded the equation of race and

---

[29] Jean-Paul Sartre, *Anti-Semite and Jew: An Exploration of the Etiology of Hate*, trans. George J. Becker (New York: Schocken Books, Inc., 1948).

national belonging was. Finding a solution to the conflict arising from these issues was not just a question of how to manage difference within state populations. It also required effective control over the ebb and flow of peoples across nation-state borders for work or for access to resources.

Sarah C. Dunstan

Rosa Luxemburg

From "The Right of Nations to Self-Determination" (1907)

Among other problems, the 1905 Revolution in Russia has brought into focus the nationality question. Until now, this problem has been urgent only in Austria-Hungary. At present, however, it has become crucial also in Russia, because the revolutionary development made all classes and all political parties acutely aware of the need to solve the nationality question as a matter of practical politics. All the newly formed or forming parties in Russia, be they radical, liberal or reactionary, have been forced to include in their programs some sort of a position on the nationality question, which is closely connected with the entire complex of the state's internal and external policies. For a workers' party, nationality is a question both of program and of class organization. The position a workers' party assumes on the nationality question, as on every other question, must differ in method and basic approach from the positions of even the most radical bourgeois parties, and from the positions of the Pseudo-socialistic [sic], petit bourgeois parties. Social Democracy, whose political program is based on the scientific method of historical materialism and the class struggle, cannot make an exception with respect to the nationality question. Moreover, it is only by approaching the problem from the standpoint of scientific socialism that the politics of Social Democracy will offer a solution which is *essentially uniform*, even though the program must take into account the wide variety of forms of the nationality question arising from the social, historical, and ethnic diversity of the Russian empire.

In the program of the Social Democratic Labor Party (RSDLP) of Russia, such a formula, containing a general solution of the nationality question in all its particular manifestations, is provided by the ninth point; this says that the party demands a democratic republic whose constitution would insure, among other things, *"that all nationalities forming the state have the right to self-determination."*

This program includes two more extremely important propositions on the same matter. These are the seventh point, which demands the abolition of classes and the full legal equality of all citizens without distinction of sex, *religion*, *race* or *nationality*, and the eighth point, which says that the several ethnic groups of the state should have the right to schools conducted in their respective national languages at state expense, and the right to use their languages at assemblies and on an equal level with the state language in all state and public functions. Closely connected to the nationality question is the third point of the program, which formulates the demand for wide self-government on the local and provincial level in areas which are characterized by special living conditions and by the special composition of their populations. Obviously, however, the authors of the program felt that the equality of all citizens before the law, linguistic rights, and local self-government were not enough to solve the nationality problem, since they found it necessary to add a special paragraph granting each nationality the "right to self-determination."

What is especially striking about this formula is the fact that it doesn't represent anything specifically connected with socialism nor with the politics of the working class. "The right of nations to self-determination" is at first glance a paraphrase of the old slogan of bourgeois nationalism put forth in all countries at all times: "the right of nations to freedom and independence." In Poland, the "innate right of nations" to freedom has been the classic formula of nationalists from the Democratic Society to Limanowski's *Pobudka*, and from the national socialist *Pobudka* to the anti-socialist National League" [sic] before it renounced its program of independence. [...] Similarly, a resolution on the "equal rights of all nations" to freedom was the only tangible result of the famous pan-Slav congress held in Prague, which was broken up in 1848 by the pan-Slavic bayonets of Windischgraetz. On the other hand, its generality and wide scope, despite the principle of "the right of nations to self-determination" which obviously can be applied not only to the peoples living in Russia but also to the nationalities living in Germany and Austria, Switzerland and Sweden, America – strangely enough is not to be found in any of the programs of today's socialist parties. This principle is not even included in the program of Austrian Social Democracy, which exists in a state with an extremely mixed population, where the nationality question is of crucial importance.

The Austrian party would solve the nationality question not by a metaphysical formula which leaves the determination of the nationality question up to each of the nationalities according to their whims, but only by means of a well-defined plan. Austrian Social Democracy demands the elimination of the existing state structure of Austria, which is a collection of "kingdoms and princely states" patched together during the Middle Ages by the dynastic politics of the Hapsburgs, and includes various nationalities mixed together territorially in a hodgepodge manner. The party rather demands that these kingdoms and states should be divided into territories on the basis of nationality, and that these national territories be joined into a state union. But because the nationalities are to some extent jumbled together through almost the entire area of Austria, the program of Social Democracy makes provision for a special law to protect the smaller minorities in the newly created national territories.

Everyone is free to have a different opinion on this plan. [...]

In the ranks of international socialism, the Russian Workers' Party is the only one whose program includes the demand that "nationalities be granted the right to self-determination."

Apart from Russian Social Democracy, we find this formula only in the program of the Russian Social Revolutionaries, where it goes hand in hand with the principle of state federalism. The relevant section of the political declaration of the Social Revolutionary Party states that "the wide application of the principle of federalism in the relations between individual nationalities is possible," and stresses the "recognition of their unlimited right to self-determination."

It is true that the above formula exists in another connection with international socialism: namely, it is a paraphrase of one section of the resolution on the nationality problem adopted in 1896 by the International Socialist Congress in London. However, the circumstances which led to the adoption of that resolution, and the way in which the resolution was formulated, show clearly that if the ninth paragraph in the program of the Russian party is taken as an application of the London Resolution, it is based on a misunderstanding.

The London resolution was not at all the result of the intention or need to make a statement at an international congress on the nationality question in general, nor was it presented or adopted by the Congress as a formula for the *practical resolution of that question* by the workers' parties of the various countries. Indeed, just the opposite was true. The London Resolution was adopted on the basis of a motion presented to the Congress by the social-patriotic faction of the Polish movement, or the Polish Socialist Party (PPS), a motion which demanded that the recon-struction of an independent Poland be recognized as one of the most urgent demands of international socialism.[30] Influenced by the criticism

---

[30] The above motion read: "Whereas, the subjugation of one nation by another can serve only the interests of capitalists and despots, while for working people in both oppressed

raised at the Congress by Polish Social Democracy and the discussion concerning this in the socialist press, as well as by the first mass demonstration of the workers' movement in Russia the memorable strike of forty thousand textile workers in Petersburg in May 1896 the International Congress did not consider the Polish motion, which was directed in its arguments and in its entire character against the Russian revolutionary movement. Instead, it adopted the London Resolution already mentioned, which signified a rejection of the motion for the reconstruction of Poland.

The Congress – the resolution states – declares itself in favor of the complete right of all nations to self-determination, and expresses its sympathy for the workers of every country now suffering under the yoke of military, national, or other despotism; the Congress calls on the workers of all these countries to join the ranks of the class-conscious workers of the whole world in order to fight together with them for the defeat of international capitalism and for the achievement of the aims of international Social Democracy.

As we can see, in its content, the London Resolution replaces the exclusive consideration of the Polish question by the generalization of the question of all suppressed nationalities, transferring the question from a national basis onto an inter-national one, and instead of a definite, completely concrete demand of practical politics, which the motion of the PPS demanded the reconstruction of independent Poland – the resolution expresses a general socialist principle: sympathy for the proletariat of all suppressed nationalities and the recognition of their *right* to self-determination. There can be no doubt that this principle was not formulated by the Congress in order to give the international workers' movement a practical solution to the nationality problem. On the contrary, a practical guideline for socialist politics is contained not in the first part of the London Resolution quoted above, but in the second part, which "calls upon the workers of all countries suffering national oppression to enter the ranks of international Social Democracy and to work for the realization of its principles and goals." It is an unambiguous way of emphasizing that the principle formulated in the first part – the right of nations to self-determination – can be put into effect only in one way:

---

and oppressor nation it is equally pernicious; and whereas, in particular, the Russian tsardom, which owes its internal strength and its external significance to the subjugation and partition of Poland, constitutes a permanent threat to the development of the international workers' movement, the Congress hereby resolves: that the independence of Poland represents an imperative political demand both for the Polish proletariat and for the international labor movement as a whole." [Apparently note by R. L.]

viz., by first realizing the principles of international socialism and by attaining its ultimate goals.

Indeed, none of the socialist parties took the London Resolution to be a practical solution of the nationality question, and they did not include it in their programs. Even Austrian Social Democracy, for which the solution of the nationality problem was a question involving its very existence, did not do this; instead, in 1899, it created for itself independently the practical "nationality program" quoted above. What is most characteristic, even the PPS did not do this, because, despite its efforts to spread the tale that the London Resolution was a formula in "the spirit" of socialism, it was obvious that this Resolution meant rather a rejection of its motion for the reconstruction of Poland, or at the very least, a dilution of it into a general formula without any practical character.[31] In point of fact, the political programs of the modern workers' parties do not aim at stating abstract principles of a social ideal, but only at the formulation of those practical social and political reforms which the class-conscious proletariat needs and demands in the framework of bourgeois society to facilitate the class struggle and their ultimate victory. The elements of a political program are formulated with definite aims in mind: to provide a direct, practical, and feasible solution to the crucial problems of political and social life, which are in the area of the class struggle of the proletariat; to serve as a guideline for everyday politics and its needs; to initiate the political action of the workers' party and to lead it in the right direction; and finally, to separate the revolutionary politics of the proletariat from the politics of the bourgeois and petit bourgeois parties.

The formula, "the right of nations to self-determination," of course doesn't have such a character at all. It gives no practical guidelines for the day to day politics of the proletariat, nor any practical solution of nationality problems. For example, this formula does not indicate to the Russian proletariat in what way it should demand a solution of the Polish national problem, the Finnish question, the Caucasian question, the Jewish, etc. It offers instead only an unlimited authorization to all interested "nations" to settle their national problems in any way they like. The only practical conclusion for the day to day politics of the working class which can be drawn from the above formula is the guideline that it is the duty of that class to struggle against all manifestations of national

---

[31] Only the German branch of the Polish Socialist Party thought it relevant to include the London Resolution in its program during its struggles with German Social Democracy. After it joined the German Party again, the PPS adopted the Erfurt program as its own without reservations ...

oppression. If we recognize the right of each nation to self-determination, it is obviously a logical conclusion that we must condemn every attempt to place one nation over another, or for one nation to force upon another any form of national existence. However, the duty of the class party of the proletariat to protest and resist national oppression arises not from any special "right of nations," just as, for example, its striving for the social and political equality of sexes does not at all result from any special "rights of women" which the movement of bourgeois emancipationists refers to. This duty arises solely from the general opposition to the class regime and to every form of social inequality and social domination, in a word, from the basic position of socialism. But leaving this point aside, the only guideline given for practical politics is of a purely negative character. The duty to resist all forms of national oppression does not include any explanation of what conditions and political forms the class-conscious proletariat in Russia at the present time should recommend as a solution for the nationality problems of Poland, Latvia, the Jews, etc., or what program it should present to match the various programs of the bourgeois, nationalist, and pseudo-socialist parties in the present class struggle. In a word, the formula, "the right of nations to self-determination," is essentially not a political and problematic guideline in the nationality question, but only a means of *avoiding that question.*

Margaret Sanger

From *Pivot of Civilization* (1922)

Motherhood, which is not only the oldest but the most important profession in the world, has received few of the benefits of civilization. It is a curious fact that a civilization devoted to mother-worship, that publicly professes a worship of mother and child, should close its eyes to the appalling waste of human life and human energy resulting from those dire consequences of leaving the whole problem of child-bearing to chance and blind instinct. It would be untrue to say that among the civilized nations of the world to-day, the profession of motherhood remains in a barbarous state. The bitter truth is that motherhood, among the larger part of our population, does not rise to the level of the barbarous or the primitive. Conditions of life among the primitive tribes were rude enough and severe enough to prevent the unhealthy growth of sentimentality, and to discourage the irresponsible production of defective children. Moreover, there is ample evidence to indicate that even among the most primitive peoples the function of maternity was recognized as of primary and central importance to the community.

If we define civilization as increased and increasing responsibility based on vision and foresight, it becomes painfully evident that the profession of motherhood as practised today is in no sense civilized. Educated people derive their ideas of maternity for the most part, either from the experience of their own set, or from visits to impressive hospitals where women of the upper classes receive the advantages of modern science and modern nursing. From these charming pictures they derive their complacent views of the beauty of motherhood and their confidence for the future of the race. The other side of the picture is revealed only to the trained investigator, to the patient and impartial observer who visits not merely one or two "homes of the poor," but makes detailed studies of town after town, obtains the history of each mother, and finally correlates and analyzes this evidence. Upon such a basis are we able to draw conclusions concerning this strange business of bringing children into the world.

Every year I receive thousands of letters from women in all parts of America, desperate appeals to aid them to extricate themselves from the trap of compulsory maternity. Lest I be accused of bias and exaggeration in drawing my conclusions from these painful human documents, I prefer to present a number of typical cases recorded in the reports of the United States government, and in the evidence of trained and impartial investigators of social agencies more generally opposed to the doctrine of Birth Control than biased in favor of it.

A perusal of the reports on infant mortality in widely varying industrial centers of the United States, published during the past decade by the Children's Bureau of the United States Department of Labor, forces us to a realization of the immediate need of detailed statistics concerning the practice and results of uncontrolled breeding. Some such effort as this has been made by the Galton Laboratory of National Eugenics in Great Britain. The Children's Bureau reports only incidentally present this impressive evidence. They fail to coordinate it. While there is always the danger of drawing giant conclusions from pigmy premises, here is overwhelming evidence concerning irresponsible parenthood that is ignored by governmental and social agencies.

I have chosen a small number of typical cases from these reports. Though drawn from widely varying sources, they all emphasize the greatest crime of modern civilization – that of permitting motherhood to be left to blind chance, and to be mainly a function of the most abysmally ignorant and irresponsible classes of the community.

Here is a fairly typical case from Johnstown, Pennsylvania. A woman of thirty-eight years had undergone thirteen pregnancies in seventeen years. Of eleven live births and two premature stillbirths, only two children were alive at the time of the government agent's visit. The second to eighth, the eleventh and the thirteenth had died of bowel trouble, at ages ranging from three weeks to four months. The only cause of these deaths the mother could give was that "food did not agree with them." She confessed quite frankly that she believed in feeding babies, and gave them everything anybody told her to give them. She began to give them at the age of one month, bread, potatoes, egg, crackers, etc. For the last baby that died, this mother had bought a goat and gave its milk to the baby; the goat got sick, but the mother continued to give her baby its milk until the goat went dry. Moreover, she directed the feeding of her daughter's baby until it died at the age of three months. "On account of the many children she had had, the neighbors consider her an authority on baby care."

Lest this case be considered too tragically ridiculous to be accepted as typical, the reader may verify it with an almost interminable list of similar cases.[32]

The statistics which show that the greatest number of children are born to parents whose[33] earnings are the lowest, that the direst poverty is associated with uncontrolled fecundity emphasize the character of the parenthood we are depending upon to create the race of the future.

A distinguished American opponent of Birth Control some years ago spoke of the "racial" value of this high infant mortality rate among the "unfit." He forgot, however, that the survival-rate of the children born of these overworked and fatigued mothers may nevertheless be large enough, aided and abetted by philanthropies and charities, to form the greater part of the population of to-morrow. As Dr. Karl Pearson has stated: "Degenerate stocks under present social conditions are not short-lived; they live to have more than the normal size of family."

Reports of charitable organizations; the famous "one hundred neediest cases" presented every year by the New York Times to arouse the sentimental generosity of its readers; statistics of public and private hospitals, charities and corrections; analyses of pauperism in town and country – all tell the same tale of uncontrolled and irresponsible fecundity. The facts, the figures, the appalling truth are there for all to read. It is only in the remedy proposed, the effective solution, that investigators and students of the problem disagree.

Confronted with the "startling and disgraceful" conditions of affairs indicated by the fact that a quarter of a million babies die every year in the United States before they are one year old, and that no less than 23,000 women die in childbirth, a large number of experts and enthusiasts have placed their hopes in maternity-benefit measures.

Such measures sharply illustrate the superficial and fragmentary manner in which the whole problem of motherhood is studied today. It seeks a *laisser faire* policy of parenthood or marriage, with an indiscriminating paternalism concerning maternity. It is as though the Government were to say: "Increase and multiply; we shall assume the responsibility of keeping your babies alive." Even granting that the administration of these measures might be made effective and effectual, which is more than doubtful, we see that they are based upon a complete ignorance or disregard of the most important fact

---

[32] U.S. Department of Labor: Children's Bureau. Infant Mortality Series, No. 3 pp. 81, 82, 83, 84.

[33] Cf. U. S. Department of Labor. Children's Bureau: Infant Mortality Series, No. 11. p. 36.

in the situation – that of indiscriminate and irresponsible fecundity. They tacitly assume that all parenthood is desirable, that all children should be born, and that infant mortality can be controlled by external aid. In the great world-problem of creating the men and women of to-morrow, it is not merely a question of sustaining the lives of all children, irrespective of their hereditary and physical qualities, to the point where they, in turn, may reproduce their kind. Advocates of Birth Control offer and accept no such superficial solution. This philosophy is based upon a clearer vision and a more profound comprehension of human life. Of immediate relief for the crushed and enslaved motherhood of the world through State aid, no better criticism has been made than that of Havelock Ellis:

"To the theoretical philanthropist, eager to reform the world on paper, nothing seems simpler than to cure the present evils of child-rearing by setting up State nurseries which are at once to relieve mothers of everything connected with the men of the future beyond the pleasure – if such it happens to be – of conceiving them, and the trouble of bearing them, and at the same time to rear them up independently of the home, in a wholesome, economical and scientific manner. Nothing seems simpler, but from the fundamental psychological point of view nothing is falser. A State which admits that the individuals composing it are incompetent to perform their most sacred and intimate functions, and takes it upon itself to perform them itself instead, attempts a task that would be undesirable, even if it were possible of achievement."[34]

It may be replied that maternity benefit measures aim merely to aid mothers more adequately to fulfil their biological and social functions. But from the point of view of Birth Control, that will never be possible until the crushing exigencies of overcrowding are removed – overcrowding of pregnancies as well as of homes. As long as the mother remains the passive victim of blind instinct, instead of the conscious, responsible instrument of the life-force, controlling and directing its expression, there can be no solution to the intricate and complex problems that confront the whole world to-day. This is, of course, impossible as long as women are driven into the factories, on night as well as day shifts, as long as children and girls and young women are driven into industries to labor that is physically deteriorating as a preparation for the supreme function of maternity.

The philosophy of Birth Control insists that motherhood, no less than any other human function, must undergo scientific study, must be voluntarily directed and controlled with intelligence and foresight. As long as we countenance what H. G. Wells has well termed "the monstrous

---

[34] Havelock Ellis, *Sex in Relation to Society*, p. 31.

absurdity of women discharging their supreme social function, bearing and rearing children, in their spare time, as it were, while they 'earn their living' by contributing some half-mechanical element to some trivial industrial product" any attempt to furnish "maternal education" is bound to fall on stony ground.

Annie Marion Maclean

From *Modern Immigration* (1925)

After having viewed the immigration situation in the seven countries selected for this study, the question naturally arises whether there are observable in these countries any common aims. One express determination does seem to be present in all, and that is to admit only such immigrants as will cause no permanent impairment of the national standards of living. Each country has its own aims and ambitions for the future, which have been derived from the type of people who first developed its resources, or from those whom each nation calls the native-born. This really means those groups who relatively early succeeded to places of importance. It is thus that Nordics prevail in one nation, and Alpines or Mediterraneans in another, and each values most its own distinctive characteristics. Besides this, for varying reasons, there is likely to be found in each country preferential alignment with certain other racial or national groups. For example, the Germans, who are predominantly Nordics, because of occupational adaptability, are desired in Brazil, which is of other basic stock. But such apparent exceptions do not obscure the fact that there has developed a national consciousness and self-appreciation in each nation which makes it openly question the wisdom of admitting into its midst aliens with standards varying widely from its own. The colored races have been the first to come under the ban, with considerable objection against the Orientals. Each nation is certain that it does not want its present character to suffer deterioration by the further admixture of unassimilable groups; and all view with suspicion those races having divergent physical, economic, and religious standards. An English-speaking white man's civilization seems to be the accepted standard in all but the South American republics where the Latin tongues take first place. Even in Brazil are now indications of a color-line. This much, then, the countries under observation have in common in respect to their immigration policies. The World War having focused attention upon the structural weakness of a nation made up of a polyglot people, greater homogeneity of population has since become the watchword. [...]

Melting-Pot Not a Population Solvent

The old American idea of the melting-pot as a population solvent has been pretty generally abandoned, and the newer idea that there is a Gresham's Law for people as well as for money is taking its place. What the biologists call poor germ plasm has a way of persisting that may well cause even the most besotted optimist to hesitate before again opening wide the national doors. Industrial development can be too costly. It is too costly when it is achieved at the expense of a strong race of men. It is platitudinous to say that physical and moral integrity should mean more to a land of free institutions than all the treasure that can be dug from the earth, and should never be sacrificed for exports. Yet our industrial practice has usually been opposed to this principle. When production at any cost becomes a nation's god, it were as well that oblivion should come quickly. Better far is the attitude of Australia when she refused to develop her sugar plantations with labor which she did not want from New Guinea. It was contended that only colored men from the tropics could raise sugar-cane on the northeast coast and survive. Then replied Australia: "We will not raise sugar-cane to the detriment of our native-born." The contention of absentee capitalists, however, proved incorrect since white men are now doing the work successfully. That is one instance where a nation put higher considerations ahead of material prosperity. It is true that racial prejudice of itself has an ugly mien, but when its semblance is born of a desire to maintain intact standards or principles for which some men have bled and died, many feel that it takes on a less sinister aspect. Each race in turn as it rises to supremacy superimposes its ideals upon the world; and if, after experimentation, these fail, they must be discarded in favor of others better adapted to the times. This is the hour of the white man's triumph and he is putting his theories of social and political control to the test.

Trend of Legislative Ideals

Immigration legislation seems to have veered away from the sentimental ideal. A distinct trend is now apparent toward regard for the future welfare of the nation, and so of the world. If self-preservation is the first law of physical life, it is as surely the first law of national life. This principle seems to be indorsed [sic] by the seven countries studied, albeit somewhat haltingly by the United States. Here the idea that this is a home for the world's oppressed dies hard, and this is historically justifiable. The United States has set the pace, both in spirit and legislation, for other immigrant-receiving countries. Her nearest neighbor, Canada, has been most affected, with the result that she has now to face most of the problems which have arisen in the United States, but with a much smaller native population to meet the impact of what might easily become a proportionately greater alien invasion. The other British dominions have guarded themselves against such an eventuality.

Diversity of Aims Appears

So far as this discussion has proceeded, the various nations may be said to have common aims. Beyond this point there are divergences. The countries belonging to the British Commonwealth of Nations not only desire to be English-speaking and white but also dominantly British, and this attitude is reflected in their legislation. This is Empire loyalty carried to its logical conclusion. If the ideals and institutions of the homeland are good, what better endorsement of their worth can there be than that 1,110 self-governing colonies should desire to perpetuate them? But British outposts can be maintained only by the protecting arm of Britain. It is thus that Australia can make good her vigorous resistance to peaceful Asiatic invasion. The eagle eyes of swarthy land-hungry millions are ever turned upon that great and sparsely settled continent, but they are turned in vain. [...]

English-Speaking Nations Desire Literacy of Immigrants

A distinct aim that is seen in our English-speaking nations is the effort to establish some standard of literacy as a prerequisite to admission into the country and to the privileges of citizenship. While no formal test of what a man knows can ever be satisfactory as a determinant of inherent worth, it reveals, after all, a hint of his perseverance amid favoring circumstances. It is not too much to expect that people seeking homes in self-governing countries should be able to read and write their own language. Australia goes even further than this and says they must be able to write from dictation in English. It took the United States many years and much acrid controversy to enact a law containing even a reading test and that in any language. Canada and South Africa have followed the United States, while New Zealand has to a degree patterned after Australia. The South American republics have not yet been in a position to insist on literacy, although they are extending opportunities for free education within their borders.

All Countries Except the United States Need Settlers

With the exception of the United States, the primary aim of all the countries included in this study is to attract settlers who will develop their agricultural resources. For this they frequently offer to desirable persons special inducements including free or assisted passage, free or low-priced land with easy terms of payment, money advances if necessary for equipment and to tide the settler over until after his first harvest. There is unanimity of opinion about the wisdom of attracting the best possible type of settlers. In these countries, industrial immigrants are not wanted. In the United States, the situation is different; here capitalists are eager for more unskilled alien labor, while labor organizations are equally eager to prohibit its entrance. The general public is divided in its opinion, with a probable majority in favor of restriction. Where there is a constant influx of unskilled aliens there is always a margin of unemployment, which, in times of business depression, assumes menacing proportions. It would seem under such circumstances, especially in view of the attitude of capital toward immigration, that unemployment should be a legitimate charge upon business itself, as industrial accidents are, and not upon the charitable agencies supported by the public. The difficulty of establishing such a policy, and enforcing it if it were established, makes our present restriction seem the only practicable plan.

Assimilation of Aliens a Problem of Greater or Less Degree in All Countries

The main problem to be observed in all lands has to do with the assimilation of aliens. There are administrative problems in every country, it is true, and these may become serious where great numbers must be handled, as in the United States. Over fifteen thousand pushing at the gates of Ellis Island in one day[35] might well paralyze a force of several hundred who, working at greatest speed, could not care for more than a third of that number. The eagerness of Europeans to reach the United States before the monthly quotas for their respective countries are full creates a situation difficult to manage, creates in fact a problem of first magnitude. Family tragedies are frequently a resulting by-product of the administration of existing laws.

Other countries do not meet a similar problem on a comparable scale; they have not yet become the longed-for Paradise of the world's unfortunates. Owing to the present policies of these countries, they may never

---

[35] July 1, 1923, the beginning of the new immigration "year".

become the Promised Land to the miscellaneous poverty-stricken crowds of Europe that the United States has been for at least two generations. If so their problems of administration as well as of assimilation will remain simpler. In any case, in all nations, the problems connected with assimilation would be less disturbing if there were a more generous recognition than there is of the worth that exists in all racial strains. A person once admitted to a strange land should not be made to feel contempt for his old allegiance. It is not in this way that new loyalties are born; it is in this way that international hatreds are fostered. Conspicuous examples of ill-judged effort to inject new national ideals into aliens were furnished by some of the undertakings known as "Americanization" during the days of war hysteria in the United States. Conscience-stricken because of years of apathy, the country seized the luckless alien, and tried to run him into a non-existent mould. The effect was disconcerting to everybody. Education and an opportunity to share in the common life, together with justice in all things, are now recognized as a more effective means of making new loyalties grow in the breast of an alien than all the formal undertakings that can be conceived.

Compared to the magnitude of the social problems due to immigration with which the United States has had to contend, the other countries included in this study can hardly be said to have problems at all. Canada, it is true, has had and still has difficulties to meet, but naturally on a much smaller scale than her southern neighbor. The United States of America, the Dominion of Canada, the Dominion of New Zealand, the Commonwealth of Australia, the Union of South Africa and the South American republics of Brazil and Argentina have much in common in their problems and in their aims with reference to immigration. Important mutual help might result if they would come together for their discussion.

Caroline Playne

From *Neuroses of the Nations* (1925)

Collective mentality can no more be reached directly than can individual mind. By their fruits ye shall know them. Behaviour, conduct, expression, action – it is these which must be weighed, as signs and symptoms of mental states.

It is under the pressure of some stress of life that groups of men break down, depart from the control of reason and the dictates of intelligent apprehension. This leads to disorder of conduct, of mind, and even of the physical organism of the individuals who, in the aggregate, compose the crowd or group. During the war-period practically no group who took part in the social or communal life of the day could be said to be free from passionate excitation or to have retained self-control and self-possession when the mischief was at its height. There was an all-round want of balance, an all-round fevered absorption in ill-considered and often futile activities, a failure in activity of the higher levels of human intelligence, a general degradation of tastes and sensibilities from which it may be said that practically no one, who participated in the life of the time, escaped. There were individuals and groups who were opposed to the nationalistic crazes of the great masses, but the method and manner of their opposition were characterized often enough by want of balance and consideration; it was apt to be pushed in irrational and feverish ways, even when original conceptions were in line with sane human thought. Whilst the groups of extremists throughout the period and the whole of the national group at the acutest stages of the disturbance, in each and every belligerent country, may be said to have been insane, the world's malady, as a whole, must be described rather as psycho-neurosis than insanity. And its insane character – as displayed in prevailing conduct and false mental and moral moods – must be regarded as a product of psycho-neurosis.

There is universal agreement that whilst bodily contagions were far less prevalent than during previous wars, owing to the successful methods of

603

modern science in combating them, nervous and mental diseases prevailed as never before, during the 1914–1918 War. On the first page of his study, *Instinct and the Unconscious*, the late Dr. Rivers says: "One of the most striking features of the war from which we have recently emerged – perhaps its most important feature from the medical point of view – has been the enormous scale on which it produced those disturbances of nervous and mental functions which are grouped together by the physician under the heading of psycho-neurosis." Although these words apply, of course, to the afflictions from which soldiers suffered during the War, evidence abounds to show that psycho-neurosis was also very common among civilians. But further than this, the records of the group-psychology of the period show the same neurosis, displayed collectively and generally. One prevailing feature may be cited as an example.

The suppression of memory is one of the most significant features of neurosis. It can be claimed that nothing was more distinctive of the war-neurosis than the way in which former happy trade and social relationships, scientific and artistic companionships, mutual religious endeavours (as in the mission-field), close intercourse of all kinds, passed away from the memory of society, were buried by the respective groups of opposed belligerents. When conflict prevails, it is normal to remember and to dwell on that which is bad or disagreeable in an enemy. It is abnormal to deny positively social relationships of long standing, to totally suppress the memory of much that has been a matter of experience. Yet such suppression was manifest at every turn whilst the war-complex lasted. Example after example might be given of the obsessing idea of the English mass-mind that the German people were and always had been hordes of savages, loosely characterized as Huns. Yet this same mass-mind had chiefly known Germans as good bakers, hairdressers, or handy, careful waiters, with all of whom they had been on the best of terms for generations, and with whom there had been much marrying and inter-marrying.[36] Nothing of this made the least difference. The memory of long-continued experience was completely blotted out, so that it was useless to try and recall such experience.

The very Frenchmen who, before the War, had promoted French–German understanding, writers and artists and scientists, forgot these wider sympathies.[37] Distinguished men who, despite ancient feuds, had

---

[36] How common were German names in England for decades before the War! Almost every List of Honour contained names of distinct German origin.

[37] See as example, *Les Coupables*, by Charles Richet, Membre de l'Institut, etc. In this book, written by a man intimately acquainted with pre-war history, there occur some notable

worked in closest relationships with their fellows beyond the Vosges, lost all consciousness of ever having been connected by any fellow-feeling or activity, or human interest. The German mass-mind forgot the English trader whom they and their forefathers had often honoured as a visitor in their midst. With few exceptions they forgot British friends, even those for whom they had cherished great affection. All the common experiences of companionship in sport, in art, in learning were buried by the opposed groups in the big conflict. The Unconscious seems to provide as convenient a lumber-room for the mass-mind as it does for the individual. National groups suppressed that portion of common knowledge and experience which hindered their desire or weakened the flow of passionate instincts, just as the individual, with morbid tendencies, suppresses realities when blinded by passion and fury, or buries memories of experience, when these conflict with instinctive forces.

The effects of suppression by the mass-mind were as baneful to the moral life of the different groups as the suppressions of psycho-neurosis are to the peace and well-being of the individual.

If it is true that "mental health depends on the presence of a state of equilibrium between instinctive tendencies and the forces by which they are controlled,"[38] it is not astonishing that serious mental failure and retrograde moral conditions characterized the war-period. And further, the natural "restorative processes which come into activity" in the course of the development of human existence (as they do in the individual life), as attempts – must they be called unhappy attempts? – to solve the conflict between instinctive on-rushings and intelligent orderings, are part of the psychoneurosis of disturbed periods.

Such attempts are very characteristic of pre-war years, as will be seen. Dr. Rivers describes these morbid processes by saying: "Again the frequency of neuroses in the recent war has certainly been due in part to the call made upon instinctive tendencies which in the usual peaceful character of our modern civilization receive no stimulus, so that the more adventurous have to resort to excessive speed, dangerous sports, big game-hunting, and other similar pursuits to excite their danger-instincts, and give that spice of conflict which redeems the monotonous calm of our modern life in times of peace. While increase in the activity of

---

examples of the obliteration of well-known facts from memory and consciousness. The murders of Serajevo [sic] are left out of count in summarizing the three immediate origins of the War. The first is thus stated: 'Austria injuriously threatens the independence of the Serb nation.' This on the part of a scientist of great eminence, shows lapse of memory as the result of emotion. It is a great pleasure to record that Dr. Richet has completely recovered his former wide sympathies.

[38] *Instinct and the Unconscious*, Rivers, p. 119.

instinctive tendencies thus plays an important part in the production of neurosis, this part is, as a rule, overshadowed by the second factor – weakening of the controlling forces. Both in peace and war the immediate factor in the production of neurosis is weakening of control by shock, strain, illness, or fatigue."[39] It seems clear that here are helpful lines on which to pursue the study of group-mental maladies during the war-period.

The origin of the trouble is really "a rolling-back into barbarism," owing to the insurgency of instinctive processes, such as, in the interests of communal life, are usually repressed, or – perhaps more fortunately – sublimated. When their suppression causes conflict, this is side-tracked by artificial stimulation, by superabundant activities producing super-abundant goods and wealth of all sorts, by ceaseless movement, journey-ings, sports of all kinds, endless social engagements and pleasures, and life is over-full.

The consequent strain and stress – especially nervous strain, stress and failure – weakened the controlling forces, put them out of gear. Reason, intelligence, social instincts were suspended – fevered, senseless, unceas-ing activities set the pace and the tone. Insurgent instincts played what havoc they might because the control of experience, race-wisdom, group-intelligence had lapsed, through overstrain. Such natural instincts as fear and suspicion gained complete ascendancy over fatigued, strained group-minds. And then, because there was much timidity and fear, excessive and unnatural efforts were made to meet the fear, or to banish the shame felt at being afraid.[40] The following description of the culminating suffering of the individual-neurosis applies also to group-neurosis, as the present generation has suffered from it. The sufferer may throw himself into still greater activity, or may attempt to drown the conflict by excesses of various kinds, but only succeeds in still further sapping his strength till some comparatively trivial shock, illness, or wound removes him from the possibilities of such attempts to solve the conflict. He becomes the victim of the fully-developed state, formerly anxiety-neurosis from the called neurasthenia, but now ... which forms one of its most special exaggerated anxiety ... striking and characteristic symp-toms [sic, whole sentence].[41]

The armed peace, the idea of keeping peace by endless preparations for war, was the perverse and excessive effort made by the various groups to meet the unwarranted fear which possessed them and to cover up the

[39] Idem, Rivers. p. 120.
[40] The tone of Henri Bordeau's novel, *La Peur de Vivre*, illustrates these sequences.
[41] Idem, Rivers, pp. 123, 124, 125.

shame they felt at being afraid. Witness the outrageous boastings of German militarists.

All the strutting, all the parading, all the glorified manoeuvres, all the vaunted naval reviews, indeed the whole complex, which exalted military life above civil life during decades before the War, was a forced and stultifying effort to meet the fear that assaulted over-stimulated and over-anxious, unstrung human beings. It was an attempt to banish the shame of such fear. It was an indication of conflict, and an attempt at rationalization, a nucleus of "morbid intellectual processes."

It was – and indeed still is – a state of confused delusion. Dr. Rivers' arguments, concerning the production of the hysteria of war through the enhanced suggestibility which results from military training, call for serious attention.[42]

When, owing to the prevailing "anxiety or repression-neurosis," military and naval preparations are increased to the extent of training practically the entirety of the able-bodied manhood of nations, this enhancement of suggestibility must be dangerously extended. Moreover, if enhanced suggestibility not only accompanies hysteria but is "an important, if not essential, factor in the production of the state,"[43] we find an explanation of the war-hysteria which attacked and undermined the constitution of such a naturally sober and intelligent nation as the Germans; also of hysterical excesses in France, Boulangism or the celebrations of the Franco-Russian alliance in 1893, which Tolstoy characterizes in *Christianity and Patriotism*;[44] also of the extraordinary suggestibility shown in Italy, when in October 1911, as the result of a short campaign of newspaper propaganda, the whole country supported the quixotic Tripoli war and wasted strength and resources in vain endeavours to subdue a vast wilderness. What examples of the abrogation of modifying principles based on intelligence, leaving in full power the other and, more or less, opposed principle of suggestion, these instances furnish!

It seemed necessary thus to indicate the underlying conceptions of group-psychology which are adopted in this study of the world's mental malady before proceeding to the study of its development, circumstances and character, as manifested in national groups.

Again, the question may be forestalled: Does not every historical period exhibit group-mental maladies? Why speak of a special mental malady displayed at this particular period? Mass-aberrations might certainly be traced in almost every age throughout the history of the human race. The contention maintained is, however, that particular mass-

---

[42] See idem, p. 130.   [43] Idem, p. 130.
[44] Translated by Constance Garnett (Jonathan Cape).

neurosis developed more generally during the pre-war decades, that it probably spread to larger proportions than previous group-psycho-neurosis attained.

In times that may be considered ordinary, delusions, confusions, distractions, and manias prevail among portions of society. Nevertheless, on the whole and ultimately, a measure of balance and control is maintained. Indeed, all taken together, sanity prevails among human collectivities, the struggle is even, or it inclines to the side of wisdom and right-mindedness. That this was not the case, but that, on the contrary, the measure of balance inclined greatly towards folly, dementia and fury, is implied in the constant admissions made by writers, holding all kinds of differing views, they speak of men as mad, of nations as mad, of the world as mad. Sociological reasons for this prevalence of human "regression" at this particular hour in the course of human development, will be advanced, when the history of the trouble has been considered. This much may be suggested at once. If conflict is to be allayed, time is needed to obtain balance to establish control. But conflict was present in an acute form, there was an uprush of primitive instincts, a rebound of natural tendencies, upsetting restrictions and suppressions. Artificialities were probably greater and more established than ever before, and the uprush, the urge for liberation, was more unwitting and stark. The consequent conflict heaved and swelled till it threw society off the tracks. For the fullness and complexity of life allowed no time for the solving of conflict on reasonable, intelligent lines. The richness of circumstance, the rush of events prompted distraction, the dodging of conflict rather than its patient solution. Wise balancing requires time for thought and quietness of mood. A distracted world knew neither. Hence the inroads of mass-hysteria and a further rolling-back into barbarism.

In order to sum up, it may be said that, as the malady comes to be further discussed in connection with one nation after another, it will be recognized that, though common to civilization, it differs in kind and degree in different regions; but that it everywhere springs from prevalent conditions of the civilization and of the mass-mentality of the period. The symptoms, in earlier stages, may, we have seen, be compared to those of psycho-neurosis and nervous breakdown. Later on these develop into something like dementia.

That this was vaguely realized by almost every contemporary speaker and writer is shown by the fact that, almost without exception, they describe the trouble as "madness." Many writers, who aver that the nation they belong to is, that they themselves and their friends and allies are perfectly sane explaining that their particular exaltations are only natural resentment of the terrible aberrations of other nations and other groups, these same writers – it is interesting to note – frequently speak of the universal madness of the time in general terms. The study of nervous and mental deterioration, whether of the individual or of the group, is never an agreeable study. Yet such study is as necessary when it is the group-mind which is affected as it is when individuals are the sufferers. The symptoms of mass-madness must be recognizable if, in future, preventive measures are to be taken at an early stage. They must be recorded, in order that methods may be devised for dealing with general disorders. It is more necessary to avoid, stem, or heal neuroses on a collective scale than it is to come to the aid of individuals suffering nervously and mentally. For this reason the remembrance of the conditions prevailing at the period of the Great War needs preserving.

It is of particular importance, of course, that the manias and depravities of one nation should not be unduly magnified, and the manias and depravities of other nations glossed over or minimized. It will be found that the subtler forms of the malady, shown in some countries, are not only more interesting to study, but that they call for closer attention, for they are less evident though, perhaps, farther reaching. The universal neurosis which endangered human society has its analogy, if not its physical counterpart, in that plague of nervous character which scourged the world during the same period – influenza. Influenza occurred repeatedly; it played havoc here, there and everywhere, assuming different forms, and displaying varying symptoms. It died down, but never quite disappeared; it flared up and ran its course, with more or less virulence, till, finally, in the midst of the World-War, it gathered full strength and ravished the farthest ends of the earth. In the 1917, 1918 outbreaks the victims, who succumbed to this nervous plague, were more in number than those slain by all the fighters in the course of the great fratricidal War of modern history.

Lucy Philip Mair

From *The Protection of Minorities* (1928)

One of the most difficult problems of present-day Europe is that which results from the mixture of heterogeneous populations within the borders of a single State. Centuries of conquests, migrations, partitionings, and dominations of one race by another have produced a tangle so inextricable that it is impossible to make political boundaries coincide completely with racial divisions. Consequently there are in each of the Central and Eastern European States groups of people who differ from the majority of the population in language, in religion, in national sentiment, or in all together. Although they are citizens of the State where they live, they feel like aliens in a country which is not theirs, and are too often so regarded by the majority. Until this sense of division has disappeared, the newly created States cannot develop any real unity. But it can only disappear gradually in the course of generations of mutual toleration. Attempts to hasten the process by force, or to carry out a superficial assimilation of the language and culture of minorities to those of the majority, defeat their own ends. Such a policy brought about the disruption of the Central European Empires, and would be even more fatal in the new Europe where so many minorities belong to races with a rich and rightly cherished inheritance. The new States do not have the same vast numbers of potential irredentists within their borders; but they have enough to make the question of their treatment a serious one from the point of view of European peace.

Oppressed and discontented minorities turn naturally for sympathy to their own people across the border; or their protection affords to some Power with aggressive intentions a pretext for a "righteous war." An ideal peace settlement, based on the principle of self-determination, ought, it might be thought, to have drawn the new frontiers so as to leave no such discontented groups on the wrong side. But even if self-determination had been given free play, even if it had been the only consideration which had to be taken into account, that would have been impossible. Geographical conditions by themselves were enough to prevent it. In some cases the minorities are established in the centre of the country, far from any State where their own race is predominant. The Saxons in Rumania are an instance. In some districts, as in Upper Silesia, where the towns are populated by Germans and the surrounding country by Poles, no economically workable division could have been made on strictly racial lines. The Ruthenians are divided in two by one of the most uncompromising natural boundaries in Europe, the Carpathians. The Croatians are not separated from the main body of their own people, but, since they cannot form an independent State, are included in Yugo-Slavia, with whose majority population they are racially akin, though their language is different. In every State there are considerable numbers of Jews, for whom "self-determination" can have no meaning, because, except for inhabitants of the Jewish National Home in Palestine, there is no Jewish nationality. Most important of all are the minorities which the application or the principle of self-determination has itself produced, where territory held by right of conquest has been restored to the people from whom it was taken, and the former dominant race has become a minority in the land of the people whom it once governed.

The Supreme Council, since it took upon itself the responsibility for redistributing the territories of Europe, felt that it was responsible also for ensuring that the settlement which it had endeavoured to make just should also be lasting. If it had not done so, it would have deserved the charge brought against it of "Balkanising Europe."

The territorial settlement, though it redressed the grave injustices that had been brought about by the growth of the Central Powers, was not by itself enough to guarantee the stability of the new order. Central Europe was being divided among new States, lacking any experience of government and exulting in the young pride of their new nationality. In most cases they held their former oppressors in the hollow of their hand. It was not to be expected that groups which for generations had regarded one another with the bitterest enmity should unite in brotherly love at a word from the Powers; there was only too much likelihood that their first thought would be of revenge.

Instead, therefore, of leaving the treatment of minorities entirely to the discretion of the Governments under whom they were placed, the Supreme Council made certain stipulations for their protection, which were embodied in treaties or declarations signed by the new and enlarged States. Such treaties are by no means without precedent in the history of the last century, though the earlier agreements were in general less definite.

People cannot be compelled by treaty to love their neighbours; and as long as they continue to hate them they will devise means of injuring them. What the treaties do is to make such injuries as far as possible illegal. The ill-treatment of minorities may range from the crude forms of massacre and mass expulsion to more refined methods, of which the most popular is the restriction of the free use of the mother-tongue. Education laws, commercial laws, and regulations for the administration of justice, are the most obvious means to this end. Agrarian reforms have been centuries overdue in all the new States, and their execution must inevitably affect principally the alien minorities which during all these centuries have possessed land out of all proportion to their numbers. This is a hardship against which the treaties could give no protection, not, as is sometimes alleged, because agrarian questions are more intrinsically domestic than any other subject of national legislation, but because the continuance of the minorities in their former privileged position would have struck at the very existence of the new States. Even here the minorities are guaranteed, as they are in all other respects, against exceptional measures directed against them as a class. There are minorities transferred from States where local autonomy is taken for granted to States where it is unheard of; and minorities who find themselves under the rule of a people whose standards of culture and civilisation are lower than their own. They can be protected against the deliberate extinction of their own culture, but not against what they feel as the indignity of being governed by persons whom they regard as their inferiors. This, after all, is a grievance not unknown in most countries.

The past cannot be altered; if it could, how easy it would be to construct an ideal future. But with the few exceptions inherent in situations which have grown up through centuries, the treaties do constitute a fairly comprehensive charter of rights, and even in some cases of privileges.

Luisa Moreno

From "Caravans of Sorrow: Noncitizen Americans of the Southwest" (1940)

One hears much today about hemisphere unity. The press sends special correspondents to Latin America, South of the Border songs are wailed by the radio, educational institutions and literary circles speak the language of cultural cooperation, and, what is more important, labor unions are seeking the road of closer ties with the Latin American working people. The stage is set. A curtain rises. May we ask you to see behind the scenery and visualize a forgotten character in this great theater of the Americas?

Long before the "grapes of wrath" had ripened in California's vineyards a people lived on highways, under trees or tents, in shacks or railroad sections, picking crops – cotton, fruits, vegetables – cultivating sugar beets, building railroads and dams, making a barren land fertile for new crops and greater riches.

The ancestors of some of these migrant and resident workers, whose home is this Southwest, were America's first settlers in New Mexico, Texas, and California, and the greater percentage was brought from Mexico by the fruit exchanges, railroad companies, and cotton interests in great need of underpaid labor during the early postwar period. They are the Spanish-speaking workers of the Southwest, citizens and noncitizens working and living under identical conditions, facing hardships and miseries while producing and building for agriculture and industry.

Their story lies unpublicized in university libraries, files of government, welfare and social agencies – a story grimly titled the "Caravans of Sorrow."

And when in 1930 unemployment brought a still greater flood of human distress, trainloads of Mexican families with children born and raised in this country departed voluntarily or were brutally deported. As a result of the repatriation drive of 1933, thousands of American-born youths returned to their homeland, the United States, to live on streets and high-ways, drifting unattached fragments of humanity. Let the annals of juvenile delinquency in Los Angeles show you the consequences.

Today the Latin Americans of the United States are seriously alarmed by the "antialien" drive fostered by certain un-American elements; for them, the Palmer days [referring to the mass arrests and expulsions of suspected Communist subversives conducted under the direction of Attorney General A. Mitchell Palmer during the height of the infamous "Red Scare" of 1919–20] have never ended. In recent years while deportations in general have decreased, the number of persons deported to Mexico has constantly increased. During the period of 1933 to 1937, of a total of 55,087 deported, 25,135 were deportations of Mexicans. This is 45.5 percent of the total and does not include an almost equal number of so-called voluntary departures.

Commenting on these figures, the American Committee for Protection of Foreign Born wrote to the Spanish-Speaking Peoples' Congress in 1939: "One conclusion can be drawn, and that is, where there is such a highly organized set-up as to effect deportations of so many thousands, this set-up must be surrounded with a complete system of intimidation and discrimination of that section of the population victimized by the deportation drive."

Confirming the fact of a system of extensive discrimination are university studies by Paul S. Taylor, Emory Bogardus, and many other professors and social workers of the Southwest. Let me state the simple truth. The majority of the Spanish-speaking peoples of the United States are victims of a setup for discrimination, be they descendants of the first white settlers in America or noncitizens.

I will not go into the reasons for this undemocratic practice, but may we state categorically that it is the main reason for the reluctance of Mexicans and Latin Americans in general to become naturalized. For you must know, discrimination takes very definite forms in unequal wages, unequal opportunities, unequal schooling, and even through a denial of the use of public places in certain towns in Texas, California, Colorado, and other Southwestern states.

Only some 5 or 6 percent of Latin American immigrants have become naturalized. A number of years ago it was stated that in a California community with fifty thousand Mexicans only two hundred had become citizens. An average of one hundred Mexicans out of close to a million become citizens every year. These percentages have increased lately. Another important factor concerning naturalization is the lack of documentary proof of entry, because entry was not recorded or because the immigrants were brought over en masse by large interests handling transportation from Mexico in their own peculiar way.

Arriving at logical conclusions the Latin American noncitizens, rooted in this country, are increasingly seeing the importance and need for naturalization. But how will the thousands of migrants establish residence? What possibility have these people had, segregated in "Little Mexicos," to learn English and meet educational requirements? How can they, receiving hunger wages while enriching the stockholders of the Great Western Sugar Company, the Bank of America, and other interests, pay high naturalization fees? A Mexican family living on relief in Colorado would have to stop eating for two and a half months to pay for the citizenship papers of one member of the family. Is this humanly possible?

But why have "aliens" on relief while the taxpayers "bleed"? Let me ask those who would raise such a question: what would the Imperial Valley, the Rio Grande Valley, and other rich irrigated valleys in the Southwest be without the arduous, self-sacrificing labor of these noncitizen Americans? Read *Factories in the Fields*, by Carey McWilliams to obtain a picture of how important Mexican labor has been for the development of California's crop after the world war. Has anyone counted the miles of railroads built by these same noncitizens? One can hardly imagine how many bales of cotton have passed through the nimble fingers of Mexican men, women, and children. And what conditions have they had to endure to pick that cotton? Once, while holding a conference for a trade union paper in San Antonio, a cotton picker told me how necessary a Spanish paper was to inform the Spanish-speaking workers that FSA [Farm Security Administration] camps were to be established, for she remembered so many nights, under the trees in the rain, when she and her husband held gunny sacks over the shivering bodies of their sleeping children – young Americans. I've heard workers say that they left their shacks under heavy rains to find shelter under trees. You can well imagine in what condition those shacks were.

These people are not aliens. They have contributed their endurance, sacrifices, youth, and labor to the Southwest. Indirectly, they have paid more taxes than all the stockholders of California's industrialized culture, the sugar beet companies and the large cotton interests that operate or have operated with the labor of Mexican workers.

Surely the sugar beet growers have not been asked if they want to dispense with the skilled labor cultivating and harvesting their crops season after season. It is only the large interests, their stooges, and some badly misinformed people who claim that Mexicans are no longer wanted.

And let us assume that 1.4 million men, women, and children were no longer wanted, what could be done that would be different from the anti-Semitic persecutions in Europe? A people who have lived twenty and thirty years in this country, tied up by family relations with the early settlers, with American-born children, cannot be uprooted without the complete destruction of the faintest semblance of democracy and human liberties for the whole population.

Some speak of repatriation. Naturally there is interest in repatriation among thousands of Mexican families in Texas and, to a lesser degree, in other states. Organized repatriation has been going on, and the net results [sic] in one year has been the establishment of the Colonia "18 de Marzo" in Tamaulipas, Mexico, for two thousand families. There are 1.4 million Mexicans in the United States according to general estimates, probably including a portion of the first generation. Is it possible to move those many people at the present rate, when many of them do not want to be repatriated?

What then may the answer to this specific noncitizen problem be? The Spanish-Speaking Peoples' Congress of the United States proposes legislation that would encourage naturalization of Latin American, West Indian, and Canadian residents of the United States and that would nurture greater friendships among the peoples of the Western Hemisphere.

The question of hemispheric unity will remain an empty phrase while this problem at home remains ignored and is aggravated by the fierce "antialien" drive.

Legislation to facilitate citizenship to all natural-born citizens from the countries of the Western Hemisphere, waiving excessive fees and educational and other requirements of a technical nature, is urgently needed. A piece of legislation embodying this provision is timely and important. Undoubtedly it would rally the support of the many friends of true hemispheric unity.

You have seen the forgotten character in the present American scene – a scene of the Americas. Let me say that, in the face of greater hardships, the "Caravans of Sorrow" are becoming the "Caravans of Hope." They are organizing in trade unions with other workers in agriculture and industry. The unity of Spanish-speaking citizens and noncitizens is being furthered through the Spanish-Speaking Peoples' Congress of the United States, an organization embracing trade unions and fraternal, civic, and cultural organizations, mainly in California. The purpose of this movement is to seek an improvement of social, economic, and cultural conditions, and for the integration of Spanish-speaking citizens and noncitizens into the American nation. The United Cannery, Agricultural, Packing, and Allied Workers of America, with thousands of Spanish-speaking workers in its membership, and Liga Obrera of New Mexico, were the initiators of the Congress.

This Congress stands with all progressive forces against the badly labeled "antialien" legislation and asks the support of this Conference for democratic legislation to facilitate and encourage naturalization. We hope that this Conference will serve to express the sentiment of the people of this country in condemnation of undemocratic discrimination practiced against any person of foreign birth and that it will rally the American people, native and foreign born, for the defeat of un-American proposals. The Spanish-speaking peoples in the United States extend their fullest support and cooperation to your efforts.

Sheila Kitzinger

From "Conditional Philanthropy towards Colored Students in Britain" (1960)

Colored students – far from being avoided and shunned in Britain – are often sought out by people who are particularly interested in their welfare. These people may have some knowledge of India or the colonies, may be particularly concerned about race relations from a religious or political point of view, or may see the lonely colored student as a willing disciple for their brand of political or religious truth. The results of such concern are not always those which the philanthropists would wish them to be.

Mr. Smith writes a note to John inviting him for coffee the following evening. The note looks all right and it is certainly very kind – but, since they have never met, what does Mr. Smith want to get out of him? – John asks himself. Is he just curious about colored people? Is he retired from the Colonial Service and nostalgic for Nigeria? Or is it religion that he is going to drag him into? With these suspicions in his mind John goes to the coffee party and sees that most of the other guests are also colored. Immediately he begins to feel uncomfortable. Again he has been put into a category – that of people with colored skins. Obviously Mr. Smith is not interested in him as a person, and this is only one better (and a good deal duller) than the sort of party at which he often finds himself where he is presented as a freak, where there is "someone who plays the flute, someone who stands on his head – and a colored man." Mr. Smith talks about an organization which he says is very interested in the welfare of colored students, hands round a few pamphlets and tries to get his guests to talk, but the conversation is not flowing very easily. Usually John comes away feeling rather depressed, hoping he can avoid the man next time he sees him in the street, and determined never to join that organization. Mr. Smith, on the other hand, is left feeling that the colored students were ungrateful and, when his next invitation is left unanswered, may begin to think that these fellows are not worth bothering about after all.

At Oxbridge there have been attempts to start clubs to enable white and colored students to meet. Of course they already meet in other clubs if they have any interests in common. On one such occasion some white undergraduates who did not know any colored students personally, and wanted to, consulted me about the formation of such a club. After some discussion it emerged that while colored women were to be allowed to join, no white women undergraduates were to be admitted to membership, on the grounds that it would be "unsuitable" for them to get to know colored men. "It might not be a good thing for white girls to get friendly with Negroes. It raises so many problems," I was told. The club never came to anything.

Within some religious groups the atmosphere is especially sanctimonious. These people are earnestly concerned to do good and to show positive Christian friendship to those less fortunate than themselves, but they often lack the understanding of human psychology – and perhaps the humility – which would enable them to see where they go wrong. A young woman undergraduate who had been friendly with a man from Ghana who had been very fond of her, came to me one day asking what his views on religion were, because she thought he was "chucking it over." Far from having personal interest in the man himself, she was motivated by group enthusiasm for a soul that was in danger of becoming lost. "What is happening to him?" she asked. "We are very worried about him in the Methodist Society. He does not come to meetings any more. Ostensibly he had a quarrel with me and that was the reason, but actually that wasn't the real reason." I suggested that he might feel that institutionalized religion did not help him much at the moment and that he might be seeking within himself. "But the trouble is," she replied, "that he has been 'seeking' for so long. That is why we are worried. We think he may be getting skeptical." This girl genuinely wanted to do all she could to help her West African friend and I do not think it had ever occurred to her that she was not treating him as a person, but only as a soul to be saved. He had thought that she was his friend, and when he gradually realized that this friendship was conditional upon his accepting certain religious beliefs, he not only felt very strongly that he did not wish to expose himself to such condescension, but suffered severe disappointment and became deeply depressed to the extent that he could probably have benefited from psychiatric help.

There is a large pseudo-religious organization which I shall call "the Force," the members of which take great pains to enlist colored people. Oxbridge undergraduates often come up against them, are offered conference holidays abroad, sometimes with fares paid, and occasionally even gifts such as cameras. Trusted members of the organization are detailed to look after a small group of prospective adherents, to pray for and with them, to care for them spiritually and physically, remember their birthdays, learn their national songs and dances, explain the aims of the organization and see that they meet the right people. They speak of "My Nigerians" or "My Thais," and see themselves as an effective bulwark against militant Communism.

Other groups active in contacting colored students in Oxbridge are international societies, Rotary, the Catholics, the Christian Union, a fundamentalist group connected with the Gospel Hall, and certain semi-political organizations, including the World Federalists. All students sponsored by the Commonwealth Office receive letters of greeting from the Conservative and Labour parties upon arrival in Britain (the Conservative being rather better done usually than the Labour letters) and a few attend conferences – free of charge – arranged by these parties. A colored man is an asset to most platforms, religious or political, nowadays, and tends to make any organization look more successful.

Emphasis on only the institutionalized aspect of this sort of philanthropy, however, may give the wrong impression. Difficulties can arise in any self-conscious friendship on an intra-personal level between white and colored people. One very kindly English lady approached me because she was perplexed and hurt by the ungrateful treatment she had received from an African girl who had been introduced to her at church and whom she had invited to tea. The girl came, but did not appear a second time. Gradually Miss Grant's hurt feeling began to turn to indignation, until she felt herself the victim of gross ingratitude. She told me that such people were inferior, primitive, and "could never be like us." The African girl, on her side, may have been irritated by an experience which seemed to her to be what Sartre, in *Portrait of an Anti-Semite*, calls "a demonstration of tolerance." It is sadly ironic that it is just these people who reach out a hand of friendship – but for the wrong reason – who may most subtly endanger easy relations between colored and white people. Some of them make a supreme effort to be broadminded and arrive at the point where they are willing to make the experiment of entertaining a Negro in their homes, but socially created barriers prove too strong for them. They become embarrassed by the Negro's self-consciousness. Neither can speak or act spontaneously and naturally because each feels that he is being evaluated. In the present state of race relations in Britain, at the outset of any acquaintance between people of different color, whatever the education or sophistication of those concerned, there is this evaluation of attitudes.

Colored students at Oxbridge are rarely faced with the more obvious problems of race prejudice. As members of the University they belong to a select group, an elite of its kind, and it is only when they leave Oxbridge during the vacations that they feel bound to assert their social identity as Oxbridge men. College and University ties and other insignia on clothing tend to be worn in London, Birmingham and Manchester rather than in Oxbridge itself. But the more subtle problems of condescension and of conditional philanthropy confront them even at Oxbridge. The Negro "wants to be greeted as a man," as Sartre says of the Jew, "and even in those circles into which he has managed to penetrate," it is as a Negro that he is received. He is the "good" Negro, the Negro "who is the exception, and whom one sees out of friendship and in spite of his race," or, equally, because of his race, which can be just as humiliating. The Negro in such a situation cannot retaliate as he can when confronted with overt aggression. It may be because this is so that students speak of it as an extremely frustrating experience which they all, at some time or another, go through. Some manage to laugh it off, and feel rather sorry for the kindly white people. Others feel ridiculed, and are suspicious that this is being done purposely to put them in an inferior position. On the whole, reactions in Oxbridge tend to be of the former kind.

Negroes at Oxbridge nearly always discuss this problem in both its institutionalized and its interpersonal aspects, in interviews, for they are on their guard and quick to notice when they are being "handled." Sometimes they are introspective and analytical concerning their own reactions. A West Indian told me that he felt "bitter" against one large socio-religious movement "because it is too patronizing an atmosphere for me." He described a meeting during which Colonial and other colored students were asked to stand up to show the international character of the gathering. Afraid that the ushers were coming round to him, he walked out quickly, and since then, he said, he had been "very wary."

Another West Indian said:

At first it is very difficult. You want to do the right thing, and if you have any pride at all you get hurt. There are certain groups of people who invite one in one's first term – church and chapel groups, international and religious societies and others. They speak to you very nicely, but all the time they seem to be thinking, "I wonder whether he can read?" or "Does he use a knife and fork?" One man came up to me in my first term and asked me if we got good books in the West Indies, and I said, "Yes." He was an ignorant man – though very kind – and he said, "Do you have Little Dorrit?" or some such silly book by Dickens which everyone knows. As if we had never heard of it out there! It is dreadfully difficult if you are at all proud. But they don't mean it. The religious people – they seem to start befriending you because they say, "Well, we all want to get to Heaven, so here is a good opportunity of exerting benevolence on this colored man." Especially for the Barbadian it is hard. Because there you have been brought up to think of yourself as coming from "Little England," as it is called – and you suddenly discover that you aren't English at all, and that all the English consider you an outsider and uncivilized. And you were so proud of belonging to "Little England" at home, and English history was your history, and you were a part of it – you thought. In our first term lots of people invited us and were kind to us like that. But we soon learned to distinguish between them. We were very sensitive at first. But now we don't go any longer. You can soon tell really. With my friends at college I never discuss race relations and color at first, and then, after I have been fairly friendly with them for about a term, I feel I want to discuss these things with them to see what they really think. And some are very embarrassed and don't want to discuss it – and say that they see no difference and can't we talk about something else? ... But there are others who are not embarrassed, and we get to talking about these problems – and then we can become good friends. And then I realize that the first sort of people were often those who just wanted a queer collection for their parties. You know – in college they invite you to a party so as to have it a bit unusual. And they think they are doing you a favour! ... Now when I go to parties and meetings I wonder why I am invited.

Thus Negroes soon acquire the art of out-maneuvering the philanthropist. The initial bewilderment is replaced by a strategy of avoidance – or, perhaps by tolerance of the philanthropist, for the sake of possible material advantages. For example, a highly skeptical member of a certain religious organization was enjoying first class air travel to and from conferences, and free holidays in a country mansion. He paid for this by becoming the conference's "exhibition Negro."

Others are too proud to accept this treatment. They may attempt some categorization of white people's behavior towards them; they feel that if they can conceptualize and "place" it, they are better able to resist its implications. Thus, a Ghanaian said, "There are three types of Englishmen who show an interest in colored people. Those who are interested and entertain you because their religious or political beliefs teach them to. Those who are curious about how you behave, and want to see what a black man does with a knife and fork ... And those who are genuinely interested in you as a person." Another man told me, "There are three types of strained interracial relationships possible. Hostility and rudeness, avoidance, and over-kindness" – and, taking it for granted that I should understand the first two, he went on to describe in greater detail the behavior which really irritated him – "'I hope you don't mind me asking, but what country do you come from?' These people are very embarrassed. They take it for granted that their skin color is superior of course. Lots of people try to be kind. I don't want them to try to be kind. They make too much of an effort – overdo it." Negro students are often concerned to understand sociological techniques which will enable them to analyze the more subtle forms of prejudice which they encounter – and, among these, conditional philanthropy is by far the most humiliating, and, although easy to detect, is the most difficult to resist openly.

The friendship which is proffered in these cases is based upon condescension and pitying interest, and is conditional upon the acceptance of inferior status by the colored man. It may find its expression in a liberal-minded paternalism in which the kindly authority and superior wisdom of the individual acting as "father" is maintained over the individual acting as "son" – a situation implied in the oft-quoted mythical words of the white man to a young Negro, "I am glad to have you as my son. But never as my son-in-law." This is not equality. The paternalist is often full of goodwill and tolerance, but he sees everything in Africa and the West Indies in terms of Western – or even purely English or English middle-class – cultural values. He sees the relation between Britain and the underdeveloped countries as one between leader and led, teacher and taught, and finds it impossible to appreciate the existence of indigenous cultural values. With this severely limited viewpoint he is likely to become disappointed when the African does not respond wholeheartedly to his outstretched hand. He is rendered incapable of the sort of understanding that might result from trying to see the world with an African's eyes. Thus it is that the Negro is divested of social personality by those people who go out of their way to befriend him. He becomes an anonymous unit in a color group towards which his white host feels benevolent sympathy. It is even difficult for him to talk about this to white people lest he should be misunderstood. But a man can feel more degraded by this enforced anonymity than by overt hostility. He is treated not as a person, but as a "thing" towards which attitudes of friendship and toleration are directed, on principle, by kindly and well-meaning people. This is a problem of race relations confronting the educated and liberal-minded British today. For to treat a man as an equal one must feel him as an equal – and that, unfortunately, is not a question of deliberate effort.

Shirley Graham

From "Minority Peoples in China" (1961)

The first overwhelming impression of the Peoples [sic] Republic of China is of its many people. They are all along the way as one drives in from the airport – on foot carrying loads on their backs, driving carts, pulling carts, driving oil tanks, in pedicarts and motor trucks, on bicycles. They are in the nearby fields, working the ground or constructing buildings beside the road. When one drives through the gap in Peking's ancient wall, the throng multiplies. And one is struck by the many different kinds of people, different colors of skin, varying sizes and contour of face. The westerner is prone to exclaim, "But they don't look Chinese!"

Density of population in China was cited in the past as excusing the crimes of the exploiters. Cheap labor was "natural" because laborers were so numerous. Floods and famine were explained as dispensations of a "divine Providence" which thinned out overcrowded cities. Today this land is rapidly coming to contain one-fourth of the total world population, but nobody in China deplores the fact. Nobody is worried about it. Where once was fear and dread is now confidence. Of all the rich resources of the land none is so highly valued, none so carefully tended, none promises so bountiful a return as its many people.

About six percent of the 680 million people in China belong to national minorities which, in the past, were driven or fled into the mountains or most distant border regions. Oppressed and exploited by the ruling majority, despised, excluded from development in the regions, hunted down by Japanese invaders and enslaved by Kuomintang despots, many of these people lived in the most primitive conditions. The new Government now names fifty-one different minority nationalities which were separated from each other and from the dominant majority by location, language, customs and rigid laws forbidding marriage, or indeed, any contact outside the community. This classification, however, will be even larger if dialects, differing religion and tribal affiliations be taken into account. The one common denominator between all these minorities was fear and hatred towards other peoples. No matter how primitive was the social system, whether tribal, slave or feudal, each nation had its own small ruling class at the top, with its mass of degraded toilers at the bottom. And each had its fierce religious taboos, superstitions and priesthood.

In some cases the minority people had been the original inhabitants of the land (as were our own Indians), but had been pushed back, though not destroyed, by the Hans who have been the dominant people for near two thousand years. When the Manchus came to power in China they imposed cruel oppression on all non-Manchu nationalities. Even the proud Hans were forced to till the earth. In time, however, Han landlords shared with Mongol princes and Manchu nobles in holding high position and ruling all other peoples. Gradually the Manchurians were absorbed by the Hans until by the beginning of the 20th Century only the Manchu dynasty could be sure of "pure" Manchurian blood and only in the Imperial Court and in a small northwest province was the language of the Manchus spoken or written. The 94 percent of majority Hans now represent the Han people plus vanished nationalities and individuals of nationalities which through hundreds of years they have absorbed.

Not all minority peoples were concentrated in a particular territory. As example, the Huis, numbering about 3,900,000 are scattered throughout China. These people are descendants of Arabs, Turks, and Persians who migrated to China between the 8th and 9th centuries. The first to come were soldiers sent by the Abbasid Caliph al Mansur in 756 to help the reigning Tang Emperor suppress a rebellion in China's northwest regions. After victory these men were granted land and settled down, marrying local women. A little later, Arab and Persian merchants began arriving in China. During the Tang and Sung dynasties many of them made their homes permanently in China. These were Muslims who brought their faith with them. Records show that in the year 878 there were 200,000 foreigners (mainly Muslims, but also Christians and Jews) in Canton alone. But the Huis have suffered long and continued persecution. Right through Kuomintang rule they were mocked as "people with queer ways". As late as 1948 two mosques – one in Peking and one in Tientsin – were destroyed by Chiang Kai-shek's troops. To escape discrimination in education and employment, many Huis, like other minority people, concealed their origin.

Such was the situation with regard to minority peoples when Peoples [sic] Republic of China was established in 1949. The years of wars and constant struggle from 1911, when the Manchu dynasty was forced to abdicate, to the victory of the People's Liberation Army in 1949, had brought little change in the regions occupied by national minorities. They had been forced to fight by warlords; boys had been dragged off to the Army and left dying on the road. War had only made their lot harder and brought famine into every home. But now it was the task of the new Government to convince these peoples that the triumph of the Liberation Army was their triumph, that they too had been liberated from the old life of hardships, to show them the path to a better way of life. This was a most difficult task. Article III of the Peoples Constitution declared:

The People's Republic of China is a single multi-national state. All nationalities are equal. Discrimination against, or oppression of any nationality, and acts which undermine the unity of nationalities are prohibited. All nationalities have freedom to use and foster the growth of their spoken and written languages, and to preserve or reform their own customs and ways. Regional autonomy applies in areas where people of national minorities live in compact communities. National autonomous areas are inalienable parts of the People's Republic of China.

Stating a policy is one thing. Carrying it out in the face of century old customs, patterns of thought, backwardness, prejudices and ignorance is something else. With the minimum of delay and the maximum of good will, the Chinese approached this task in the simplest and most direct manner. The areas where minority peoples lived were the poorest in all China. And so the first representatives of the new Government brought food and clothing. They brought salt. Doctors, most of them women, without lectures or criticism, began helping mothers with their children, began tending the sick and old people. The first reaction to these newcomers was suspicion, hatred and distrust. Sometimes the head of a village or clan flew into a rage and ordered them away or isolated them. But then came others with seed for planting, in some cases they brought in the first plows ever seen in the area and here and there were bands of strong, young workers who began opening roads and building bridges. Even the most ferocious animal in time recognizes a friend. And these minority peoples were not animals. Silently they watched the newcomers hastily build a big house – bigger than any house they had ever seen. Timidly, they asked questions. "This is a school for your children," they were told. But they did not know the meaning of the word "school."

In 1951, on the outskirts of Peking, the College of Nationalities was opened. "College" was a rather ambitious designation, reflecting the plan for the school rather that [sic] what, at the time, it actually was. In the beginning, the College of Nationalities was simply an institution offering schooling to anyone who because he or she was a member of a minority nationality, had been denied education. The schooling was given on whatever level was required. From the outlying minority regions were sent the brightest and most alert of the young people who, in addition to being taught fundamentals of reading, writing and arithmetic, were taught how to analyze and renew worn out soil, improved planting and harvesting methods, land drainage and land irrigation. Each student was also given some understanding of his own nation's history and a realization of why his people were as they were. Backwardness was shown as the result of oppression and superstition. No attempt was made to change the students [sic] cultural patterns or religion. Because there are eating taboos for adherents of certain faiths, special kitchens were set up in the College of Nationalities where cooks prepared different foods in carefully separated pots.

Within an amazingly short time these students were returning home to become teachers in the newly built schools. Westerners might look with disdain upon these young teachers, many of them still in their teens, who only the year before could neither read nor write. But they knew their job. Where a schoolhouse had been built, they assembled the children. If there was no schoolhouse they set about building one. They went to the fields and talked quietly to the workers, gave them handfuls of fresh seed and suggested how it *might* be handled. Old methods are not easily uprooted, especially in a land where what ones [sic] ancestors did was regarded as sacred, but when the new ways were shown to be easier and to produce more crops, the elders began taking notice. The young teachers were patient and steadfast. Slowly, at first, and then more rapidly, changes became apparent.

Among the most backward peoples of the world were the Yis who lived along the northeastern border of Yunnan. An unsatisfactory census taken in 1950 estimated 70,000 people of Yi nationality. Some five percent were slave-owners, holding more than two thirds of all land. Fourteen per cent were outright slaves, living about the households of their masters, who could sell, give away or kill them. Thirty-three per cent were serfs who had the use of small patches of land on which to grow, but who had to work in the master's fields. Their children were not regarded as freeborn, but as slaves. The Yis were divided into two castes – Black Yis (Nosu) and White Yis (Punosu). The minority of Black Yis was the ruling caste, while White Yis were the slaves who worked under the whip and ate the leavings from their masters [sic] meals. Some masters fettered the feet of the slaves after work at night. And the distinction of Black and White Yis did not come from skin coloring. But because, down through the ages, it was said and believed that *Black Yis had black bones!*

This was one of the more difficult minority regions and the new Peoples [sic] Government approached the problem on a level which took into account the powerful ruling class. It encouraged the settling of ancient feuds and attempted to bring together contending nobles who lived in constant fear of each other. They too were ignorant, backward and lived without comfort. Masters were helped to understand that change would benefit their entire nation and thus provide them with the opportunity to advance themselves. Some were soon willing to try out the plans offered by the People's Government. This called for the freeing of all slaves and more time was necessary for persuasion and arguments. When the slaves were freed and the land redivided, the owners were allowed to keep a reasonable number of fields, all their cattle, houses, farm implements and stores of grain. Most nobles were not too unhappy about this. But it would be unreasonable to suppose that *all* were willing to be separated from any part of their lands or to give up one slave. Some resisted to the bitter end. The last resort of the new People's Government was to *invoke the law*. The new Constitution *abolished* slavery within the borders of the People's Republic of China. The slaves had to have land. The Government redivided the land, provided the liberated slaves with building material for homes, draught animals, seed grain and farm tools. By the summer of 1957, agriculture among the Yis was proceeding through mutual cooperation. Former masters and former slaves today point to the marvelous improvements in their mode of living.

The minority nationalities concentrated on the border areas of Yunnan Province had no written language. China's linguists are now compiling outlines of about four-fifths of the minority languages throughout the country, with phonetics, grammar, vocabulary and development. The seven nationality languages whose outlines have been completed are those of the Hani, Tai, Kawa, Nahsi, Lahu, Lisu and Chingpo peoples. This includes altogether about 1,800,000 people. Since liberation linguists have designed scripts for the language and created written languages where they did not exist. Editors are now compiling simple books and dictionaries to facilitate study by minority peoples.

One of the smallest national groups in China are the Olunchuns. They were formerly wandering tribes of hunters whose hunting grounds were on the northern spurs of the small Khingan Mountains, in northeast China. Cone-like birch bark tents were their only homes. They migrated from place to place according to their hunting activities. Primitive life in this cold, mountainous region were [sic] extremely hard even without Japanese invaders and cruel oppression from war-lords. As it was, the

Olunchuns almost dwindled away. In 1949 the People's Government gave their figure as 910.

The new government provided the Olunchuns with grain, guns, cartridges and clothing. They paid them for serving as forest fire protection squads. In time houses were built for them to settle down in. They were also taught farming which had heretofore been unknown among them. Seed and farm implements were provided. As the peoples' [sic] interest developed hunting and farming "parties" were organized. Gradually they learned to eat cereal and cloth took the place of animal skins as their clothing.

The new Olunchun Autonomous Hsiang is a settlement located in Hsunke County, Heilungkiang Province. It consists of sixty-seven households with Olunchuns comprising eighty per cent of the population. Early in 1958 the settlement formed four brigades for hunting, agriculture, deer breeding and subsidiary occupations. By the end of the year, the settlement's earnings rose 159 per cent. The area under crops has been expanded, giving an output of nearly 600 kilogrammes for each person. These people are now not only self-sufficient in cereals, but are even able to sell some grain. It is a notable fact that during the recent months when so much of China's cultivated land was washed away and famine threatened certain regions, the Olunchuns of the northeast were able to rush grain to stricken areas.

The Olunchuns have now developed fur and leather tanning. They have a maternity home, nursery, school and library. All school-age children have free education. Some are in Middle Schools, others have been sent to the College of Nationalities in Peking.

Though there are now Nationality Institutes in nearly every province in China where students may receive Normal School or Technical Training, in February of 1959 there were 2,498 students from forty-six national minorities registered at the College of Nationalities in Peking. This institution is now a college in every sense of the word and only students who have completed Secondary and Middle Schools are admitted. Instruction here is given in the Han language which these advanced students must now thoroughly master. A number also attend the Foreign Language Institute which is close by where they broaden their education by learning Russian, French, English or German. These young people of differing national backgrounds are now being trained for leadership in the entire Peoples [sic] Republic of China. They may go into advanced scientific study, engineering – the whole world is theirs! Wherever they are and whatever they do, they will be integrating their people into the cultural and scientific advancement of the whole country. And wherever they go or whatever they become they will carry with them the rich, cultural background of their national heritage, which in the days now forever gone, it was wisest and safest to hide.

They are the favored ones, today, these young people of once despised national minorities. And other Chinese smile indulgently, and say softly, "We are all Chinese! China has endured and is itself because of its many people."

12

Technology, Progress, and Environment
Introduction by Kimberly Hutchings

The study of international relations is intertwined with questions of technology and progress (or regress). In the late nineteenth and early twentieth centuries, liberal internationalists celebrated the globalizing potential of technological developments such as the railway and telegraph.[1] At the same time, they worried about the development of lethal technologies and argued for international legislation to limit the use of weapons such as poison gas or aerial bombing. In the latter half of the twentieth century, modernization theories, in which all societies could play catch up to the affluent west through technological transformation, existed in parallel with apocalyptic imaginings of nuclear war and ecological disaster. In the twenty-first century scholars identify similar paradoxes in relation to digital and cyber-technologies for world politics. On the one hand, these new technologies may usher in a realm of global democracy and peace, on the other hand they may condemn us to an era of post-truth, global surveillance, autonomous weapons, permanent war, and environmental devastation.[2] Underlying this utopia/dystopia dialectic is a gendered narrative in which "man" uses technology to recreate the world and then finds himself the victim of technology's power. Some of the thinkers discussed below embrace the terms of this gendered imaginary. Others incorporate reflection on how men's and women's relation to scientific, industrial, communication, and military technologies is, or should be, different.[3]

---

[1] See D. R. McCarthy (ed.), *Technology and World Politics: An Introduction* (London: Routledge, 2018), and for a more complex account of the different meanings of technology see E. Schatzberg, *Technology: Critical History of a Concept* (Chicago, IL: Chicago University Press, 2018).

[2] See K. D. Haggerty and V. Ericson (eds.), *The New Politics of Surveillance and Visibility* (London: University of Toronto Press, 2006); Corien Prin, *Digital Democracy in a Globalised World* (London: Edward Elgar, 2017); Benjamin R. Barber, "Three Scenarios for the Future of Technology and Strong Democracy," *Political Science Quarterly*, 113:4 (1998): 573–589.

[3] For a recent account of the different ways in which men's and women's relation to technology is mediated by patriarchal stereotypes and a sexually segregated labour

The lives of the thinkers represented in this section span an era of intense technological change, with transformative effects on international (and household) political economy, colonial administration, international communication, travel, migration, bureaucracy, and surveillance, as well as on the logistics and weapons of war and revolution. The texts take us from the very earliest uses of aeroplanes in warfare prior to the First World War (Suttner's *Barbarization of the Skies*, 1912) to the era of the Vietnam War (Sontag's "On Photography," 1973). Although some of the thinkers embrace straightforwardly progressive or apocalyptic narratives, none of them endorse the idea of technological determinism, and most of them are nuanced in their approach to technology in relation to world politics.

In addition to strong endorsements of industrialization and modernization (Rand) and pioneering arguments about ecological destruction (Carson), we find normative ambivalence about the relation between technology and progress, and an interest in the detail of how different types of international actor approach and understand different technologies. For example, Mead and her team of UNESCO researchers address the question of technological progress in development policy from a perspective of cultural relativism that undermines standard accounts of the "advanced" and the "backward." Matossian develops a classification of different ways in which intellectuals in decolonized or decolonizing states respond ideologically to the industrial "backwardness" of their nations. Gowing meticulously plots the interactions between scientists, bureaucrats, and politicians that first led to the development of the Atomic Bomb, and then to its detonation at Hiroshima and Nagasaki. Sontag reflects on how photography is used, and how it transforms navigating and understanding a world in which both passport photographs and pictorial war journalism are normalized.

The 1899 and 1907 Hague conferences saw the first sustained effort to enshrine the banning of certain weapons in international law.[4] Bertha von Suttner (1843–1914), a founder of the Austrian Peace Society, was a major player amongst European activists that had lobbied for this development. She attended both conferences and had high hopes that they signaled what she saw as a catching up of "civilized" people's *moral* development with their *technological* development. Von Suttner was at

market, see Marie Hicks, *Programmed Inequality: How Britain Discarded Women Technologists and Lost the Edge in Computing* (Cambridge, MA: MIT Press, 2017).

[4] Nobuo Hayashi, "The Role and Importance of the Hague Conferences: A Historical Perspective," UNDIR Resource, 2017, www.unidir.org/files/publications/pdfs/the-role-and-importance-of-the-hague-conferences-a-historical-perspective-en-672.pdf (accessed February 1, 2021).

this time one of the most famous peace activists in the world.[5] She had become famous in the wake of the publication of her novel, translated as *Lay Down Your Arms* (1894, first published 1889). The novel chronicled the gradual realization by its heroine, Martha, of the horror and futility of war, and built on Suttner's knowledge of Austria's aristocratic military class. In her memoirs she notes: "There was at that time as little talk of an anti-duelling league as of a league in opposition to duels between nations. To be exposed to murdering and being murdered was simply one of the chivalraic and patriotic necessities that life brings to men."[6]

Suttner typified predominant views about her age as an age of progress. She was enthusiastic about the idea of European civilization and about the ways in which science and technology could enable the improvement of economic and political life. In her view, however, technological advances were too often perverted by lack of moral progress, in particular when it came to what she saw as attachment to the "barbaric" and "brutal" mores of inter-state competition and war. In this respect, the "conquest of the air," which became increasingly certain during the period of the Hague conferences, with the invention of viable airships and aeroplanes, posed particularly difficult dilemmas.[7]

Suttner explored the dilemmas of flying in two publications, her novel *When Thoughts Will Soar: A Romance of the Immediate Future*[8] and the short pamphlet excerpted below, *The Barbarization of the Skies*.[9] The novel is written in a much more hopeful spirit than the pamphlet. In the novel, Suttner waxes lyrical about the beauties of flying, links it to feminine moral sensibility, and celebrates the ways in which it renders borders irrelevant. In *Barbarization of the Skies*, however, the tone is much more pessimistic. She points to the horrors attendant on the weaponization of the air, drawing on the example of the first ever aerial bombing, of Tripoli in 1911 during the Italian invasion of Libya, and the competitive acquisition of military dirigibles and aeroplanes by rival states. The pamphlet is a plea that at the next Hague conference the prohibition against aerial bombing originally introduced at the first conference for a five-year period should be renewed. But there is a strong

---

[5] See Kimberly Hutchings and Patricia Owens, "Women Thinkers and the Canon of International Thought: Recovery, Rejection, and Reconstitution," *American Political Science Review*, 115:2 (2021): 347–359.

[6] Bertha von Suttner, *Memoirs: The Records of an Eventful Life, Volume I* (Boston, MA and London: Ginn & Co., 1910), 138.

[7] Ibid., 401.

[8] Bertha von Suttner, *When Thoughts Will Soar: A Romance of the Immediate Future* (London: Constable & Co. Ltd, 1914), 61.

[9] Bertha von Suttner, *The Barbarization of the Skies*, trans. Belinda Cooper, ed. Hope Elizabeth May (Mount Pleasant, MI: The Bertha von Suttner Project, 2016 [1912]).

sense that Suttner's earlier optimism about the power of international law has disappeared.

Air power did not, in the end, play a decisive military role in the First World War; instead it emerged as a key civilian and commercial, as well as a military, technology in the interwar period. As flying became more familiar to much larger publics, a massive popular enthusiasm for aviation developed and became part of new kinds of internationalist thinking, which we represent with Elizabeth Lippincott McQueen (1878–1958).[10] McQueen is not easy to classify as an international thinker and activist.[11] Information about McQueen's earlier life is scant. An American, from New Jersey, her father was a Methodist minister, but at some stage she became a licensed Christian Science practitioner and her faith was crucial to her particular brand of imperialist liberal internationalism and "air-mindedness." According to her own report, McQueen experienced a kind of epiphany when visiting Palestine (established as a British mandate in the Versailles settlement) on a relief mission, as a member of the US branch of an Anglo-American Society, based in London, in 1919/20, when she saw seven aeroplanes substitute for two regiments of soldiers.[12] This experience inspired a vision of flying as the antidote to war and led her to research into aeronautics, and to develop the idea of air-mindedness, in particular of women's air-mindedness, as the key to international peace. In fact, it is not clear that McQueen did make the connection she claims in 1920 in Palestine.[13] Evidence suggests that it was more likely her own first experience of flight and the successful Atlantic crossing by Lindberg that encouraged her to put together her existing, religiously grounded belief in Anglo-American power as the guarantor of world peace with the notion of air-mindedness.[14]

McQueen founded the Women's International Aeronautical Association (WIAA) in 1929, which, in addition to encouraging and publicizing women aviators, also spread the gospel of air-mindedness, one that McQueen continued to proselytize into the 1950s. For her, flying was not linked to peace simply because of the ways in which it

[10] Waqar Zaidi, "Liberal Internationalist Approaches to Science and Technology in Interwar Britain and the US," in Daniel Laqua (ed.), *Internationalism Reconfigured: Transnational Ideas and Movements between the World Wars* (New York: I. B. Tauris, 2011), 17–44.

[11] Tamson Pietsch, "Elizabeth Lippincott McQueen: Thinking International Peace in an Air-Minded Age," in Patricia Owens and Katharina Rietzler (eds.), *Women's International Thought: A New History* (Cambridge: Cambridge University Press, 2021), 174–206.

[12] Ibid., 179.   [13] Ibid., 182.   [14] Ibid., 186.

enabled international friendship through making it easier to travel and communicate across borders. Rather, thinking the values of universality and non-territoriality, as embodied in flying, actively constructed a peaceful world. Air-mindedness could heal the world's conflicts in the same way as prayer could heal the body. Air-minded *thinking* did the work of peace, rather than aviation technology.

The interwar period was a time in which internationalist organizations, such as the WIAA, had significant influence on popular understandings of international relations. However, as internationalist optimism about the future of world politics faded in the 1930s, the high tide of internationalist international associations and societies also receded. Most contemporary students of IR will be aware that the period of the late 1930s into the 1950s Cold War era saw the rise in importance of social science and realist ideologies in popular and expert analyses of international relations. Less well-known is that this was also a period in which anthropologists sought to influence the general public's as well as international policy-makers' understanding of the factors that conditioned conflict and peace.

By the 1930s, cultural relativism had become the dominant approach within the discipline of Anthropology, of which Margaret Mead (1901–1978) was a prominent representative.[15] Mead is now most famous for the controversies surrounding her classic 1928 anthropological study *Coming of Age in Samoa*, in which she appeared to prefigure Beauvoir (see the section on Men, Women, and Gender) in claiming that gender identities were predominantly cultural constructions. However, during the Second World War in the United States, Mead became a celebrated public figure for her popularly written book *And Keep Your Powder Dry*,[16] in which she used America to exemplify her views about "national character" and the link between culture and personality. Mandler argues that Mead and her fellow anthropologists were remarkably successful in embedding assumptions about the links between individual and national character in popular understanding and policy approaches to dealing with allies and enemies in the wartime context, for example in propaganda and intelligence operations.[17]

However, in a post-war context in which deterrence and modernization theories and a battle between rival universal ideologies

---

[15] Peter Mandler, *Return from the Natives: How Margaret Mead Won World War Two and Lost the Cold War* (New Haven, CT and London: Yale University Press, 2013).

[16] Margaret Mead, *And Keep Your Powder Dry: An Anthropologist Looks at America* (New York and London: Berghahn Books, 2000 [1942]).

[17] Mandler, *Return from the Natives*, 85.

were dominating the international agenda, Mead found that cultural relativism had lost its purchase on the imaginations of social scientists, policymakers, and the general public. She soon gave up on policy work, after producing a report for UNESCO on technological change in non-industrialized cultures.[18] This report challenged the premises of modernization theory and technological determinism, and associated vocabulary: "Phrases like 'under-developed,' 'backward,' 'simple' – to the extent that they cover a whole culture – are equally defeating" (654–655). Instead, Mead's work on technology and development envisages a creative encounter between foreign expertise, material techniques, and cultures. She argues that using "modernized" locals is not necessarily the most helpful way to encourage the embrace of new technologies to cultures. In fact, she is dismissive of the "native" actor, educated in or by the colonial metropole, seeing them as lacking in cultural authenticity. For analysts such as Mary Matossian (b. 1930) however, the Westernized leader in industrially backward countries provided a key to understanding the new ideological dynamics of nationalism in world politics.[19]

Matossian's analysis replicates elements of Mead's "culture and personality" idea, but in a way that universalizes rather than contextualizes the psychology of the nationalist and/or anticolonial intellectual. In "Ideologies of Delayed Industrialization," originally published in 1958,[20] she argues that nationalist leaders, including Gandhi, Sun Yat Sen, Atatürk, Stalin, Mussolini, Nehru, and Nasser, forge their sense of self and their nationalist/anticolonial ideologies through their ambivalent relation to the industrialized "West." This ambivalence has common implications in contradictory attitudes towards industrialized modernity, and being caught between archaism (looking back to a golden age) and futurism (looking forward to a revolutionary new order).

Matossian's generalizations echo earlier Euro-American civilizational discourses, in which Russians, Turks, and southern Europeans represent inferior positions in a racialized hierarchy with Anglo-Saxons at the apex and Africans at the base. She notes: "the Kemalists glorify their ancestors

---

[18] *Cultural Patterns and Technical Change: A Manual Prepared by the World Federation for Mental Health and Edited by Margaret Mead.* UNESCO Tensions and Technology Series (Paris: UNESCO, 1953).

[19] The historian Mary Matossian's earlier work was focused on the USSR, Armenia, and modern authoritarian ideologies. Although her work on delayed industrialization has been influential, she has become more well-known for her later work, in particular Mary Kilbourne Matossian, *Poison of the Past: Molds, Epidemics and History* (New Haven, CT and London: Yale University Press, 1989).

[20] Mary Matossian, "Ideologies of Delayed Industrialization: Some Tensions and Ambiguities," *Economic Development and Cultural Change*, 6:3 (1958): 217–228.

as brave, tolerant, realistic, generous, peaceful, and respectful of women: in short 'spiritual' examplars of the well-bred Western European gentleman" (660). The fact that her argument became a reference point for scholarship on processes of industrialization and economic development in "underdeveloped" states testifies to continuities between Matossian's Cold War context and those of Suttner and McQueen, who also took Western civilizational superiority for granted.

Matossian rejected the idea of technological determinism and was interested in the ideational and affective dimension of human relations to technology. Her argument is essentially about a love/hate relationship with the "West" on the part of leaders of industrially "backward" countries and cultures, and it assumes an intimate link between individual psychology, political ideology, and domestic and foreign policy. Matossian's thesis about ideologies of delayed industrialization contrasts sharply with the contemporaneous rise in the United States of rationalist strategic and deterrence theories, quantitative and formal methodologies in the study of military strategy and foreign policy from the 1950s onwards. This was particularly evident in the analysis of the nuclear arms race in US universities and think tanks following the USSR's development of the atomic bomb in 1949, which gave rise to the breed of (almost always male) "defense intellectuals" that became the object of Carol Cohn's ethnographic research in the 1980s.[21]

The UK tradition of thinking about military and strategic matters remained more empirical and historical than that of the United States during the Cold War. The UK had developed its own independent deterrent in 1952, and the UK Atomic Energy Authority commissioned a history of Britain's atomic energy program, the first volume of which dealt with the Anglo-American relationship in the development of the first atomic weapon. This volume, *Britain and Atomic Energy*, was published in 1964.[22] It established the reputation of its author, Margaret Gowing (1921–1998), as a world authority on nuclear technology, weapons, and policy. Gowing's subsequent two-volume *Independence and Deterrence*, co-researched with Lorna Arnold, was published in 1974.[23] Gowing was a historian and civil servant, eventually an academic, first at the University of Kent and then as the first Professor of the History of Science at Oxford in 1973.

---

[21] Carol Cohn, "Sex and Death in the Rational World of Defense Intellectuals," *Signs*, 12:4 (1987): 687–718.

[22] Margaret Gowing, *Britain and Atomic Energy 1939–45* (London: Macmillan, 1964).

[23] Margaret Gowing, with contributions from Lorna Arnold, *Independence and Deterrence: Britain and Atomic Energy 1945–52: Volume I. Policy Making; Volume II. Policy Execution* (London: Macmillan, 1974).

Gowing's work typifies approaches to military and strategic studies in the UK, in contrast to formal and quantitative approaches in the United States. Nevertheless, her work became a reference point on both sides of the Atlantic for what it revealed about the Anglo-American relationship, including America's side-lining of Britain in 1945 and in the immediate post-war period. Although she had no scientific training, Gowing explained nuclear science in layman's terms and detailed the internal logic of scientific research in relationship to the world of policy. She had access to an extraordinary range of government papers as well as to oral testimony from many of the scientists, soldiers, bureaucrats, and politicians involved. Her work explained the importance of scientific and technological challenges as well as of interpersonal relations in the development of atomic weapons, but also told a bigger story about Anglo-American relations and shifts in geopolitical dynamics as the United States looked beyond the end of the Second World War. Gowing is clear that the fundamental reason for using the bomb was to end the war with Japan, but she also indicates that, with hindsight, a different strategic calculation might have been made as to the conditions for Japan's surrender. Even accepting that the use of the bomb was strategically justified, she captures the sense of unease and foreboding shared by scientists in the aftermath of Hiroshima and Nagasaki.

Although casualty figures and horrific injuries were as great in the mass bombings of Dresden and Tokyo as in the bombings of Hiroshima and Nagasaki, atomic bombs generated new kinds of distant and long-term destructive effects. These effects are cited by the marine biologist Rachel Carson (1907–1964) as part of the human "war" against nature that is destroying the earth's ecology in her 1962 book *Silent Spring*.[24] After its publication in the United States and UK, *Silent Spring* was published rapidly in translation in France, Germany, Italy, Norway, Denmark, Sweden, Finland, Spain, Brazil, Japan, Iceland, Portugal, and Israel.[25] Although the focus of the book was on environmental damage in the United States, it inspired environmental activism across the world.

At the time that *Silent Spring* appeared, there was virtually no acknowledgment of the relevance of ecology to international relations in dominant discourses, whether as an aspect of international policy or as a focus of social scientific research or of normative analysis.[26] In this respect,

---

[24] Rachel Carson, *Silent Spring* (Boston, MA: Houghton Mifflin, 1962).

[25] Paul Brooks, *The House of Life: Rachel Carson at Work* (Boston, MA: Houghton Mifflin, 1972), 311–312.

[26] An exception is the work of Margaret and Harold Sprout, who appear elsewhere in this volume.

Carson's work did not fit into an existing body of activism or scholarship, though it developed some of the ideas of a woman scientist from an earlier generation, Ellen Swallow Richards (1842–1911), arguably the originator of ecological theory in its modern sense.[27] Carson criticized instrumental and piecemeal approaches to using technology because they neglected the holistic relationship between physical and social environments. Industrial technology altered the environment in a negative feedback loop.

Carson was a scientist, but her language in *Silent Spring* is highly affective. She draws on familiar rhetorical tropes that contrast the harmony and peace of nature with the disharmony of technological intervention. She also explicitly masculinizes her targets of big business, industrialized agriculture, and the state. Her critics accused her of a feminine lack of rationality and logic, and, falsely, of criticizing all forms of technology.[28] Within the United States, her arguments had a significant impact not only on the beginnings of environmental social movements and policy development, but also on a developing critique of materialism and capitalist consumerism in the later 1960s and 1970s. Ayn Rand (1905–1982) has this latter development in her sights in her polemical defense of capitalist industrialization.[29]

Of all the thinkers discussed in this section, Rand is the one who most explicitly defends and celebrates industrial technology. Like Matossian, she also links technological advance with moral and political progress, and treats the world as split between the "West" and the "rest." Rand had fled the nascent USSR in the wake of the 1917 Revolution. She was ideologically committed to a particular version of American values of liberty and individualism, which, she argued, could thrive only in a capitalist free market economy. In stark contrast to Carson, she argues for a dichotomy between humanity and nature, in which only humanity has intrinsic value. A prolific novelist, as well as a public intellectual, Rand's philosophy is encapsulated in her novel *Atlas Shrugged*, which pits a technological elite of inventors against the ignorant masses.[30] She quotes extensively from this novel in her argument against environmental legislation and anti-consumerist lifestyles. She compares the latter to a racist stereotype of feudal decadence in India, and argues that

[27] Robert Clark, *Ellen Swallow: The Woman Who Founded Ecology* (Chicago, IL: Follett Publishing Co., 1973).
[28] Brooks, *The House of Life.*
[29] Ayn Rand, *The New Left: The Anti-industrial Revolution* (New York: Signet Books, 1971), 145–148.
[30] Ayn Rand, *Atlas Shrugged* (New York: Penguin Books, 1992 [1957]).

anti-technological ideologies are designed to perpetuate elite control of the masses by keeping them tied to a struggle for subsistence.

Carson and Rand replay a familiar dystopia/utopia opposition between technology as a source of destruction on the one hand and of liberation on the other. In contrast, Susan Sontag (1933–2004) offers a nuanced analysis of the nature and political effects of one particular technology, that of photography. At one point in her narrative, Gowing records how the British, having been increasingly excluded from American research and decision making, had adapted a camera to get a photograph of "the fireball and the blast wave in order to get an approximate estimate of the yield" in the bombing of Nagasaki. No photograph was taken because of weather and logistical issues.[31] As far as I am aware, Sontag never commented on this particular vignette, but it illustrates several of the points that Sontag makes in her essay.[32]

Sontag was reflecting on photography at a high point of photo-journalism in situations of war and conflict. Her essay offers a careful analysis of the effects of photography on photographer and viewer. She examines the way that taking a photograph seems to "capture" reality, and how this objectifies and thereby distorts the truth of the subject photographed. Although we think that the image of the child fleeing the napalm attack is equivalent to knowing the nature of the attack, in fact the image tells us nothing about the experience, the context, or the temporal dimension that are necessary for understanding. Yet we presume that through seeing such images "we can hold the whole world in our heads." In contexts of violence, Sontag argues that photographic images can reinforce and build moral positions. However, she denies the idea that a photographic image has political effects purely in itself: "Without a politics, photographs of the slaughter bench of history are not identifiable as such" (687). In fact, as just another image, one photograph easily becomes equivalent to another, so that pictures of "colonial wars and winter sports – are equalized by the camera" (682). She agrees that photographs can jolt political awareness, yet they are more likely to depoliticize atrocities by making them familiar.

Sontag points to the role of photographic technologies in the international management of populations, from espionage to passport control: "The 'realistic' view of the world compatible with bureaucracy redefines knowledge – as techniques and information. Photographs are valued because they give information" (688). Overall, Sontag's analysis veers towards the dystopian in her assessment of photographic technology,

---

[31] Gowing, *Britain and Atomic Energy*, 380.
[32] Susan Sontag, "On Photography," *New York Review of Books*, October 18, 1973.

but she also insists that this is not about technological determinism, in which the image controls reality, but about how human beings respond to images. We do not have to accept the image as given, our interpretation of it is our responsibility: "Strictly speaking, there is never any understanding in a photograph, but only an invitation to fantasy and speculation" (689).

Traditional framings of the question of technology in IR interpret "man" in masculine rather than generic terms. The technologies in question are large-scale industrial or military technologies, invented and managed by men, operated by workers and soldiers, instruments for the reshaping of the world and perhaps also of those that manipulate them. Some of the thinkers in this section challenge this gendered rendition of the meanings of technology and progress. Both von Suttner and McQueen argue for the feminization of airpower through the transformation of the predominant masculinist imagination of what it means to take to the skies. Carson explicitly plays on the association of feminine qualities with organic nature as opposed to the destructive masculinism of the "war" against nature. More subtly, Mead's discussion shows how international/intercultural politics plays itself out in domestic contexts and argues for a collaborative and creative approach to technological change. In contrast, Rand is enthusiastic about the human capacity for invention and the control of nature, and Matossian identifies the superiority of the "West" with advanced industrialization. Gowing's analysis, whilst acknowledging a range of chance and affective factors, ultimately understands the bomb as an instrument for policy. Within this selection of texts, therefore, we find a range of thinking about how technology has an impact on different aspects of world politics and vice versa, and the role of different kinds of international actor in mediating that relationship.

Kimberly Hutchings

Bertha von Suttner

From *The Barbarization of the Skies* (1912)

Fifteen or twenty years ago, the penniless inventors who carried with them plans for construction of steerable balloons or flying machines approached the leaders of the peace movement. Help us to conquer the air, they said, and war will be overcome. The reasons they gave were more or less the following: borders would be obliterated, since neither barriers, nor toll fences, nor fortifications can be erected in the air; traffic, simplified and accelerated tenfold, would bring nations even closer than railroads and steamers already do; through this closeness, hostilities would vanish; and through the general rejoicing that such a wonderful achievement would arouse, people would rise above their petty hatreds and jealousies.

These arguments made perfect sense to the pacifists, and they would have liked to provide the inventors' experiments with the necessary funds. As we know, however, the coffers of peace are empty; only in the ministries of war can financial support be had.

What in theory is so clear, so logical, and so mathematically certain, and seems as incontrovertible as the formula $2 \times 2 = 4$, suddenly transforms in practice into its opposite, and two times two yields any other figure as easily as four.

Now the air had been conquered; we can fly over every border and soar ... and war has yet another weapon.

And a weapon that may prove to be the most diabolical of all those yet employed.

Ultimately, logic and mathematics are right after all. Two times two is – though in roundabout ways – infallibly four, and the art of flight – even if it is used for war – will destroy war.

In what way? This will be explored later. For now, we will give a concise historical review. Not all the way back to Icarus, but only to the first Hague Peace Conference.

In 1899, when delegates from 26 nations met in The Hague to discuss the prevention of war (but unfortunately also the waging of war), in Paris work was proceeding diligently on the construction of airships that solved the problem of steerability. Rumors arose that a solution had been found; then it was said that the attempts had failed, and recently news of renewed success has surfaced. I recall that W. T. Stead wrote in his conference chronicle, which appeared in a Hague newspaper, that "the French are going to circle the 'Haus im Busch,' where the meetings are taking place, with a steerable balloon and thus prove in one fell swoop that in the future, it will no longer be possible to wage war."

The Conference considered the question, and the Convention on the Customs of War adopted a prohibition on dropping explosives from the air. Duration of this treaty: five years. Even the aficionados of war by any conceivable means who signed this limitation might have thought, 'There's no hurry with dirigibility; the problem certainly won't be solved in the next five years, if ever, so we can sign safely'.

Eight years later, in 1907, when the second Hague Conference met, France already possessed a number of dirigibles, and Zeppelin had triumphed in Germany. The five-year treaty term was over, and the prohibition was renewed but not ratified.

So was bombardment from the air permitted?

"My God," went the reassuring answer (one cannot imagine anything more calming, soothing, pouring-oil-on-troubled-waters than the assurances of military experts when they are questioned by anxious civilians about the future results of their precautions) – "My god, the airships are only used for reconnaissance; it's not possible to aim and hit from such altitudes while eying by – it would be easier to spit on nickel coin on the pavement from a balcony on the fifth floor than to bombard a target on the ground or a body of water from a balloon. No, no, only lay people could go on about shooting from above; the dirigibles will only be used for reconnoitering, and for that they are invaluable."

Invaluable – for whom? For us or the others? In extolling "improved" methods and tools, it is always forgotten that the so-called merits and advantages of weapons neutralize each other, and all that remains is greater harm on both sides.

In the meantime, news came from America that the Wright Brothers had constructed flying machines, heavier than air. This would have been the real conquest of the heights; flying machines. But what a dream, what a utopia. The news from America was apparently a humbug. Or if a couple of pitiful jumps in the air had really succeeded, how far was this from real flight, from the practical use of the aeroplane in war and peace – in how many decades (if ever) would one really achieve anything with it. Once again, there was "no hurry". But look: aeronautics and aviation spread at a furious pace – the Eiffel Tower was circled, the English Channel crossed. This was in 1909.

A brief three years, and where are we today?

In every country, bureaucracies of war are introducing air troops. Even the Republic of China has purchased Etrich monoplanes in Wienerneustadt for military purposes. Where will we be in ten years if things continue at this pace? The experts refuse to answer such questions. The issue is always the current task. Our neighbor has an airship, ergo I have to build one too; the other neighbor ordered two aeroplanes, I have to have two or if possible three. Every other consideration and prudence is pushed aside with this calculation.

Incidentally, any arguments about whether airships or flying machines should be introduced as weapons of attack have been overtaken by the facts – the weapon has already been introduced. The Italians used the first "torpedine del cielo" in the Tripoli war, and ever since, dropping bombs from the sky has been part of the experience and customs of war, and thus of international law.

From the point of view of the science and philosophy of war itself, the conquest of the air is a tremendous upheaval. For a time, people will attempt to transfer old methods and old concepts to this entirely new field; thus they now speak, for example, of the battle for "control of the air." Even the "so-called control of the sea" was an illusory concept transferred from the field of actual control of a piece of ground to the unconquerable stretches of the ocean; but what can be owned and controlled in the endless realm of the air, no one can say.

The whole system of war – all its rules, one could say – is built upon the following prerequisites:

two opponents face each other at their borders and strive to cross them, or to prevent the other from doing so; seek to gain and maintain positions; perhaps march on the capital, and if they succeed, dictate the peace.

Even in peacetime, to make this game more difficult, forts are built on the borders and the ground countermined; farther inland more fortifications, each of which must be taken before an advance is possible, and in addition each village, each estate, each cemetery where they clash is turned into a firm position.

At sea, the same game is facilitated by fleets reaching the coast, the crossing of which is made more difficult by external fortifications and mines. And now these new forces – the flying ones – are added. Now the crossing of borders is child's play. One need not be held back by fortifications for long. Not only because they can be destroyed from above with a couple of loads of piroxin; they can simply be ignored.

Death rains down from the clouds on troops deployed and in camp; railroad bridges are destroyed from above, squadrons eliminated; in the sky, however, the boundless, unobstructed sky, there are no positions to gain, and thus there can be no decision. If, under all newly created conditions, states still want to go to war with all the types of weapons previously introduced, it is as if two chess players were to sit down at the board and declare:

We want all the old rules to apply: the pawn still moves only one square, the knight jumps as before; the queen retains the most power, the king can still safely castle; but we are adding a new rule: each of us can drop something on the board from above and upset all the pieces. A nice game – the chess masters will be grateful.

The pieces have been grateful all along.

Elizabeth Lippincott McQueen

From "Talk at Aviation Luncheon" (1934)

Our hostess, Mrs. Hutchings, has requested me to speak on Women's International Association of Aeronautics and on Peace. These two are synonymous, for my objective has been 'Peace By Air' since my return to the U.S.A. from Egypt in 1920.

A word about our officers might be interesting to you.

Our President Lady Hay-Drummond-Hay, has recently returned from a visit to Marshal Italo Balbo at Tripoli, now Governor General of Libya, Italy's African colony. Her strikingly interesting interviews with the Marshal were printed in the Brittania magazine.

Our Vice Presidents are: Ruth R. Nichols, the Hon. Mrs. Victor Bruce, Thea Rasche and Lady Isobel Chaytor.

The smiling, sweet Ruth Nichols speaks for herself. She is one of the outstanding fliers in the United States.

The Hon. Mrs. Bruce has been flying for charity in England, for the benefit of hospitals there.

Thea Rasche, "the most respected and popular pilot in Germany" as Lady Hay writes, is editor of a Berlin aviation magazine.

Our Secretary, Amy Somermeir, is now touring Central Europe and will finish, in eight months, a round-the-world tour in the interests of our association. Our Treasurer is Mrs. Lloyd Stearman, wife of the President of the Lockheed Manufacturing Company.

For myself, as Founder, I can only say that I give most of my time and money to the service of aviation for the great cause of Peace which is in the depths of my heart. Peace for all the world is my high ambition.

Christ's message: "Peace on earth, good will toward men": can be realized today. Peace and love are the same and war and hate are the same. The great thinkers of all ages have tried to teach us the greater potency of love. If women would concentrate on peace, give up the petty things of life and devote their time and energy to working for peace they could turn the thoughts and acts of nations toward that great goal. It is

647

sane thinking that will bring peace. War is insanity, and the millions of men who have been killed in wars have not helped the world to progress.

Right now every one listening to me can decide to become an advocate of peace and spread the good propaganda.

If the individual would work for peace in the home, in the office and in the club, there would be no wars nor rumours of wars.

Myriad wings in the air will make for peace. The more wings the greater assurance of peace for the country who has the wings.

Our unruly member, the tongue, can be taught to speak the word of peace on all occasions. Proverbs tells us that: "Death and Life are in the power of the tongue."

When I was in Tein-Sin, China, the very intellectual Chinese president of the Chamber of Commerce, called our attention to the name of the vast ocean stretching between China and the United States. "The Pacific, – the peaceful tie," he said. "An example and behest to all people that peace should exist forever between us." Let us hope the $ 5,000,000 airplane plant being built in China by the Curtiss-Wright Corporation will spread wings of good will over that country.

An army officer told me this week that aviation has taken on a new stride and instructions have just come from Washington to make night flying a major study. He remarked there is not a chance for immediate war as the countries are not financially fit. "If they did try it", he said, "lack of resources would make them stop." He also stated that France is the best equipped of all countries and she does not want war.

Mrs. Roosevelt, on her visit to California in 1933, said to me that it was her opinion that wars would cease when there was a better understanding between nations.

Permit me to thank you women pilots at this luncheon today for your splendid esprit de corps. In the determination to make aviation a sound, safe mode of sport travel I hope you will be the leaders, and will soon surpass England who now leads in private flying.

With our 211 airports here in California, and with 1460 passengers being carried on air transports every 24 hours, flying at almost 200 miles per hour, we can well be proud of our air-wise country.

As there were only 8 passenger fatalities on transport lines in 1933 we are assured of safe flying. With only 539 women pilots in the U.S.A. there is much work to be done to increase this number and encourage timid women to try the safety of air travel.

Many women pilots carry mascots because they think they will bring good luck. There is one fine woman who doesn't worry about mascots. I asked Amelia Earhart what mascots she carried when she was flying and with characteristic directness, she answered: "I prefer a good mechanic to a mascot."

The aerial police of our association are comprised of outstanding, expert birdwomen in the large cities of the U.S.A. and in the following foreign countries: Argentine, Australia, Austria, Belgium, Canada, Czecho-Slovakia, Denmark, England, Finland, Germany, Hungary, Japan, New Zealand, South Africa, Switzerland and Turkey.

The initials are S.S. – Secret Service. Service:– Assistance is offered to pilots lost or in distress. These police learn first aid; keep scrap books of press clippings of air records made by women in the various countries; supply information as to air laws, air maps, air routes and airports. Pistol target practice is recommended for them. Secret Service:– They keep records of press clippings of any criminal proceedings against women fliers.

These women are outstanding figures in their communities, and some are in the employ of their governments.

In case of fires, floods, earthquakes or disasters of any kind, these aerial police women can be called upon by the Chief of Police of their respective cities.

The women's aerial police was organized July 29, 1933 with Amy Johnson Millison accepting the first membership.

Our members of the WIAA throughout the world know that Peace is our objective, our real goal, and I am delighted to be able to co-operate with Mr. Frank Miller and Mr. and Mrs. Hutchings of Mission Inn for a Shrine of Friendship that will bring fliers from all over the world to meet at this charming spot in amity and peace.

Thoughts and words are a powerful vibratory force moulding the world's affairs, so why not put our minds in the air for Peace.

We have had thousands of years of war. Let us now look up and forward to centuries of peaceful development.

Margaret Mead

From *Cultural Relations and Technical Change* (1953)

Where specific technical practices are to be introduced into a culture or a part of a society which has not hitherto used them, it is desirable to strip these technical practices of as many extraneous cultural accretions (from the lands of origin) as possible. This recommendation applies to such varied matters as mass production, methods of immunization, development of alphabets for unwritten languages, methods of antisepsis or of sanitation, etc. It is realized that the technologies and inventions of modern science are themselves the outgrowth of a very particular historically limited type of culture – a culture in which the focus of interest has been upon the observable, the repeatable, the measurable, upon using the external world as a model even when processes within the body were concerned.

[...]

Western trained professionals carry about with them an enormous amount of cultural baggage which could very well be discarded. [...] Extraneous and culturally destructive effects can be avoided by stripping each scientific technique to the bone, to the absolute essentials which will make it possible for other people to learn to use it, and to handle it in a living, participating, creative way.

This recommendation applies not only to stripping scientific practices bare of the particular habits of the members of the Western society within which a practice was developed, but also to the advisability of leaving behind the particular rationalizations and sanctions, both religious and scientific, with which a specific practice may have been associated in a given Western country. For example, the insistence that individual will power should be invoked in teaching good nutritional usage is the result of a blend of Protestant Christian conceptions of the human will and scientific findings as to the best way to utilize a given set of food resources. In another culture, pleasure in eating, or customary compliance with ritual arrangements of food, may be invoked instead.

650

[...]

The model for such a procedure, by which the end product of modern technology is reinterpreted in terms of particular cultures, was established in the United States during World War II, when the question was raised how recipes were to be developed for using new dried food products which resembled no known kind of food. As long as recognized food staples were distributed by the nationals of a country carrying out a food relief programme, a question like this was seldom raised, and the result was the kind of misery and ill feeling which came from assuming that European populations would eat maize. But these new synthetic foods were as strange to Americans as they would be to Greeks or Japanese. Because they were relatively unencumbered with traditional sentiments, were in fact stripped down to the barest essentials, the question of what to do with them could be asked. Experimental groups were set up among women from different countries for whom these were designed as relief foods, to explore the range of different ways in which the same synthetic food might be used as hot soup or cold dessert, or simply as an ingredient in a made dish. Once this exploration was completed, although it did yield suggestive recipes and insights about differences in cultural practice, it seemed clear that the best advice was: (a) Do not set up any fixed way of using the new foods which will inevitably be special to American food habits and; (b) in each country get local cooks, who may be trusted, if given support and latitude, to work out ways of adopting the new strange materials, of turning what was food only in the scientific sense – in that it had been demonstrated to contain the necessary nutrients for human beings – into food in the cultural sense, something that people would eat and be nourished by.

In this instance, the synthetic food, because it was new, had as yet little weight of cultural meaning, except in matters like colour. But for most of the technological change which is introduced from one part of the world to another, the burden of the habits and beliefs of the people who developed a particular technique is heavy. It will be necessary to set about stripping each practice down, as well as building up training and development methods which permit each new culture which takes over a particular technique to contribute new patterns of use. This means a style of analysis which asks of each procedure: What is the scientifically essential, the minimum core of this operation? In regard to a thermometer questions would be asked about size, shape, colour, the use of the particular system of measurement, the way "normal" was marked; the preference for a mouth or a rectal thermometer: the phrasing of high and low temperatures; the phrasing of the meaning of temperature deviations as showing that an individual was sick, or that an individual was putting up a fight against disease, etc.

In building a factory questions would be asked about such matters as size and shape – Does a factory have to have walls? Should the assembly line move the object or should a moving platform move the men along with the objects? How long is a shift? What should control the tempo of the operation? – as well as the more obvious question of how an operation of a factory type should be set up in a society with entirely different patterns of human relations.

But one of the great advantages of first stripping each technological change to the core, of querying the most time-honoured accretions and practices, is that the experts then genuinely need constructive thinking by members of the culture where they are going to work. Because the situation is new, no one can give them a recipe, and usually the culturally workable answer can only be arrived at by experiment – with living human beings from the culture in question. If a thermometer is not even to look like our thermometer, then what is it to look like? If a factory is not a building with walls, what is it? If dried beans are not bean soup, what are they? The scene is then set for the participation of the members of the other culture, in which the experts with experience – knowing their helplessness in this area of re-design – will welcome help, and the gifted members of the culture in which the device or process has never been used will be able to contribute imaginatively. By this very contribution they will lay the groundwork for the mental health of all the members of their society who must learn to take temperatures or work in factories.

Obversely, a sensitive attention to the way in which the existing techniques of the country to which change is being brought are interwoven with the local value system is also important. So it may be found that agricultural practices are tied up with an image of the earth as a mother who gives food and is fed, and an image of mutual giving – by man, care and fertilizer; by the earth, food for man – may be used for the new agricultural techniques.

When the particular values of a given culture are to be used as vehicles for change, such a use should be planned and applied by those members of the culture who share the belief or the aspiration which is to be used. Those who are engaged either in introducing technological change or in providing for a cushioning or muting of the effects of technological change, have become increasingly aware, during the last few years, of the advantages of couching a change in terms which are familiar to a given society, in supporting a new practice by quoting an old sacred text. At the same time, many discussions among experts reveal a deep disquiet about such a procedure, a disquiet which manifests itself in questions, such as whether it is possible to imbed modern scientific practices in age-old systems of religious values. [...] These questions reveal a dilemma, in which the secularized expert asks how in fact he – who does not believe in a particular system of values, and shows, by his every act, his adherence to a secularized scientific system of values – can with any integrity use these values, which he believes to be outmoded and wrong, to accomplish such ends as the introduction of literacy and public health.

This problem, however, is also soluble if it is referred to the general principles of cultural integrity. If members of the group of people who are to use the new technology themselves do the planning, then they will be adapting their own beliefs, and quoting their own sacred texts, restructuring their own lives, in accordance with the common sub-goal of infant welfare or universal literacy, which they share with the technical experts from the city, from the modernizing sector of the population, from another country, or from an international agency. For a man who himself believes in no God to search the Koran for an appropriate text to support methods of preventing well polution [sic] will, at best, limit his efficiency and make his commitment to the effort of guaranteeing a population pure water less whole-hearted. At worst, it introduces an element of manipulation into the operation which reduces the dignity of those whose holy texts are quoted to the level of puppets, whose strings are pulled by an arrogant and alien hand. But if the people themselves, steeped in the traditional wisdom of their scriptures, transform the new knowledge into a new expression of an ancient and beloved revelation, then the dangers of lack of spontaneity, falseness, manipulation and degradation are avoided.

Careful attention to this principle of participation will also help to deal with one of the most serious dangers in the purposive introduction of new technologies among peoples who have newly come to trust in and desire the scientifically based achievements and values of the West. Among such peoples a great many of those who acquire an education in medicine, or engineering, or agriculture, will have had to make a considerable break with their own traditions, and will have compensated for this by embracing – with the self-protective zeal and blindness of the convert – the beliefs and practices which they associate with the new knowledge. Their willingness to assume a whole series of symbols – from fountain pens, raincoats and brief cases to an insistence upon marriage for love, and the disregard of traditional patterns of inter-personal relations – is often an essential step in the particular path of modernization or westernization on which they have determined, or for which their own society has selected them. But they are, for this very reason, seldom the appropriate persons to adapt the new practices to the traditions which are still shared by the masses of the people.

[…]

For example, a critical observer, watching from a distance, may be impressed with the way in which local officials in the Indonesian Republic have adapted the traditional shadow play to their programmes of keeping the people of the villages informed about the changes which are being vigorously pursued throughout Indonesia. This new shadow play has ordinary human characters and has been stripped of supernatural elements. But this use of the shadow play is viewed with deep and genuine scepticism by young political leaders, who feel that the shadow play itself should be eradicated as lending inevitably an inappropriate aura of religious awe to the modern national leadership. For an educator who felt this way to plan to use the shadow play would mean either a compromise with his principles or an expression of pessimism and contempt for the villagers who, from his point of view, are steeped in age-old mysticism. If, however, some programme of information is entrusted to village leaders, who entertain no such scepticism and who themselves feel the shadow play to be a most appropriate way of educating the people to take part in the work of developing their country, then there is no such question as compromise or insincerity. […] a new synthesis will take place, which is organic because it has occurred within the same human organisms, which is harmonious because it is an expression of individual human beings' efforts to make sense of their own lives.

As each culture is a whole, however sorely torn at the moment – whole in the sense that it is the system by which and through which its members live – in all relationships between cultures, each must be accorded dignity and value. Much of the present phrasing of technical assistance planning, and much of the present evaluation of change within a country, is conducted with explicit or implicit denial of the dignity of members of those countries which, while often the inheritors of much older traditions, have not been in the vanguard of those aspects of culture which stem from modern science. This is self-defeating, in that it arouses violent resistances and attempts at compensation and retaliation from those whose feelings of self-esteem have been violated; it is also contrary to the findings of modern psychiatric practice, which insist on the recognition of the patient's validity as a human being. Phrases which divide the world into the "haves" and the "have nots", overvalue bread and plumbing and devalue music and architecture. Those whose status is defined as a "have not" may come to repudiate the possibility of learning anything at all, or of sharing anything at all except "bread" with those who have so denigrated their cherished ways of life. Phrases like "under-developed", "backward", "simple" – to the extent that they cover a whole culture – are equally defeating. If, instead, we draw on an image in which two adults – one experienced in one skill, another in a different skill – pool their knowledge so that each can use the skill of the other for a particular task, as when foreign explorer and local guide venture together into a forest, much more viable relationships can be set up. Leaders of the newest countries, only recently established by revolution or mandate or negotiation, are young adults, not children – less experienced but not less adult than those upon whose skills and resources they need to draw. […] A very little scrutiny, if the whole culture is taken into account, is enough to do away with assumptions of superiority, and to permit the establishment of working partnerships, in which engineer and architect, scientist and sage, pool their different but not incompatible wisdoms. The most complex invention of the Western world – radar or psychoanalytic therapy – is still only part of a way of life, to which others, skilled in ways of life which have developed differently, may be expected to contribute new insights. The sensitive application of a gadget, or the rejection of some use to which it has callously been put, may be as great or even greater a contribution than the invention of the gadget itself.

Mary Matossian

From "Ideologies of Delayed Industrialization" (1962)

It is difficult to discern, at first glance, any important common characteristics in ideologies such as Gandhism and Marxism-Leninism,
Kemalism, and Shintoism. If they have anything in common, it seems
to be a strong infusion of self-contradiction. But on second glance the
diverse characteristics and geographic origins of these ideologies fade
into the background. In their very self-contradictions one may detect
recurrent patterns.

The recurrent patterns can, I think, be accounted for by the similarity
of context in which these ideologies have emerged. This context is the
industrially backward country which has the following characteristics:
(1) it has been in contact with the industrial West for at least fifty years;
(2) in it there has emerged a native intelligentsia composed of individuals with at least some Western education; and (3) large-scale industrialization is currently being contemplated or has been in progress for no
more than twenty-five years. The ideologies which have emerged in such
conditions would include Marxism-Leninism, Shintoism, Italian
Fascism, Kemalism, Gandhism, the current Egyptian Philosophy of
the Revolution, Sun Yat-sen's Three Principles of the People, the
Indonesian Pantjasila, and many others.

Industrially backward countries have two common problems: the
destruction of traditional institutions and values, sometimes even before
the impact of industrialism is felt; and the challenge of the modern West.
The "assaulted" individual must reorient himself in at least three directions: (1) in his relationship to the West, (2) in his relationship to his
people's past, and (3) in his relationship to the masses of his own people.
It is the "assaulted" intellectual, and his relationship to the uneducated
masses, which will be considered here in particular: for although everyone has ideas and wishes, only intellectuals devise ideologies.

Ideology may be defined as a pattern of ideas which simultaneously
provides for its adherents: (1) a self-definition, (2) a description of the

current situation, its background, and what is likely to follow, and (3) various imperatives which are "deduced" from the foregoing. In ideology there is a strong tendency to merge fact and value, to superimpose upon "things as they are" the things that are desired. Sjahrir, the Indonesian socialist, said that the weaker the intellect, the greater the element of wish in the formulation of a man's thought. He has held that the element of wish is strongest among "backward" persons. Perhaps it would be more accurate to say that the intellectual in an industrially backward country cleaves to contradictory propositions because of the situation in which he finds himself. His experience and his present problems tend to direct his reasoning into certain channels. His ego needs protection which science and logic cannot provide. This seems to be true of all men to some extent. If the intellectual is to lead the masses of an industrially backward country in the undertaking of great endeavors, he must provide them with incitement balanced by comfort, with self-criticism balanced by self-justification.

To seek a "morphology" and "natural history" of ideologies of delayed industrialization seems premature, given the present state of Western knowledge. The following analysis is not intended to provide neat answers to big questions, but to indicate some areas where further probing might be productive. [...] Thus, all ideologies of delayed indus-trialization are essentially revolutionary – in Mannheim's usage, utopian. They direct activity toward changing a social order which is already changing. Even the superficially conservative ideologies turn out to be pseudo-conservative in the sense that they advocate a change in the status quo. Pseudo-conservative or radical, these ideologies advocate the manipulation of the disagreeable Present. In this sense, *Les extremes se touchent.*

The first problem of the "assaulted" intellectual is to assume a satis-factory posture vis-a-vis the West. The position taken is frequently ambiguous, embracing the polar extremes of xenophobia and xenophilia. The intellectual may resent the West, but since he is already at least partly Westernized, to reject the West completely would be to deny part of himself. The intellectual is appalled by discrepancies between the standard of living and "culture" of his own country, and those of modern Western nations. He feels that something must be done, and done fast. He is a man on the defensive, searching for new defensive weapons. As Gamal Abdul Nasser wrote to a friend in 1935: Allah said, "Oppose them with whatever forces you can muster!" But what are these forces we are supposed to have in readiness for them?

Another characteristic of the "assaulted" intellectual is his uneasy attitude toward himself and his own kind – the intelligentsia and middle classes. Often he scorns his kind (and by implication, himself) as "pseudo", "mongrel", neither truly native nor truly Western. In order to find self-respect, he goes in search of his "true self"; he tries to "discover India"; he revisits the West. For example, Gandhi wrote in 1908:

"You, English, who have come to India are not good specimens of the English nation, nor can we, almost half-Anglicized Indians, be considered as good specimens of the real Indian nation."

[...] The "assaulted" intellectual works hard to make invidious comparisons between his own nation and the West. He may simply claim that his people are superior, as did Gandhi: "We consider our civilization to be far superior to yours". Or he may hold that his ancestors had already rejected Western culture as inferior. But these assertions can elicit conviction only among a few and for a short while. More often the intellectual says, "We are equal to Westerners", or "You are no better than I am." Around this theme lies a wealth of propositions: (1) "In the past you were no better (or worse) than we are now". (2) "We once had your good qualities, but we were corrupted by alien oppressors". (3) "We have high spiritual qualities despite our poverty, but you are soulless materialists". (4) "Everything worthwhile in your tradition is present or incipient in ours". The slogan, "trade, not aid", when used metaphorically, is another variation on this theme, The nationalist claims to seek a blend of the "best" in East and West. But why must both East and West inspire the new culture? Behind this there is perhaps the implicit wish to see the "East" a genuine partner, an equal, of the West.

The foregoing postures vis-a-vis the West may be comforting to the intellectual, but they will not stimulate action unless certain imperatives are "deduced" from them. For example, "We must purge our national culture of alien corruptions and realize our true character which has been lying dormant within us." But doses of self-criticism are equally important incentives to action, because they make it impossible to relax in complacency. [...]

Another man who administered blunt criticism was Mustafa Kemal Ataturk, who told the Turkish Grand National Assembly in 1920, "We have accepted the principle that we do not, and will not, give up our national independence. Although we always respect this basic condition, when we take into consideration the level of prosperity of the country, the wealth of the nation, and the general mental level, and when we compare it with the progress of the world in general, we must admit that we are not a little, but very backward."

Ataturk praised the Turkish nation, however, for high moral qualities and great past achievements. Although he was probably a xenophile by conviction, he succeeded to a remarkable degree in overcoming the xenophobia of his people by means of his ideological rhetoric.

[...]

Ataturk justified the importation of specific alien inventions, such as terms from non-Turkish languages, with the assertion that the so-called import was actually indigenous: according to the Sun Language Theory, Turkish was the mother of all the languages of the world, so that "borrowed" words were actually prodigal sons come home. This technique of encouraging an import by calling it indigenous was complemented by the technique of eradicating the indigenous by calling it imported, For example, Ataturk pointed out that the fez was a head-gear imported from Europe a hundred years before.

When the intellectual in an industrially backward country surveys modern Western civilization, he is confronted with five hundred years of scientific, artistic, social, economic, political, and religious developments. He sees a flood of heterogeneous Western cultural elements, from jazz to steel mills, pouring into his country. Then, fearing that he will be "swamped" by the deluge, and lose his own identity, he tries to control cultural imports, In order to do this, he must find a standard to determine exactly what should be borrowed. The standard used by the nationalist is that the element to be imported should be in "conformity" with his own national culture and should serve to strengthen his nation. This formula is very elastic, and can be used to justify the borrowing or rejection of practically anything.

The tension between archaism and futurism is another ambiguity in ideologies of delayed industrialization. It is closely related to the xenophobia–xenophilia tension, because the West is "the new" and the native culture is "the old" at the onset of contact. Archaism is an attempt to resurrect a supposed "golden age", or some part of it. This "golden age" is usually not in the disagreeable recent past, but in a more remote period, and it can only be recovered by historical research and interpretation.

For example, Mussolini gloried in imperial Rome and the medieval "corporate state"; the Slavophiles glorified the peasant mir and the indigenous Christian Orthodox practices in Russia; the Shintoists revived an ancient mythology that deified the Emperor; Sun Yat-sen and Chiang Kai-shek exhorted the Chinese to revive Confucian ethics; Gandhi urged that India return to the age of "Rama Raj"; and Ataturk exulted in the barbaric virtues of the Osmanli nomads. [...]

But Nehru condemns archaism:

"We have to come to grips with the present, this life, this world, this nature which surrounds us with its infinite variety. Some Hindus talk of going back to the Vedas; some Moslems dream of an Islamic theocracy. Idle fancies, for there is no going back, there is no turning back even if this was thought desirable. There is only one-way traffic in Time."

Archaism may slip into a futuristic ideology, such as Marxism, and create an ambiguity. Adam Ulam has suggested that Marxism has its greatest appeal for semi-proletarianized or uprooted peasants who are nostalgic for the "good old days" when their actions were governed by nature, the village elders, the family patriarch, and the religious authorities – instead of the less congenial factory boss and the State. To the uprooted peasant Marxism offers a comforting strain of archaism: that is, it envisions a utopia in which state and factory, as coercive institutions, have "withered away".

Whenever a resurrection of the past is contemplated, the question arises, "What part of the past?" or "Which age was our golden age, and why?" Sometimes the age selected is an imperial age, when the people in question enjoyed their greatest authority over others. Sometimes a period of "pristine simplicity" is admired. But new imperial conquests are incompatible with the weak political and economic position of industrially backward countries, and a return to the "simple life" is incompatible with industrialization. In such cases archaism is not a solution to the problem at hand, but an escape from it.

However, there are more constructive uses of the past. The intellectual may discover that in the remote past his people possessed the very virtues which are supposed to make a modern nation great. For example, the Kemalists glorify their ancestors as brave, tolerant, realistic, generous, peaceful, and respectful of women; in short, "spiritual" exemplars of the well-bred Western European gentleman. These "genuine" Turks were temporarily "corrupted" by Arab–Persian–Byzantine culture, but they are now due to take their rightful place among "civilized" nations. The manifest content of such an ideological position may be archaistic, but its latent content is futuristic.

The Communists also use the past in this way. But they have characteristic standards for determining what elements of the past are desirable. The Chinese Communists have cultivated peasant literature and art because they are "progressive", being products of a "progressive" class; whereas gentry culture is rejected as "feudal". In the Soviet Union the pre-revolutionary leaders most cherished by the Communist regime are those it considers "progressive" for their time (such as Peter the Great), whereas "reactionaries" (such as Dostoyevsky, until recently) have been under a cloud.

Nationalists, when selecting elements from their past, ask, "What will tend to strengthen the nation?" But tradition has lost its natural charm, and traditionalism is something the nationalist must "work at". He uses the shared traditions of his people as raw material with which to build national morale; but tradition is a means, existing only for the sake of national strength, and not as an axiomatic, self-justified good. [...]

There are other uses of the past besides escapism, the sanctioning of innovations, the glorification of "progressive" individuals and groups, and national self-strengthening. The past may be used to eradicate what the intellectual feels to be undesirable in the present and for the future. By publicizing the results of historical research, showing that a supposedly indigenous cultural element (like the fez) is of foreign origin, he may thereby stigmatize it. He may use other grounds to stigmatize the Ottoman and Chinese literary languages; they are the languages of reactionary and oppressive ruling classes who have cared only for their own welfare, rather than the welfare of the people.

The concern of both nationalists and Communists for vernacular languages and peasant arts is closely related to a third problem of the "assaulted" intellectual: his relationship with the uneducated masses. Some intellectuals have a sentimental, patronizing, or contemptuous attitude toward the masses. [...]

Other intellectuals, like Nehru, wonder if the peasants are the "true" Indians, while they (the intellectuals) are only "pseudos". The Russian Narodniki went "back to the people" to learn from them and to teach them; and so have Turkish intellectuals in our own century. Undeniably, many intellectuals have felt sincere compassion for the sufferings of the peasants and sincere respect for the folk arts. But it is unlikely that the attitude of an intellectual toward the uneducated masses in an industrially backward country (or in any country) is free from ambiguity: he looks up to "the people" and down on "the masses".

However he may feel about the majority of his compatriots, the intellectual must face the practical problems of industrialization and modernization. The intellectual knows that a government which really *represents* the thinking of the uneducated masses will not attack these problems boldly and comprehensively. The peasant may long for riches, but he is not eager to give up his traditional ways. To attain its ends, the intelligentsia must arouse the masses to strenuous effort, or, as Alexander Gerschenkron puts it, give them an emotional "New Deal".

[...]

In most cases, when an ideology of delayed industrialization emerges, the traditional rulers (king, sultan, tsar, etc.) have been overthrown, or are on the verge of being overthrown. But when traditional rulers remain in power, as in Japan, they are supported by new social groups and assume new social functions. They must now mobilize the masses to meet the challenge of the modern industrial West. Whether there has been a massive social revolution or a "circulation of elites", the cultural revolution is inevitable.

[...]

In order to understand an ideology it is important to determine what problems its initiators are trying to solve. In the case of intellectuals in industrially backward countries, the three main problems are: (1) What is to be borrowed from the West? (2) What is to be retained from the nation's past? (3) What characteristics, habits, and products of the masses are to be encouraged? It is remarkable that intellectuals in widely separate parts of the world have reacted similarly to these problems.

Rachel Carson

From *Silent Spring* (1962)

THE HISTORY OF LIFE on earth has been a history of interaction between living things and their surroundings. To a large extent, the physical form and the habits of the earth's vegetation and its animal life have been molded by the environment. Considering the whole span of earthly time, the opposite effect, in which life actually modifies its surroundings, has been relatively slight. Only within the moment of time represented by the present century has one species – man – acquired significant power to alter the nature of his world.

During the past quarter century this power has not only increased to one of disturbing magnitude but it has changed in character. The most alarming of all man's assaults upon the environment is the contamination of air, earth, rivers, and sea with dangerous and even lethal materials. This pollution is for the most part irrecoverable; the chain of evil it initiates not only in the world that must support life but in living tissues is for the most part irreversible. In this now universal contamination of the environment, chemicals are the sinister and little-recognized partners of radiation in changing the very nature of the world – the very nature of its life. Strontium 90, released through nuclear explosions into the air, comes to earth in rain or drifts down as fallout, lodges in soil, enters into the grass or corn or wheat grown there, and in time rakes up its abode in the bones of a human being, there to remain until his death. Similarly, chemicals sprayed on croplands or forests or gardens lie long in soil, entering into living organisms, passing from one to another in a chain of poisoning and death. Or they pass mysteriously by underground streams until they emerge and, through the alchemy of air and sunlight, combine into new forms that kill vegetation, sicken cattle, and work unknown harm on those who drink from once pure wells. As Albert Schweitzer[33] has said, "Man can hardly even recognize the devils of his own creation."

It took hundreds of millions of years to produce the life that now inhabits the earth – eons of time in which that developing and evolving and diversifying life reached a state of adjustment and balance with its surroundings. The environment, rigorously shaping and directing the life it supported, contained elements that were hostile as well as supporting. Certain rocks gave out dangerous radiation; even within the light of the sun, from which all life draws its energy, there were short-wave radiations with power to injure. Given time – time not in years but in millennia – life adjusts, and a balance has been reached. For time is the essential ingredient; but in the modern world there is no time.

The rapidity of change and the speed with which new situations are created follow the impetuous and heedless pace of man rather than the deliberate pace of nature. Radiation is no longer merely the background radiation of rocks, the bombardment of cosmic rays, the ultraviolet of the sun that have existed before there was any life on earth; radiation is now the unnatural creation of man's tampering with the atom. The chemicals to which life is asked to make its adjustment are no longer merely the calcium and silica and copper and all the rest of the minerals washed out of the rocks and carried in rivers to the sea; they are the synthetic creations of man's inventive mind, brewed in his laboratories, and having no counterparts in nature.

To adjust to these chemicals would require time on the scale that is nature's; it would require not merely the years of a man's life but the life of generations. And even this, were it by some miracle possible, would be futile, for the new chemicals come from our laboratories in an endless stream; almost five hundred annually find their way into actual use in the United States alone. The figure is staggering and its implications are not easily grasped – 500 new chemicals to which the bodies of men and animals are required somehow to adapt each year, chemicals totally outside the limits of biologic experience.

Among them are many that are used in man's war against nature. Since the mid-1940's over 200 basic chemicals have been created for use in killing insects, weeds, rodents, and other organisms described in the modern vernacular as "pests"; and they are sold under several thousand different brand names.

---

[33] Albert Schweitzer: German-Alsatian theologian, philosopher, music scholar, and physician (1875–1965), who won the Nobel Peace Prize in 1952 for his lifelong devotion to providing medical services in Africa.

These sprays, dusts, and aerosols are now applied almost universally to farms, gardens, forests, and homes – nonselective chemicals that have the power to kill every insect, the "good" and the "bad," to still the song of birds and the leaping of fish in the streams, to coat the leaves with a deadly film, and to linger on in soil – all this though the intended target may be only a few weeds or insects. Can anyone believe it is possible to lay down such a barrage of poisons on the surface of the earth without making it unfit for all life? They should not be called "insecticides," but "biocides."

The whole process of spraying seems caught up in an endless spiral. Since DDT was released for civilian use, a process of escalation has been going on in which ever more toxic materials must be found. This has happened because insects, in a triumphant vindication of Darwin's principle of the survival of the fittest, have evolved super races immune to the particular insecticide used, hence a deadlier one has always to be developed – and then a deadlier one than that. It has happened also because, for reasons to be described later, destructive insects often undergo a "flareback," or resurgence, after spraying, in numbers greater than before. Thus the chemical war is never won, and all life is caught in its violent crossfire.

Along with the possibility of the extinction of mankind by nuclear war, the central problem of our age has therefore become the contamination of man's total environment with such substances of incredible potential for harm – substances that accumulate in the tissues of plants and animals and even penetrate the germ cells to shatter or alter the very material of heredity upon which the shape of the future depends.

Some would-be architects of our future look toward a time when it will be possible to alter the human germ plasm by design. But we may easily be doing so now by inadvertence, for many chemicals, like radiation, bring about gene mutations. It is ironic to think that man might determine his own future by something so seemingly trivial as the choice of an insect spray.

All this has been risked – for what? Future historians may well be amazed by our distorted sense of proportion. How could intelligent beings seek to control a few unwanted species by a method that contaminated the entire environment and brought the threat of disease and death even to their own kind? Yet this is precisely what we have done. We have done it, moreover, for reasons that collapse the moment we examine them. We are told that the enormous and expanding use of pesticides is necessary to maintain farm production. Yet is our real problem not one of *over-production?* Our farms, despite measures to remove acreages from production and to pay farmers not to produce, have yielded such a staggering excess of crops that the American taxpayer in 1962 is paying out more than one billion dollars a year as the total carrying cost of the surplus-food storage program. And is the situation helped when one branch of the Agriculture Department tries to reduce production while another states, as it did in 1958, "It is believed generally that reduction of crop acreages under provisions of the Soil Bank will stimulate interest in use of chemicals to obtain maximum production on the land retained in crops."

All this is not to say there is no insect problem and no need of control. I am saying, rather, that control must be geared to realities, not to mythical situations, and that the methods employed must be such that they do not destroy us along with the insects.

The problem whose attempted solution has brought such a train of disaster in its wake is an accompaniment of our modern way of life. Long before the age of man, insects inhabited the earth – a group of extraordinarily varied and adaptable beings. Over the course of time since man's advent, a small percentage of the more than half a million species of insects have come into conflict with human welfare in two principal ways: as competitors for the food supply and as carriers of human disease.

Disease-carrying insects become important where human beings are crowded together, especially under conditions where sanitation is poor, as in time of natural disaster or war or in situations of extreme poverty and deprivation. Then control of some sort becomes necessary. It is a sobering fact, however, as we shall presently see, that the method of massive chemical control has had only limited success, and also threatens to worsen the very conditions it is intended to curb.

Under primitive agricultural conditions the farmer had few insect problems. These arose with the intensification of agriculture – the devotion of immense acreages to a single crop. Such a system set the stage for explosive increases in specific insect populations. Single-crop farming does not take advantage of the principles by which nature works; it is agriculture as an engineer might conceive it to be. Nature has introduced great variety into the landscape, but man has displayed a passion for simplifying it. Thus he undoes the built-in checks and balances by which nature holds the species within bounds. One important natural check is a limit on the amount of suitable habitat for each species. Obviously then, an insect that lives on wheat can build up its population to much higher levels on a farm devoted to wheat than on one in which wheat is intermingled with other crops to which the insect is not adapted.

The same thing happens in other situations. A generation or more ago, the towns of large areas of the United States lined their streets with the noble elm tree. Now the beauty they hopefully created is threatened with complete destruction as disease sweeps through the elms, carried by a beetle that would have only limited chance to build up large populations and to spread from tree to tree if the elms were only occasional trees in a richly diversified planting.

Another factor in the modern insect problem is one that must be viewed against a background of geologic and human history: the spreading of thousands of different kinds of organisms from their native homes to invade new territories. This world-wide migration has been studied and graphically described by the British ecologist Charles Elton in his recent book *The Ecology of Invasions*. During the Cretaceous Period, some hundred million years ago, flooding seas cut many land bridges between continents and living things found themselves confined in what Elton calls "colossal separate nature reserves." There, isolated from others of their kind, they developed many new species. When some of the land masses were joined again, about 15 million years ago, these species began to move out into new territories – movement that is not only still in progress but is now receiving considerable assistance from man.

The importation of plants is the primary agent in the modern spread of species, for animals have almost invariably gone along with the plants, quarantine being a comparatively recent and not completely effective innovation. The United States Office of Plant Introduction alone has introduced almost 200,000 species and varieties of plants from all over the world. Nearly half of the 180 or so major insect enemies of plants in the United States are accidental imports from abroad, and most of them have come as hitch hikers on plants.

In new territory, out of reach of the restraining hand of the natural enemies that kept down its numbers in its native land, an invading plant or animal is able to become enormously abundant. Thus it is no accident that our most troublesome insects are introduced species.

These invasions, both the naturally occurring and those dependent on human assistance, are likely to continue indefinitely. Quarantine and massive chemical campaigns are only extremely expensive ways of buying time. We are faced, according to Dr. Elton, "with a life-and-death need not just to find new technological means of suppressing this plant or that animal"; instead we need the basic knowledge of animal populations and their relations to their surroundings that will "promote an even balance and damp down the explosive power of outbreaks and new invasions."

Much of the necessary knowledge is now available but we do not use it. We train ecologists in our universities and even employ them in our governmental agencies but we seldom take their advice. We allow the chemical death rain to fall as though there were no alternative, whereas in fact there are many, and our ingenuity could soon discover many more if given opportunity.

Have we fallen into a mesmerized state that makes us accept as inevitable that which is inferior or detrimental, as though having lost the will or the vision to demand that which is good? Such thinking, in the words of the ecologist Paul Shepard, "idealizes life with only its head out of water, inches above the limits of toleration of the corruption of its own environment ... Why should we tolerate a diet of weak poisons, a home in insipid surroundings, a circle of acquaintances who are not quite our enemies, the noise of motors with just enough relief to prevent insanity. Who would want to *live* in a world which is just not quite fatal?"

Yet such a world is pressed upon us. The crusade to create a chemically sterile, insect-free world seems to have engendered a fanatic zeal on the part of many specialists and most of the so-called control agencies. On every hand there is evidence that those engaged in spraying operations exercise a ruthless power. "The regulatory entomologists ... function as prosecutor, judge and jury, tax assessor and collector and sheriff to enforce their own orders," said Connecticut entomologist Neely Turner. The most flagrant abuses go unchecked in both state and federal agencies.

It is not my contention that chemical insecticides must never be used. I do contend that we have put poisonous and biologically potent chemicals indiscriminately into the hands of persons largely or wholly ignorant of their potentials for harm. We have subjected enormous numbers of people to contact with these poisons, without their consent and often without their knowledge. If the Bill of Rights contains no guarantee that a citizen shall be secure against lethal poisons distributed either by private individuals or by public officials, it is surely only because our forefathers, despite their considerable wisdom and foresight, could conceive of no such problem.

I contend, furthermore, that we have allowed these chemicals to be used with little or no advance investigation of their effect on soil, water, wildlife, and man himself. Future generations are unlikely to condone our lack of prudent concern for the integrity of the natural world that supports all life.

There is still very limited awareness of the nature of the threat. This is an era of specialists, each of whom sees his own problem and is unaware of or intolerant of the larger frame into which it fits. It is also an era dominated by industry, in which the right to make a dollar at whatever cost is seldom challenged. When the public protests, confronted with some obvious evidence of damaging results of pesticide applications, it is fed little tranquilizing pills of half truth. We urgently need an end to these false assurances, to the sugar coating of unpalatable facts. It is the public that is being asked to assume the risks that the insect controllers calculate. The public must decide whether it wishes to continue on the present road, and it can do so only when in full possession of the facts. In the words of Jean Rostand,[34] "The obligation to endure gives us the right to know."

---

[34] Jean Rostand: French biologist and playwright (1894–1997).

Margaret Gowing

From *Britain and Atomic Energy, 1939–1945* (1964)

The atomic bomb which fell on Hiroshima killed 64,000 people within four months and the bomb on Nagasaki 39,000 people. In addition, 72,000 people were injured in Hiroshima and 25,000 in Nagasaki.[35] At Hiroshima four square miles were totally devastated and nine square miles were very badly damaged. [...] The morality and wisdom of the use of these bombs will be disputed throughout our lives and for such time as they remain the only ones to be used in warfare.

[...]

It is true that the pattern of injury and cause of death from the first atomic bombs were different from those in conventional bombing. For example, burns caused over half the deaths in Hiroshima, radiation thirty per cent, and blast eighteen per cent.[36] It is difficult to assert, however, that it is worse to be killed by radiation than by burns. For those with strong stomachs who care to look at photographs of corpses and survivors, those of the atomic bomb casualties suffering from burns are the most horrible.[37] No doubt the photographs of casualties in Hamburg, Dresden and Tokyo are equally shocking.

[...]

The one type of casualty from the atomic bombs which can be put on a different moral level from those of conventional bombs is the casualty maimed or injured even though he was not present in the towns when the bombs were dropped. This kind of casualty could arise in two ways, and it is important to distinguish clearly between them. Radioactivity from bomb fall-out might linger and cause disease in new inhabitants of the bombed areas. Or children might be born malformed in some way

---

[35] Ashley W. Oughterson and Shields Warren, *Medical Effects of the Atomic Bombs on Japan* (New York: McGraw Hill, 1956).

[36] Oughterson and Warren, *op. cit*. pp. 95–6. These figures are actually for deaths among the first-day injured survivors but they give orders of magnitude.

[37] Oughterson and Warren, *op. cit.*

because their parents or grandparents or remoter ancestors were irradiated by the bombs. The scientists who made the bombs were from the outset, from the time of the Peierls and Frisch memorandum, conscious of the dangers of radioactivity from fall-out. There was concern about radioactive contamination of the ground by the bombs, because this might be described as chemical warfare and be contrary to the Geneva Convention. The height from which the bombs in Japan were released was in fact determined primarily by the wish to make the blast damage as great as possible, but it did also mean that there was very little radioactive contamination in Hiroshima and Nagasaki. Delayed casualties from the bombs, more cases of leukemia for example than there would otherwise have been, are indeed still appearing but these are among people who were themselves irradiated by the bombs when they fell.

[...]

The first atomic bombs were, it seems, wholly comparable with conventional mass bombing attacks in terms of casualties. Why then were they so effective and so terrible? Their effectiveness was largely psychological – the bombs destroyed so quickly and so completely such a large area that defence was hopeless. The mass air raids were not concealed and at least there was warning and a sense of temporary safety. But now one plane carrying one bomb could destroy a city in seconds, without warning. It was this that made the atomic bomb 'unendurable'.[38]

The Second World War and the nightmares that preceded and accompanied it – not only the air raids but the gas chambers and the Japanese prison camps – seemed to have brought mankind to a low pitch of degradation. Total war is inseparable from horror. Since this was so, those American and British scientists of Los Alamos who felt a brief elation when their bombs dropped were not amoral. At least they could feel that their weapon, unlike some other exercises in killing and destruction, was effective. The raids on Hamburg and Dresden, for example, which caused casualties that were greater than those of Hiroshima and Nagasaki, had no decisive effect on the war. But the atomic bombs did at least end the six years' agony.

But however justifiable, even inevitable, the Hiroshima and Nagasaki bombs were, in the light of what had happened in the past, the scientists and the politicians had to face the future. The scientists, helped by the engineers, had drawn a line across history so that the centuries before August 6th, 1945, were sharply separated from the years to come. And though perhaps they did not contemplate the technical 'escalation' of the

---

[38] Testimony of Dr. Philip Morrison, of Los Alamos. (U.S. Congress, Hearings before the Special Committee on Atomic Energy, Pt. 2, p. 233 *et seq.*)

next fifteen years nor think in terms of megatons and megadeaths, of weapons that could obliterate not a single town but half a country, they knew that the atomic age had only begun. They might feel some hope of the bomb as a deterrent to war, and some hope of the peaceful uses of atomic energy. Bur their main feeling on the morrow of Hiroshima and Nagasaki was one of dark foreboding.

Ayn Rand

From *The New Left* (1971)

In today's drugged orgy of boastfully self-righteous swinishness, the masks are coming down and you can hear all but explicit confessions of that hatred. For example, five years ago, on the occasion of the East Coast's massive power failure and blackout, *Life* magazine published the following in its issue of November 19, 1965: "It shouldn't happen every evening, but a crisis like the lights going out has its good points. In the first place, it deflates human smugness about our miraculous technology, which, at least in the area of power distribution and control, now stands revealed as utterly flawed ... and it is somehow delicious to contemplate the fact that all our beautiful brains and all those wonderful plans and all that marvelous equipment has combined to produce a system that is unreliable."

Currently, the *Newsweek* survey criticizes the spectacular progress of the United States, as follows:

"The society's system of rewards favored the man who produced more, who found new ways to exploit nature. There were no riches or prestige for the man who made a deliberate decision to leave well enough alone – in this case, his environment."

Observe that this "system of rewards" is treated as if it were an arbitrary whim of society, not an inexorable fact of nature. Who is to provide the riches – or even the minimum sustenance – for the man who does not choose "to exploit nature"? What is "prestige" to be granted for – for nonproduction and nonachievement? For holding man's life cheaper than his physical environment? When man had to "leave well enough alone" – in prehistoric times – his life expectancy was 15 to 20 years.

This phrase, "'to leave well enough alone," captures the essence of the deaf, blind, lethargic, fear-ridden, hatred-eaten human ballast that the men of the mind – the prime movers of human survival and progress – have had to drag along, to feed and to be martyred by, through all the millennia of mankind's history.

The Industrial Revolution was the great breakthrough that liberated man's mind from the weight of that ballast. The country made possible by the Industrial Revolution – The United States of America – achieved the magnificence which only free men can achieve, and demonstrated that reason is the means, the base, the precondition of man's survival.

[...]

The demand to "restrict" technology is the demand to restrict man's mind. It is nature – i.e., reality – that makes both these goals impossible to achieve. Technology can be destroyed, and the mind can be paralyzed, but neither can be restricted. Whenever and wherever such restrictions are attempted, it is the mind – not the state – that withers away.

Technology is applied science. The progress of theoretical science and of technology – i.e., of human knowledge – is moved by such a complex and interconnected sum of the work of individual minds that no computer or committee could predict and prescribe its course. The discoveries in one branch of knowledge lead to unexpected discoveries in another; the achievements in one field open countless roads in all the others. The space exploration program, for instance, has led to invaluable advances in medicine. Who can predict when, where or how a given bit of information will strike an active mind and what it will produce?

To restrict technology would require omniscience – a total knowledge of all the possible effects and consequences of a given development for all the potential innovators of the future. Short of such omniscience, restrictions mean the attempt to regulate the unknown, to limit the unborn, to set rules for the undiscovered.

And more: an active mind will not function by permission. An inventor will not spend years of struggle dedicated to an excruciating work if the fate of his work depends, not on the criterion of demonstrable truth, but on the arbitrary decision of some "authorities." He will not venture out on a course where roadblocks are established at every turn, in the form of the horrendous necessity to seek, to beg, to plead for the consent of a committee. The history of major invention, even in semi-free societies is a shameful record, as far as the collective wisdom of an entrenched professional consensus is concerned.

As to the notion that progress is unnecessary, that we know enough, that we can stop on the present level of technological development and maintain it, without going any farther – ask yourself why mankind's history is full of the wreckage of civilizations that could not be maintained and vanished along with such knowledge as they had achieved; why men who do not move forward, full back into the abyss of savagery.

Even a primitive, pre-industrial economy, run primarily on muscle power, cannot function successfully through the mere repetition of a routine of motions by passively obedient men who are not permitted to think.

How long would a modern factory last if it were operated by mechanics trained to a routine performance, without a single engineer among them? How long would the engineers last without a single scientist? And a scientist – in the proper meaning of the term – is a man whose mind does not stand still.

Machines are an extension of man's mind, as intimately dependent on it as his body, and they crumble, as his body crumbles, when the mind stops.

A stagnant technology is the equivalent of a stagnant mind. A "restricted" technology is the equivalent of a *censored* mind.

But – the ecologists claim – men would not have to work or think, the computers would do everything. Try to project a row of computers programmed by a bunch of hippies.

Now observe the grim irony of the fact that the ecological crusaders and their young activist followers are vehement enemies of the status quo – that they denounce middle-class passivity, defy conventional attitudes, clamor for action, scream for "change" – and that *they are cringing advocates of the status quo in regard to nature.*

In confrontation with nature, their plea is: "Leave well enough alone." Do not upset the balance of nature – do not disturb the birds, the forests, the swamps, the oceans – do not rock the boat (or even build one) – do not experiment – do not venture out – what was good enough for our anthropoid ancestors is good enough for us – adjust to the winds, the rains, the man-eating tigers, the malarial mosquitoes, the tsetse flies – do not rebel – do not anger the unknowable demons who rule it all.

In their cosmology, man is infinitely malleable, controllable and dispensable, nature is sacrosanct. It is only man – and his work, his achievement, his mind – that can be violated with impunity, while nature is not to be defiled by a single bridge or skyscraper. It is only human beings that they do not hesitate to murder, it is only human schools that they bomb, only human habitations that they burn, only human property that they loot – while they crawl on their bellies in homage to the reptiles of the marshlands, whom they protect from the encroachments of human airfields, and humbly seek the guidance of the stars on how to live on this incomprehensible planet.

They are worse than conservatives – they are "conservationists." What do they want to conserve? Anything, except man. What do they want to rule? Nothing, except man.

[…]

Whom and what are they attacking? It is not luxuries or the "idle rich," but the availability of "luxuries" to the broad masses of people. They are denouncing the fact that automobiles, air conditioners and television sets are no longer toys of the rich, but are within the means of an American worker – a beneficence that does not exist and is not fully believed anywhere else on earth.

What do they regard as the proper life for working people? A life of unrelieved drudgery, of endless, gray toil, with no rest, no travel, no pleasure – above all, no pleasure. Those drugged, fornicating hedonists do not know that man cannot live by toil alone, that pleasure is a necessity, and that television has brought more enjoyment into more lives than all the public parks and settlement houses combined.

What do they regard as luxury? Anything above the "bare necessities" of physical survival – with the explanation that men would not have to labor so hard if it were not for the "artificial needs" created by "commercialism" and "materialism." In reality, the opposite is true: the less the return on your labor, the harder the labor. It is much easier to acquire an automobile in New York City than a meal in the jungle. Without machines and technology, the task of mere survival is a terrible, mind-and-body-wrecking ordeal. In "nature," the struggle for food, clothing and shelter consumes all of a man's energy and spirit; it is a losing struggle – the winner is any flood, earthquake or swarm of locusts. (Consider the 500,000 bodies left in the wake of a single flood in Pakistan; they had been men who lived without technology.) To work only for bare necessities is a *luxury* that mankind cannot afford.

Who is the first target of the ecological crusade? No, not big business. The first victims will be a specific group: those who are young, ambitious and poor. The young people who work their way through college; the young couples who plan their future, budgeting their money and their time; the young men and women who aim at a career; the struggling artists, writers, composers who have to earn a living, while developing their creative talents; any purposeful human being – i.e., the best of mankind. To them, *time* is the one priceless commodity, most passionately needed. *They* are the main beneficiaries of electric frozen foods, washing machines and labor-saving devices. And if the production and, above all, the invention of such devices is retarded or diminished by the ecological crusade, it will be one of the darkest crimes against humanity – particularly because the victims' agony will be private, their voices will not be heard, and their absence will not be noticed publicly until a generation or two later (by which time, the survivors will not be able to notice anything).

But there is a different group of young people, the avant-garde and cannon fodder of the ecological crusade, the products of "Progressive" education: the purposeless. These are the concrete-bound, mentally stunted youths, who are unable to think or to project the future, who can grasp nothing but the immediate moment. To them, time is an enemy to kill – in order to escape a confrontation with inner emptiness and chronic anxiety. Unable to generate and carry out a goal of their own, they seek and welcome drudgery – the drudgery of mere physical labor, provided, planned and directed by someone else. You saw it demonstrated on their so-called "Earth Day," when young people who did not take the trouble to wash their own bodies, went out to clean the sidewalks of New York.

[...]

What do the leaders hope to gain in practice? I shall answer by quoting a passage from *Atlas Shrugged*. It was published in 1957 – and I must say that I am not happy about having been prophetic on this particular issue.

It is a scene in which Dagny Taggart, at a conference with the country's economic planners, begins to grasp their motives.

[...]

She had thought that industrial production was a value not to be questioned by anyone; she had thought that these men's urge to expropriate the factories of others was their acknowledgment of the factories' value. She, born of the industrial revolution, had not held as conceivable, had forgotten along with the tales of astrology and alchemy, what these men knew in their secret, furtive souls: that so long as men struggle to stay alive, they'll never produce so little but that the man with the club won't be able to seize it and leave them still less, provided millions of them are willing to submit – that the harder their work and the less their gain, the more submissive the fiber of their spirit – that men who live by pulling levers at an electric switchboard, are not easily ruled, but men who live by digging the soil with their naked fingers, are – that the feudal baron did not need electronic factories in order to drink his brains away out of jeweled goblets, and neither did the rajahs of the People's State of India.

(January–February 1971)

Susan Sontag

"On Photography" (1973)

We linger unregenerately in Plato's cave, still reveling, our age-old habit, in mere image of the truth. But being educated by photographs isn't like being educated by older, more crafted images. For one thing, there are a great many more images around claiming our attention. Daguerre started the inventory, with faces, and since then just about everything has been photographed; or so it seems. This very instability of the photographing eye changes the terms of confinement in the cave, our world. In teaching us a new visual code, photographs alter and enlarge our notions of what is worth looking at and what we have a right to observe. The most grandiose result of the photographic enterprise is to give us the sense that we can hold the whole world in our heads – as anthology of images.

Movies and television programs light up walls, flicker, and go out; but with still photographs the image is also an object, lightweight, cheap to produce, easy to carry about, accumulate, store. In Godard's *Les Carabiniers* (1963), two sluggish lumpenpeasants are lured into joining the King's Army by the promise that they will be able to loot, rape, kill, or do whatever else they please to the enemy, and get rich. But the suitcase of booty that Michel Ange and Ulysse triumphantly bring home, years later, to their wives turns out to contain only picture postcards, hundreds of them, of monuments, department stores, mammals, wonders of nature, methods of transport, works of art, and other classified treasures from around the globe. Godard's gag vividly parodies the equivocal magic of the photographic image. Photographs are perhaps the most mysterious of all the objects that make up, and thicken, the environment we recognize as "modern." Photographs really are experience captured, and the camera is the ideal arm of consciousness in its acquisitive mood.

To photograph is to appropriate the thing photographed. It means putting oneself into a certain relation to the world that feels like knowledge – and, therefore, like power. A now notorious first fall into alienation, habituating people to abstract the world into printed words, is supposed to have engendered that surplus of Faustian energy and psychic damage needed to build modern, inorganic societies. But print seems a less treacherous form of leaching out the world, of turning it into a mental object, than photographic images, which provide most of the knowledge people have about the look of the past and the reach of the present. What can be read about the world is frankly an interpretation, as are older kinds of flat-surface visual statements, like paintings and drawings, Photographed images do not seem to be statements about the world so much as pieces of it: miniatures of reality that anyone can make or acquire.

Photographs, which fiddle with the scale of the world, themselves get reduced, blown up, cropped, retouched, doctored, trickled out. They age, plagued by the usual ills of other objects made of paper. They are lost, or become valuable, are bought and sold; they are reproduced. Photographs, which package the world, seem to invite packaging. They are stuck in albums, tacked on walls, printed in newspapers, collected in books. Cops alphabetize them; museums exhibit them.

Photographs furnish evidence. Something we hear about but doubt seems "proven" when we're shown a photograph of it. In one version of its utility, the camera record incriminates. Starting with their use by the Paris police in the murderous round-up of Communards in June, 1871, photographs become a useful tool of modern states in the surveillance and control of their increasingly mobile populations. In another version of its utility, the camera record passes for incontrovertible proof that a given thing happened. The picture may distort; but there is always a presumption that something exists, or did exist, which is "like" what's in the picture.

Whatever the limitations (through amateurism) or pretensions (through artistry) of the individual photographer, a photograph seems to have a more innocent, and therefore more accurate, relation to visible reality than do other mimetic objects. Virtuosi of the noble image like Paul Strand and Edward Steichen, composing mighty, unforgettable photographs decade after decade, still want, first of all, to show something "out there," just like the Polaroid owner for whom photographs are a handy, fast form of note-taking, or the shutterbug with a Brownie who takes snapshots as souvenirs of daily life.

Despite the presumption of veracity that gives all photographs authority, interests, seductiveness, the work that photographers do is also part of the usually shady commerce between art and truth. Even when photographers do serve reality, they're still haunted by tacit imperatives of taste and conscience. The immensely gifted members of the Farm

Security Administration photographic project of the late 1930s (among them Walker Evans, Dorothea Lange, Ben Shahn, Russell Lee) would take dozens of frontal pictures of one of their sharecropper subjects until satisfied that they had gotten just the right look on film – the precise expression on the subject's face that supported their own notions about poverty, despair, exploitation, dignity, light, texture, and space.

In deciding how a picture should look, in preferring one exposure to another, standards are always being imposed on the subject. Although there is a sense in which the camera does indeed capture reality, not just interpret it, photographs are as much an interpretation of the world as any other work of art. Those occasions when taking photographs is relatively undiscriminating, promiscuous, or self-effacing do not lessen the didacticism of the whole enterprise. This very passivity – and ubiquity – of the photographic record is photography's "message," its aggression.

Images which idealize (like most fashion and animal photography) are no less aggressive than work which makes a virtue of plainness (like class pictures, still lifes of the bleaker sort, and mug shots). There is an aggression implicit in every use of the camera. This is as evident in the 1840s, that brief period which Walter Benjamin considers photography's greatest, the mere ten years that preceded its "industrialization," as in all the succeeding decades, during which technology made possible an ever-increasing spread of that mentality which looks at the world as a set of potential photographs. Even for these masters of the first decade, David Octavius Hill and Julia Margaret Cameron, Hugo and Nadar, who used the camera as a means of getting painterly images, the point of taking photographs was a vast departure from the aims of painters. From its start, photography implied the capture of the largest possible number of subjects. Painting never had so imperial a scope. The subsequent "industrialization" of camera technology only continues a promise inherent in photography from its very beginning: to democratize all experiences by translating them into images.

The "industrialization" of photography that Benjamin deplores in his essay of 1931 is much further advanced now, forty years later, than even he could have imagined. That age when taking photographs required a cumbersome and expensive contraption – the toy of the clever, the wealthy, and the obsessed – seems remote indeed from the era of sleek pocket cameras which anyone can use. The first cameras, made in France and England in the late 1830s, had only inventors and buffs to operate them. Since there were then no professional photographers, there could not be amateurs either. In this first decade, taking photographs had no clear social use; it was a gratuitous, that is, an artistic activity, without yet being an art. Contrary to what Benjamin argues, it was only with "industrialization" that photography became an art. As "industrialization" provided social uses for the operations of the photographer, so the reaction against these uses inspired the self-consciousness and taste for stylistic experiments of photography-as-art.

Recently photography has become almost as widely practiced as sex and dancing – which means that, like every other mass art form, photography is not practiced by most people as an art. It is mainly a social rite, a defense against anxiety, and a tool of power. Memorializing the achievements of individuals considered as members of families (as well as of other groups) is the earliest popular use of photography. For at least a century, the wedding photograph has been as much a part of the ceremony as the prescribed verbal formulas. Cameras are part of family life. According to a sociological study made in France, most households have a camera, but a household with children is twice as likely to have at least one camera as a household in which there are no children. Not to take pictures of one's children, particularly when they are small, is a sign of parental indifference, just as not turning up for one's graduation picture is a gesture of adolescent rebellion.

Through photographs, each family constructs a portrait of itself – a kit of images that bears witness to its connectedness. It hardly matters what activities are photographed so long as photographs get taken and are cherished. Photography becomes a rite of family life just when, in the industrializing countries of Europe and America, the very institution of the family starts undergoing radical surgery. As that claustrophobic unit, the nuclear family, was being carved out of the much larger traditional family, photography came along to reinforce symbolically the imperiled family life. Those ghostly traces, photographs, supply the token presence of the dispersed relatives. A family's photograph album is generally "about" the extended family – and, often, is all that's left of it.

As photographs give people an imaginary sense of possession of a past that is unreal, they also help people to take possession of space in which they are insecure. Thus, photography is linked with one of the most influential of modern activities: tourism. It seems positively unnatural to travel for pleasure without taking a camera along. For the bemused and somewhat anxious vacationer, the photograph offers indisputable evidence that the trip was made, that fun was had. Photographs document consumption carried on outside the view of family, friends, neighbors. Dependence on the camera as the device that makes real what one is experiencing doesn't fade when people travel more. Taking photographs fills the same need for the sophisticates accumulating photograph-trophies of their boat trip up the Albert

Nile or their fourteen days in China as it does for vacationers taking snapshots of the Eiffel Tower.

A way of certifying experience, taking photographs is also a way of refusing it – by converting experience into an image, a souvenir. Travel becomes a strategy for accumulating photographs. The very activity of taking pictures is soothing. Most tourists feel compelled to put the camera between themselves and whatever is remarkable that they encounter. Lacking other responses, they take a picture. This gives shape to experience: stop, take a photograph, and move on. The method especially appeals to people handicapped by a ruthless work ethic – Germans, Japanese, and Americans. They have something to do that is like a friendly imitation of work: they can take pictures.

People robbed of their past seem to be the most fervent picture takers, at home and abroad. Everyone who lives in an industrialized society has lost the past to some degree, but in certain countries, such as the United States and Japan, the break with the past has been particularly traumatic. Right now, the fabled American tourist of the Fifties and Sixties, rich with dollars and Babbittry, is being replaced by the Japanese tourist, newly released from his island prison by the miracle of overvalued yen, who is generally armed with two cameras, one on each hip.

In a full-page ad currently running in many European weeklies, a small group of people stand pressed together, peering out of the photograph, all but one looking stunned, excited, upset. The one who wears a different expression holds a camera to his eye; he seems self-possessed, almost smiling. While the others are passive, clearly alarmed spectators, having a camera has transformed one person into something active, a voyeur. Only he has mastered the situation.

What do these people see? We don't know. And it doesn't matter. It is an Event: something worth seeing – and therefore worth photographing. The ad copy, white letters across the dark lower third of the photograph like news coming over a teletype machine, consists of just six words: "... Prague ... Woodstock ... Vietnam ... Sapporo ... Londonderry ... LEICA." Crushed hopes, youth antics, colonial wars, and winter sports are alike – are equalized by the camera.

Part of the horror of such recent coups of photojournalism as the pictures of bonzes reaching for the gasoline can, of a Pakistani prisoner on his back about to be impaled, comes from the awareness of how plausible it has become, in situations where the photographer has the choice between a photograph and a life, to choose the photograph. The person who intervenes cannot record; the person who is recording cannot intervene. The omnipresence of cameras persuasively suggests that time consists of interesting events, events worth photographing.

This, in turn, makes it easy to feel that any event, once underway [sic], and whatever its moral character, ought to be allowed to complete itself – so that something else can be brought into the world, the photograph. After the event has ended, the picture will still exist. Thus on the event is conferred a kind of immortality (and importance) it would never otherwise have enjoyed. While real people are out there killing themselves or other real people, the photographer stays behind his camera, creating a tiny element of another world: the image-world that bids to outlast us all.

While the camera is an observation station, the act of photographing is more than passive observing. Taking pictures, like sexual voyeurism, is a way of tacitly – often explicitly – encouraging whatever is going on to keep on happening. To take a picture is to have an interest in things as they are, in the status quo remaining unchanged (at least for as long as it takes to get a good picture), to be in complicity with whatever makes a subject interesting, worth photographing – including, when that's the interest, another person's pain or misfortune.

"I have always thought of photography as a naughty thing to do – that was one of my favorite things about it," Diane Arbus wrote, "and when I first did it I felt very perverse." Being a professional photographer can be thought of as naughty, to use Arbus's Pop word, if the photographer seeks out subjects considered to be naughty, taboo, marginal. But naughty subjects are harder to find these days. And what is the perverse part of taking pictures? Professional photographers must often have sexual fantasies when they are behind the camera. Perhaps the perversion lies in the fact that these fantasies are both plausible and inappropriate.

In *Blow-Up* (1967), Antonioni has the fashion photographer played by David Hemmings convulsively writhing above Veruschka's body with his camera clicking. Naughtiness, indeed. In fact, using a camera is not a very good way of pushing someone around sexually. Between photographer and subject there has to be distance. The camera doesn't rape, or even possess, though it may presume, intrude, trespass, distort, exploit, and, at the farthest reach of metaphor, assassinate – all activities that, unlike the sexual push and shove, can be conducted from a distance, and with some detachment.

There is a much odder sexual fantasy in Michael Powell's extraordinary movie *Peeping Tom* (1958), which is not about a peeping tom but about a homicidal photographer who kills women while photographing them, with a weapon concealed in his camera; he develops the films, and runs them off at night for his solitary pleasure. Not once does he touch his subjects. He doesn't desire their bodies; he wants their photographed images, particularly those showing them experiencing their own death. The film assumes connections between impotence and aggression, professionalized "looking" and cruelty, which point to the central fantasy connected with the camera. The camera as phallus is, at most, a flimsy variant of the inescapable metaphor that everyone unselfconsciously employs. However hazy our awareness of this fantasy, it is named without subtlety whenever we talk about "loading" and "aiming" a camera, about "shooting" a film.

The old-fashioned camera was clumsier and harder to reload than a Brown Bess musket. The modern camera is trying to be a ray gun. One ad reads:

The Yashica Electro-35 GT is the spaceage camera your family will love. Take beautiful pictures day or night. Automatically. Without any nonsense. Just aim, focus and shoot. The GT's computer brain and electronic shutter will do the rest.

Like a car, a camera is sold as a predatory weapon – one that's as automated as possible, ready to spring. Popular taste expects an easy, invisible technology. Manufacturers reassure their customers that taking pictures demands no skill, that the machine is all-knowing, and responds to the slightest pressure of the will. It's as simple as turning the ignition key or pulling the trigger.

Like guns and cars, cameras are fantasy machines whose use is addictive. However, contrary to the rhetoric of ordinary language and advertising, they are not as lethal as guns and cars. For cars being marketed like guns there is at least this much truth in the hyperbole: except in wartime, cars kill more people than guns do. The camera does not kill, so it seems to be all a bluff – like a man's fantasy of having a gun, knife, or tool between his legs. Still, there is something predatory in the act of taking a picture. To photograph people is to violate them, by seeing them as they never see themselves, by having knowledge of them they can never have. To photograph is to turn people into objects that can be symbolically possessed. To photograph someone is a sublimated murder, just as the camera is the sublimation of a gun. Taking pictures is a soft murder, appropriate to a sad, frightened time.

Perhaps people will learn to act out more aggressions with cameras and fewer with guns, with the price being an even more image-choked world. One situation where people are switching from bullets to film is the photographic safaris that are replacing gun safaris in East Africa. The hunters have Hasselblads instead of Winchesters; instead of looking through the telescopic sight to aim a rifle, they look through a viewfinder. In end-of-the-century London, Samuel Butler complained that "there is a photographer in every bush, going about like a roaring lion seeking whom he may devour." The photographer is now charging real beasts, beleaguered and getting too rare to kill.

Guns have metamorphosed into cameras in this unique comedy, the ecology safari, because nature has ceased to be what it always was – what people needed protection from. Now nature – discovered to be pathetic, endangered, mortal – needs to be protected from people. When we are afraid, we shoot. But when we are nostalgic, we take pictures.

It is a nostalgic time right now, and likely to remain so for a while. Photography is an elegiac art, a twilight art. There is no subject the photographer might attempt that could not be touched with pathos. All photographs are *memento mori*. To take a photograph is to participate in another person's (or thing's) mortality, vulnerability, mutability. Precisely by slicing out this moment and freezing it, all photographs testify to time's relentless melt.

Cameras begin duplicating the world at the time when the human landscape starts to undergo a vertiginous rate of change. Just when the greatest number of forms of life are being destroyed in the shortest space of time, a device is invented to record what is disappearing. The textured Paris of Atget and Brassai is mostly gone. Like the dead relatives and friends preserved in the family album, whose presence in photographs exorcises some of the horror and guilt of their disappearance, so the photographs of neighborhoods now torn down, rural places disfigured and made barren, supply our pocket relation to the past.

A photograph is both a pseudo-presence and a token of absence. Like a wood fire in a room, photographs – especially those of people, of distant landscapes and faraway cities, of the vanished past – are incitements to reverie. The sense of the unattainable that can be set off by photographs feeds directly into the erotic feelings of those for whom desirability is enhanced by distance. The lover's photograph in a woman's wallet, the poster photograph of a rock star over an adolescent's bed, the snapshots of a cabdriver's children above his dashboard – all such talismanic uses of photographs express a feeling both sentimental and implicitly magical, attempts to contact another reality.

Photographs can be aids to desire in the most direct, utilitarian way – as when someone keeps photographs of anonymous archetypes of desire as an aid to masturbation. The situation is more complex when photographs are used to stimulate the moral impulse. Desire has no history. It is made up of archetypes and in that sense is abstract. But moral feelings are embedded in history, whose persona are always concrete, whose situations are always specific. Thus, almost opposite rules hold true for the use of the photograph to awaken desire and its use to awaken conscience. The images that mobilize conscience are always specific to a given historical situation. The more general they are, the less likely they are to be effective.

A photograph that brings news of some unsuspected zone of misery can't make a dent in public opinion unless there is an appropriate context of feeling and attitude. The photographs Matthew Brady took of the horrors of the battlefields did not make people any less keen to go on with the Civil War. The photographs of skeletal prisoners held at Andersonville inflamed Northern public opinion – against the South. (The effect of the Andersonville photographs must have been partly due to the very novelty, at that time, of seeing photographs.) The political understanding that many Americans came to in the 1960s would allow them, looking at the photographs Dorothea Lange took of Nisei on the West Coast being transported to internment camps in 1942, to recognize their subject for what it was – a crime committed by the government against a large group of American citizens. Few people who saw the photographs in the 1940s could have had so unequivocal a reaction; the ground for such a judgment barely existed then. Photographs cannot create a moral position, but they can reinforce one – and can help build a nascent one.

Photographs may be more memorable than moving images – because they are a neat slice of time. Television is a stream of under-selected images, each of which cancels its predecessor. A still photograph is a "privileged moment," turned into a slim object that one can keep and look at again. Photographs like the one taken in 1971 and put on the front page of most newspapers in the world – a naked child running down a South Vietnamese highway toward the camera, having just been hit by American napalm, her arms open, screaming with pain – were of great importance in mobilizing antiwar sentiment in this country from 1967 on. And each one was certainly more memorable than a hundred hours of televised barbarities.

One would like to believe that the American public would not have been so unanimous in its acquiescence to the Korean War if it had been confronted with photographic evidence of the devastation of Korea, an ecocide and genocide in some respects even more thorough than the ones inflicted on the Vietnamese a decade later. But the supposition is trivial. The public did not see such photographs because there was, ideologically, no space for them. Americans did have access to photographs of the sufferings of the Vietnamese because journalists felt backed in their efforts to get those photographs, some people having redefined the event as a savage colonialist war. The Korean War was understood differently – as another struggle of the Free World against the Soviet Union and China – and, given that characterization, photographs of the cruelty of unlimited firepower would have been irrelevant. If an event is now defined as something worth photographing, it is still ideology (in the broadest sense) that tells us what constitutes an event. And it is never photographic evidence which can construct – more properly, invent – events. Without a politics, photographs of the slaughter-bench of history are not identifiable as such.

The quality of feeling, including moral outrage, that people can muster in response to photographs of the oppressed, the exploited, the starving, and the napalmed also depends on the degree of their familiarity with these images. The photographs of Biafrans starving in the 1960s had less impact for some people than Werner Bischof's photographs of Indian famine victims in the 1950s because those images had become banal, and the photographs appearing now in magazines of Tuareg families dying of starvation in the Southern Sahara may seem to many like an unbearable replay of a now familiar atrocity exhibition.

Photographs shock us in so far as they show us something novel. Unfortunately, the ante keeps getting raised – partly through the very proliferation of such images of horror. One's first encounter with the photographic inventory of ultimate horror is a kind of revelation, perhaps the only revelation people are granted now, a negative epiphany. For me, it was photographs of Bergen-Belsen and Dachau which I came across by chance in a bookstore in Santa Monica in July, 1945. Nothing I have seen – in photographs or in real life – ever cut me as sharply, deeply, instantaneously. Ever since then, it has seemed plausible to me to think of my life as being divided into two parts: before I saw those photographs (I was twelve) and after. My life was changed by them, though not until several years later did I understand what they were about. What good was served by seeing them? They were only photographs – of an event I had scarcely heard of and could do nothing to affect, of suffering I could hardly imagine and could do nothing to relieve. When I looked at those photographs, something was broken. Some limit had been reached, and not only that of horror; I felt irrevocably grieved, wounded, but a part of my feelings started to lighten, something went dead; something is still crying.

To suffer is one thing; another thing is living with the photographed images of suffering, which does not necessarily strengthen conscience and the ability to be compassionate. It can also corrupt them. Once one has seen such images, one has started down the road of seeing more – and more. Images transfix. Images anesthetize. An event known through photographs certainly becomes more real than it would have been if one had never seen the photographs – think of the Vietnam war. But, after repeated exposure to images, it also becomes less real.

There is the same law for evil as for pornography. The shock of photographed atrocities wears off with repeated viewings, just as the surprise and bemusement one feels the first time one sees a pornographic movie wear off after seeing a few more. The sense of taboo which makes us indignant and sorrowful is not much sturdier than the sense of taboo that regulates our definition of what is obscene. And both have been sorely tried in recent years. The vast photographic catalogue of misery and injustice throughout the world has given everyone a certain familiarity with atrocity, making the horrible seem more ordinary – making it appear familiar, remote ("It's only a photograph"), inevitable. At the time of the first photographs of the Nazi camps, there was nothing banal about these images. After almost thirty years, we may be reaching a saturation point. In these last decades, "concerned" photography has done at least as much to deaden conscience as to arouse it.

The ethical content of photographs is fragile. With the exception of certain photographs, like the camps and Vietnam, most photographs don't keep their emotional charge. A photograph of 1900 that was affecting then because of its subject would, today, be more likely to move us because it is a photograph taken in 1900. The particular qualities and intentions of photographs tend to be swallowed up in the generalized pathos of time past. Aesthetic distance seems built into the very experience of looking at photographs, if not right away, then with the passage of time. Time eventually positions most photographs, even the very amateurish, at the level of art.

The "industrialization" of photography permitted its rapid absorption into rational – i.e., bureaucratic – ways of running society. No longer toy images, photographs became part of the furniture of the environment – a touchstone and confirmation of that reductive approach to reality which is called "realistic." Photographs were enrolled in the service of important institutions of control, notably the family and the police, as symbolic objects and pieces of information. Thus, in the bureaucratic cataloguing of the world, many important documents are not valid unless they have affixed to them a photograph-token of the citizen's face.

The "realistic" view of the world compatible with bureaucracy redefines knowledge – as techniques and information. Photographs are valued because they give information. They tell one what there is: they make an inventory. In fact, except to cops, novelists, and historians, even their value as information is trivial. The information that photographs can give starts to seem more important than it really is at that moment in cultural history when everyone is thought to have a right to something called "news." Photographs were seen as a way of giving information to people who do not take easily to reading. The *Daily News* still calls itself "New York's Picture Newspaper," its bid for populist identity. At the opposite end of the scale, *Le Monde*, a newspaper designed for skilled, well-informed readers, runs no photographs at all. The presumption is that, for such readers, a photograph could only illustrate the analysis contained in an article.

A new sense of the notion of "information" has been constructed around the photographed image. The photograph is a thin slice of space as well as time. In a world ruled by photographic images, all borders ("framing") seem arbitrary. Anything can be separated from anything else. All that is necessary is to frame the subject differently. Through photographs, the world becomes a series of unrelated, free-standing particles; and history, past and present, a set of anecdotes and *faits divers*. It makes reality atomic, "manageable," and opaque. It is a view of the world which denies interconnectedness. The ultimate wisdom of the photographed image is to say: "There is the surface. Now, think – or, rather, feel, intuit – what is beyond it, what the reality must be like if it looks this way." Strictly speaking, there is never any understanding in a photograph, but only an invitation to fantasy and speculation.

Photography implies that we know about the world if we accept it as the camera records it. But this is the opposite of understanding, an approach which starts from not accepting the world as it looks. All possibility of understanding is rooted in the ability to say no. Strictly speaking, it is doubtful that a photograph can help us to understand anything. The simple fact of "rendering" a reality doesn't tell us much about that reality. A photograph of the Krupp factory, as Brecht points out, tells us little about this institution. The "reality" of the world is not in its images, but in its functions. Functioning takes place in time, and must be explained in time. Only that which narrates can make us understand.

The limit of photographic knowledge of the world is that, while it can arouse conscience, it can, finally, never be ethical or political knowledge. In itself, the knowledge gained through still photographs will always be some kind of sentimentalism – whether cynical or humanist. It will always be knowledge at bargain prices – a semblance of knowledge, a semblance of appropriation, a semblance of rape, a semblance of wisdom. Photographs have a great effect on our ethical sensibility, by making us feel that the world is more available than it really is. By furnishing this already crowded world with a duplicate world of images, photography subtly devalues the world and undermines the possibility of having fresh responses to it.

Being involved with photographs is an aesthetic consumerism to which we are all, understandably, addicted. We are image-junkies now. It is a glorious form of mental pollution. Poignant longings for beauty, for an end to probing below the surface, for a redemption and celebration of the body of the world – all these good feelings are expressed in the pleasures we take in photographs. But other, more doubtful longings get expressed as well.

13

Religion and Ethics
Introduction by Kimberly Hutchings

One conventional history of international relations traces it back to the 1648 Peace of Westphalia that marked the end of European wars of religion. On this account, international relations are the product of the end of an era in which a common value system was a key element of world order. In contrast to "Christendom," the post-Westphalian European society or system of sovereign states was compatible with religious and ethical pluralism and was therefore capable of expanding to include states from a variety of different religious and ethical traditions. For this reason, students attempting to explain and understand international relations should be able to bracket out religion and ethics as essentially "domestic" matters. As many scholars have pointed out, this account of the history of international relations is more myth than reality.[1] It neglects the fact that European states were also empires and the limits of Post-Westphalian religious pluralism. It neglects the ways in which international law and norms carry the legacy of religious universalism. It neglects the role of values in IR theories. It also neglects longstanding traditions of international ethics, and of religion as an object of, as well as motivation for, inquiry for scholars of international relations.

The high point of the influence of the Westphalian myth was the Cold War period in the United States, when a combination of commitment to liberal ideology and social scientific method was mutually reinforcing with assumptions about historical secularization and value-free academic inquiry. On the other side of the Atlantic, IR scholars were much more open to seeing the relevance of religious and ethical values to the

---

[1] See Andreas Osiander, "Sovereignty, International Relations, and the Westphalian Myth," *International Organization*, 55:2 (2001): 251–287; Benno Teschke, *The Myth of 1648: Class, Geopolitics, and the Making of Modern International Relations* (London: Verso, 2003); Sebastian Schmidt, "To Order the Minds of Scholars: The Discourse of the Peace of Westphalia in International Relations Literature," *International Studies Quarterly*, 55:3 (2011): 601–623.

maintenance of world order, although there was a shift from more explicitly Christian language to the more neutral terminology of "international society" during the Cold War period.[2] In practice, however much IR analysis might claim to distance itself from religion and ethics it is always entangled with both. As Barbara Ward argues below, the idea of the "West," which became essentialized during the Cold War as a package of liberal values and an analytic category, is bound up with a particular reading of the legacy of Christianity. Even the explicit renunciation of "idealism" by realist thinkers after the Second World War was driven by a commitment to ethical and, often, religious values.[3] The difficulty in tracing themes of religion and ethics in IR scholarship is that they are everywhere, and it is not always easy to disentangle claims made about the significance of religious or ethical values as components of international politics from the religious or ethical commitments of the scholars themselves.

Prior to the Cold War, in the decades in which IR began its formation as an intellectual field, as we have seen, ethical and religious values were often explicitly embedded in explanatory and normative arguments from the imperial core about war, foreign policy, and trade, whether from imperial or anticolonial, revolutionary standpoints. The experience of the First World War sparked off the development of pacifism as an ethico-political doctrine, inspiring international policy and activism as well as a renewed interest in the ethics of war (see our section on World Peace). In turn, the use of aerial bombardment and of atomic weapons at Hiroshima and Nagasaki in the Second World War created new dilemmas about the possibilities of just war, and inspired new antinuclear activist movements. Developments in international law and norms since the end of the Cold War, in particular in relation to humanitarian intervention and the "Responsibility to Protect" have inspired a major revival in international ethics as a subfield of IR. Outside of the context of war, the idea of international human rights has become a crucial element of development and democratization agendas, as well as the focus of an enormous ethical literature. The 9/11 attacks put religion back onto the explicit IR agenda, provoking scholars to notice longstanding challenges to secularization theory and encouraging more

---

[2] See Nukhet A. Sandal and Patrick James, "Religion and IR Theory: Towards a Mutual Understanding," *European Journal of International Relations*, 17:1 (2010): 3–25.

[3] See Nicolas Guilhot, "American Katechon: When Political Theology Became International Relations," *Constellations*, 17:2 (2010): 224–253; Vassilis Paipais, "Overcoming 'Gnosticism'? Realism and Political Theology," *Cambridge Review of International Affairs*, 29:4 (2015): 1603–1623.

work on religion as a causal factor in international relations and, more radically, the development of post-secular IR.[4]

Against this very complex backdrop, the texts featured below offer snapshots of the ways in which different women incorporated issues of ethics and religion in their international thinking in the first half of the twentieth century, from Addams's 1902 *Democracy and Social Ethics* to Anscombe's 1956 "Mr Truman's Degree." The texts are doing quite different things. Addams (1860–1935) is making an argument about the nature of ethical reasoning in an age of transnationalism and democracy, whereas Anscombe (1919–2001) is making an ethical argument about how we differentiate between legitimate killing and murder in the context of war. Buck (1892–1973) is defending the transformational international potential of a particular mode of Christian missionary work, and Ward (1914–1981) is lamenting secularization as the road to totalitarianism. Weil (1909–1943) is using one understanding of Christianity to lambast Christianity as imperialist and destructive, while Hurston (1891–1960) is undermining the global narrative of Christian triumphalism, as well as drawing attention to religious practice as a fundamentally transnational phenomenon. Goldman (1869–1940) identifies religion with the destructive power of the state and capital and Cooper (1858–1964) draws on Christianity to undermine theories of racial supremacy.

We have already encountered Jane Addams as a leader of the international women's peace movement (see the section on World Peace). In addition to her work as a peace activist, Addams was a founder of the settlement movement in the United States and deeply involved in the "progressive" politics of the time. She was also part of the pragmatist movement, along with thinkers such as John Dewey and William James.[5] Her work in the settlement house in Chicago (Hull House) engaged her directly with impoverished immigrant communities working and living in appalling conditions and adapting to an alien way of life. Her experience at Hull House confirmed her view that life in a modern, industrialized city was throwing up ethical and political challenges that could not be

---

[4] For a comprehensive overview of the field of international ethics, see Brent J. Steele and Eric A. Heinze (eds.), *Routledge Handbook of Ethics and International Relations* (London: Routledge, 2017). See also Fabio Petito and Pavlos Hatzopoulos (eds.), *Religion in International Relations: The Return from Exile* (Basingstoke and New York: Palgrave Macmillan, 2003); Luca Mavelli and Fabio Petito (eds.), *Towards a Postsecular International Politics: New Forms of Community, Identity and Power* (Basingstoke and New York: Palgrave Macmillan, 2014).

[5] M. Cochran, "The 'Newer Ideals' of Jane Addams's Progressivism," in M. Cochran and C. Navari (eds.), *Progressivism and US Foreign Policy between the World Wars* (Basingstoke: Palgrave Macmillan, 2017).

adequately dealt with through established moral paradigms. What was needed, she argued, was a transformation from individual ethics, in which particular moral standards are embedded in the individual conscience, to social ethics oriented around the ideal of democracy: "We slowly learn that life consists of processes as well as of results, and that failure may come quite as easily from ignoring the adequacy of one's method as from selfish or ignoble aims" (705).

For Addams, then, ethics had to be "prefigurative," meaning that the way in which one engaged with others in formulating moral values and judgments needed to be democratic, in keeping with the moral ideal of democracy that, she argued, was the appropriate response to the challenges of coexistence in mass, multicultural, unequal societies. For her, this meant that ethics required experimentation and broadening of experience: "Partly through this wide reading of human life, we find in ourselves a new affinity with all men, which probably never existed in the world before" (706). In this respect, she suggested that it was the immigrant communities that she worked with that provided the best examples of how to live with others according to a democratic ethos, rather than the educated moralists who agonized over the righteousness of their own actions. Addams's moral theory in *Democracy and Social Ethics* is the basis for her later argument for pacifism. She draws analogies between her experience of relations between different immigrant communities and between them and city authorities, especially the police, and the context of international conflict. In the same way as the commandment of conscience or law is in tension with the ideal of democracy when it comes to questions of justice in the modern city, so is the ethos of military life in tension with the idea of democracy. A democratic, social ethics is necessarily pacifist.

The desperate poverty and violence of inner-city Chicago in the late nineteenth century led thinkers such as Addams and Emily Greene Balch into founding settlements and pioneering social work. But it was also a context in which more radical responses to the appalling inequities of industrial capitalism emerged. By the 1890s, anarchism was a well-established transnational anti-capitalist movement, grounded in a fundamental rejection of the state and committed to world-wide revolution.[6] Emma Goldman, a Jewish woman born in the Russian empire, emigrated to the United States with her family from what is now Lithuania when she was seventeen. She became a leading figure in the anarchist movement in

---

[6] For a discussion of the significance of anarchism for the study of international relations see Alex Prichard, *Justice, Order and Anarchy: The International Political Theory of Pierre Joseph Proudhon* (Abingdon: Routledge, 2013).

the United States and internationally, becoming notorious for her (unwitting) involvement in the assassination of President McKinley. Along with other anarchists, she campaigned against US involvement in the First World War, and was part of an anti-conscription league. She was imprisoned on several occasions, and was eventually deported from the United States in 1919 and never allowed to return. Like Luxemburg, she was extremely suspicious of the centralist tendencies of Bolshevism. She wrote critically about the development of the Russian Revolution, supported the anarchist parties in the Spanish Civil War, and saw the collapse of the League of Nations and the imminence of a second world war as vindicating her views about the destructive nature of the state.

Goldman and her family were the kind of people that Hull House was set up to help. Goldman, however, disparages Addams in her autobiography. For Goldman, Addams was part of a middle class do-gooding social democracy that failed to grasp the radical change needed to revolutionize individual as well as social life. In her setting out of her anarchist ethical ideal, Goldman identifies God, Property, and the State as the three phantoms keeping humanity from freedom. She is scathing about religion, and the way it attempts to control human thought and feeling. She argues for a world in which the tensions between individual and society, artificially constructed by the institutions of religion, property, and state, will disappear. Anarchism "stands for the liberation of the human mind from the dominion of religion; the liberation of the human body from the dominion of property; liberation from the shackles and restraint of government" (711). Her ethical philosophy here overlaps to some extent with Addams, since Goldman also argued that anarchism needed to be prefigurative. In contrast to Bolshevism, anarchist revolution should not depend on top-down centralized structures, a fact that eventually caused her to despair of a successful international anarchist revolution.

From the beginnings of European colonization of the Americas from 1492 onwards, Christian missionaries served as tools for the socialization and domination of subject populations before and after colonial and imperial conquest. Christian doctrine was used as an excuse for enslavement and extermination in European empires (and of course also within Europe itself). It was also a site in which human and civilizational hierarchies could be put into question. International thinkers in the late nineteenth and early twentieth centuries were conscious that missionary activity was a way of extending and entrenching imperial power. They were also conscious of new anthropological work that challenged the old hierarchy of civilizations (see the discussion of Mead in the section on Technology, Progress, and Environment). Pearl Buck came from a missionary family and spent much of her early life in China, where as a child she was embedded in local cultures. In her 1933 text *Is There a Case for Foreign Missions?* she wrestles with the question of the legitimacy of missionary work.

Given her radical credentials (see the section on Men, Women, and Gender), it is perhaps surprising that Buck does not simply reject the validity of Christian missions. Instead, she supports the potential of legitimate missionary work within a context in which, she says, "I do not believe that any religion is comprehensive enough to exclude all others" (719). Buck argues that Christianity does have something to offer other religions/civilizations: "In nations where the figure of Christ has been perceived, however dimly, I find something I do not find elsewhere" (718). However, she does not think that Christian missions should be evangelical. Their aim should not be conversion; rather the point of the mission should be to share in the life of the people: "It seems to me this is the only possible basis for missions. It removes from us the insufferable stigma of moral arrogance, and it gives us besides a test of our own worth" (720–721). Buck is suggesting, then, an ethic of exemplarity, but one that should work in all directions, and open up all civilizations to learn from each other. In this sense, it recalls Addams's democratic social ethics and aims to detach missionary work from the idea of a civilizing mission.

The idea of missionary work as part of an imperial or ethical civilizing mission relies on an understanding of religious traditions as fundamentally spatially and temporally contained. In the discussion of the role of Christianity in international society in the nineteenth and twentieth centuries, international thinkers treat Christianity as coming from Europe and traveling to Africa, Asia, the Americas, and Australasia. Although there are arguments about different forms of Christianity, Catholic or Protestant, and how they may link to different modes of imperialism or settler colonialism, for good or ill, Christianity travels from west to east and south, and begins its global travels in 1492. Of course, this account is false, and was well known to be false. Christianity originated in Palestine and there were established Christian communities in Africa well before there were in northern Europe, and ones in India that predate European imperialism. The entrenchment of the idea that Christianity is fundamentally European helps to contextualize the failures of the League of Nations in its response to the Italian invasion and colonization of Ethiopia in 1935, the context for several other selections in this volume. Ethiopia was a Christian country and a recognized state, but this did not fit with the predominant European imaginary. At the time of that invasion, Zora Neale Hurston was engaged in anthropological research into "Hoodoo" religious practices in the American South, and three years afterwards researched "Voodoo" religious practices in Haiti.

Hurston is a controversial figure in African American intellectual history. She was a key figure in the Harlem renaissance in the 1920s, but many of her peers found her representation of African American folklore in her anthropological and fictional work as confirming white stereotypes of Black people. There have also been questions raised about the accuracy of her accounts of religious rituals, and about how much she relied on the work of others. Hurston was the daughter of a Baptist preacher, and religion was a key theme in all of her writings, though commentators differ in their assessment of her faith, or lack of it. In her autobiography and in letters, she firmly denied any allegiance to organized religion. However, she was clearly fascinated by religious ritual. For our purposes, what is important about her thinking is that it overturns the standard imaginary of Christianity as a European export. Prevalent views about Voodoo practices at the time understood it as a bastardized version of Catholicism. But Hurston is adamant that Haitian gods are "not the catholic calendar of saints done over in black" (724). Rather, she suggests that the resonances between Voodoo and Christianity emerge out of a much longer story, in which African belief systems influenced Christianity: "It [Voodoo] adapts itself like Christianity to its locale, reclaiming some of its [Christianity's] borrowed characteristics to itself. Such as fire worship as signified in the Christian church by the altar and the candles. And the belief in the power of water to sanctify as in baptism" (722).

Hurston was also insistent that Voodoo departed from Christian, Greek, and Norse traditions in identifying Damballah not with "God the Father," but as a figure combining both sexes. In her anthropological and fictional work, her portrayal of Black women celebrated their strength and creativity in a context of racist and patriarchal oppression. Her work is now cited as a reference point for Black feminist and womanist ethics and theology.[7] Simone Weil is, like Hurston, a controversial thinker. A child of the secularized French Jewish middle classes, she renounced an affiliation with Judaism and converted to Christianity.[8] She denounced Judaism in the strongest terms and has, as with other

---

[7] See Katie Geneva Cannon, Emilie M. Townes, and Angela D. Sims (eds.), *Womanist Theological Ethics: A Reader* (Louisville, KY: WJK Press, 2011).

[8] See Helen M. Kinsella, "Of Colonialism and Corpses: Simone Weil on Force," in Patricia Owens and Katharina Rietzler (eds.), *Women's International Thought: A New History* (Cambridge: Cambridge University Press, 2021), 72–92; and the section on Anticolonialism.

Jewish thinkers such as Arendt and Luxemburg, been accused of anti-semitism. In "Letter to a Priest," written in 1942 shortly before she died of malnutrition, she grapples with the question of the relation between Christianity and imperialism. In contrast to Hurston, her story of Christianity reproduces the idea of Christianity as a European export. She is, however, even more critical than Buck in her evaluation of the effects of exporting her faith: "Missionary zeal has not Christianized Africa, Asia and Oceania, but has brought these territories under the cold, cruel and destructive domination of the white race, which has trodden down everything" (727).

Weil connects Christianity's imperial history to "Israel," meaning Judaism, and to the Roman Empire (see also the discussion of and selection by Weil in the section on Anticolonialism). This is explained in terms of a heritage of "ineradicable nationalism" and a will to compel obedience. Nationalism entrenches an "us/them" mentality that devalues the outsider. In the Roman context, Christianity becomes adopted as the state religion only after it has passed its disruptive, millenarian phase and can be used as a tool to "uproot" colonized peoples and keep them under control.[9] Weil's analysis, like Goldman's, treats Christianity as a set of ideas and a political tool that is tied to the bloody history of the state from its inception. Nazism and modern European colonialism and imperialism are an extension of this history.[10] In her view, the history of modern international order could not be understood without reference to Christianity. But Weil is also making another argument, very much akin to Buck's, which is that Christianity can be thought of and practiced in another way. For Weil, this is a possibility inherent in all religious traditions and to attempt to bolt on Christianity to other religions is a profound mistake. The spiritual and ethical substance of Weil's alternative to rule-based religious and ethical doctrine has been subject to much debate. Like Buck and Addams, Weil's Christian ethos seems to center around responsiveness to the needs of others and the virtue of moral humility.

The work of Buck and Weil testifies directly to the role that Christianity has played in the oppressive histories of the relations between peoples, empires, and states. But Christianity also provided a resource for them to contest those histories. By 1945, the ideas that became enshrined in the 1948 UN Declaration of International Human

---

[9] See Kinsella, "Of Colonialism and Corpses," 72–92.
[10] See Helen M. Kinsella, "Simone Weil: An Introduction," in Felix Roesch (ed.), *Emigré Scholars and the Genesis of American International Relations* (New York: Palgrave Macmillan, 2014): 176–196.

Rights were already being formulated. Cooper's text speaks to the idea of human rights as fundamentally universal and transnational, and she directly locates the origins of modern political values of equality, rights, and justice in Christian doctrine. It was originally written in French as part of the defense of her doctoral thesis in 1925, at the request of her white supremacist examiner, Bouglé. She translated and amended it in 1945 to use with her students. We have already encountered Cooper's work on gender, race, and class in *A Voice from the South* and on the French and Haitian revolutions (see the sections on Imperialism and Men, Women, and Gender). In the text below, Cooper uses the standard narrative of the link between Christianity and Western civilization to challenge Bouglé's claim that democracies could evolve only in "Nordic" countries.

In addition to pointing to the various factual mistakes and inconsistencies in Bouglé's argument, Cooper deploys the Christian origins of ideas of individual moral worth to point to the failures of the "West" and how far it has departed from those ideas. She comments bitingly on the paradox that "Nations who adore the principles of Democracy, of Equality, of fraternity" (715) are unable to comply with the simplest Gospel injunction to provide a cup of water if the one who needs it is Black. She points to the decline of Western civilization in which progress is now associated with who has the most destructive power: "The banner today is borne by the men or the nation who invents the most marvelous project of destruction, the most powerful and irresistible instrument of war" (716). And she briskly reminds Bouglé that if individuals have moral worth, deriving from "a shadow mark of the Creator's image," then: "The concept of Equality as it is the genuine product of the idea of inherent value in the individual derived from the essential worth of Humanity must be before all else unquestionably of universal application" (716).

Cooper's moral cosmopolitanism is reflected in the UN 1948 Declaration, but the geopolitical context of the Cold War limited the expansion and development of international human rights regimes. Rather than enabling a more inclusive ethical imagination in world politics, Christian thinkers based in the United States and UK became preoccupied with their own moral identity and its resilience to threats of Communism and totalitarianism. Ward was a Catholic who moved in elite lay and Church circles. She was on friendly terms with British and US politicians and policymakers, with postcolonial leaders, such as Nkrumah, and with the Catholic Church hierarchy.[11] She worked for

---

[11] Jean Gartlan, "Barbara Ward – Lay Woman *Extraordinaire*," *US Catholic Historian*, 29:3 (2011): 9–16.

the *Economist* magazine from the late 1930s and was Foreign Editor from 1945 to 1950, working with Susan Strange, later moving on to a variety of positions in universities, charities, and think tanks. She was made a life peer in the UK House of Lords in 1976. Ward was a prolific writer and commentator, whose faith played a key part in her abiding interest in issues of international justice, and her pioneering work on the idea of sustainable development.[12] Her book *Faith and Freedom* (1954) became at the time an influential reference point for attempts to clarify the meaning of "Western" identity in a Cold War context. In it, she argues for the return to a "values"-led understanding of the meaning of Western civilization: "The West will prove more vulnerable than any other society if it abandons the pursuit of visions and ideals for, more than any other community, it is the product not of geographical and racial forces but of the moulding power of the human spirit" (733).

It is interesting to juxtapose Ward's argument to Cooper's. Both thinkers are concerned by the ways in which Christianity's legacy has been lost. Cooper connects this loss to racism, colonialism, slavery, and exploitation of other peoples. Ward connects this loss rather to enlightenment rationalism, which she suggests leads to the worship of the state and to fascist and communist totalitarianisms: "Even the most doubtful must confront the fact that totalitarian government in its extremest form has returned when the waning of religion left the altars of the soul empty and turned men back to the oldest gods of all – the idols of the tribe" (734). Ward's religious genealogy overturns Hurston's argument for the interconnection of African and Christian religious practices, it re-inscribes an exceptionalist narrative for the West. Having done this, it also makes a plea for the translatability of Christianity into other religious traditions, and the possibility of an international common cause across different spiritual identities against the entirely secular and rationalist behemoth of communism. In order for this to happen, the West has to reassert its vision of a free and just society and reject identification with instrumental rationality, consumerism, and the market.

A crucial factor in the Cold War was, of course, the development of nuclear weapons technologies, and the build-up of nuclear arsenals justified by reference to deterrence theory (see the section on Technology, Progress, and Environment). The use of atomic weapons was one of the events of the Second World War that provoked reflection both on the laws of war and on just war theory amongst theologians and philosophers. One of the earliest contributors to these debates was

---

[12] See Barbara Ward, *The Rich Nations and the Poor Nations* (New York: W. W. Norton, 1962); Barbara Ward, *Spaceship Earth* (New York: Columbia University Press, 1966).

Elizabeth Anscombe. Like Ward, she was a Catholic, and her moral views reflect her commitment to certain Catholic values, including the intrinsic value of human life, but her approach to moral argument is very different from Ward's. In her text, Anscombe famously takes issue with the award by Oxford of an honorary degree to President Truman, the man who had authorized the bombings of Hiroshima and Nagasaki.[13] The way in which she makes her case, however, is not straightforwardly political or polemical, but by using the tools of analytic philosophy to attack and defend particular moral positions.

In the article, Anscombe argues for a principle of discrimination that enables us to (at least most of the time) draw a line between war and murder. War may encompass the deaths of innocents, but only if this is as a by-product of action that is aimed at military targets. Here she is invoking the doctrine of "double effect" often traced back to Saints Augustine and Thomas Aquinas, that the moral meaning of an action is driven by its intention. In the case of the bombings of Hiroshima and Nagasaki, however, there was no military target. The point of the action was to decimate the cities in order to force Japan into an earlier surrender. This indiscriminately instrumentalizes people who pose no threat for another purpose and has to be understood as murder not war. It is their indiscriminate nature that Anscombe sees as the moral key to the immorality of atomic weapons of mass destruction. Interestingly, she considers pacifism to be immoral for similar reasons, because it also fails to draw a line between war and murder, though with the opposite implication of no one counting as a legitimate target. "Mr Truman's Degree" (1956) is still frequently referenced in contemporary debates about the ethics of war. It provides a model not just for a particular position on *in bello* justice (meaning justice in the conduct of war), but more broadly for a way of doing moral philosophy at a time when moral philosophy was very much out of fashion.

The texts explored in this section make different arguments about religion, ethics, and international relations. Nevertheless, there are thematic connections between them. Several of them identify Christianity as having a crucial role in the formation of imperial and inter-state world order and conceptions of justice. Only Hurston stands out as telling a different history than the dominant "West" to "rest" narrative. Although for thinkers such as Goldman, the role of all religions is to support

[13] See Rachael Wiseman, "G. E. M. Anscombe: The False Hypocrisy of the Ideal Standard," in Charlotte Aston, Amber Carpenter, and Rachael Wiseman (eds.), *Portraits of Integrity: 26 Case Studies for History, Literature and Philosophy* (London: Bloomsbury Academic, 2020).

hierarchy and exploitation, for other thinkers the identification of the significance of Christianity for world politics is often normatively ambivalent. Theorists such as Buck and Weil set one interpretation of the meaning of Christianity against another, so that it is simultaneously a force for oppression and for liberation or justice. Addams, Buck, and Weil also contest the idea of a rationalist or rule-based approach to religious practice or ethical judgment, in contradistinction to Cooper and Anscombe, who rely on the power of reason to make their particular ethical cases. They all see ethics and/or religious values as central to international politics, but they do not treat ethics or religion as a causal variable that can be separated from broader conditions and structures, and neither do they see the articulation and defense of values as a matter of private conscience. For all of them, ethical and religious dimensions of international life are public and shared, whether through recording Voodoo rituals or picketing President Truman. It may be that this latter quality is particularly characteristic of women's international thought across all of the topics considered in this volume.

Kimberly Hutchings

Jane Addams

From Introduction to *Democracy and Social Ethics* (1902)

It is well to remind ourselves, from time to time, that "Ethics" is but another word for "righteousness," that for which many men and women of every generation have hungered and thirsted, and without which life becomes meaningless.

Certain forms of personal righteousness have become to a majority of the community almost automatic. It is as easy for most of us to keep from stealing our dinners as it is to digest them, and there is quite as much voluntary morality involved in one process as in the other. To steal would be for us to fall sadly below the standard of habit and expectation which makes virtue easy. In the same way we have been carefully reared to a sense of family obligation, to be kindly and considerate to the members of our own households, and to feel responsible for their well-being. As the rules of conduct have become established in regard to our self-development and our families, so they have been in regard to limited circles of friends. If the fulfilment of these claims were all that a righteous life required, the hunger and thirst would be stilled for many good men and women, and the clew of right living would lie easily in their hands.

But we all know that each generation has its own test, the contemporaneous and current standard by which alone it can adequately judge of its own moral achievements, and that it may not legitimately use a previous and less vigorous test. The advanced test must indeed include that which has already been attained; but if it includes no more, we shall fail to go forward, thinking complacently that we have "arrived" when in reality we have not yet started.

To attain individual morality in an age demanding social morality, to pride one's self on the results of personal effort when the time demands social adjustment, is utterly to fail to apprehend the situation.

It is perhaps significant that a German critic has of late reminded us that the one test which the most authoritative and dramatic portrayal of the Day of Judgment offers, is the social test. The stern questions are not in regard to personal and family relations, but did ye visit the poor, the criminal, the sick, and did ye feed the hungry?

All about us are men and women who have become unhappy in regard to their attitude toward the social order itself; toward the dreary round of uninteresting work, the pleasures narrowed down to those of appetite, the declining consciousness of brain power, and the lack of mental food which characterizes the lot of the large proportion of their fellow-citizens. These men and women have caught a moral challenge raised by the exigencies of contemporaneous life; some are bewildered, others who are denied the relief which sturdy action brings are even seeking an escape, but all are increasingly anxious concerning their actual relations to the basic organization of society.

The test which they would apply to their conduct is a social test. They fail to be content with the fulfilment of their family and personal obligations, and find themselves striving to respond to a new demand involving a social obligation; they have become conscious of another requirement, and the contribution they would make is toward a code of social ethics. The conception of life which they hold has not yet expressed itself in social changes or legal enactment, but rather in a mental attitude of maladjustment, and in a sense of divergence between their consciences and their conduct. They desire both a clearer definition of the code of morality adapted to present day demands and a part in its fulfilment, both a creed and a practice of social morality. In the perplexity of this intricate situation at least one thing is becoming clear: if the latter day moral ideal is in reality that of a social morality, it is inevitable that those who desire it must be brought in contact with the moral experiences of the many in order to procure an adequate social motive.

These men and women have realized this and have disclosed the fact in their eagerness for a wider acquaintance with and participation in the life about them. They believe that experience gives the easy and trustworthy impulse toward right action in the broad as well as in the narrow relations. We may indeed imagine many of them saying: "Cast our experiences in a larger mould if our lives are to be animated by the larger social aims. We have met the obligations of our family life, not because we had made resolutions to that end, but spontaneously, because of a common fund of memories and affections, from which the obligation naturally develops, and we see no other way in which to prepare ourselves for the larger social duties." Such a demand is reasonable, for by our daily experience we have discovered that we cannot mechanically hold up a moral standard, then jump at it in rare moments of exhilaration when we have the strength for it, but that even as the ideal itself must be a rational development of life, so the strength to attain it must be secured from interest in life itself. We slowly learn that life consists of processes as well as results, and that failure may come quite as easily from ignoring the adequacy of one's method as from selfish or ignoble aims. We are thus brought to a conception of Democracy not merely as a sentiment which desires the well-being of all men, nor yet as a creed which believes in the essential dignity and equality of all men, but as that which affords a rule of living as well as a test of faith.

We are learning that a standard of social ethics is not attained by travelling a sequestered byway, but by mixing on the thronged and common road where all must turn out for one another, and at least see the size of one another's burdens. To follow the path of social morality results perforce in the temper if not the practice of the democratic spirit, for it implies that diversified human experience and resultant sympathy which are the foundation and guarantee of Democracy.

There are many indications that this conception of Democracy is growing among us. We have come to have an enormous interest in human life as such, accompanied by confidence in its essential sound- ness. We do not believe that genuine experience can lead us astray any more than scientific data can.

We realize, too, that social perspective and sanity of judgment come only from contact with social experience; that such contact is the surest corrective of opinions concerning the social order, and concerning efforts, however humble, for its improvement. Indeed, it is a conscious- ness of the illuminating and dynamic value of this wider and more thorough human experience which explains in no small degree that new curiosity regarding human life which has more of a moral basis than an intellectual one.

The newspapers, in a frank reflection of popular demand, exhibit an omniverous [sic] curiosity equally insistent upon the trivial and the important. They are perhaps the most obvious manifestations of that desire to know, that "What is this?" and "Why do you do that?" of the child. The first dawn of the social consciousness takes this form, as the dawning intelligence of the child takes the form of constant question and insatiate curiosity.

Literature, too, portrays an equally absorbing though better adjusted desire to know all kinds of life. The popular books are the novels, dealing with life under all possible conditions, and they are widely read not only because they are entertaining, but also because they in a measure satisfy an unformulated belief that to see farther, to know all sorts of men, in an indefinite way, is a preparation for better social adjustment – for the remedying of social ills.

Doubtless one under the conviction of sin in regard to social ills finds a vague consolation in reading about the lives of the poor, and derives a sense of complicity in doing good. He likes to feel that he knows about social wrongs even if he does not remedy them, and in a very genuine sense there is a foundation for this belief.

Partly through this wide reading of human life, we find in ourselves a new affinity for all men, which probably never existed in the world before. Evil itself does not shock us as it once did, and we count only that man merciful in whom we recognize an understanding of the criminal. We have learned as common knowledge that much of the insensibility and hardness of the world is due to the lack of imagination which prevents a realization of the experiences of other people. Already there is a conviction that we are under a moral obligation in choosing our experiences, since the result of those experiences must ultimately determine our understanding of life. We know instinctively that if we grow contemptuous of our fellows, and consciously limit our intercourse to certain kinds of people whom we have previously decided to respect, we not only tremendously circumscribe our range of life, but limit the scope of our ethics.

We can recall among the selfish people of our acquaintance at least one common characteristic, – the conviction that they are different from other men and women, that they need peculiar consideration because they are more sensitive or more refined. Such people "refuse to be bound by any relation save the personally luxurious ones of love and admiration, or the identity of political opinion, or religious creed." We have learned to recognize them as selfish, although we blame them not for the will which chooses to be selfish, but for a narrowness of interest which deliberately selects its experience within a limited sphere, and we say that they illustrate the danger of concentrating the mind on narrow and unprogressive issues.

We know, at last, that we can only discover truth by a rational and democratic interest in life, and to give truth complete social expression is the endeavor upon which we are entering. Thus the identification with the common lot which is the essential idea of Democracy becomes the source and expression of social ethics. It is as though we thirsted to drink at the great wells of human experience, because we knew that a daintier or less potent draught would not carry us to the end of the journey, going forward as we must in the heat and jostle of the crowd.

The six following chapters are studies of various types and groups who are being impelled by the newer conception of Democracy to an acceptance of social obligations involving in each instance a new line of conduct. No attempt is made to reach a conclusion, nor to offer advice beyond the assumption that the cure for the ills of Democracy is more Democracy, but the quite unlooked-for result of the studies would seem to indicate that while the strain and perplexity of the situation is felt most keenly by the educated and self-conscious members of the community, the tentative and actual attempts at adjustment are largely coming through those who are simpler and less analytical.

Emma Goldman

From "Anarchism: What It Really Stands for" (1911)

"Property is robbery," said the great French Anarchist Proudhon. Yes, but without risk and danger to the robber. Monopolizing the accumulated efforts of man, property has robbed him of his birthright, and has turned him loose a pauper and an outcast. Property has not even the time-worn excuse that man does not create enough to satisfy all needs. The A B C student of economics knows that the productivity of labor within the last few decades far exceeds normal demand. But what are normal demands to an abnormal institution? The only demand that property recognizes is its own gluttonous appetite for greater wealth, because wealth means power; the power to subdue, to crush, to exploit, the power to enslave, to outrage, to degrade. America is particularly boastful of her great power, her enormous national wealth. Poor America, of what avail is all her wealth, if the individuals comprising the nation are wretchedly poor? If they live in squalor, in filth, in crime, with hope and joy gone, a homeless, soilless army of human prey.

[...]

Anarchism cannot but repudiate such a method of production: its goal is the freest possible expression of all the latent powers of the individual. Oscar Wilde defines a perfect personality as "one who develops under perfect conditions, who is not wounded, maimed, or in danger." A perfect personality, then, is only possible in a state of society where man is free to choose the mode of work, the conditions of work, and the freedom to work. One to whom the making of a table, the building of a house, or the tilling of the soil, is what the painting is to the artist and the discovery to the scientist, – the result of inspiration, of intense longing, and deep interest in work as a creative force. That being the ideal of Anarchism, its economic arrangements must consist of voluntary productive and distributive associations, gradually developing into free communism, as the best means of producing with the least waste of human energy. Anarchism, however, also recognizes the right of the individual, or numbers of individuals, to arrange at all times for other forms of work, in harmony with their tastes and desires.

Such free display of human energy being possible only under complete individual and social freedom, Anarchism directs its forces against the third and greatest foe of all social equality; namely, the State, organized authority, or statutory law, – the dominion of human conduct.

Just as religion has fettered the human mind, and as property, or the monopoly of things, has subdued and stifled man's needs, so has the State enslaved his spirit, dictating every phase of conduct. "All government in essence," says Emerson, "is tyranny." It matters not whether it is government by divine right or majority rule. In every instance its aim is the absolute subordination of the individual.

[…]

Indeed, the keynote of government is injustice. With the arrogance and self-sufficiency of the King who could do no wrong, governments ordain, judge, condemn, and punish the most insignificant offenses, while maintaining themselves by the greatest of all offenses, the annihilation of individual liberty.

[…]

Yet even a flock of sheep would resist the chicanery of the State, if it were not for the corruptive, tyrannical, and oppressive methods it employs to serve its purposes. Therefore Bakunin repudiates the State as synonymous with the surrender of the liberty of the individual or small minorities, – the destruction of social relationship, the curtailment, or complete denial even, of life itself, for its own aggrandizement. The State is the altar of political freedom and, like the religious altar, it is maintained for the purpose of human sacrifice.

In fact, there is hardly a modern thinker who does not agree that government, organized authority, or the State, is necessary only to maintain or protect property and monopoly. It has proven efficient in that function only.

Even George Bernard Shaw, who hopes for the miraculous from the State under Fabianism, nevertheless admits that "it is at present a huge machine for robbing and slave-driving of the poor by brute force." This being the case, it is hard to see why the clever prefacer wishes to uphold the State after poverty shall have ceased to exist.

Unfortunately, there are still a number of people who continue in the fatal belief that government rests on natural laws, that it maintains social order and harmony, that it diminishes crime, and that it prevents the lazy man from fleecing his fellows. I shall therefore examine these contentions.

A natural law is that factor in man which asserts itself freely and spontaneously without any external force, in harmony with the requirements of nature. For instance, the demand for nutrition, for sex gratification, for light, air, and exercise, is a natural law. But its expression needs not the machinery of government, needs not the club, the gun, the handcuff, or the prison. To obey such laws, if we may call it obedience, requires only spontaneity and free opportunity. That governments do not maintain themselves through such harmonious factors is proven by the terrible array of violence, force, and coercion all governments use in order to live. Thus Blackstone is right when he says, "Human laws are invalid, because they are contrary to the laws of nature."

Unless it be the order of Warsaw after the slaughter of thousands of people, it is difficult to ascribe to governments any capacity for order or social harmony. Order derived through submission and maintained by terror is not much of a safe guaranty; yet that is the only "order" that governments have ever maintained. True social harmony grows naturally out of solidarity of interests. In a society where those who always work never have anything, while those who never work enjoy everything, solidarity of interests is non-existent; hence social harmony is but a myth. The only way organized authority meets this grave situation is by extending still greater privileges to those who have already monopolized the earth, and by still further enslaving the disinherited masses. Thus the entire arsenal of government – laws, police, soldiers, the courts, legislatures, prisons, – is strenuously engaged in "harmonizing" the most antagonistic elements in society.

[...]

The deterrent influence of law on the lazy man is too absurd to merit consideration. If society were only relieved of the waste and expense of keeping a lazy class, and the equally great expense of the paraphernalia of protection this lazy class requires, the social tables would contain an abundance for all, including even the occasional lazy individual. Besides, it is well to consider that laziness results either from special privileges, or physical and mental abnormalities. Our present insane system of production fosters both, and the most astounding phenomenon is that people should want to work at all now. Anarchism aims to strip labor of its deadening, dulling aspect, of its gloom and compulsion. It aims to make work an instrument of joy, of strength, of color, of real harmony, so that the poorest sort of a man should find in work both recreation and hope.

To achieve such an arrangement of life, government, with its unjust, arbitrary, repressive measures, must be done away with. At best it has but imposed one single mode of life upon all, without regard to individual and social variations and needs. In destroying government and statutory laws, Anarchism proposes to rescue the self-respect and independence of the individual from all restraint and invasion by authority. Only in freedom can man grow to his full stature. Only in freedom will he learn to think and move, and give the very best in him. Only in freedom will he realize the true force of the social bonds which knit men together, and which are the true foundation of a normal social life.

But what about human nature? Can it be changed? And if not, will it endure under Anarchism?

Poor human nature, what horrible crimes have been committed in thy name! Every fool, from king to policeman, from the flatheaded parson to the visionless dabbler in science, presumes to speak authoritatively of human nature. The greater the mental charlatan, the more definite his insistence on the wickedness and weaknesses of human nature. Yet, how can any one speak of it today, with every soul in a prison, with every heart fettered, wounded, and maimed?

John Burroughs has stated that experimental study of animals in captivity is absolutely useless. Their character, their habits, their appetites undergo a complete transformation when torn from their soil in field and forest. With human nature caged in a narrow space, whipped daily into submission, how can we speak of its potentialities?

Freedom, expansion, opportunity, and, above all, peace and repose, alone can teach us the real dominant factors of human nature and all its wonderful possibilities.

Anarchism, then, really stands for the liberation of the human mind from the dominion of religion; the liberation of the human body from the dominion of property; liberation from the shackles and restraint of government. Anarchism stands for a social order based on the free grouping of individuals for the purpose of producing real social wealth; an order that will guarantee to every human being free access to the earth and full enjoyment of the necessities of life, according to individual desires, tastes, and inclinations.

[...]

As to methods. Anarchism is not, as some may suppose, a theory of the future to be realized through divine inspiration. It is a living force in the affairs of our life, constantly creating new conditions. The methods of Anarchism therefore do not comprise an iron-clad program to be carried out under all circumstances. Methods must grow out of the economic needs of each place and clime, and of the intellectual and temperamental requirements of the individual. The serene, calm character of a Tolstoy will wish different methods for social reconstruction than the intense, overflowing personality of a Michael Bakunin or a Peter Kropotkin.

Equally so it must be apparent that the economic and political needs of Russia will dictate more drastic measures than would England or America. Anarchism does not stand for military drill and uniformity; it does, however, stand for the spirit of revolt, in whatever form, against everything that hinders human growth. All Anarchists agree in that, as they also agree in their opposition to the political machinery as a means of bringing about the great social change.

[...]

The political superstition is still holding sway over the hearts and minds of the masses, but the true lovers of liberty will have no more to do with it. Instead, they believe with Stirner that man has as much liberty as he is willing to take. Anarchism therefore stands for direct action, the open defiance of, and resistance to, all laws and restrictions, economic, social, and moral. But defiance and resistance are illegal. Therein lies the salvation of man. Everything illegal necessitates integrity, self-reliance, and courage. In short, it calls for free, independent spirits, for "men who are men, and who have a bone in their backs which you cannot pass your hand through."

[...]

Direct action, having proven effective along economic lines, is equally potent in the environment of the individual. There a hundred forces encroach upon his being, and only persistent resistance to them will finally set him free. Direct action against the authority in the shop, direct action against the authority of the law, direct action against the invasive, meddlesome authority of our moral code, is the logical, consistent method of Anarchism.

Will it not lead to a revolution? Indeed, it will. No real social change has ever come about without a revolution. People are either not familiar with their history, or they have not yet learned that revolution is but thought carried into action.

Anarchism, the great leaven of thought, is today permeating every phase of human endeavor. Science, art, literature, the drama, the effort for economic betterment, in fact every individual and social opposition to the existing disorder of things, is illumined by the spiritual light of Anarchism. It is the philosophy of the sovereignty of the individual. It is the theory of social harmony. It is the great, surging, living truth that is reconstructing the world, and that will usher in the Dawn.

Anna Julia Cooper

From "Equality of Races and the Democratic Movement" (1925)

In his Thesis "Les Idées Égalitaires," Monsieur Bouglé declares quite decisively that the notion of Equality manifests itself only in our Western Civilization. "It is only in two parts of the glove [sic], Europe and America, at points where Latin, German and Anglo Saxon Races have developed a certain culture known as Occidental Civilization that we discover a general evolution towards Democracy" (p. 37).

In a word Mr. Bouglé's Thesis holds that Human Equality is a man-made concept resulting as a natural product of the transformations in Nordic Society. That his method in tracing its origin and growth must be purely realistic and dissociated from moral sanctions as to whether it is either right or realizable.

This decision is in my judgment as cold as the Russian Steppes and as bleak-barren as the peaks of the Himalayas. Can we – ought we to – analyze human society as if it were a question of minerals or of vegetation? Perhaps. But even so it is necessary in every case to beware of arbitrary preconceptions, and especially is it necessary to note well the importance of every exception which may vitiate the argument.

The subject which has been imposed upon me is, as worded, too vast and too vague for a thesis. To do it justice would require the life work of a Grote and another of a Gibbon, not to speak of the modern democracies to which James Bryce has devoted two big volumes of more than a thousand pages in treating only six examples of [them]; nor of the classic work of Tocqueville who limits himself quite simply to the U.S.A. ending with 1830.

"Les Idées Égalitaires et le Mouvement Démocratique." (The Concept of Equality and the Democratic Movement.) Where? And at what Epoch?

It is necessary to set up some sort of metes and bounds for the terrain even if the flight contemplates only the stratosphere.

I have read carefully and with deep and lively interest the learned and scientific work of Dr. Bouglé of the Sorbonne Faculté and I would like if I dared such a liberty to place beside it some facts in actual life from a single one of the nations who bear aloft with assurance the banner of Equality in Democracy, who are privileged as the most advanced to the torch of civilization for the enlightenment of the "Backward" races but who, to the world's amazement, show up some deplorable lapses away from the formula proposed by the philosopher. And right here may be the danger spot.

If one approaches the subject by pure reason it becomes necessary to accept the conclusion in its entirety without personal or local bias and without exception taken to suit any embarrassing fact. If for example the conditions for equality as defined by the author are achieved by some nations not included in the term "occidental," we cannot imagine some fictitious lines in order to exclude the ones or to include the others. A case in point may be noted in the Franco-Japanese Treaty of August 4, 1896, which affirms:

Among the legislative enactments of countries of the Orient, a place apart, a place of honor must be conceded to that of the Empire of Japan. Most recent monuments bear the imprint of Western civilizations, the principles with which they are inspired are those of the most advanced codes of the Old Europe, and nowhere perhaps does this characteristic loom up more conspicuously than in the regulations which at the present moment govern the status in Japan of foreigners living there or who carry on business there. Equality of rights before the law between nationals and foreigners is openly and formally proclaimed, etc., etc.

Is it not reasonable to grant that if our theory regarding the elite of nations is not sufficiently comprehensive to include a nation with such a creditable recommendation, ... we should either enlarge our definition to harmonize with the facts or else treat the subject of Equality not as an abstraction but as it manifests itself uniquely in Europe and in America? A better hypothesis it seems to me, would be the postulate that progress in the democratic sense is an inborn human endowment – a shadow mark of the Creator's image, or if you will an urge-cell, the universal and unmistakable hall-mark traceable to the Father of all, That

> In the mud and scum of things
> There alway, alway something sings

and it is that "Something" – that *Singing* Something, which distinguishes the first Man from the last ape, which in a subtle way tagged him with the picturesque Greek title *anthropos*, the *upward face*, and which justifies the claim to equality by birthright to the inheritance from a common Father for the "Backward" no less than the "Advanced" among his varying but undeniable progeny. The sense of "belonging" may seem to slumber more or less indefinitely here or there for racial groups and it may be blatantly denied and successfully ignored by aggressive usurpers who assert with conviction: "We are *the people*! Beside us there is none other." But the divine Spark is capable of awakening at the most unexpected moment and it never is wholly smothered or stamped out. Therefore the racial group or nation that undertakes the role to play God and dominate the earth, has an awful, a terrific responsibility.

To assume that the ideas inherent in social progress descend by divine favor upon the Nordic people, a Superior Race chosen to dominate the Earth, assuredly pampers the pride of those believing themselves the Elect of God. But one may as well anticipate Surprises. For example note the situation in Russia today (1925) little dreamed of 20 years ago, likewise in China, Turkey, in Egypt, the Gandhi movement in India.

"There are some instants," says Bryce, "when it would be wiser to bestow free institutions even if they are liable to be misused than to foment discontent by withholding them."

Might we not go so far as to say *a priori* that we ought to admit for all peoples the possibility of establishing these institutions without withholding them from any.

I trust my audacity may be pardoned in daring to take exception to certain conclusions of one of my judges, the learned Dr. Bouglé whose thesis [on] Egalité has been assigned me for questioning.

It is necessary, whatever the conditions to speak the truth as one sees it even if from a somewhat blurred viewpoint one is not able to follow exactly the shining pathway of the Master.

At page 44 the author [Bouglé] demands: "Would any one dare assert that in a given modern society there exist at the same time two different standards of justice fixing for the same act a heavy penalty if it has been committed by an artisan, a light penalty if it has been committed by a property holder?"

Two different laws inscribed as statutes? No. But custom which defies the law and makes of it a scrap of paper is so notorious that even for the nation where we love to picture the foyer of democracy, equality and justice, it is a common saying in advance of trials: "You can't put a million dollars in jail, or free a poor devil without a cent, particularly if the latter happens to be of race proscribed." ...

It is a curious fact that the nations calling themselves Christian under the banner of the Prince of Peace, devoted ostensibly to the progress of civilization, proudly named Christian civilization, Nations who adore the principles of Democracy, of Equality, of fraternity, who, among their congeners practice the noblest philanthropies, statesmen, philosophers, literati, preachers, teachers of the finest, most exalted ideas have to arraign themselves stoically against the simplest amenities of the Gospel, such as "a cup of cold water in the name of a Disciple," as soon as the question of color presents itself.

What is the trouble?

Is it that the Hand of the Potter has slipped? Must we blame God because He made of one blood all peoples that dwell on earth but went to sleep during the firing when some millions were tanned yellow, some brown and some even black. Or rather may we not rejoice that our civilization is to learn and finally apply this last and noblest lesson, the most difficult of all taught by the Master and so sacred that it should be studied, learned and inwardly digested till graven on the hearts of men and emblazoned on the suffering pathway of the Cross: "By this shall men know that ye are my disciples, that ye love one another," and that so much the more because on receiving the least of my brethren ye are receiving Me.

The concept of Equality as it is the genuine product of the idea of inherent value in the individual derived from the essential worth of Humanity must be before all else unquestionably of universal application. It operates not between such and such places, – such or such shape of the cranium, such and such theories of civilization. In my opinion, which makes no pretensions to scientific sanctions on either sociological or psychological grounds, instead of being the Special product of any unique cult, the idea of human equality is the result of the final equilibrium of all the human forces of the entire world.

So far the civilization called occidental has attained partial equilibrium only of the physical and perhaps of the intellectual forces. The banner today is borne by the men or the nation who invents the most marvelous project of destruction, the most powerful and irresistible instrument of War. The Death Ray Atomic Bomb (1945) – is tops. But unless I am greatly mistaken, this poor world has need of a second incarnation of Divine Love to teach compassion, to erect anew the ideal already so ancient but so little comprehended even by the most advanced of today: To love mercy, to practice justice and to walk humbly before God. Then equality will become no longer the equilibrium of the jungle where one concedes the equality of another only when he cannot crush or exploit him. For equality, as I understand it, is objective, not subjective. It is not for the little fellow who swells up with the idea I am as good as the other fellow; but for the big fellow with all the power and all the controls to stop and consider: The other fellow is as good as I am. Both human, both mortal, both entitled to a place in the sun. The veritable equality will then be the harmony of a well tuned orchestra where each from the greatest to the smallest contributes at his best according to the part assigned by the conductor who can do no wrong, each player striving no longer to destroy but to serve the music of the spheres: and I have the assurance to believe that the contribution of the brother in black may be considerable in a normal world. He has the Heart Talent which perhaps the civilization "called occidental" might take on to advantage; and let not our world despise the one-talent man, and let him not despise himself and hide his lord's gift because he knows the Master is an austere man: Each at his best, reverencing the Self in the All. The Master hath need of thee! Here you have my religion and my philosophy.

Pearl S. Buck

From *Is There a Case for Foreign Missions?* (1933)

Would I, even if I were a Buddhist, be willing to see Christ die out altogether from the hearts of men? Would I be willing to have men forget that He ever lived, forget His words, imperfectly as they are given to us? Even though it is proved in some future time that there never lived an actual Christ and what we think of as Christ should some day be found to be the essence of men's dreams of simplest and most beautiful goodness, would I be willing to have that personification of dreams pass out of men's minds?

What would it mean to have Him we call Christ pass away from our country, from ourselves? I know that for each of us Christ means something, some one different. But that does not matter. We all think when we speak that name of a quality of humanity which is tinged with divinity, for some of us actual and physical, for some of us with the divinity of the whole vast and unknown universe which we cannot understand and perhaps shall never understand. That quality of humanity is made up of simplicity and sincerity in all behaviour, of a perfect sympathy with others even where there is not complete agreement and understanding, of hatred and intolerance of hypocrisy, yes, and, above all, of a bearing of the burdens of the weak, a love even for one's enemies. These ideals – the noblest of which we are capable even of thinking about – are inseparably connected with the figure of Christ, veiled in a measure as He must ever be to us all.

[...]

Are we willing that these ideals should fade from our memories, our life ? They have borne too little fruit, it is true, both in us as individuals and in us as a nation. They have borne a poor diseased fruit at best. But even at times against my will I have been compelled to acknowledge that they have borne fruit. In nations where the figure of Christ has been perceived, however dimly, I find something I do not find elsewhere. To some degree the sick are cared for, the weak and defective are housed and cared for with tenderness, women are more honoured, people do struggle somewhat for goodness; somehow the poor are helped a little. It is all too little, too badly done, and there are many failures and much suffering, but – here is the point – it is better than where the figure of Christ has never been known. Somehow where Christ has been once truly seen at all, either by an individual or by a people, there remains a spirit of some sort, a memory. The memory may be weakened, the spirit may fail. But there is a difference.

This difference is both tangible and intangible. It is tangible in such instances as catastrophes of flood or accident where help is given generously and quickly even to strangers. I have lived long in a great and lofty civilization, but one where there is not this universal attitude to the poor and suffering. There is the tangible result that, even though corruption and crime endure for a time there are efforts to stay it. There are things that are done for children, for the aged, for insane persons. These are all differences, it seems to me, in a civilization which has had the figure of Christ as a part of its spiritual thought.

[...]

I am forced, therefore, to the question: Am I willing to have this happen? Am I willing to have the figure of Christ, however veiled, pass from the earth?

I know that I am not willing. I know that active goodness is the most beautiful thing in the universe to me. The stars and suns and the mystery of creation are not so wonderful to me as this mystery – that we human creatures know good and evil and can choose between them. To me the most exciting life in the world is the life that struggles towards personal goodness, which is beauty. The most wonderful spectacle is to see some one making that struggle. The most triumphant moment in life is the moment when I realize, whether for myself or for another, that a choice has been made, strength gained, a deeper content achieved by one step more along that hard and stirring adventure – the life of a man or woman who is determined to find the best he knows and do it. This struggle is made manifest in the Christian life. Others live it also, many who never have heard the name of Christ; but to know the meaning of Christ's life, to know how He lived and died, is an inestimable support and help. It has so proved to those peoples who have had Him, even though they have understood Him very little.

This does not mean that I consider all other religions worthless beside Christianity. I do not believe that any religion is comprehensive enough to exclude all others. I should be loath to see the best of any pass away from men's knowledge. I do not believe we can spare anything that is good. How much less then, can we spare that union of inner mystic spirit combined with social dynamic which we recognize as the highest form of Christianity! It is not necessary to discover or assert the superiority of Christianity over other religions. It is only necessary to recognize that we cannot do without Christ, and to decide to live by what we believe.

Then the case becomes very simple. If I am not willing for Christ to die, what hypocrisy is mine if I will do nothing to keep Him alive in the hearts and understandings of men; what selfishness if I keep Him for myself alone, or for my race! If I could so keep Him I would lose Him, in truth. His whole Spirit would evade me. My smallness could not hold Him, as no smallness has ever held Him. I must be great enough to share Christ if I would keep Christ mine.

For me, therefore, there is a case for foreign missions.

So I have retraced my own path of reasoning. It will not, perhaps, be satisfactory to others. What satisfies one person may not satisfy another. I have compressed in this brief space a spiritual experience which has extended over many years. It went of course into many intellectual ramifications and investigations into other religions of which I cannot take space to tell now. But the end was simply what I have given in simple terms.

My feelings in regard to the missionary body remain to-day the same. We must send abroad a higher type of person than the average American, even though he be above the average Christian – it will mean fewer, but it will be worth while if those few are better fitted for their opportunity. I believe the whole organization of foreign missions needs intelligent study, and it is probable that in the light of such study the basis of organization will need to be changed. We must know better the needs of the people to whom we go, and we must see how or if we can supply those needs whatever they are. This inevitably means a missionary of higher and more specific training and experience, suited to some particular place or need. Nor is this impossible. I have been impressed with the number of men of high training and reputation who would willingly for a period of years or perhaps for the rest of their lives give their time to some other country than their own.

I should like to see every missionary sent to satisfy a special need of a community – not the artificial need of a mission station for a clerical man or a woman evangelist or what not, but a real need of the people. I should like him to feel that in satisfying this need he was fulfilling the primary purpose of his religion, and not that he was to use it as a bait for enticing any one into belief in a creed or into belonging to an organization. This, of course, changes at once the whole basis of missions. It shifts the emphasis from preaching to a people to sharing a life with them, the best life we know. It seems to me this is the only possible basis for missions. It removes from us the insufferable stigma of moral arrogance, and it gives us besides a test of our own worth. Before we can share anything with benefit we must have tried it ourselves. The present situation of being able to go and preach to other peoples what we do not practise is intolerable to persons of any sensitivity.

At the same time, I do not believe in that common retort that I hear made, in answer to the question of foreign missions, 'When everything in my own country is as it ought to be I will do something about other countries.' My experience of the sort of person who says this is that he usually does nothing about his own country either. It is a mere excuse. I do not believe that we shall have at any time any country which is wholly Christian. The Christian group must strengthen in all countries at the same time if it is to continue at all. But it is essential that we strive to apply to ourselves those principles which we are asking others to apply. One of the great indignations of my life was to find certain women in Christian churches in America who would give money and time to a foreign missionary society for work among peoples ten thousand miles away but who would not open the doors of their homes to students and persons of other races in their own cities, strangers and foreigners in America. What is the use of preaching Christ abroad when we deny Him by such acts as these at home?

Above all, then, let the Spirit of Christ be manifested by mode of life rather than by preaching. I am wearied unto death with this preaching. It deadens all thought, it confuses all issues, it is producing, in China at least, a horde of hypocrites, and in the theological seminaries a body of Chinese ministers which makes one despair for the future, because they are learning how to preach about Christianity rather than how to live the Christian life. Let us cease our talk for a time and cut off our talkers, and let us try to express our religion in terms of life. The spoken word ought to be only a bit of fuel added to a flame already burning.

Zora Neale Hurston

From "Hoodoo" (1935)

New Orleans is now and has ever been the hoodoo capital of America. Great names in rites that vie with those of Hayti in deeds that keep alive the powers of Africa.

Hoodoo, or Voodoo, as pronounced by the whites, is burning with a flame in America, with all the intensity of a suppressed religion. It has its thousands of secret adherents. It adapts itself like Christianity to its locale, reclaiming some of its borrowed characteristics to itself. Such as fire-worship as signified in the Christian church by the altar and the candles. And the belief in the power of water to sanctify as in baptism.

Belief in magic is older than writing. So nobody knows how it started.

The way we tell it, hoodoo started way back there before everything. Six days of magic spells and mighty words and the world with its elements above and below was made. And now, God is leaning back taking a seventh day rest. When the eighth day comes around, He'll start to making new again.

Man wasn't made until around half past five on the sixth day, so he can't know how anything was done. Kingdoms crushed and crumbled whilst man went gazing up into the sky and down into the hollows of the earth trying to catch God working with His hands so he could find out His secrets and learn how to accomplish and do but no man yet has seen God's hand, nor yet His fingernails. All they could know was that God made everything to pass and perish except stones.

[...]

Moses was the first man who ever learned God's power-compelling words and it took him forty years to learn ten words. So he made ten plagues and ten commandments. But God gave him His rod for a present, and showed him the back part of His glory. Then too, Moses could walk out of the sight of man. But Moses never would have stood before the Burning Bush, if he had not married Jethro's daughter.

Jethro was a great hoodoo man. Jethro could tell Moses could carry power as soon as he saw him. In fact he felt him coming. Therefore, he took Moses and crowned him and taught him. So Moses passed on beyond Jethro with his rod. He lifted it up and tore a nation out of Pharaoh's side, and Pharaoh couldn't help himself. Moses talked with the snake that lives in a hole right under God's foot-rest. Moses had fire in his head and a cloud in his mouth. The snake had told him God's making words. The words of doing and the words of obedience. Many a man thinks he is making something when he's only changing things around. But God let Moses make. And then Moses had so much power he made the eight winged angels split open a mountain to bury him in, and shut up the hole behind them.

And ever since the days of Moses, kings have been toting rods for a sign of power. But it's sham-polish because no king has ever had the power of even one of Moses' words. Because Moses made a nation and a book, a thousand million leaves of ordinary men's writing couldn't tell what Moses said.

Then when the moon had dragged a thousand tides behind her, Solomon was a man. So Sheba, from her country where she was, felt him carrying power and therefore she came to talk with Solomon and hear him.

The Queen of Sheba was an Ethiopian just like Jethro, with power unequal to man. She didn't have to deny herself to give gold to Solomon. She had gold-making words. But she was thirsty, and the country where she lived was dry to her mouth. So she listened to her talking ring and went to see Solomon, and the fountain in his garden quenched her thirst.

So she made Solomon Wise and gave him her talking ring.

And Solomon built a room with a secret door and everyday he shut himself inside and listened to his ring. So he wrote down the ring-talk in books.

That's what the old ones said in ancient times and talk it again.

It was way back there – the old folks told it – that Raw-Head-And-Bloody-Bones had reached down and laid hold of the tap-root that points to the center of the world. And they talked about High Walker too. But they talked in people's language and nobody knew them but the old folks.

Nobody knows for sure how many thousands in America are warmed by the fire of hoodoo, because the worship is bound in secrecy. It is not the accepted theology of the Nation and so believers conceal their faith. Brother from sister, husband from wife. Nobody can say where it begins or ends. Mouths don't empty themselves unless the ears are sympathetic and knowing.

That is why these voodoo ritualistic orgies of Broadway and popular fiction are so laughable. The profound silence of the initiated remains what it is. Hoodoo is not drum beating and dancing. There are no moon-worshippers among the Negroes in America.

From "Voodoo" (1938)

DR. HOLLY says that in the beginning God and His woman went into the bedroom together to commence creation. That was the beginning of everything and Voodoo is just as old as that. It is the old, old mysticism of the world in African terms. Voodoo is a religion of creation and life. It is the worship of the sun, the water and other natural forces, but the symbolism is no better understood than that of other religions and consequently is taken too literally.

Thus the uplifted forefinger in greeting in Voodoo is really phallic and that means the male attributes of the Creator. The handclasp that ends in the fingers of one hand encircling the thumb of the other signifies the vulva encircling the penis, denoting the female aspect of deity. "What is the truth?" Dr. Holly asked me, and knowing that I could not answer him he answered himself through a Voodoo ceremony in which Mambo, that is the priestess, richly dressed is asked this question ritualistically. She replies by throwing back her veil and revealing her organs. The ceremony means that this is the infinite, the ultimate truth. There is no mystery beyond the mysterious source of life.

[...]

Some of the other men of education in Haiti who have given time to the study of Voodoo esoterics do not see such deep meanings in voodoo practices. They see only a pagan religion with an African pantheon. And right here, let it be said that the Haitian gods, mysteres, or loa are not the catholic calendar of saints done over in black as has been stated by casual observers. This has been said over and over in print because the adepts have been seen buying the lithographs of saints, but this is done because they wish some visual representation of the invisible ones, and as yet no Haitian artist has given them an interpretation or concept of the loa. But even the most illiterate peasant knows that the picture of the saint is only an approximation of the loa. In proof of this, most of the houngans require those who place themselves under their tutelage in order to become hounci to bring a composition book for notes, and in this they must copy the houngan's concept of the loa. I have seen several of these books with the drawings, and none of them even pretend to look like the catholic saints. Neither are their attributes the same. Who are the loa, then? I would not pretend to call the name of every mystere in Haiti. *No one* knows the name of every loa because every major section of Haiti has its own local variation. It has gods and goddesses of places and forces that are unknown fifty miles away. The heads of "families" of gods are known all over the country, but there are endless variations of the demigods even in the same localities. It is easy to see the unlettered meeting some unknown natural phenomenon and not knowing how to explain it, and a new local demigod is named. It is always added to the "family," to which it seems, by the circumstances, to belong. Hence, the long list of Ogouns, Erzulies, Cimbies, Irgbas, and the like. All over Haiti, however, it is agreed that there are two *classes* of deities, the Rada or Arada and the Petro. The Rada gods are the "good" gods and are said to have originated in Dahomey. The Petro gods are the ones who do evil work and are said to have been brought over from the Congo, some say Guinea and the Congo have provided the two sets of gods but place names of Dahomey are included in the names of the Rada deities. Perhaps there is a mingling of several African localities and spirits under the one head in Haiti. Damballah or Dambala Ouedo Freda Tocan Dahomey, to give him his full name, heads the Rada gods. Baron Samedi (Lord of Saturday), Baron Cimeterre (Lord of the Cemetery), and Baron Crois (Lord of the cross), one spirit with three names is the head of the Petro loa.

[…]

Damballah Ouedo is the supreme Mystere and his signature is the serpent. Though the picture that is bought of him is that of St. Patrick, he in no way resembles that Irish saint. The picture of St. Patrick is used because it has the snakes in it which no other saint has. All over Haiti it is well established that Damballah is identified as Moses, whose symbol was the serpent. This worship of Moses recalls the hard-to-explain fact that wherever the Negro is found, there are traditional tales of Moses and his supernatural powers that are not in the Bible nor can they be found in any written life of Moses. The rod of Moses is said to have been a subtle serpent and hence came his great powers. All over the Southern States, the British West Indies and Haiti there are reverent tales of Moses and his magic. It is hardly possible that all of them sprang up spontaneously in these widely separated areas on the blacks coming in contact with Christianity after coming to the Americas. It is more probable that there is a tradition of Moses as the great father of magic scattered over Africa and Asia. Perhaps some of his feats recorded in the Pentateuch are the folk beliefs of such a character grouped about a man for it is well established that if a memory is great enough, other memories will cluster about it, and those in turn will bring their suites of memories to gather about this focal point, because perhaps, they are all scattered parts of the one thing like Plato's concept of the perfect thing.

[…]

Damballah is the highest and most powerful of all the gods, but never is he referred to as the father of the gods as was [sic] Jupiter, Odin and great Zeus and while he is not spoken of as the father of the gods, whenever any of the other gods meet him they bow themselves and sing,

"Ohe', Ohe'! Ce Papa nous qui pe' passe'!" (It is our papa who passes.) He is the father of all that is powerful and good. The others are under him in power, that is all. He never does "bad" work. If you make a ceremony to any of the other gods and ask favors, they must come to Damballah to get the permission and the power to do it. Papa Damballah is the *great source.*

Around Damballah is grouped the worship of the beautiful in nature. One must offer him flowers, the best perfumes, a pair of white chickens; his "mange" sec (dry food) consisting of corn meal and an egg which must be placed on the altar on a white plate. He is offered cakes, french melons, watermelons, pineapples, rice, bananas, grapes, oranges, apples and the like. There must be a porcelain pot with a cover on the altar, desserts and sweet liquors, and olive oil. There must be a representation of Damballah within the oratory, a small crucifix, a bouquet, a bottle of liquor, a glass of oil to keep his lamps burning on his day. He brings good luck to those who make offerings to him regularly and faithfully. "It is possible for you to have a grand situation and it is even possible to become a minister or the president if you serve Papa Damballah faithfully. But yes!" His day is Wednesday in the afternoon of every week and his sacrifice is pair of white chickens, hen and cock. The average houngan says that he is given the white cock and hen because he guards domestic happiness. Dr. Holly says it is another acknowledgment of the bi-sexual concept of the Creator, and that Damballah with the subtle wisdom and powers represented by the snake is to the Africans something of a creator, if not actively, certainly The Source.

[...]

There is in Voodoo worship a reverent remoteness where Damballah is concerned. There are not the numerous personal anecdotes about him as about some of the lesser and more familiar gods. I asked why they did not ask more things of him, and I was told that when they make "services" to the other gods they are making them to Damballah indirectly for none of the others can do anything unless he gives them the power. There is the feeling of awe. One approaches the lesser gods and they in turn approach the great one. The others must listen and take sides in the neighborhood disputes, jealousies and feuds. One comes to Damballah for advancement and he is approached through beauty. Give Damballah his sweet wine and feed his wisdom with white pigeons.

Simone Weil

From *Letter to a Priest* (1951)

The Church has borne too many evil fruits for there not to have been some mistake made at the beginning.

Europe has been spiritually uprooted, cut off from that antiquity in which all the elements of our civilization have their origin; and she has gone about uprooting the other continents from the sixteenth century onwards.

After twenty centuries, Christianity has, practically speaking, not penetrated outside the white race; Catholicism is much more limited still in extent. America remained for sixteen centuries without hearing Christ spoken of (yet St. Paul had said: Glad Tidings which have been announced to the *whole* of creation) and the nations living there were destroyed in the midst of the most appalling cruelties before ever having had the time to know Him. Missionary zeal has not Christianized Africa, Asia and Oceania, but has brought these territories under the cold, cruel and destructive domination of the white race, which has trodden down everything.

It would be strange, indeed, that the word of Christ should have produced such results if it had been properly understood.

Christ said: 'Go ye, and teach all nations and baptize those who believe', that is to say, those who believe in Him. He never said: 'Compel them to renounce all that their ancestors have looked upon as sacred and to adopt as a holy book the history of a small nation unknown to them.' I have been assured that the Hindus would in no way be prevented by their own tradition from receiving baptism, were it not for the fact that the missionaries make it a condition that they must renounce Vishnu and Shiva. If a Hindu believes that Vishnu is the Word and Shiva the Holy Spirit, and that the Word was incarnate in Krishna and in Rama before being so in Jesus, by what right can he be refused baptism? In the same way, in the quarrel between the Jesuits and the Papacy over the missions in China, it was the Jesuits who were carrying out the words of Christ.

Missionary action in the way in which it is, in fact, conducted (especially since the condemnation of Jesuit policy in China in the seventeenth century) is bad, save perhaps in certain individual cases. The missionaries – even the martyrs amongst them – are too closely accompanied by guns and battleships for them to be true witnesses of the Lamb – I have never heard that the Church has ever officially condemned punitive expeditions undertaken to avenge the missionaries.

Personally, I should never give even as much as a sixpence towards any missionary enterprise. I think that for any man a change of religion is as dangerous a thing as a change of language is for a writer. It may turn out a success, but it can also have disastrous consequences.

The Catholic religion contains explicitly truths which other religions contain implicitly. But, conversely, other religions contain explicitly truths which are only implicit in Christianity. The most well-informed Christian can still learn a great deal concerning divine matters from other religious traditions; although inward spiritual light can also cause him to apprehend everything through the medium of his own tradition. All the same, were these other traditions to disappear from the face of the earth, it would be an irreparable loss. The missionaries have already made far too many of them disappear as it is.

St. John of the Cross compares faith to reflections of silver, truth being gold. The various authentic religious traditions are different reflections of the same truth, and perhaps equally precious. But we do not realize this. Each of us lives only one of these traditions and sees the others from the outside. But, as Catholics are forever repeating – and rightly – of unbelievers, a religion can only be known from the inside.

[...]

A third mystery is that of the relations between Christianity and the Empire. Tiberius wanted to have Christ placed in the Pantheon and refused first of all to persecute the Christians.

Later on his attitude changed. Piso, Galba's adopted son, probably belonged to a Christian family [...]. How are we to explain the fact that men like Trajan and above all Marcus Aurelius should have so relentlessly persecuted the Christians? Yet Dante places Trajan in paradise. On the other hand Commodus and other villainous emperors rather favoured them. And in what circumstances did the Empire later on come to adopt Christianity as the official religion? And on what conditions? What degradation? Was the latter made to suffer by way of exchange? In what circumstances was accomplished that collusion between the Church of Christ and the Beast? For the Beast of the Apocalypse is almost certainly the Empire.

The Roman Empire was a totalitarian and grossly materialistic regime, founded upon the exclusive worship of the State, like Nazism. A thirst for spirituality was latent amongst the wretched ones subjected to this regime. The Emperors realized from the very beginning how necessary it was to assuage it with some false mysticism, for fear that a true mysticism should arise and upset everything.

An attempt was made to transfer the Eleusinian Mysteries to Rome. These mysteries had almost certainly – convincing indications point to this – lost all genuine spiritual content.

The atrocious massacres which had so frequently taken place in Greece and especially in Athens since the Roman conquest, and even before, had very likely caused their transmission to be interrupted; the Mysteries were perhaps re-manufactured by initiates of the first degree. This would explain the scorn with which Clement of Alexandria talks about them, although he may at one time have been an initiate himself. However, the attempted transfer failed.

To make up for this, the Druids and the followers of the secret cult of Dionysus were exterminated, the Pythagoreans and all the philosophers pitilessly persecuted, the Egyptian cults prohibited, the Christians treated as we know.

The pullulation of oriental cults in Rome at that time resembles exactly that of sects of a theosophical order at the present day. As far as one is able to make out, then as now, they were not the genuine article, but artificial creations designed for snobs.

The Antonines represent something like an oasis in the appalling history of the Roman Empire. How is it that they were able to persecute the Christians?

One may ask oneself whether under cover of the enforced under-ground existence genuinely criminal elements had not insinuated them-selves among the Christians.

Above all it is necessary to bear in mind the apocalyptic spirit which inspired them. The expectation of the imminent coming of the Kingdom exalted them and gave them courage to perform the most extraordinary acts of heroism, just as the imminent expectation of the Revolution does nowadays in the case of the Communists. There must be many points of resemblance between these two psychologies.

But, in both cases, such expectancy also constitutes a very great social danger.

The historians of antiquity are full of stories about cities where, as a result of certain slaves having been granted their freedom by some tyrant for one reason or another, it became impossible for masters to make themselves obeyed by those that remained.

Slavery was such an unnatural State that it was only bearable for those whose souls were crushed by the total absence of hope. As soon as a ray of hope appeared, disobedience became rife.

What an effect must have been produced by the hope contained in the Glad Tidings! The Glad Tidings meant not only the Redemption; they meant even more the practically certain fact of the very imminent coming on earth of Christ in all his Glory.

In St. Paul, for every recommendation to be kind and just addressed to the masters, there are perhaps ten recommendations addressed to the slaves, enjoining them to work and be obedient. This might, if necessary, be explained by the remains of social prejudices left in him in spite of Christianity. But it is far more likely that it was much easier to persuade Christian masters to show kindness than it was to persuade Christian slaves, intoxicated by the expectation of the Last Day, to show obedience.

Marcus Aurelius perhaps disapproved of slavery; for it is not true that Greek philosophy, with the exception of Aristotle, acted as the apologist of that institution. According to Aristotle himself, certain philosophers condemned it as being 'absolutely contrary to nature and reason'. Plato, in the Statesman, only conceives of it being legitimately employed in dealing with criminals, in the same way as we do in the matter of imprisonment and forced labour. But Marcus Aurelius had as his business that of keeping order above all other things. He would remind himself bitterly of the fact.

Catholics readily justify the massacres of heretics by citing the social dangers inherent in heresy. It never occurs to them that the persecutions of the Christians in the early centuries are open to the same justification, with at least as great a show of reason. Much greater no doubt, for no heresy contained an idea so profoundly disturbing as the practically certain right to expect the imminent coming of Christ the King. It is certain that a wave of disobedience among the slaves of the Empire would have brought the whole edifice toppling down in the midst of frightful disorders.

By the time of Constantine, the state of apocalyptic expectation must have worn rather thin. Besides, the massacres of Christians, by hindering the transmission of the most profound doctrine, had perhaps – and even probably – emptied Christianity of a great part of its spiritual content. Constantine was able to carry out successfully in the case of Christianity the operation Claudius had been unsuccessful in carrying out in the case of Eleusis.

But it was neither in the interests nor in keeping with the dignity of the Empire that its official religion should appear as the continuation and crowning point of the centuries-old traditions of countries conquered, crushed and degraded by Rome – Egypt, Greece and Gaul. In the case of Israel, that did not matter; in the first place the new law was very far removed from the old law; and then, above all, Jerusalem no longer existed any more. Besides, the spirit of the old law, so widely separated from all mysticism, was not so very different from the Roman spirit itself. Rome could come to terms with the God of Hosts.

Even the Jewish national spirit, by preventing a great many Christians, from the start, from recognizing the affinity between Christianity and the authentic spirituality of the gentiles, was for Rome a favourable element in Christianity. This spirit, strangely enough, had even communicated itself to converted 'pagans'.

Rome, like every colonizing country, had morally and spiritually uprooted the conquered countries. Such is always the effect of a colonial conquest. It was not a question of giving them back their roots. It was necessary they should be still a little bit further uprooted.

[...]

Christianity, subjected to the combined influence of Israel and Rome, succeeded brilliantly in this task. Even today, wherever it is carried by missionaries, it exercises the same uprooting effect.

Barbara Ward

From *Faith and Freedom: A Study of Western Society* (1954)

However rational, however compelling, however logical the arguments for Western unity may be, however obvious the benefits of economic cooperation, however hopeful the promise of amity between the nations, one may still question whether reason or logic, of themselves, are enough to change the direction of Western development. The vitalities that must be mastered are the fiercest in the world. They appeal to the ultimate instincts in mankind – the protection of the tribe and the struggle for physical survival. Reason may be outmatched in its struggle with such giants. Has Western man other forces to summon to his aid?

There is, of course, the fact of fear. It is not to be despised.

[...]

But fear alone is a poor counsellor because it is essentially negative. The Western world cannot combat Communism on such a basis. A people guided only by fear leaves all the initiative and all the advantage with the other side and is reduced to a blind defensive maneuvering in order to counter the other's positive actions, to inferiority, to loss of control and in all probability to ultimate defeat. Throughout history, the men with a positive goal and a persistent aim have had their way. Like artists at work on the raw material of stone or wood or canvas, they have imposed their vision and drawn the rough vitalities of human existence together into new patterns of society. True, the materials have often proved recalcitrant and the vision has been distorted. Yet such ideals as the Greek polis, the "chosen people" of Jewry, the unity of Christendom, the American Republic – or indeed the Dictatorship of the Proletariat – have proved instruments in the hands of men by virtue of which the forces of hunger and power and fear, which are the inchoate stuff of existence, have been moulded into something nearer the visionaries' desire. If, in the second half of the twentieth century, the Western peoples have lost all their visions and dreamed all their dreams, then the world is open to the powerful myths of the totalitarians. The society which they picture may be in many respects a nightmare, but nightmares are potent in a world without good dreams.

The West will prove more vulnerable than any other society if it abandons the pursuit of visions and ideals for, more than any other community, it is the product not of geographical and racial forces but of the moulding power of the human spirit. [...] Both European society and its extension into the New World have been sustained by a unique faith in man – in his freedom, in his responsibility, in the laws which should safeguard him, in the rights that are his and in the duties by which he earns those rights. So accustomed are we to this view of man that we do not realize the audacity which was needed to bring it into being. At a time when humanity was subject to every physical calamity, when perpetual labour was needed to wring a livelihood from the soil, when the fatalities of tempest and sickness and the general recalcitrance of matter lay heavily upon man's spirit, and when the world, unpenetrated by rational discovery, was a vast unknown – in such a time, the Greek and Jewish forebears of our own civilization made their tremendous acts of faith in man and in his destiny. They declared him to be the crown of the universe. They saw nature as a field open to his reason and his dominion. The Greeks affirmed his power to build a rational order, the Jews proclaimed him a co-worker in the coming reign of righteousness.

It was because this picture of man was so high and so untrammeled and its ambition so vast that it led to the discovery of material instruments of mastery, to science and industry and all the material means of our own day. Man is not master of the universe because he can split the atom. He has split the atom because he first believed in his own unique mastery. Faith led to the material achievement, not the achievement to the faith. In fact, now that the means of mastering the environment, of building – physically – a better world, are more complete than ever before, it is a paradox that the faith is slackening.

[...]

The human heart has both appetites and despairs which rational codes alone are unable to control. Man is lonely. He is not self-sufficient. He rebels against meaninglessness in life. He is haunted by death. He is afraid. He needs to feel himself part of a wider whole and he has unassuageable powers of dedication and devotion which must find expression in worship and service. If, therefore, there is no other outlet for these powers, then the community in which he lives, the tribe, the state, Caesar, the dictator, become the natural and inevitable objects of his religious zeal.

Religion is not abolished by the "abolition" of God; the religion of Caesar takes its place. And since, for a few men, the need to worship is satisfied in hubris, in the worship of the self, the multitudes who look for a god can nearly always be certain of finding a willing candidate. In times of crisis, when insecurity, anxiety, loneliness and the meaninglessness of life become well nigh insupportable – how can a man tolerate years without work in modern industrial society? – the hunger for godlike leadership, for religious reassurance, for a merging of the self in the security of the whole becomes irresistible. Even when faith in God survives, the desire wells up for strong government. Where religious faith has vanished, all the energies of the soul are poured into the one channel of political faith. In our own day, Communism and National Socialism have proved to be powerful religions and have brought back into the world the identification of state and Church, city and temple, king and god which made up the monolithic unity of archaic society and the universal servitude of archaic man.

Few deny the historical role of Christianity in creating a double order of reality and a division of power out of which the possibility of freedom has grown. Even the most doubtful must confront the fact that totalitarian government in its extremest form has returned when the waning of religion left the altars of the soul empty and turned men back to the oldest gods of all – the idols of the tribe. Nor is it easy to conceive of any means other than religious faith for preserving a genuine division of power in society; for if man is no more than the creature of his environment and a product of his social order, on what foundations can he base claims and loyalties which go beyond the social order? From what source can he draw the strength to resist the claims of society?

[...]

It is, however, one thing to argue that a recovery of faith in God is necessary as a safeguard of Western freedom. It is quite another to put forward sociological and political and historical facts as the basis for a revival of faith. Such a procedure runs the risk of resembling the hypocrisy of eighteenth-century cynics who argued that religion was good for the poor because it kept them contented. Faith is not a matter of convenience nor even – save indirectly – a matter of sociology. It is a question of conviction and dedication and both spring from one source only – from the belief in God as a fact, as the supreme Fact of existence. Faith will not be restored in the West because people believe it to be useful. It will return only when they find that it is true.

[...] we may hope that the reunion of Christendom may begin at the point at which the greatest harm has been done – at the point where mutual charity has been lost. We do not know what form such a return to

Christian unity may take. We do not know what diversity of rite or discipline will be compatible with the essential oneness of Christian truth. But it seems clear at least that argument and reasoning will not produce unity if the desire for unity is lacking. And how can such a desire be born among men who still cannot distinguish between rejection of an error and profound dislike for the one who errs? It is charity that is the bond of perfection, it is by love that the Christian is to be known. Those who pray for the restoration of Christian unity have to pray first of all for the restoration of mutual love.

If the future of a reunited Christendom is obscure to us, how much more uncertain is the prospect of religious unity in the world at large. The strength of the outward thrust of the West in the last four hundred years has driven many non-Western peoples to defend their identity not only by imitating Western nationalism but by clinging with a new fanaticism to their old religious traditions. In the Moslem world, the asceticism and orthodoxy of the Wahabites was as much a reaction to the West as was the modernizing temper of Kemal Ataturk. British influence in India provided one impulse toward the nineteenth-century revival of Hindu religion and philosophy. In Japan, Shintoism has been fostered by the government to prevent the adoption of Western technology from extinguishing the separateness of Japanese culture. The decision of the Far Eastern rulers in the seventeenth century to exclude the Christian missionaries of the West would have been repeated in the nineteenth, if the local governments had still enjoyed the power to do so. The preaching of Christianity has seemed to them the Trojan horse of Western control. Today in China, the Communists persecute Christians on the ground that they are the fifth column of "Western American imperialism".

Yet this fact of Communist persecution is a reminder that one era of Western relationships with the East has come to an end and that a new phase is at least conceivable in the contracts between the great religions of the world. It may be that, to generate the physical and intellectual energy necessary for the great task of unifying the world, the peoples of the West needed the intolerance, the pride in their own achievement, the deep sense of superiority which, between the sixteenth and the nineteenth century, made them irresistible – and largely intolerable – to the other nations of the world. Now that, physically, the task is done and mankind must learn to consider itself a single family inhabiting its one small home in infinite space, the Western people have lost their unquestioned predominance. But they are likely, as a result, to lose their power of arousing intense resentment.

On their own side, there is infinitely more understanding and respect for other traditions and cultures than was the case even a hundred years ago when "the heathen Chinese" was a figure of fun and the religions of the East were dismissed as darkest superstition. There is now, with greater learning and greater humility, a new readiness to follow the wisdom of those Jesuit missionaries who held that the essence of Christianity could be given to Indians and Chinese only if Christianity were restated in terms of their own religious tradition and philosophy. We in the West, who are convinced that time has meaning and that God works in history, cannot believe that the thousands of years of Confucian social discipline, of Hindu mysticism, of Buddhist charity and compassion, have had no significance and were not intended to give their own special light to the general illumination of mankind. For the philosophers and scholars of Christianity today the task is, then, still the task of Paul interpreting Greek philosophy to the Hebrews and Hebrew tradition to the Greeks.

[...]

The reconciliation in Christ of the great traditions of a Mediterranean world united under Roman rule may be repeated in the wider world of our own day, which the energy of the West has drawn into closer physical contact than the peoples of Rome ever knew. And it may be, too, that the task of interpretation and understanding will be undertaken with all the greater fervour and charity since now for the first time all the religions of the world confront in Communism a secular faith based upon the explicit denial of God and upon the worship of the material order.

It cannot be too often repeated that one of the chief reasons why Communism exercises such power in the modern world is because it has unashamedly made a religion of its political objectives. Some of the jargon may be scientific. The aims may seem, in many ways, highly prosaic – fifty new power stations, a hundred per cent rise in coal production, canals across the desert, irrigation to make the wastelands fertile. But behind these material aims there lurks a lyrical passion for physical expansion, an impassioned belief that men will be brothers and society a classless paradise once the problems of production are mastered and every man works, not for "monopolists and exploiters", but for the single master, the state. There is no fear of enthusiasm, no deprecation of faith and vision in Soviet propaganda, and the appeal it has often made in the West has been above all to those who feel intensely the need in life for an explanation of reality, for an ideal and for a path to follow. [...] And in the world of Asia, these attractions are doubled by the old deep-rooted suspicion of the West, the belief that its way of life is imperialist and exploitative, and the desire to assert a new-found independence even if it involves imminent risk from the Soviet side.

In this contest with the attractions of Communism the Western world cannot rely on the momentum of past achievements and relationships. It has to reassert its vision of a free and just society, of a humanity united as brother under the Fatherhood of God. The reason for bringing the great vitalities of nationhood and of material possessions under rational control is not only that survival demands a re-ordering of Western institutions. It is, above all, because new experiments in international and social relations will show to the world at large – to the young, to the students, to the new voters in Asia and Africa, to the natural leaders of the world's masses – that the traditional faith of the West is strong enough to remould society, strong enough to fulfil the promise of brotherhood which, whatever the blindness of nationalism or the selfishness of property, remains imbedded in our society as a judgment and a challenge.

Nor can we doubt, as the Western world shows signs of recovering the faith which lies at its foundation, that Communism will begin to give ground even in the territories it has already conquered. Whatever the material achievements of the Communist system – and they are likely to be immense – a society which is imprisoned within the limits of time and which systematically debars its citizens from any sense of a more than human destiny will, when the first excitement of material creation has worn away, become a closed order of deadening monotony. [...] How much more certain would be the infiltration and reconversion of Soviet society if the Western world were not only free but patently generous and brotherly and unafraid. It is useless to suppose that a reversal of pressure can come about solely through material competition. Today, the vast material superiority of the United States is not felt, in the rest of the world, as a moral as well as a physical challenge. The West will reassert its powers of attraction only if its material achievements are seen to express a vision of spiritual order.

No one can forecast the possibility of such a renewal of the springs of faith in the West.

G. Elizabeth Anscombe

From *Mr Truman's Degree* (1956)

Choosing to kill the innocent as a means to your ends is always murder. Naturally, killing the innocent as an end in itself is murder too: but that is no more than a possible future development for[14] in our part of the globe it is a practice that has so far been confined to the Nazis. I intend my formulation to be taken strictly: each term in it is necessary. For killing the innocent, even if you know as a matter of statistical certainty that the things you do involve it, is not necessarily murder. I mean that if you attack a lot of military targets, such as munitions factories and naval dockyards, as carefully as you can, you will be certain to kill a number of innocent people; but that is not murder. On the other hand, unscrupulousness in considering the possibilities turns it into murder.

I here print as a case in point a letter which I received lately from Holland:

"We read in our paper about your opposition to Truman. I do not like him either, but do you know that in the war the English bombed the dykes of our province Zeeland, an island where nobody could escape anywhere to. Where the whole population was drowned, children, women, farmers working in the field, all the cattle, everything, hundreds and hundreds, and we were your allies! Nobody ever speaks about that. Perhaps it were well to know this. Or, to remember."

That was to trap some fleeing German military. I think my correspondent has something.

It may be impossible to take the thing (or people) you want to destroy as your target; it may be possible to attack it only by taking as the object of your attack what includes large numbers of innocent people. Then you cannot very well say they died by accident. Here, your action is murder.

"But where will you draw the line? It is impossible to draw an exact line". This is a common and absurd argument against drawing any line; it

---

[14] This will seem a preposterous assertion; but we are certainly on the way, and I can think of no reasons for confidence that it will not happen.

738

may be very difficult, and there are obviously borderline cases. But we have fallen into the way of drawing no line, and offering as justifications what an uncaptive mind will find only a bad joke. Wherever the line is, certain things are certainly well to one side or the other of it.

Now who are "the innocent" in war? They are all those who are not fighting and not engaged in supplying those who are with the means of fighting. A farmer growing wheat which may be eaten by the troops is not "supplying them with the means of fighting". Over this, too, the line may be difficult to draw. But that does not mean that no line should be drawn, or that, even if one is in doubt just where to draw the line, one cannot be crystal clear that this or that is well over the line.

"But the people fighting are probably conscripts! In that case they are just as innocent as anyone else". "Innocent" here is not a term referring to personal responsibility at all. It means rather "not harming". But the people fighting are "harming", so they can be attacked; but if they surrender they become in this sense innocent and so may not be maltreated or killed. Nor is there ground for trying them on a criminal charge; not, indeed, because a man has no personal responsibility for fighting, but because they were not the subjects of the state whose prisoners they are.

There is an argument which I know from experience it is necessary to forestall at this point, though I think it is visibly captious. It is this: on my theory, would it not follow that a soldier can only be killed when he is actually attacking? Then, e.g., it would be impossible to attack a sleeping camp. The answer is that "what someone is doing" can refer either to what he is doing at the moment or to his role in a situation. A soldier under arms is "harming" in the latter sense even if he is asleep. But it is true that the enemy should not be attacked more ferociously than is necessary to put them *hors de combat*.

These conceptions are distinct and intelligible ones; they would formerly have been said to belong to the Law of Nations. Anyone can see that they are good, and we pay tribute to them by our moral indignation when our enemies violate them. But in fact they are going, and only fragments of them are left. General Eisenhower, for example, is reported to have spoken slightingly once of the notion of chivalry towards prisoners – as if that were based on respect for their virtue or for the nation from which they come, and not on the fact that they are now defenceless.

It is characteristic of nowadays to talk with horror of killing rather than of murder, and hence, since in war you have committed yourself to killing – i.e. "accepted an evil" – not to mind whom you kill. This seems largely to be the work of the devil; but I also suspect that it is in part an effect of the existence of pacifism, as a doctrine which many people respect though they would not adopt it. This effect would not exist if people had a distinct notion of what makes pacifism a false doctrine.

It therefore seems to me important to show that for one human being deliberately to kill another is not inevitably wrong. I may seem to be wasting my time, as most people do reject pacifism. But it is nevertheless important to argue the point because if one does so one sees that there are pretty severe restrictions on legitimate killing. Of course, people accept this within the state, but when it comes to war they have the idea that any restrictions are something like the Queensbury Rules – instead of making the difference between being guilty and not guilty of murder. [...]

But the state actually has the authority to order deliberate killing in order to protect its people or to put frightful injustices right. (For example, the plight of the Jews under Hitler would have been a reasonable cause of war.) The reason for this is pretty simple: it stands out most clearly if we first consider the state's right to order such killing within its confines. I am not referring to the death penalty, but to what happens when there is rioting or when violent malefactors have to be caught. Rioters can sometimes only be restrained, or malefactors seized, by force. Law without force is ineffectual, and human beings without laws miserable (though we, who have too many and too changeable laws, may easily not feel this very distinctly). So much is indeed fairly obvious, though the more peaceful the society the less obvious it is that the force in the hands of the servants of the law has to be force up to the point of killing. It would become perfectly obvious any time there was rioting or gangsterism which had to be dealt with by the servants of the law fighting. [...]

Thus the malefactor who has been found guilty is the only defenceless person whom the state may put to death. It need not: it can choose more merciful laws. (I have no prejudice in favour of the death penalty.) Any other defenceless person is as such innocent, in the sense "not harming". And so the State can only order to kill others of its subjects besides convicted criminals if they are rioting or doing something that has to be stopped, and can only be stopped by the servants of the law fighting them.

Now, this is also the ground of the state's right to order people to fight external enemies who are unjustly attacking them or something of theirs. The right to order to fight for the sake of other people's wrongs, to put right something affecting people who are not actually under the protection of the state, is a rather more dubious thing obviously, but it exists because of the common sympathy of human beings whereby one feels for one's neighbour if he is attacked. So in an attenuated sense it can be said that something that belongs to, or concerns, one is attacked if anybody is unjustly attacked or maltreated.

Pacifism, then, is a false doctrine. Now, no doubt, it is bad just for that reason, because it is always bad to have a false conscience. In this way the doctrine that it is a bad act to lay a bet is bad: it is all right to bet what it is all right to risk or drop in the sea. But I want to maintain that pacifism is a harmful doctrine in a far stronger sense than this. Even the prevalence of the idea that it was wrong to bet would have no particularly bad consequences; a false doctrine which merely forbids what is not actually bad need not encourage people in anything bad. But with pacifism it is quite otherwise. It is a factor in that loss of the conception of murder which is my chief interest in this pamphlet.

I have very often heard people say something like this: "It is all very well to say 'Don't do evil that good may come'. But war is evil. We all know that. Now, of course, it is possible to be an Absolute Pacifist. I can respect that, but I can't be one myself, and most other people won't be either. So we have to accept the evil. It is not that we do not see the evil. And once you are in for it, you have to go the whole hog".

This is much as if I were defrauding someone, and when someone tried to stop me I said: "Absolute honesty! I respect that. But of course absolute honesty really means having no property at all ..." Having offered the sacrifice of a few sighs and tears to absolute honesty, I go on as before.

The correct answer to the statement that "war is evil" is that it is bad – *i.e.* a misfortune – to be at war. And no doubt if two nations are at war at least one is unjust. But that does not show that it is wrong to fight or that if one does fight one can also commit murder.

Naturally my claim that pacifism is a very harmful doctrine is contingent on its being a false one. If it were a true doctrine, its encouragement of this nonsensical "hypocrisy of the ideal standard" would not count against it. But given that it is false, I am inclined to think it is also very bad, unusually so for an idea which seems as it were to err on the noble side.

When I consider the history of events from 1939 to 1945, I am not surprised that Mr. Truman is made the recipient of honours. But when I consider his actions by themselves, I am surprised again. Some people actually praise the bombings and commend the stockpiling of atomic weapons on the ground that they are so horrible that nations will be afraid ever again to make war. "We have made a covenant with death, and with hell we are at an agreement". There does not seem to be good ground for such a hope for any long period of time.

Pacifists have for long made it a point in their propaganda that men must grow more murderous as their techniques of destruction improve, and those who defend murder eagerly seize on this point, so that

I imagine by now it is pretty well accepted by the whole world. Of course, it is not true. In Napoleon's time, for example, the means of destruction had much improved since the time of Henry V; but Henry, not Napoleon, was a great massacrer of civilians, saying when he did particularly atrocious things that the French were a sinful nation and that he had a mission from God to punish them. And, of course, really large scale massacre up to now has belonged to times with completely primitive methods of killing. Weapons are now manufactured whose sole point is to be used in massacre of cities. But the people responsible are not murderous because they have these weapons; they have them because they are murderous. Deprived of atomic bombs, they would commit massacres by means of other bombs.

Protests by people who have not power are a waste of time. I was not seizing an opportunity to make a "gesture of protest" at atomic bombs; I vehemently object to our action in offering Mr. Truman honours, because one can share in the guilt of a bad action by praise and flattery, as also by defending it. When I puzzle myself over the attitude of the Vice-Chancellor and the Hebdomadal Council, I look round to see if any explanation is available why so many Oxford people should be willing to flatter such a man.

[...]

It is possible still to withdraw from this shameful business in some slight degree: it is possible not to go to Encaenia: if it should be embarrassing to someone who would normally go to plead other business, he could take to his bed. I, indeed, should fear to go, in case God's patience suddenly ends.

Index